BE KIND, MY NEIGHBOR

By Yugo Limbo

CONTENT WARNING

This book contains sensitive material relating to:

Blood, Cults, Death, Drugs, Gore, Kidnapping, Manipulation/Abuse, Murder, Sexual Situations & BDSM, and Unreality

Please take care of yourself, and take breaks if needed.

Be Kind, My Neighbor
By Yugo Limbo

Copyright © 2022 Yugo Limbo. All rights reserved.

ISBN 978-1-945509-92-6
First Printing, August 2022
Printed in China

Published by:
Silver Sprocket | 1018 Valencia St, San Francisco, CA 94110, USA
Avi Ehrlich, Publisher | Josh PM, General Manager | Ari Yarwood, Managing Editor | Carina Taylor, Production Designer | Simon Jane Crowbrock, Shop Goblin | Daniel Zhou, Shop Rat | Raul Higuera-Cortez, Big Head Bandit | Yasmeen Abedifard, Shop Shroom | Sarah Maloney, Shop Cat | Sol Cintron, Fruit Bat | www.silversprocket.net

PREFACE

Howdy there.

Whoof, it's been quite the journey makin' this comic- almost one and a half years, huh? Extremely fun, and extremely cathartic, too. Finally being able to unabashedly express myself. . . wow! As a trans artist, it felt good to finally write about people like me- and imbue my identity and struggles into them. There is no one universal "right way" to be trans- your individual experience is your own!

Don't forget that! Exist as you want!

Ah, I'm rambling. This story isn't JUST about the trans experience of course. . . it's about a lot of things, and I think people of all kinds can have a blast with it. Psychedelic horror! Puppets! Cults! Love! Music! Finding your community! Processing trauma! All these ingredients make a nice gumbo, I think- and I hope you have as much fun eating this gumbo as I did cooking it.

-Yugo Limbo

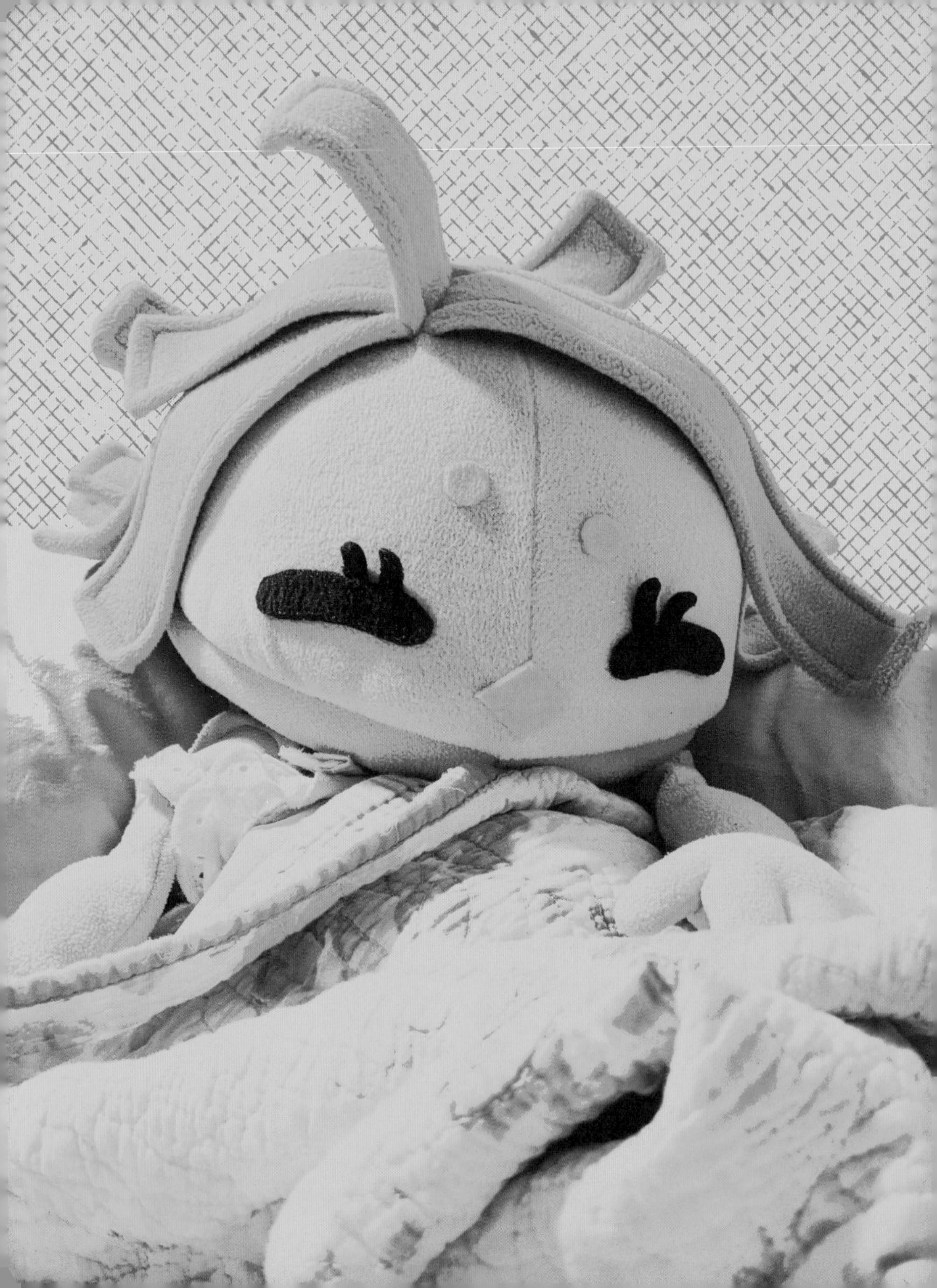

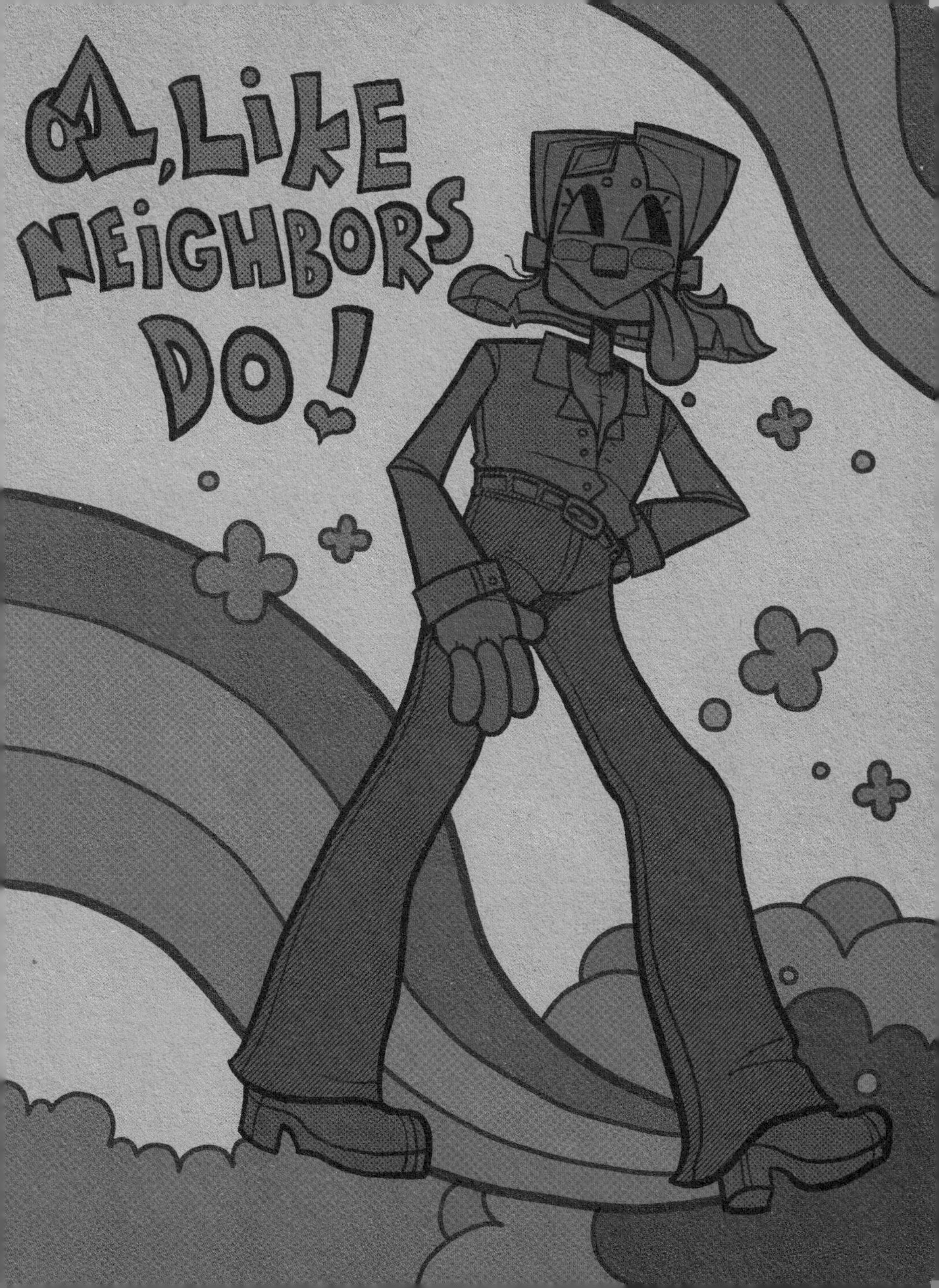

A LIKE NEIGHBORS DO!

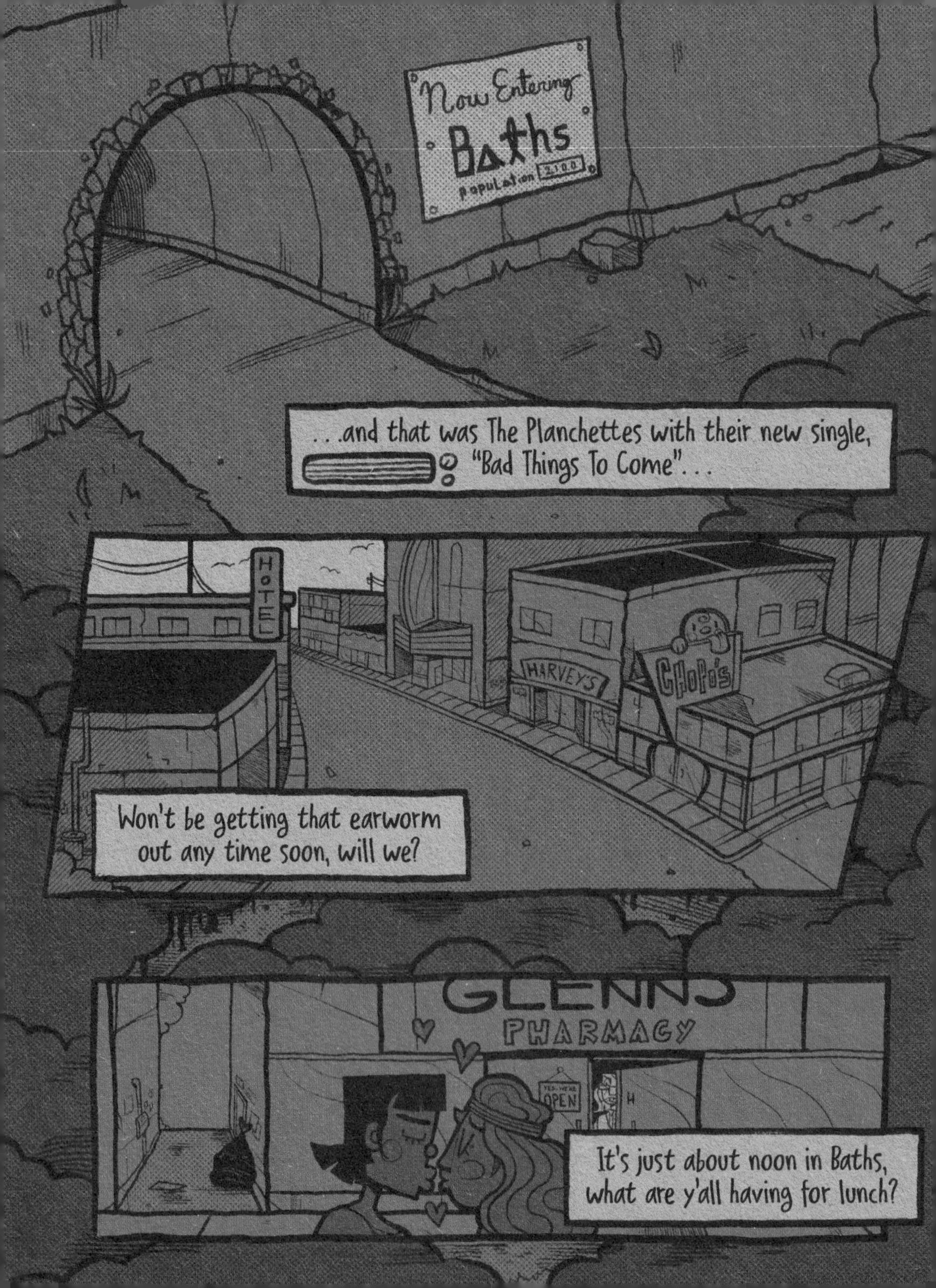

Now Entering
Baths
population
...and that was The Planchettes with their new single, "Bad Things To Come"...
HOTEL
HARVEY'S
CHOPO'S
Won't be getting that earworm out any time soon, will we?
GLENNS
PHARMACY
OPEN
It's just about noon in Baths, what are y'all having for lunch?

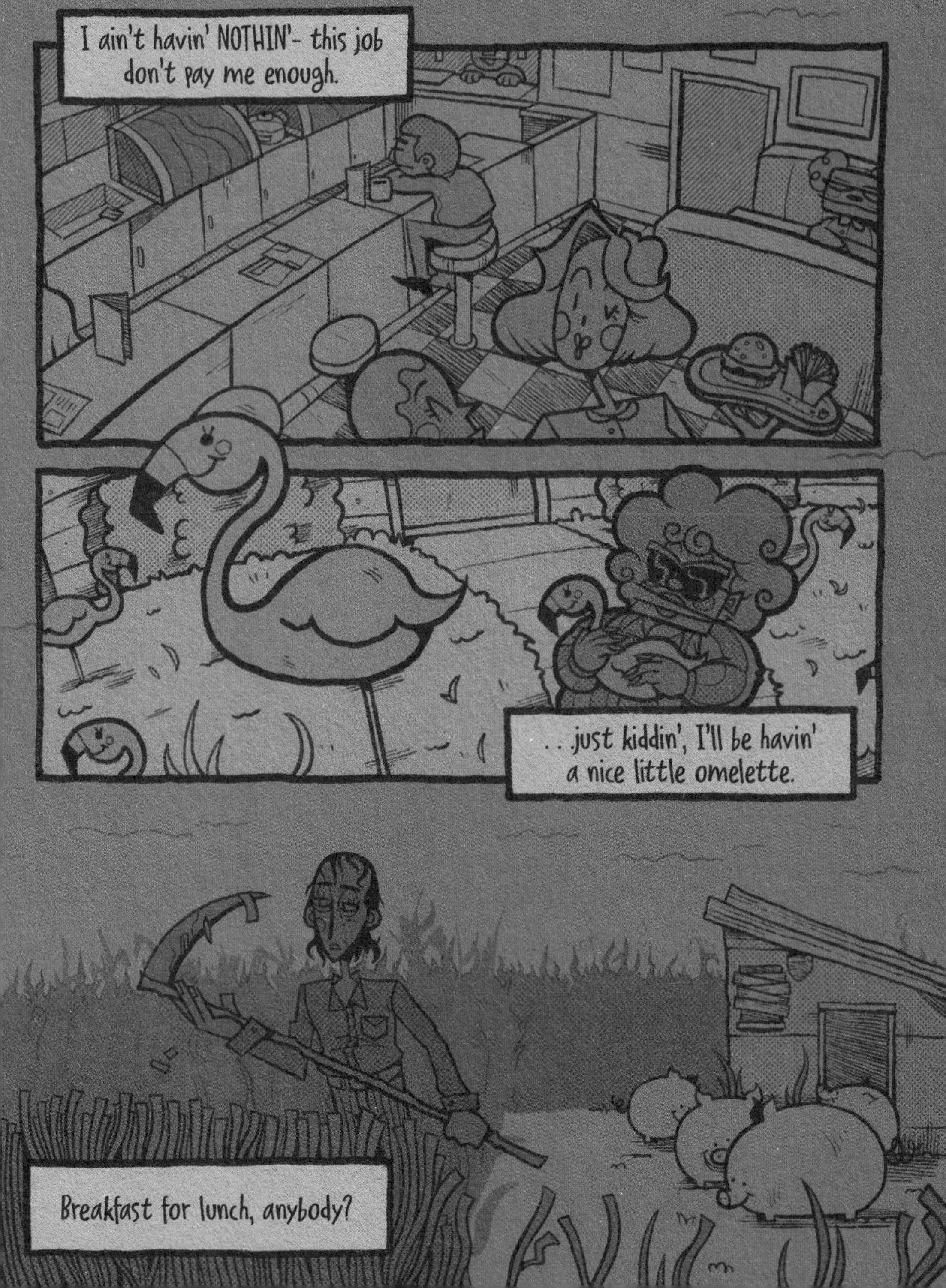

I ain't havin' NOTHIN'- this job don't pay me enough.
. . .just kiddin', I'll be havin' a nice little omelette.
Breakfast for lunch, anybody?

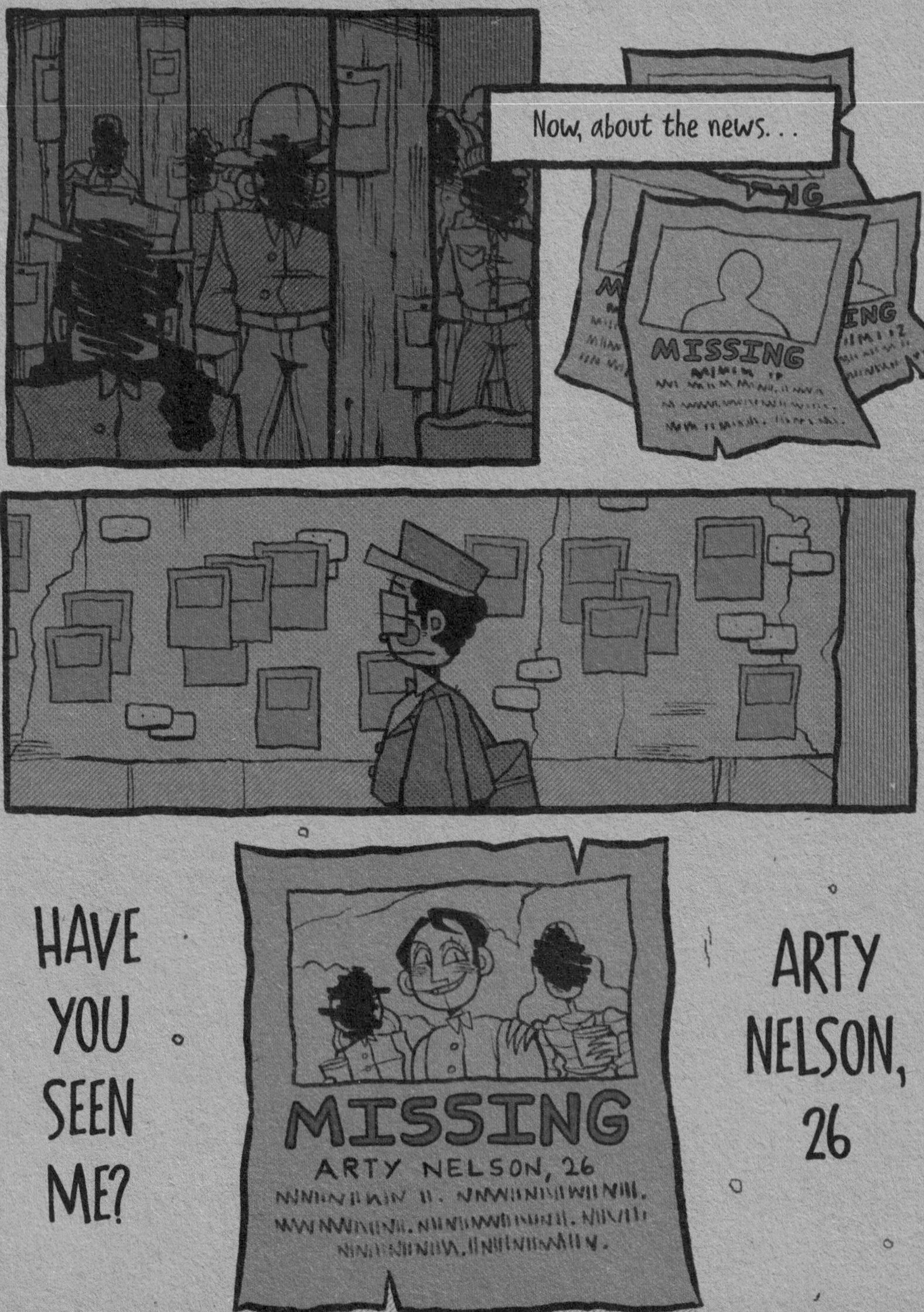
Now, about the news. . .
MISSING
HAVE YOU SEEN ME?
MISSING
ARTY NELSON, 26
ARTY NELSON, 26

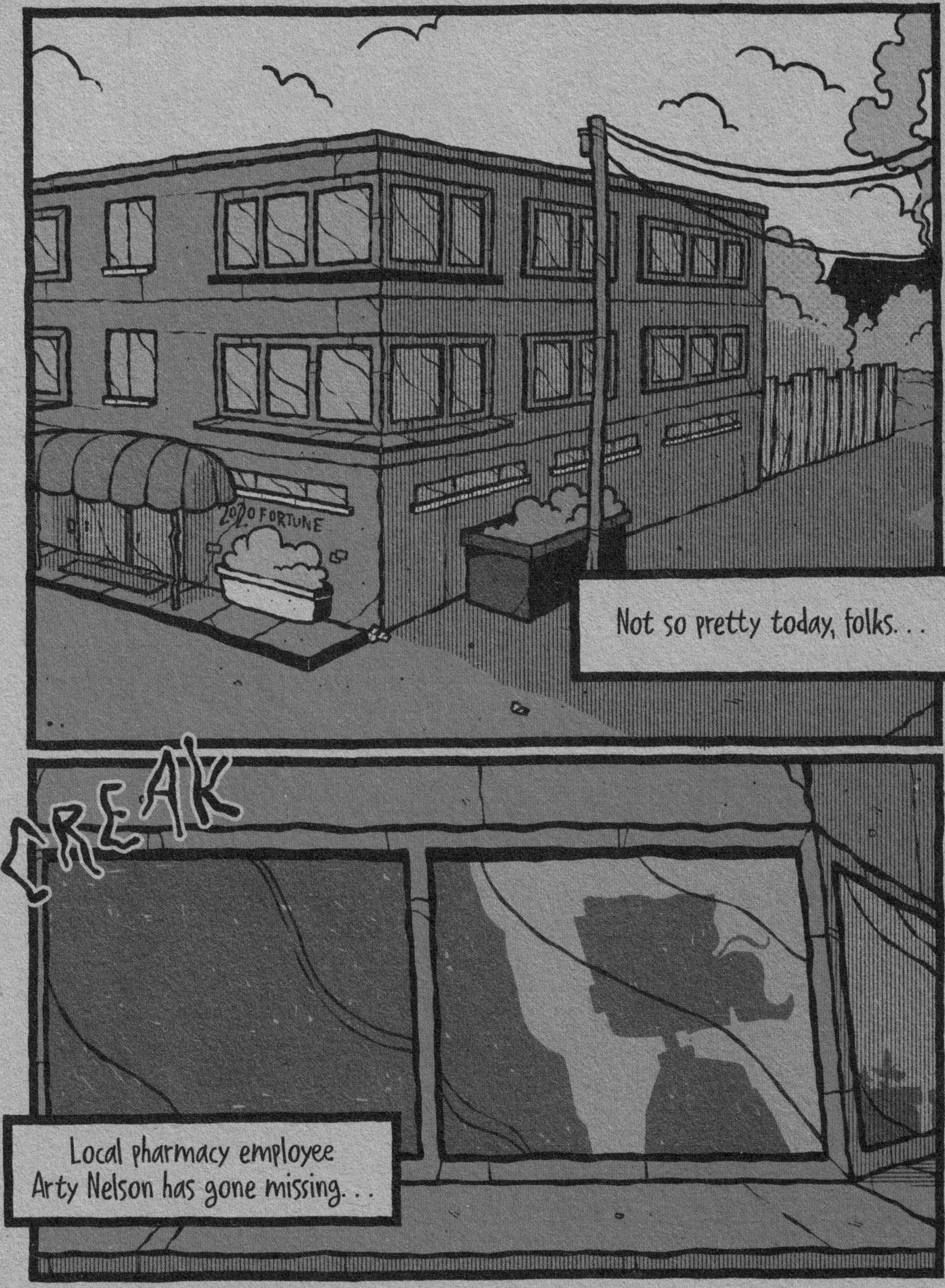
2020 FORTUNE
Not so pretty today, folks. . .
CREAK
Local pharmacy employee
Arty Nelson has gone missing. . .

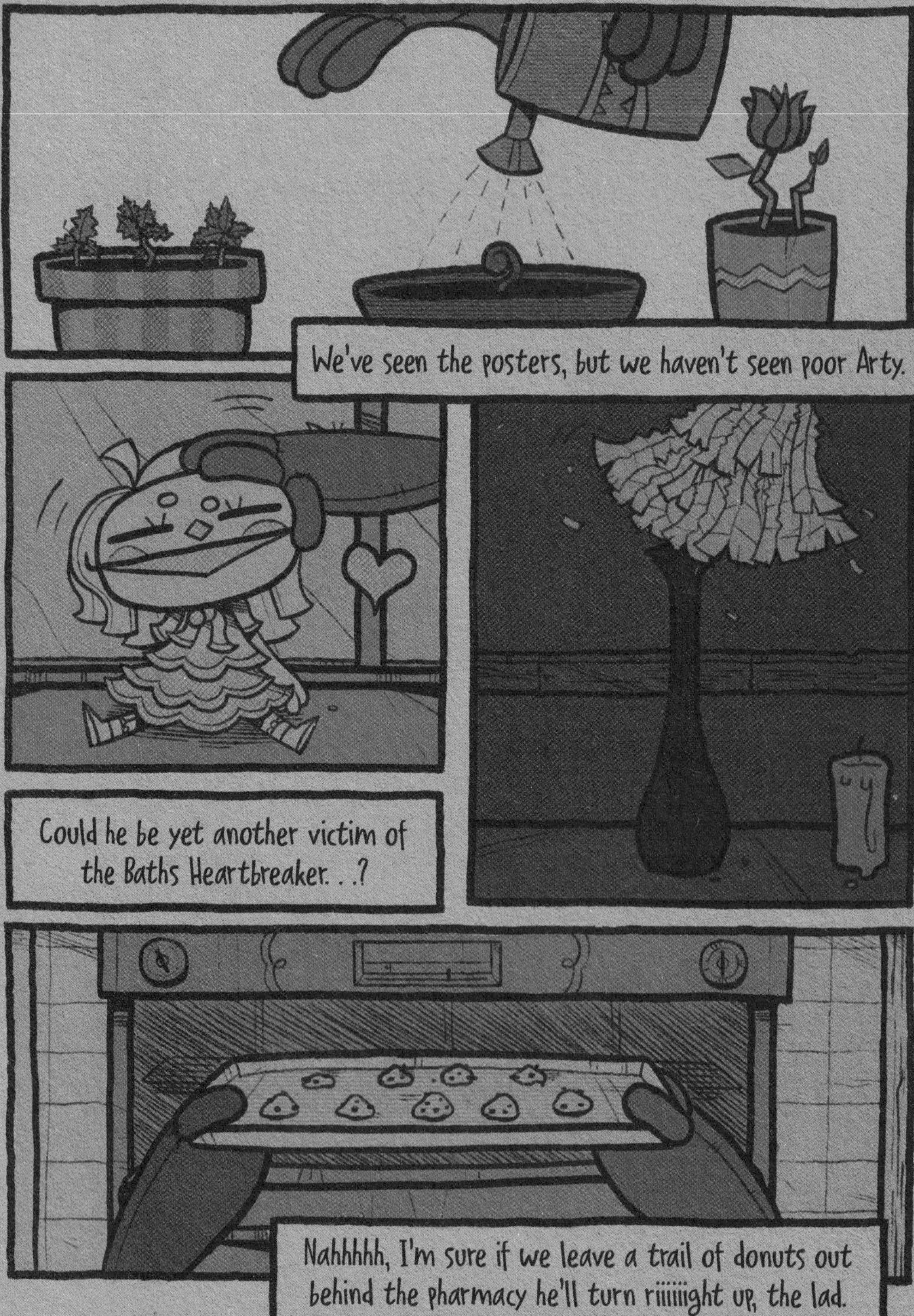
We've seen the posters, but we haven't seen poor Arty.
Could he be yet another victim of the Baths Heartbreaker. . .?
Nahhhhh, I'm sure if we leave a trail of donuts out behind the pharmacy he'll turn riiiiiight up, the lad.

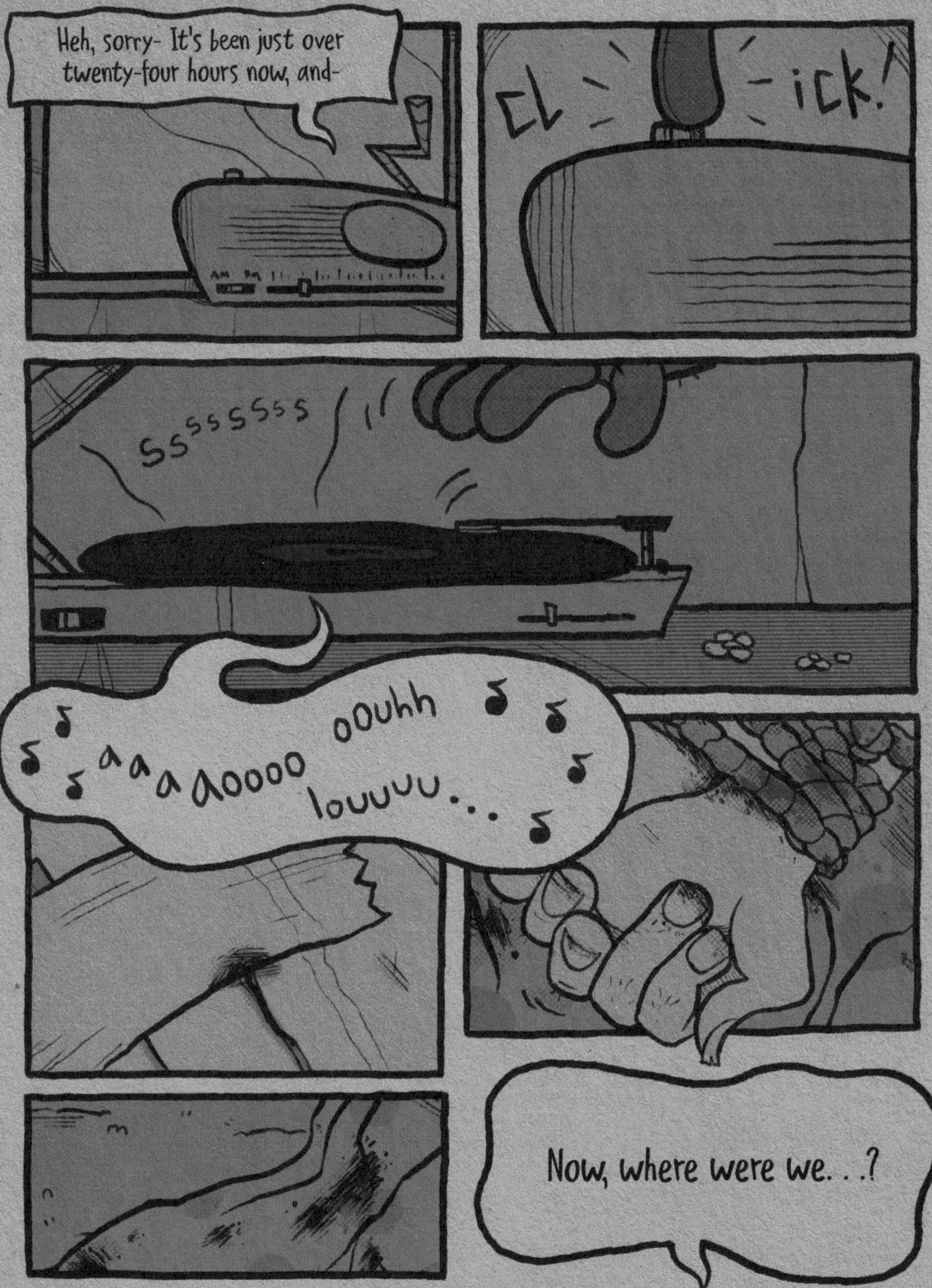
Heh, sorry- It's been just over twenty-four hours now, and-
CL -ick!
Ssssssss
aaaaoooo oouhh louuuu...
Now, where were we...?

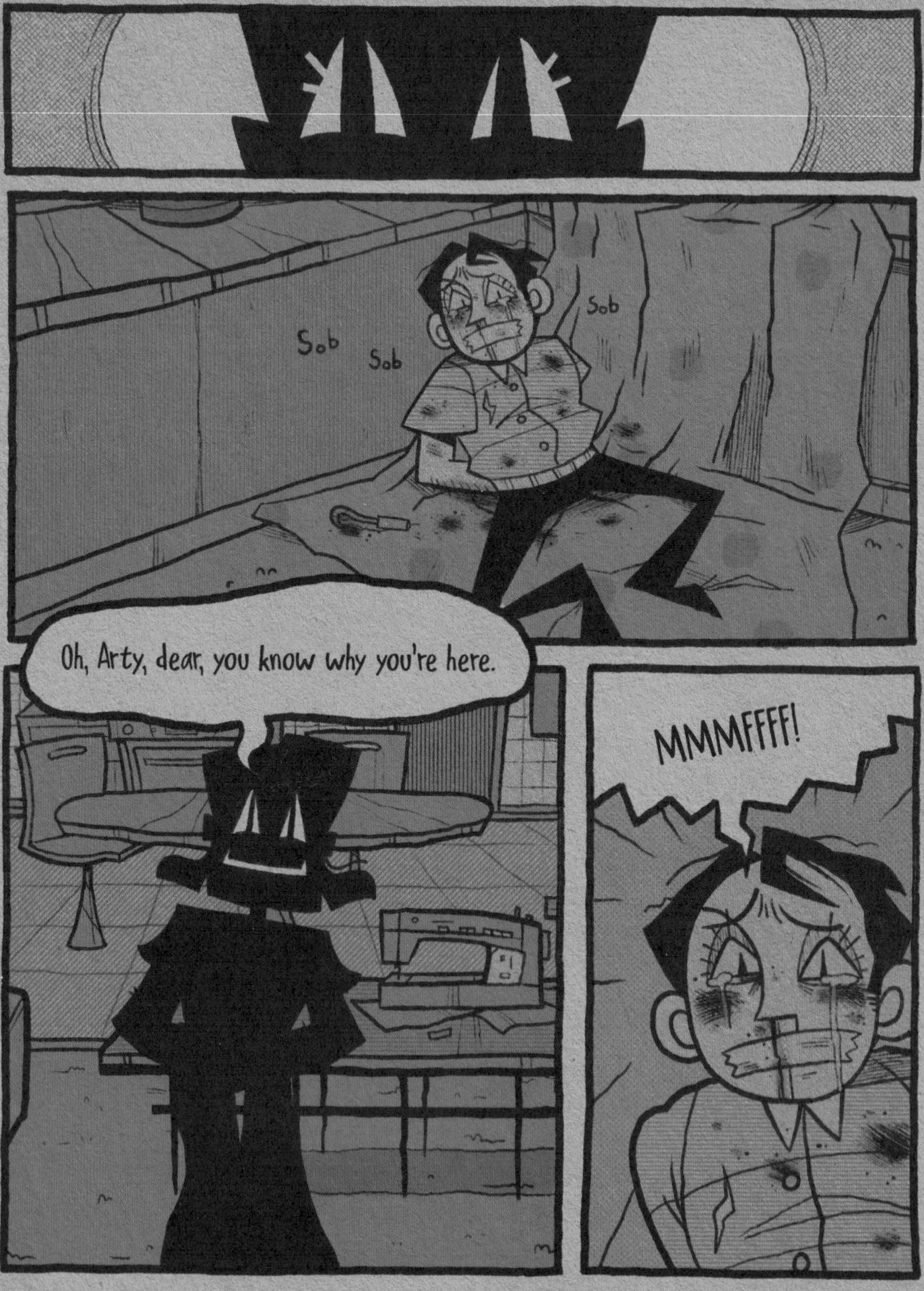
Sob
Sob
Sob
Oh, Arty, dear, you know why you're here.
MMMFFFF!

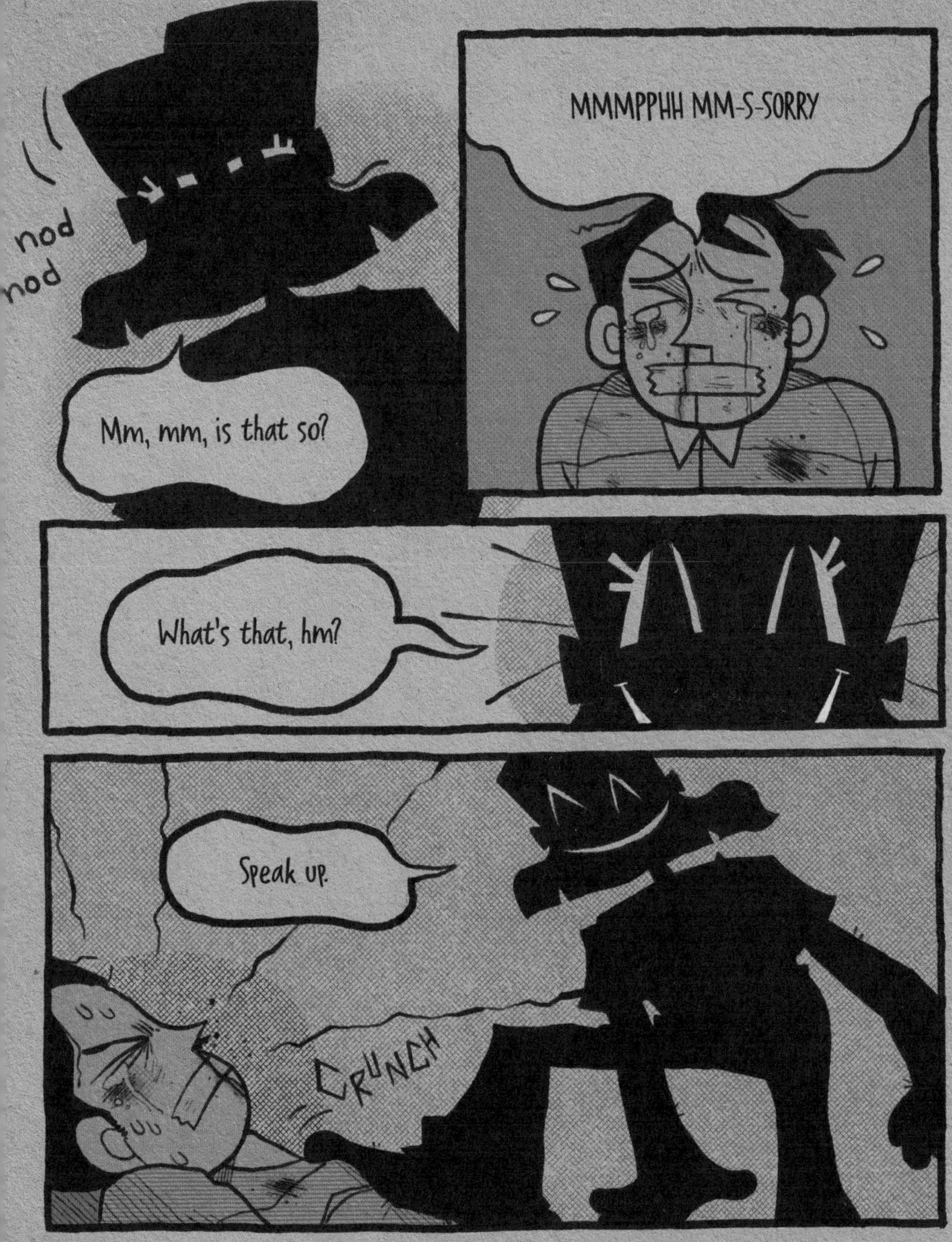
nod
nod
Mm, mm, is that so?
MMMPPHH MM-S-SORRY
What's that, hm?
Speak up.
CRUNCH

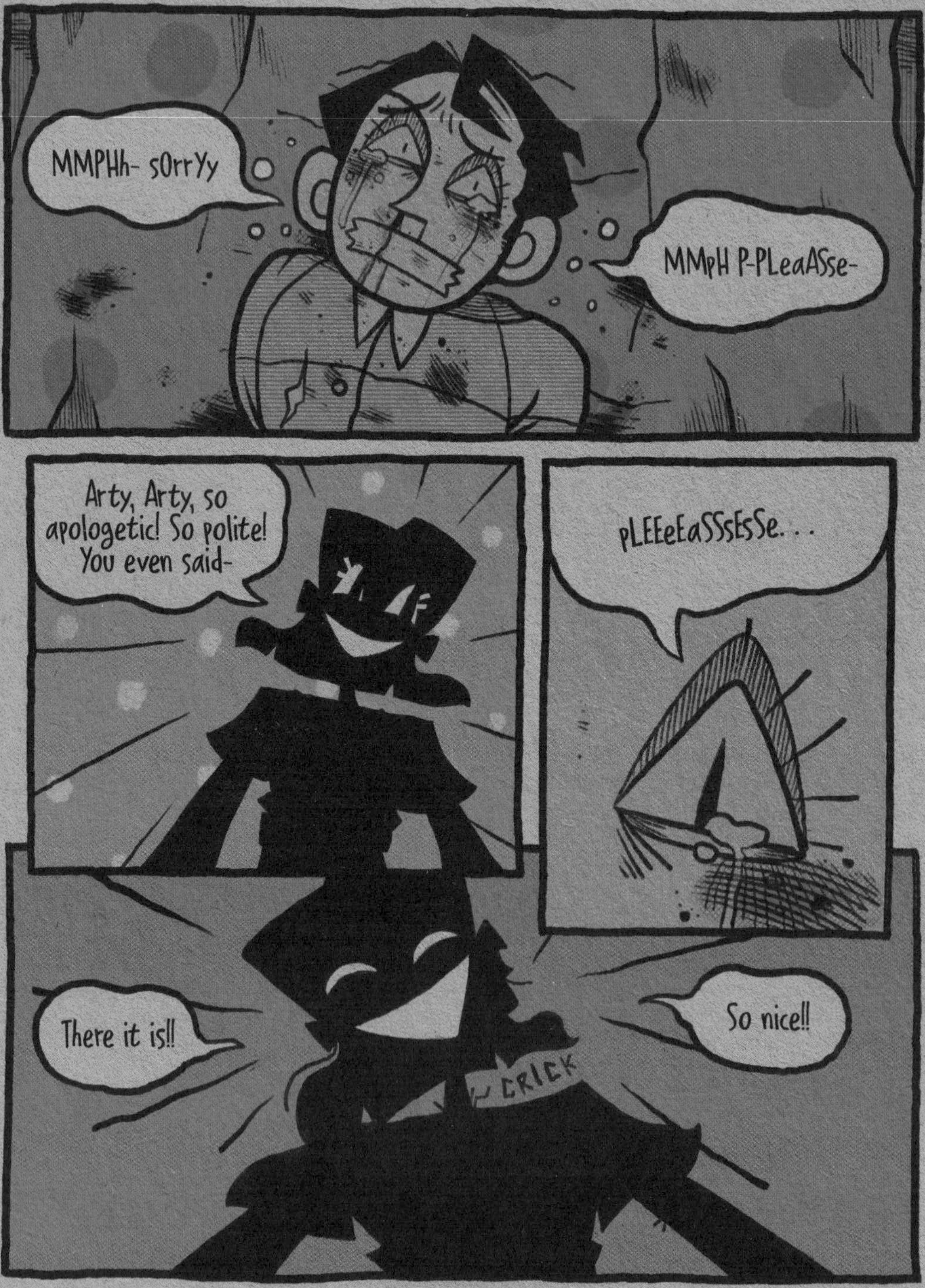
MMPHh- sOrrYy
MMpH P-PLeaASse-
Arty, Arty, so apologetic! So polite! You even said-
pLEEeEaSSsEsSe. . .
There it is!!
So nice!!
CRICK

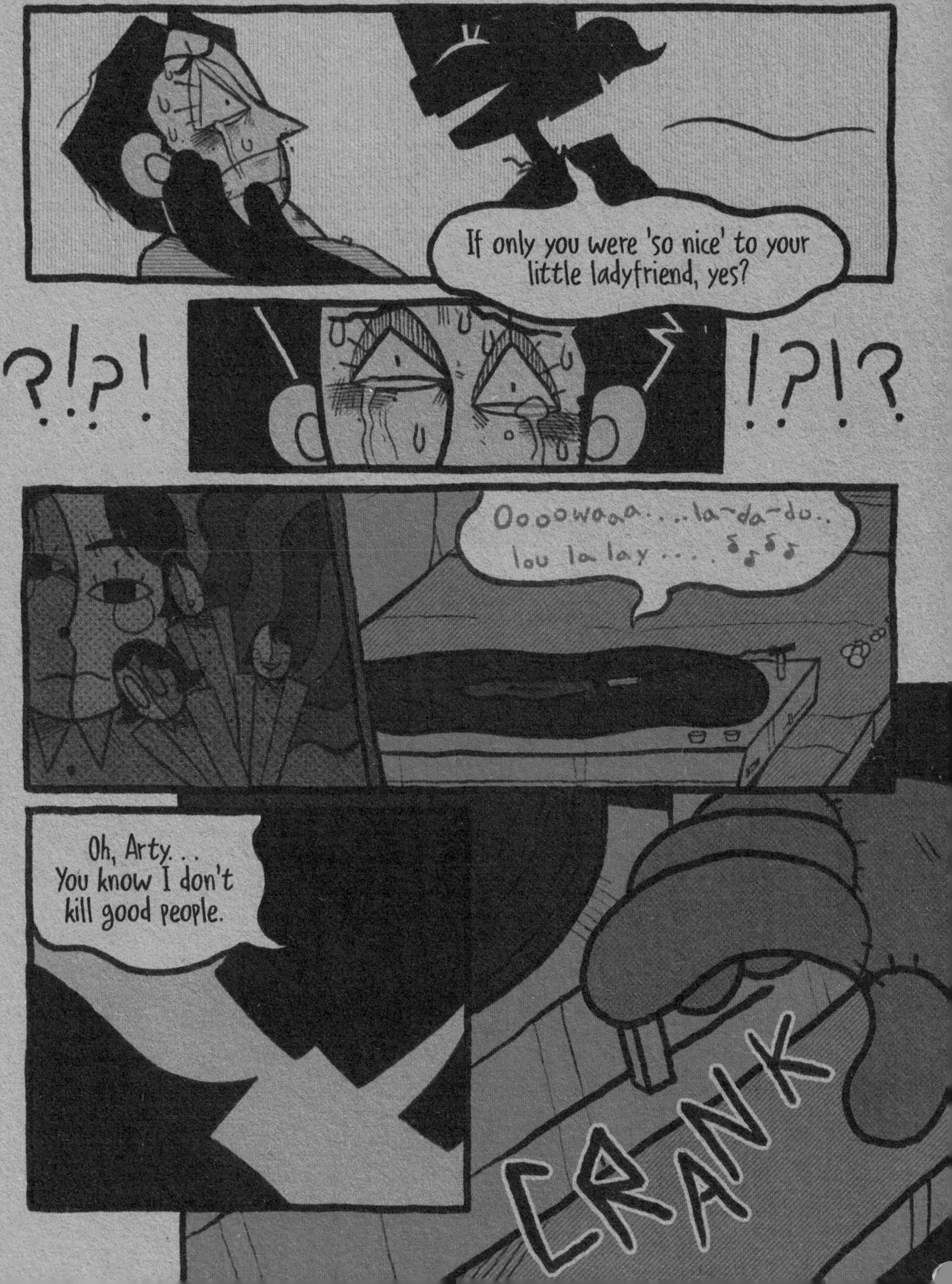
If only you were 'so nice' to your little ladyfriend, yes?
?!?!
!?!?
Oooowaaa.....la~da~do..
lou la lay.....
Oh, Arty...
You know I don't kill good people.
CRANK

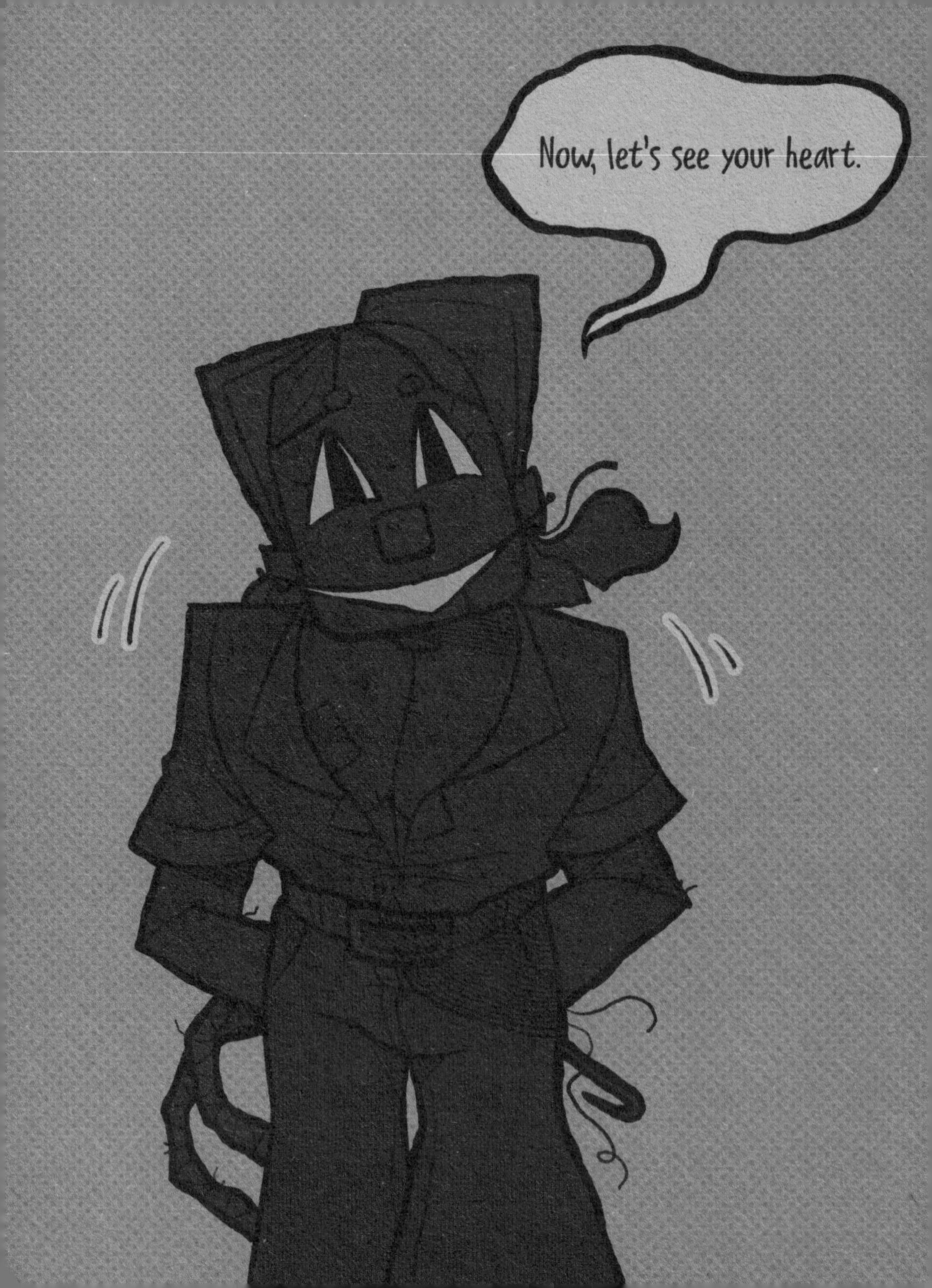
Now, let's see your heart.

Hi, how are you?

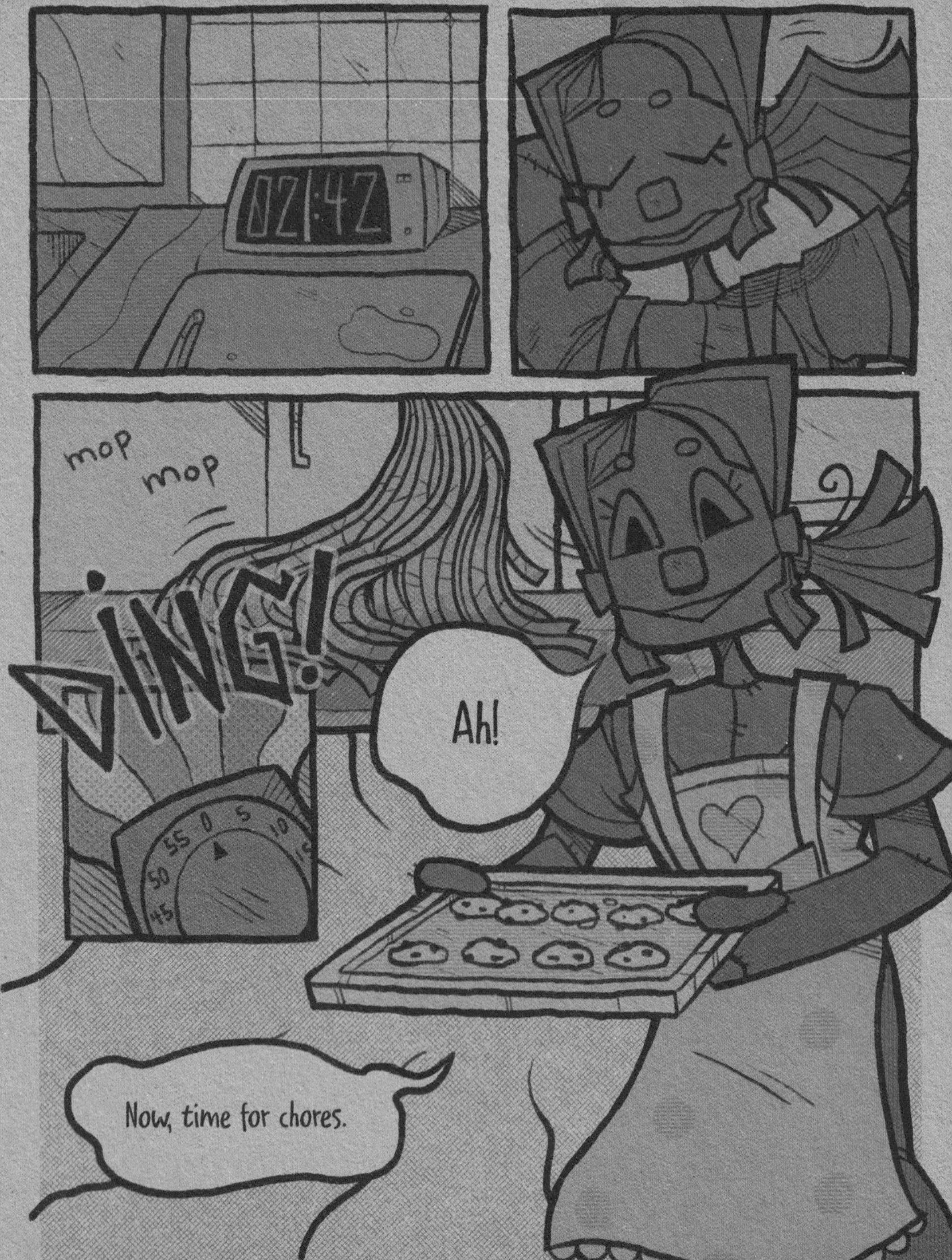
02:42
mop
mop
DING!
Ah!
Now, time for chores.

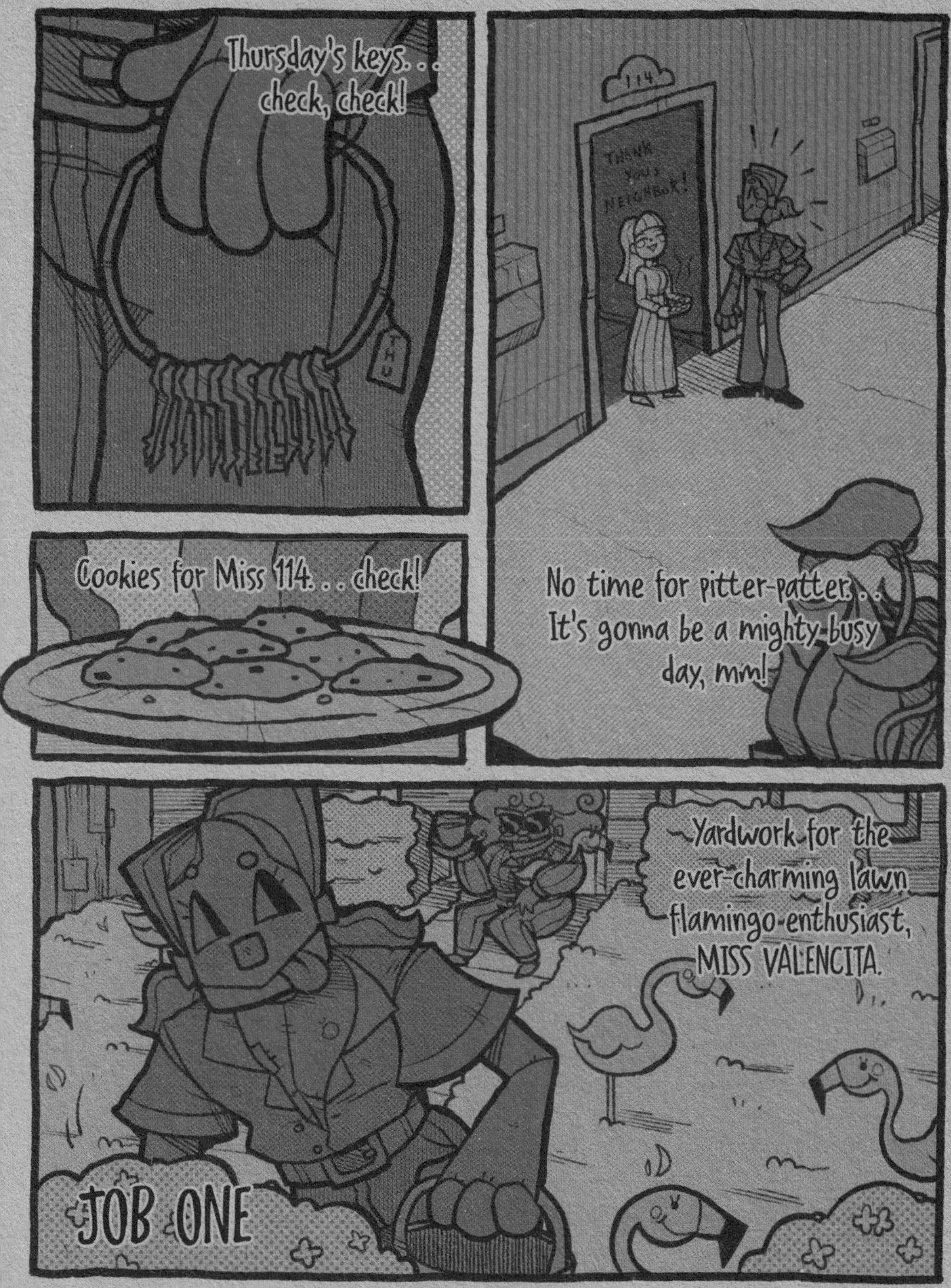
Thursday's keys. . .
check, check!
THU
114
THANK YOU, NEIGHBOR!
Cookies for Miss 114. . . check!
No time for pitter-patter. . .
It's gonna be a mighty busy day, mm!
Yardwork for the ever-charming lawn flamingo-enthusiast, MISS VALENCITA.
JOB ONE

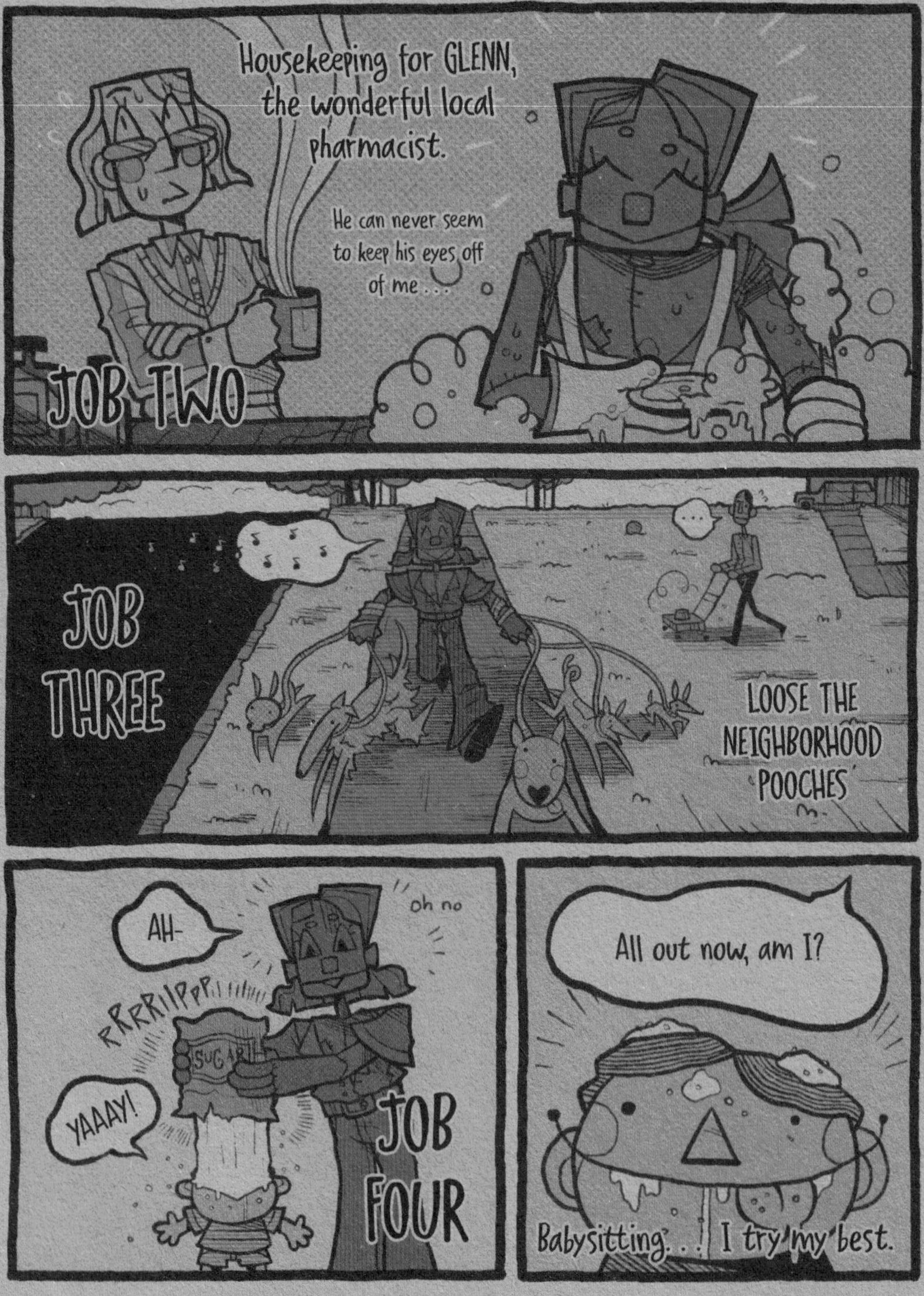
Housekeeping for GLENN, the wonderful local pharmacist.
He can never seem to keep his eyes off of me . . .
JOB TWO
JOB THREE
LOOSE THE NEIGHBORHOOD POOCHES
...
AH-
oh no
RRRRIPPP
SUGAR
YAAAY!
JOB FOUR
All out now, am I?
Babysitting. . . I try my best.

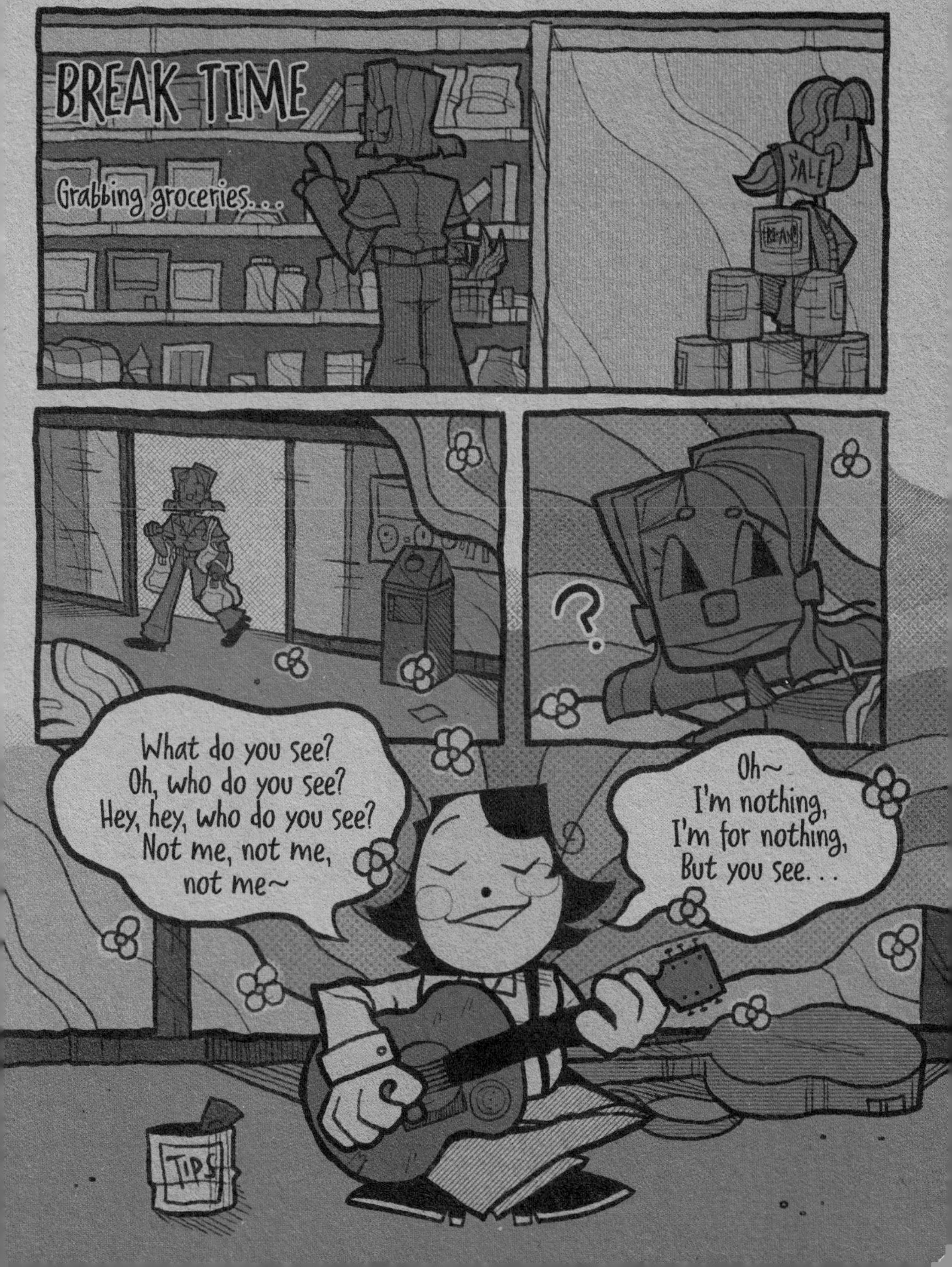
BREAK TIME
Grabbing groceries. . .
SALE
?
What do you see? Oh, who do you see? Hey, hey, who do you see? Not me, not me, not me~
Oh~ I'm nothing, I'm for nothing, But you see. . .
TIPS

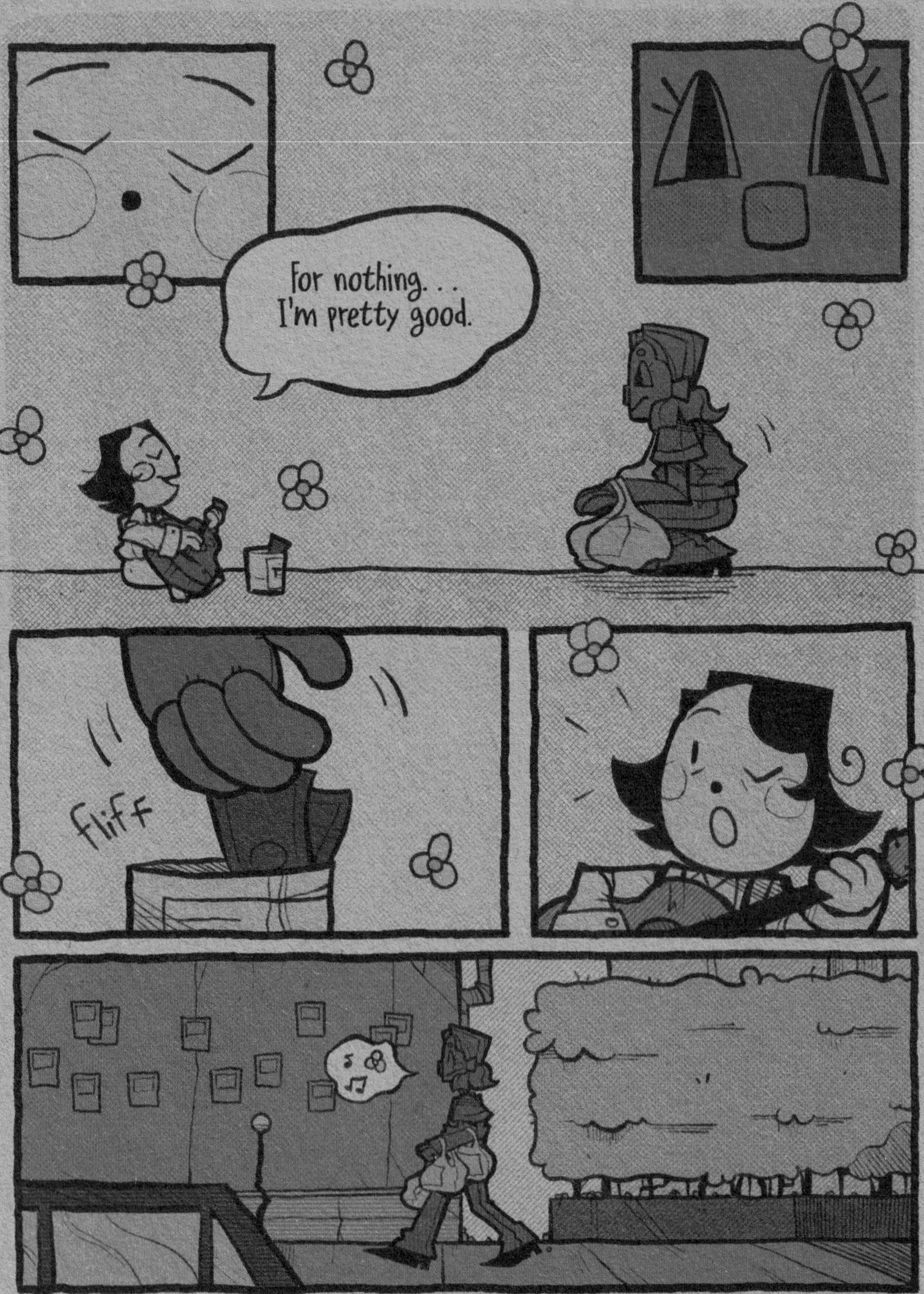
For nothing...
I'm pretty good.
fliff

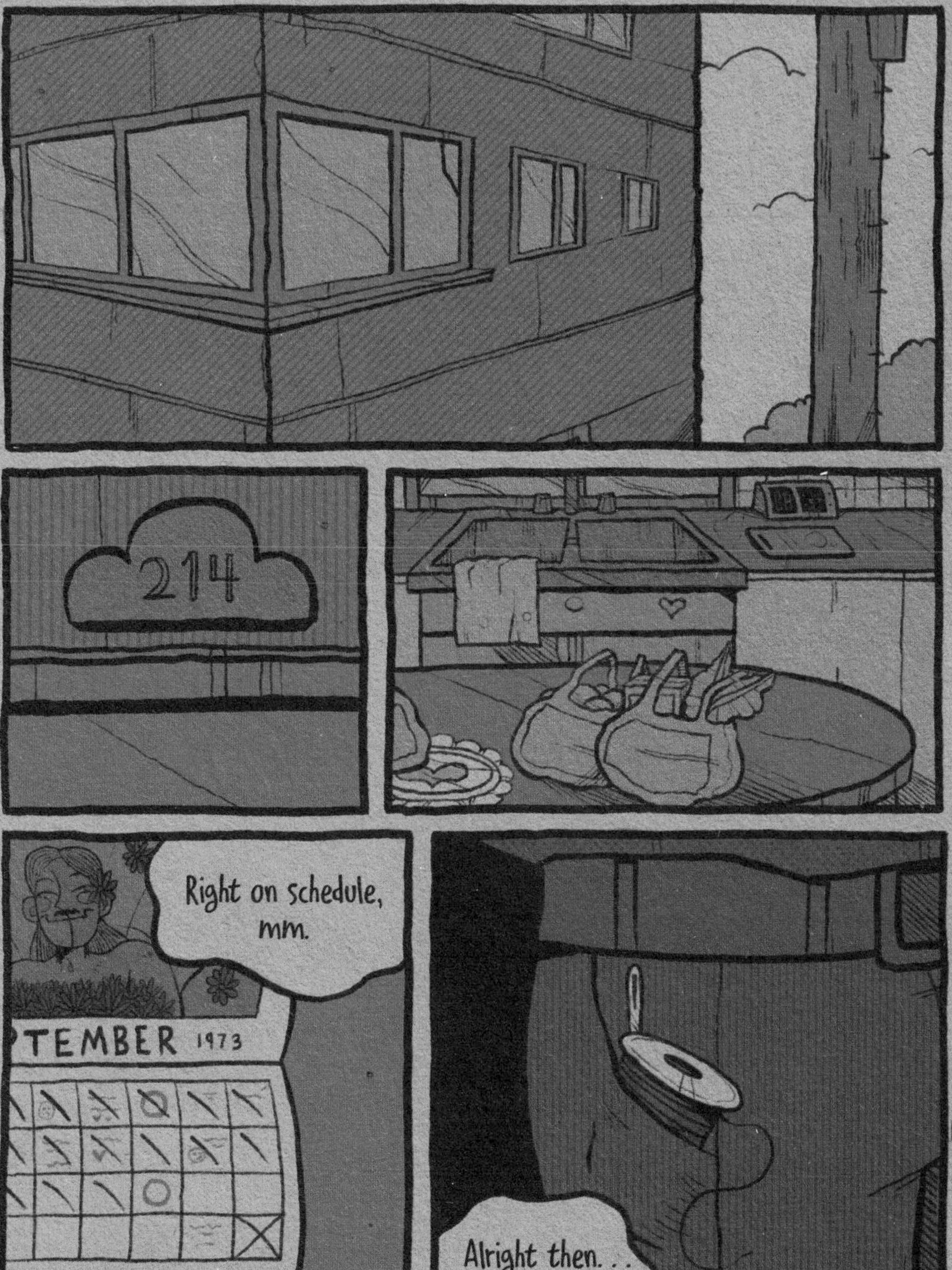
214
Right on schedule, mm.
TEMBER 1973
Alright then. . .

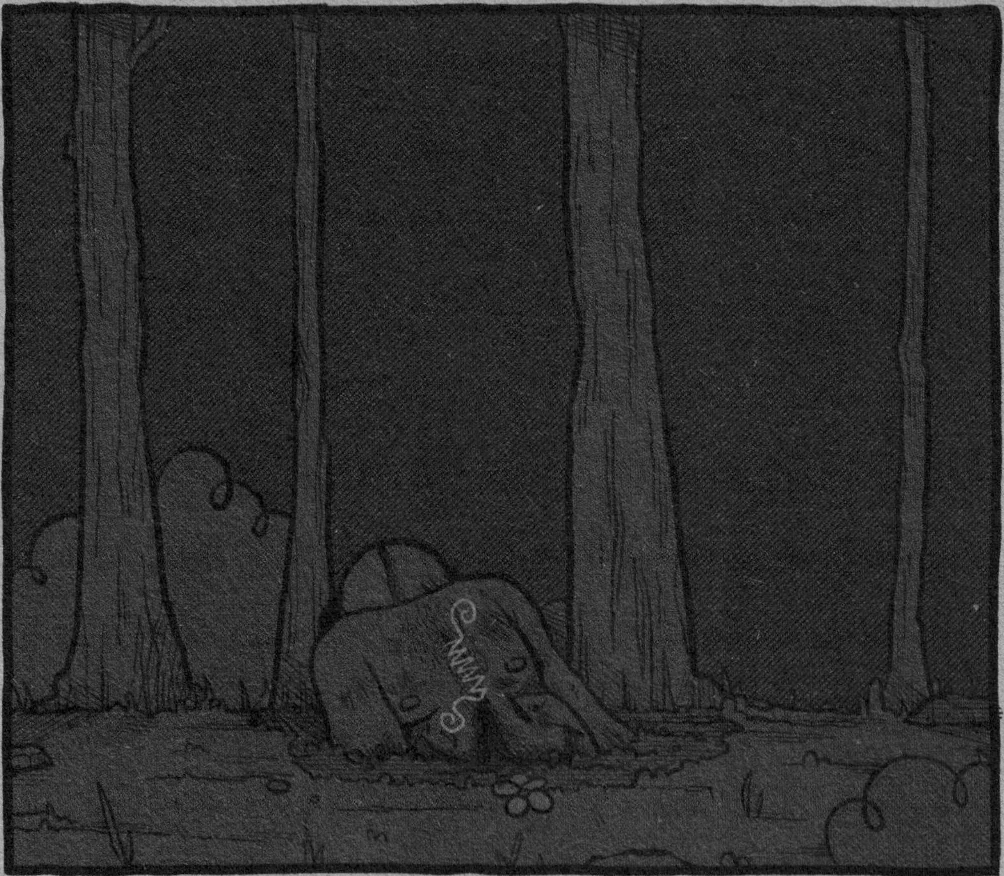

Bye now, Arty.

Vrrrr. . .click!
Hey!
I told you not to record me!
I'm not ready yet. . .
I gotta practice a little more, baby!

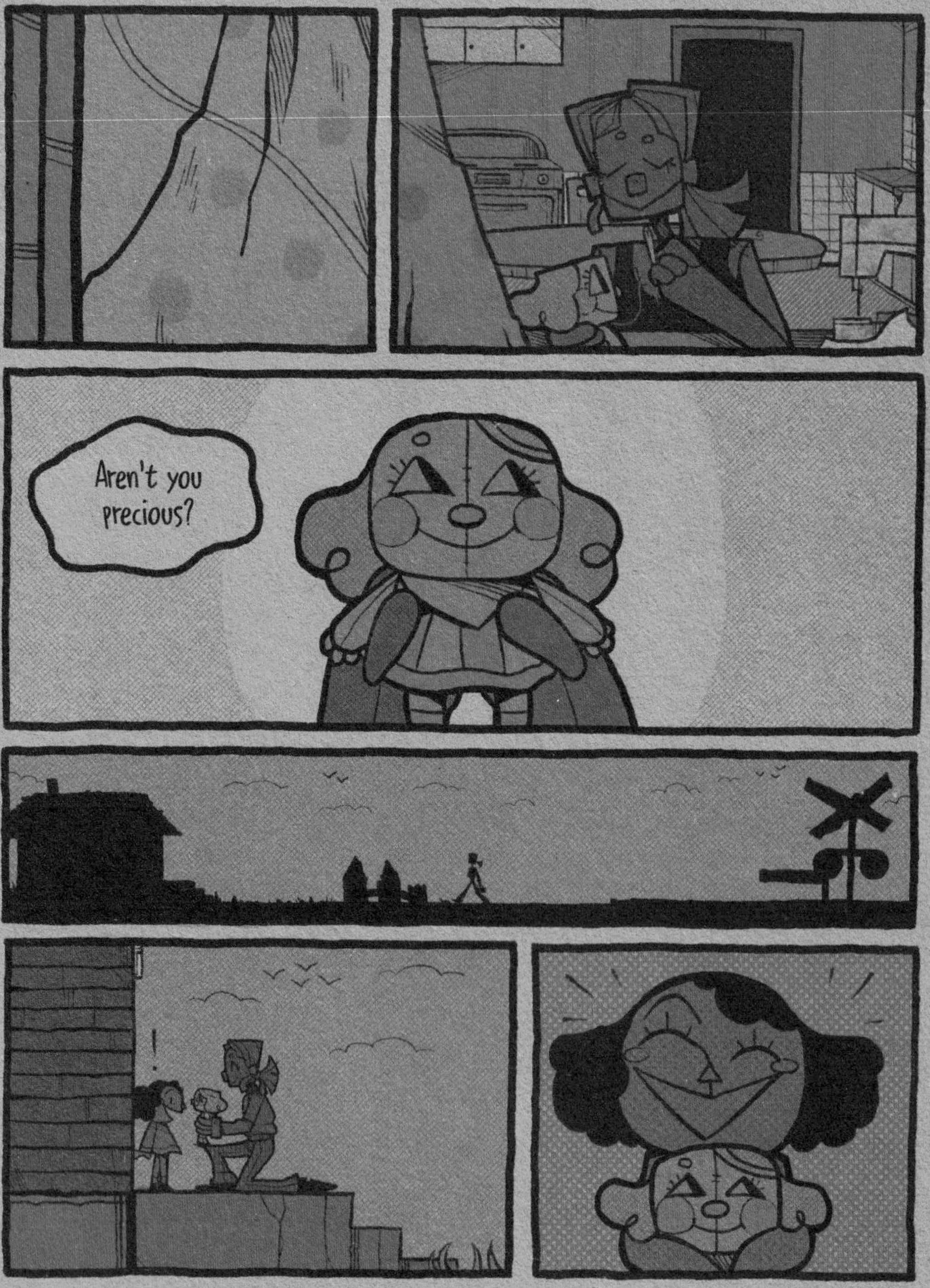
Aren't you precious?
!

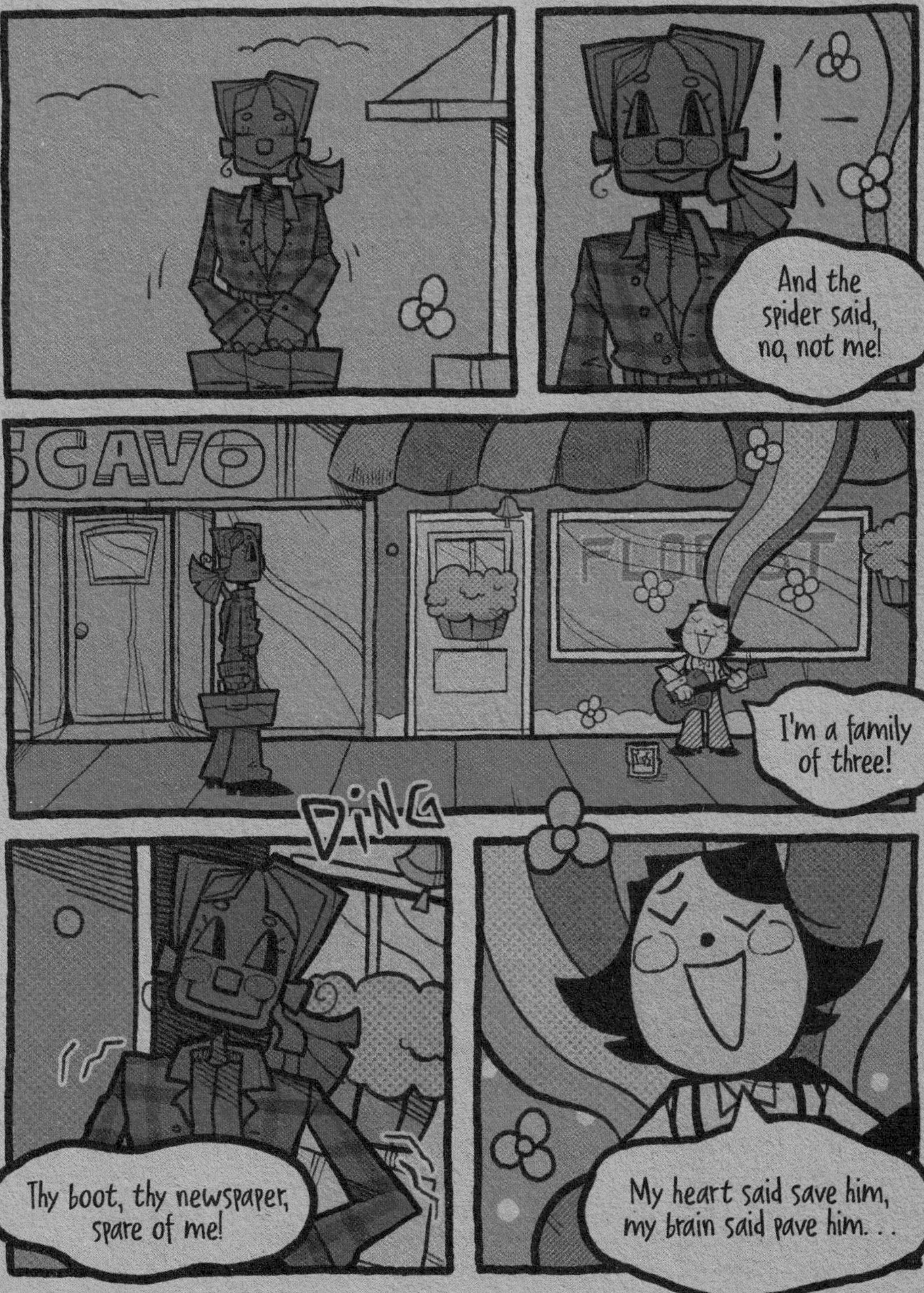
And the spider said, no, not me!
SCAVO
FLORIST
I'm a family of three!
DING
Thy boot, thy newspaper, spare of me!
My heart said save him, my brain said pave him. . .

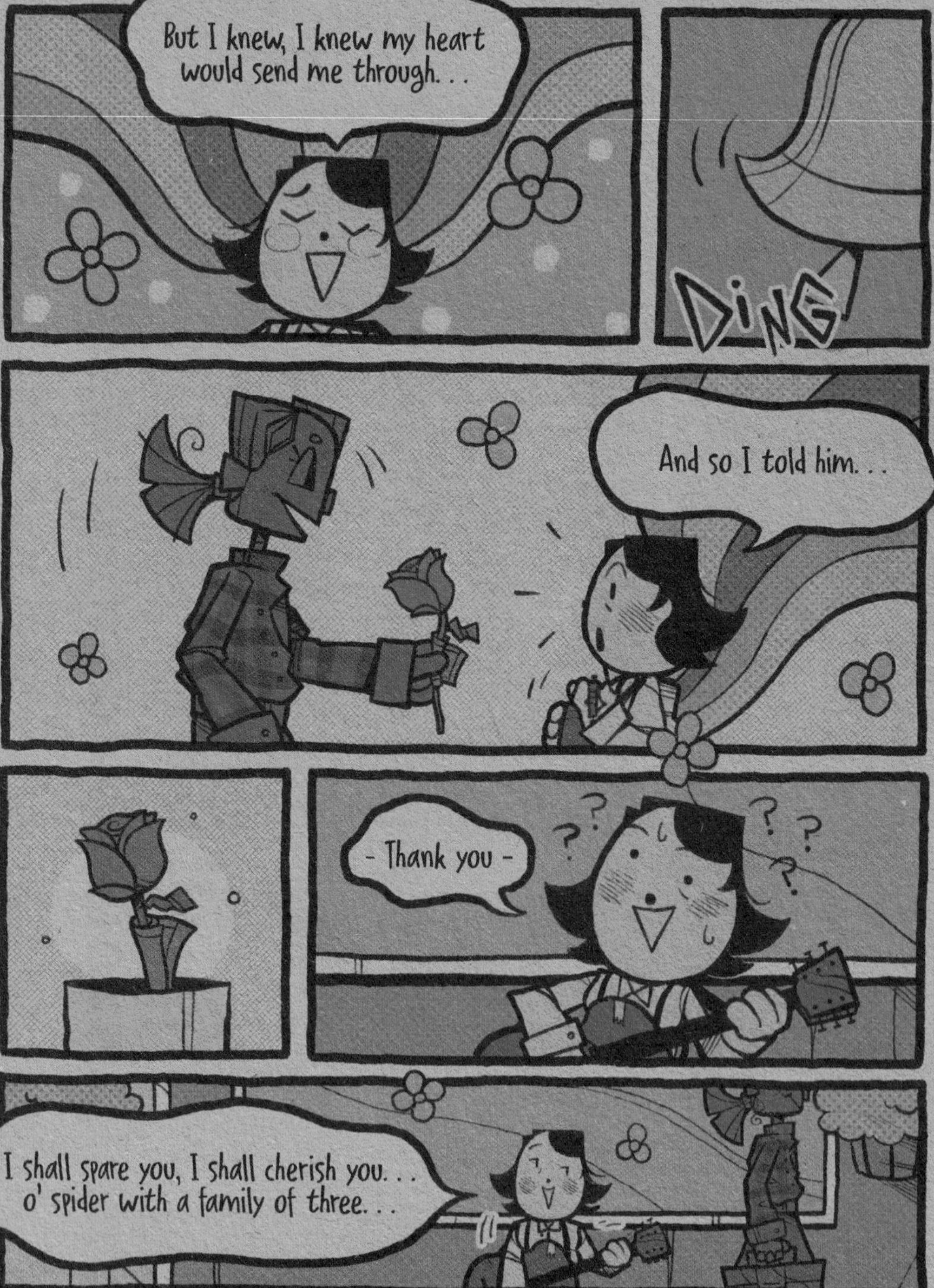
But I knew, I knew my heart would send me through. . .
DING
And so I told him. . .
- Thank you -
I shall spare you, I shall cherish you. . . o' spider with a family of three. . .

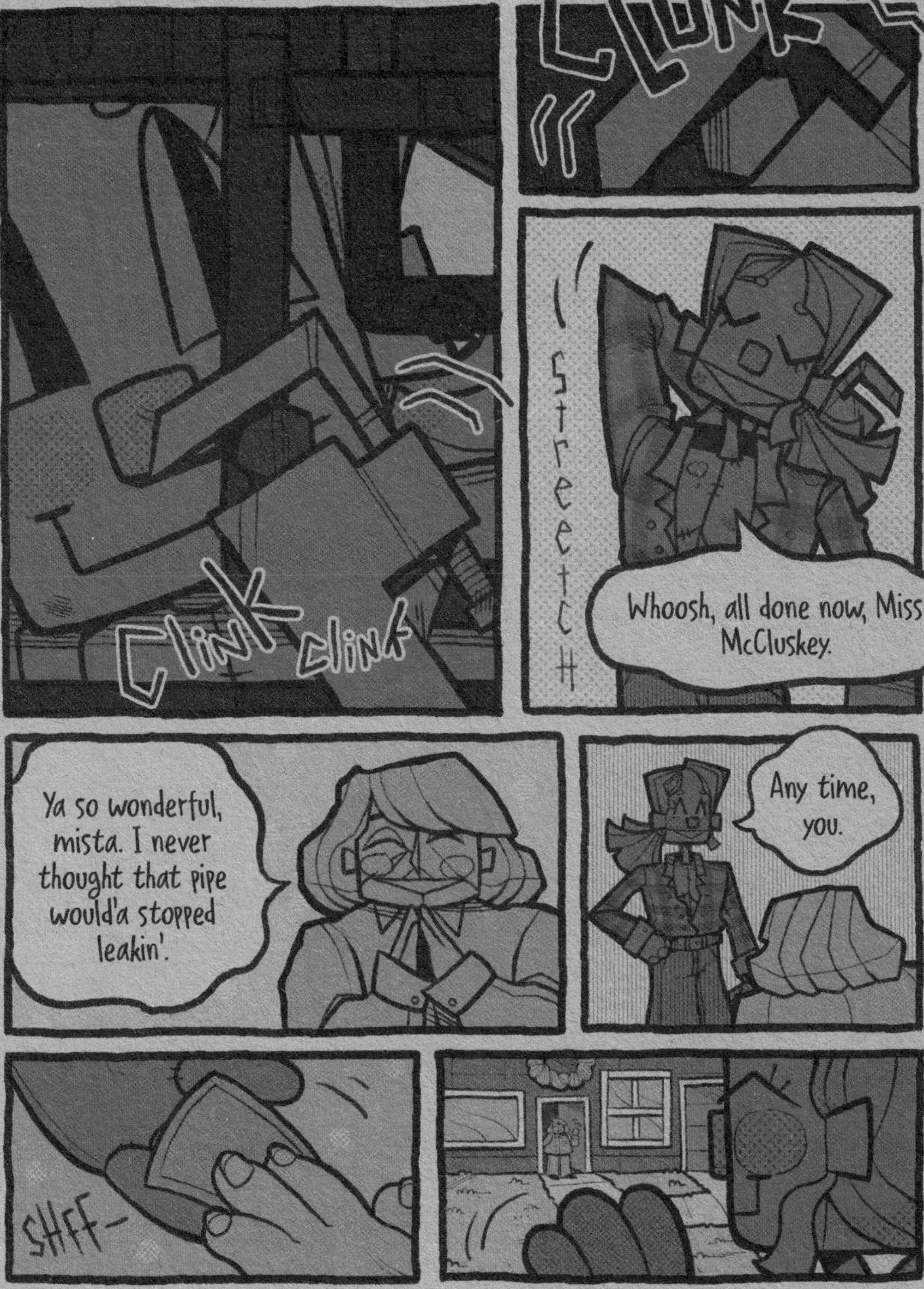
CLUNK
Clink clink
stretch
Whoosh, all done now, Miss McCluskey.
Ya so wonderful, mista. I never thought that pipe would'a stopped leakin'.
Any time, you.
SHFF-

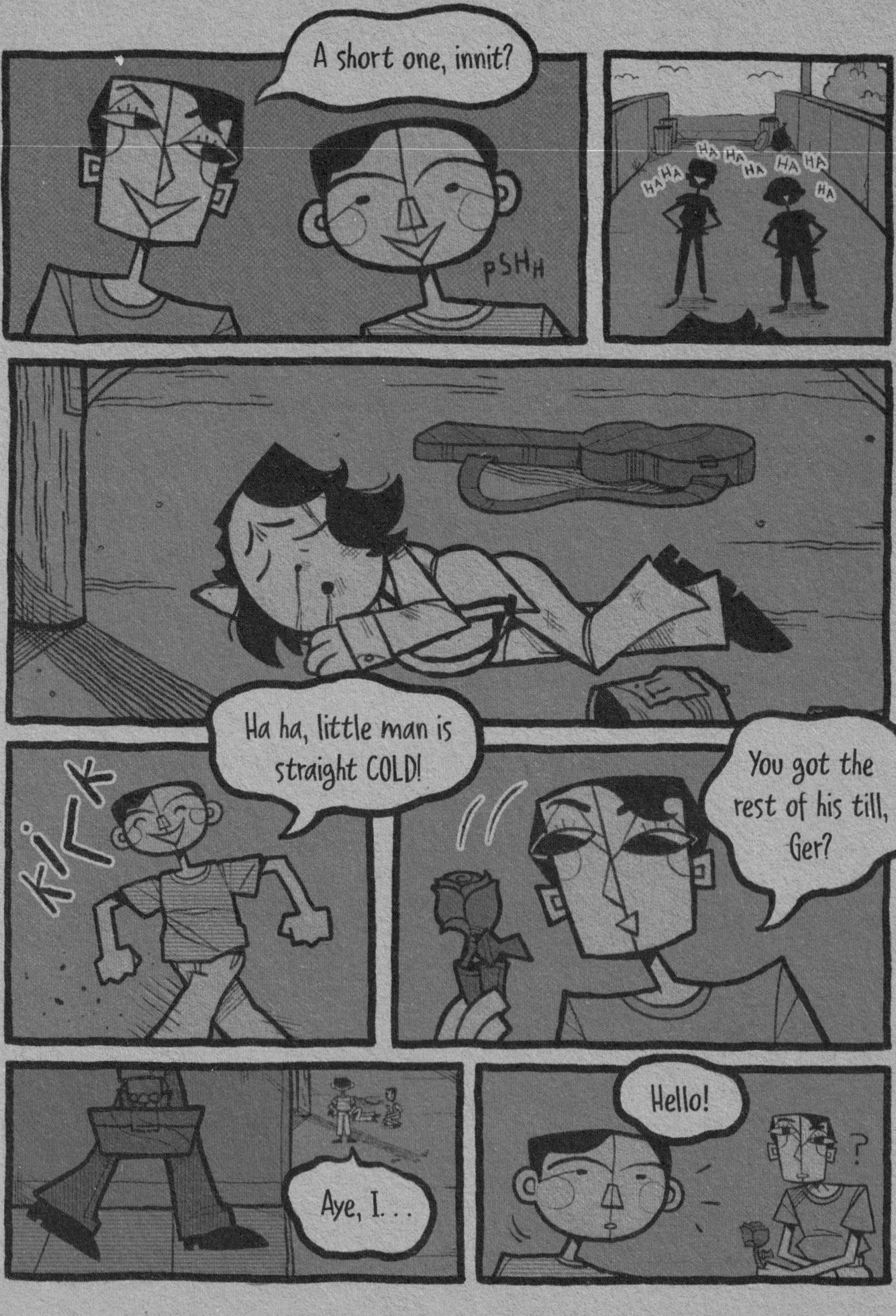
A short one, innit?
PSHH
HA HA HA HA HA HA HA HA HA
Ha ha, little man is straight COLD!
KICK
You got the rest of his till, Ger?
Aye, I. . .
Hello!
?

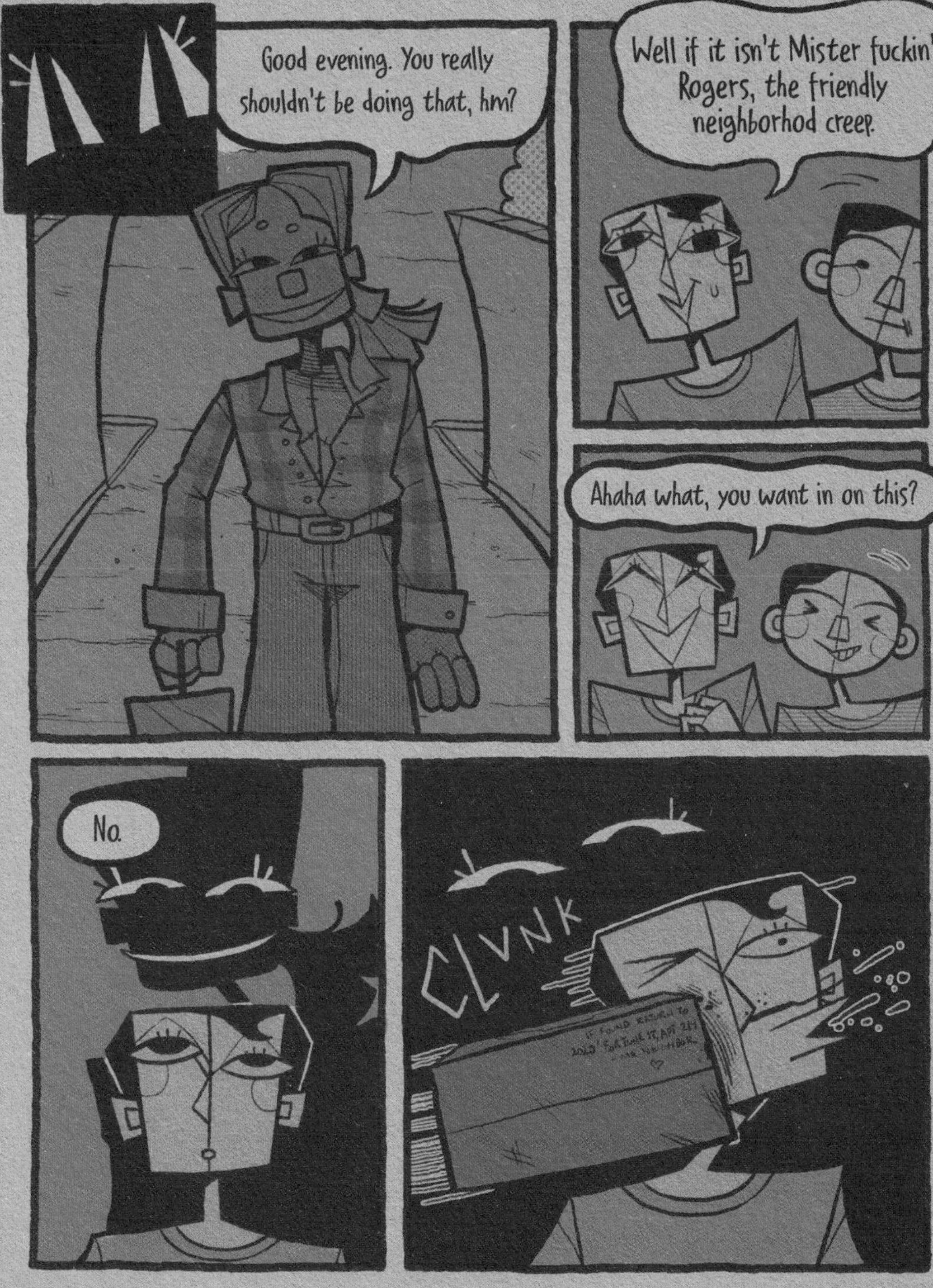
Good evening. You really shouldn't be doing that, hm?
Well if it isn't Mister fuckin' Rogers, the friendly neighborhod creep.
Ahaha what, you want in on this?
No.
CLUNK
IF FOUND RETURN TO

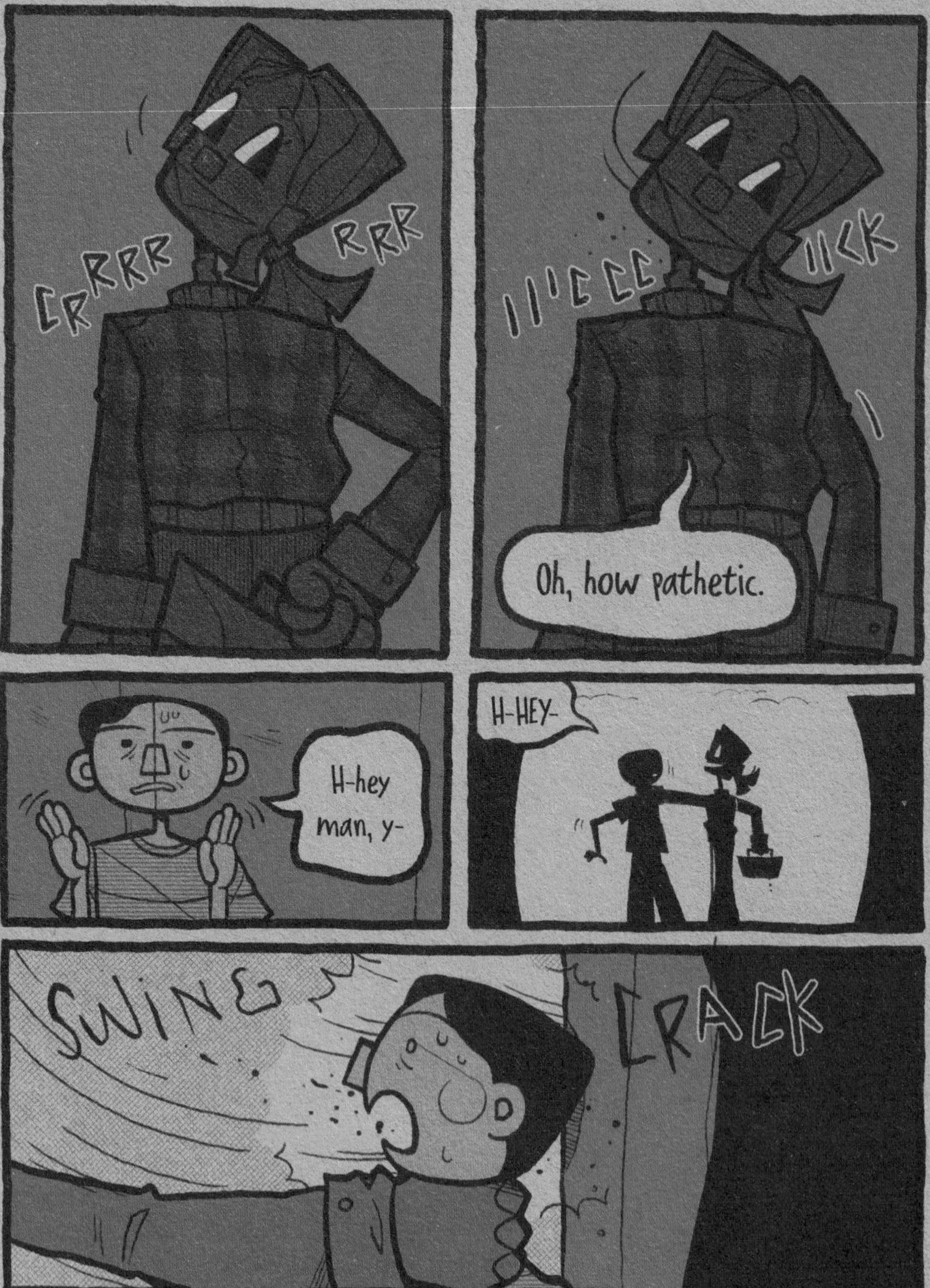
CRRRR RRR
II'CCC IICK
Oh, how pathetic.
H-hey man, y-
H-HEY-
SWING
CRACK

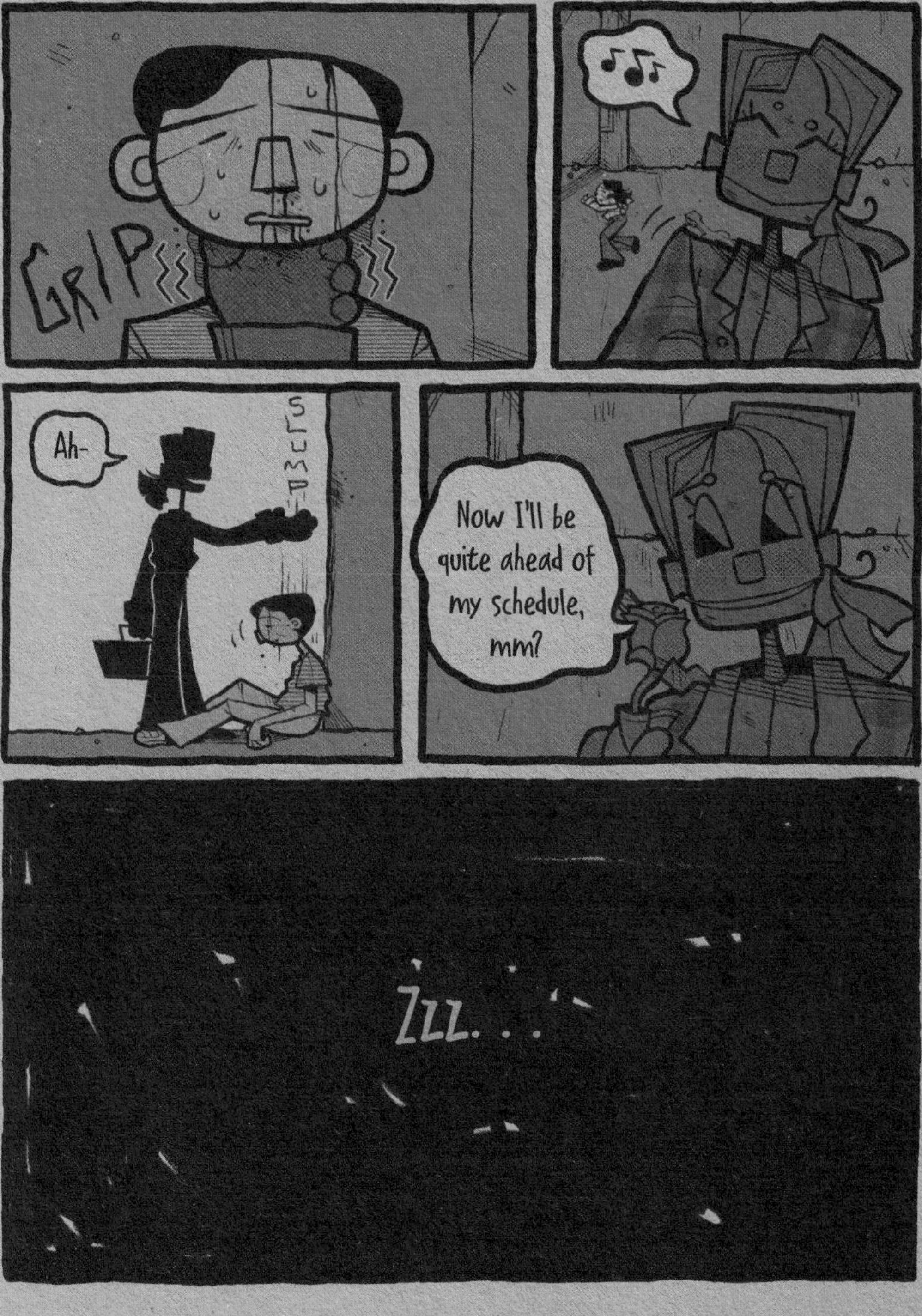
GRIP
Ah-
SLUMP
Now I'll be quite ahead of my schedule, mm?
Zzz. . .

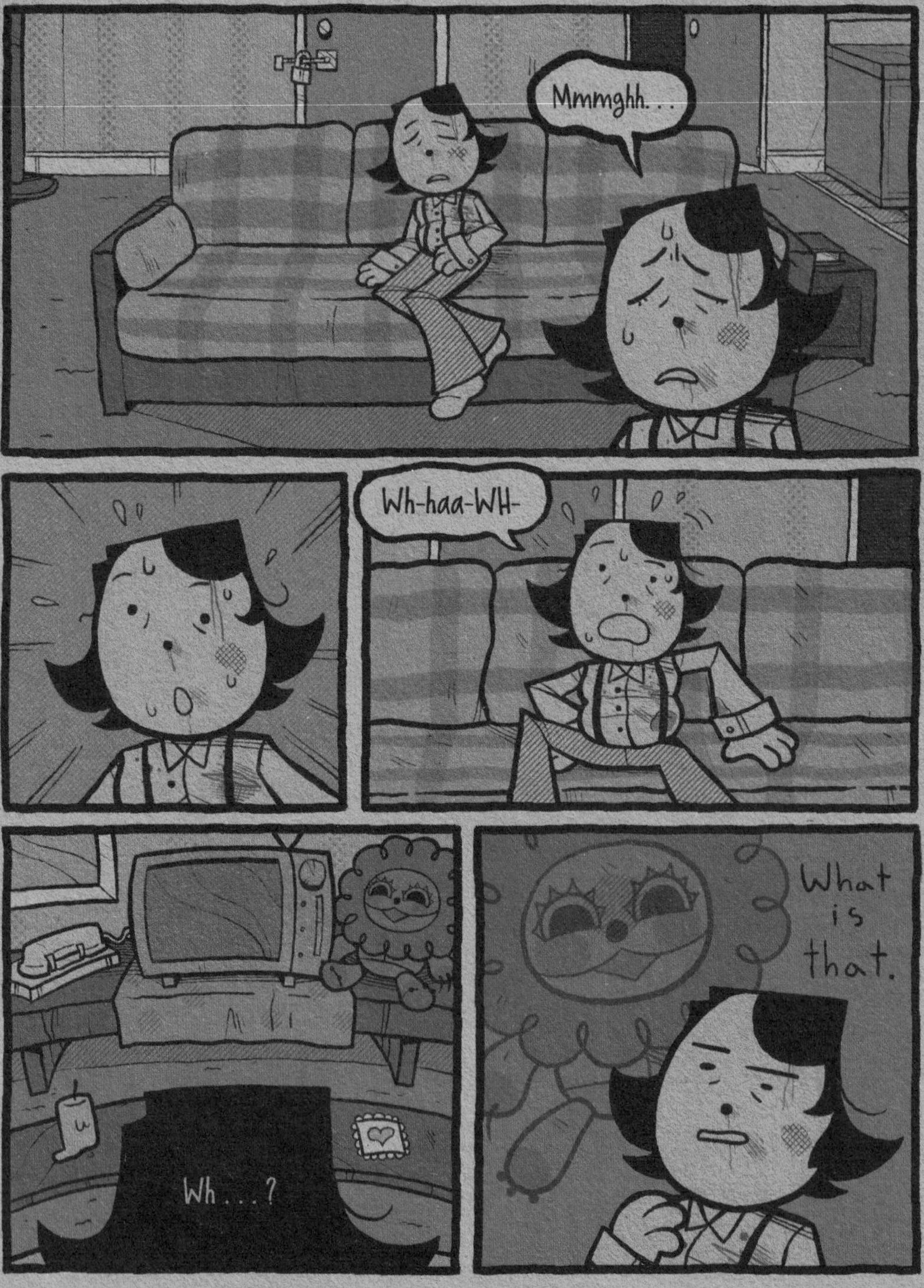
Mmmghh...
Wh-haa-WH-
Wh...?
What is that.

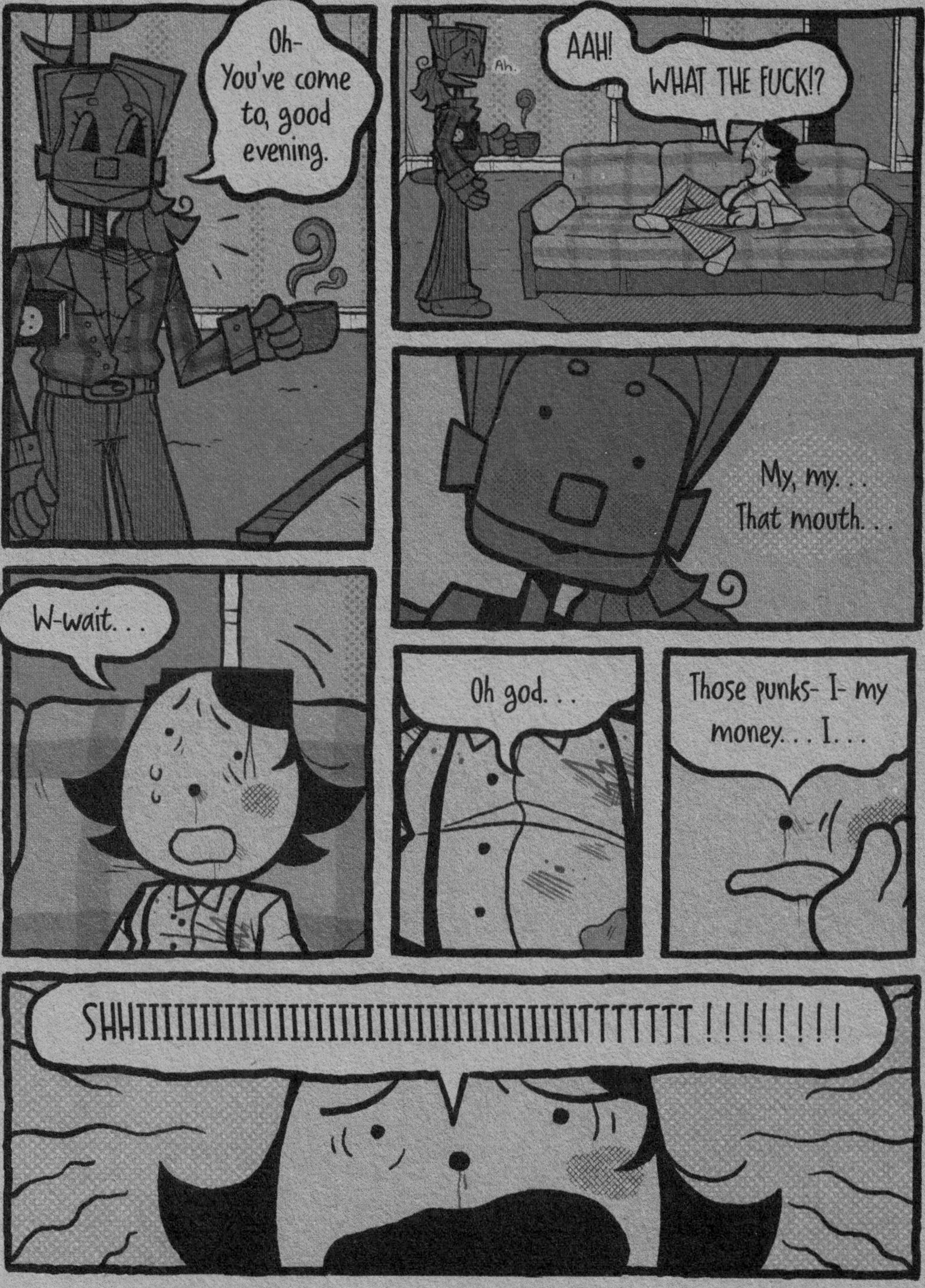
Oh-
You've come to, good evening.
Ah.
AAH!
WHAT THE FUCK!?
My, my. . .
That mouth. . .
W-wait. . .
Oh god. . .
Those punks- I- my money. . . I. . .
SHHIIIIIIIIIIIIIIIIIIIIIIIIIIIIIIIIIIIIIIIIIIITTTTTTT!!!!!!!!

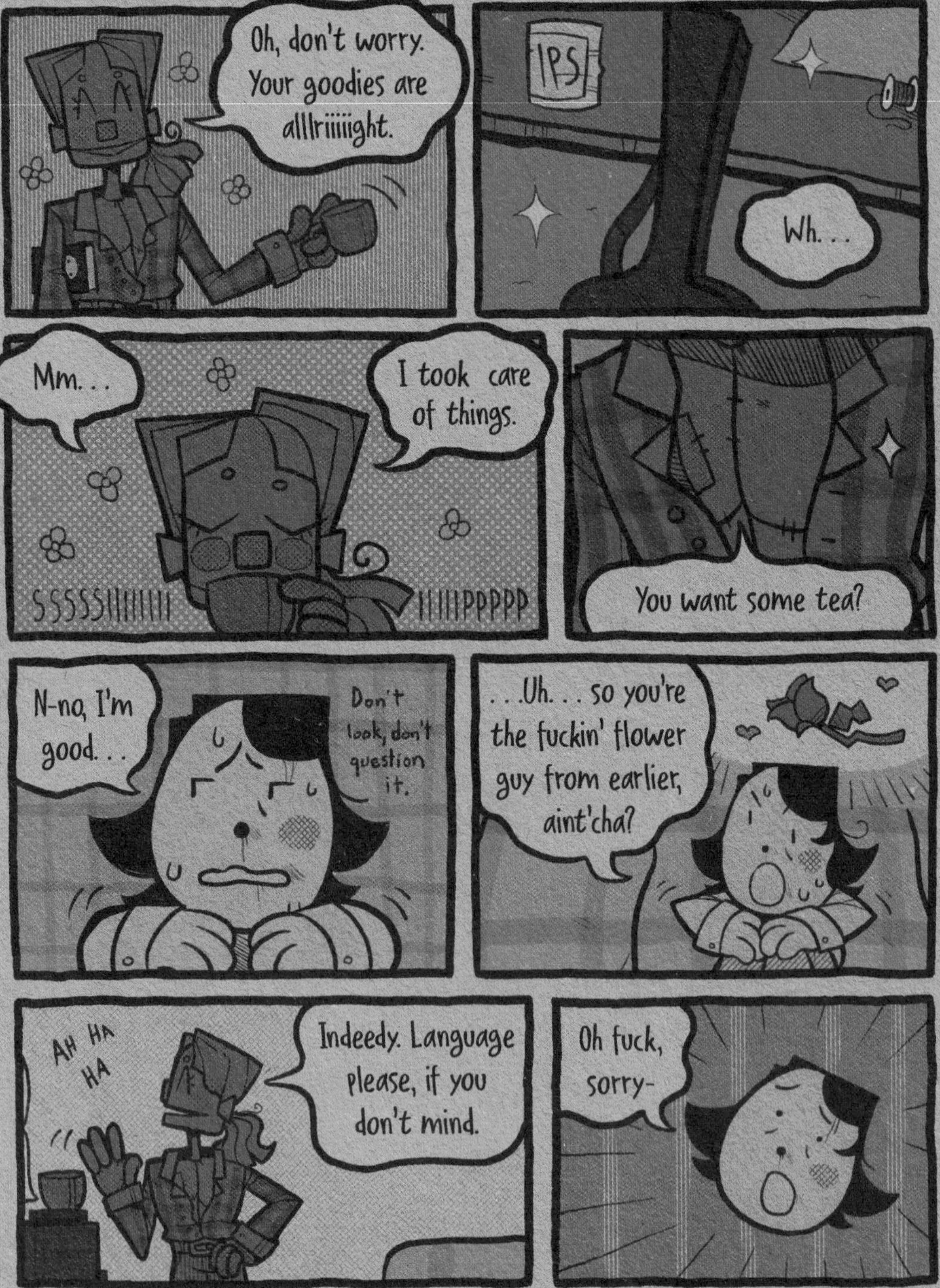
Oh, don't worry. Your goodies are alllriiiiight.
IPS
Wh. . .
Mm. . .
I took care of things.
SSSSSIIIIIII
IIIIIPPPPP
You want some tea?
N-no, I'm good. . .
Don't look, don't question it.
. . .Uh. . . so you're the fuckin' flower guy from earlier, aint'cha?
AH HA HA
Indeedy. Language please, if you don't mind.
Oh fuck, sorry-

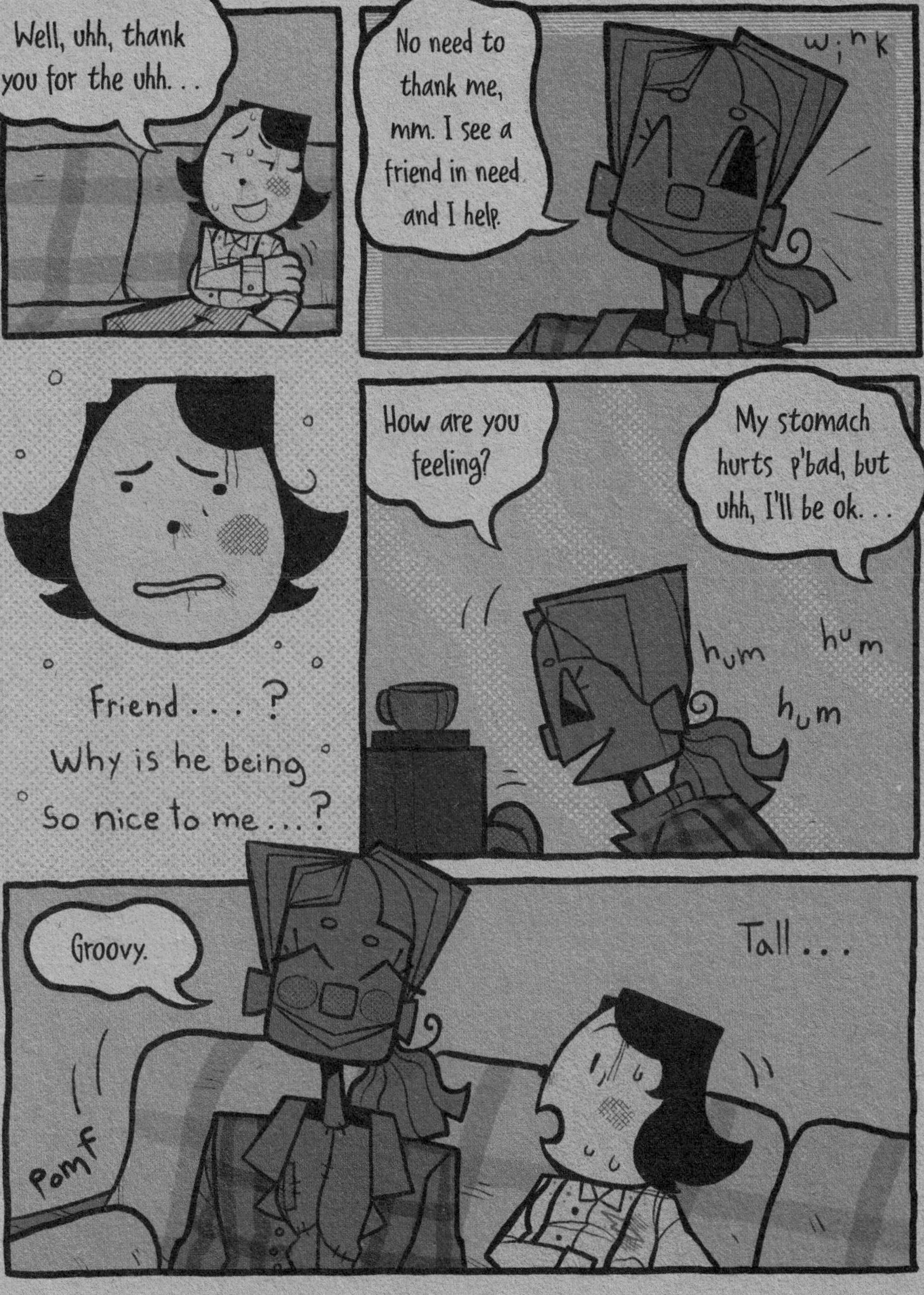
Well, uhh, thank you for the uhh. . .
No need to thank me, mm. I see a friend in need and I help.
wink
Friend . . . ?
Why is he being so nice to me . . . ?
How are you feeling?
My stomach hurts p'bad, but uhh, I'll be ok. . .
hum
hum
hum
Groovy.
Tall . . .
pomf

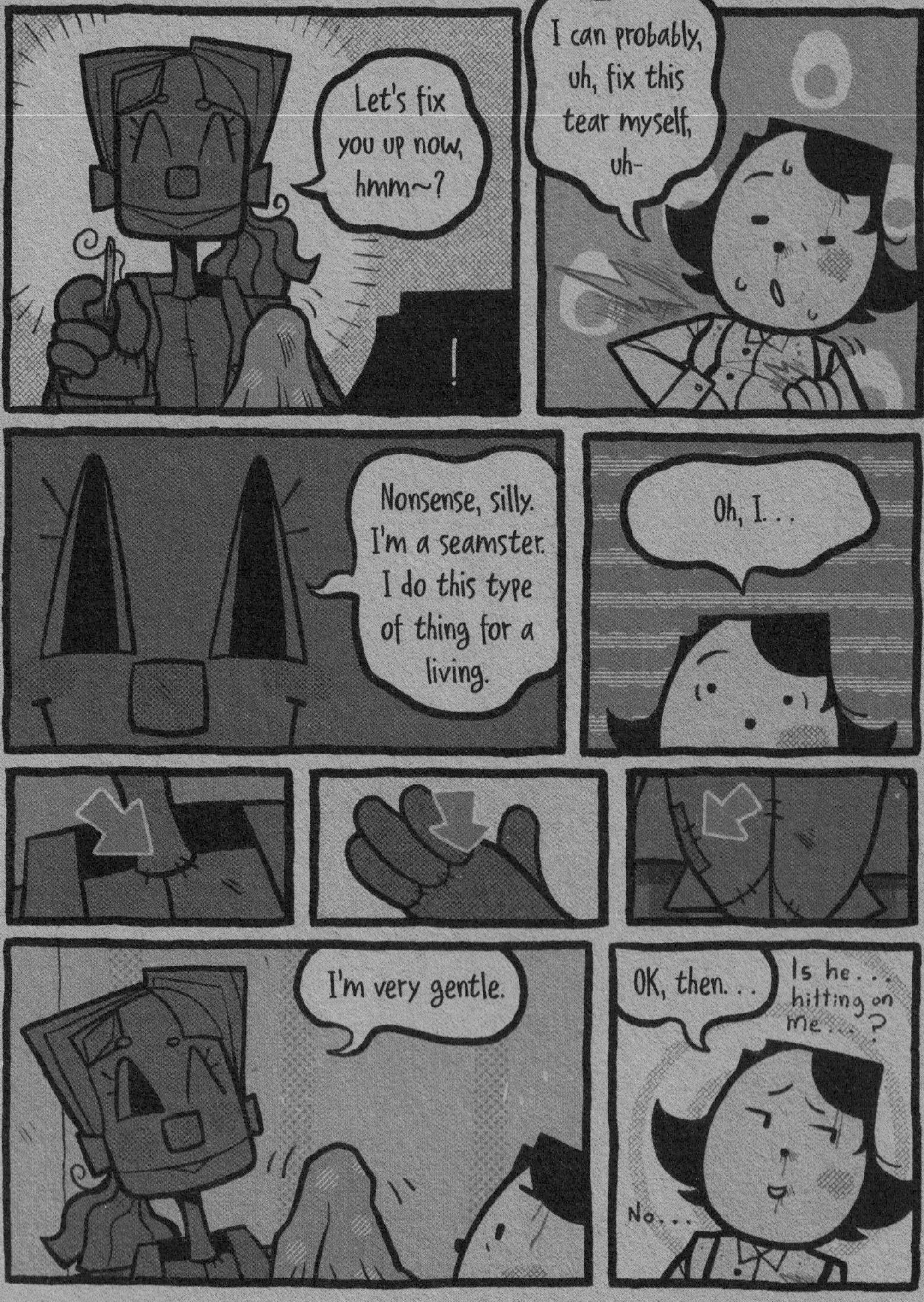
Let's fix you up now, hmm~?
!
I can probably, uh, fix this tear myself, uh-
Nonsense, silly. I'm a seamster. I do this type of thing for a living.
Oh, I. . .
I'm very gentle.
OK, then. . .
Is he. . . hitting on me. . . ?
No. . .

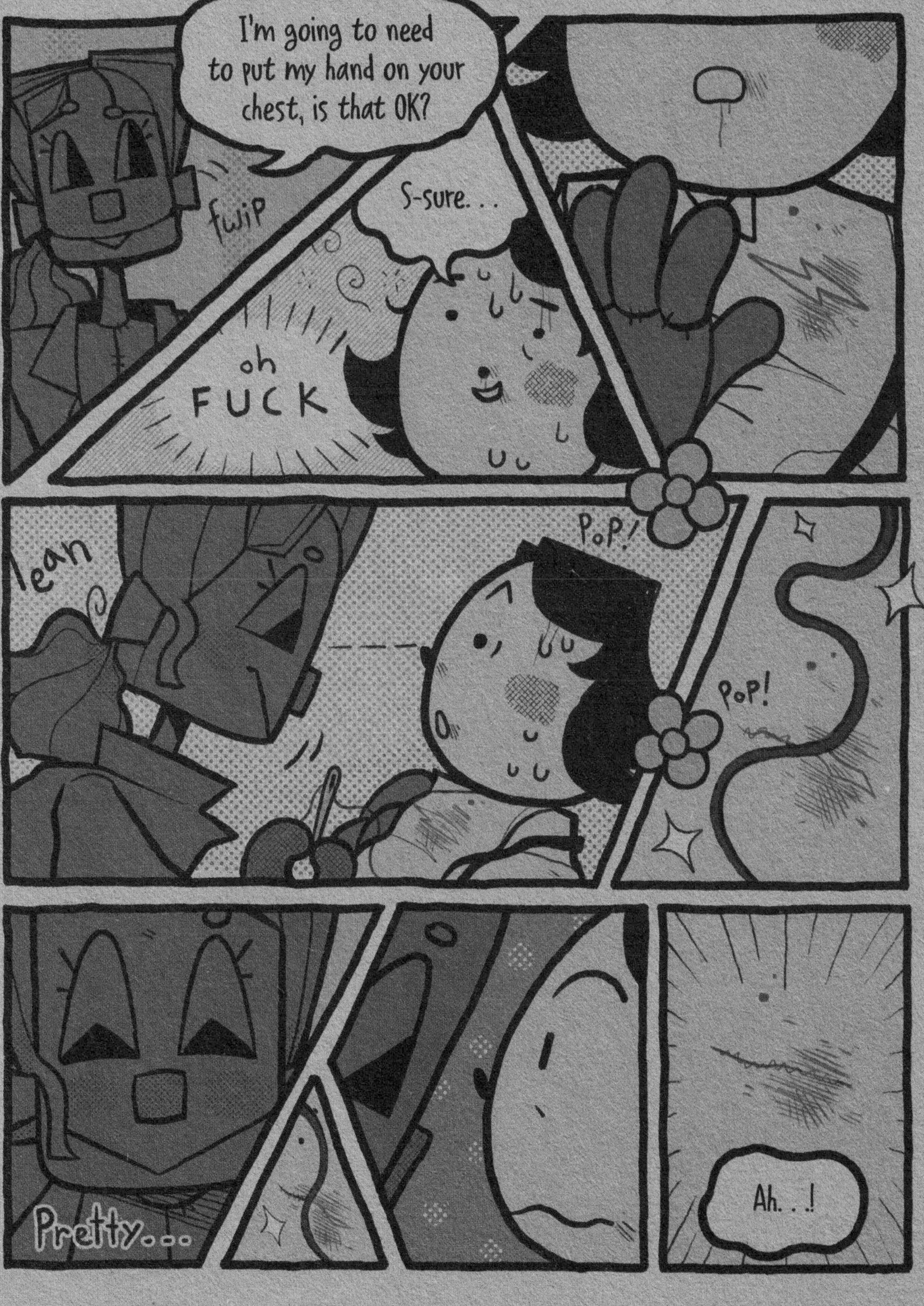
I'm going to need to put my hand on your chest, is that OK?
fwip
S-sure. . .
oh FUCK
lean
PoP!
PoP!
Pretty...
Ah. . .!

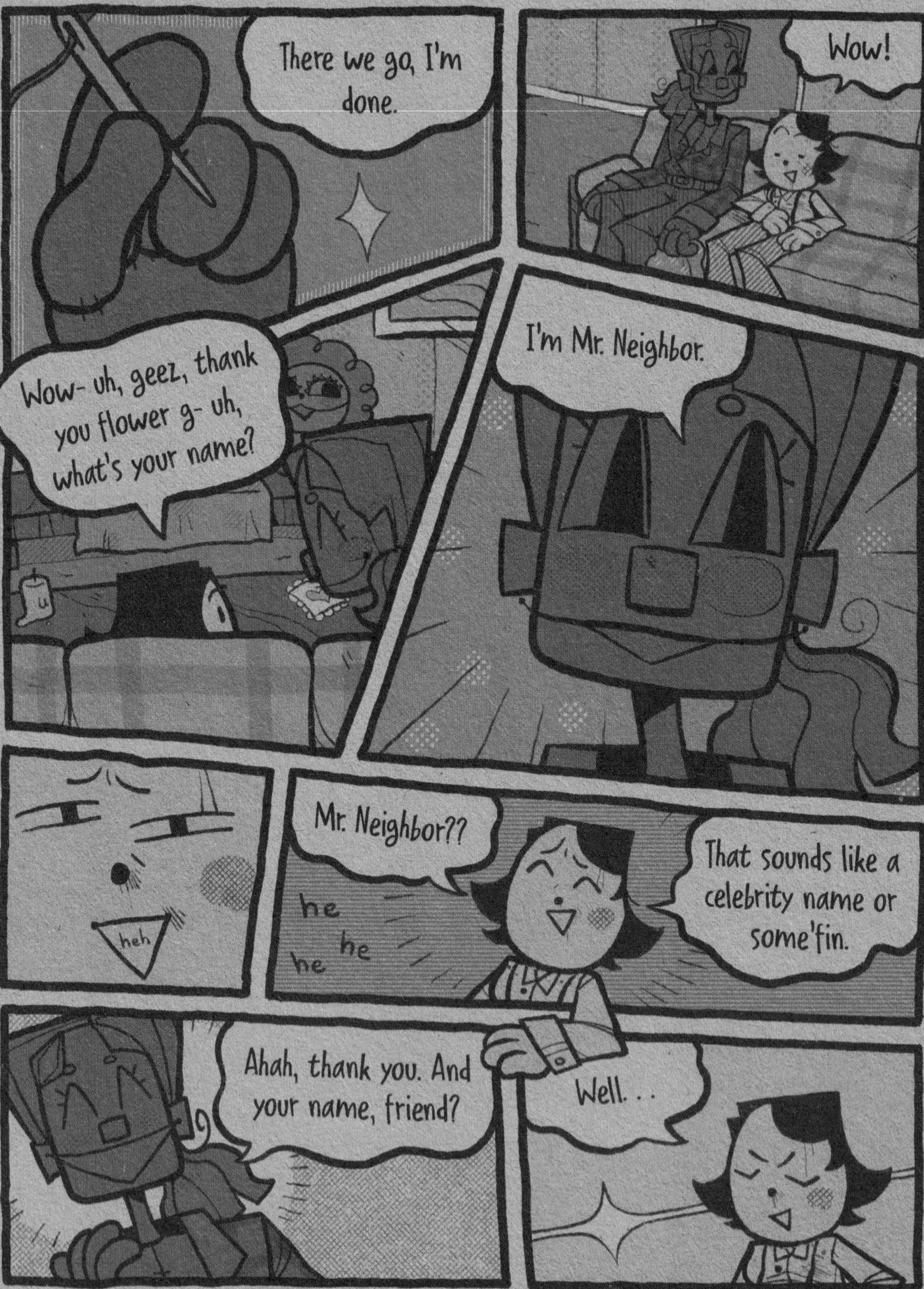
There we go, I'm done.
Wow!
Wow- uh, geez, thank you flower g- uh, what's your name?
I'm Mr. Neighbor.
heh
Mr. Neighbor??
he he he
That sounds like a celebrity name or some'fin.
Ahah, thank you. And your name, friend?
Well. . .

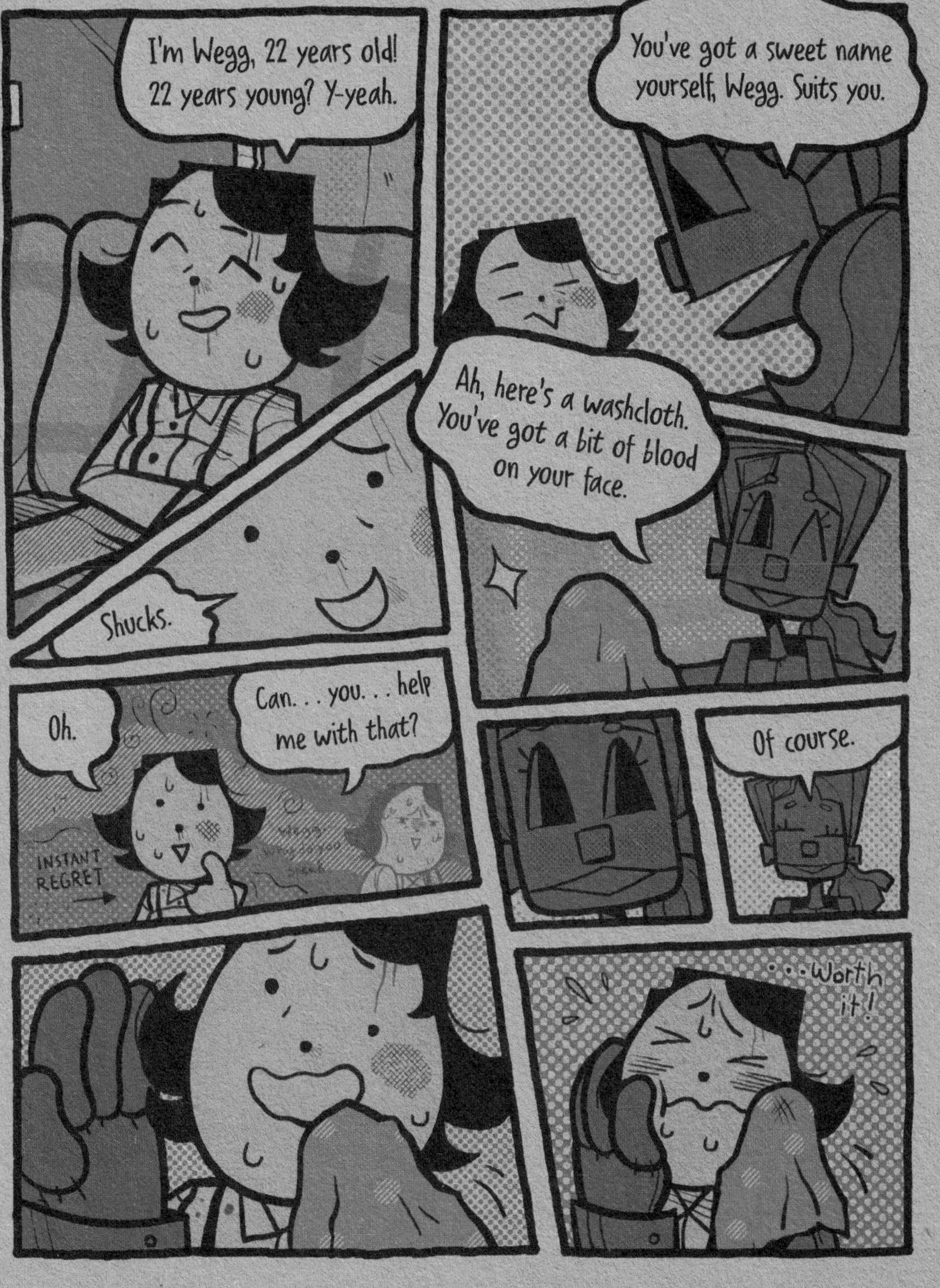
I'm Wegg, 22 years old! 22 years young? Y-yeah.
You've got a sweet name yourself, Wegg. Suits you.
Shucks.
Ah, here's a washcloth. You've got a bit of blood on your face.
Oh.
Can. . . you. . . help me with that?
INSTANT REGRET
Of course.
. . . Worth it!

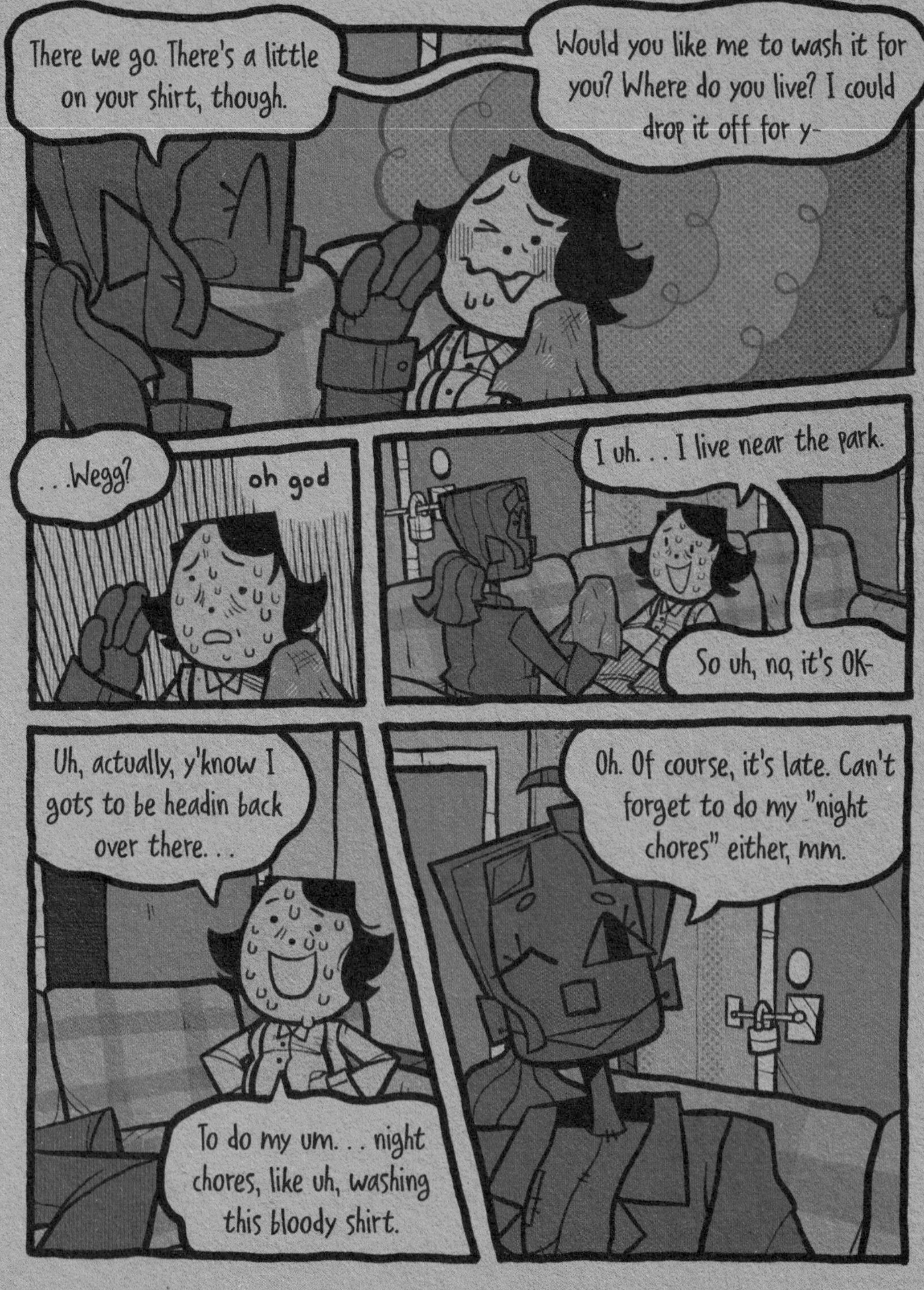
There we go. There's a little on your shirt, though.
Would you like me to wash it for you? Where do you live? I could drop it off for y-
. . .Wegg?
oh god
I uh. . . I live near the park.
So uh, no, it's OK-
Uh, actually, y'know I gots to be headin back over there. . .
To do my um. . . night chores, like uh, washing this bloody shirt.
Oh. Of course, it's late. Can't forget to do my "night chores" either, mm.

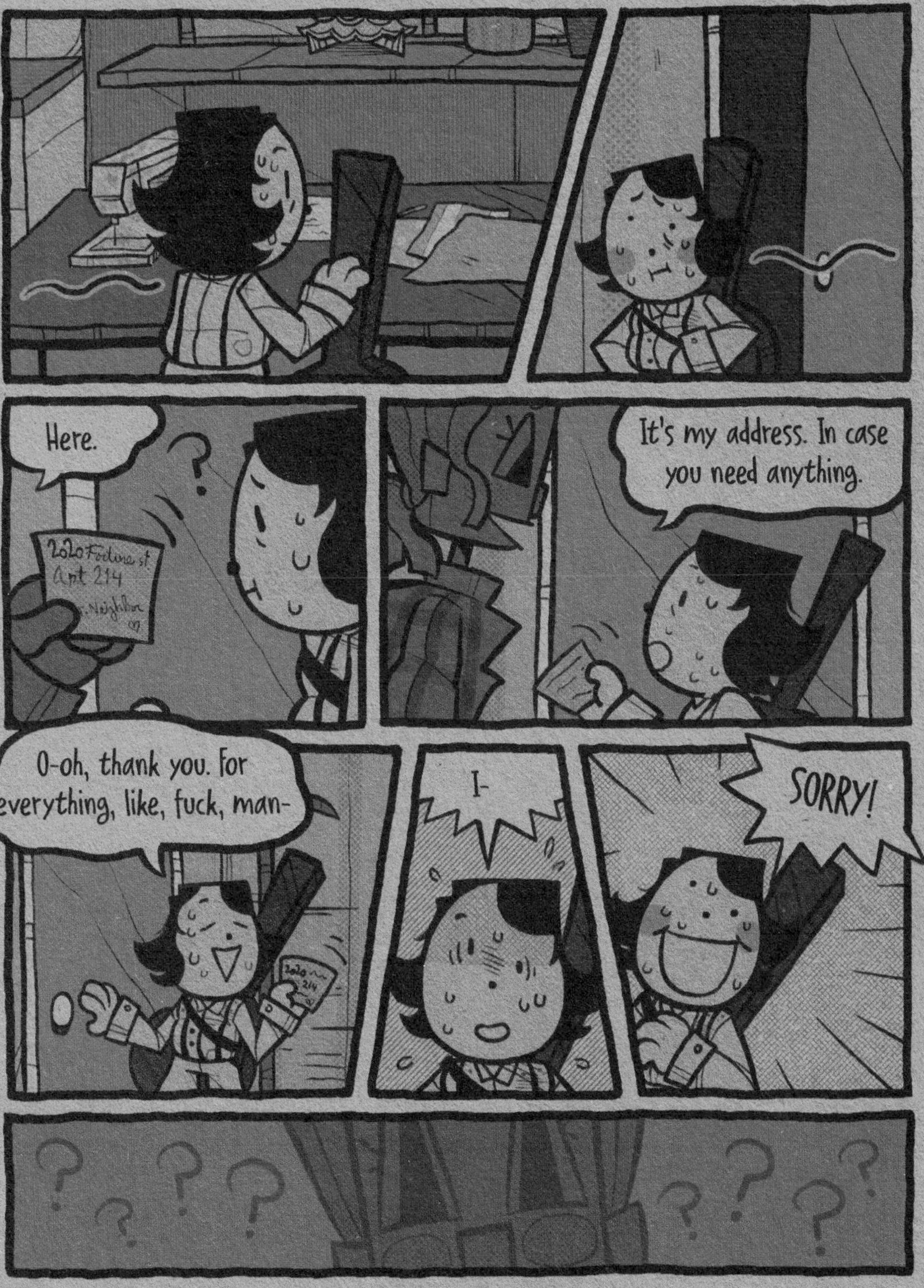
Here.
2020 Fortune st.
Apt 214
Neighbor
It's my address. In case you need anything.
O-oh, thank you. For everything, like, fuck, man-
I-
SORRY!

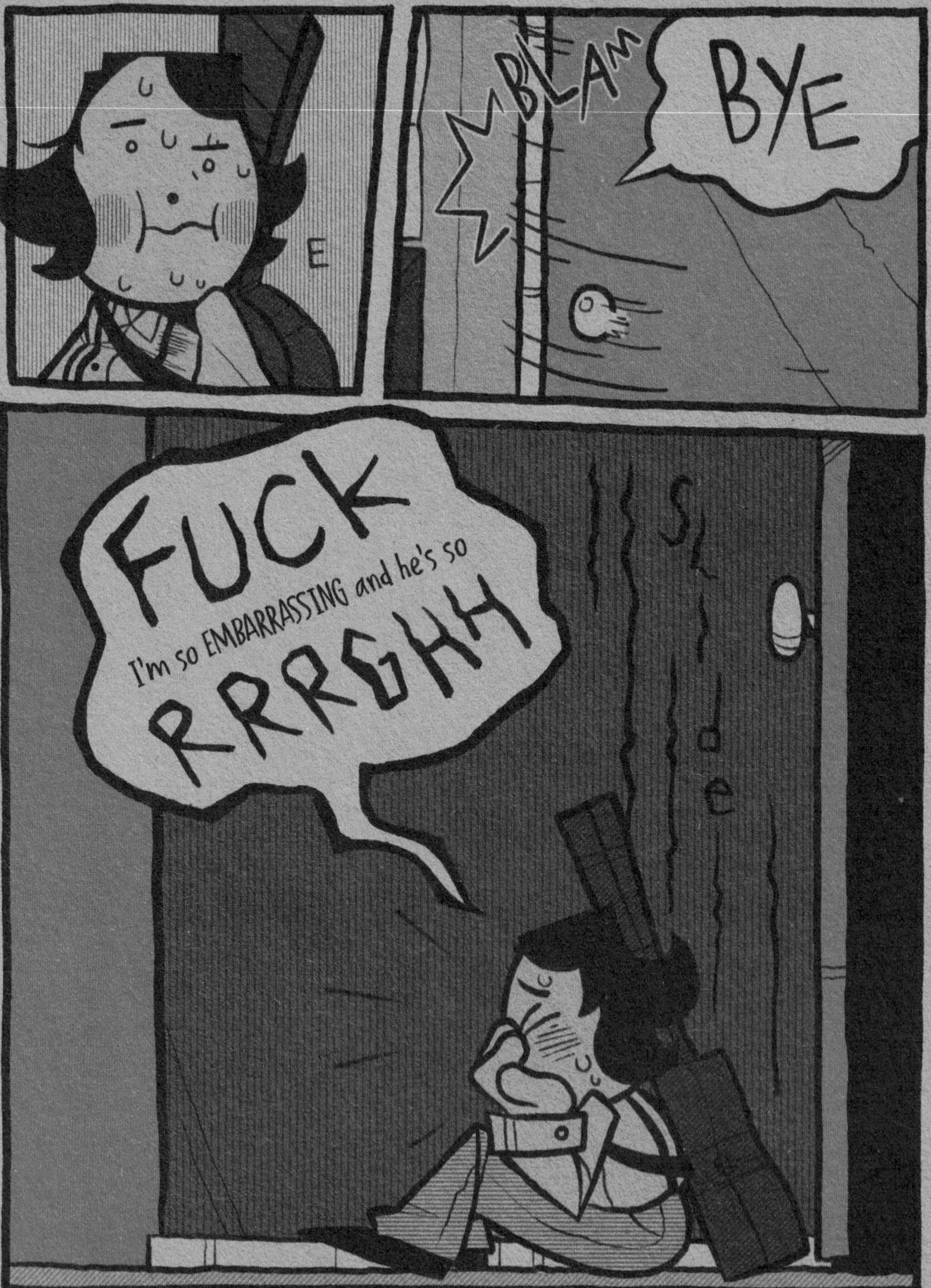
E
BLAM
BYE
FUCK
I'm so EMBARRASSING and he's so
RRRGHH
slide

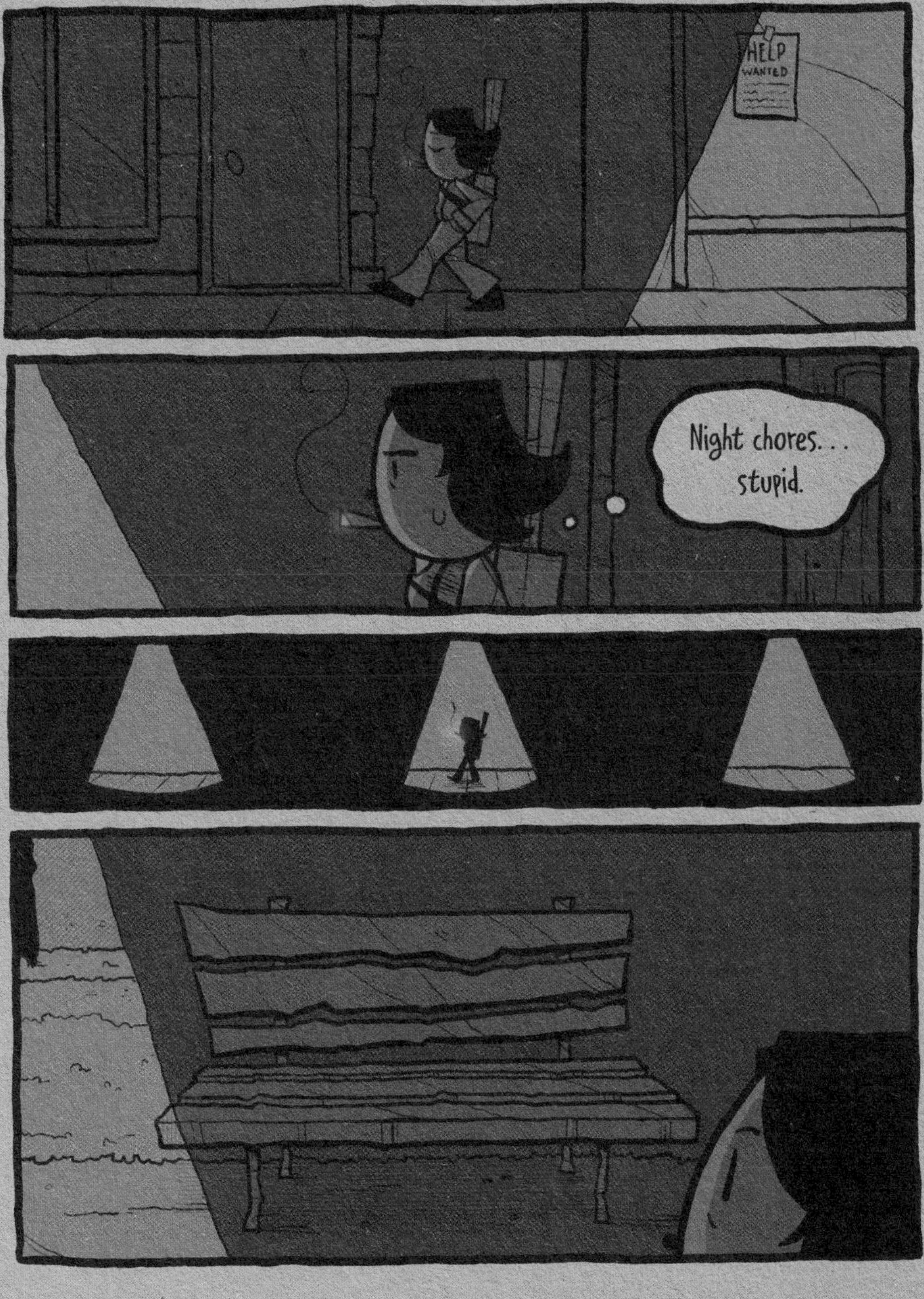
HELP WANTED
Night chores...
...stupid.

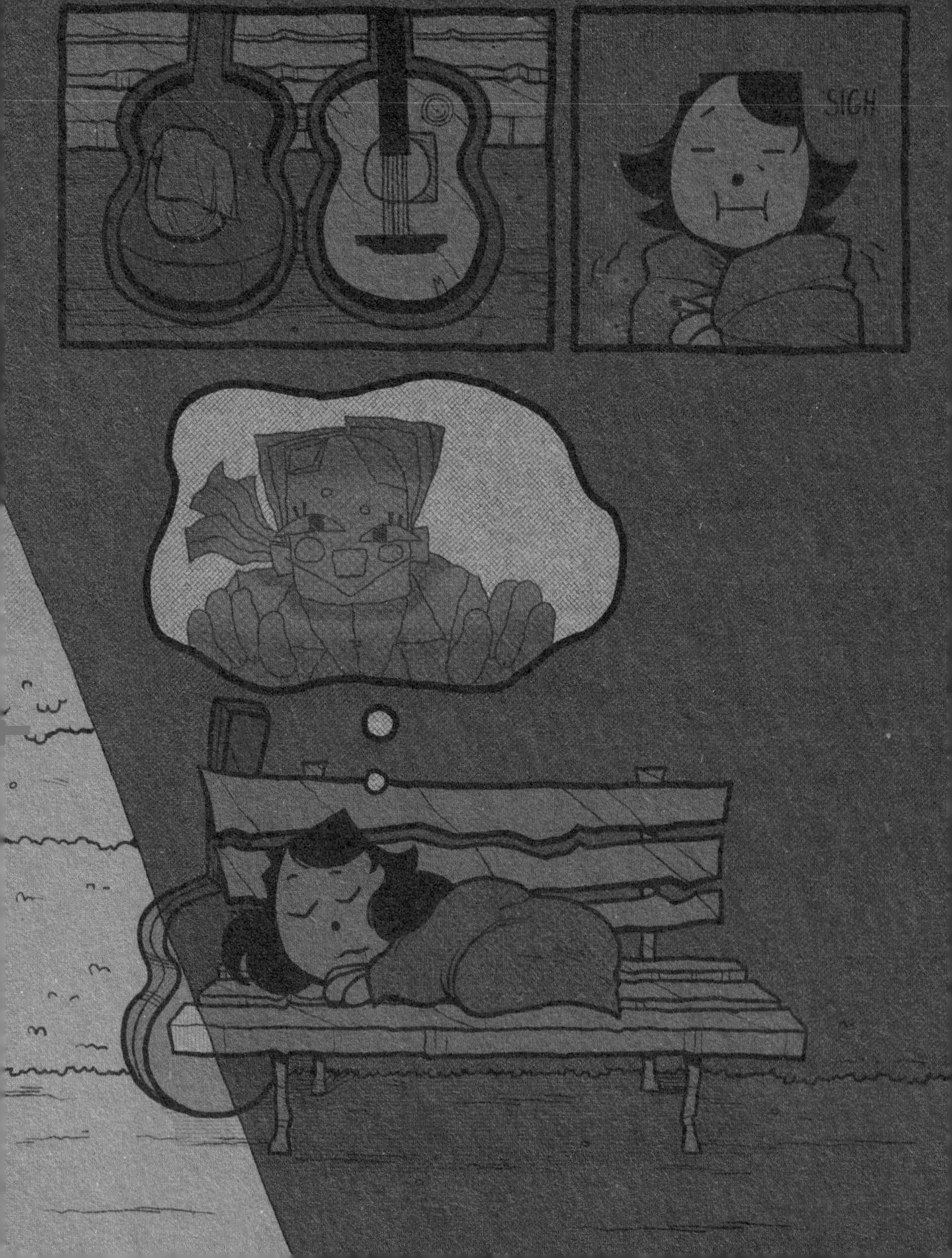
SIGH

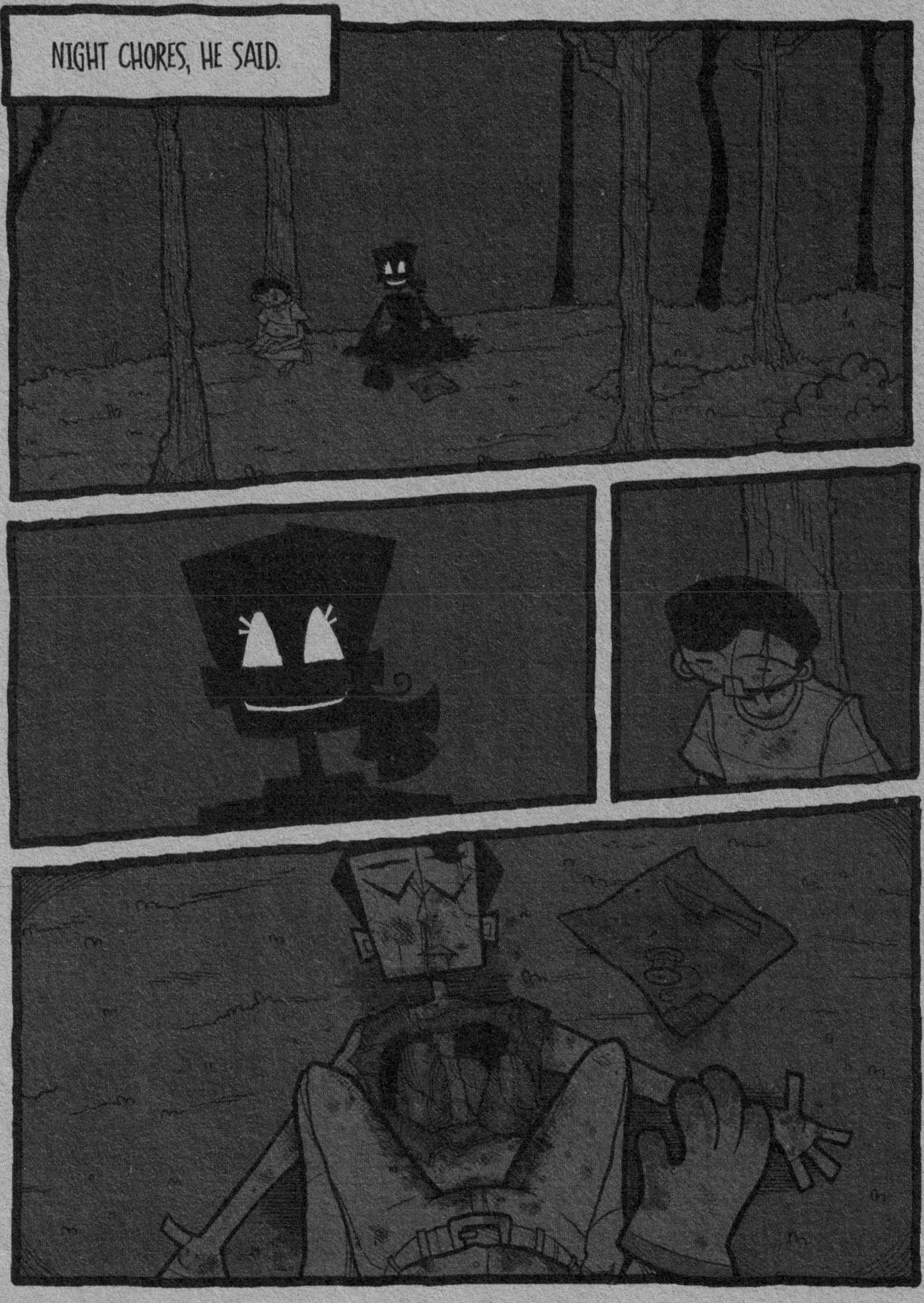
NIGHT CHORES, HE SAID.

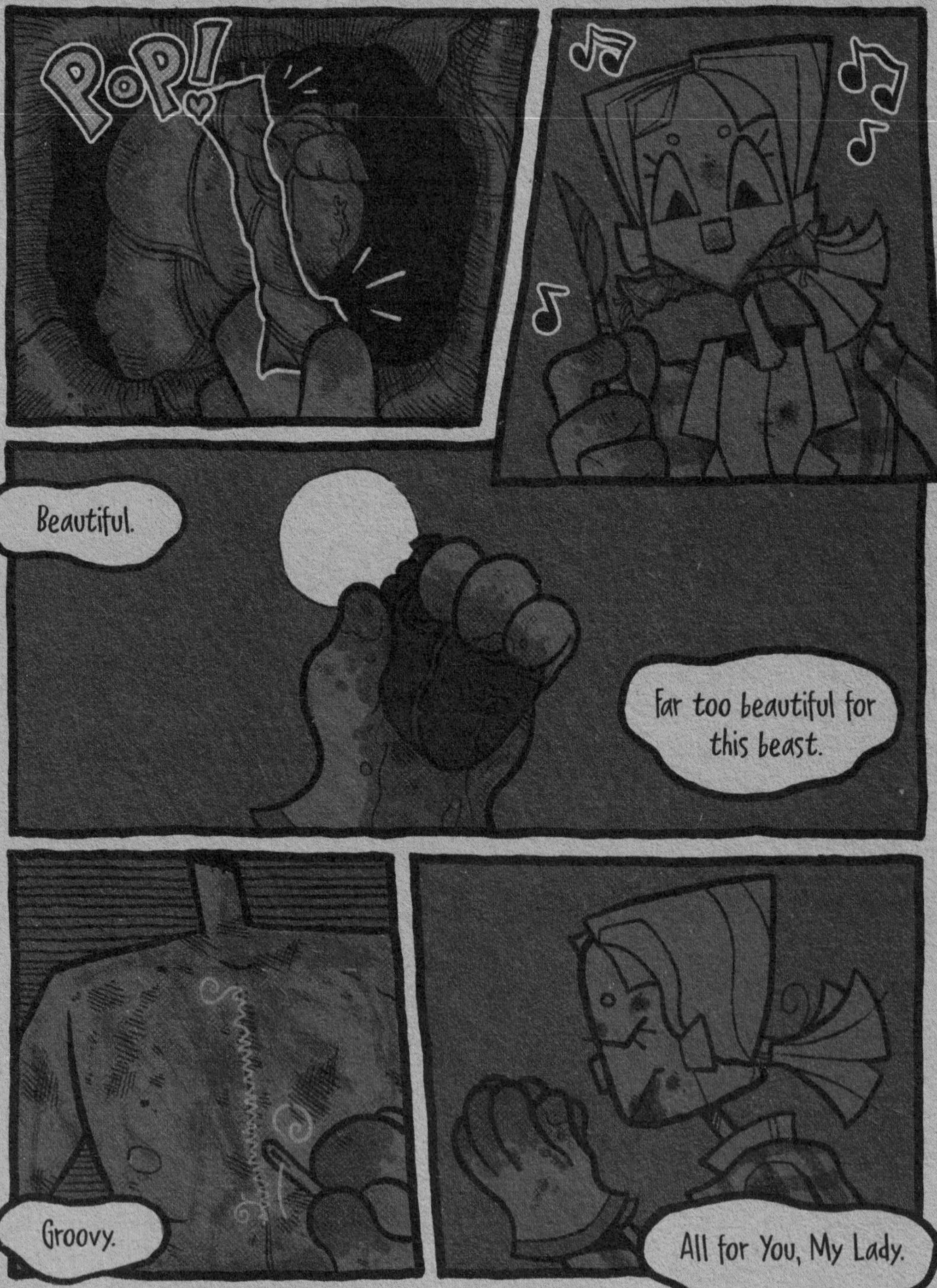
POP!
Beautiful.
Far too beautiful for this beast.
Groovy.
All for You, My Lady.

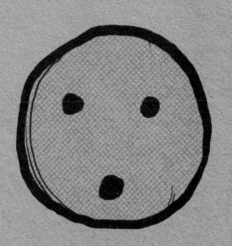

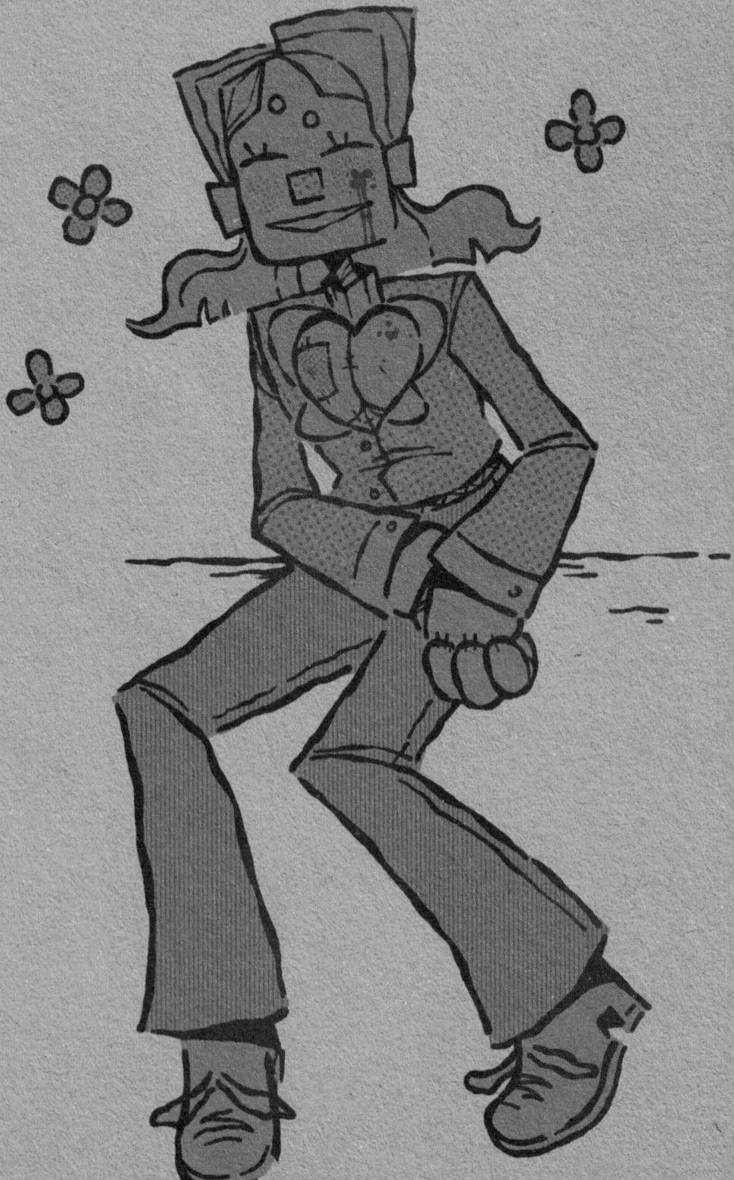

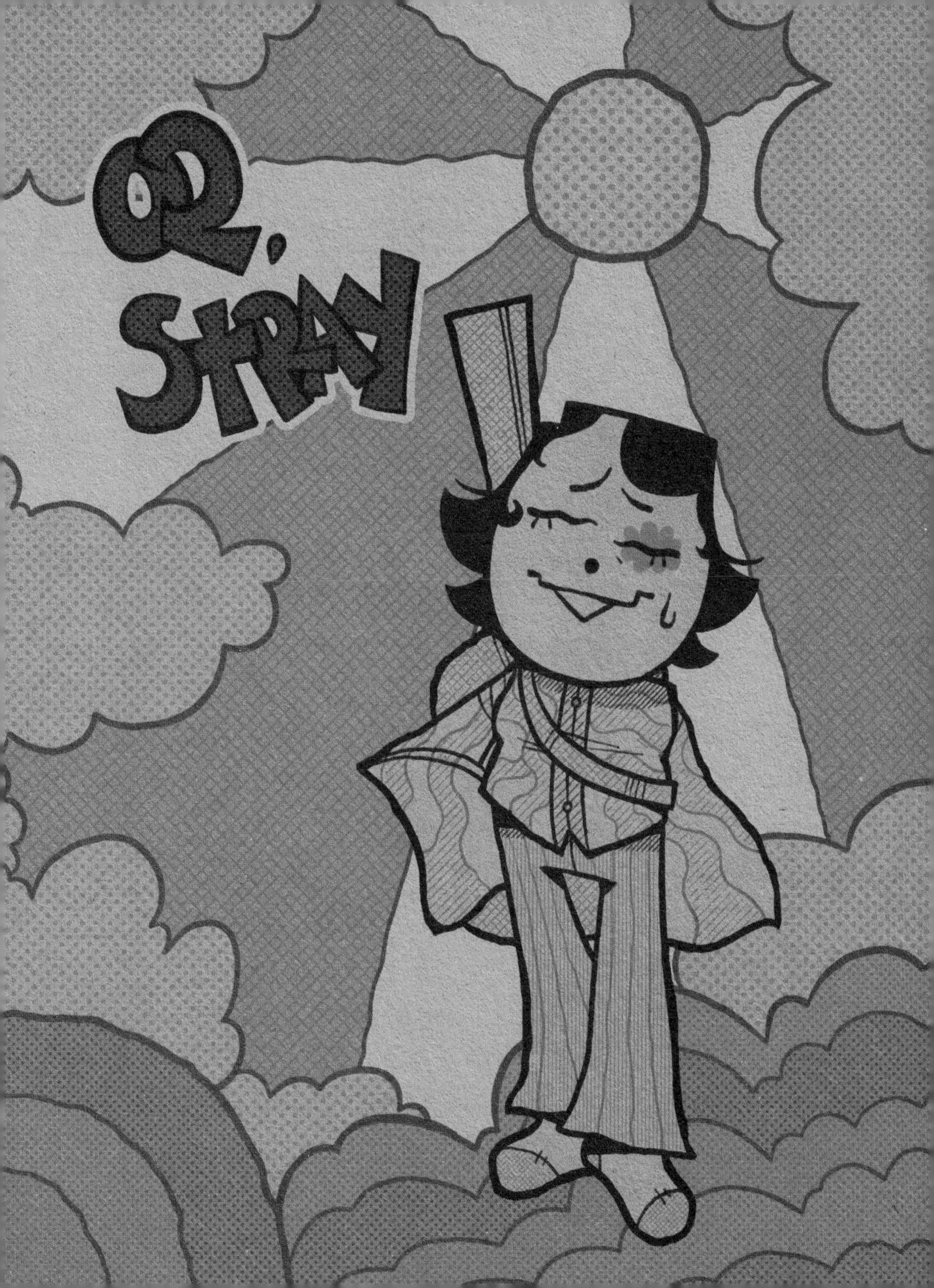
02. STRAY

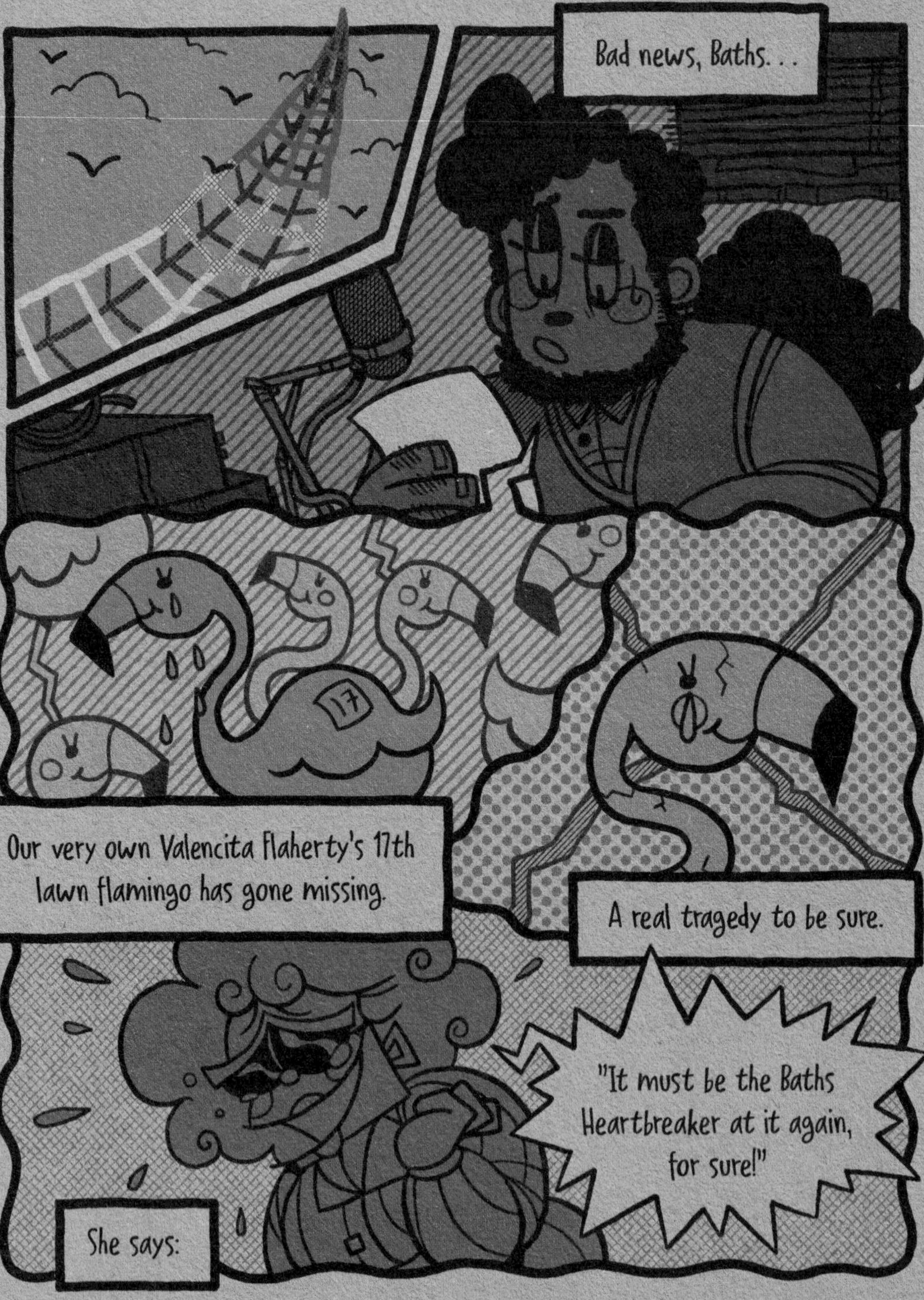
Bad news, Baths. . .
Our very own Valencita Flaherty's 17th lawn flamingo has gone missing.
17
A real tragedy to be sure.
She says:
"It must be the Baths Heartbreaker at it again, for sure!"

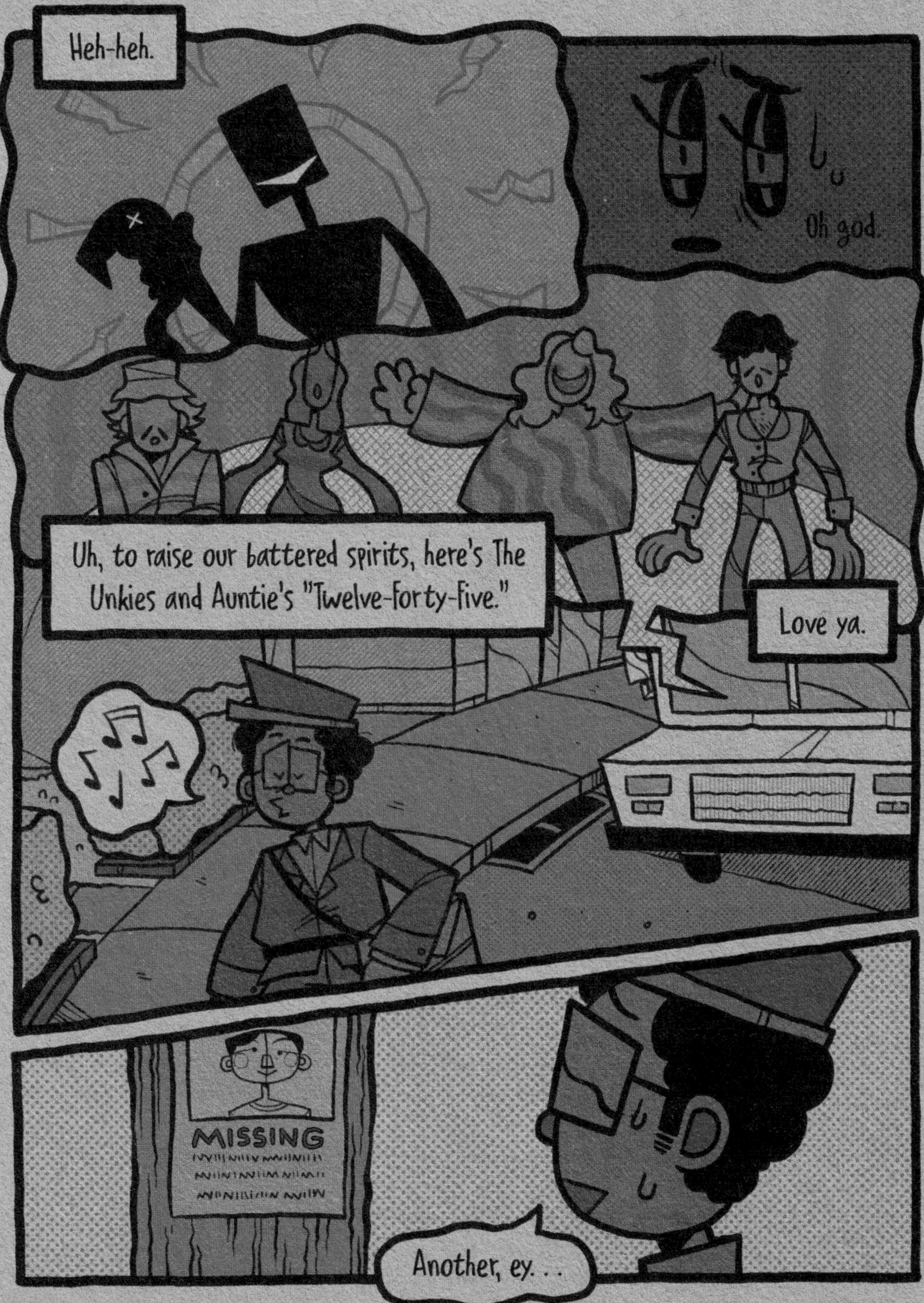
Heh-heh.
Oh god.
Uh, to raise our battered spirits, here's The Unkies and Auntie's "Twelve-Forty-Five."
Love ya.
MISSING
Another, ey. . .

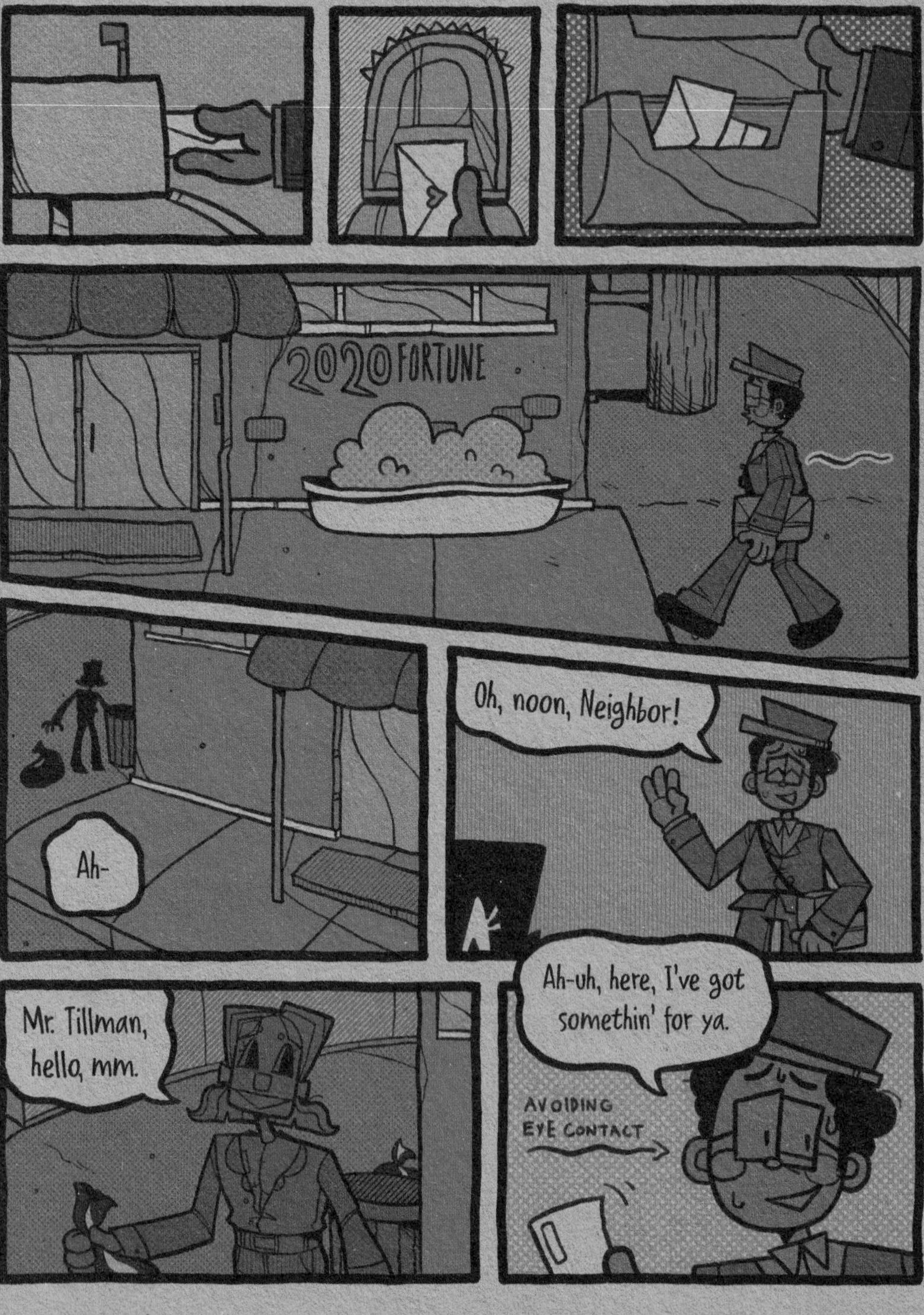
2020 FORTUNE
Ah-
Oh, noon, Neighbor!
Mr. Tillman, hello, mm.
Ah-uh, here, I've got somethin' for ya.
AVOIDING EYE CONTACT

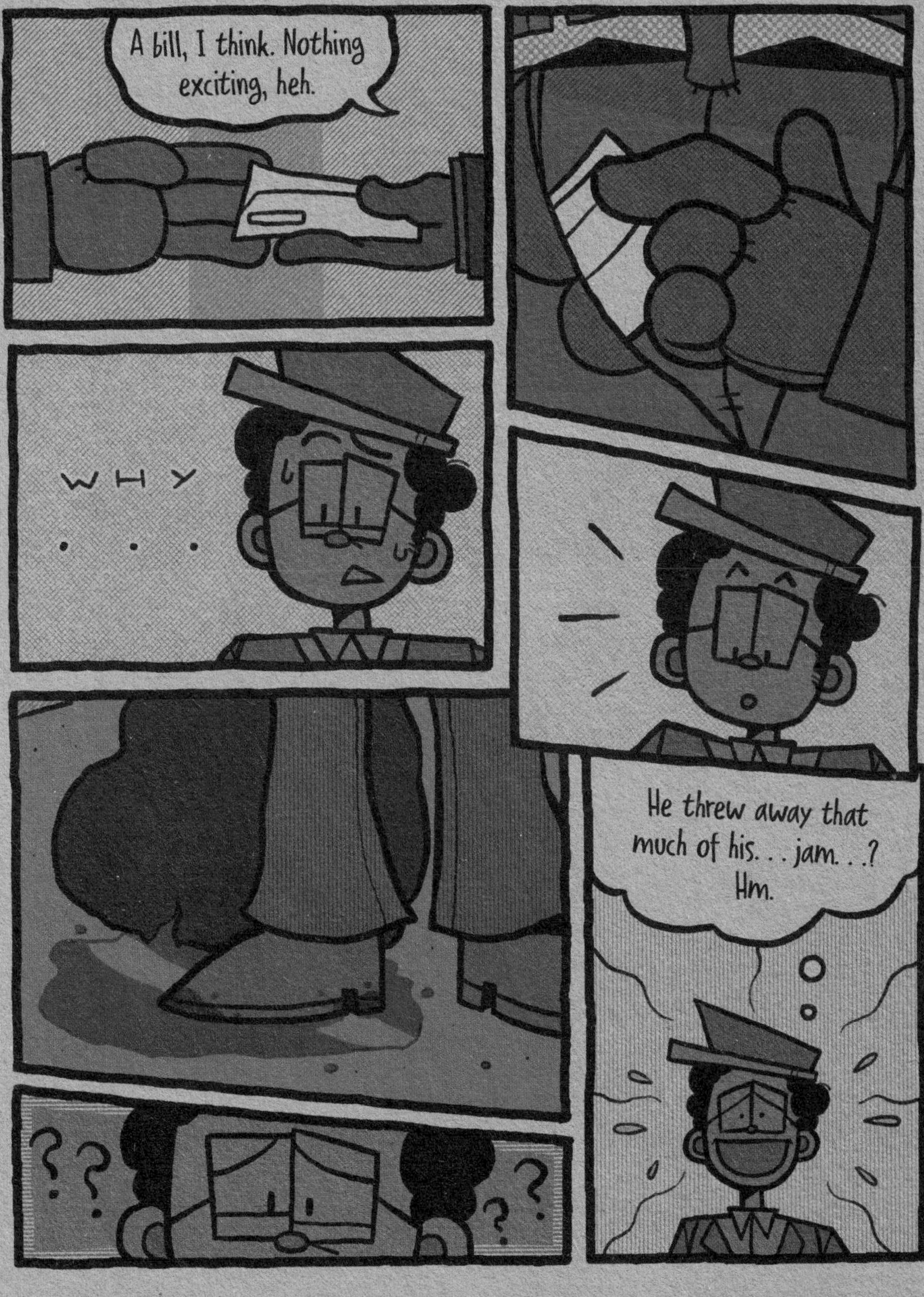
A bill, I think. Nothing exciting, heh.
WHY . . .
He threw away that much of his. . . jam. . .? Hm.

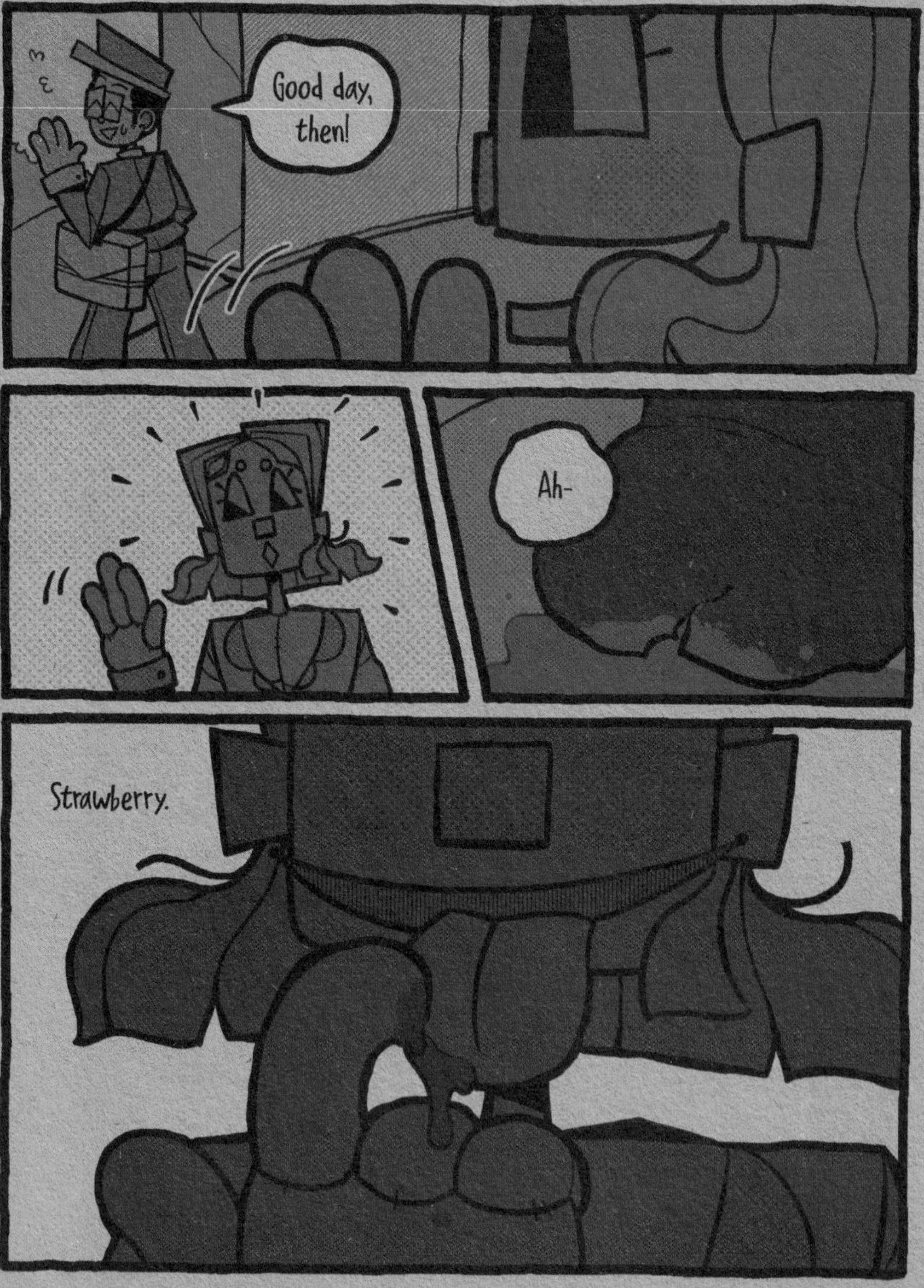
Good day, then!
Ah-
Strawberry.

Do you think I could make it
out there on my own?
No . . ?
I'm safe here?
I guess you're right. . .

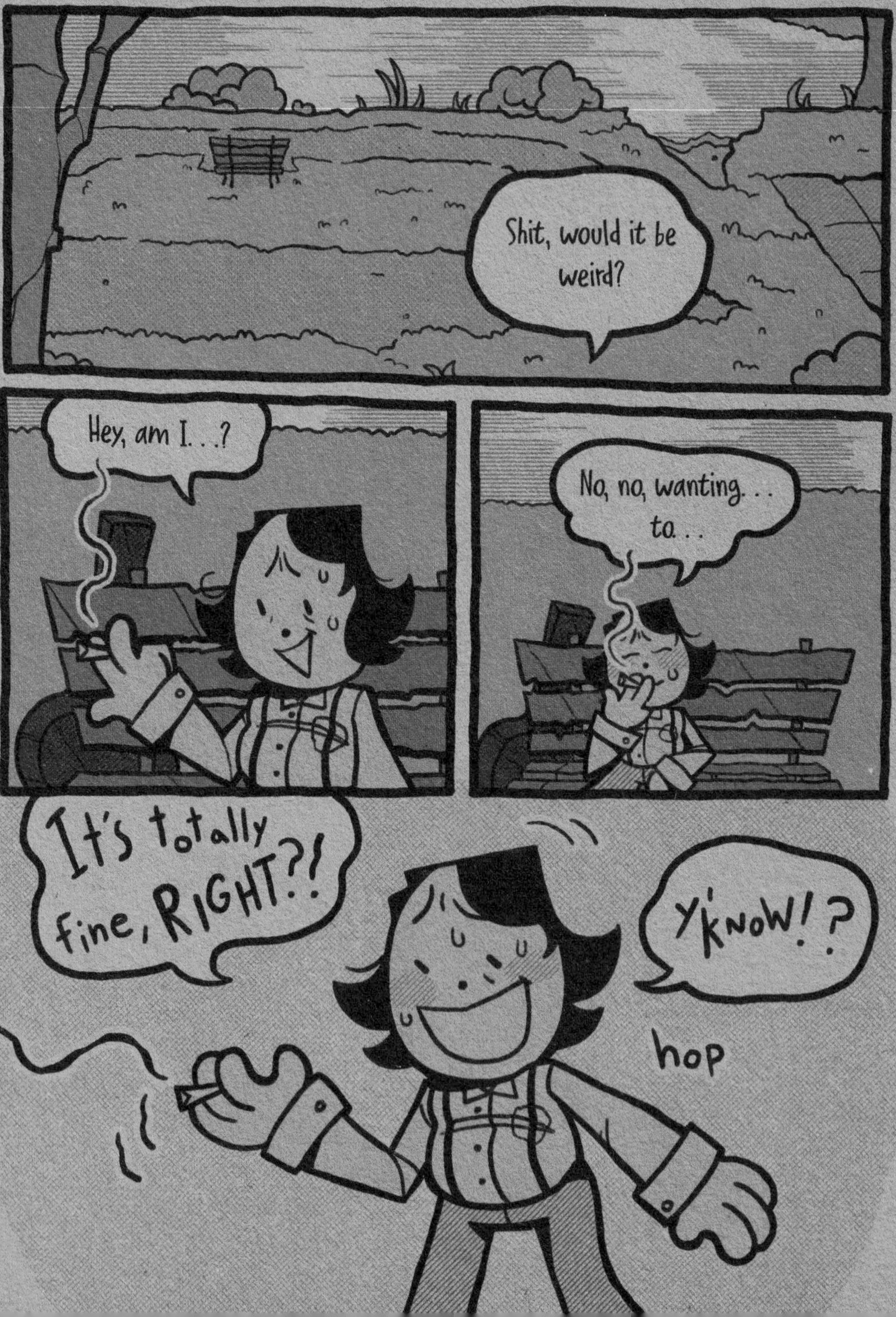
Shit, would it be weird?
Hey, am I. . .?
No, no, wanting. . . to. . .
It's totally fine, RIGHT?!
Y'KNOW!?
hop

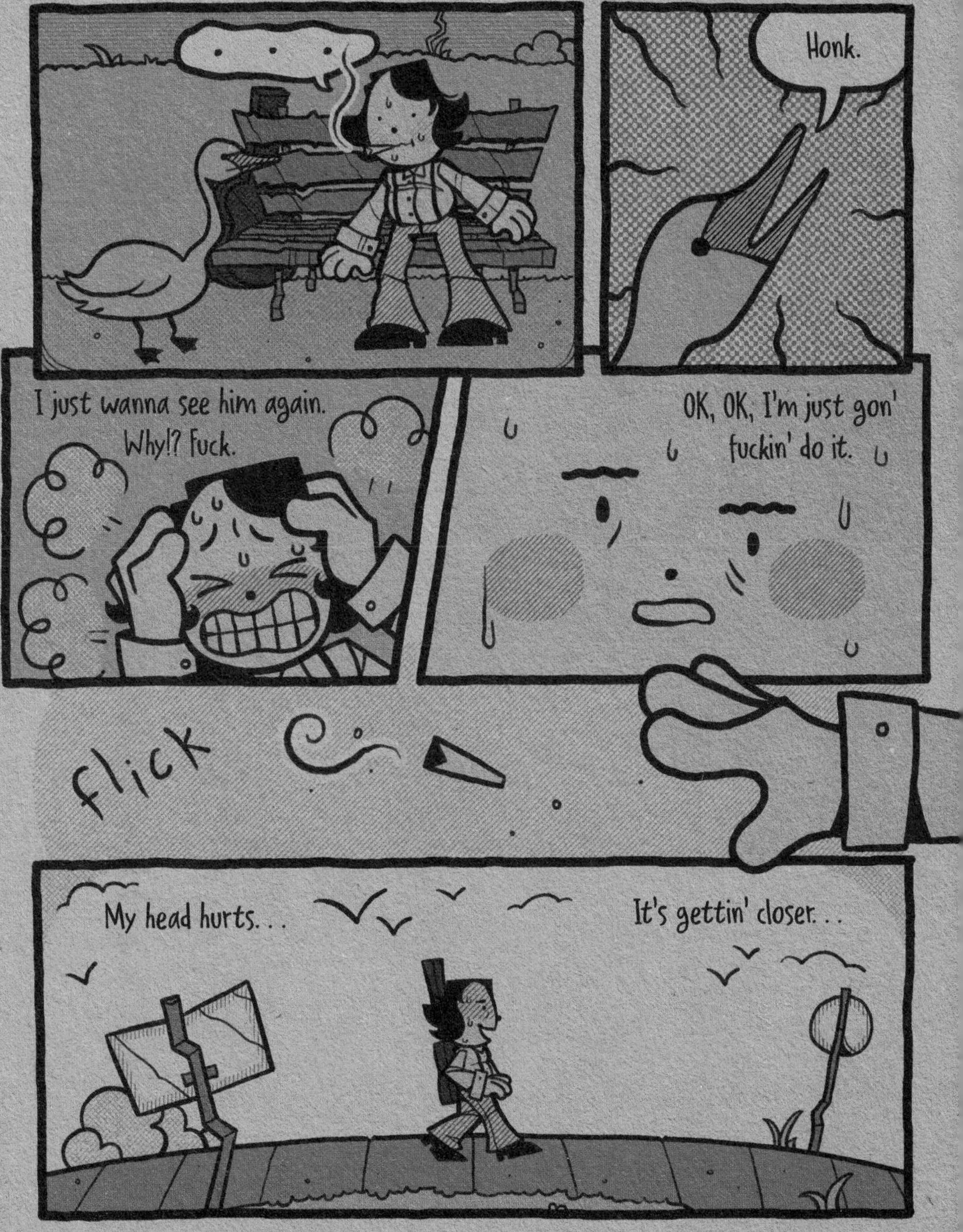
. . .
Honk.
I just wanna see him again.
Why!? Fuck.
OK, OK, I'm just gon' fuckin' do it.
flick
My head hurts. . .
It's gettin' closer. . .

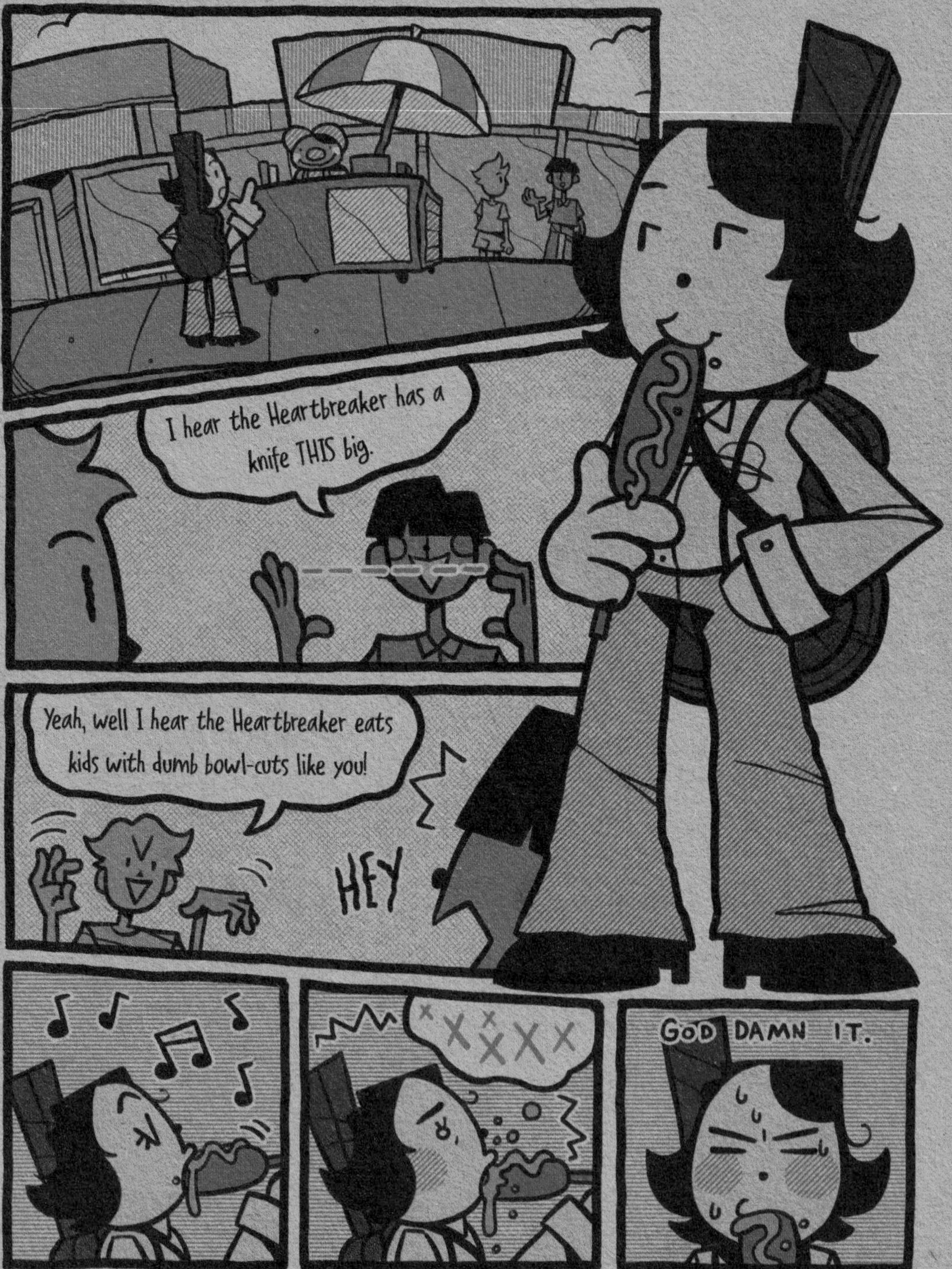
I hear the Heartbreaker has a knife THIS big.
Yeah, well I hear the Heartbreaker eats kids with dumb bowl-cuts like you!
HEY
GOD DAMN IT.

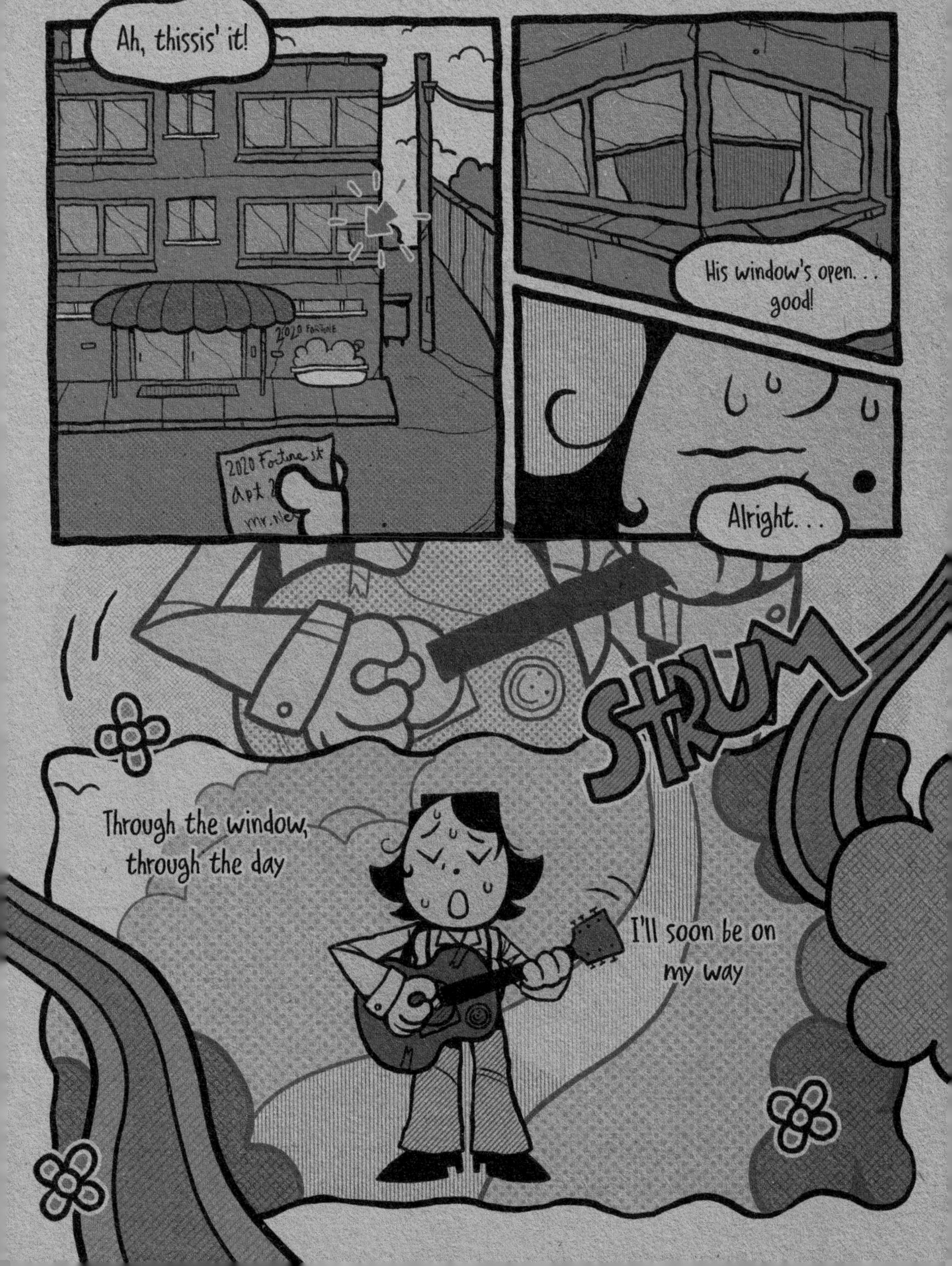
Ah, thissis' it!
2020 FORTUNE
2020 Fortune st
Apt 2
mr. Ne
His window's open. . . good!
Alright. . .
STRUM
Through the window, through the day
I'll soon be on my way

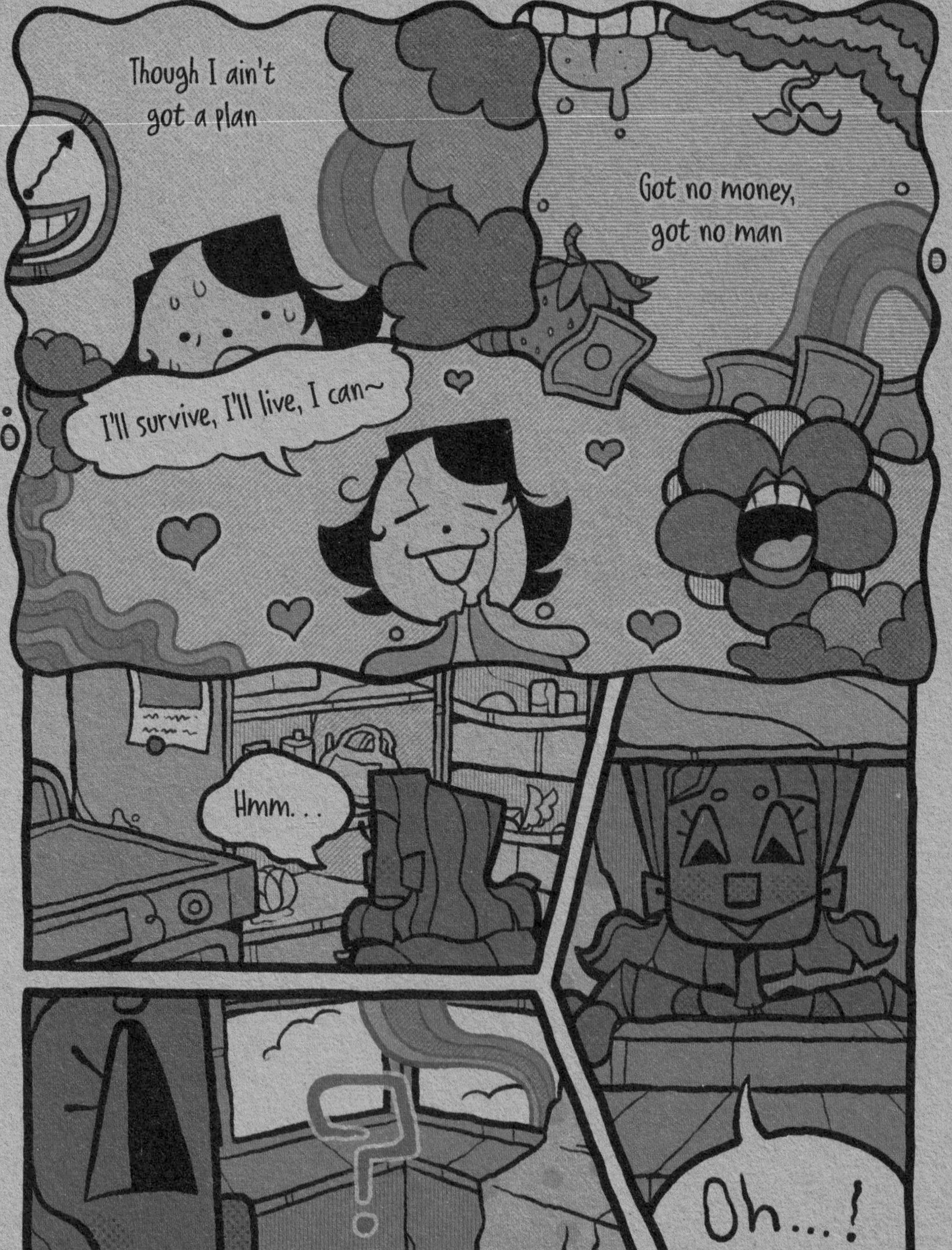
Though I ain't
got a plan
Got no money,
got no man
I'll survive, I'll live, I can~
Hmm. . .
Oh...!

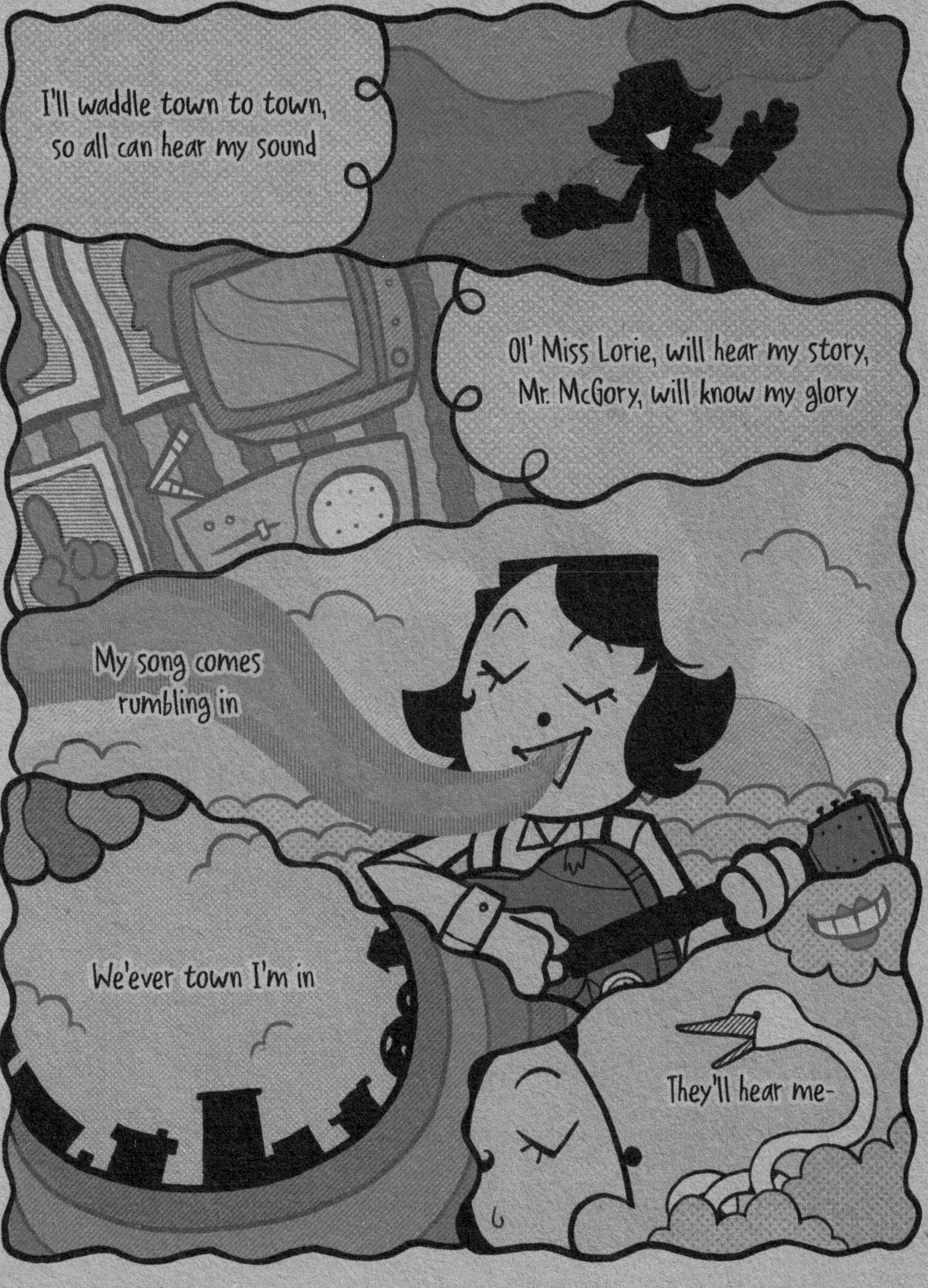
I'll waddle town to town,
so all can hear my sound
Ol' Miss Lorie, will hear my story,
Mr. McGory, will know my glory
My song comes
rumbling in
We'ever town I'm in
They'll hear me-

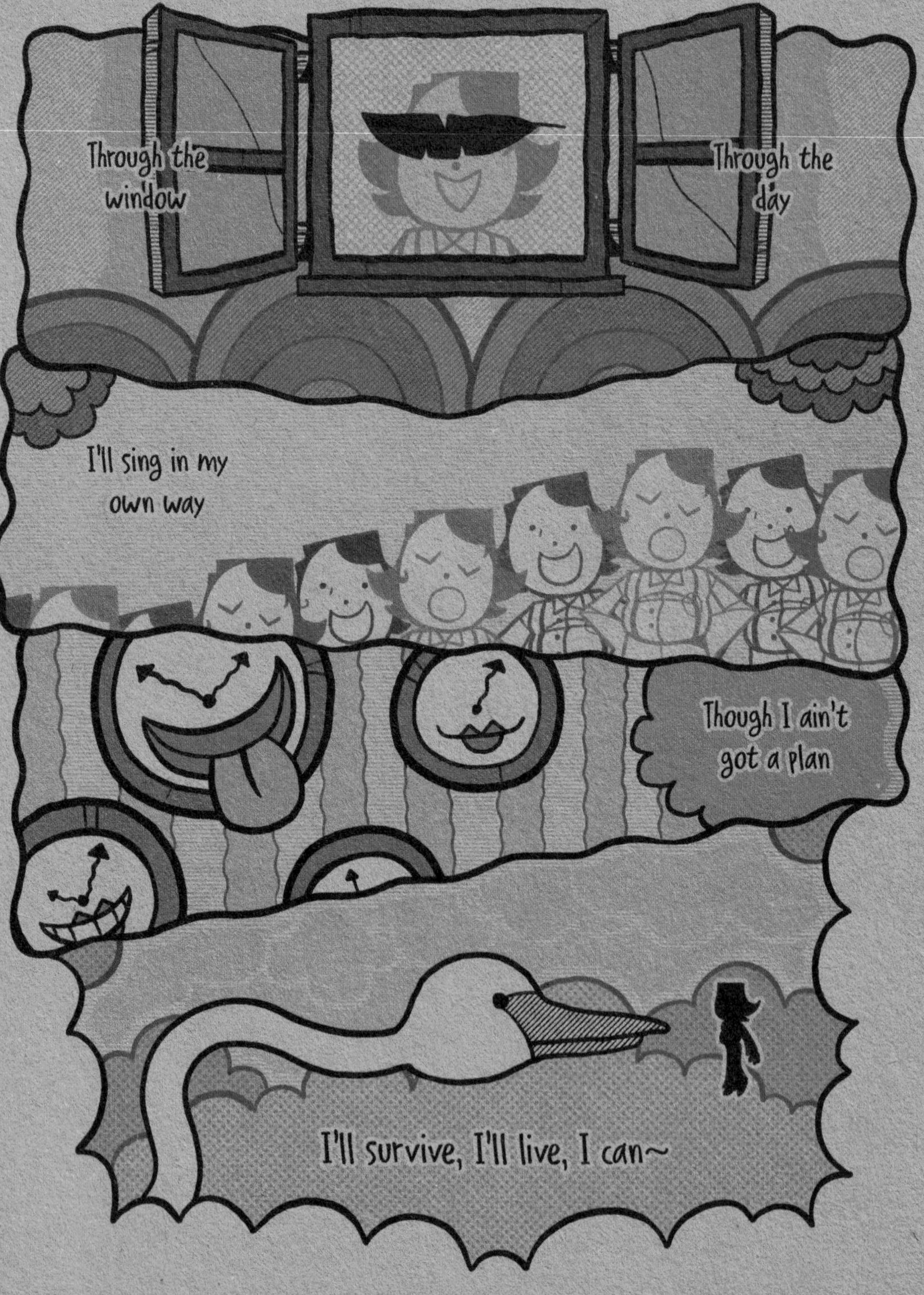
Through the window
Through the day
I'll sing in my own way
Though I ain't got a plan
I'll survive, I'll live, I can~

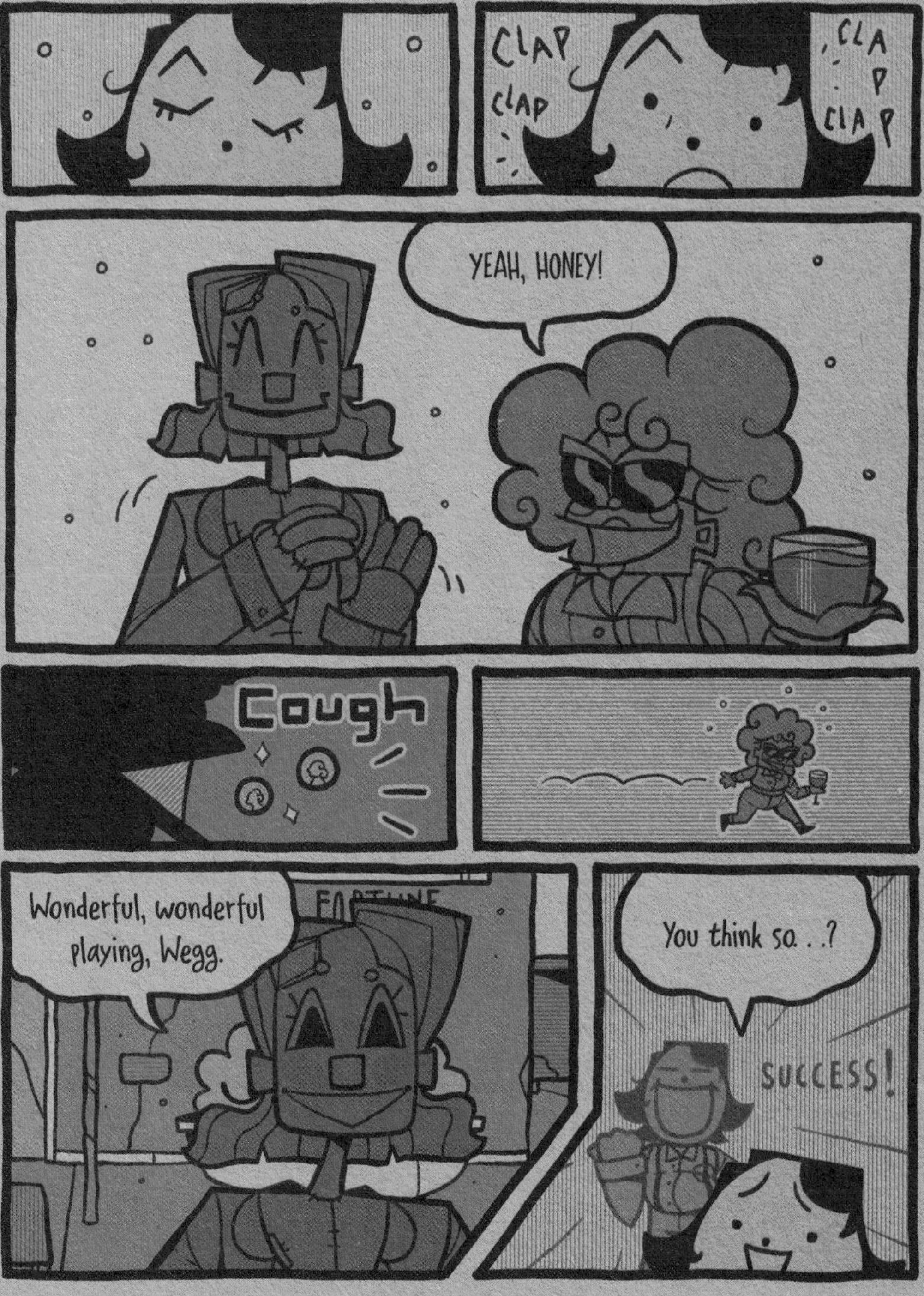
CLAP
CLAP
CLAP
CLAP
YEAH, HONEY!
Cough
FORTUNE
Wonderful, wonderful playing, Wegg.
You think so. . .?
SUCCESS!

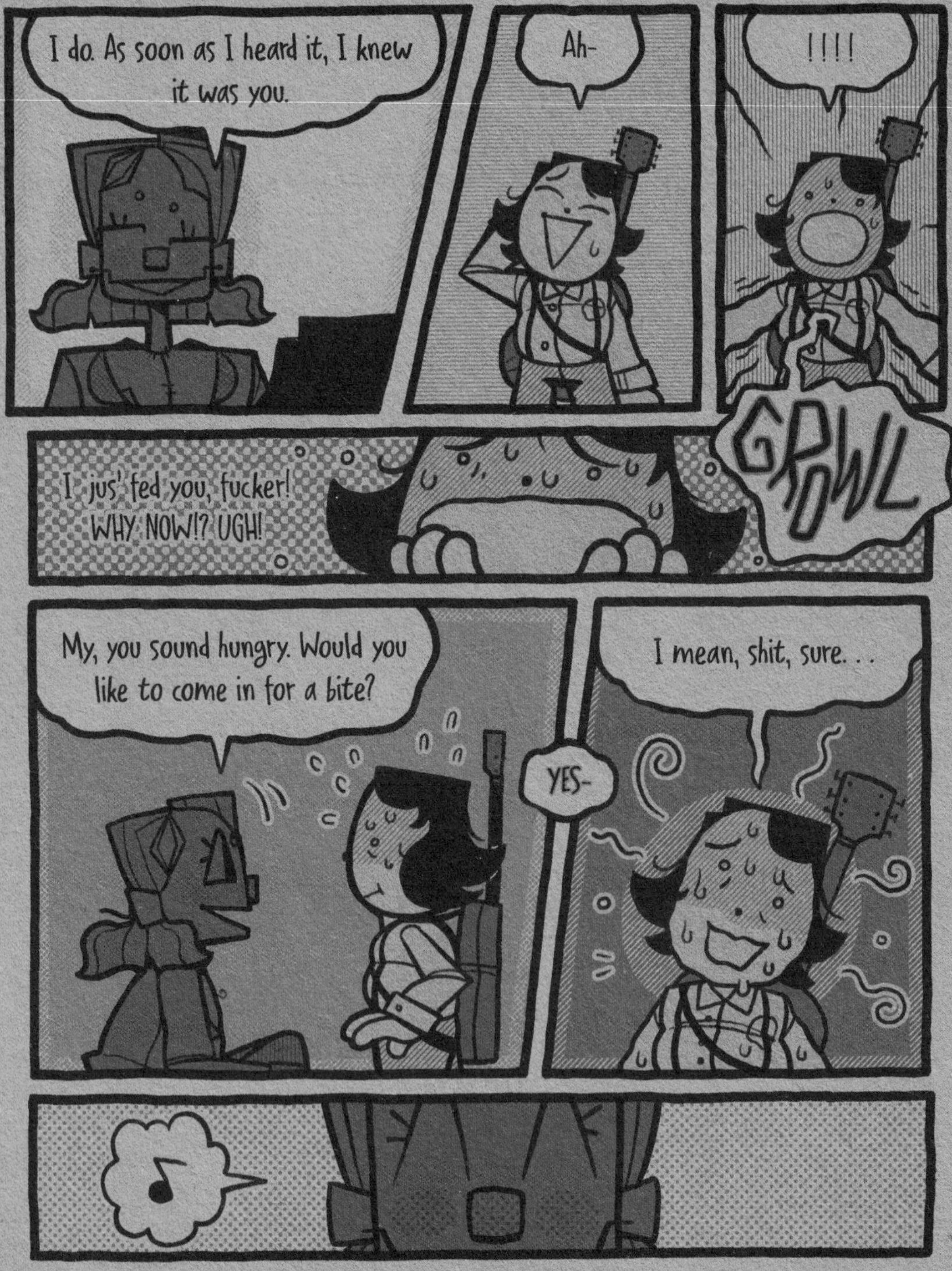
I do. As soon as I heard it, I knew it was you.
Ah-
!!!!
GROWL
I jus' fed you, fucker! WHY NOW!? UGH!
My, you sound hungry. Would you like to come in for a bite?
YES-
I mean, shit, sure. . .

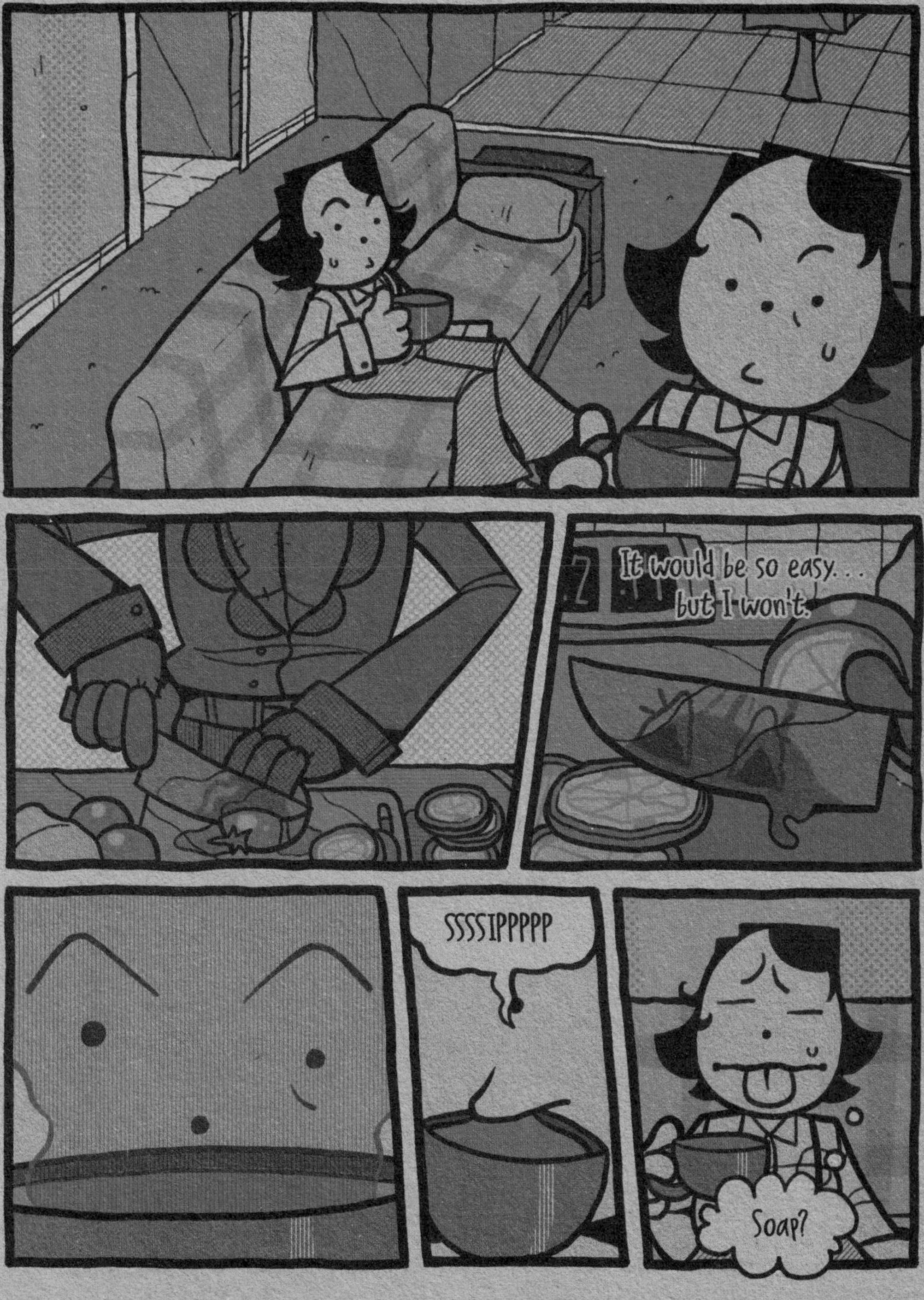

It would be so easy. . .
but I won't.
SSSSIPPPPP
Soap?

HOLY SHIT

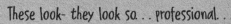

These look- they look so. . . professional. . .

They're just sandwiches, but thank you, Wegg.

Wowww. . .

My, my, you were hungry. . .

Oh. . . .

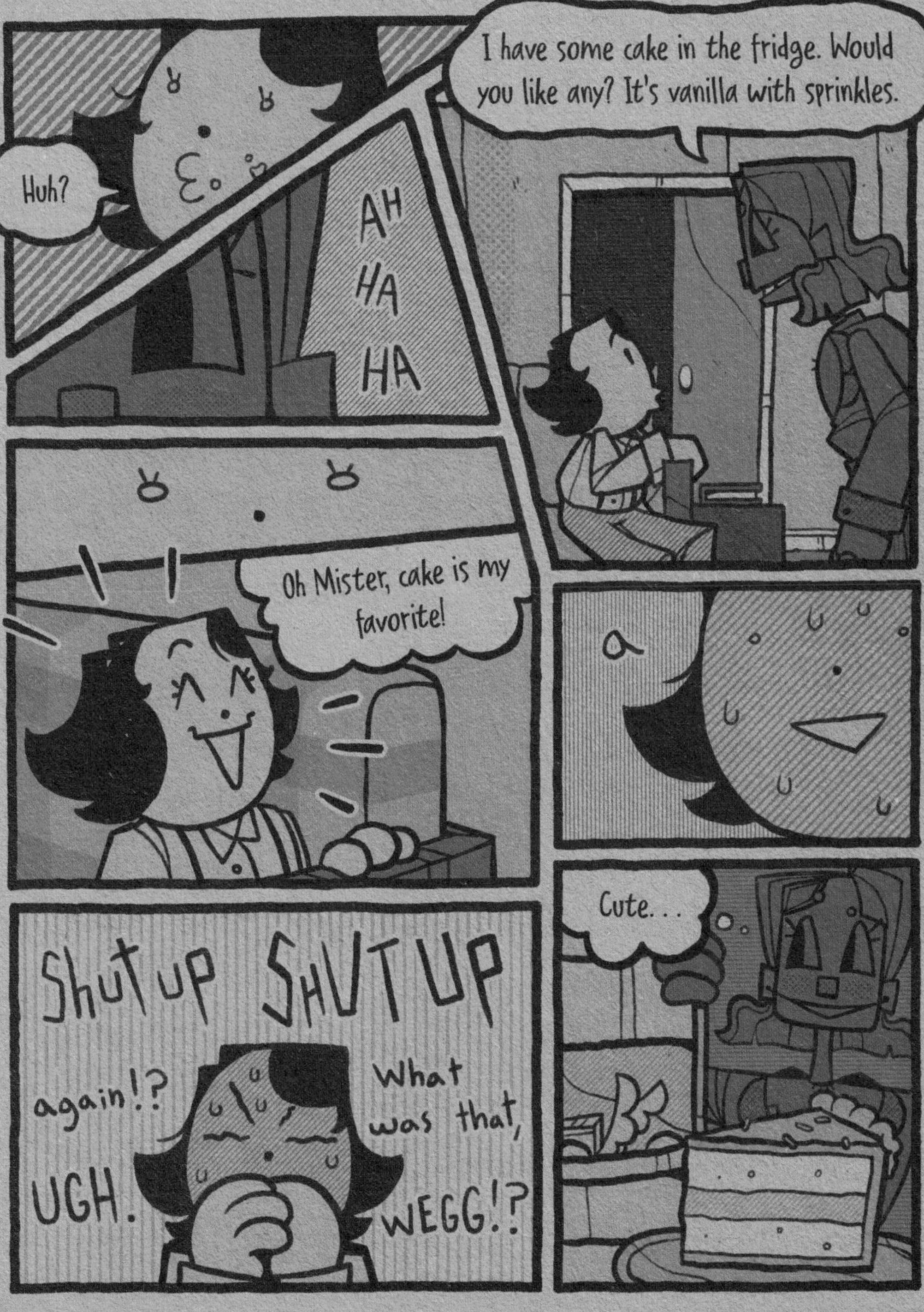
Huh?
AH HA HA HA
I have some cake in the fridge. Would you like any? It's vanilla with sprinkles.
Oh Mister, cake is my favorite!
Cute...
SHUT UP SHUT UP
What was that, WEGG!?
again!?
UGH.

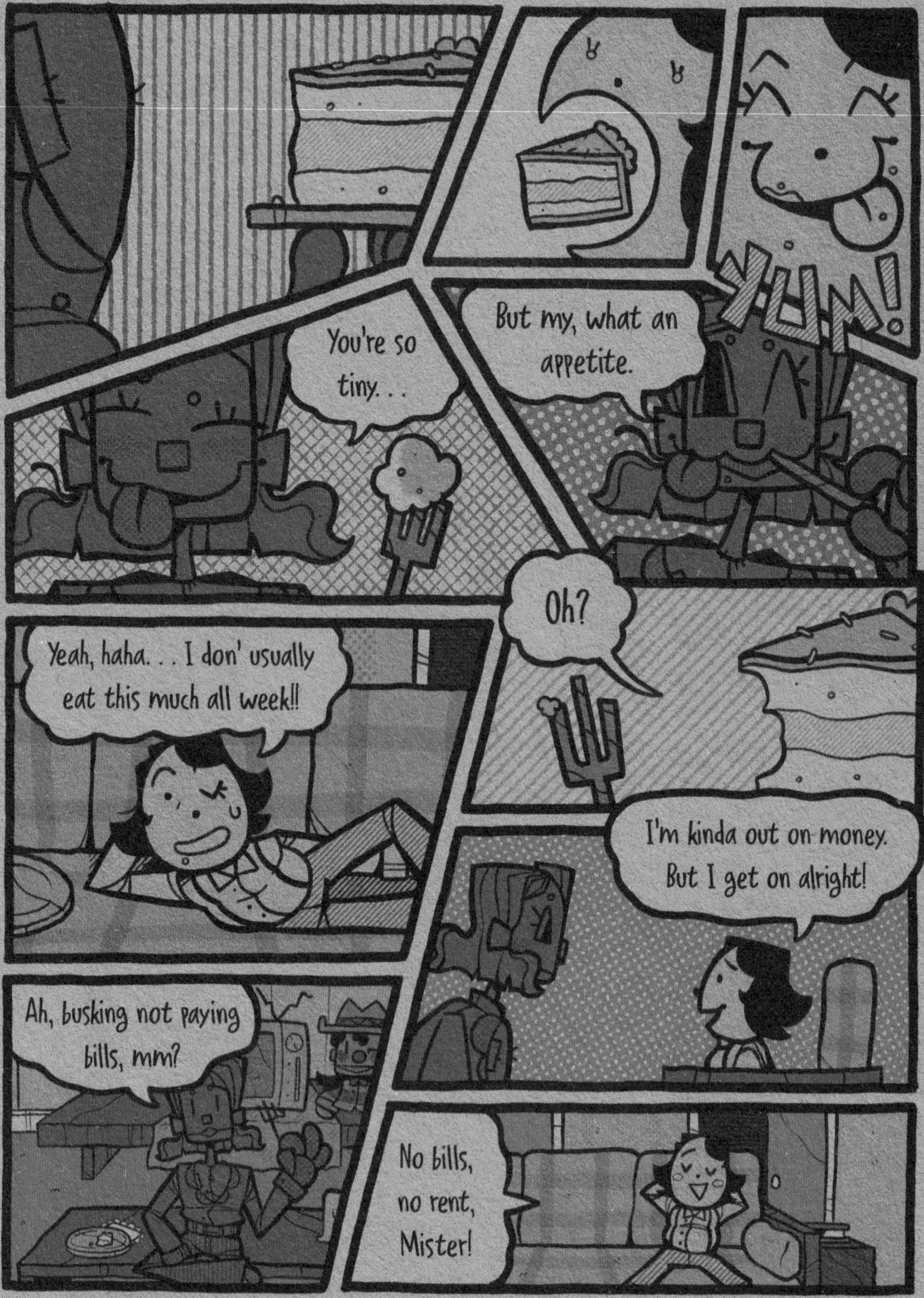
YUM!
You're so tiny...
But my, what an appetite.
Oh?
Yeah, haha... I don' usually eat this much all week!!
I'm kinda out on money. But I get on alright!
Ah, busking not paying bills, mm?
No bills, no rent, Mister!

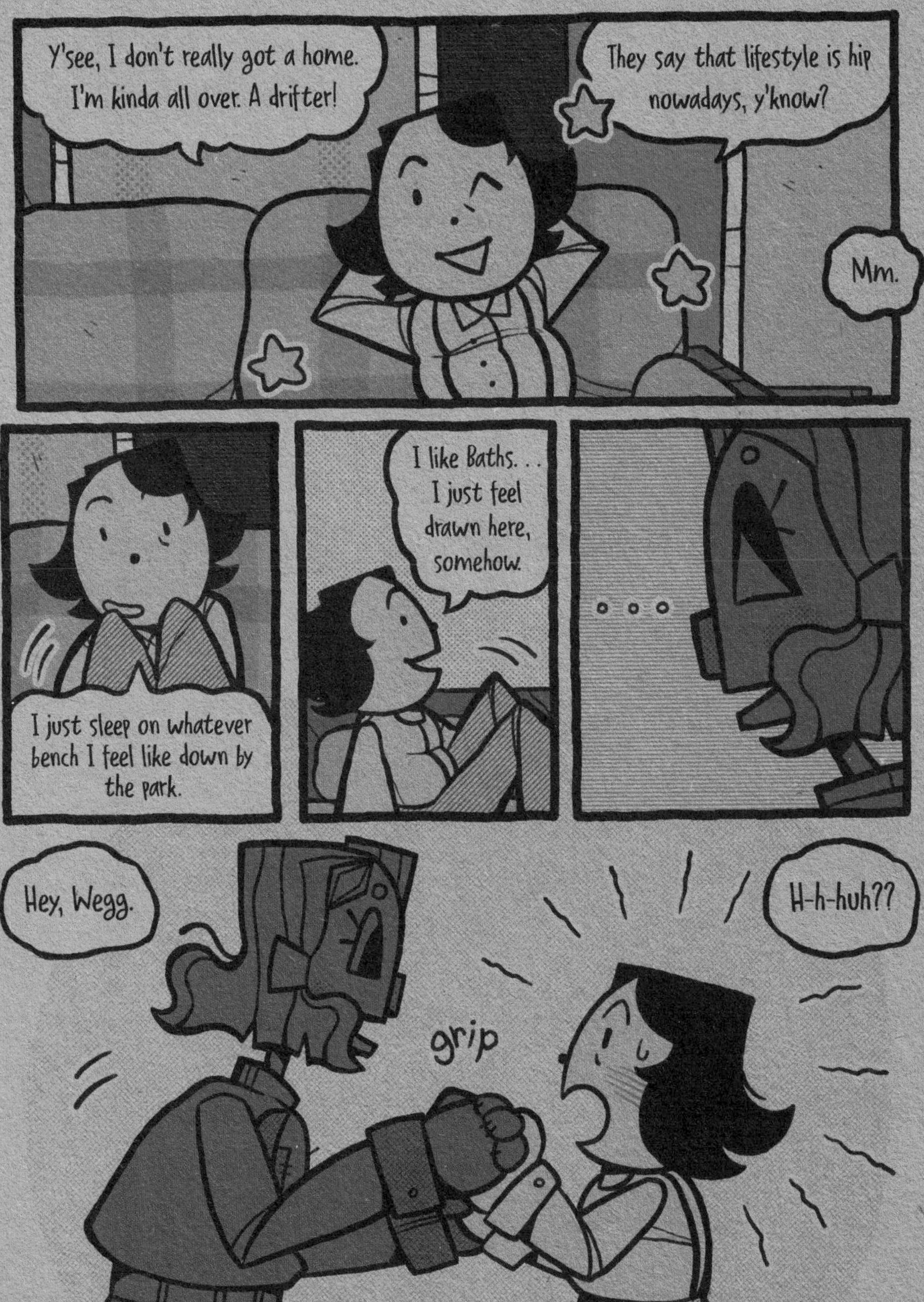
Y'see, I don't really got a home. I'm kinda all over. A drifter!
They say that lifestyle is hip nowadays, y'know?
Mm.
I just sleep on whatever bench I feel like down by the park.
I like Baths. . . I just feel drawn here, somehow.
. . .
Hey, Wegg.
H-h-huh??
grip

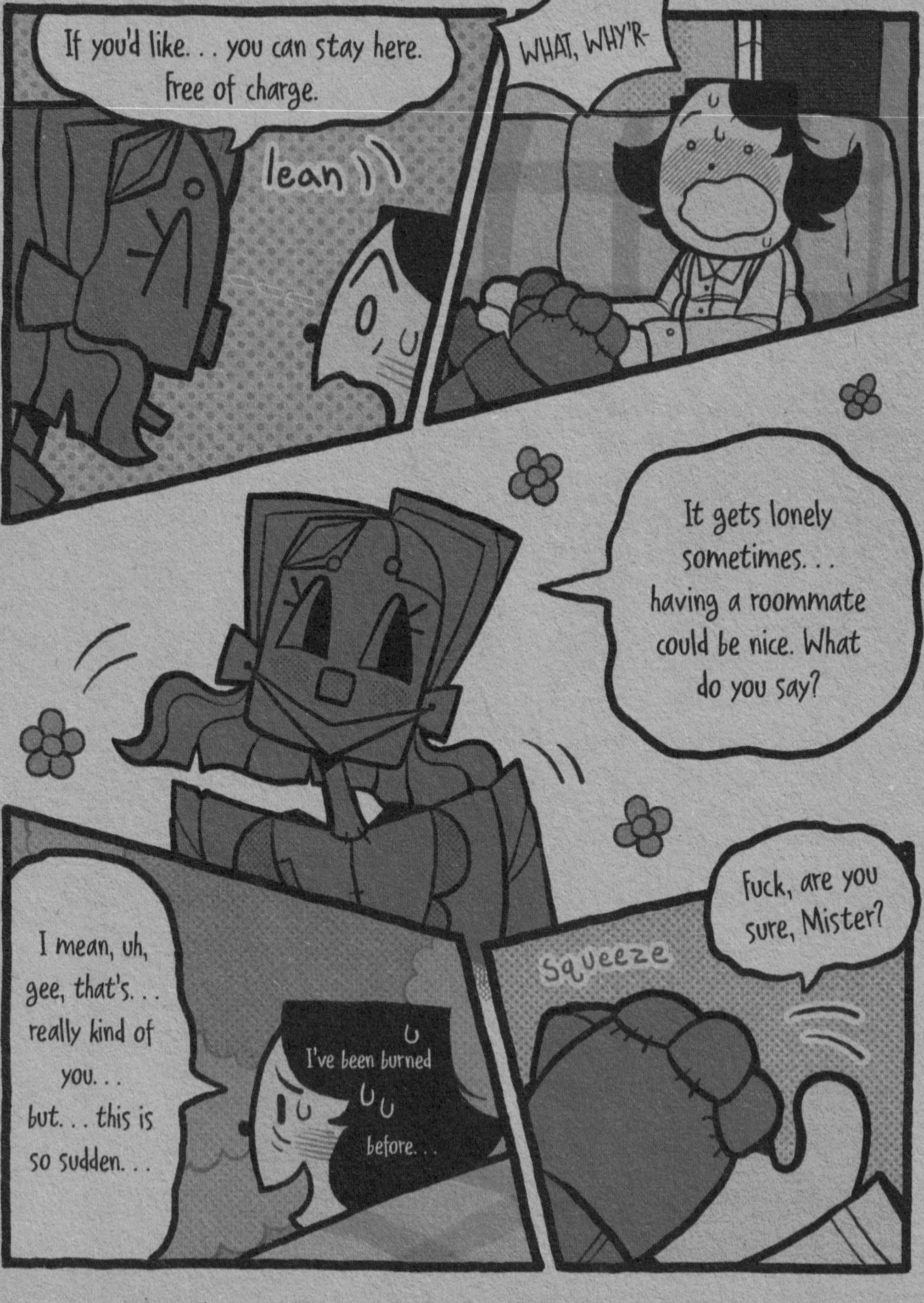
If you'd like... you can stay here. Free of charge.
lean
WHAT, WHY'R-
It gets lonely sometimes... having a roommate could be nice. What do you say?
I mean, uh, gee, that's... really kind of you... but... this is so sudden...
I've been burned before...
Fuck, are you sure, Mister?
squeeze

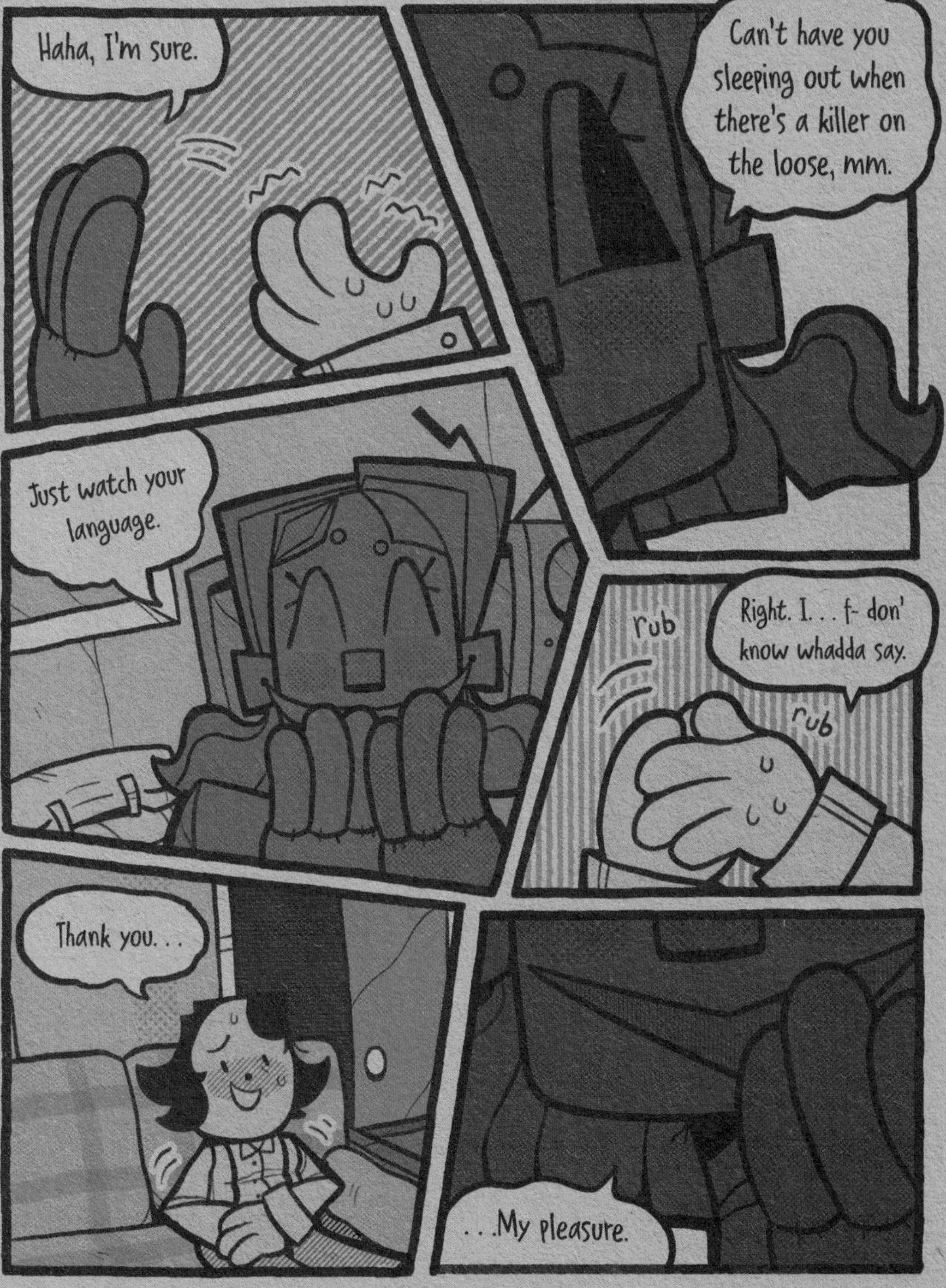
Haha, I'm sure.
Can't have you sleeping out when there's a killer on the loose, mm.
Just watch your language.
Right. I. . . f- don' know whadda say.
rub
rub
Thank you. . .
. . .My pleasure.

Ow, ow, OW! That hurts!
What are you doing to me!?
Wait. . . I feel. . . good.
Ohhhhhhhh. . .
I love you guys. . .

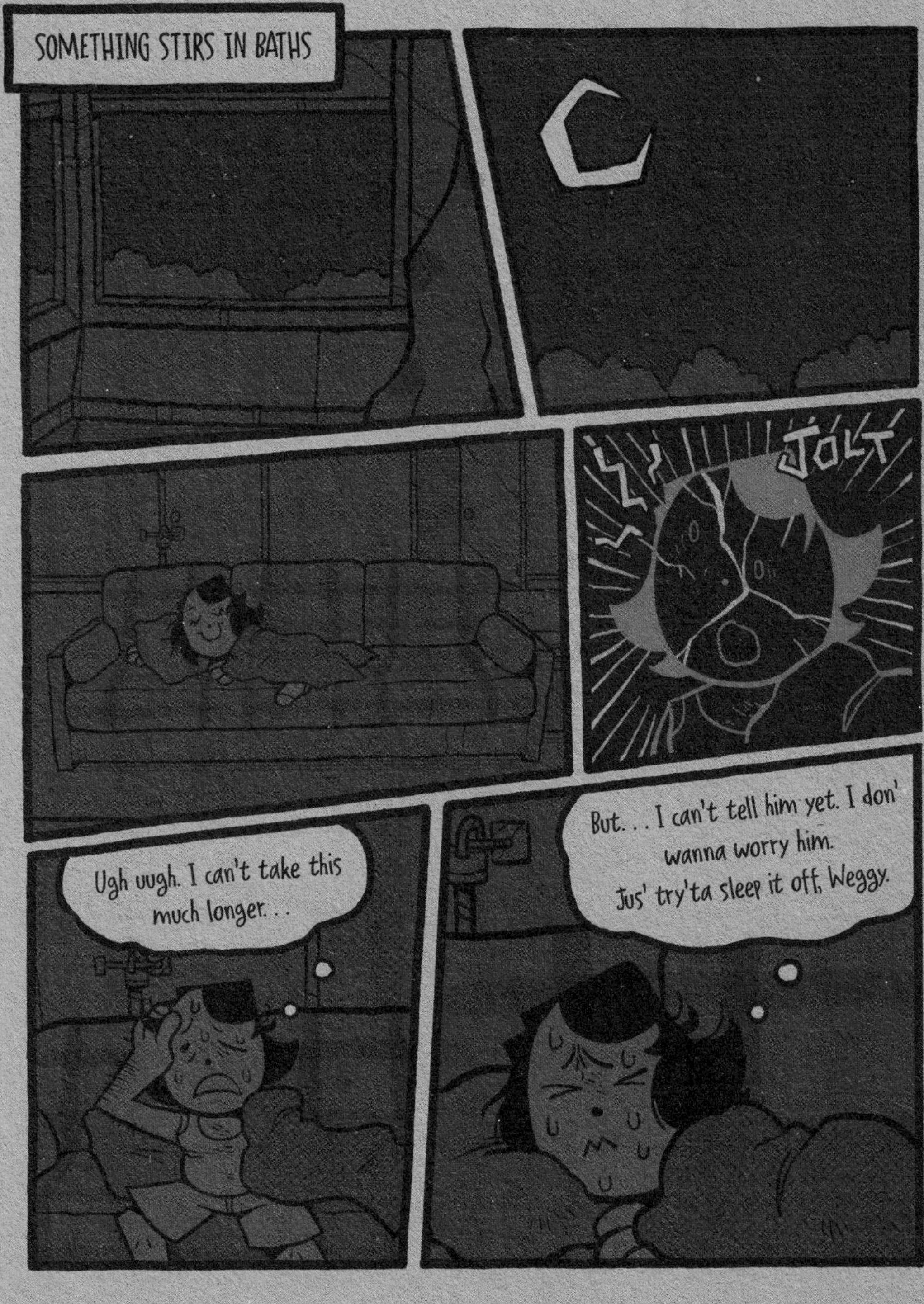
SOMETHING STIRS IN BATHS
JOLT
Ugh uugh. I can't take this much longer. . .
But. . . I can't tell him yet. I don' wanna worry him.
Jus' try'ta sleep it off, Weggy.

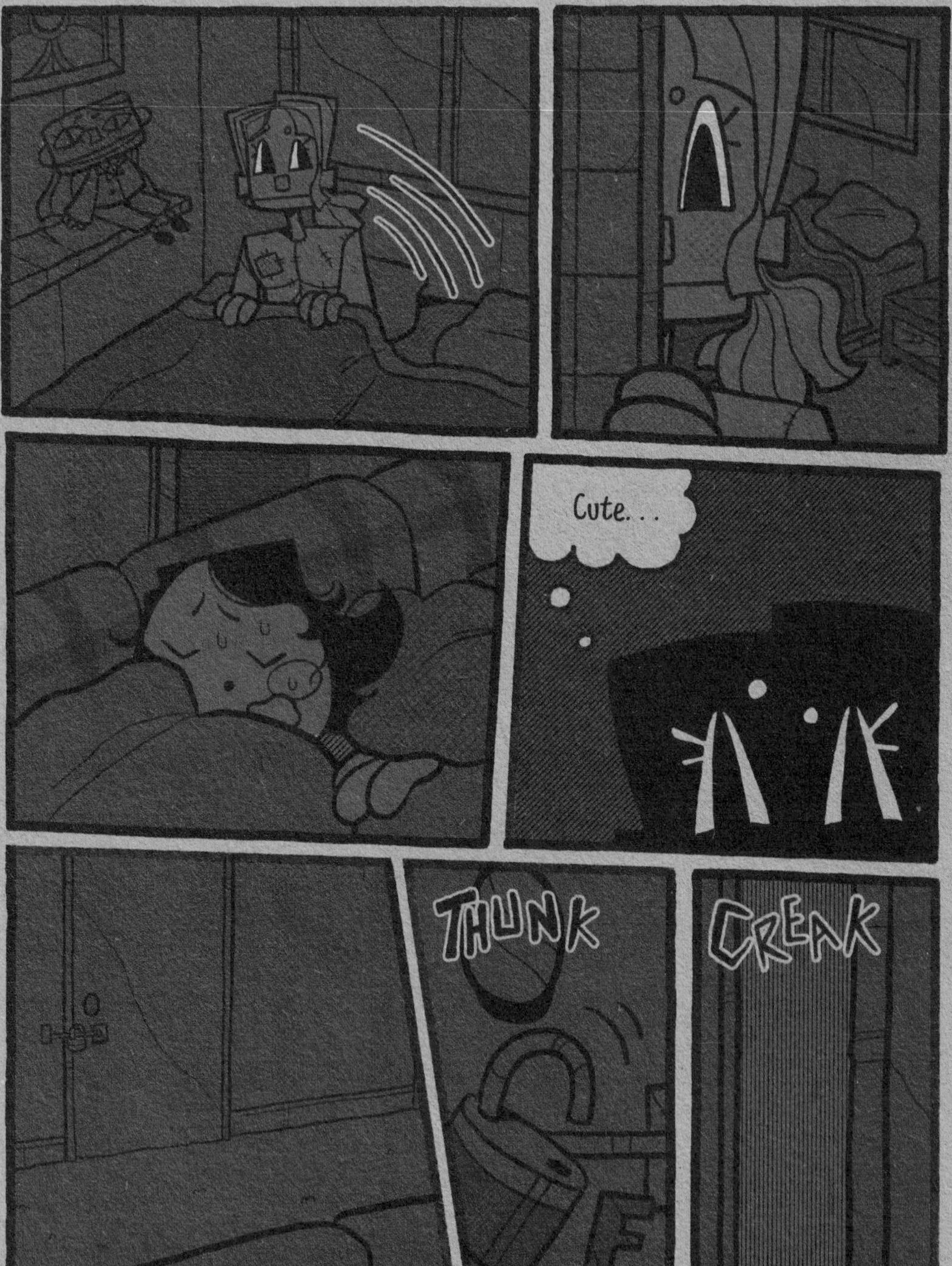
Cute...
THUNK
CREAK

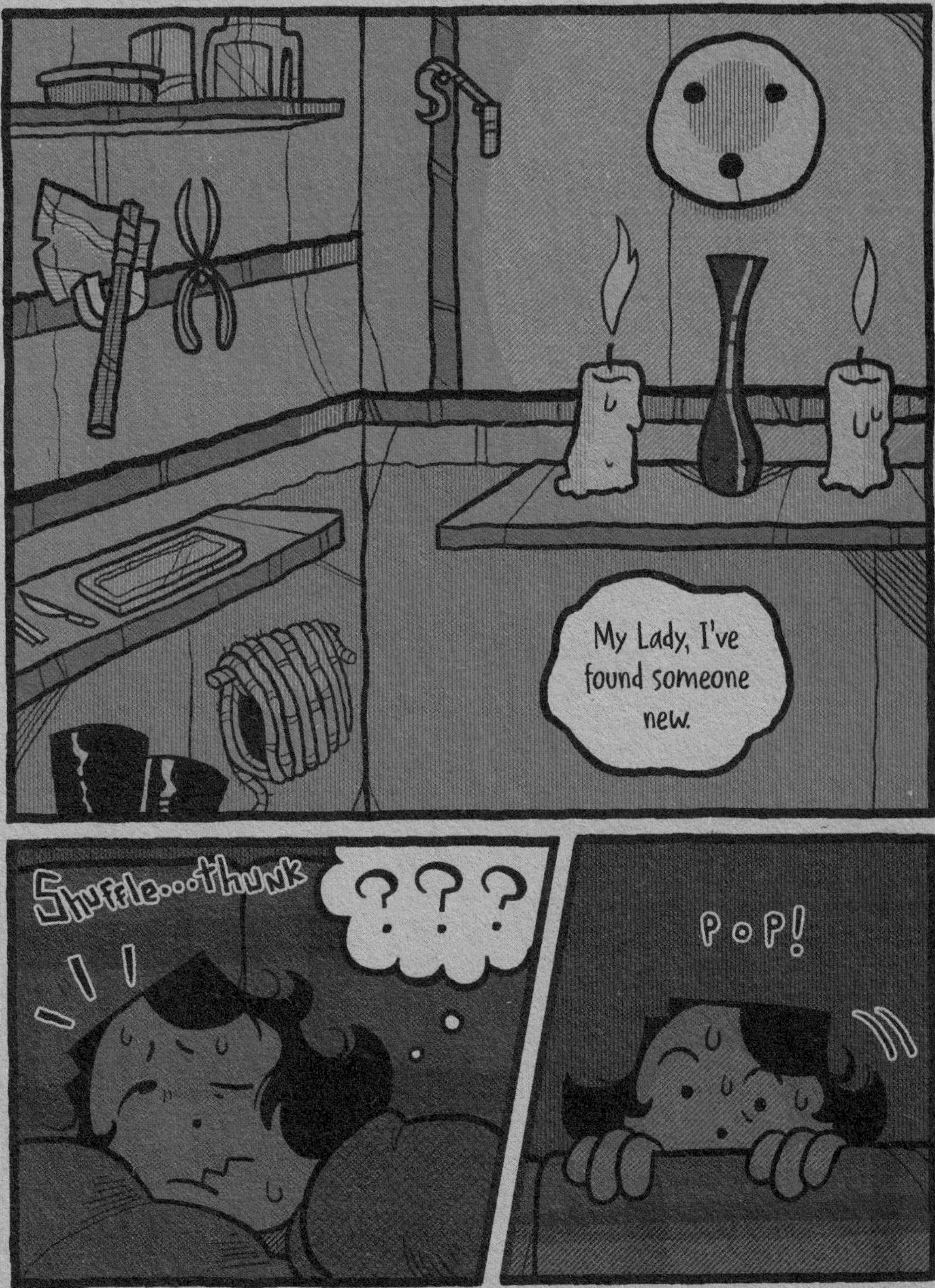
My Lady, I've found someone new.
Shuffle...thunk
???
POP!

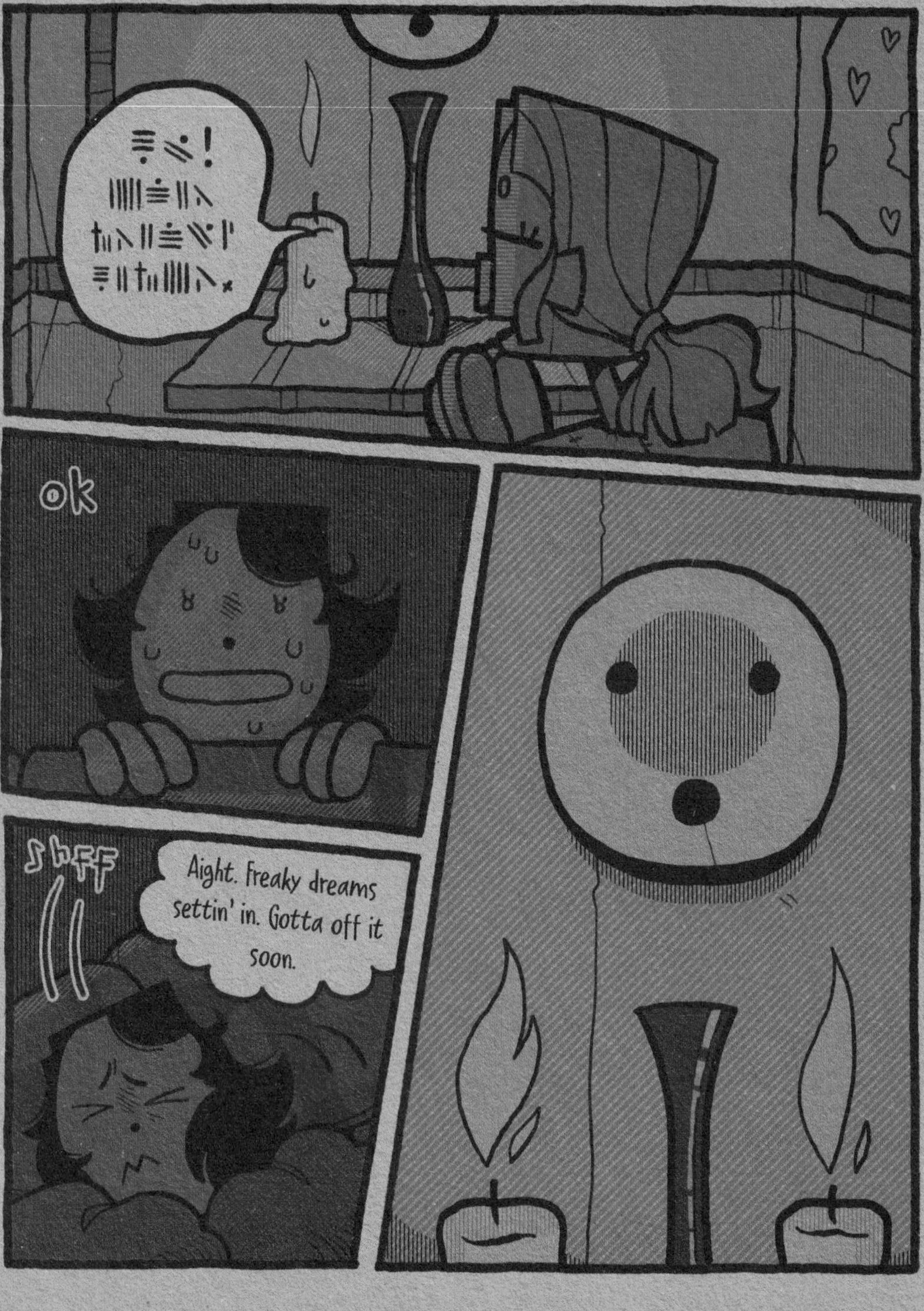
ok
shff
Aight. Freaky dreams settin' in. Gotta off it soon.

Thank you.

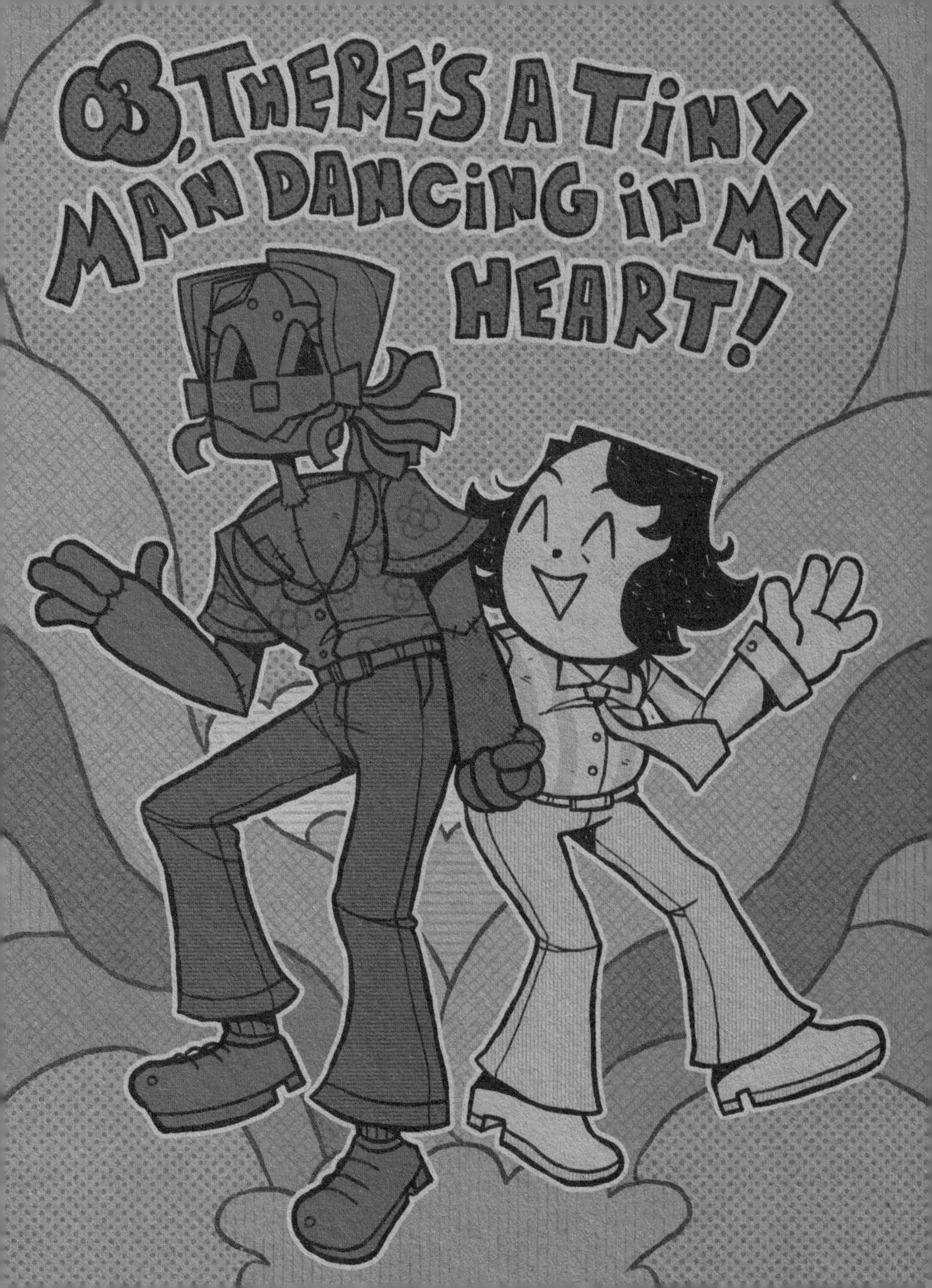
03. THERE'S A TINY MAN DANCING IN MY HEART!

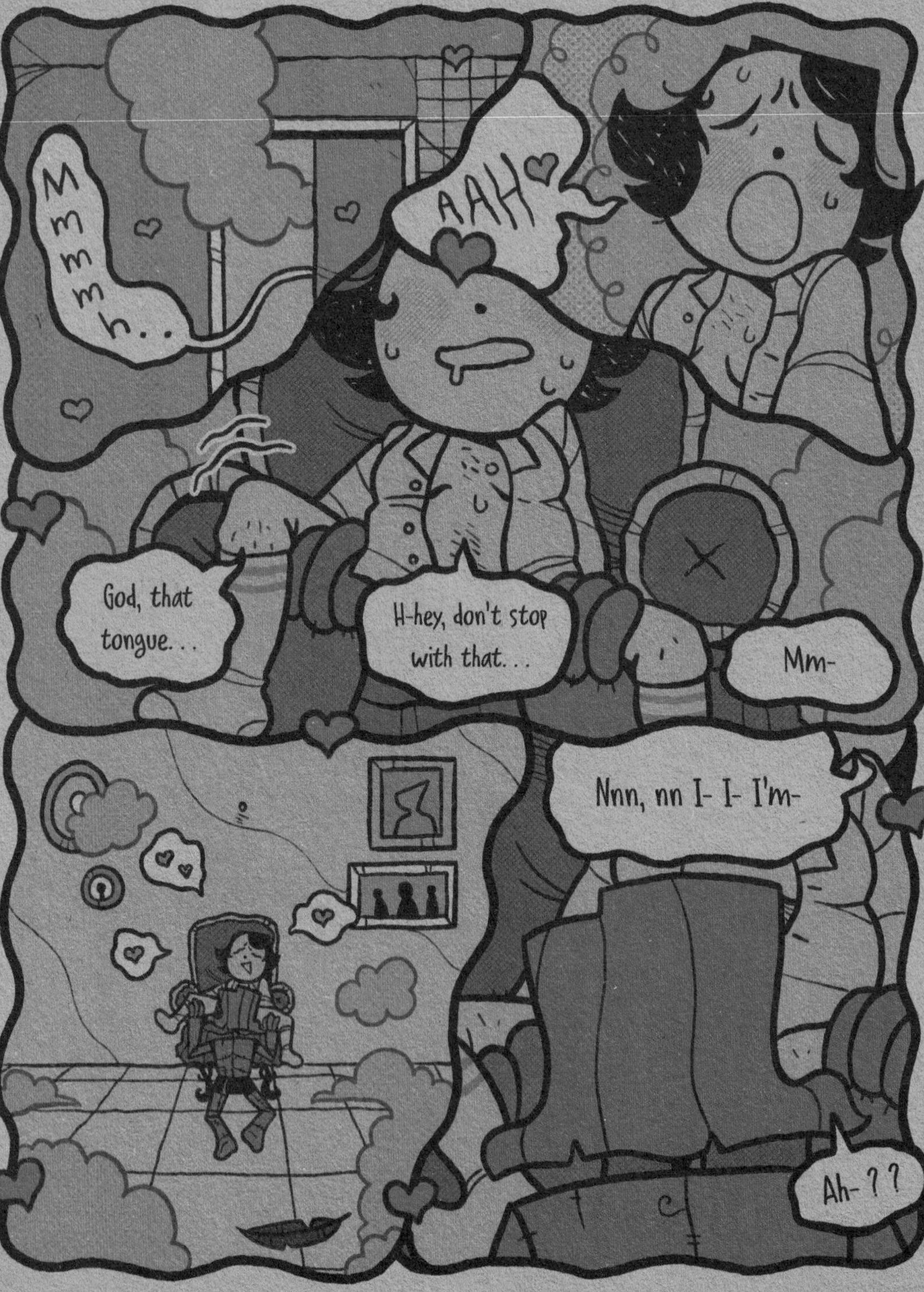
Mmmmh...
AAH
God, that tongue...
H-hey, don't stop with that...
Mm-
Nnn, nn I- I- I'm-
Ah-??

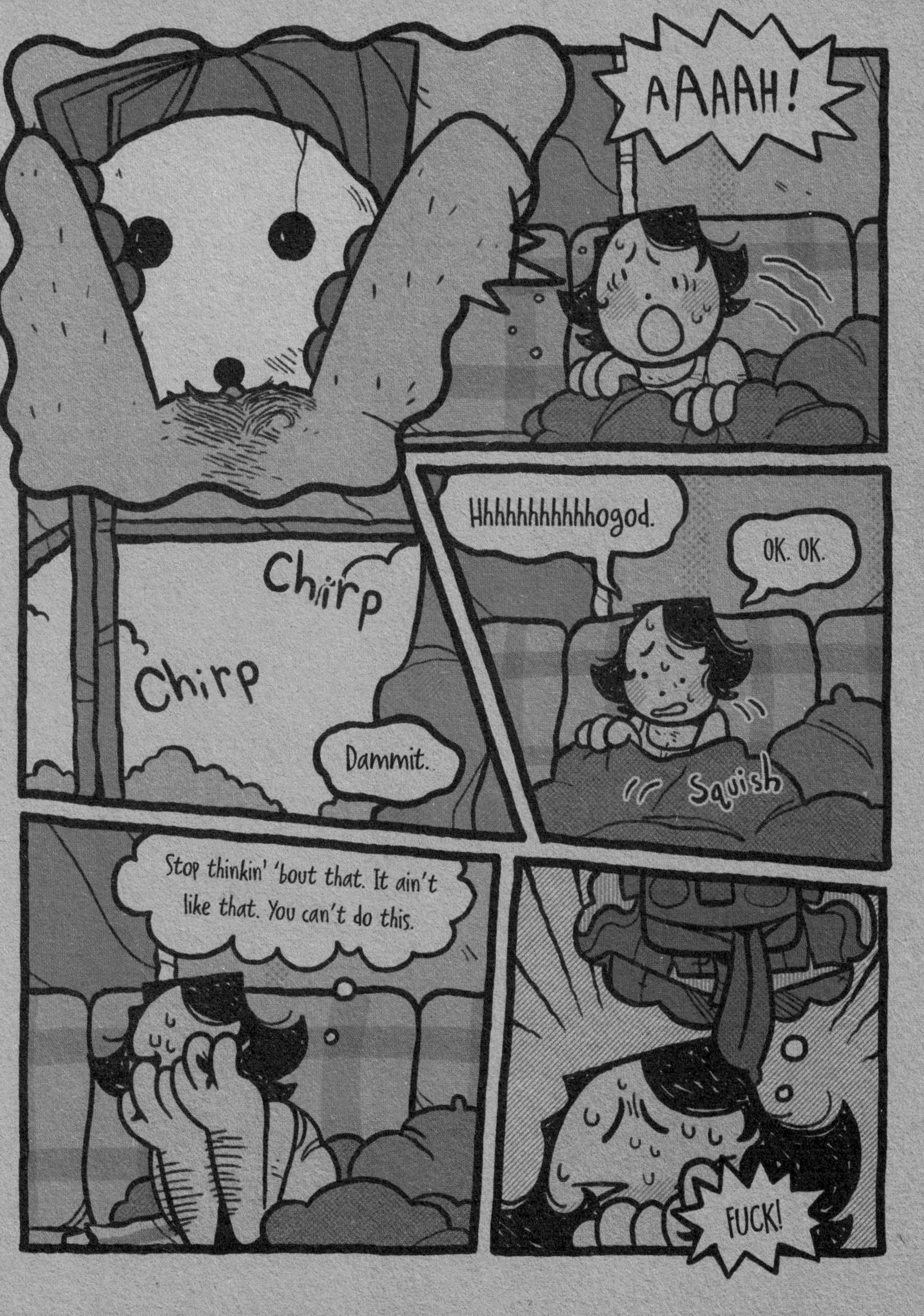
AAAAH!
Chirp
Chirp
Dammit.
Hhhhhhhhhhhogod.
OK. OK.
Squish
Stop thinkin' 'bout that. It ain't like that. You can't do this.
FUCK!

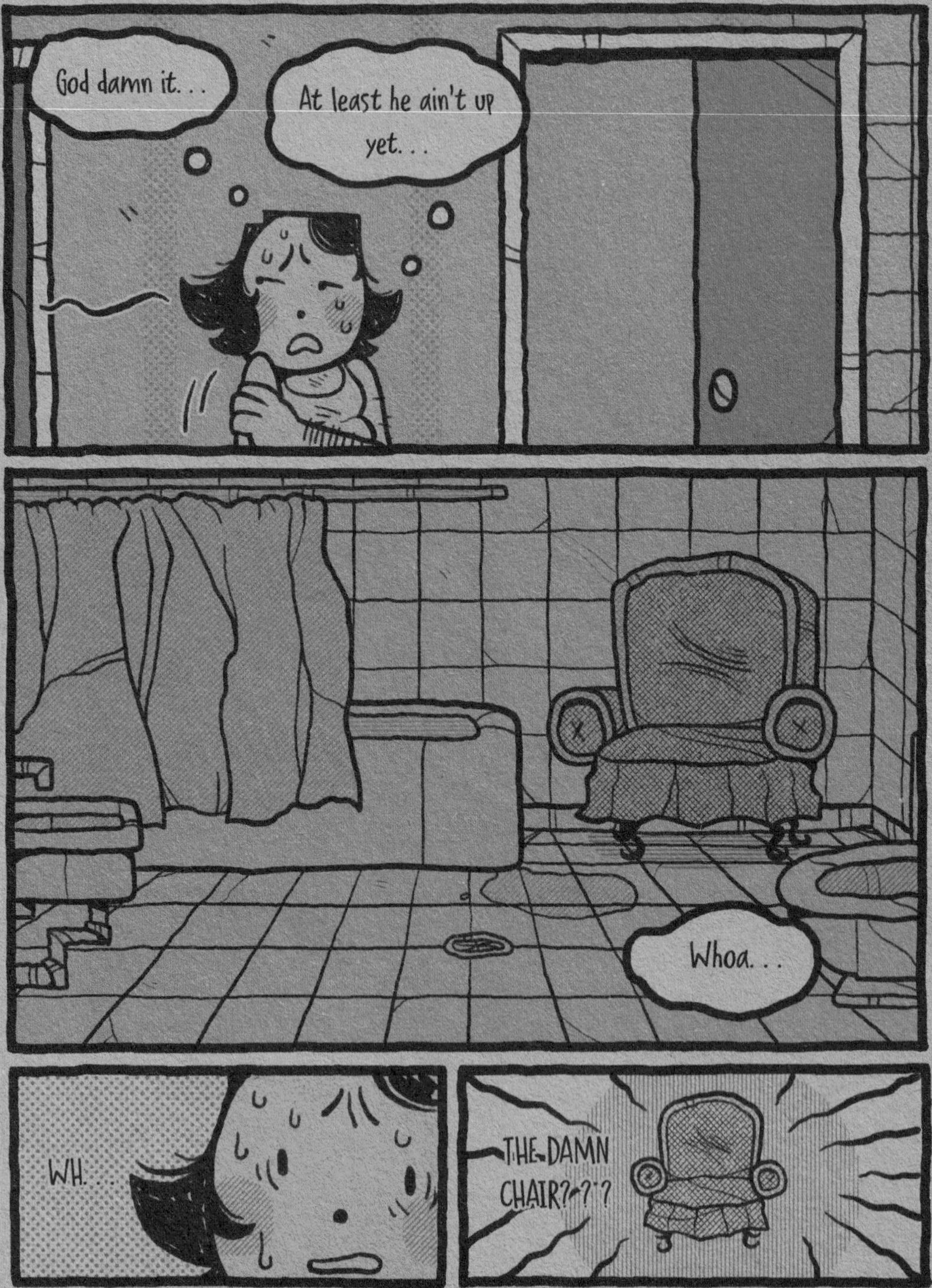
God damn it. . .
At least he ain't up yet. . .
Whoa. . .
WH. . .
THE DAMN CHAIR???

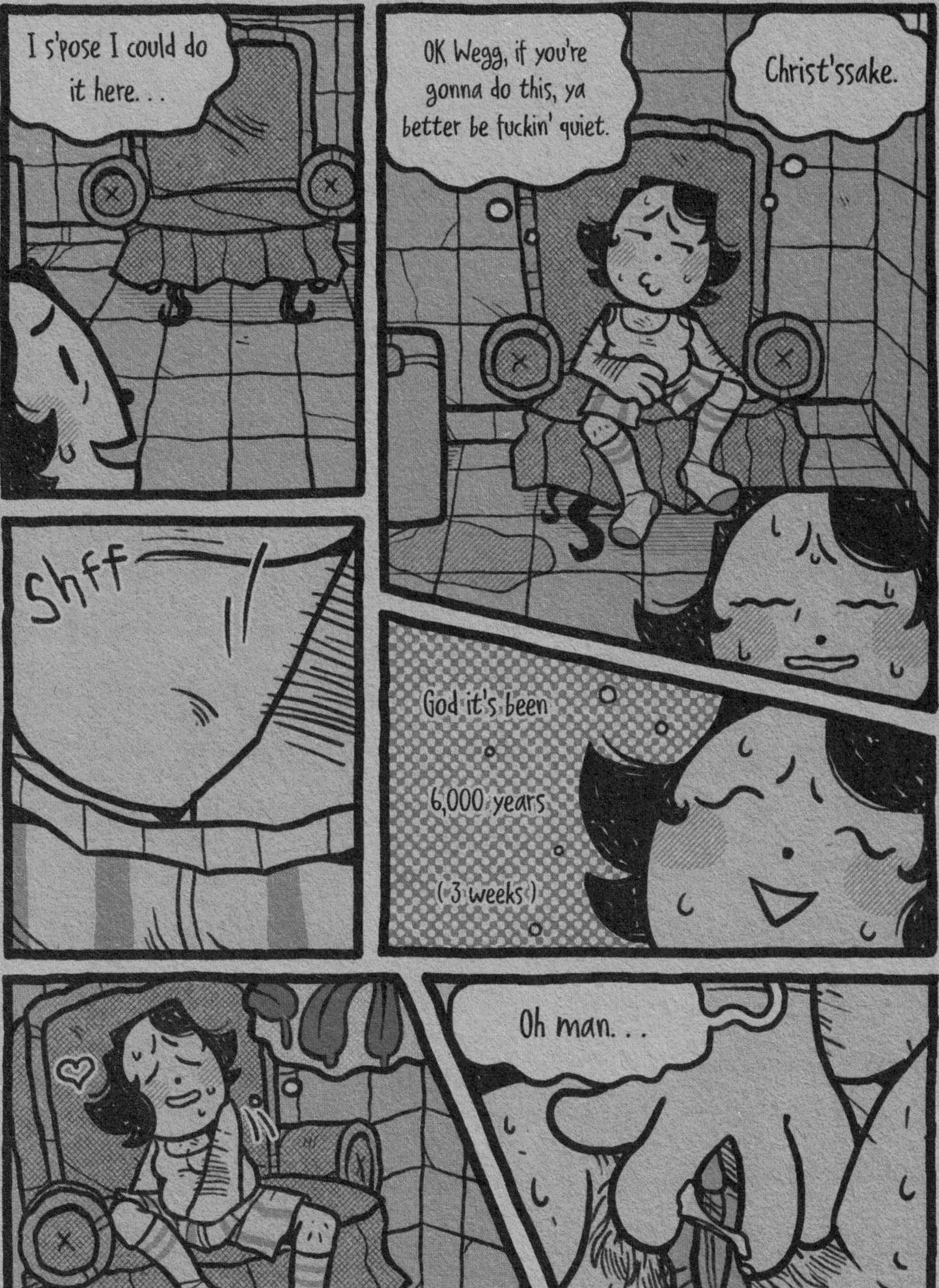

I s'pose I could do it here. . .
OK Wegg, if you're gonna do this, ya better be fuckin' quiet.
Christ'ssake.
Shff
God it's been
6,000 years
(3 weeks)
Oh man. . .

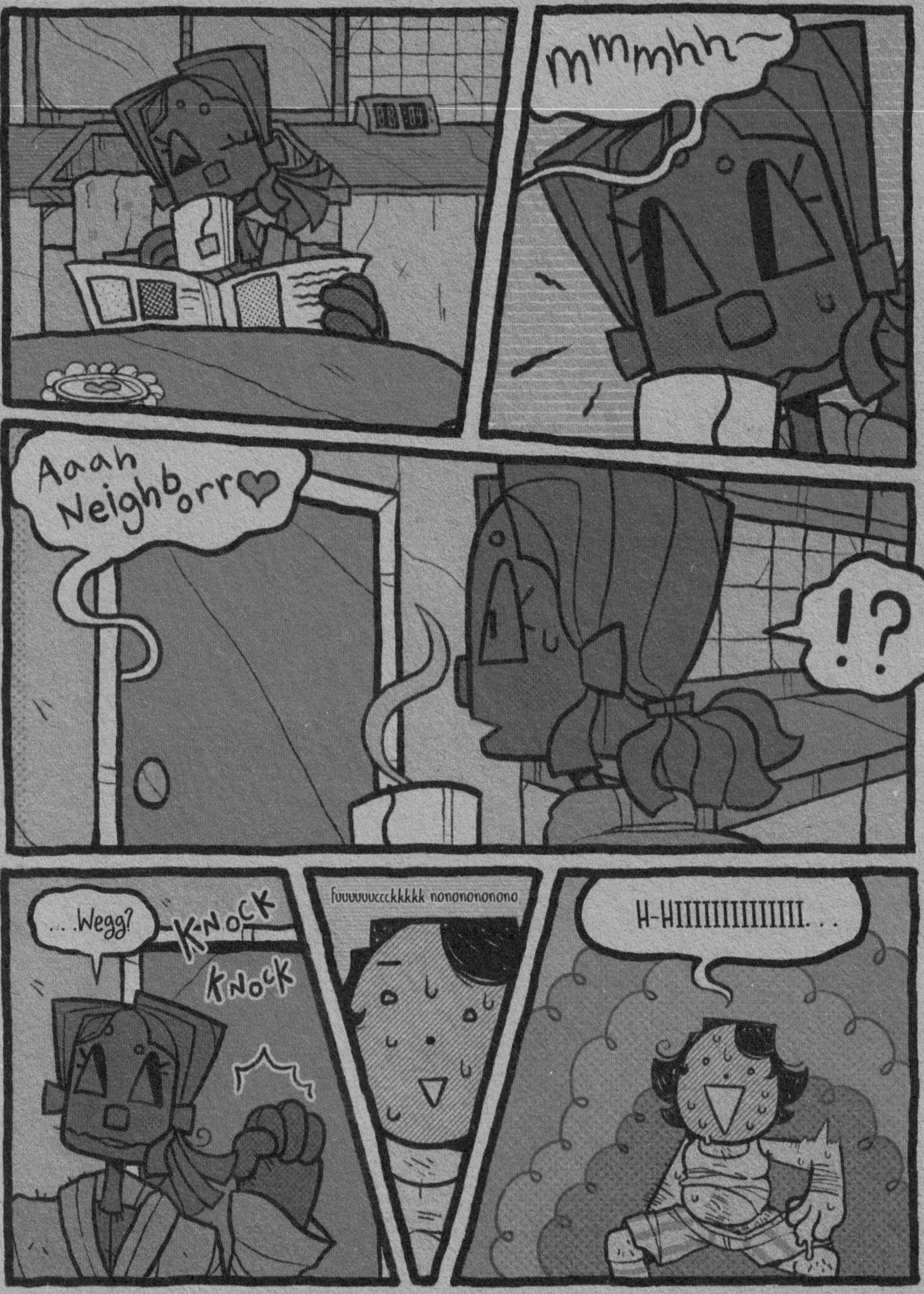
mmmhh~
Aaah Neighborr♥
!?
. . .Wegg?
KNOCK
KNOCK
fuuuuuucccckkkkk nononononono
H-HIIIIIIIIIIIIIII. . .

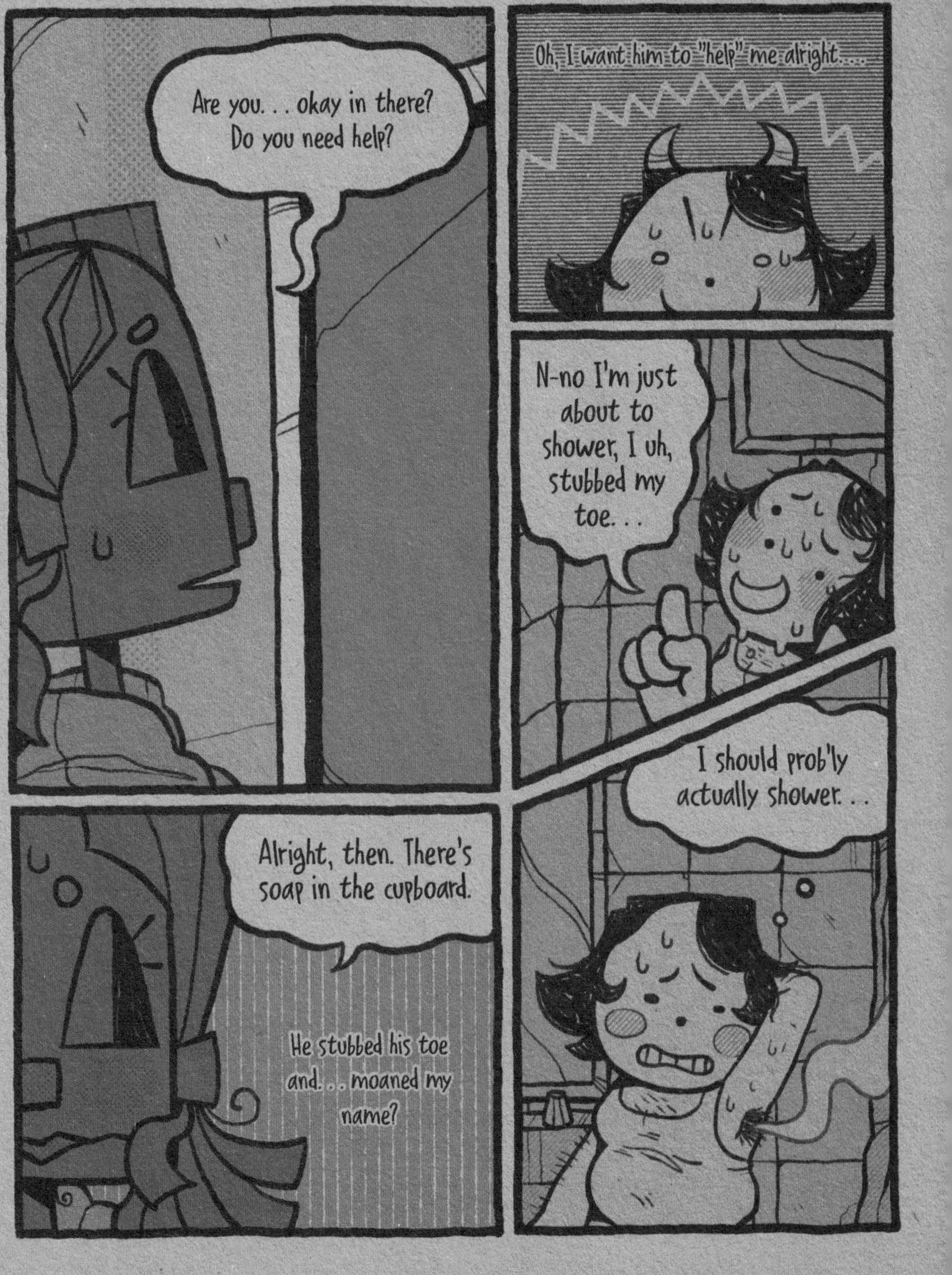
Are you. . . okay in there? Do you need help?
Oh, I want him to "help" me alright. . . .
N-no I'm just about to shower, I uh, stubbed my toe. . .
I should prob'ly actually shower. . .
Alright, then. There's soap in the cupboard.
He stubbed his toe and. . . moaned my name?

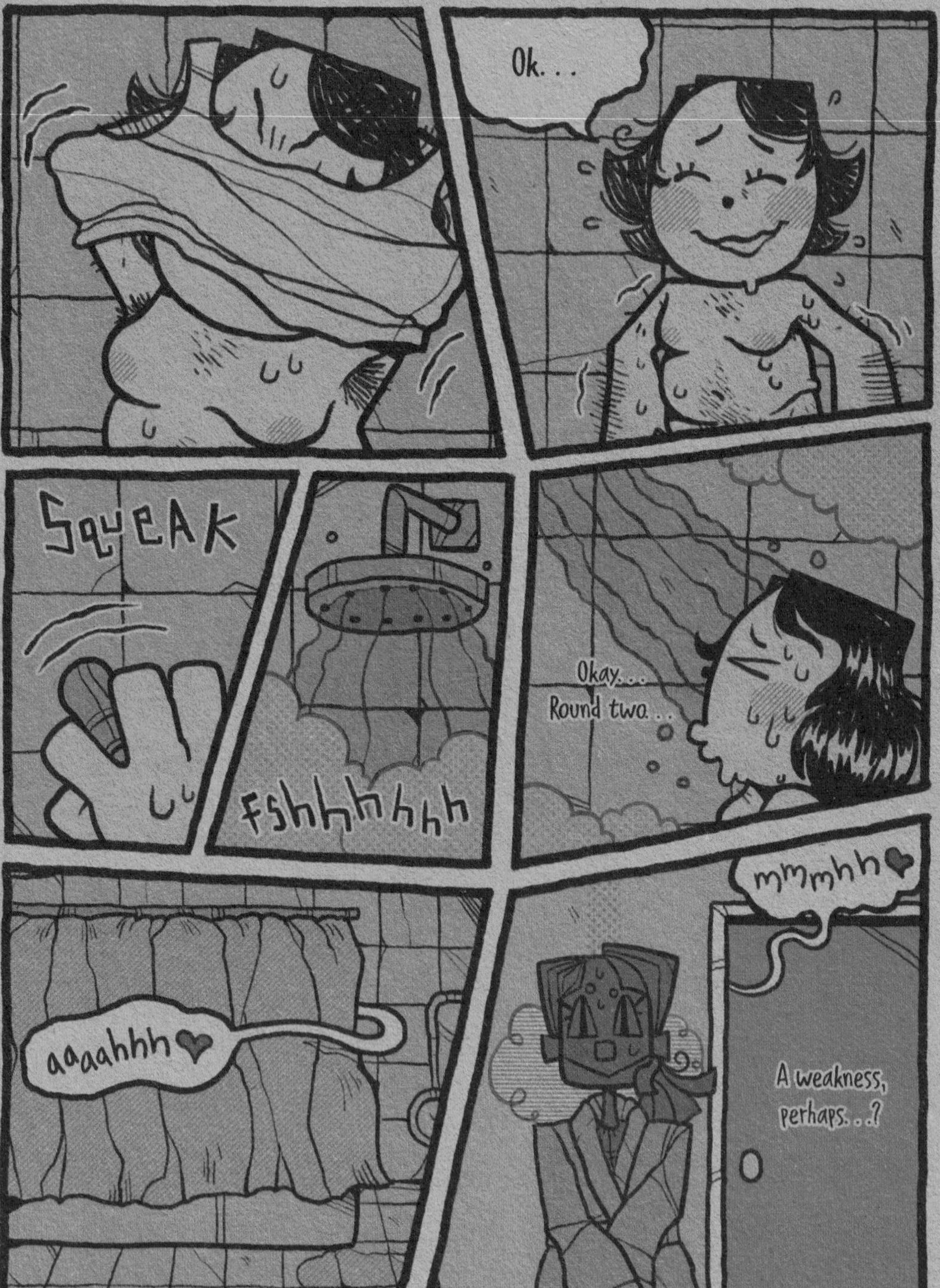
Ok. . .
Squeak
Fshhhhhhh
Okay. . .
Round two. . .
aaaahhh
mmmhh
A weakness,
perhaps. . .?

Wait, you're. . . like me, too?
No way.
That makes me. . . really happy.
We're in this together.

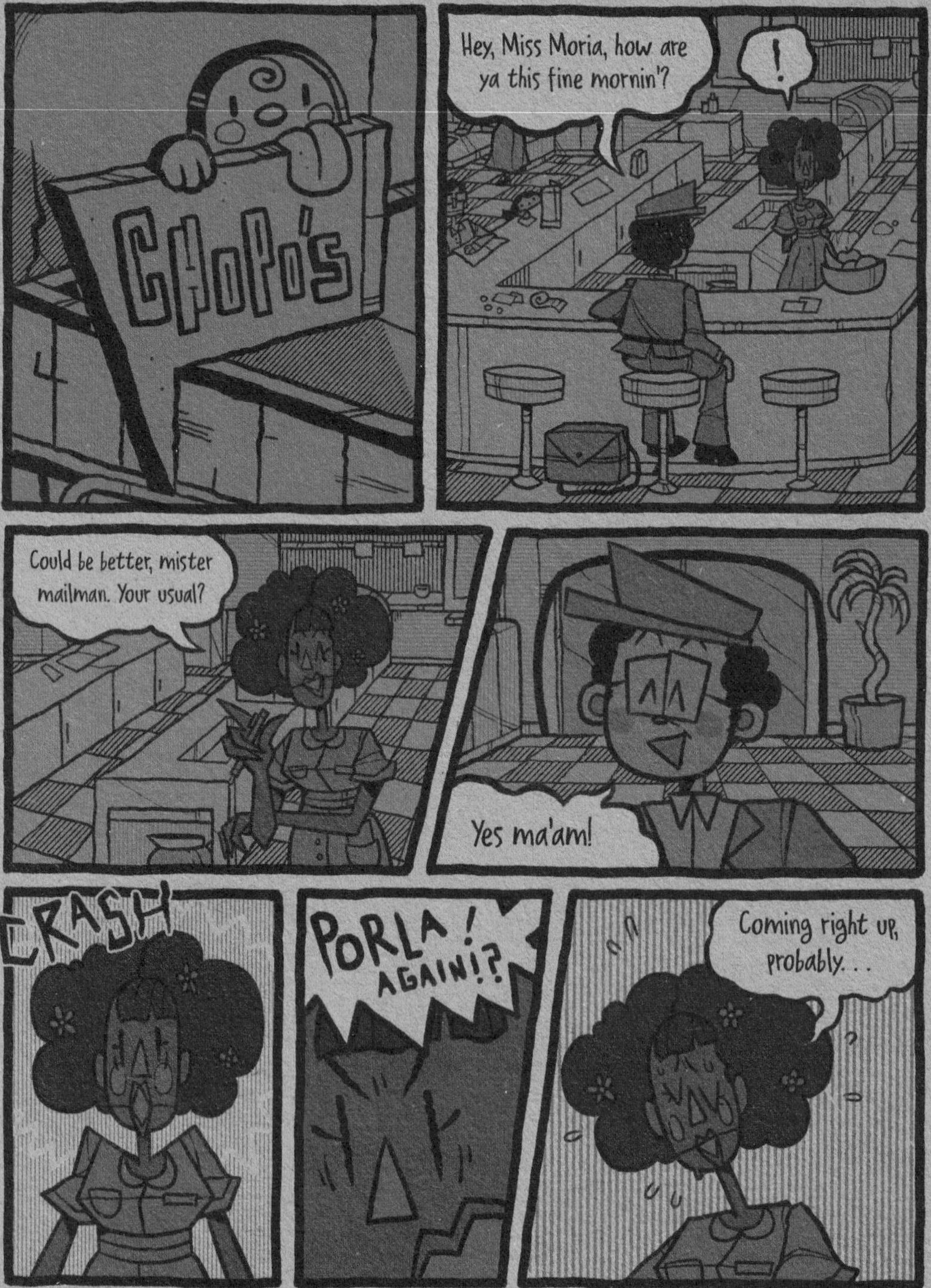
CHOPO'S
Hey, Miss Moria, how are ya this fine mornin'?
!
Could be better, mister mailman. Your usual?
Yes ma'am!
CRASH
PORLA! AGAIN!?
Coming right up, probably...

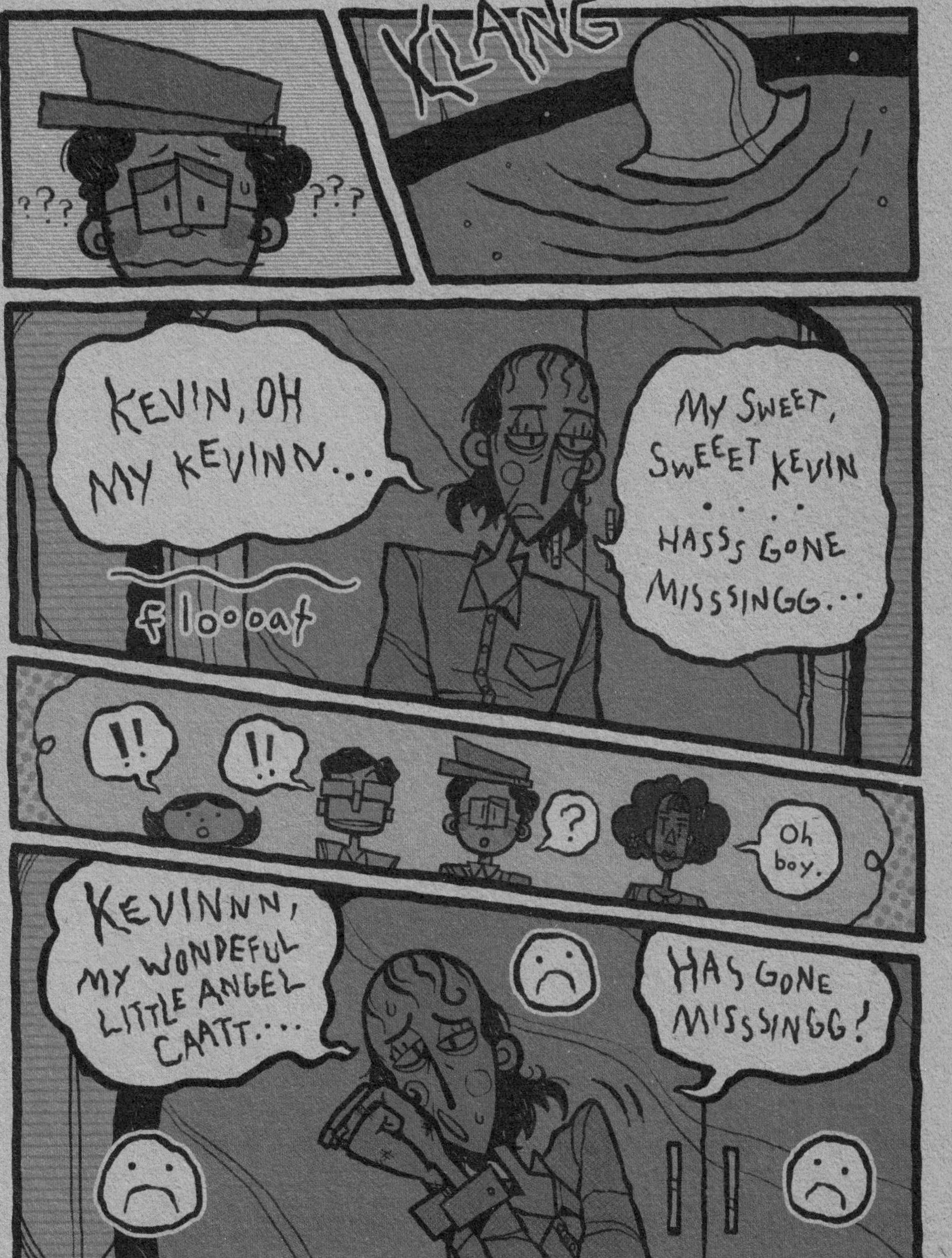
???
???
KLANG
KEVIN, OH MY KEVINN...
floooat
MY SWEET, SWEEET KEVIN . . . HASSS GONE MISSSINGG...
!!
!!
?
Oh boy.
KEVINNN, MY WONDEFUL LITTLE ANGEL CAATT....
HAS GONE MISSSINGG!

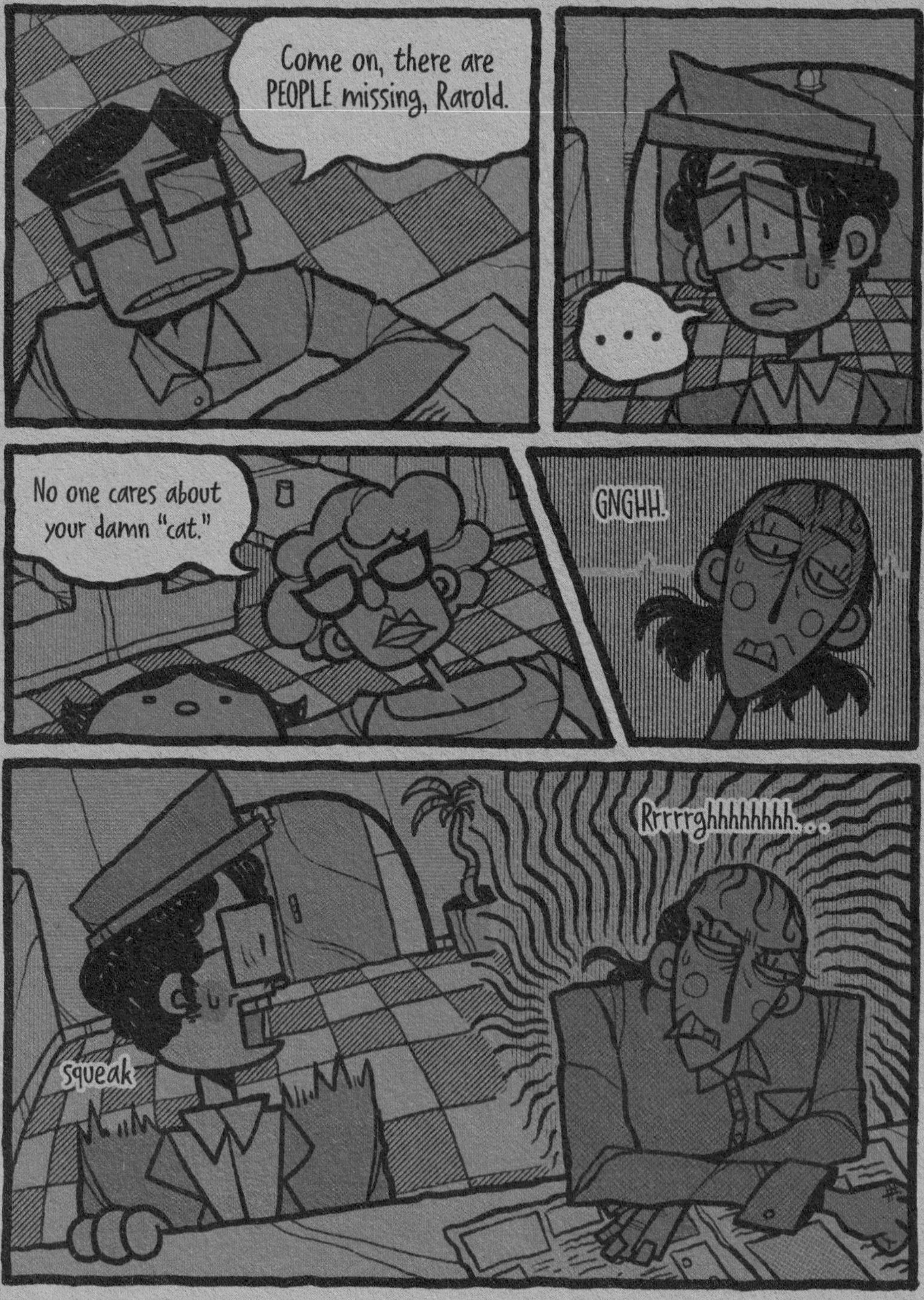
Come on, there are PEOPLE missing, Rarold.
...
No one cares about your damn "cat."
GNGHH.
Rrrrrghhhhhhhh...
squeak

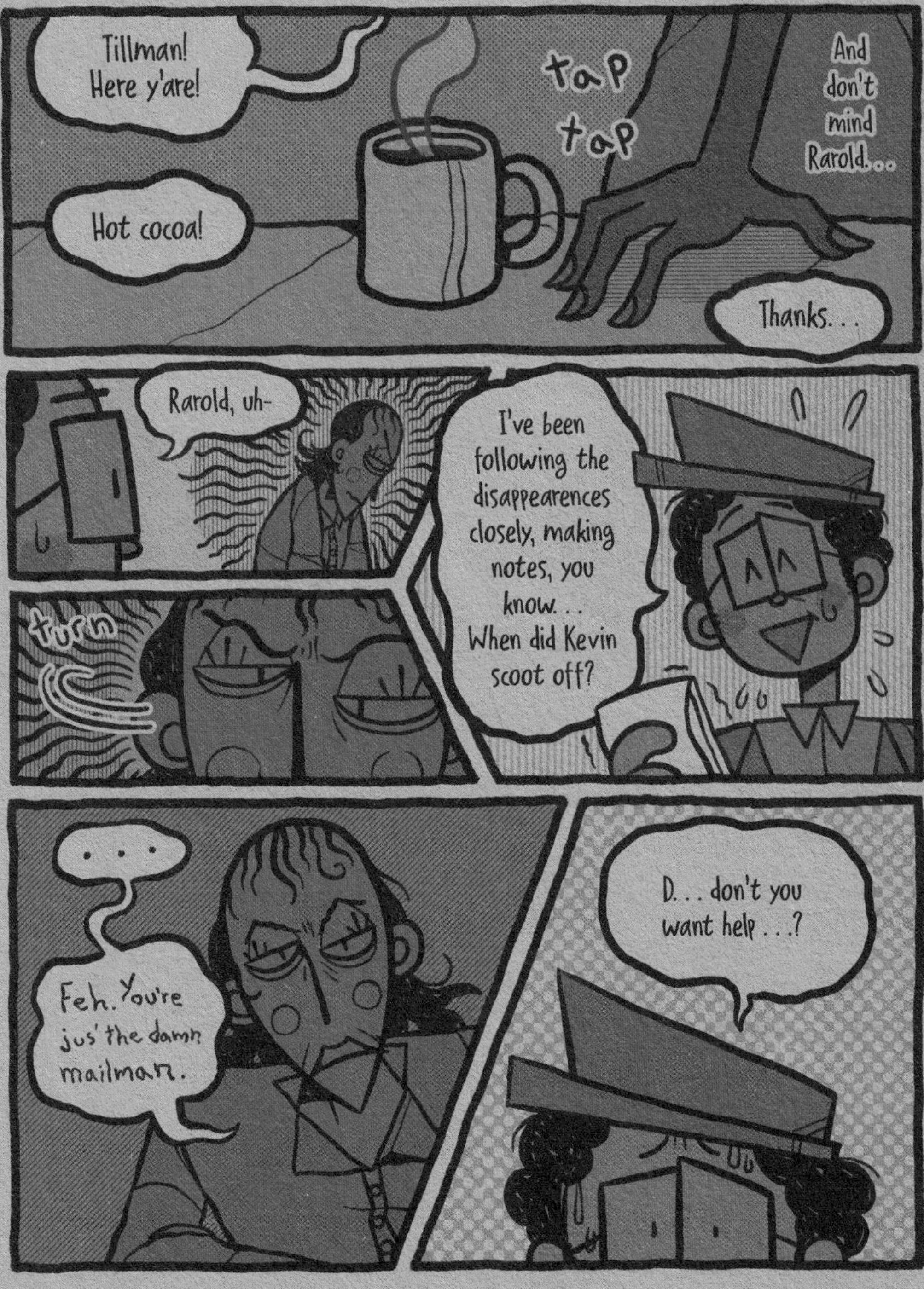
Tillman! Here y'are!
Hot cocoa!
tap tap
And don't mind Rarold...
Thanks...
Rarold, uh-
turn
I've been following the disappearences closely, making notes, you know... When did Kevin scoot off?
...
Feh. You're jus' the damn mailman.
D... don't you want help...?

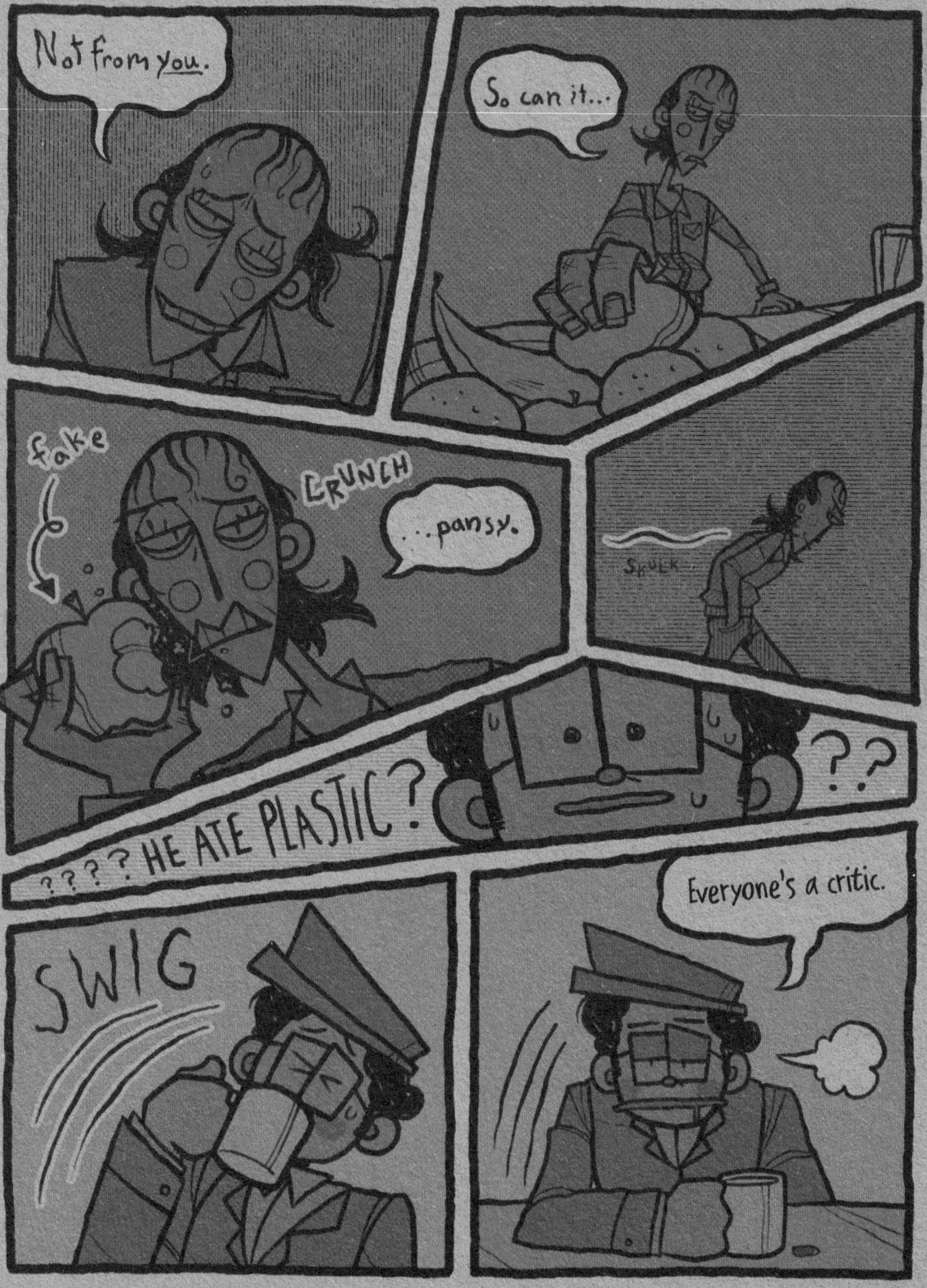
Not from you.
So can it...
fake
CRUNCH
...pansy.
SKULK
??
????HE ATE PLASTIC?
SWIG
Everyone's a critic.

. . .does it hurt?
. . .wow, OK!
Well, I'm not very good at
sewin'. . .
. . .but I'll try my best, ya big
lug. . .

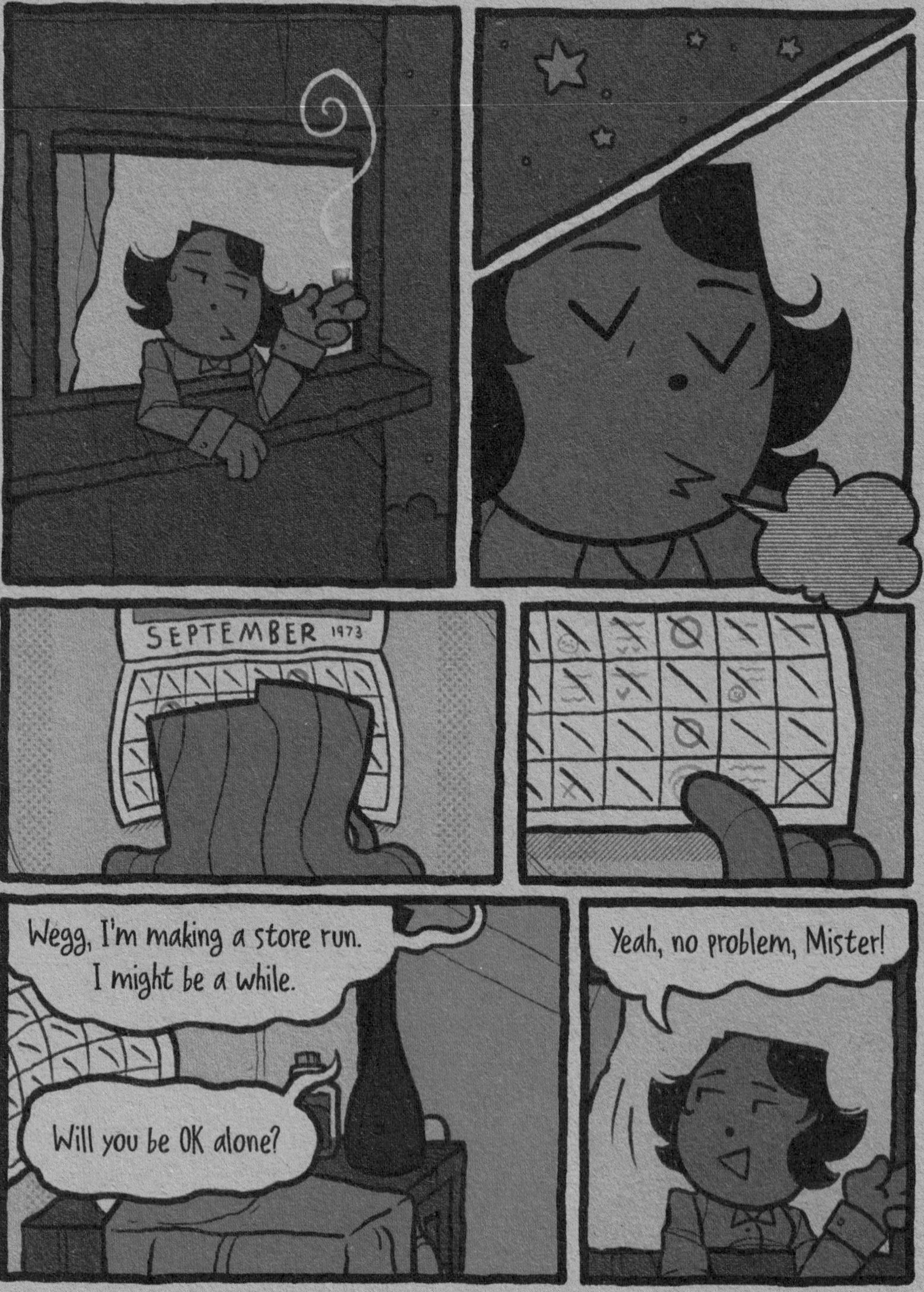
SEPTEMBER 1973
Wegg, I'm making a store run. I might be a while.
Will you be OK alone?
Yeah, no problem, Mister!

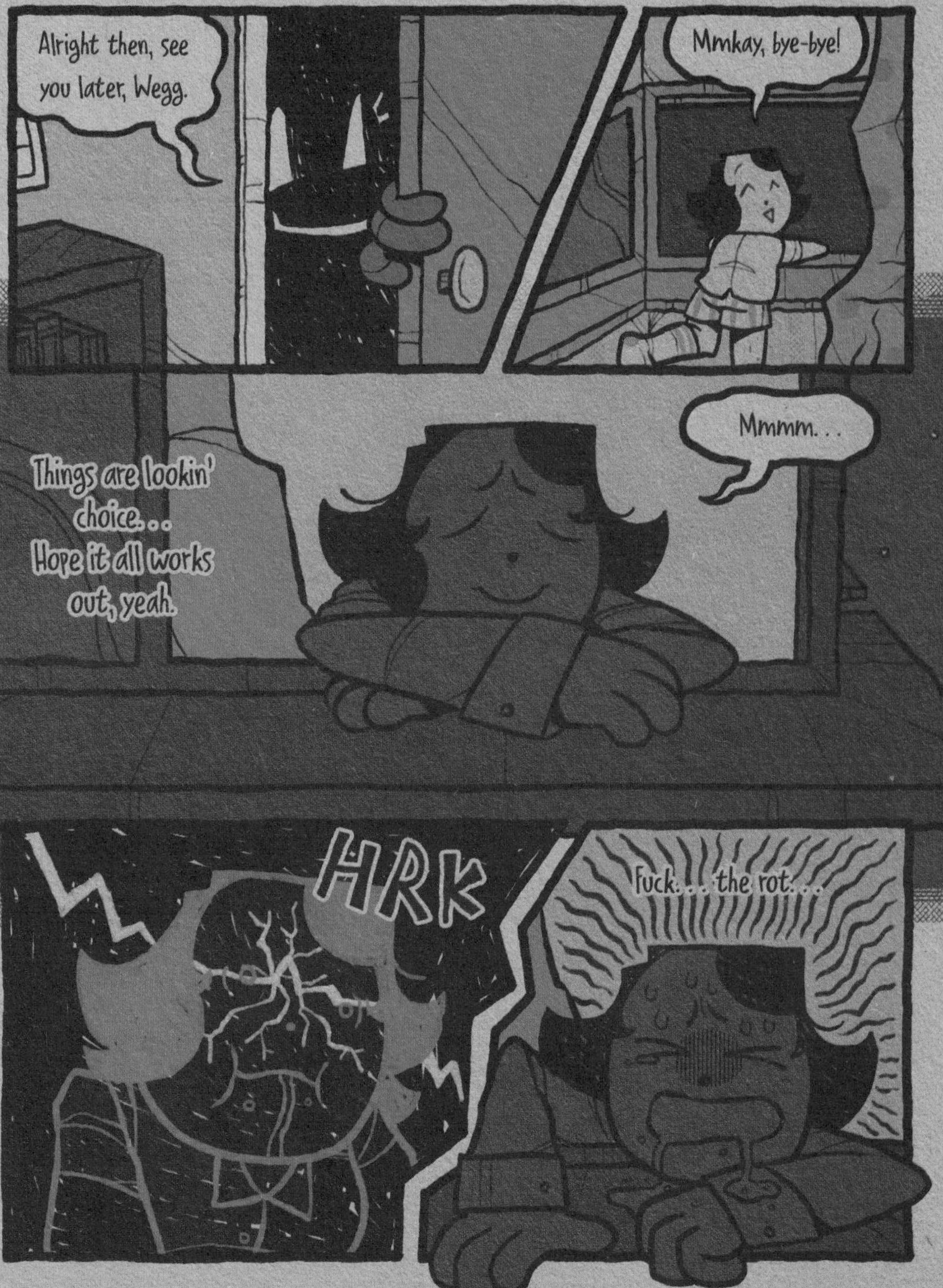
Alright then, see you later, Wegg.
Mmkay, bye-bye!
Mmmm. . .
Things are lookin' choice. . . Hope it all works out, yeah.
HRK
Fuck. . . the rot. . .

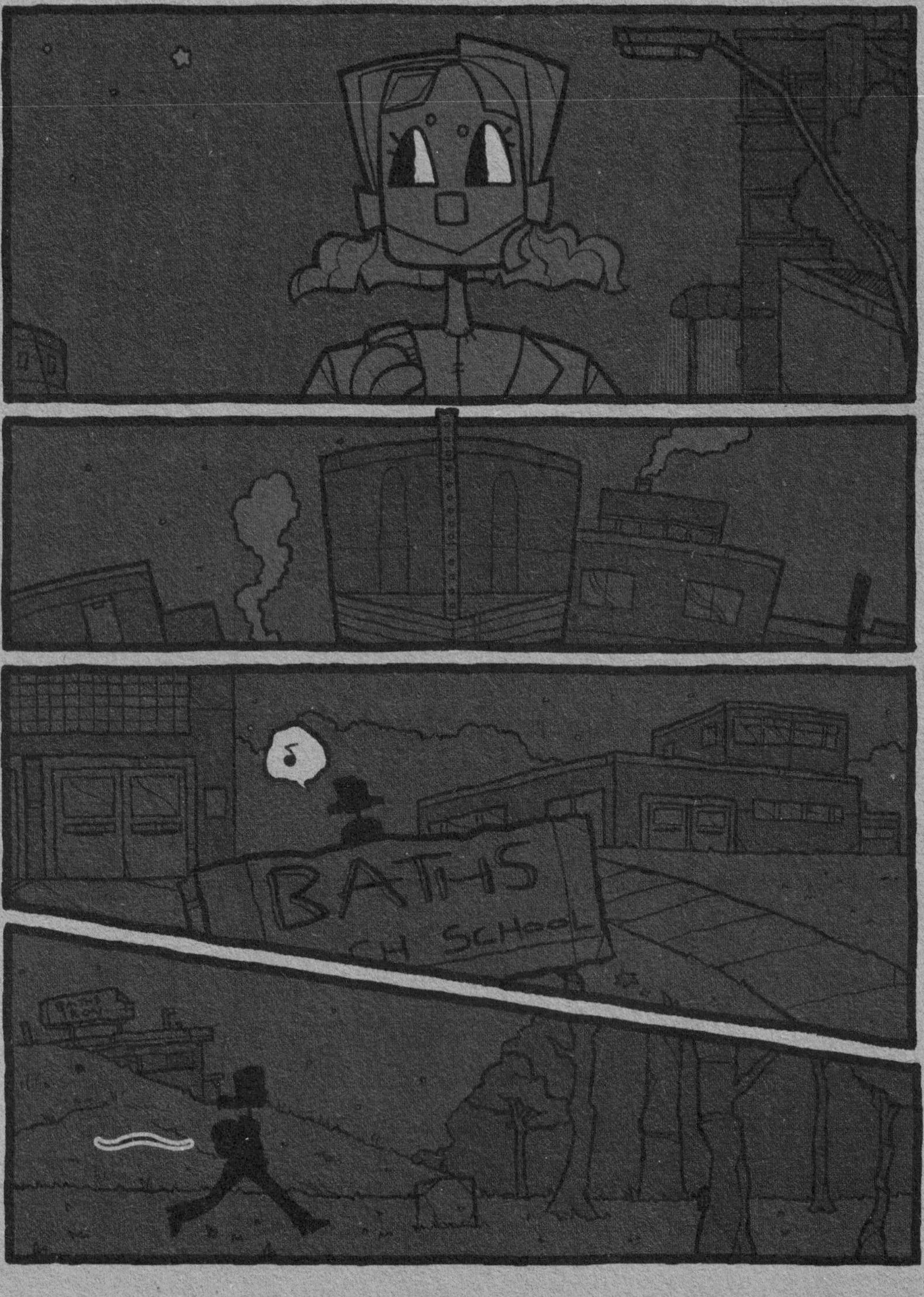
BATHS
CH SCHOOL

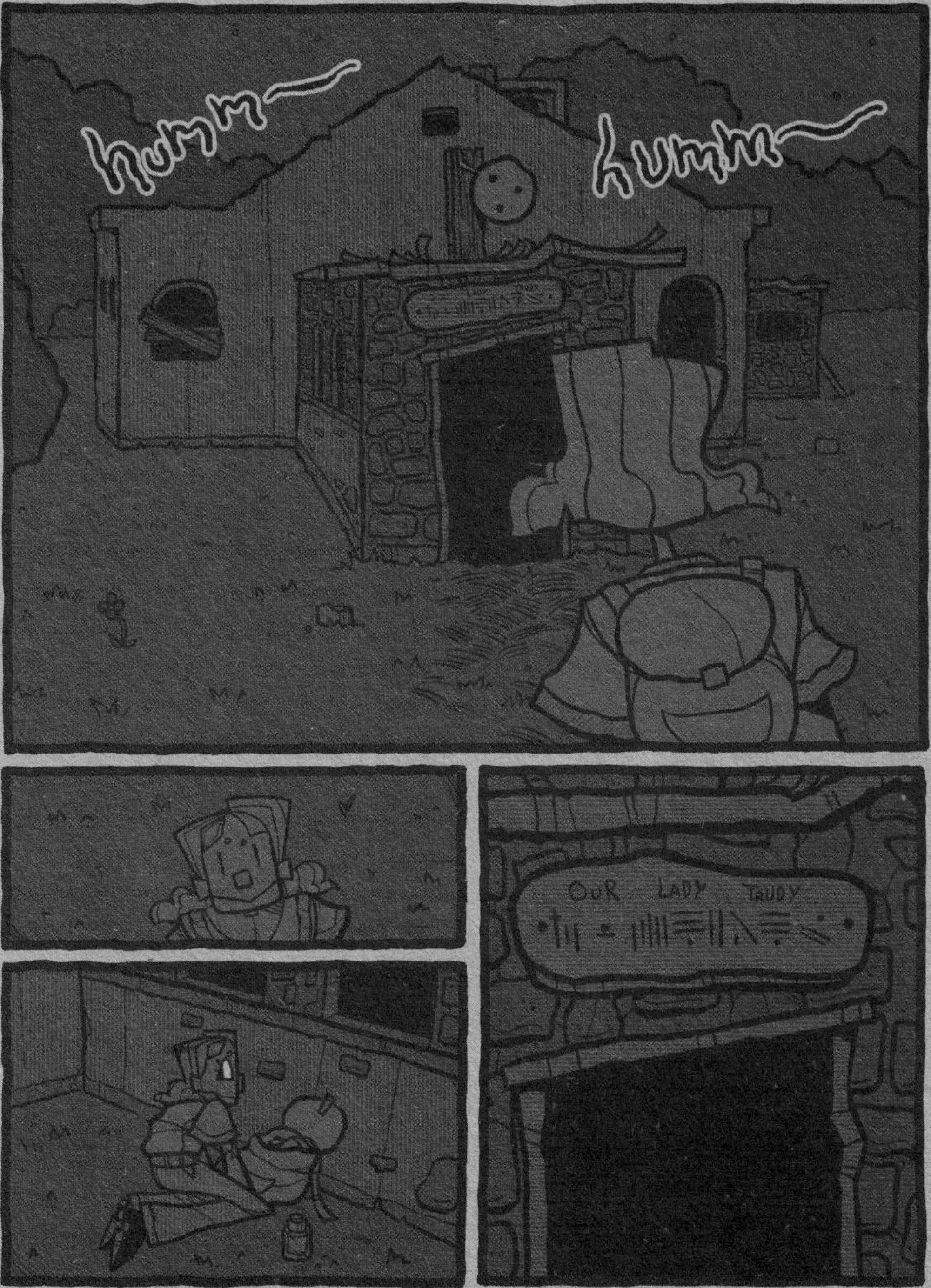
humm—
humm—
OUR LADY TRUDY

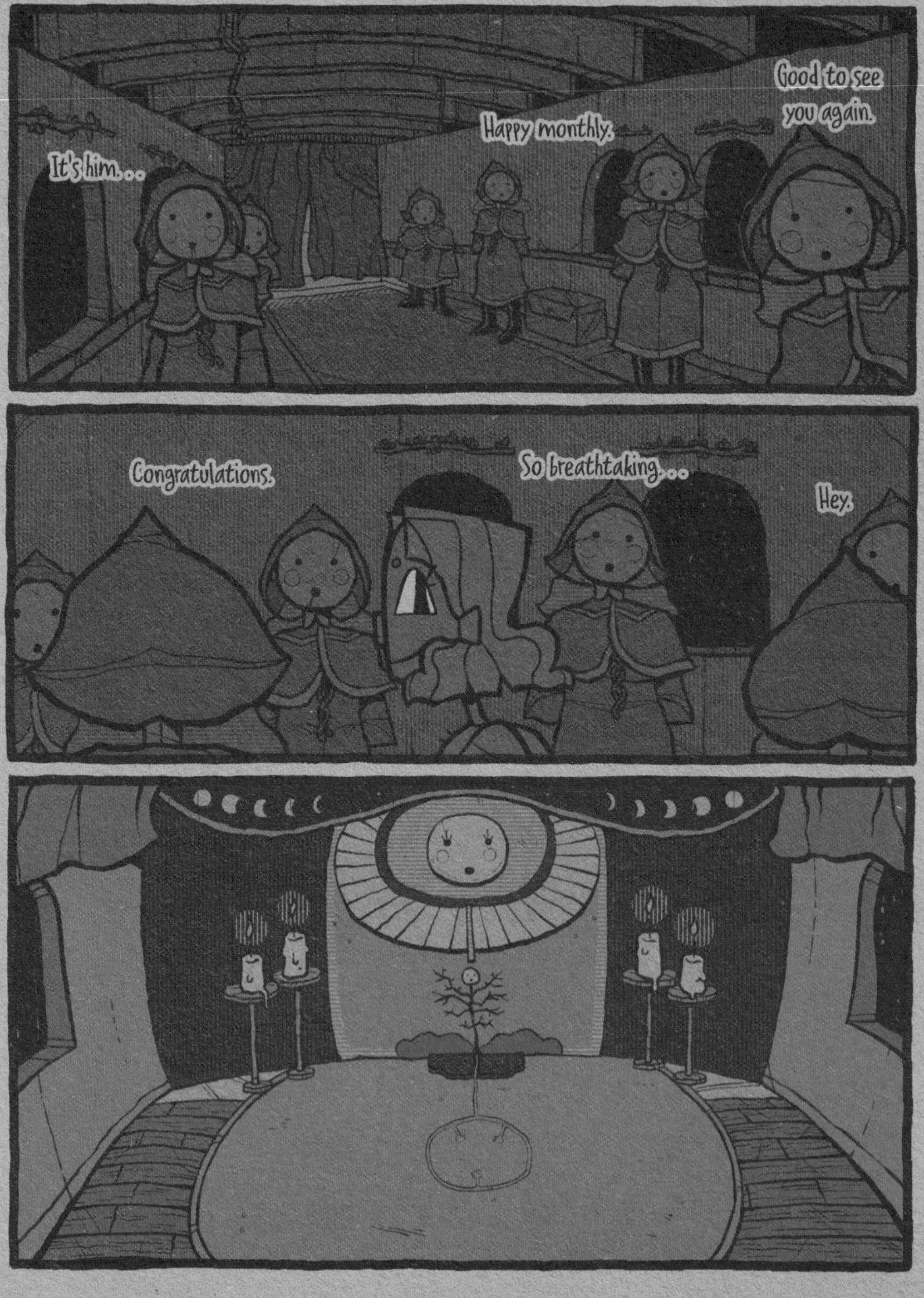
It's him. . .
Happy monthly.
Good to see you again.
Congratulations.
So breathtaking. . .
Hey.

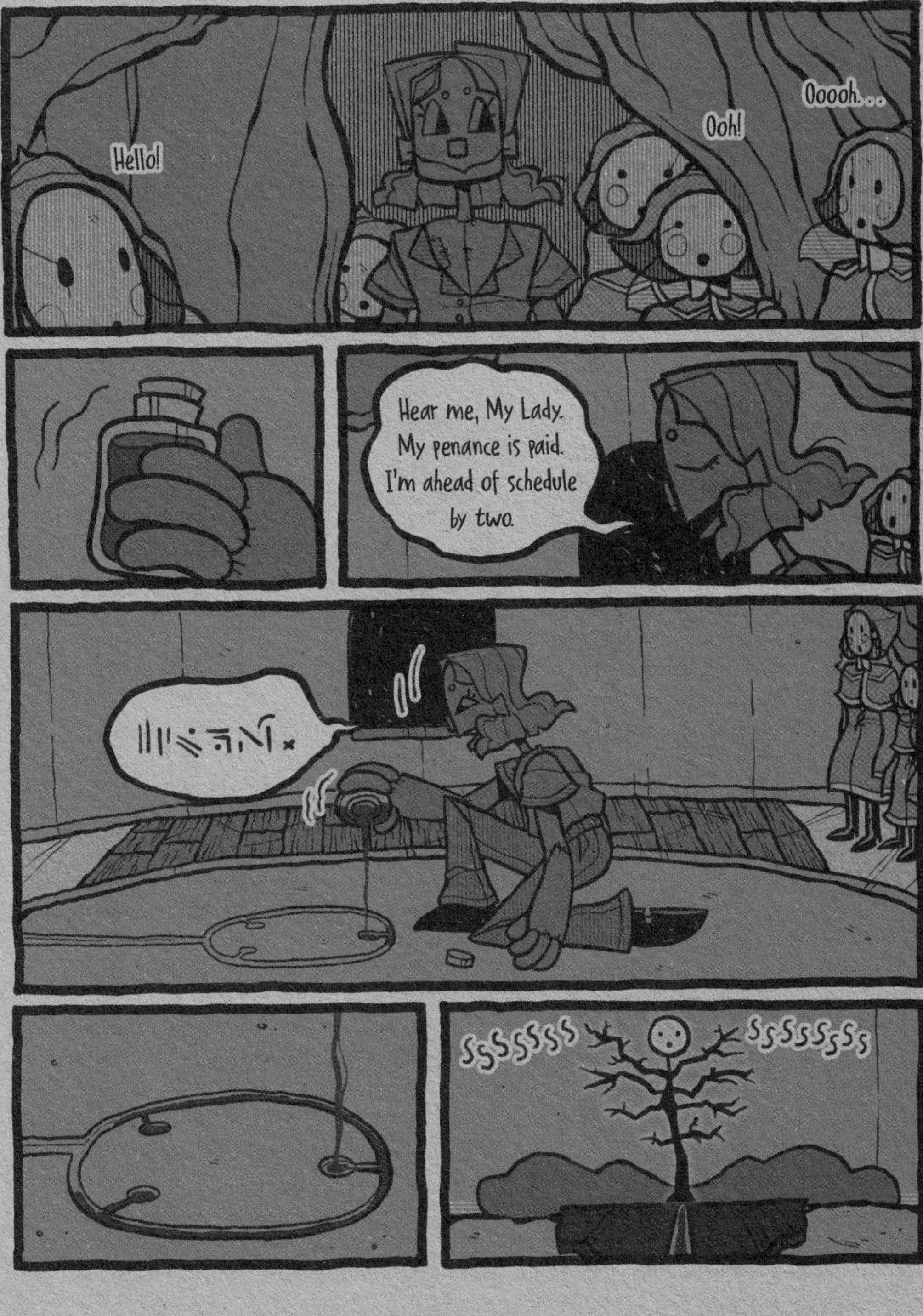
Hello!
Ooh!
Ooooh...
Hear me, My Lady. My penance is paid. I'm ahead of schedule by two.
SSSSSSS
SSSSSSSS

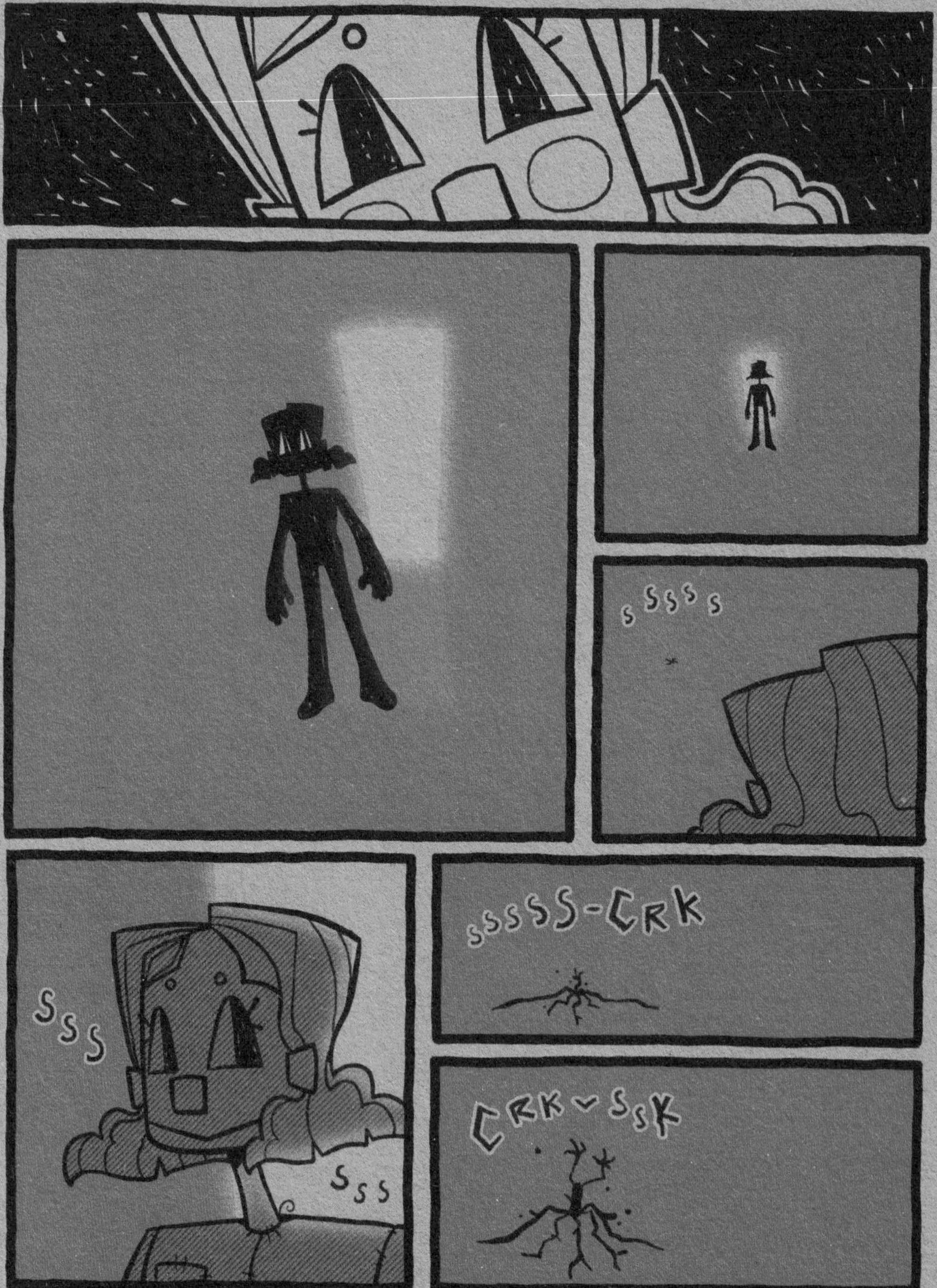

sSSSs
SSS
SSS
sssSS-CRK
CRK-SSK

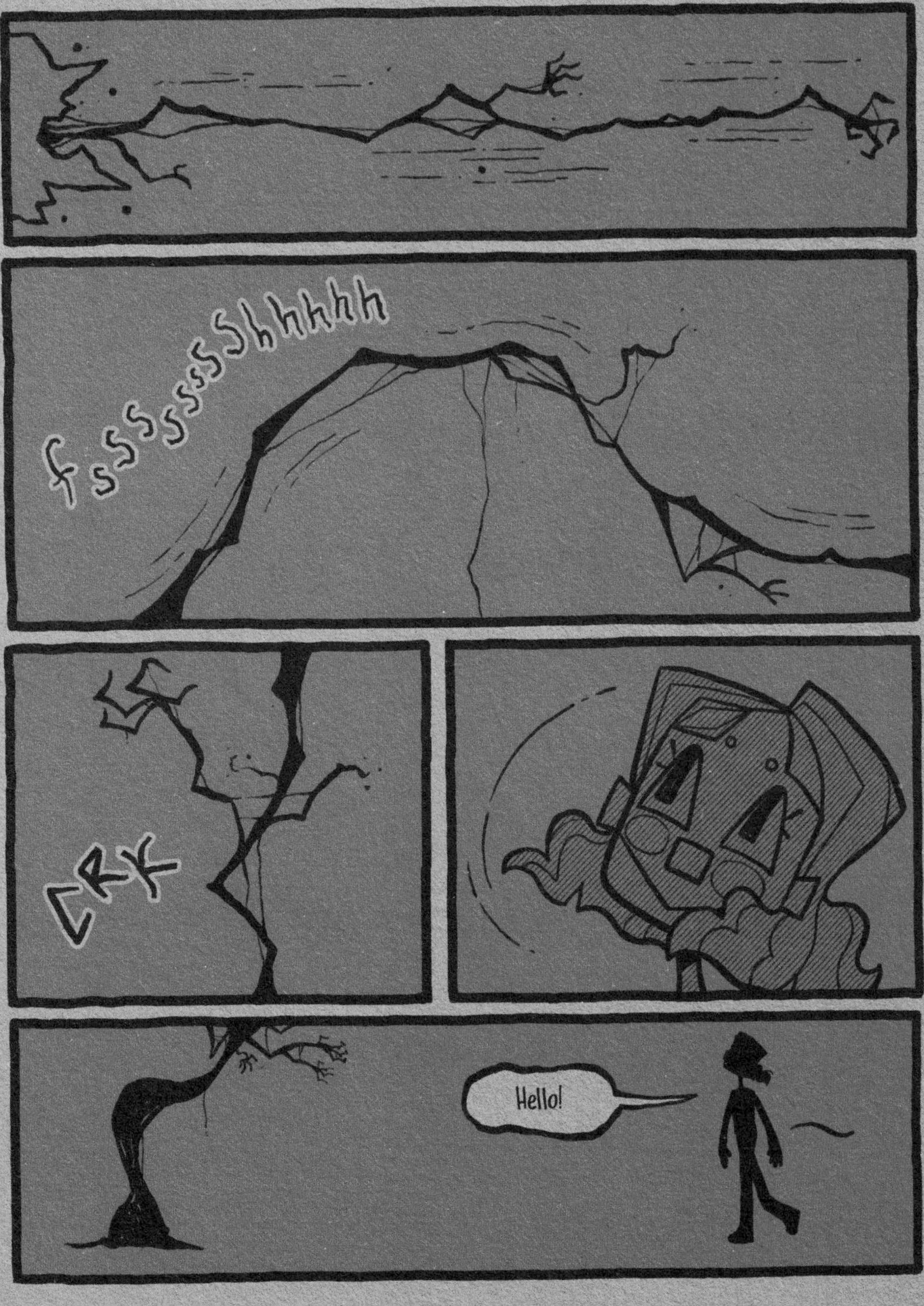
fsssssssShhhhh
CRK
Hello!

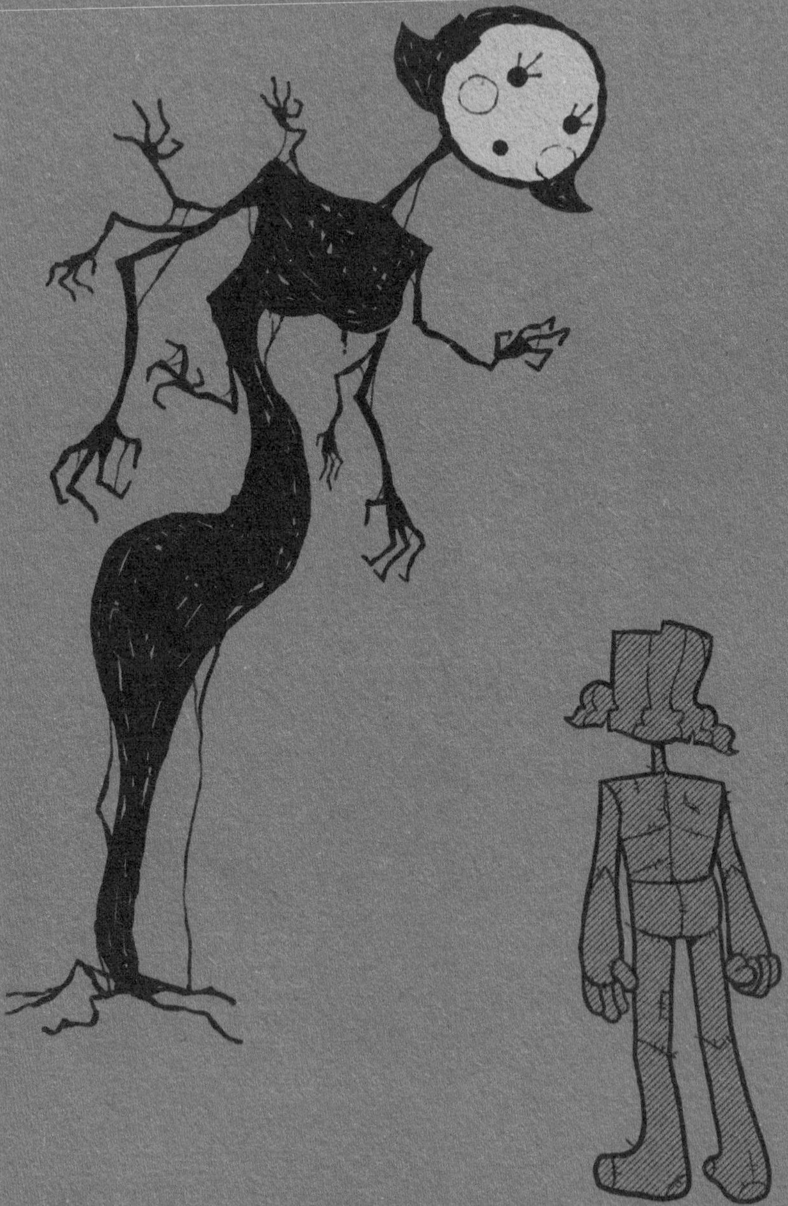

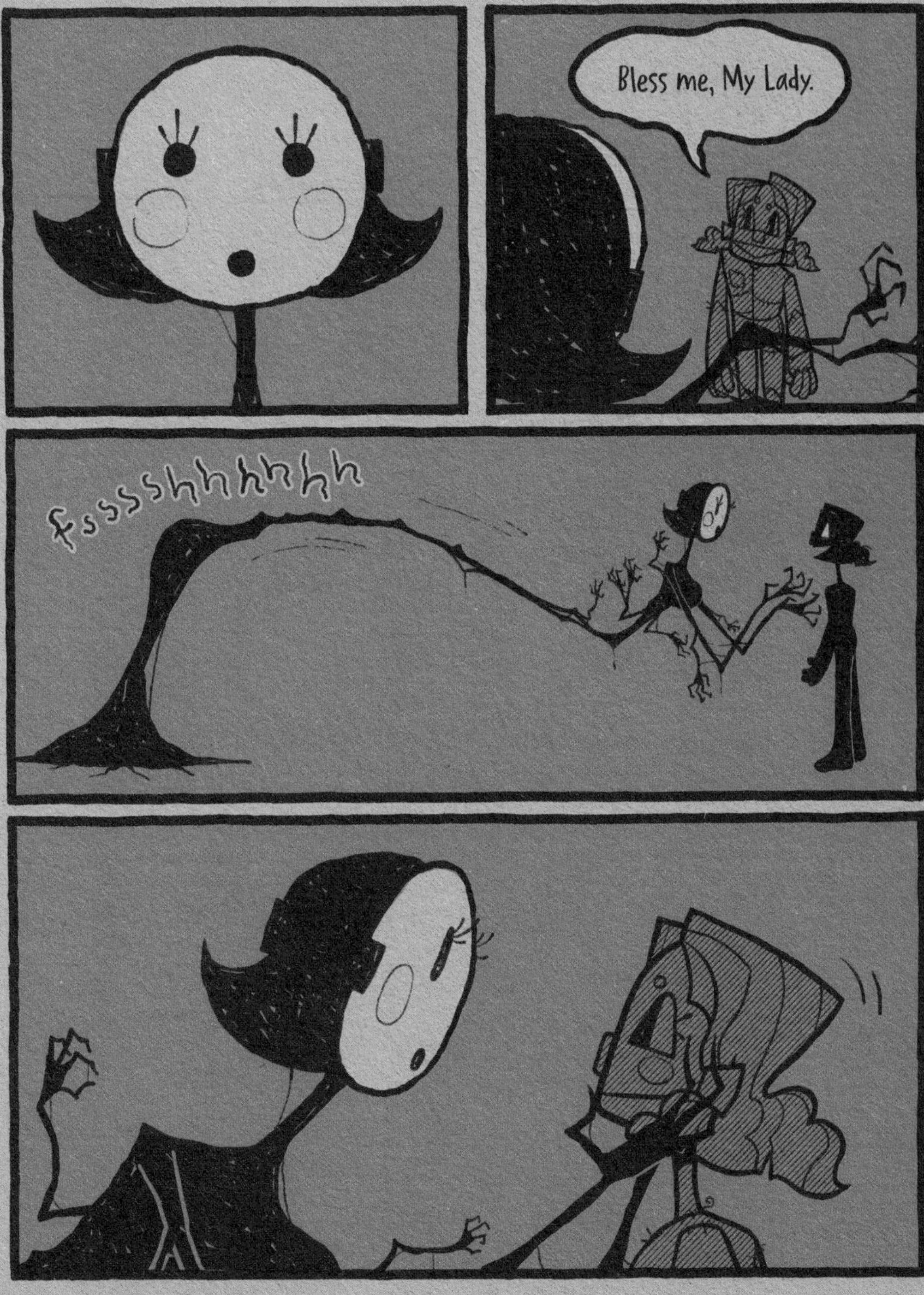
Bless me, My Lady.
fssssshhhhhh

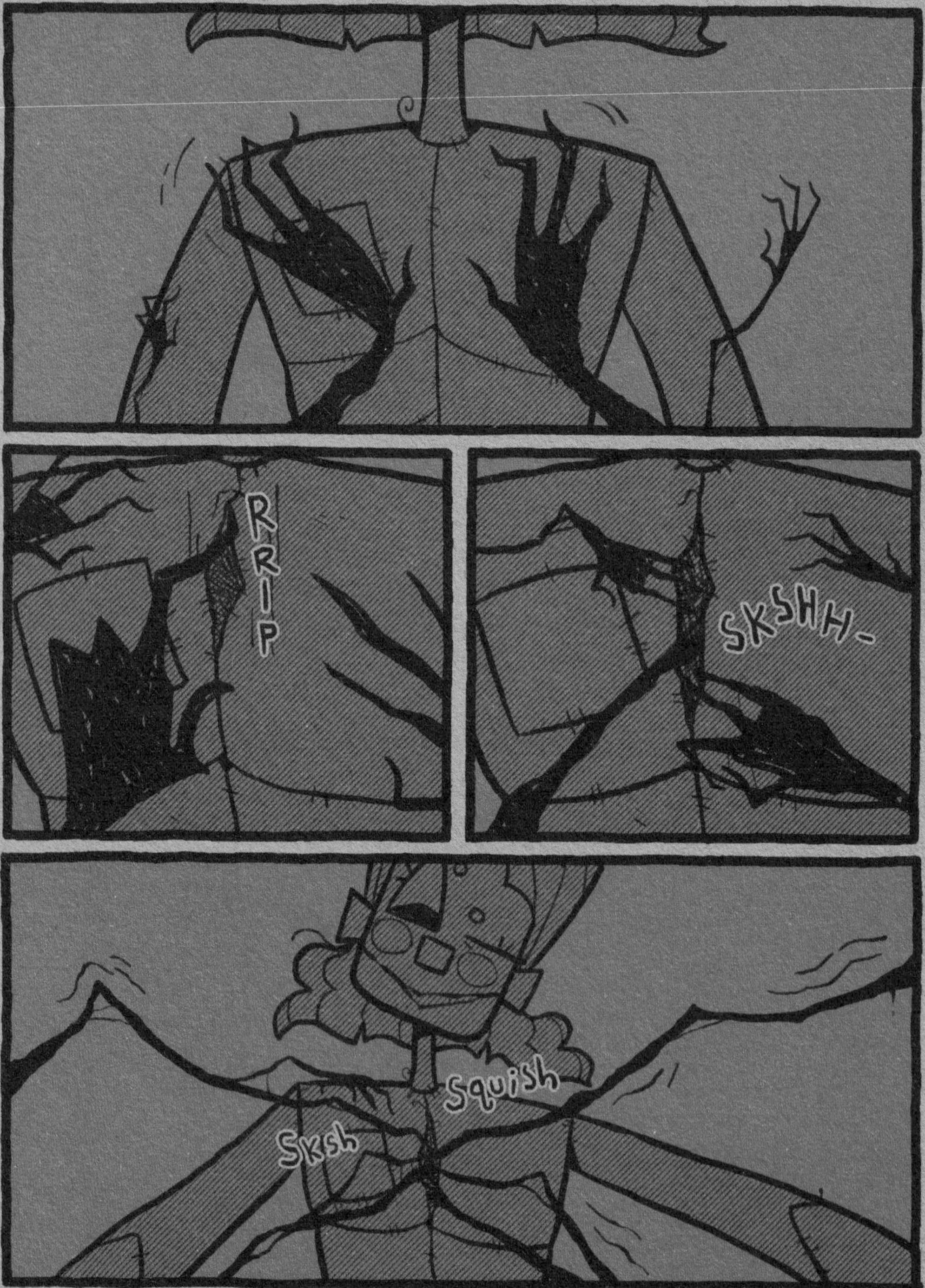
RRIP
SKSHH-
Squish
Sksh

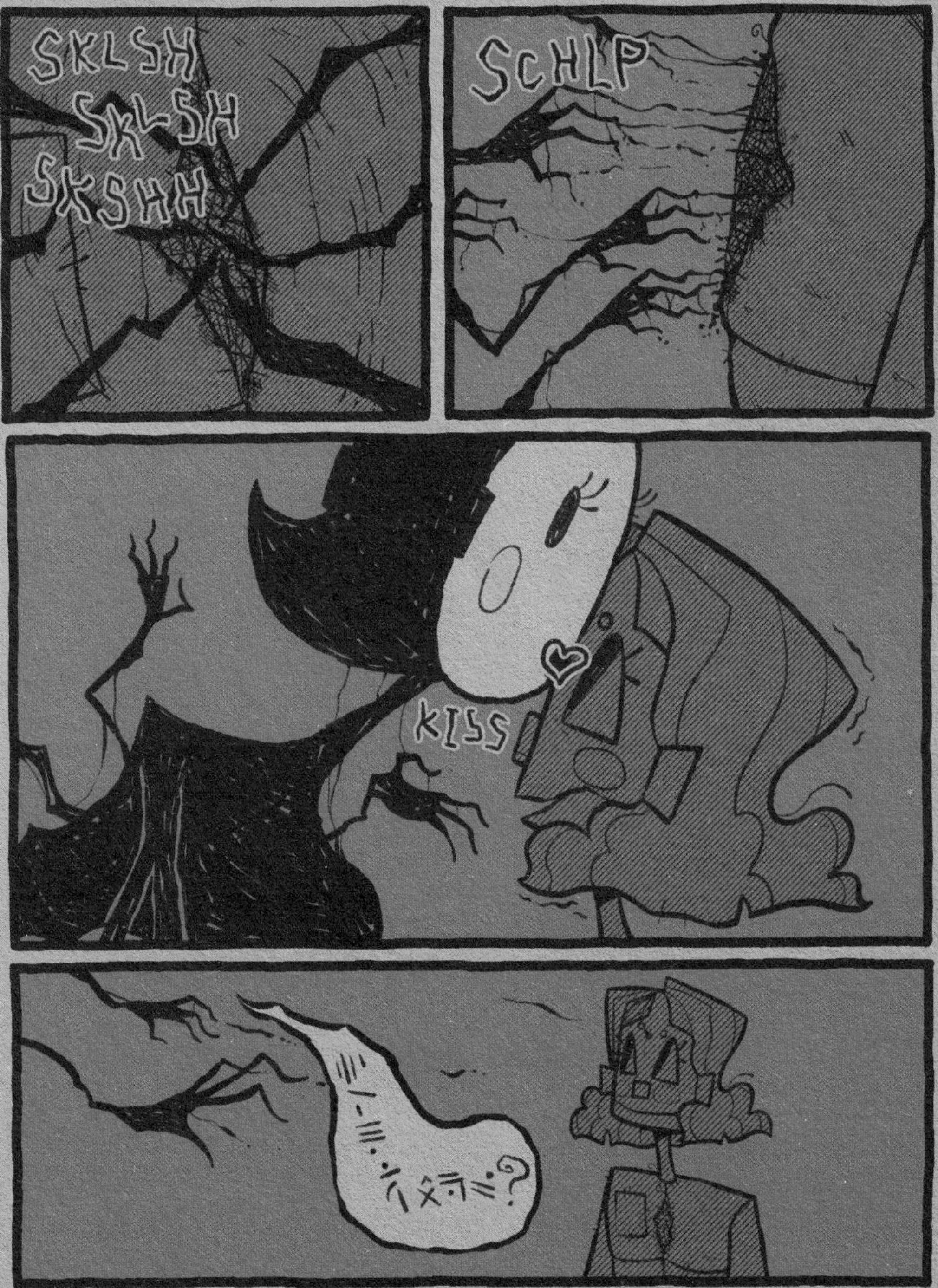
SKLSH
SKLSH
SKSHH
SCHLP
KISS

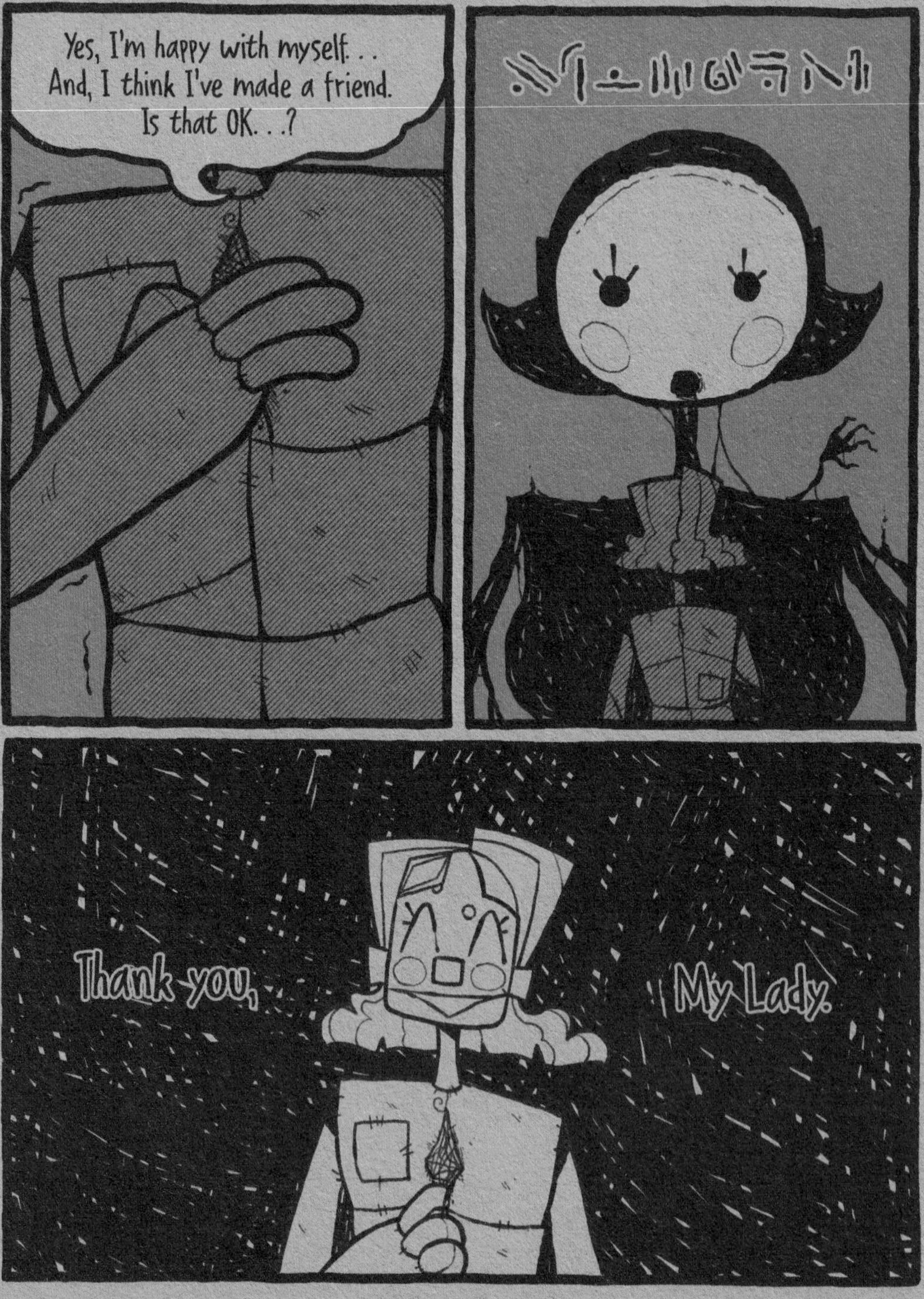

Yes, I'm happy with myself. . .
And, I think I've made a friend.
Is that OK. . .?
Thank you,
My Lady.

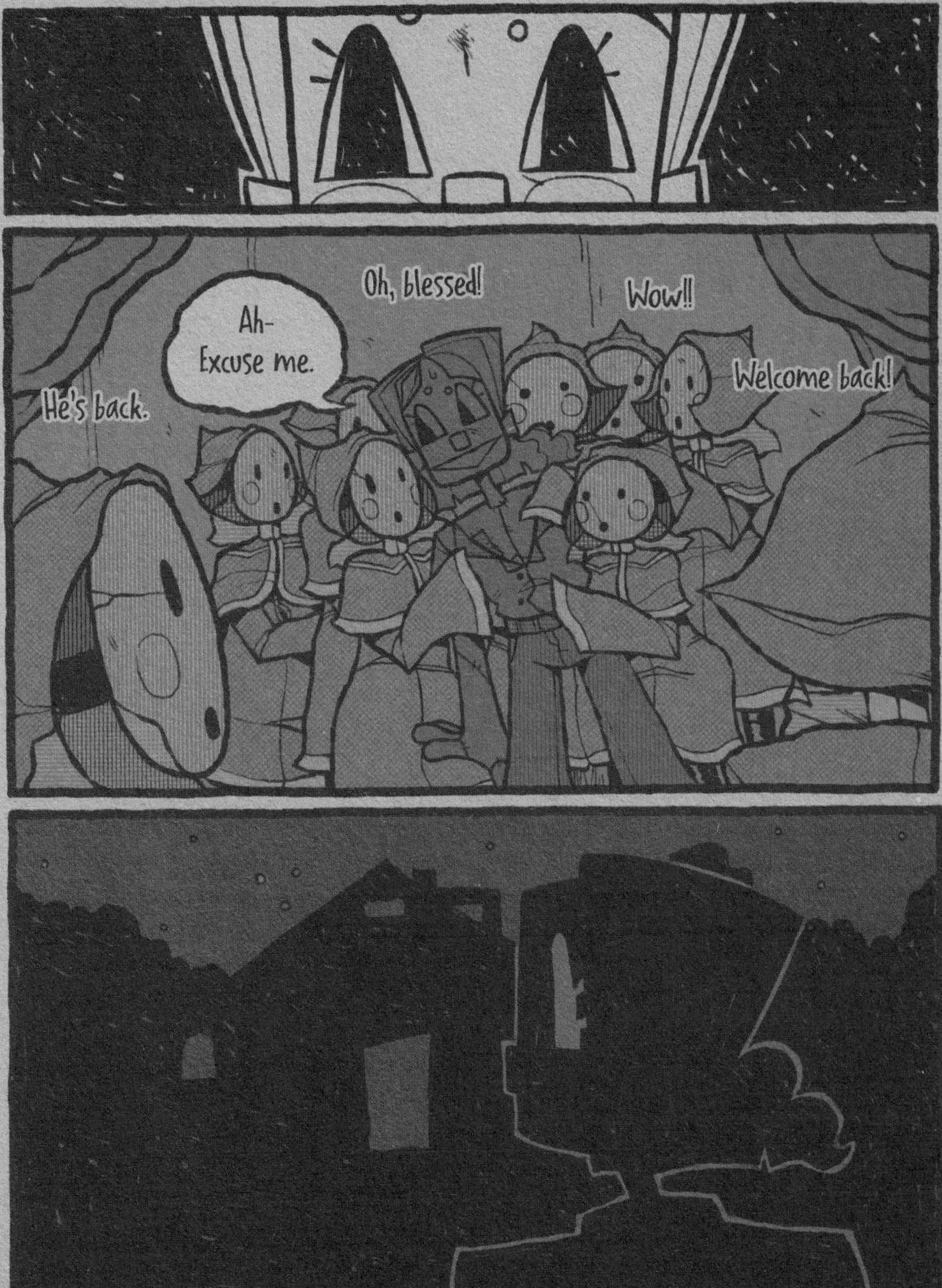
He's back.
Ah- Excuse me.
Oh, blessed!
Wow!!
Welcome back!

CLUNK

Wegg. . . ah.

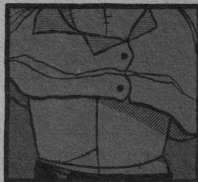

. . .another month. . .

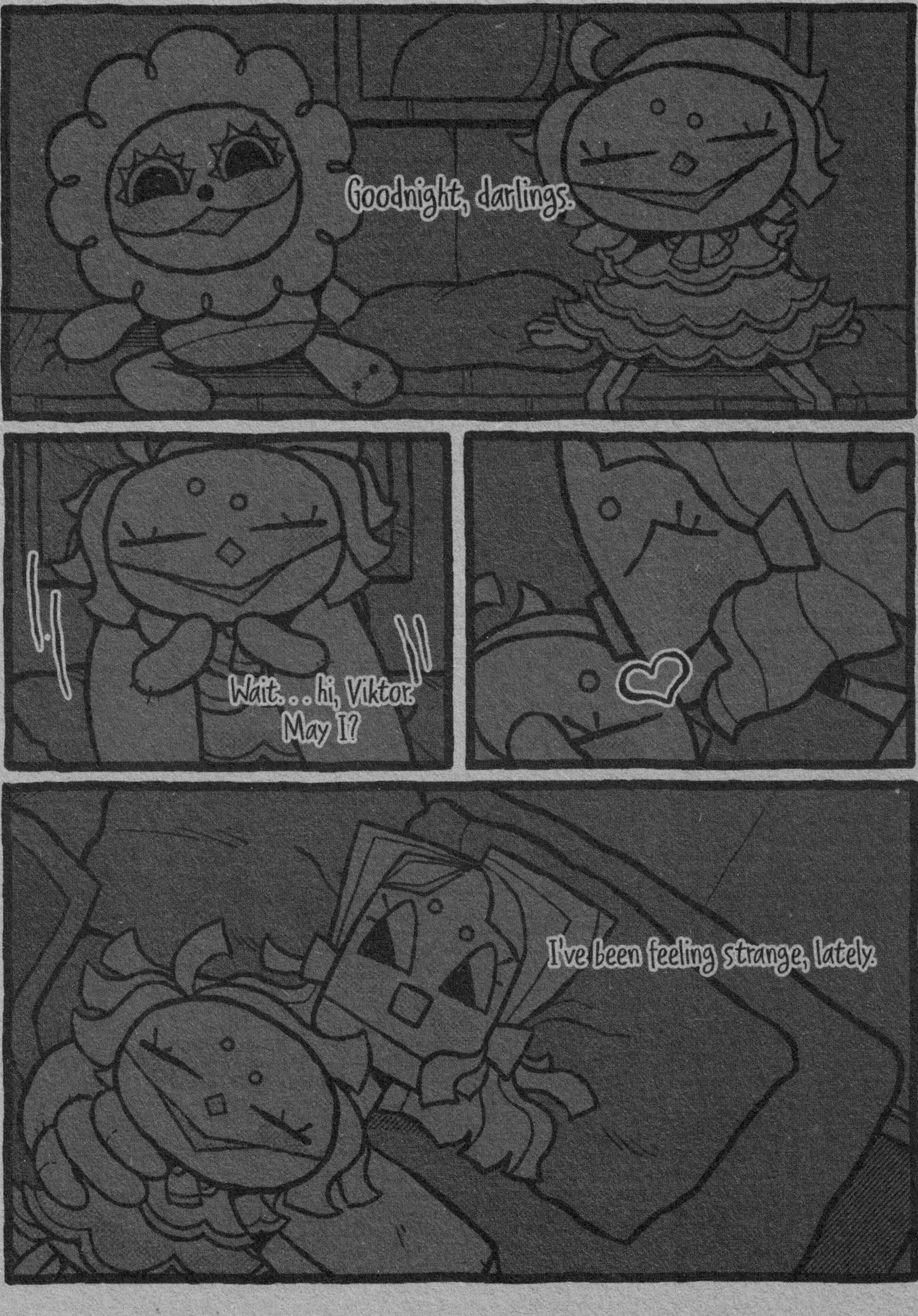
Goodnight, darlings.
Wait. . . hi, Viktor.
May I?
I've been feeling strange, lately.

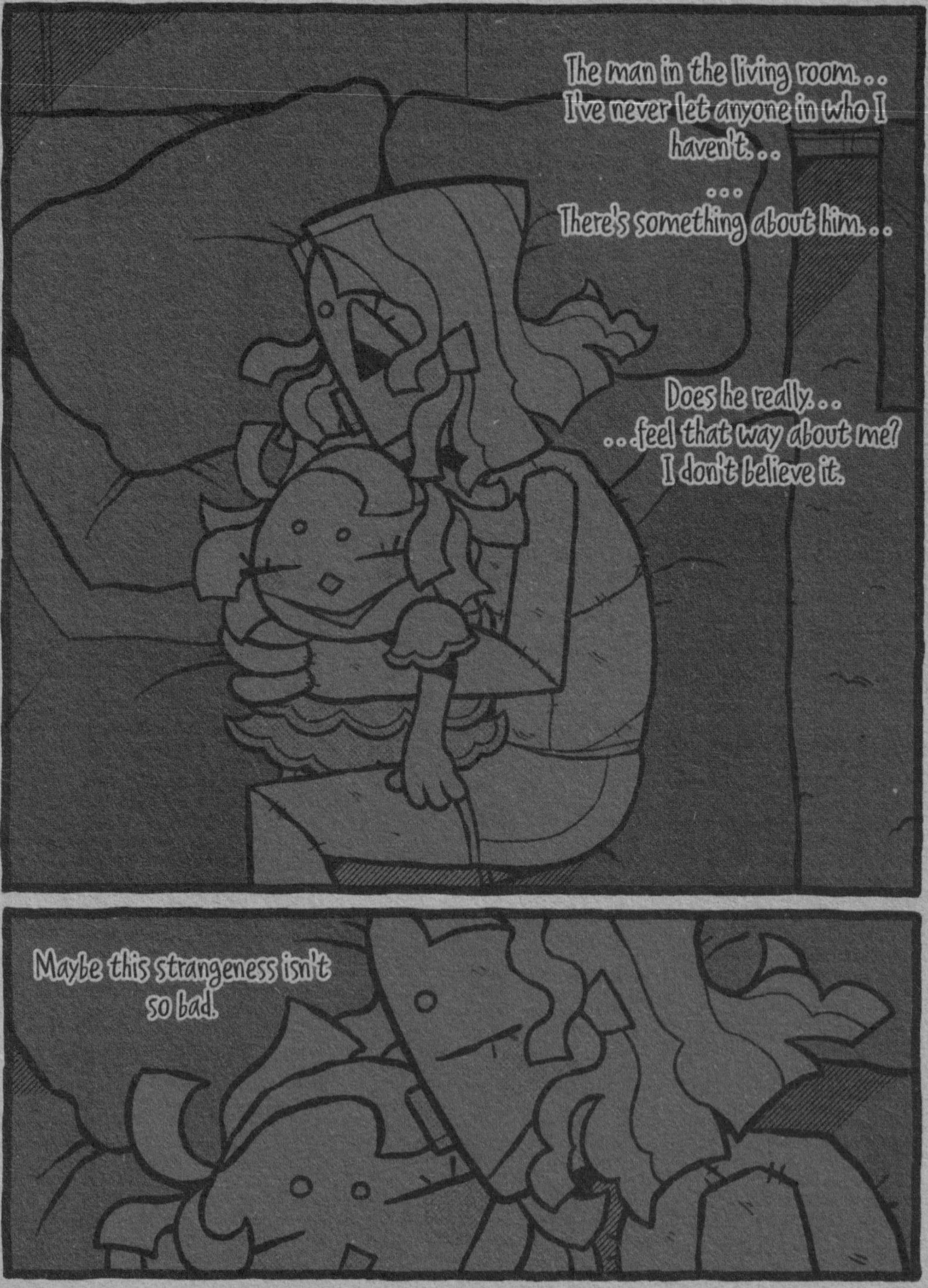
The man in the living room. . .
I've never let anyone in who I haven't. . .
. . .
There's something about him. . .
Does he really. . .
. . .feel that way about me?
I don't believe it.
Maybe this strangeness isn't so bad.

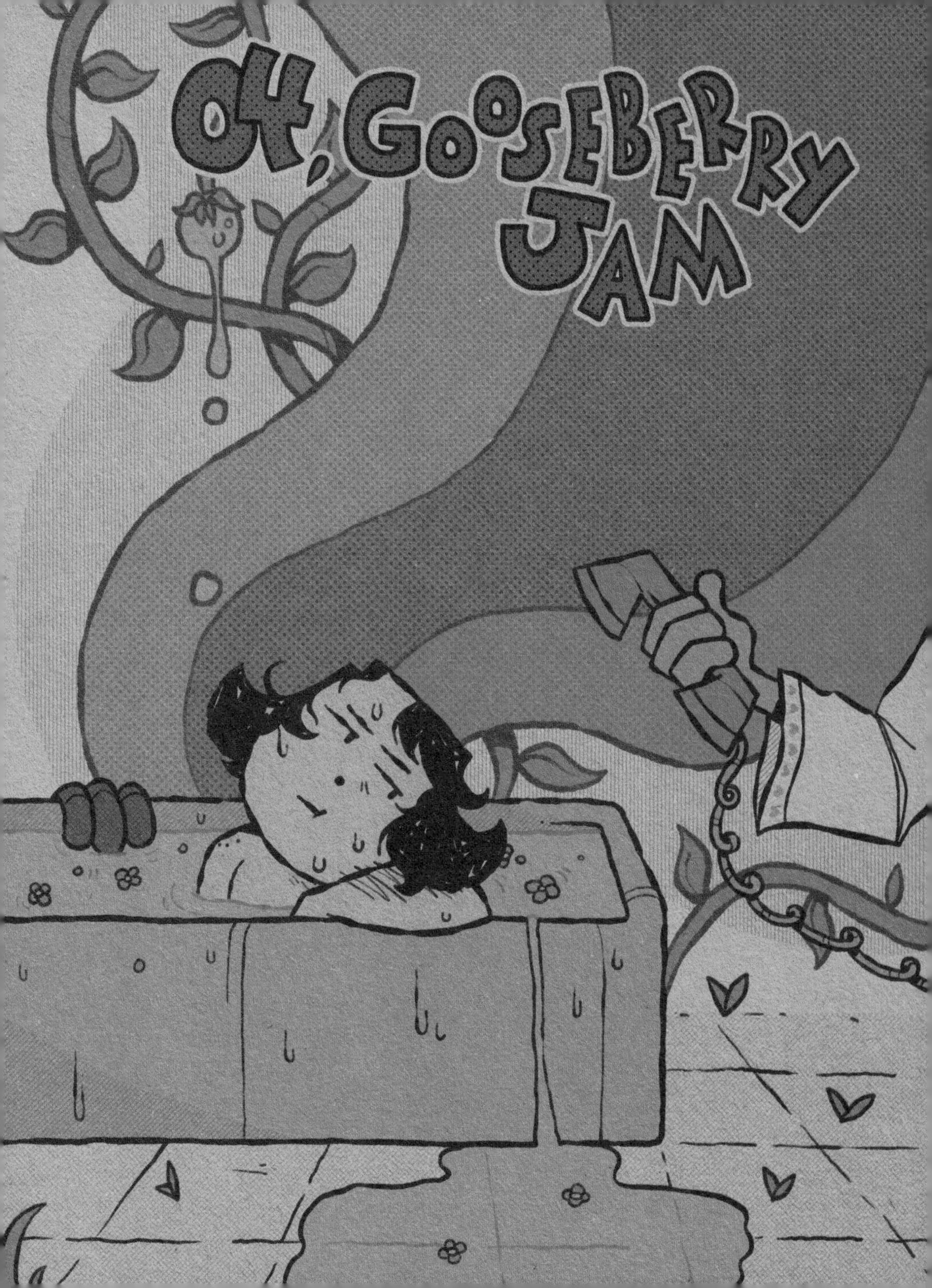
04, GOOSEBERRY JAM

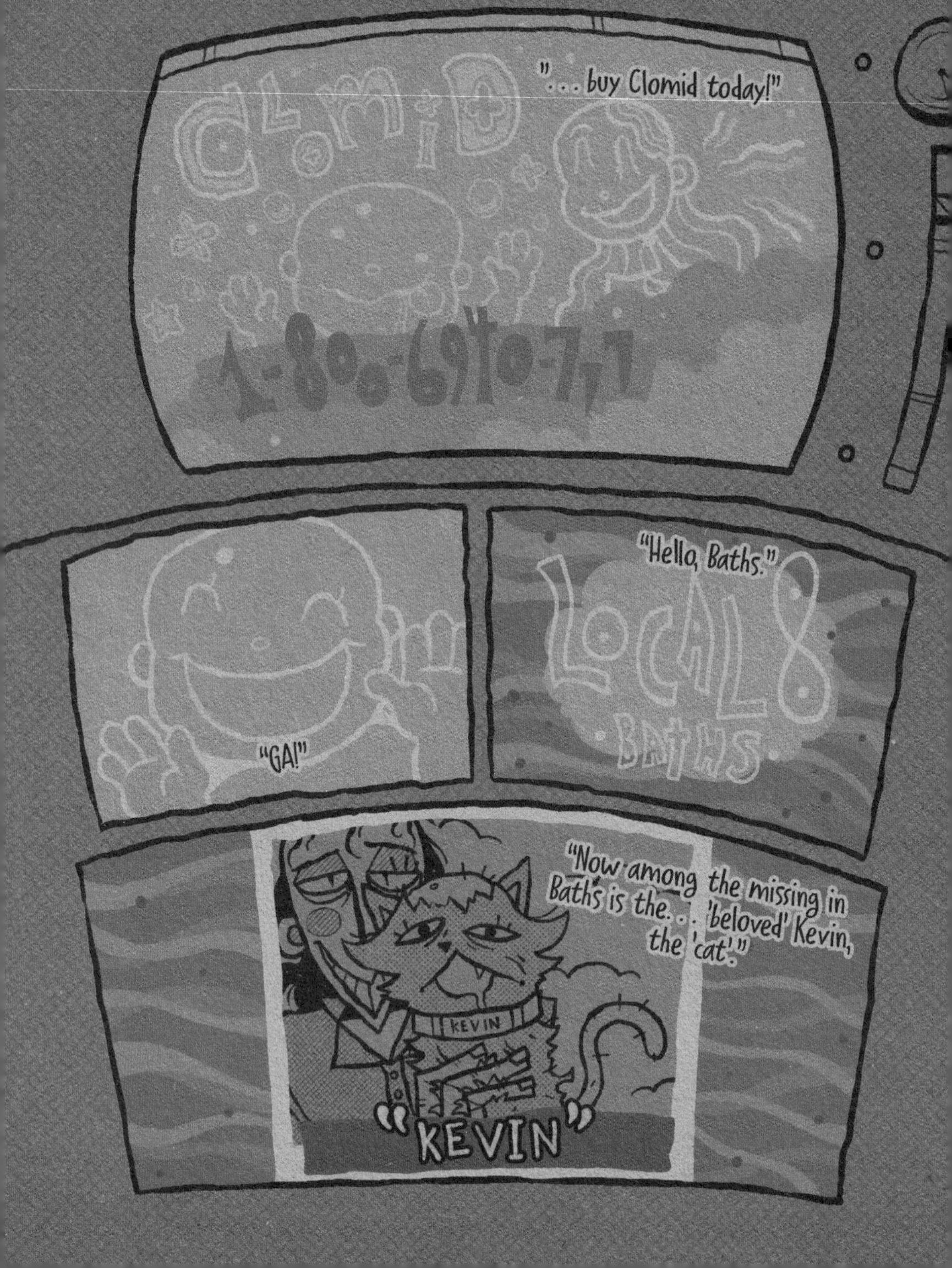
Clomid
"... buy Clomid today!"
1-800-69-TO-7-7
"GA!"
"Hello, Baths."
LOCAL 8
BATHS
"Now among the missing in Baths is the... 'beloved' Kevin, the 'cat'."
KEVIN
KEVIN

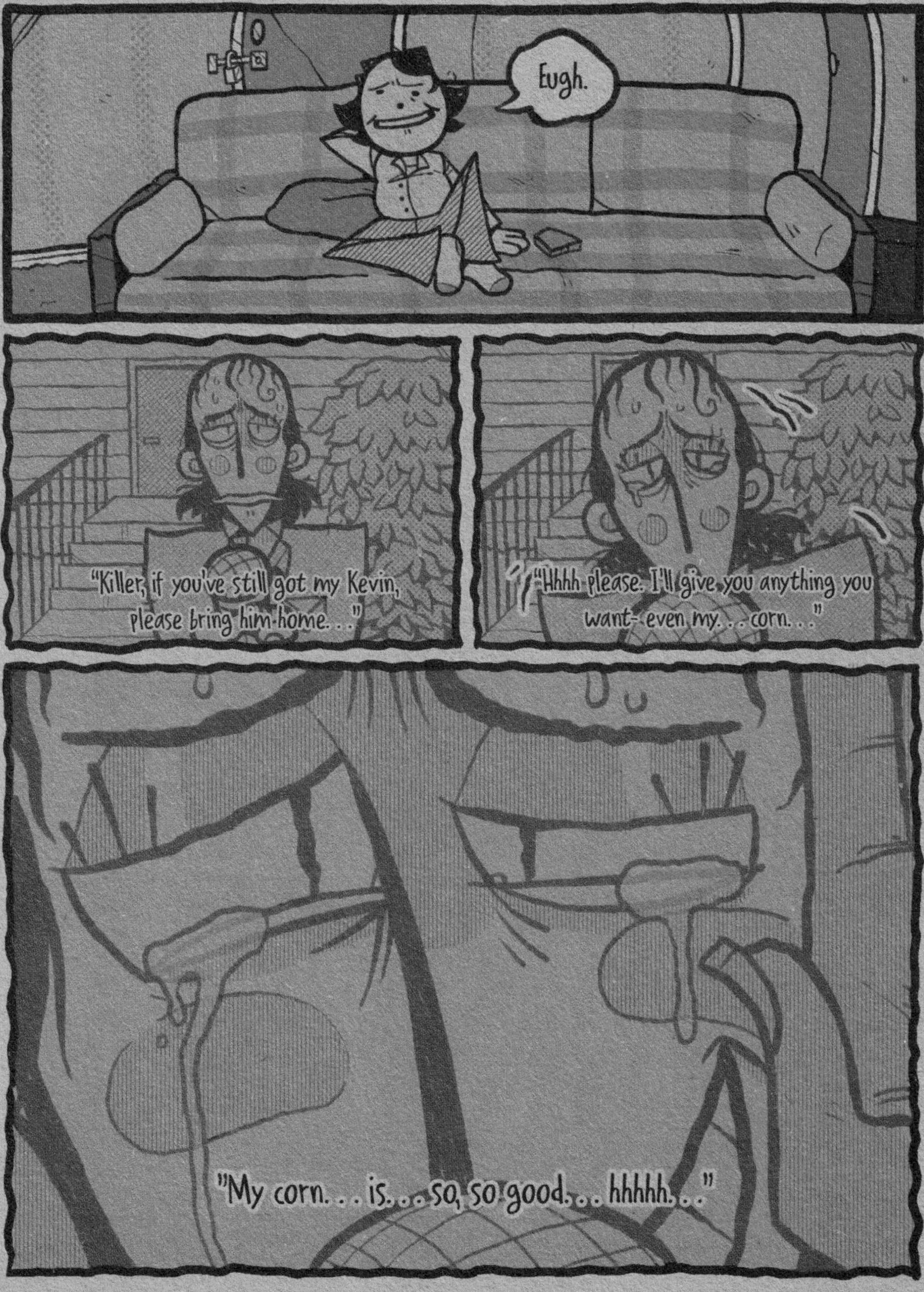
Eugh.
"Killer, if you've still got my Kevin, please bring him home. . ."
"Hhhh please. I'll give you anything you want- even my. . . corn. . ."
"My corn. . . is. . . so, so good. . . hhhhh. . ."

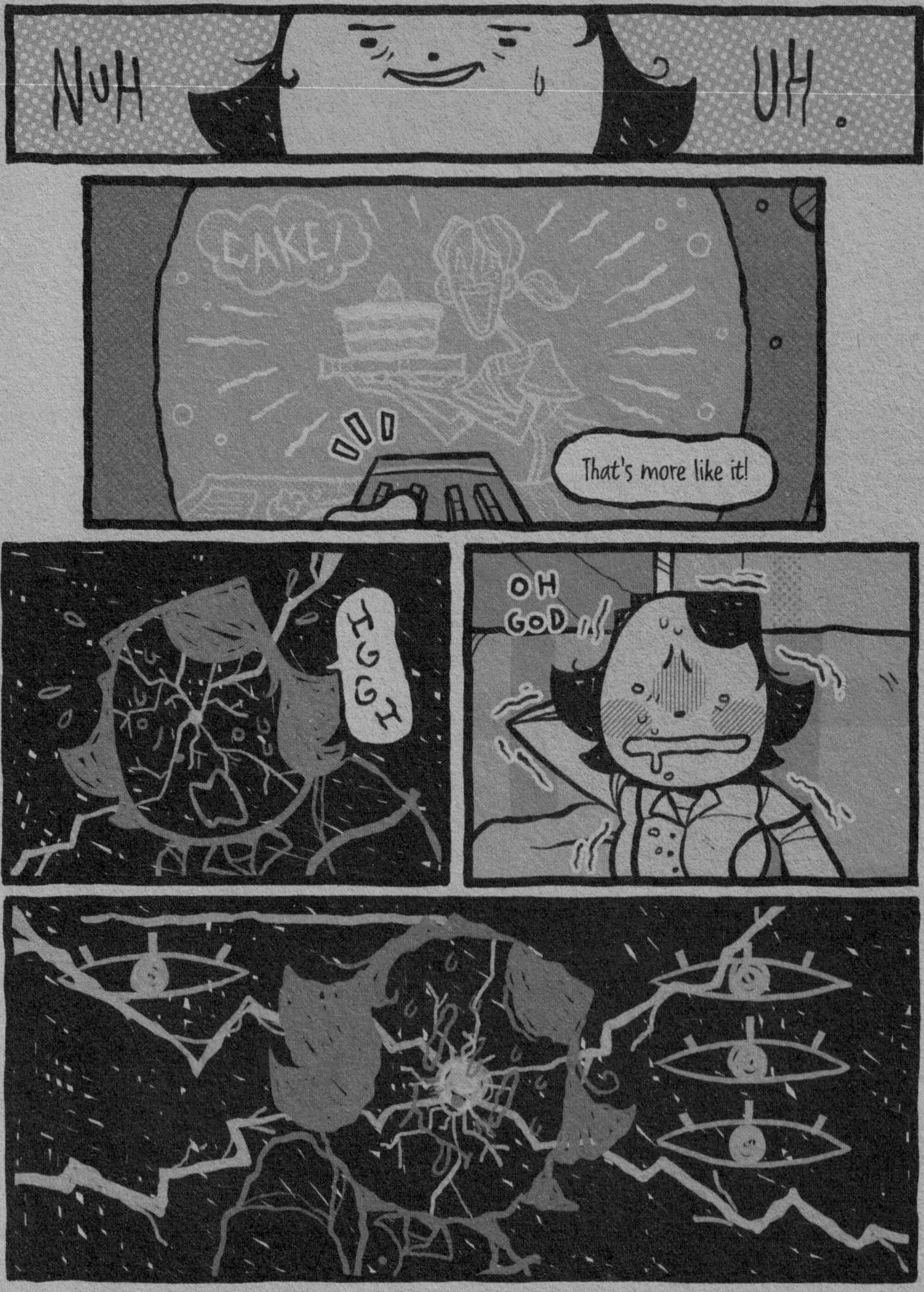
NUH
UH.
CAKE!
That's more like it!
IGGI
OH GOD

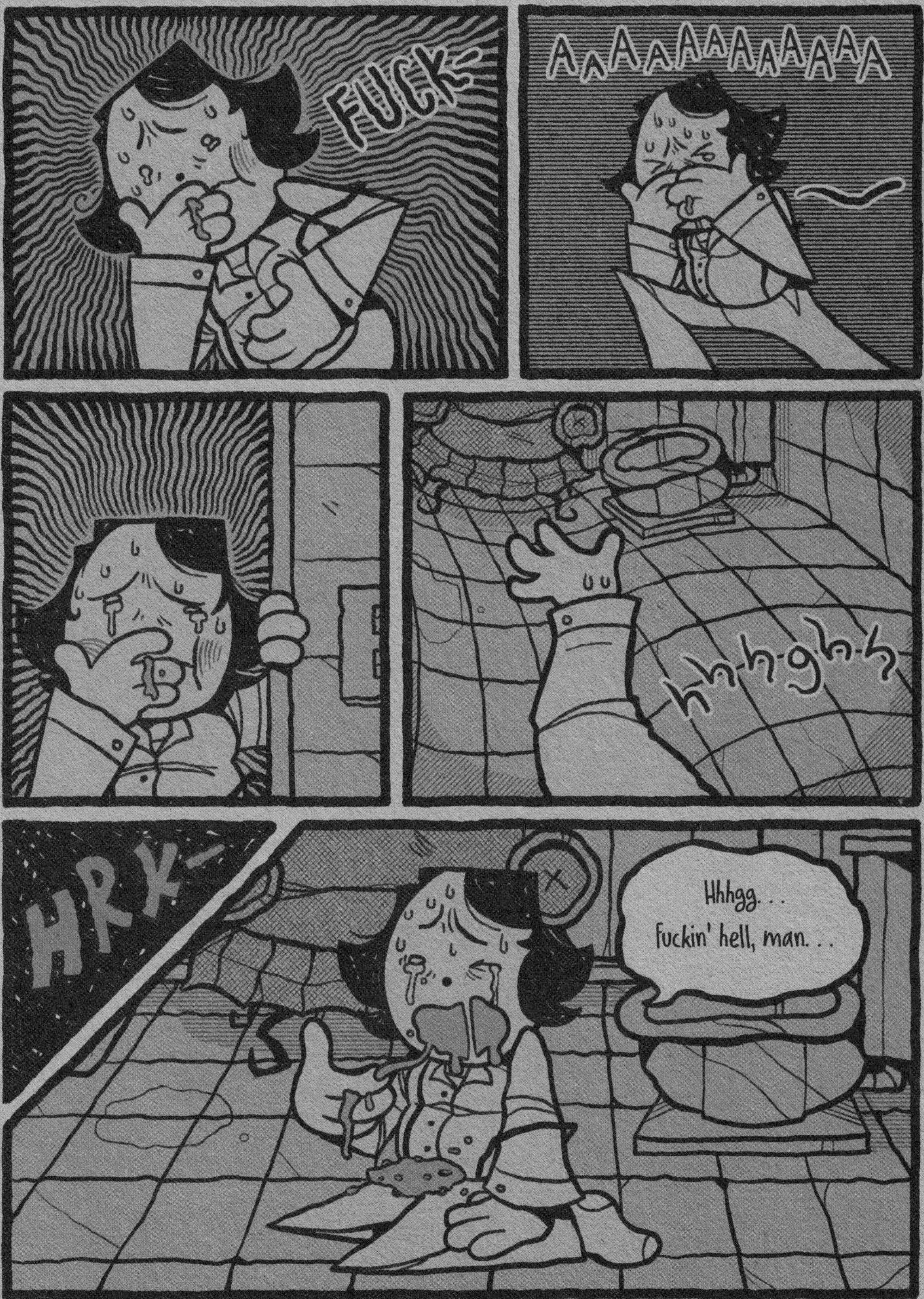
FUCK-
AAAAAAAAAAAAA
hh-h-g-h-h
HRK-
Hhhgg. . .
Fuckin' hell, man. . .

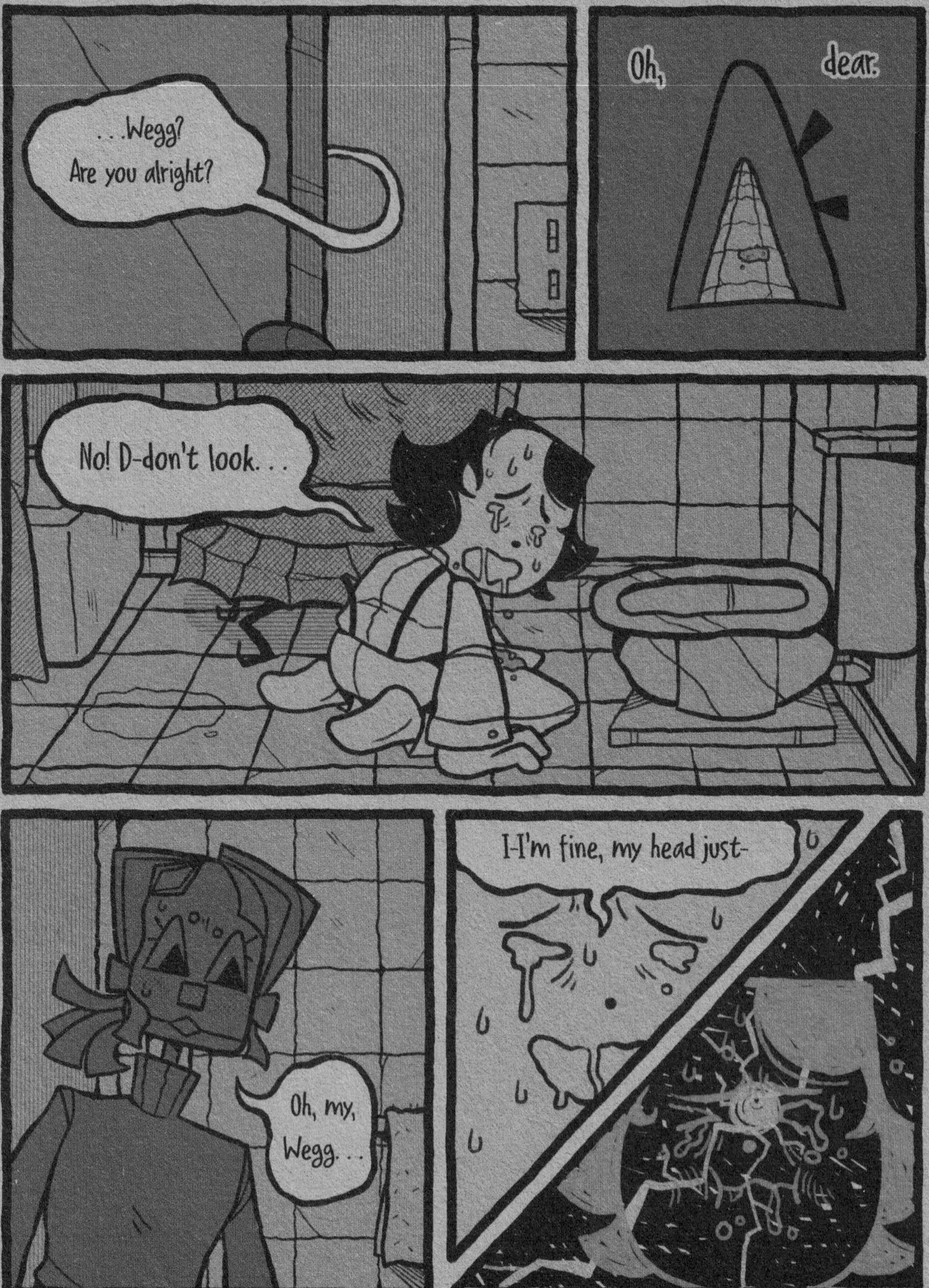
...Wegg?
Are you alright?
Oh,
dear.
No! D-don't look...
Oh, my,
Wegg...
I-I'm fine, my head just-

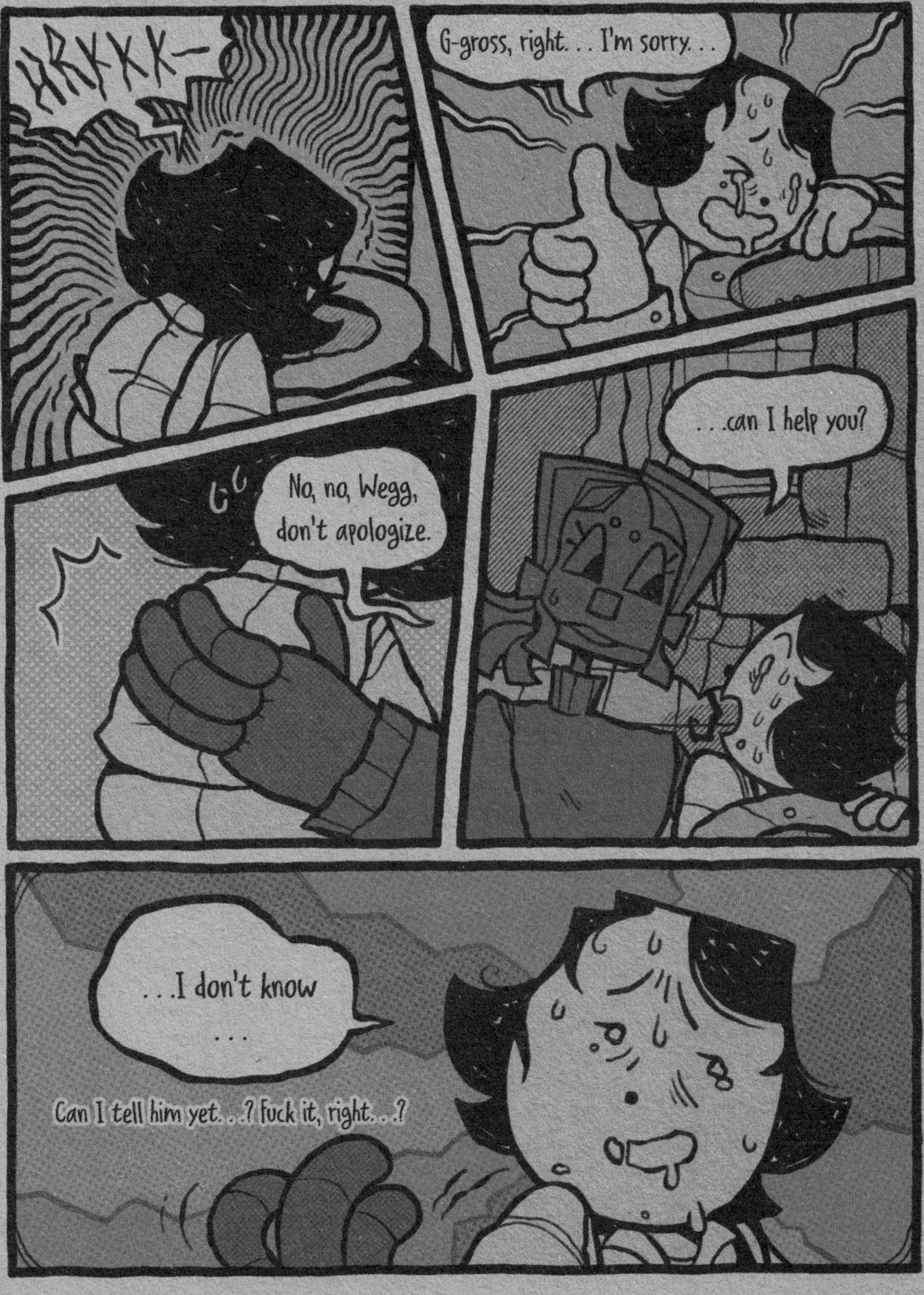
HRKKK—
G-gross, right. . . I'm sorry. . .
No, no, Wegg, don't apologize.
. . .can I help you?
. . .I don't know . . .
Can I tell him yet. . .? Fuck it, right. . .?

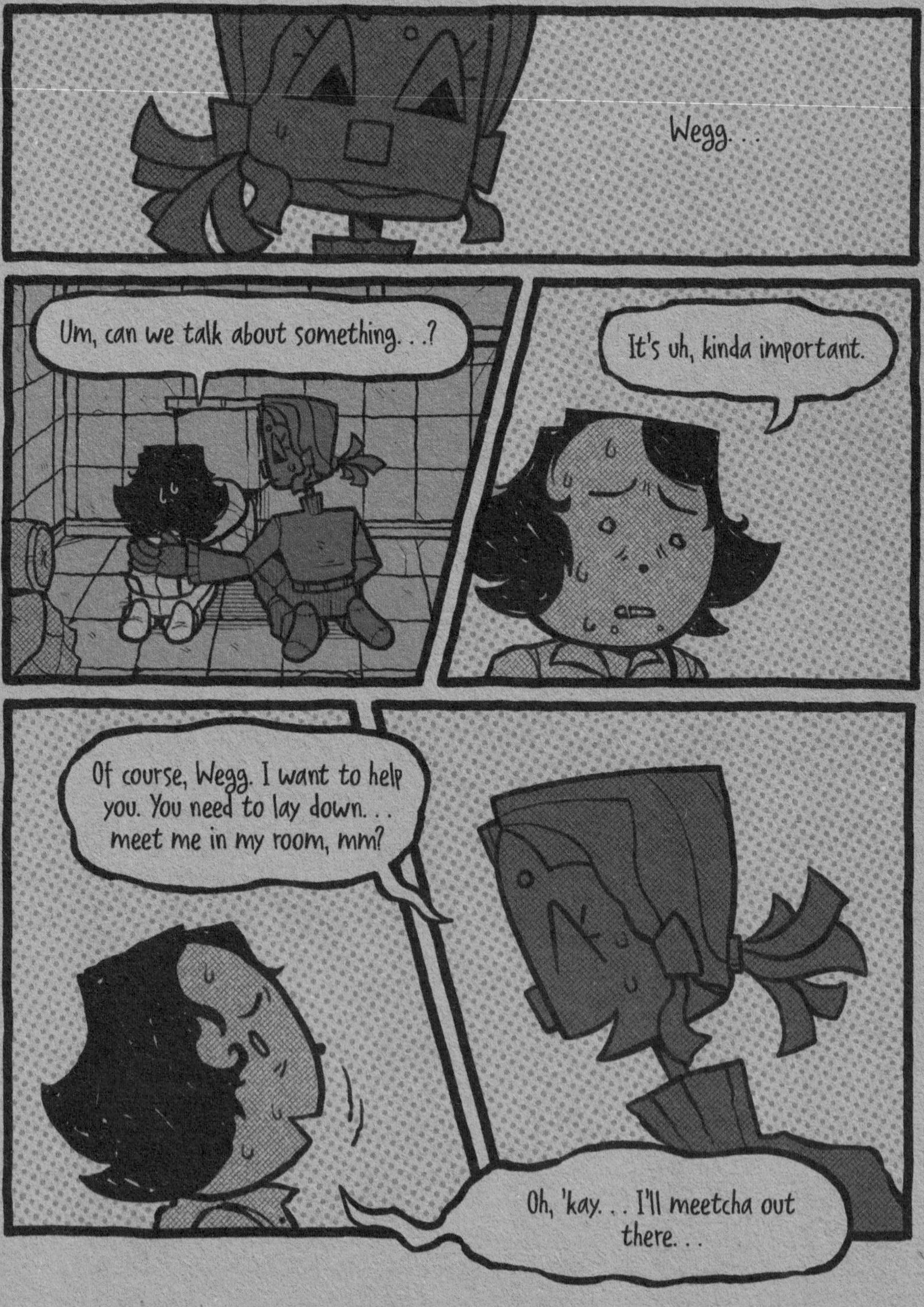
Wegg. . .
Um, can we talk about something. . .?
It's uh, kinda important.
Of course, Wegg. I want to help you. You need to lay down. . . meet me in my room, mm?
Oh, 'kay. . . I'll meetcha out there. . .

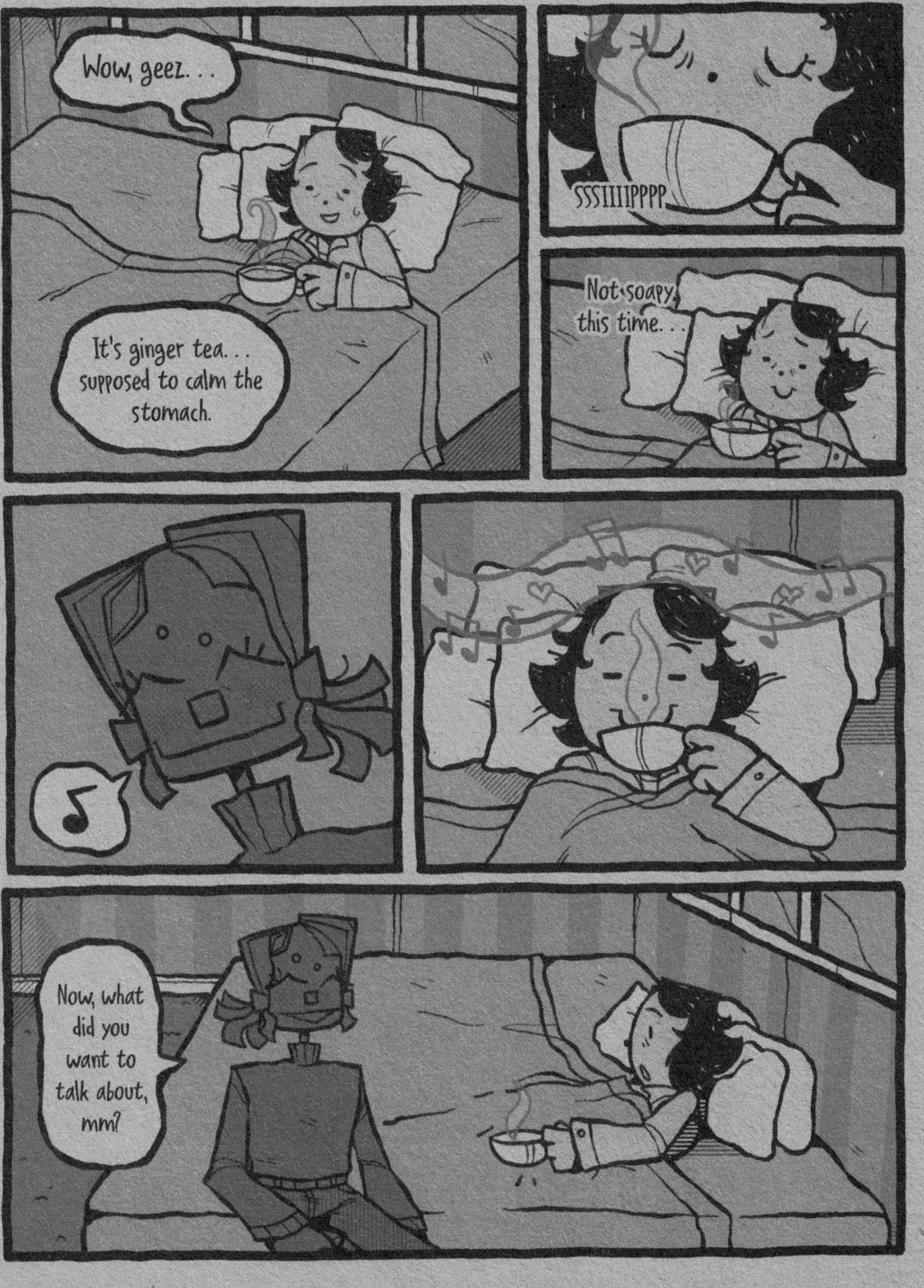
Wow, geez. . .
It's ginger tea. . . supposed to calm the stomach.
SSSIIIIPPPP
Not soapy this time. . .
♪
Now, what did you want to talk about, mm?

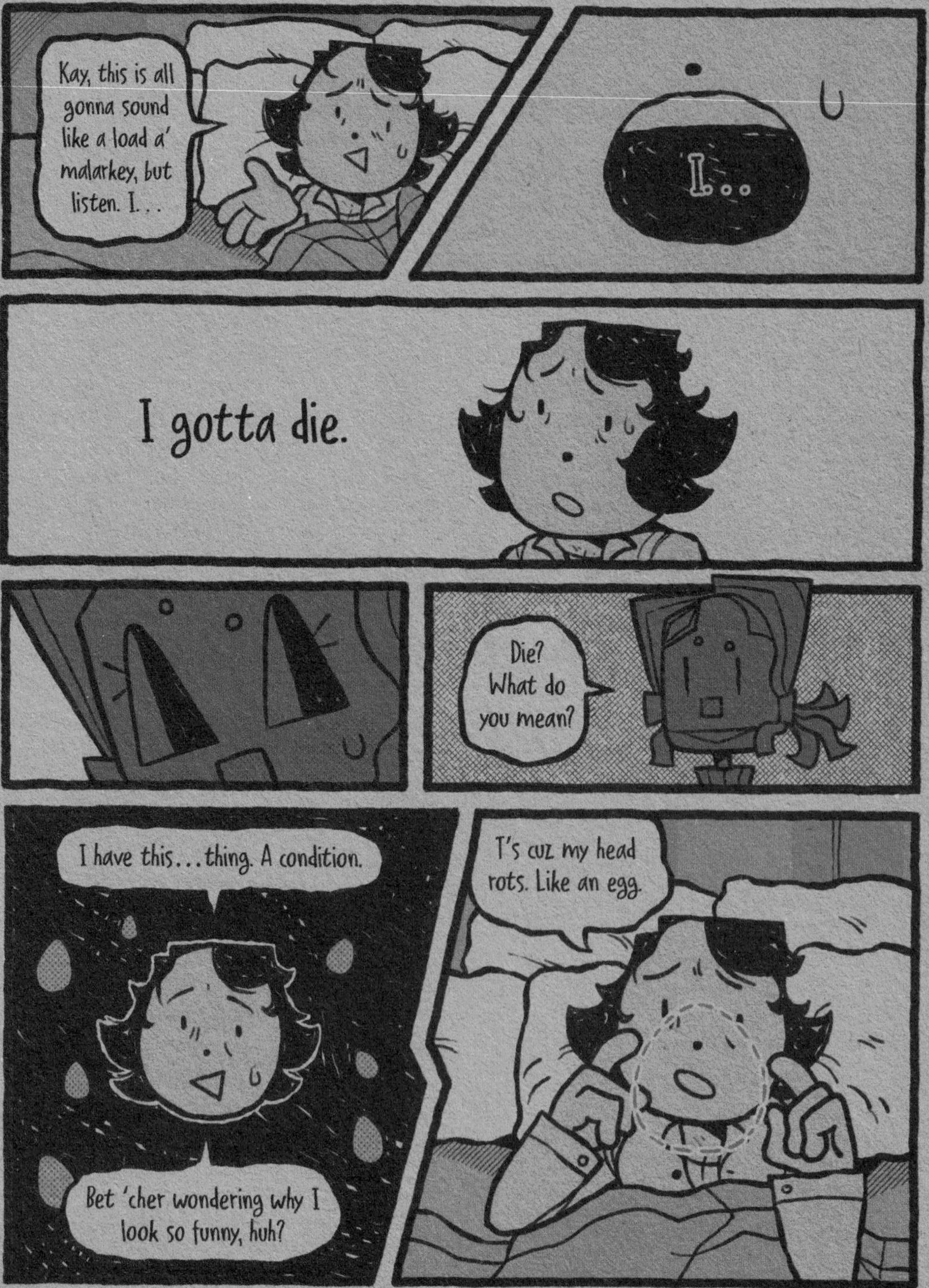
Kay, this is all gonna sound like a load a' malarkey, but listen. I. . .
I. . .
I gotta die.
Die? What do you mean?
I have this. . . thing. A condition.
Bet 'cher wondering why I look so funny, huh?
T's cuz my head rots. Like an egg.

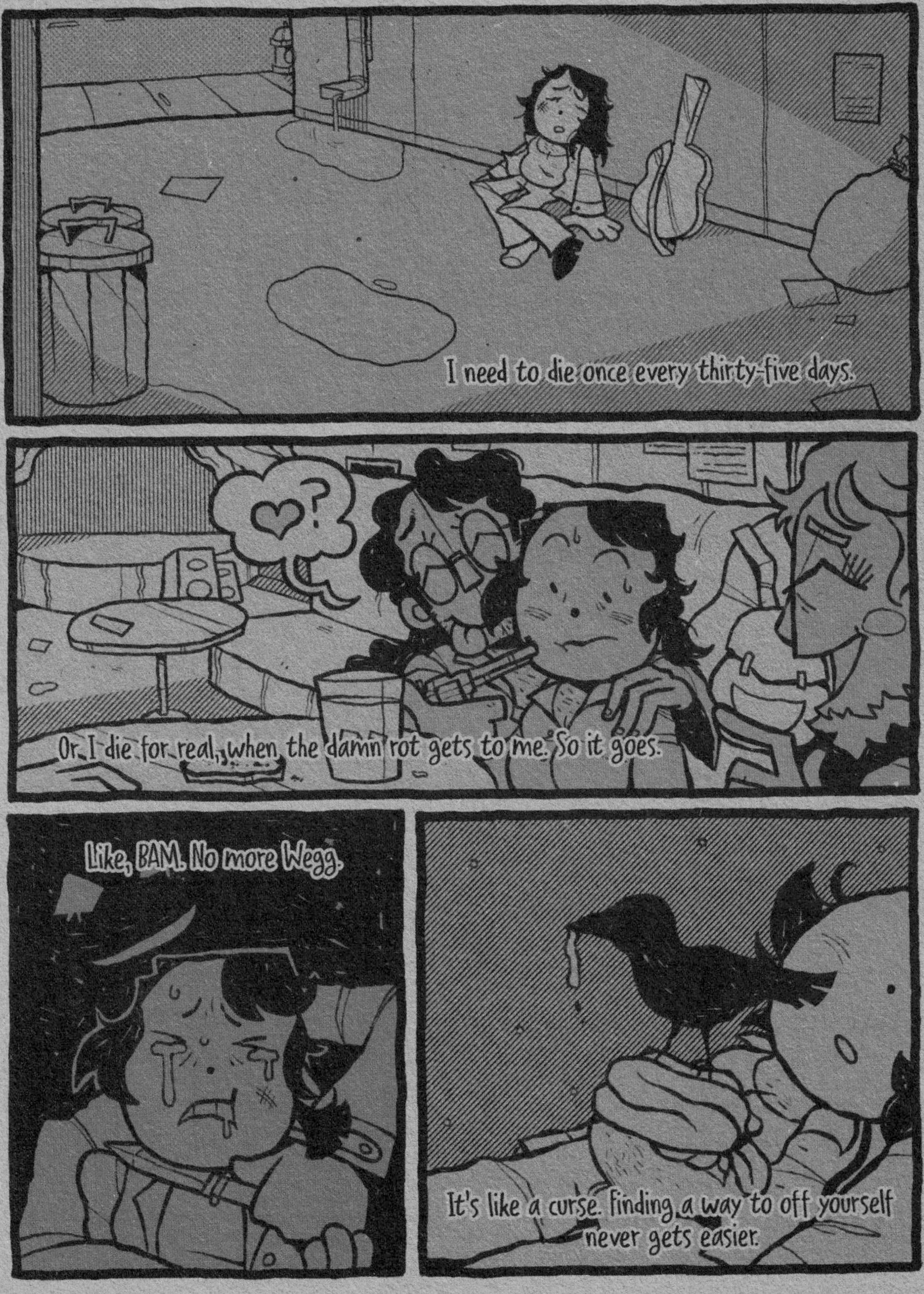
I need to die once every thirty-five days.
Or I die for real, when the damn rot gets to me. So it goes.
Like, BAM. No more Wegg.
It's like a curse. Finding a way to off yourself never gets easier.

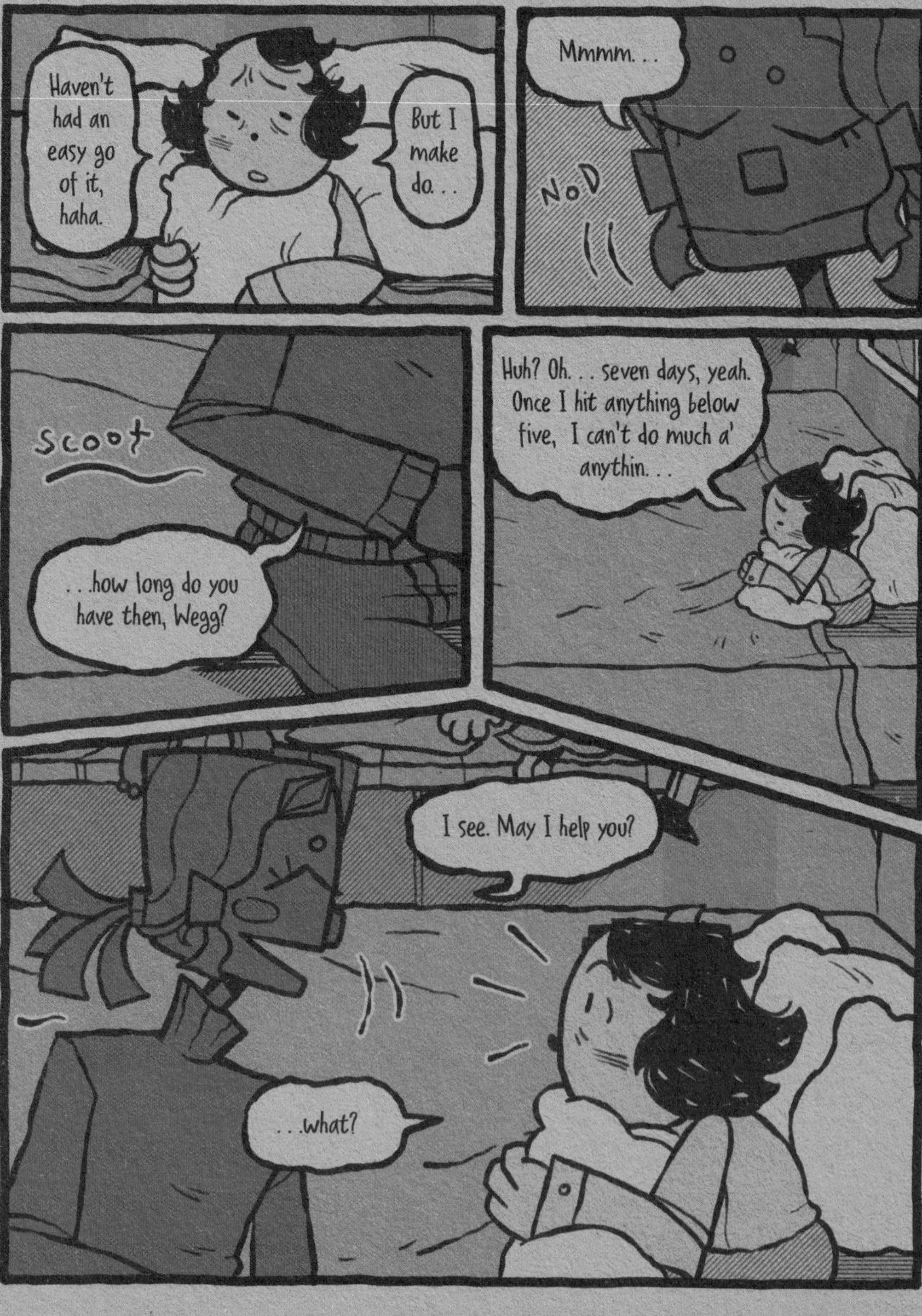
Haven't had an easy go of it, haha.
But I make do. . .
Mmmm. . .
NoD
scoot
. . .how long do you have then, Wegg?
Huh? Oh. . . seven days, yeah. Once I hit anything below five, I can't do much a' anythin. . .
I see. May I help you?
. . .what?

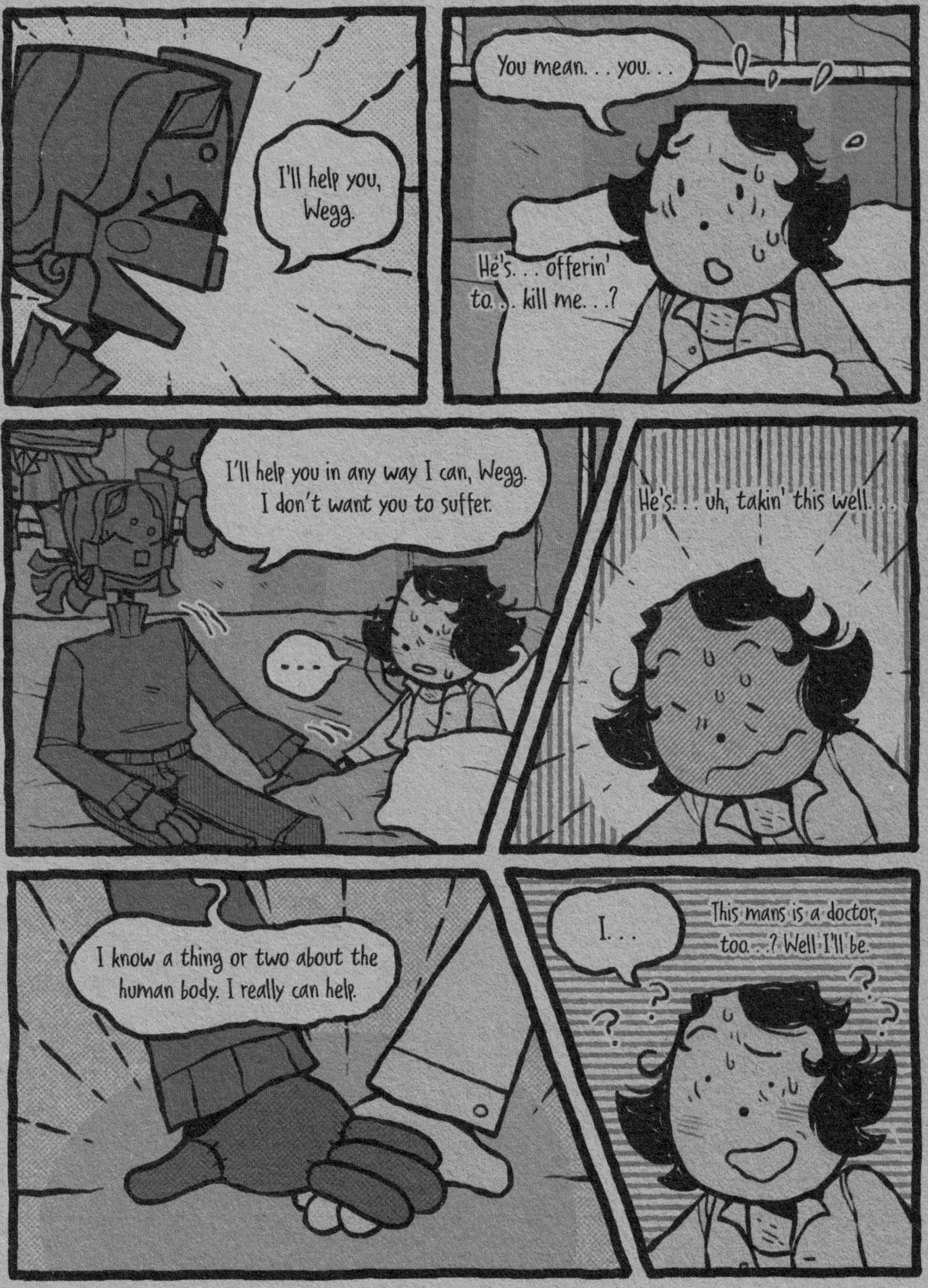

I'll help you, Wegg.
You mean. . . you. . .
He's. . . offerin' to. . . kill me. . .?
I'll help you in any way I can, Wegg. I don't want you to suffer.
. . .
He's. . . uh, takin' this well. . .
I know a thing or two about the human body. I really can help.
I. . .
This mans is a doctor, too. . .? Well I'll be.

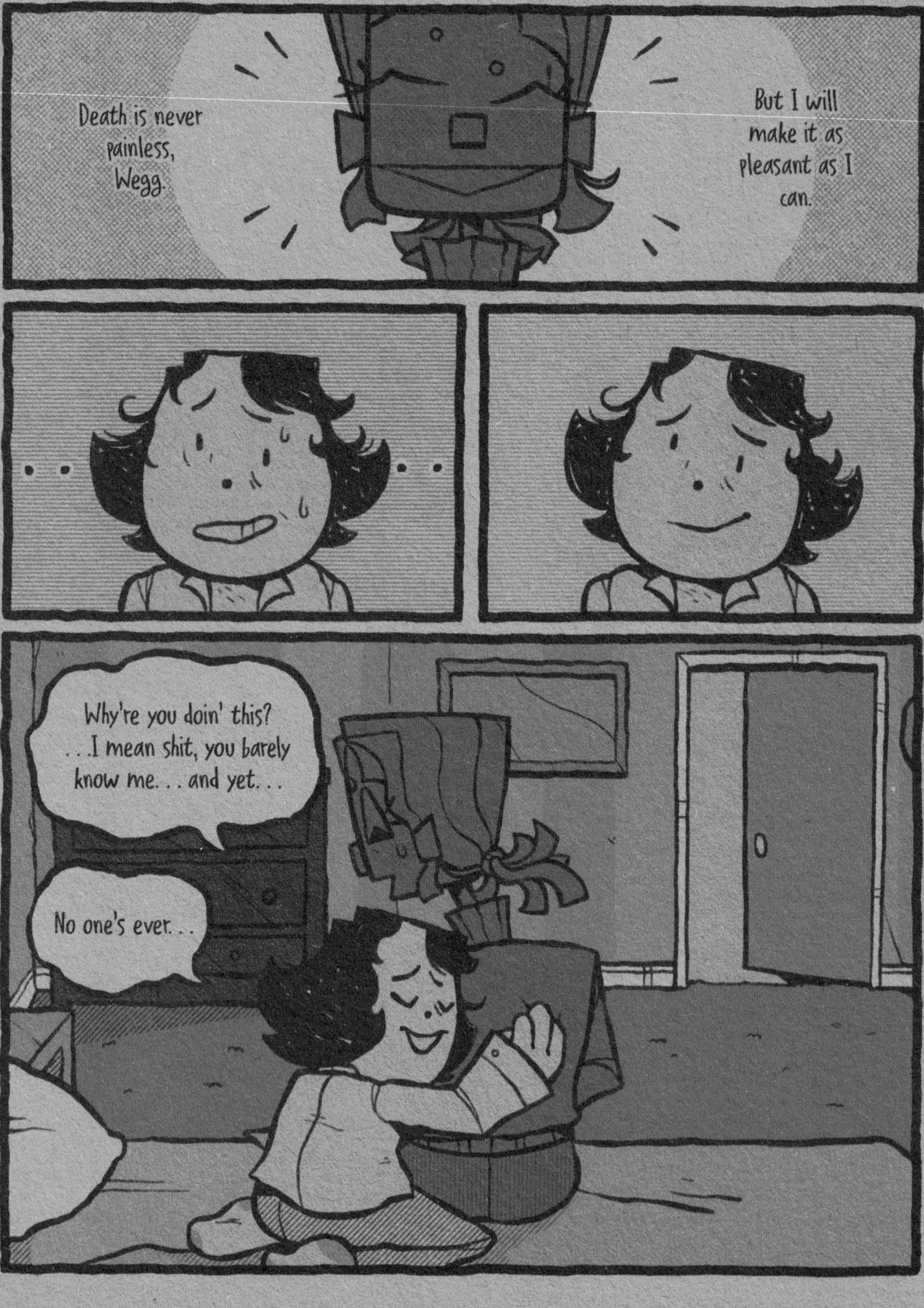
Death is never painless, Wegg.
But I will make it as pleasant as I can.
. . .
. . .
Why're you doin' this? . . .I mean shit, you barely know me. . . and yet. . .
No one's ever. . .

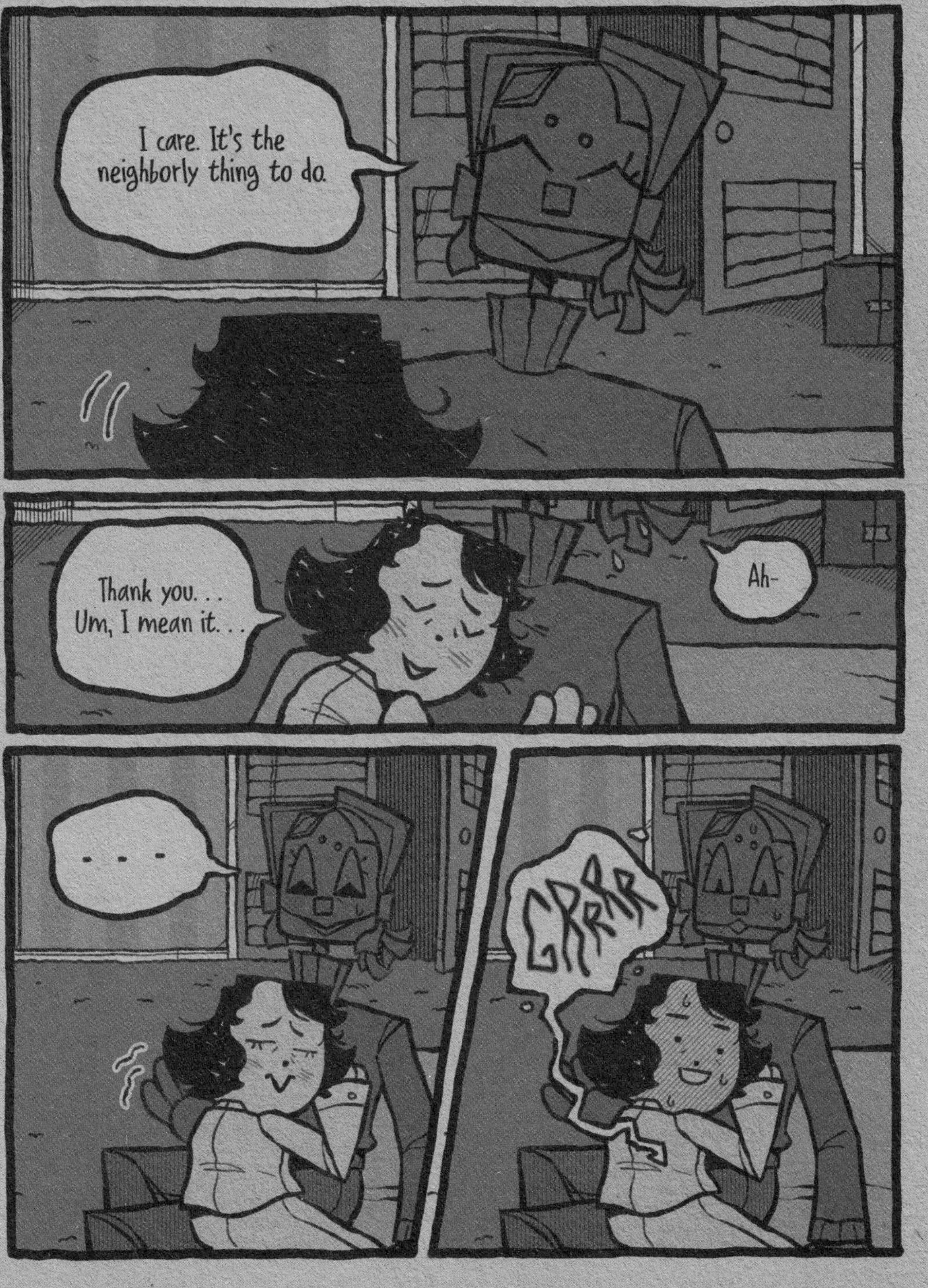
I care. It's the neighborly thing to do.
Thank you... Um, I mean it...
Ah-
...
GRRRR

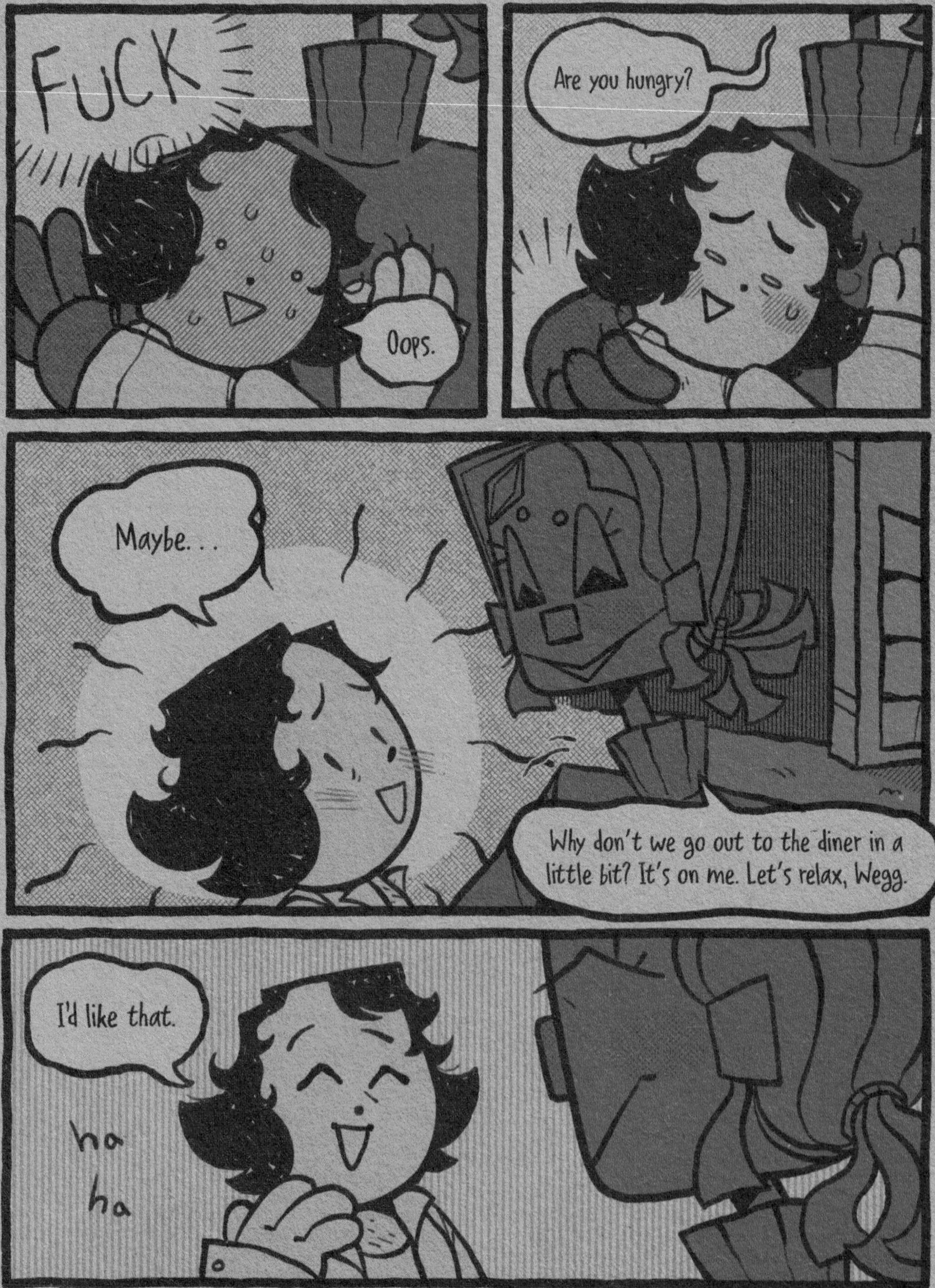
FUCK
Oops.
Are you hungry?
Maybe. . .
Why don't we go out to the diner in a little bit? It's on me. Let's relax, Wegg.
I'd like that.
ha ha

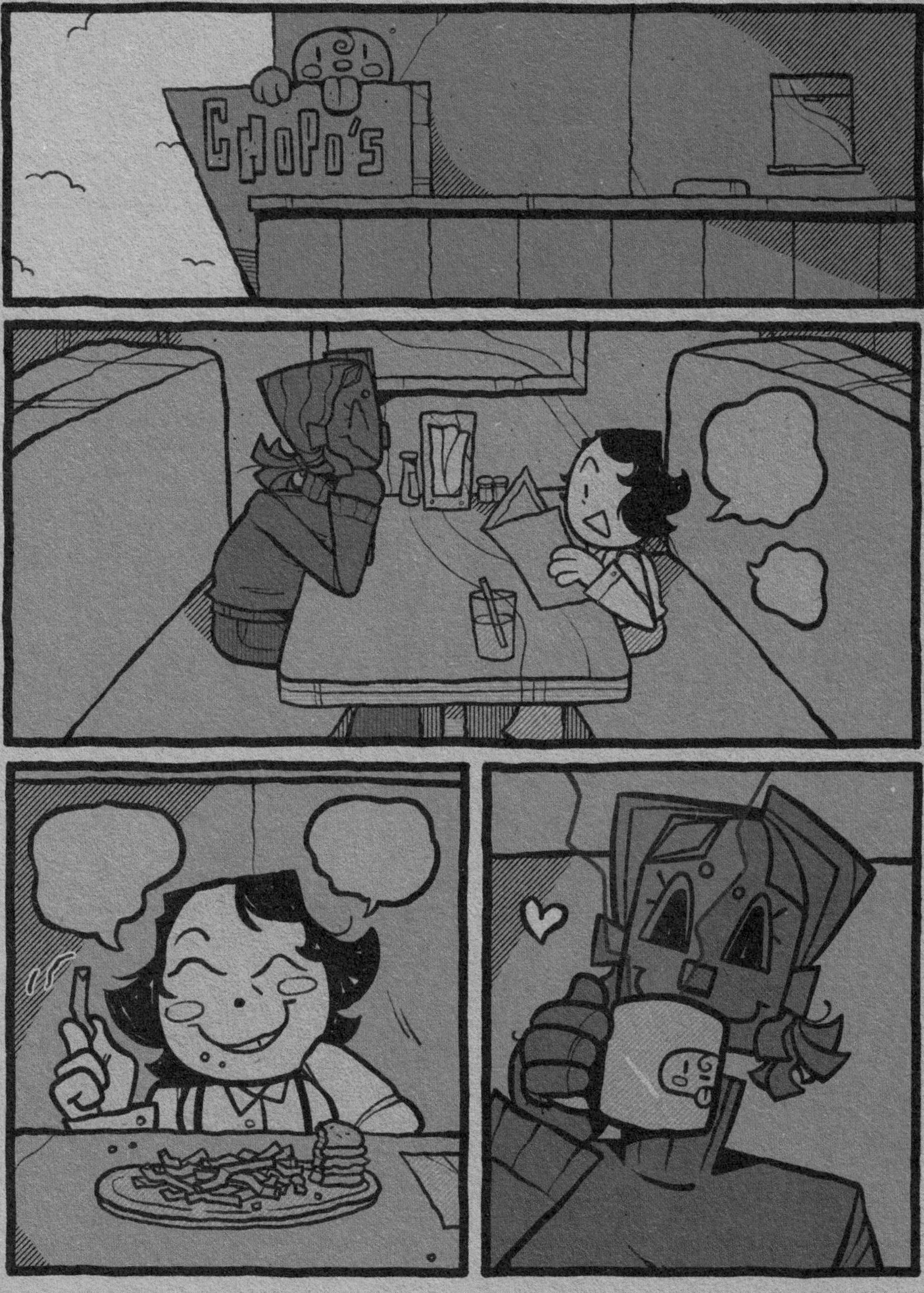
CHOPO'S

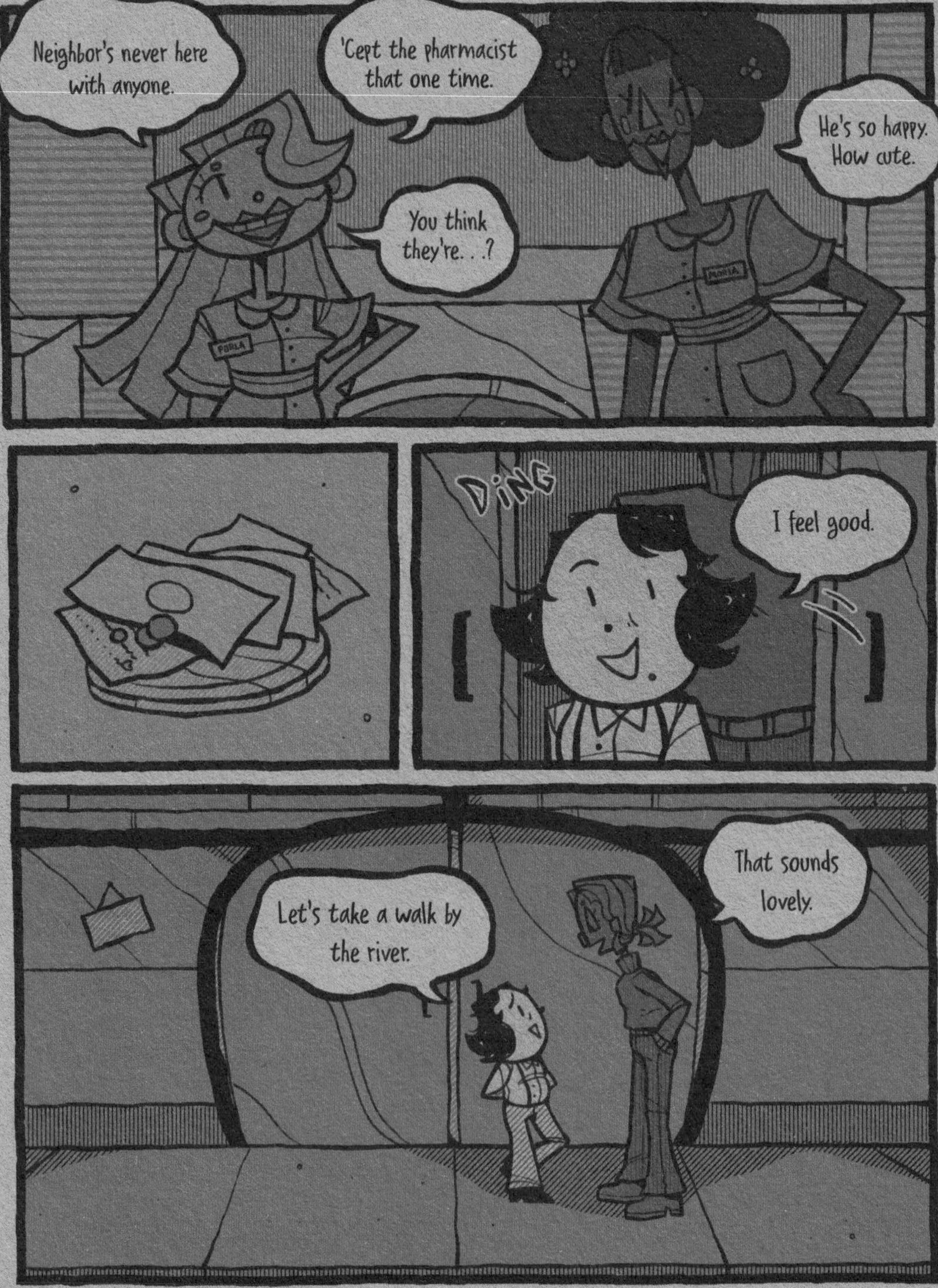
Neighbor's never here with anyone.
'Cept the pharmacist that one time.
You think they're. . .?
He's so happy. How cute.
DiNG
I feel good.
Let's take a walk by the river.
That sounds lovely.

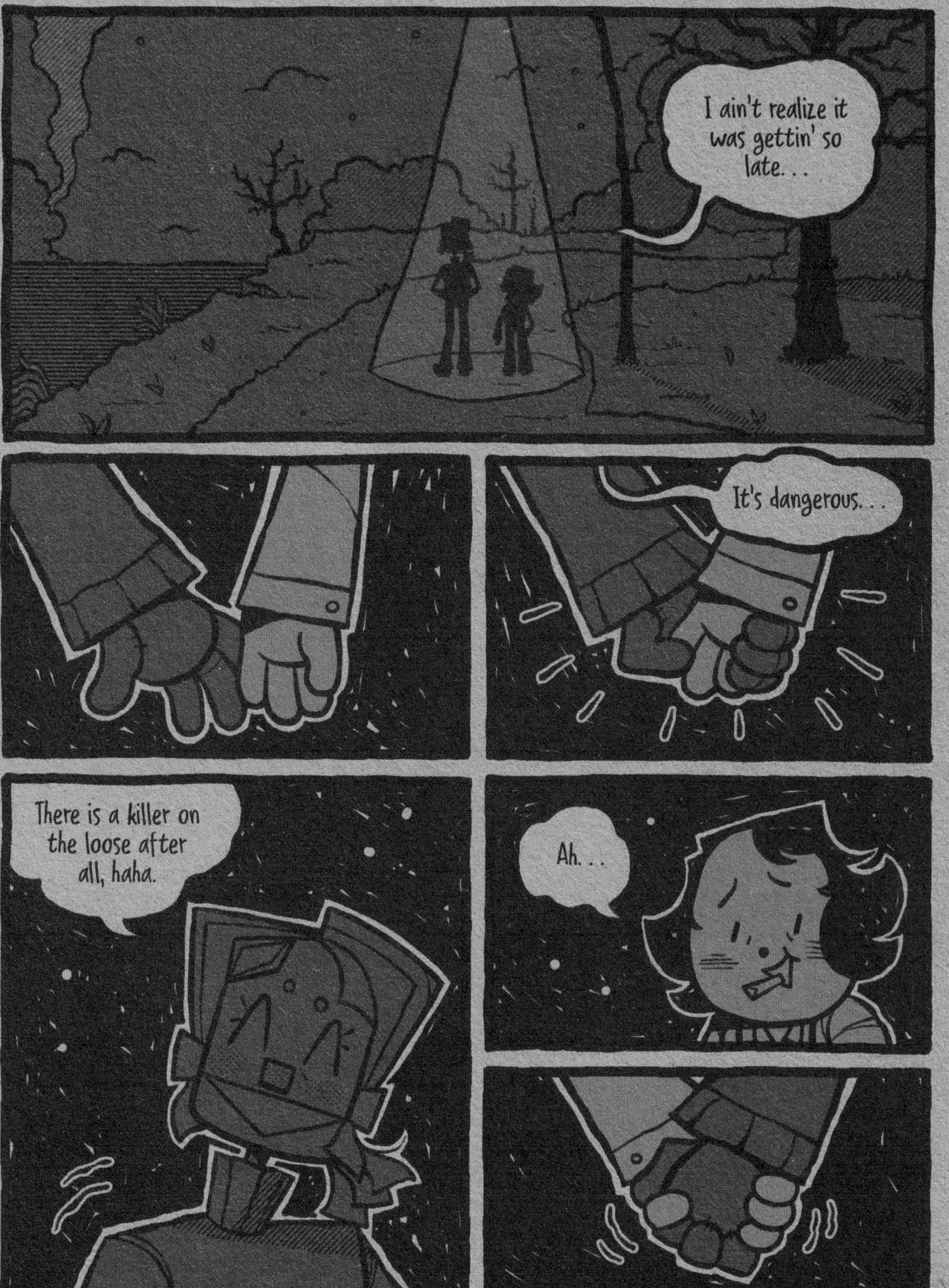
I ain't realize it was gettin' so late. . .
It's dangerous. . .
There is a killer on the loose after all, haha.
Ah. . .

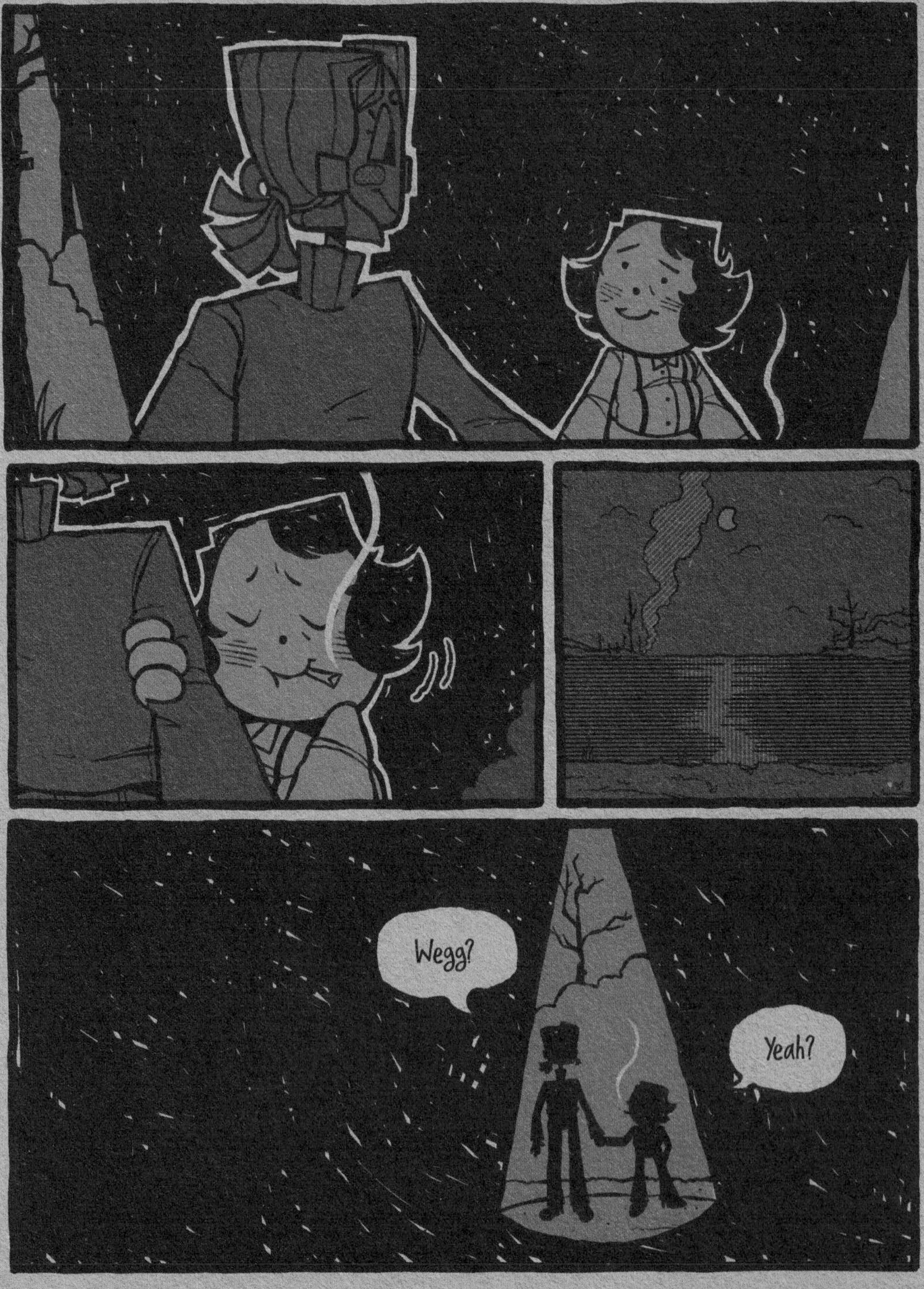
Wegg?
Yeah?

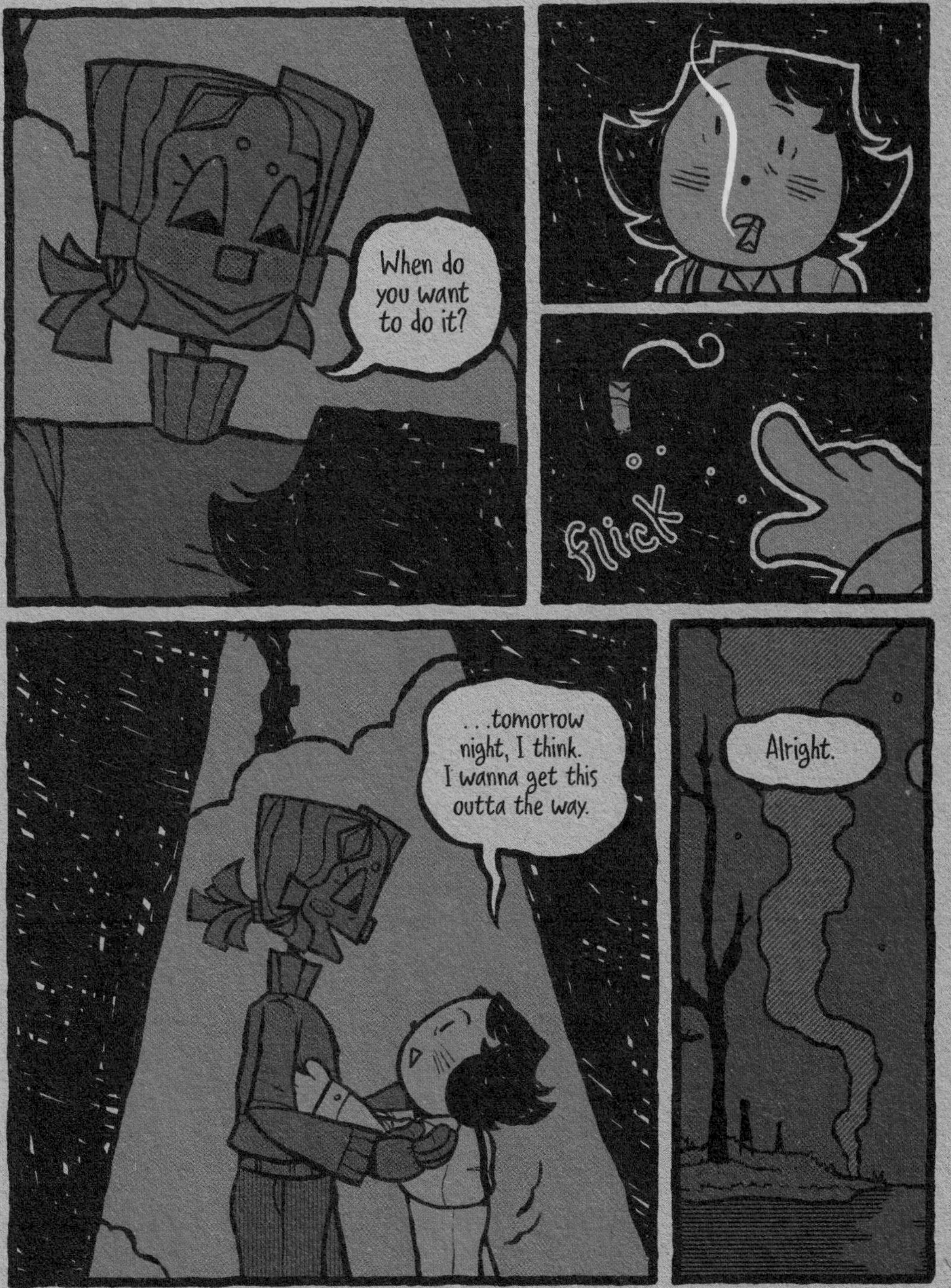
When do you want to do it?
flick
...tomorrow night, I think. I wanna get this outta the way.
Alright.

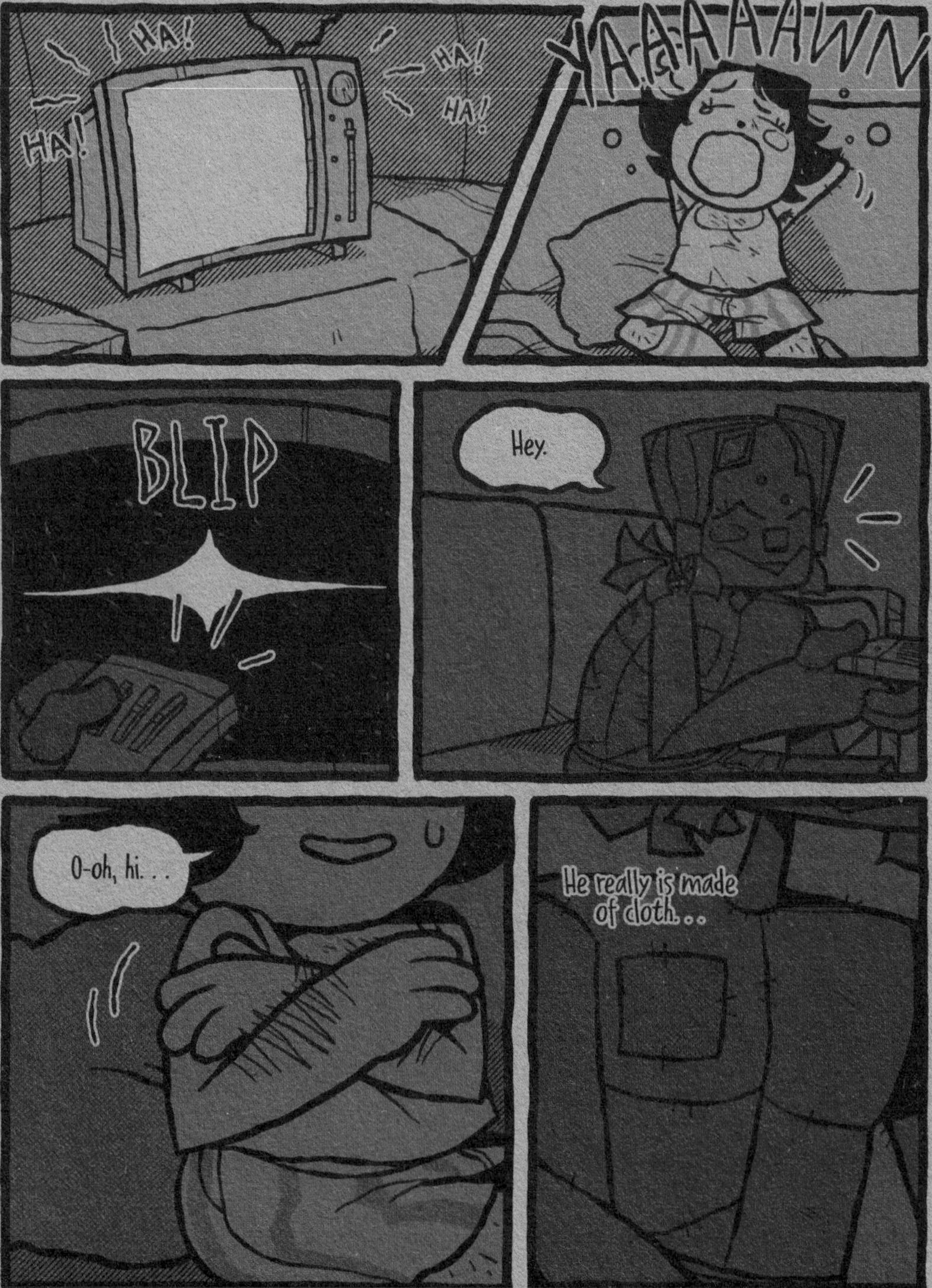
HA!
HA!
HA!
HA!
YAAAAAAWN
BLIP
Hey.
O-oh, hi. . .
He really is made of cloth. . .

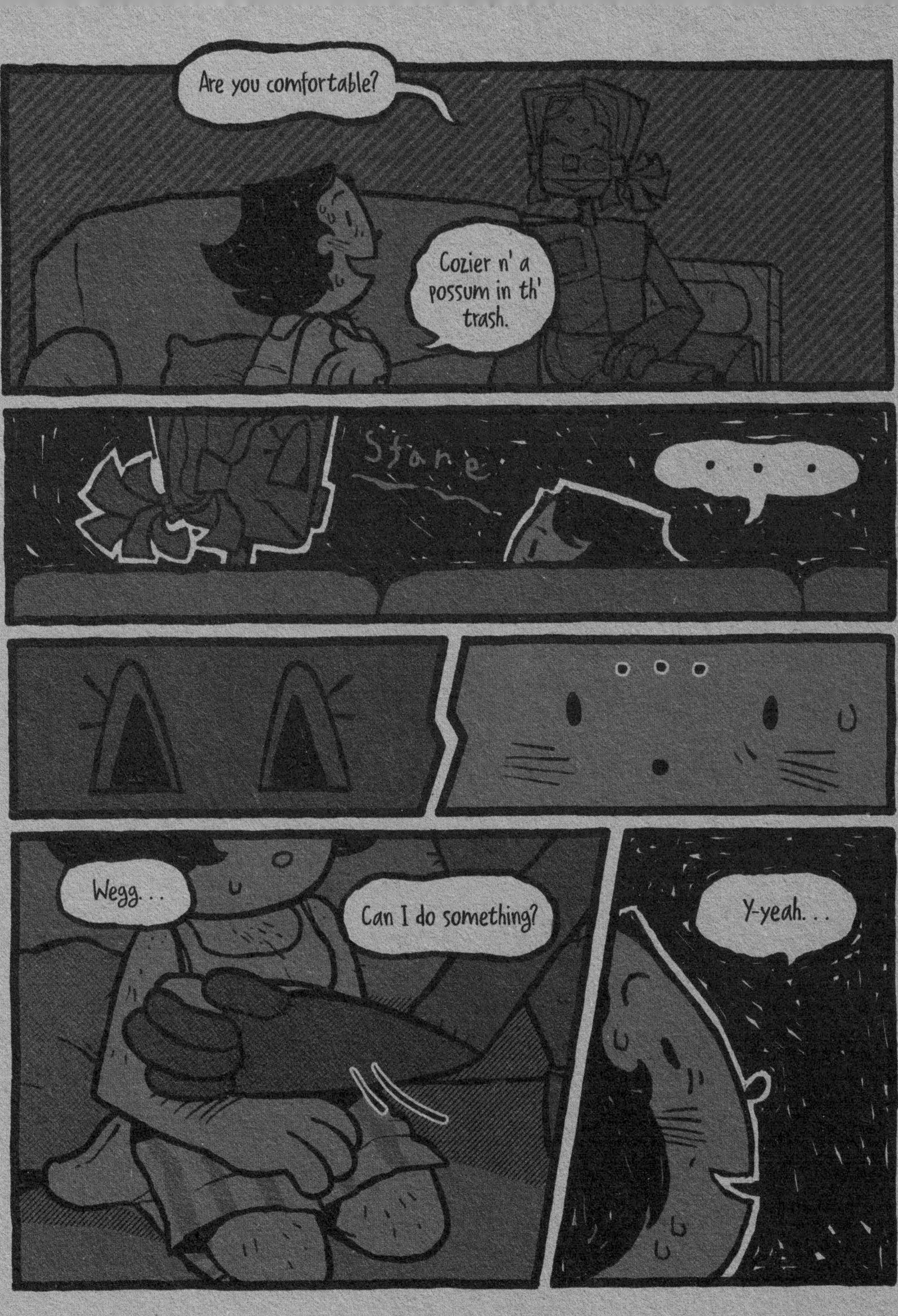
Are you comfortable?
Cozier n' a possum in th' trash.
Stare
. . .
Wegg. . .
Can I do something?
Y-yeah. . .

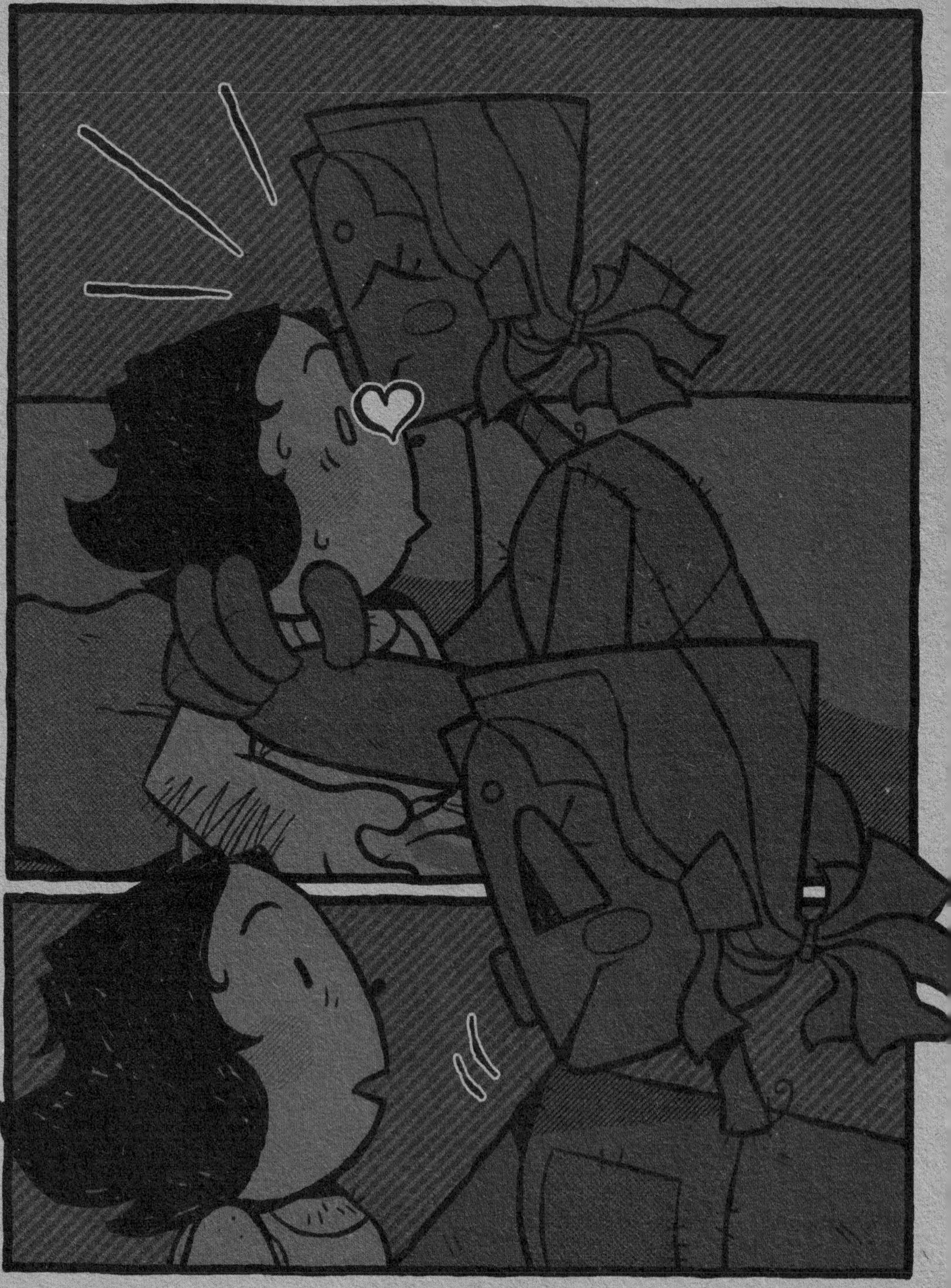

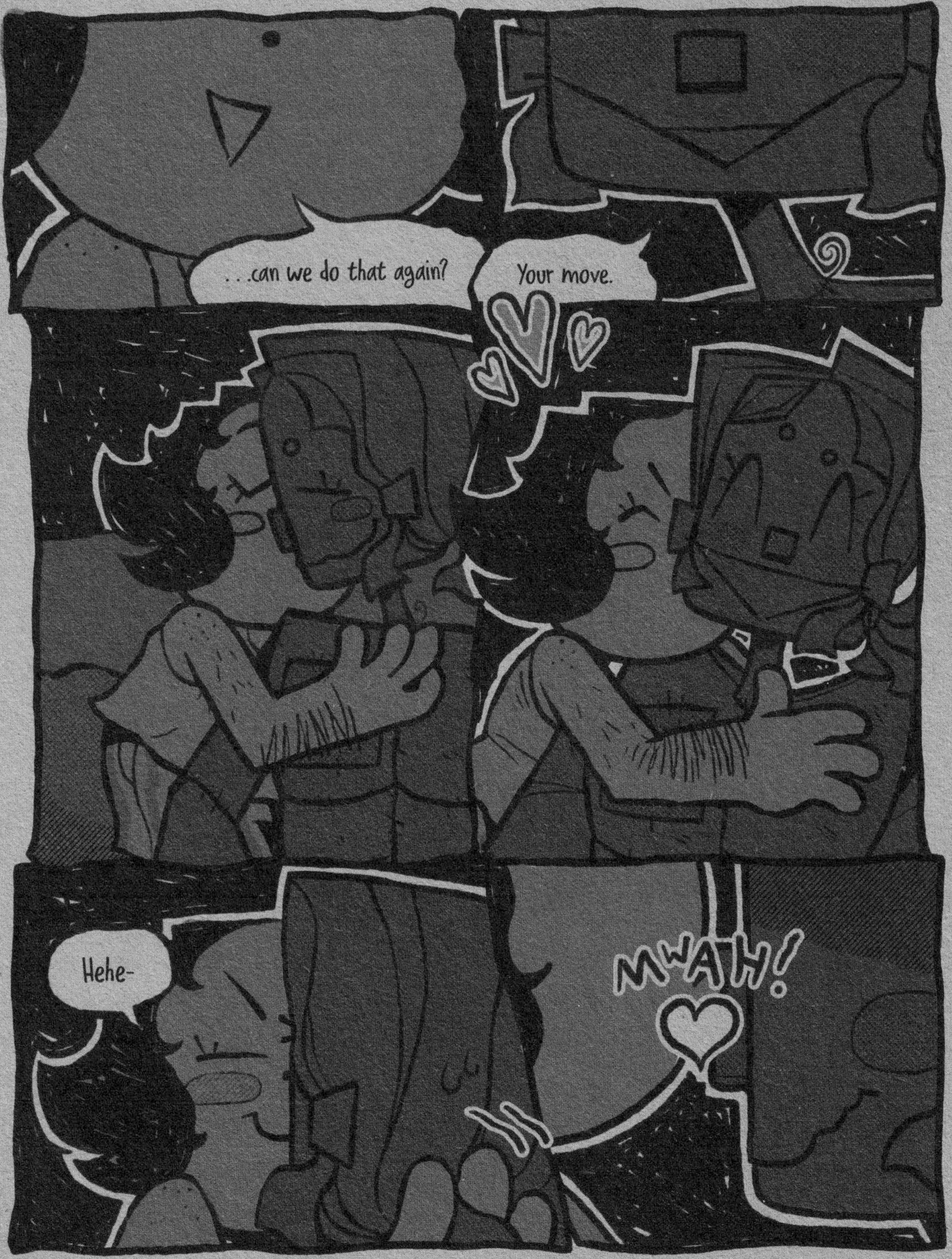

. . .can we do that again?
Your move.
Hehe-
MWAH!

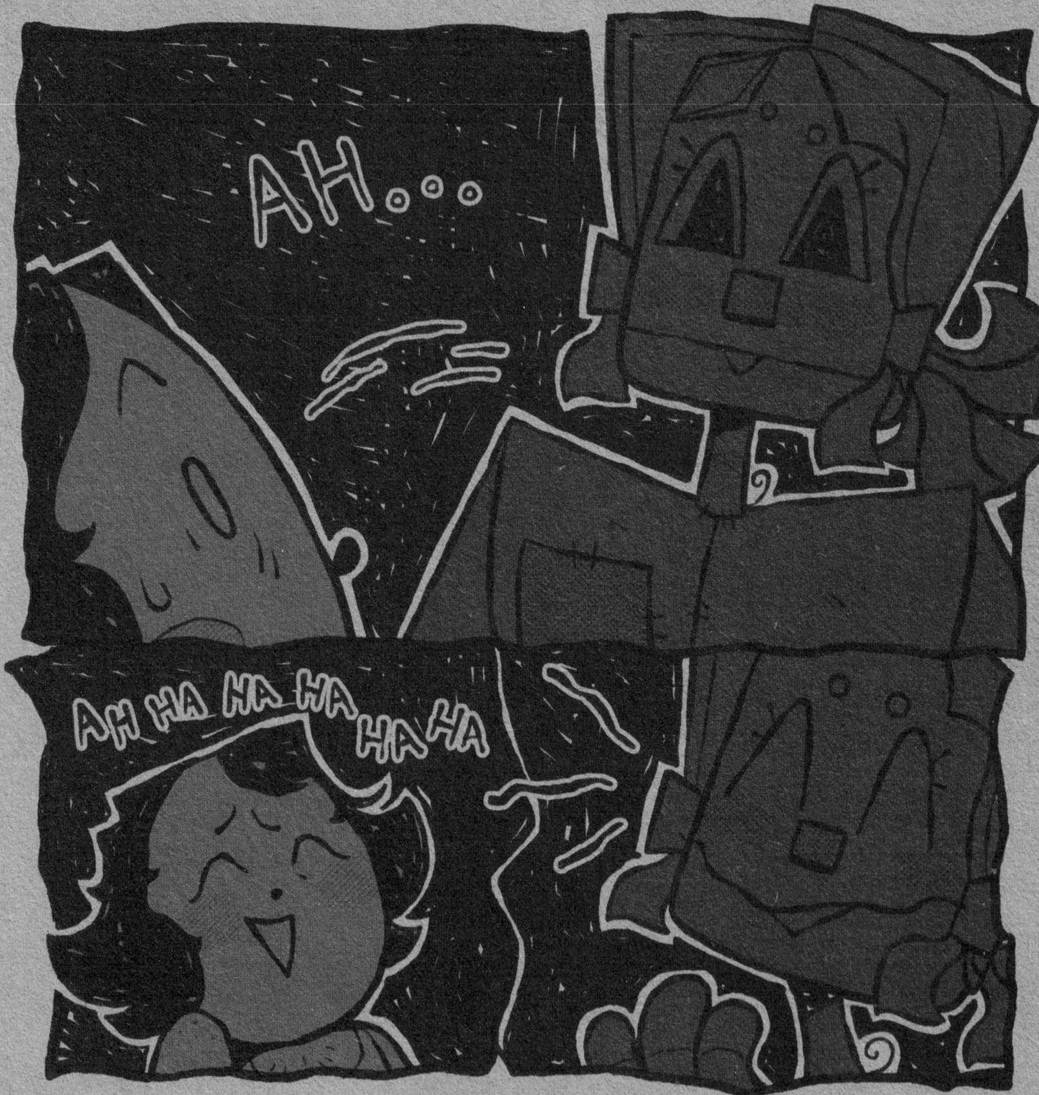
AH...
AH HA HA HA HA HA HA

Good night, Wegg. I'll see you in the morning.

I had that dream again.
Water. Feathers. Blood.
Kisses. More.
Why'm I cryin'?

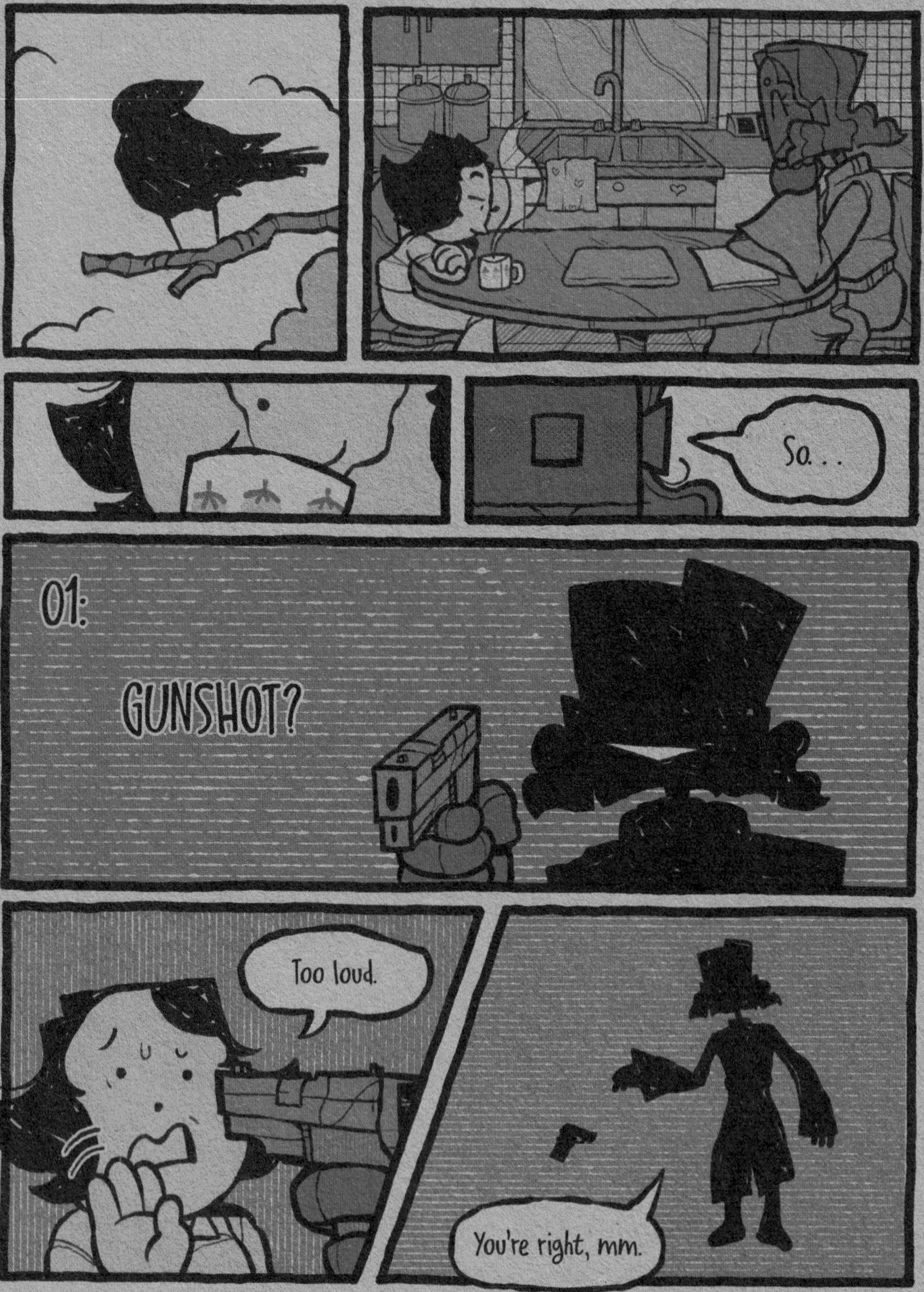
So. . .
01:
GUNSHOT?
Too loud.
You're right, mm.

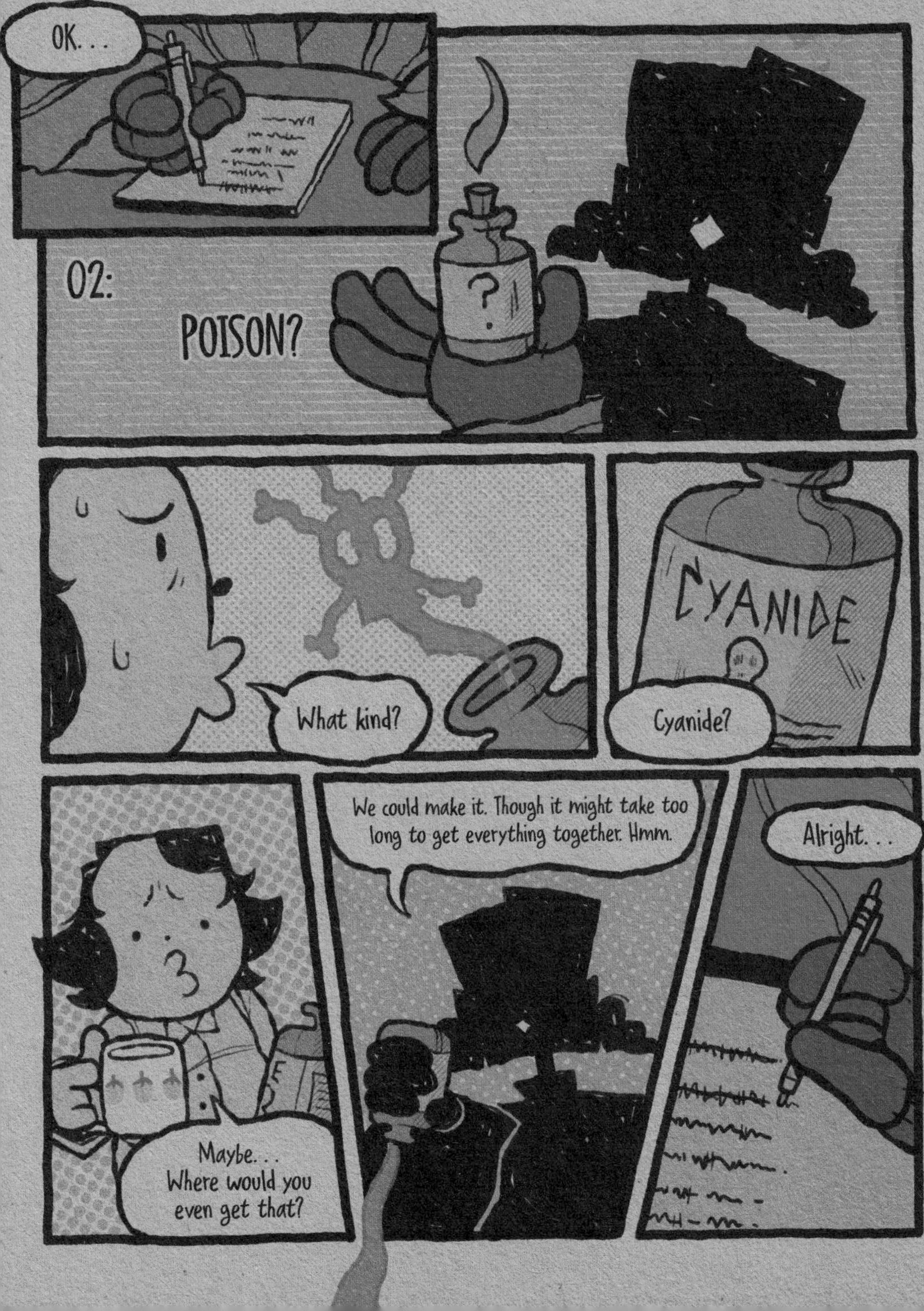
OK. . .
02:
POISON?
What kind?
CYANIDE
Cyanide?
Maybe. . .
Where would you even get that?
We could make it. Though it might take too long to get everything together. Hmm.
Alright. . .

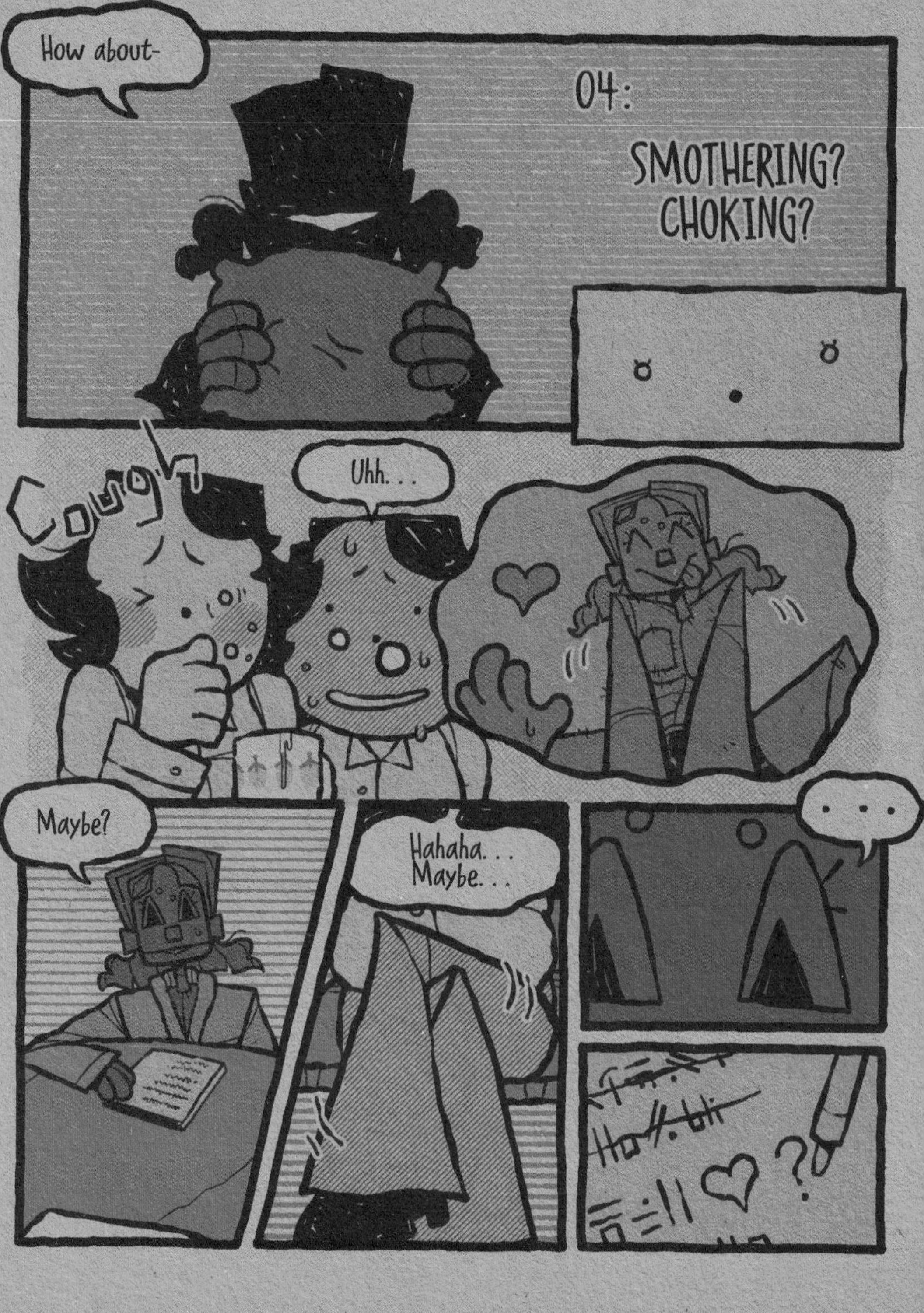
How about-
04:
SMOTHERING?
CHOKING?
Uhh. . .
Maybe?
Hahaha. . .
Maybe. . .
. . .

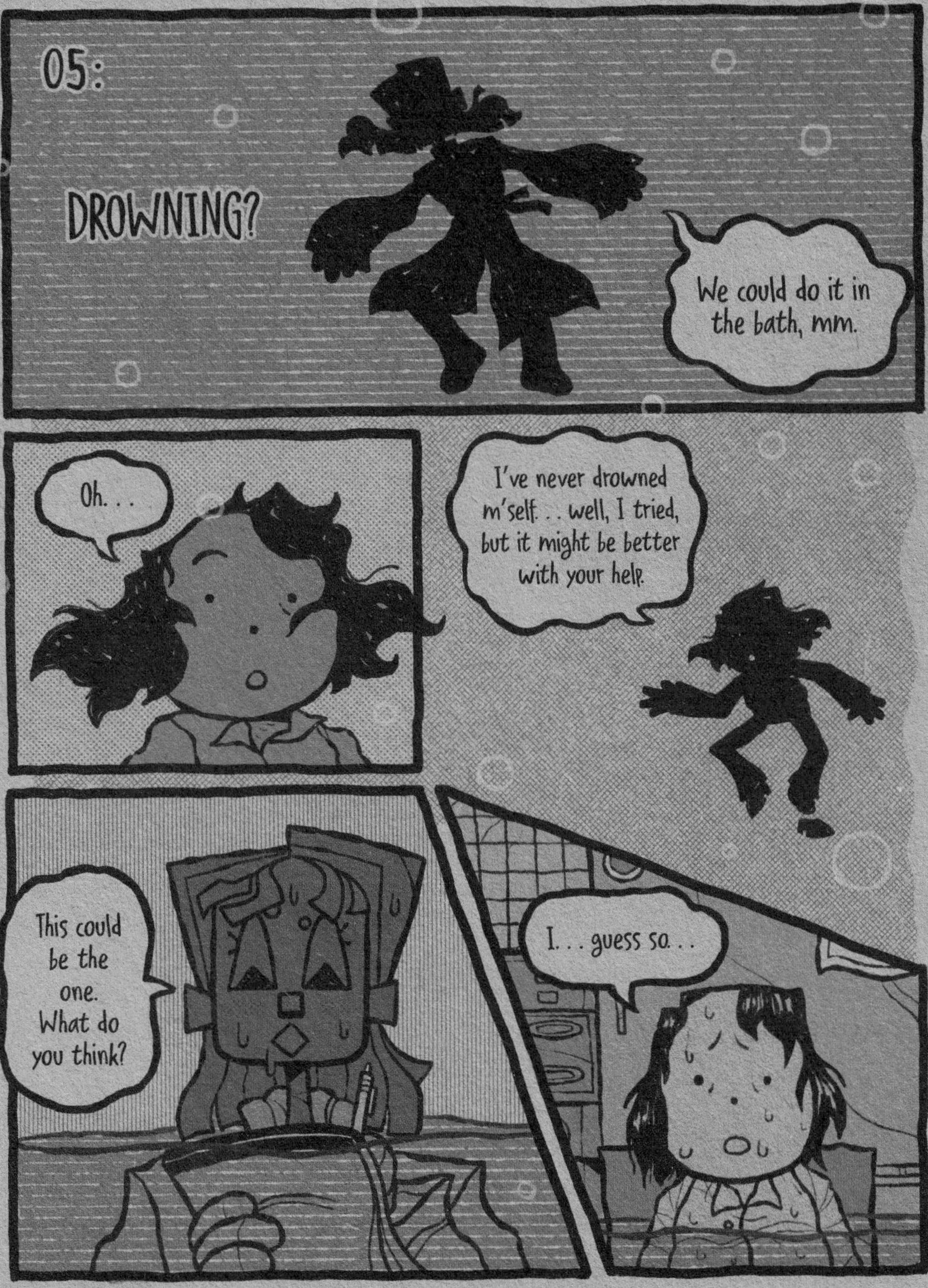
05:
DROWNING?
We could do it in the bath, mm.
Oh. . .
I've never drowned m'self. . . well, I tried, but it might be better with your help.
This could be the one. What do you think?
I. . . guess so. . .

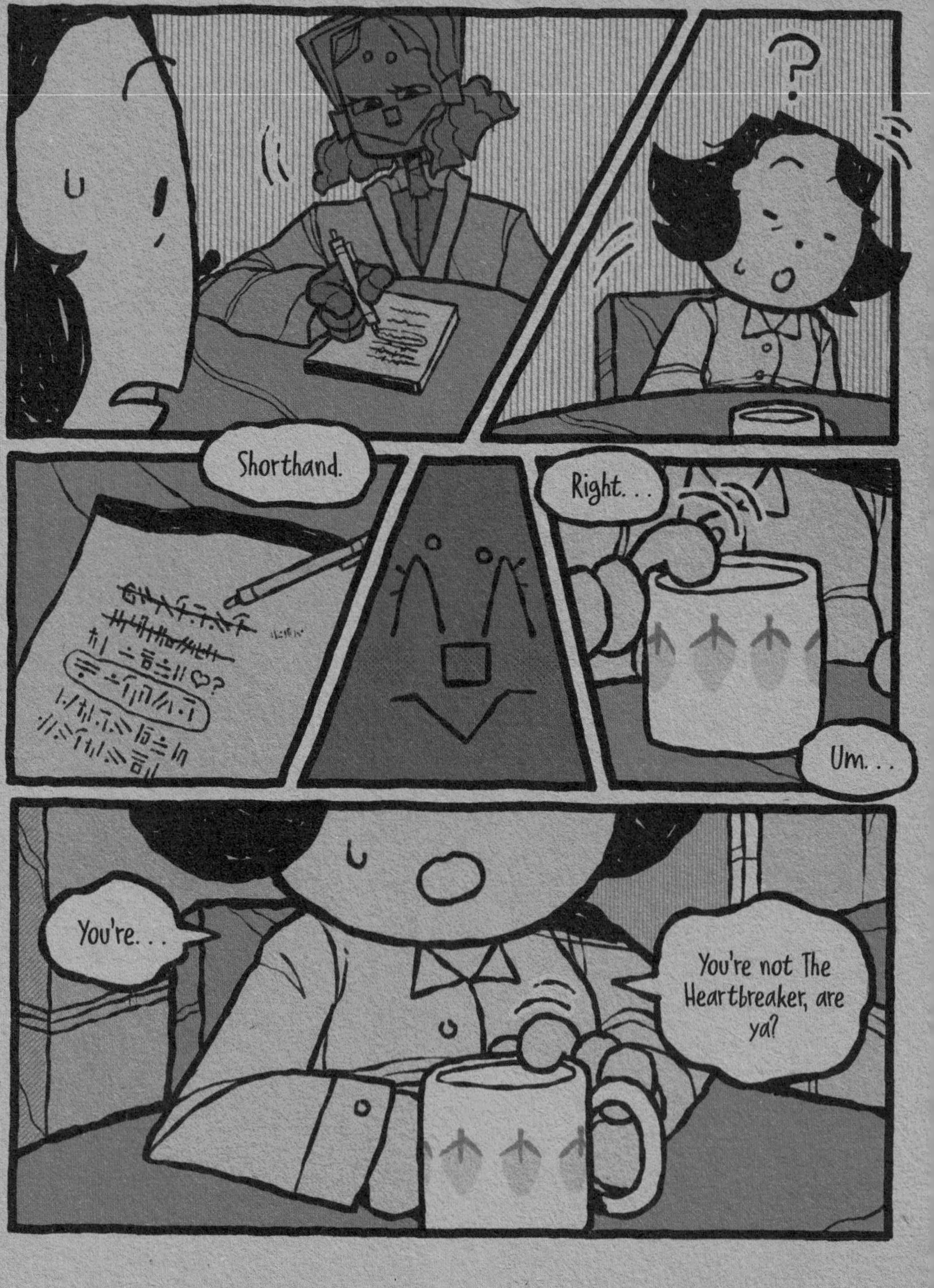
?
Shorthand.
Right...
Um...
You're...
You're not The Heartbreaker, are ya?

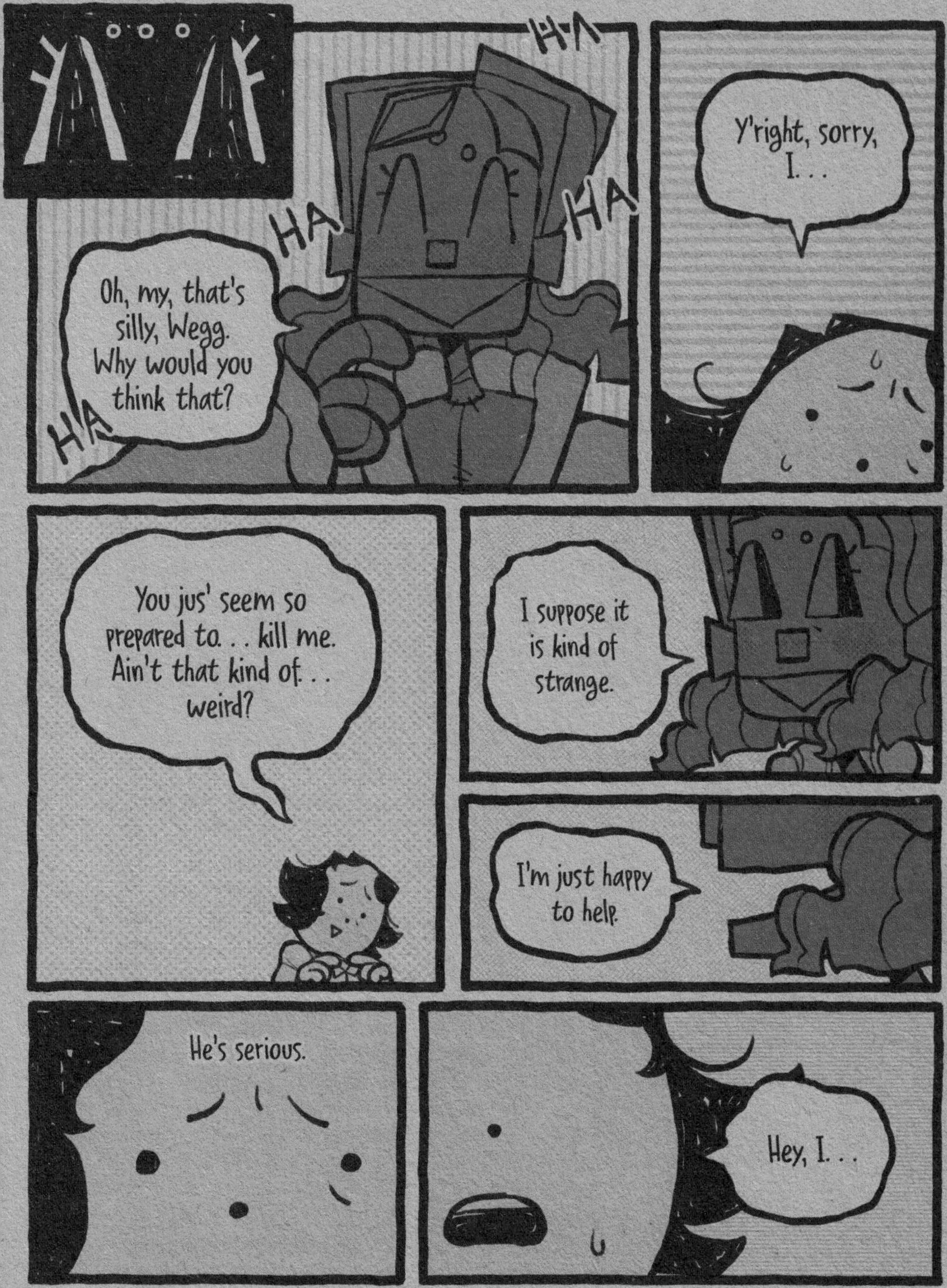
HA
HA
HA
HA
Oh, my, that's silly, Wegg. Why would you think that?
Y'right, sorry, I. . .
You jus' seem so prepared to. . . kill me. Ain't that kind of. . . weird?
I suppose it is kind of strange.
I'm just happy to help.
He's serious.
Hey, I. . .

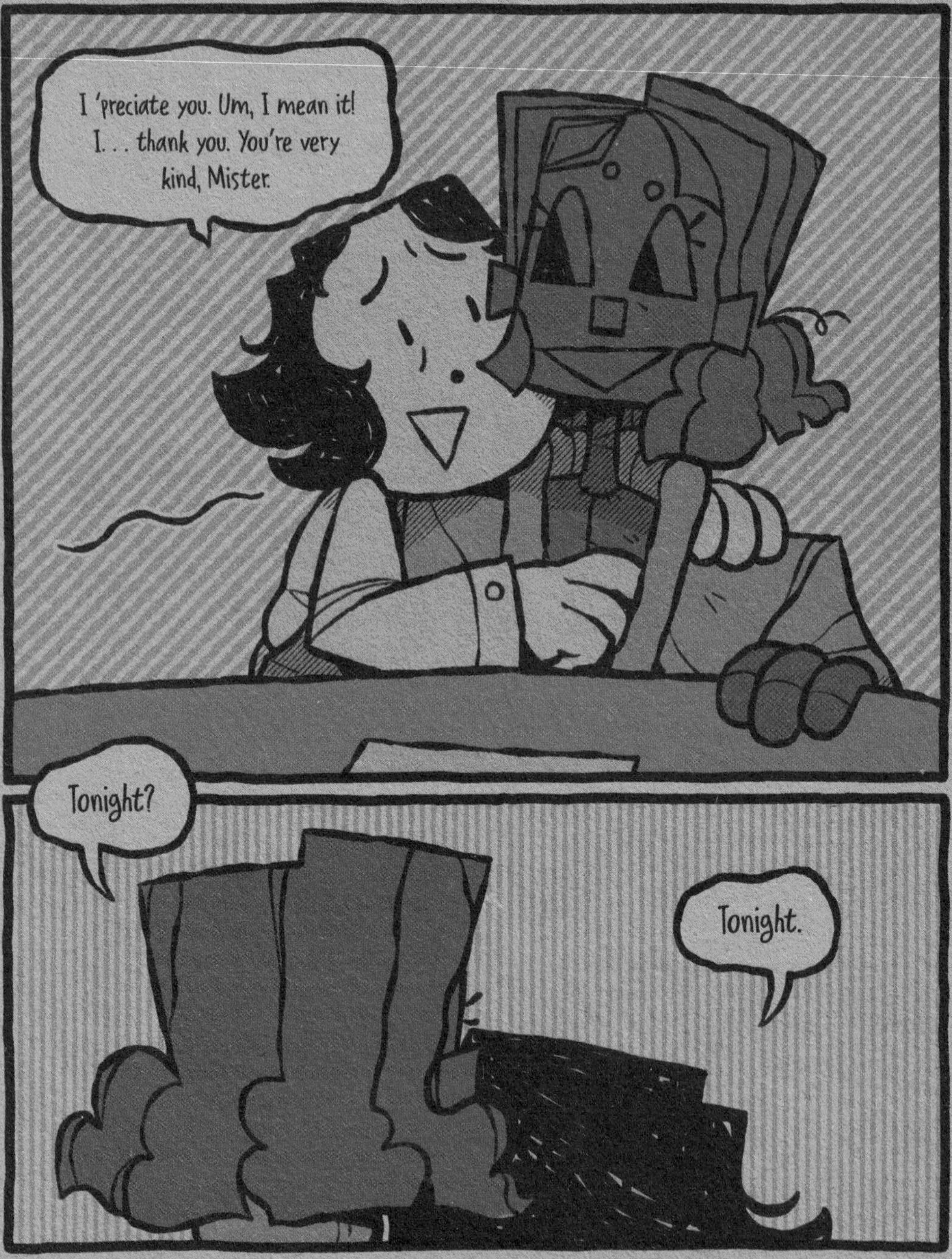
I 'preciate you. Um, I mean it! I. . . thank you. You're very kind, Mister.
Tonight?
Tonight.

Am I really ready for this?

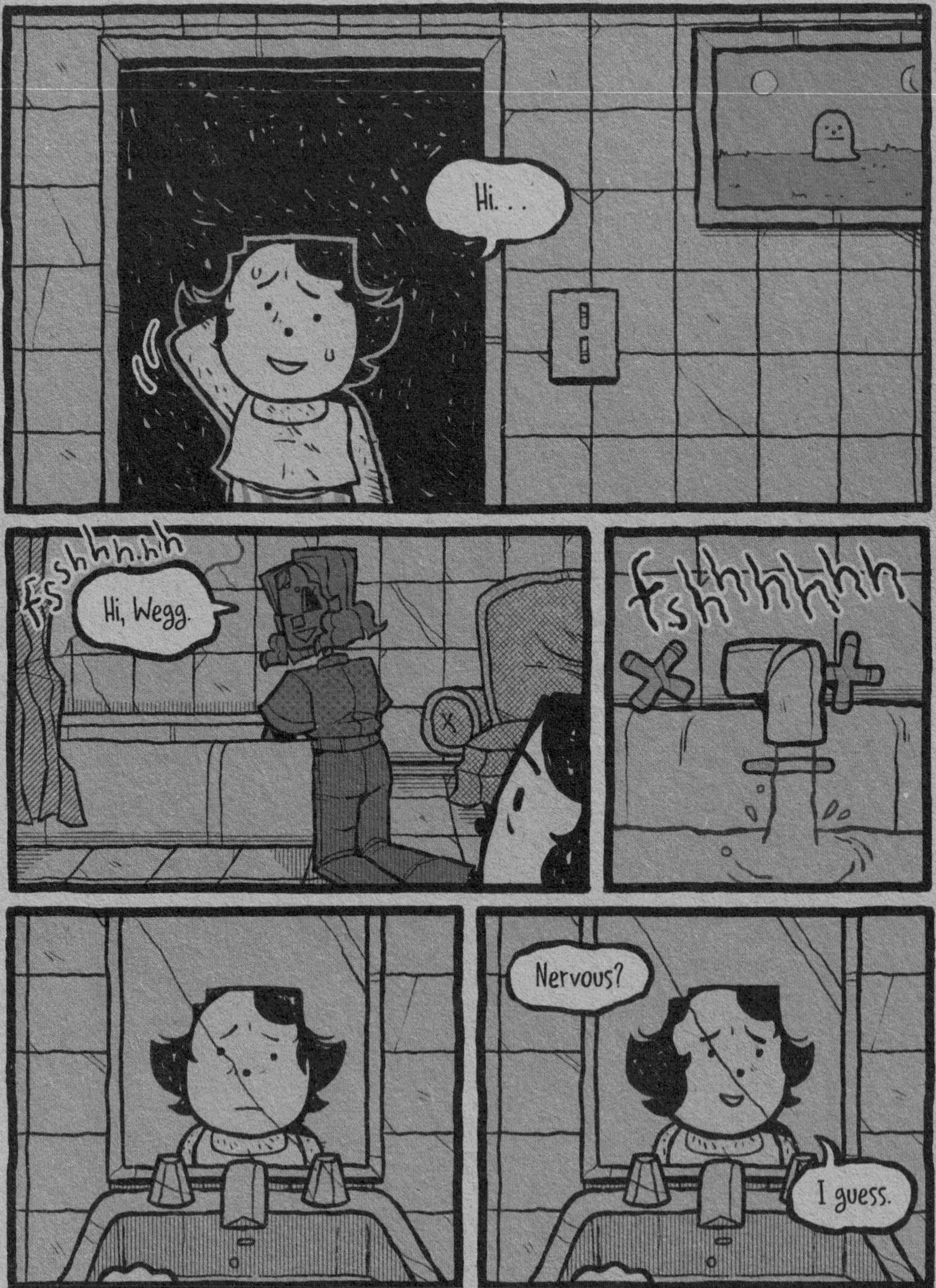
Hi. . .
fshhhhh
Hi, Wegg.
fshhhhhh
Nervous?
I guess.

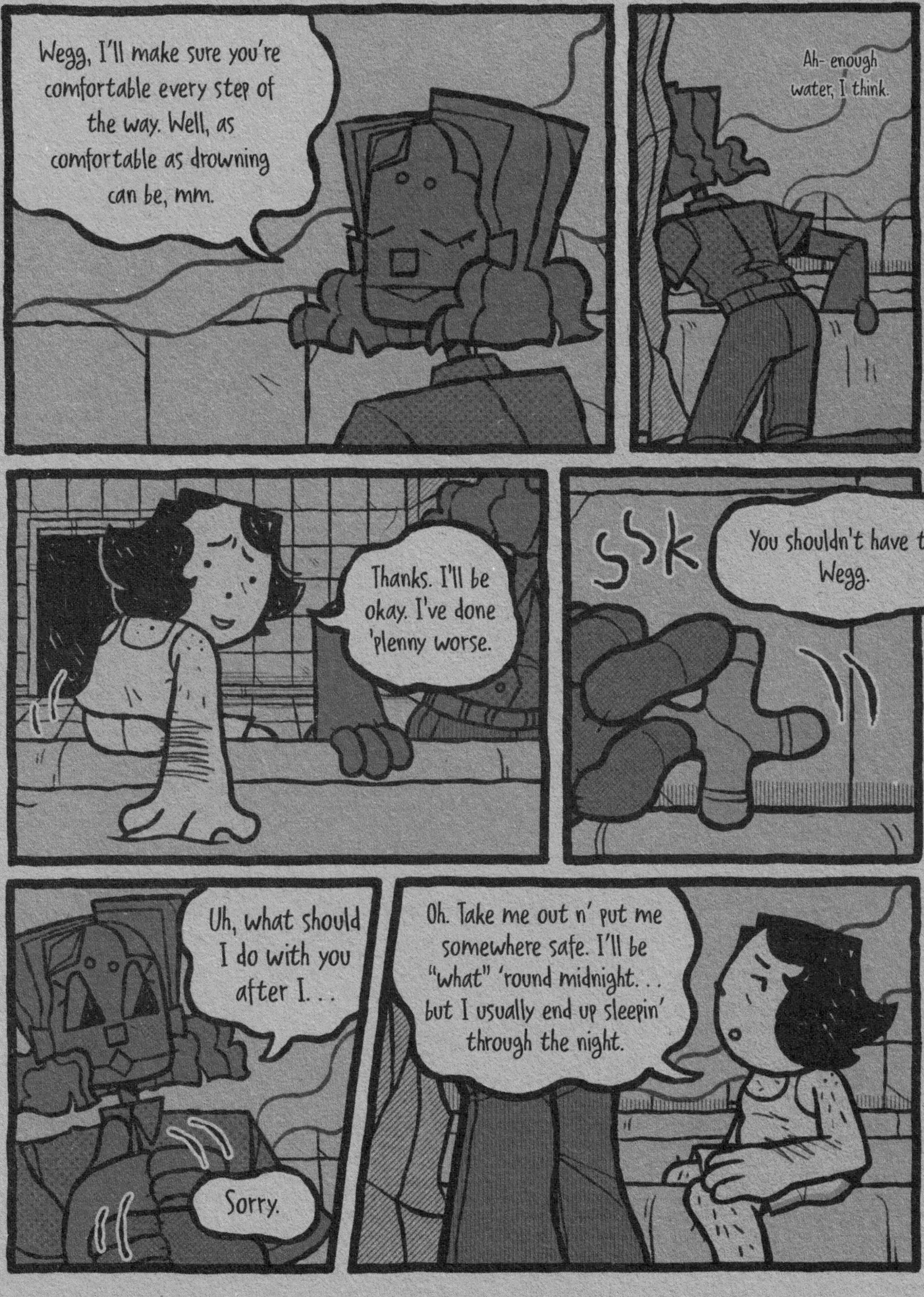
Wegg, I'll make sure you're comfortable every step of the way. Well, as comfortable as drowning can be, mm.
Ah- enough water, I think.
Thanks. I'll be okay. I've done 'plenny worse.
SSK
You shouldn't have to, Wegg.
Uh, what should I do with you after I. . .
Sorry.
Oh. Take me out n' put me somewhere safe. I'll be "what" 'round midnight. . . but I usually end up sleepin' through the night.

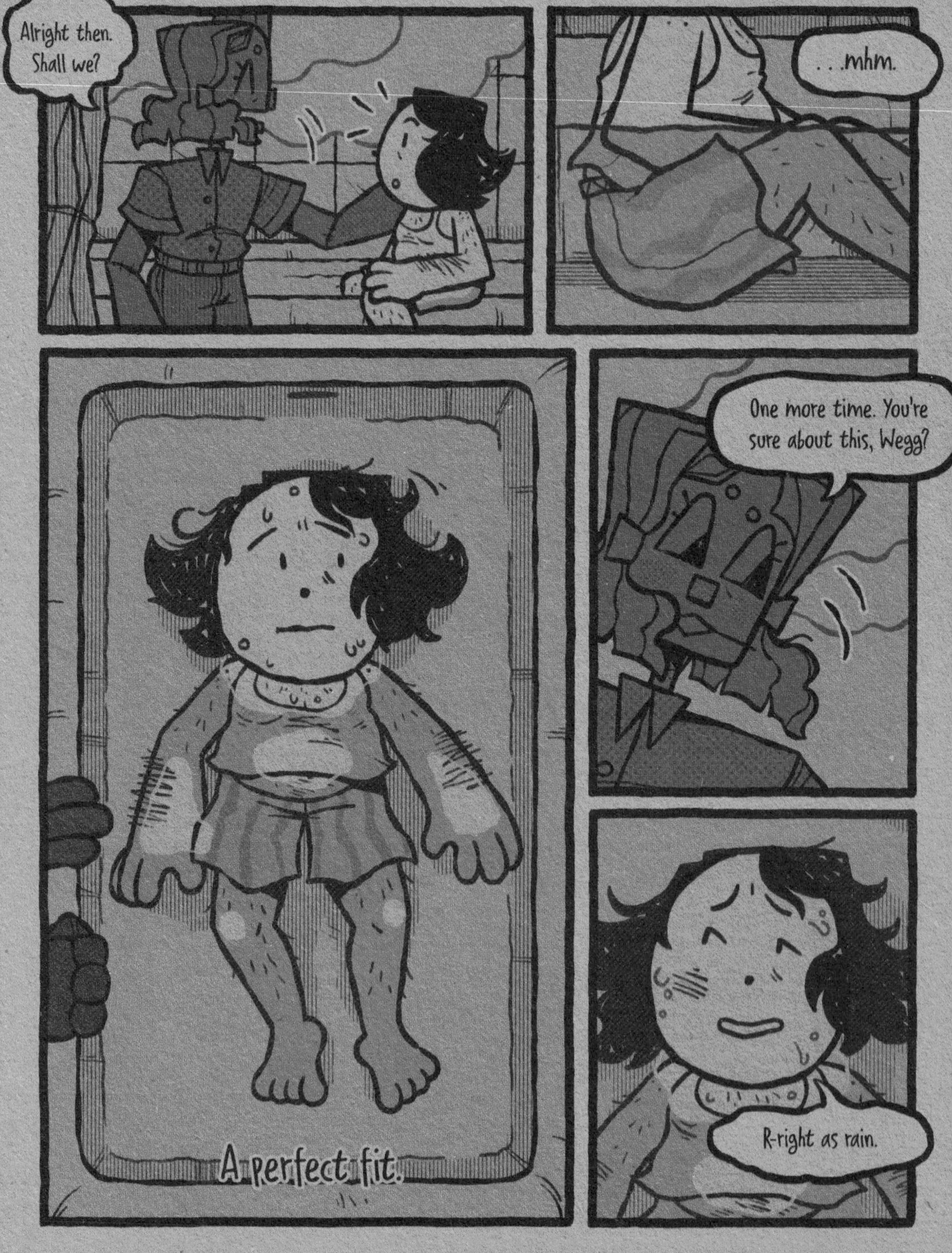
Alright then. Shall we?
. . .mhm.
A perfect fit.
One more time. You're sure about this, Wegg?
R-right as rain.

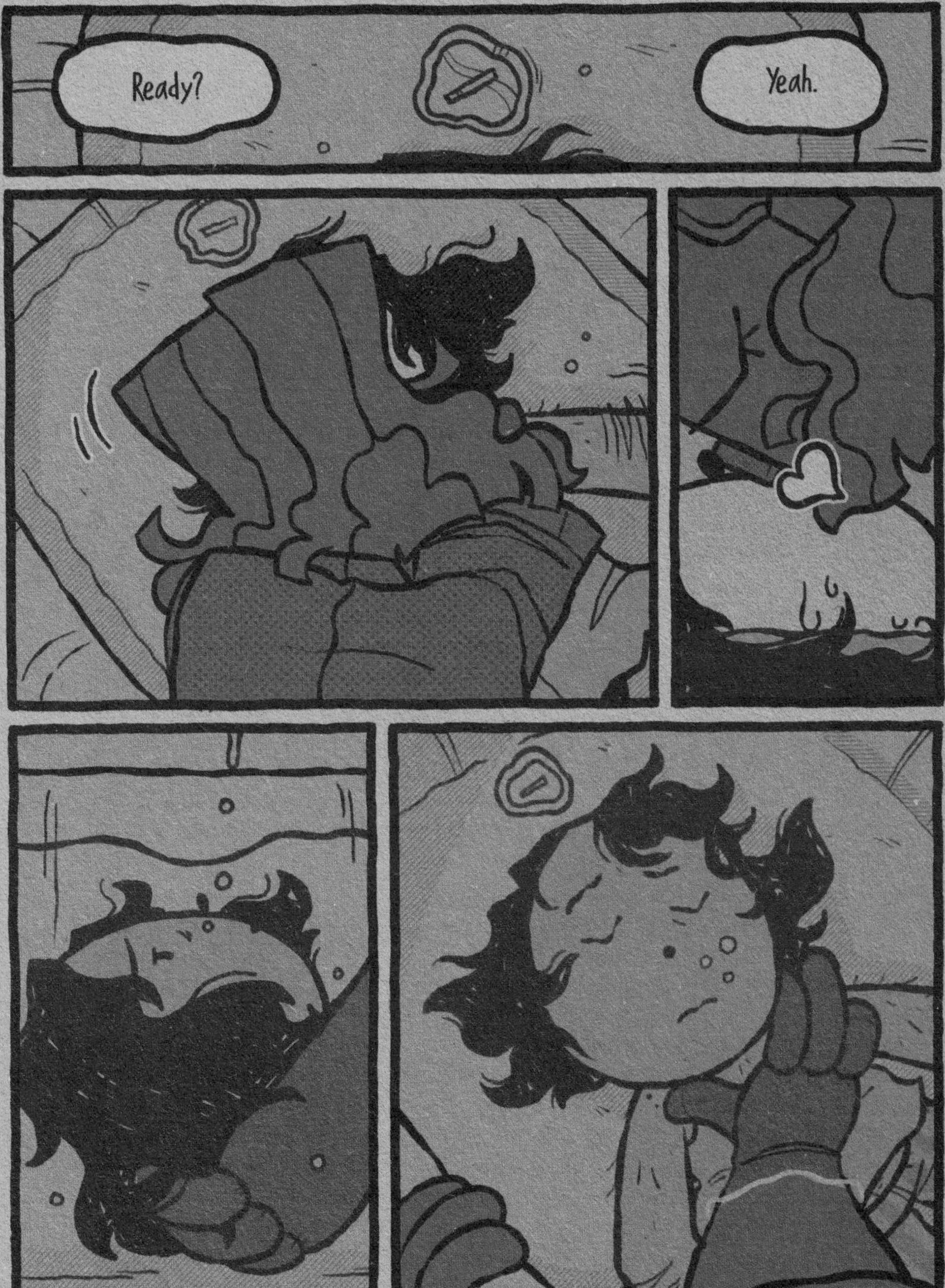
Ready?
Yeah.

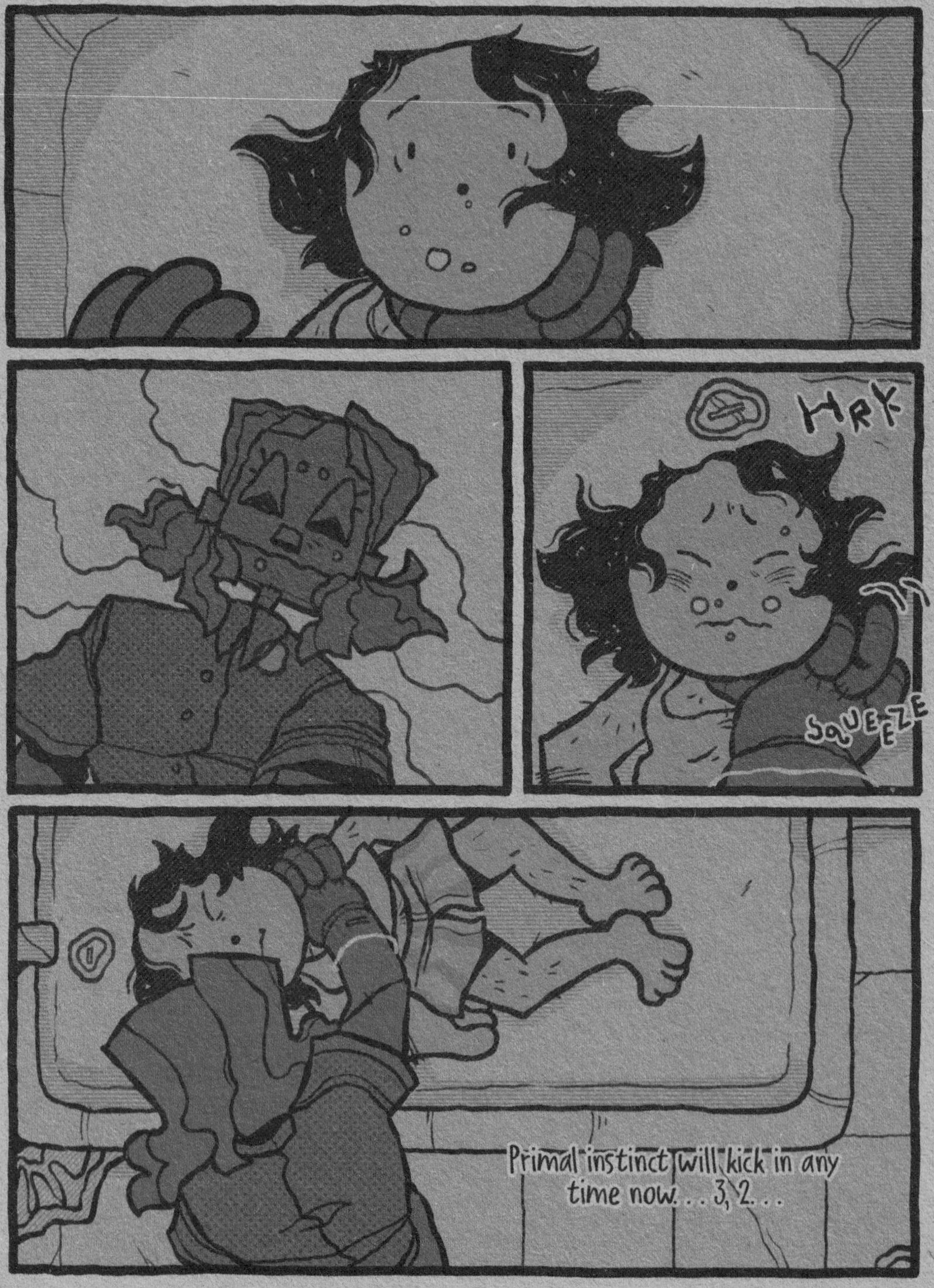
HRK
SQUEEZE
Primal instinct will kick in any time now. . . 3, 2. . .

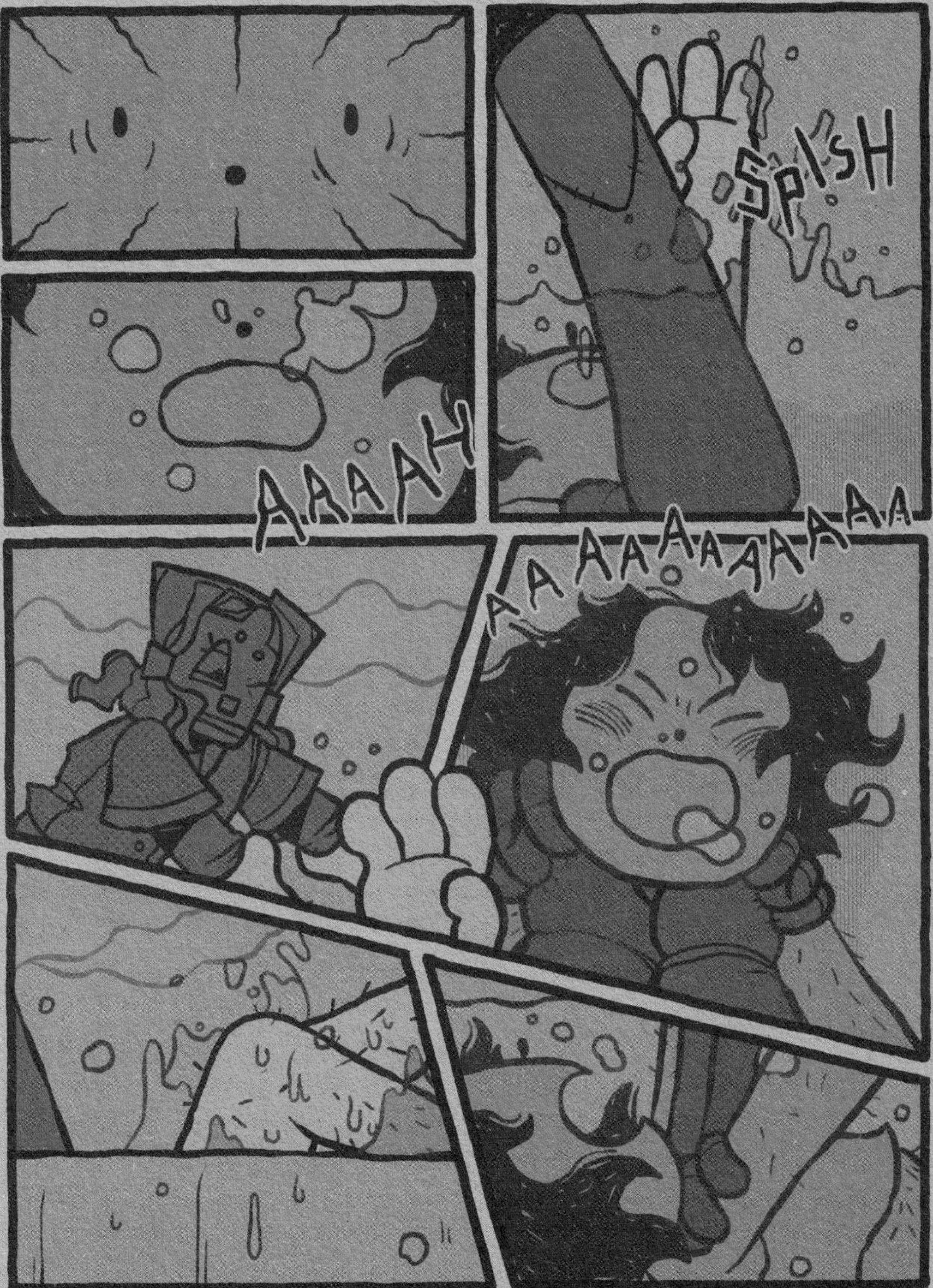
SPISH
AAAAH
AAAAAAAAAAAAA

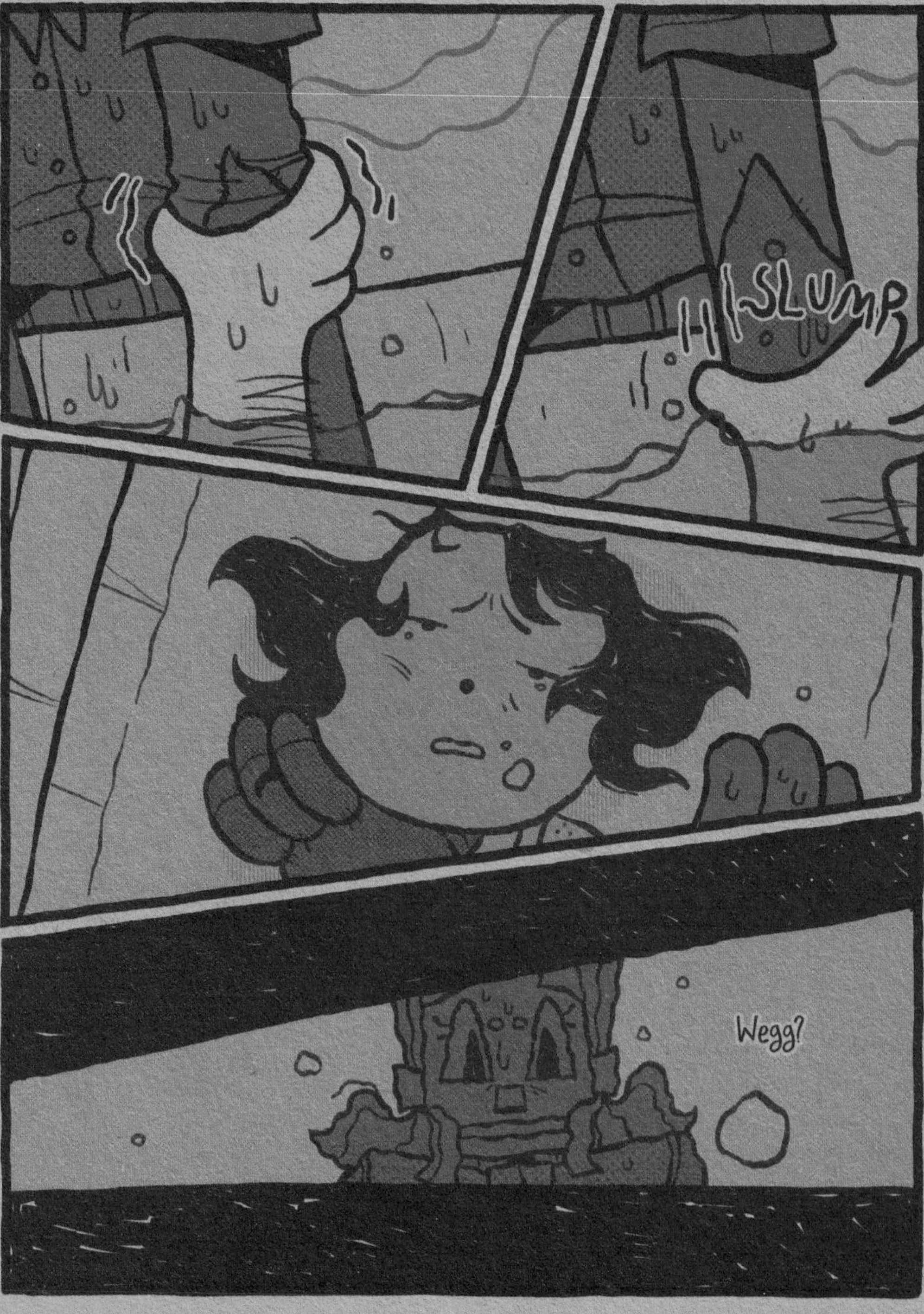
SLUMP
Wegg?

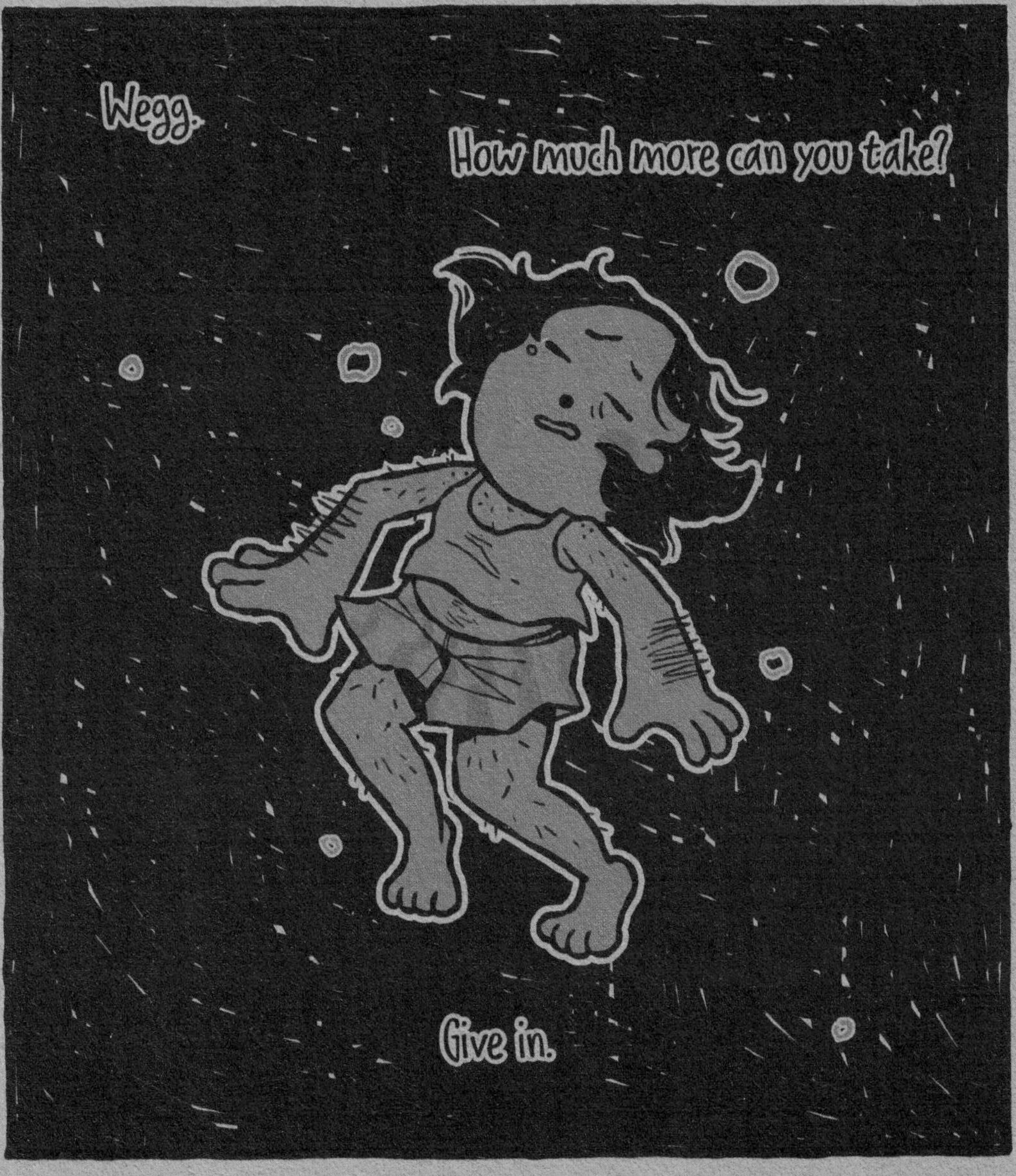
Wegg.
How much more can you take?
Give in.

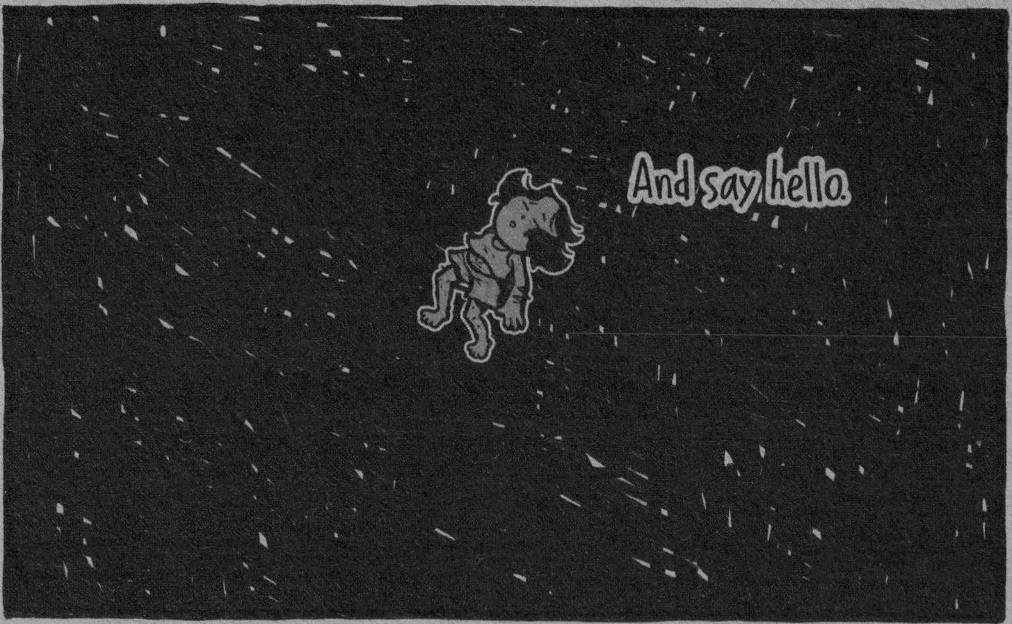
And say hello.

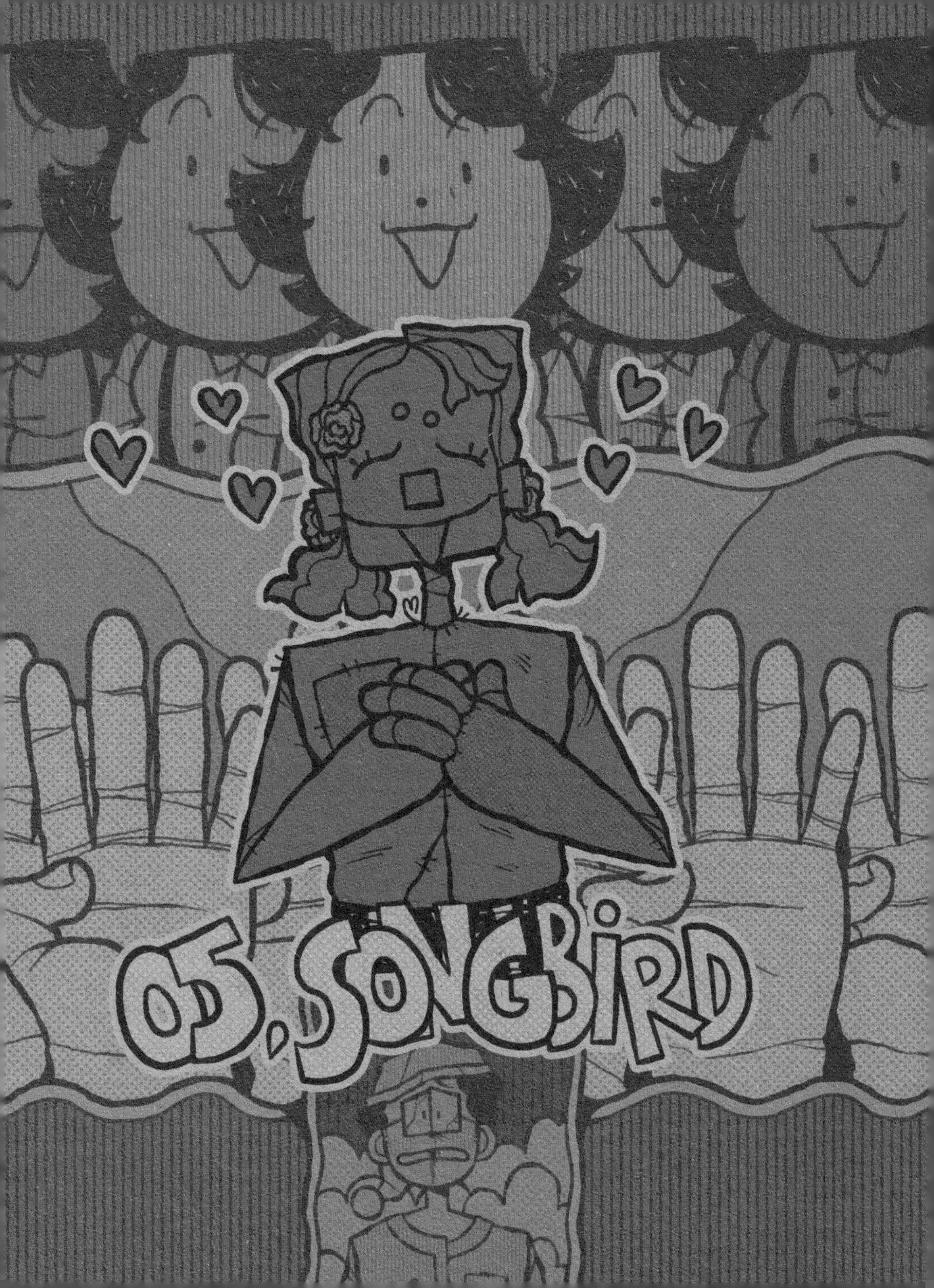
05. SONGBIRD

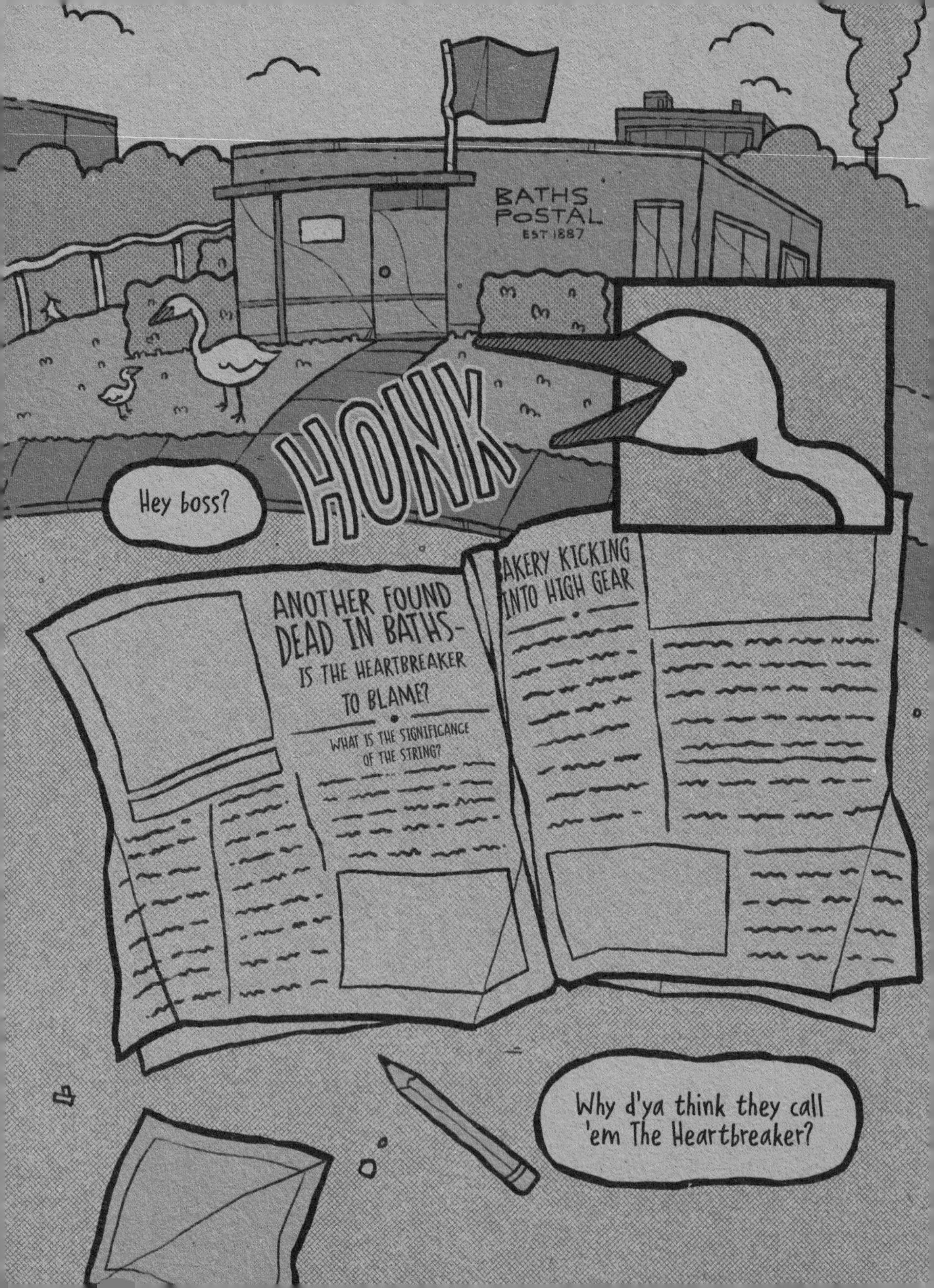

BATHS POSTAL EST 1887
HONK
Hey boss?
ANOTHER FOUND DEAD IN BATHS- IS THE HEARTBREAKER TO BLAME?
WHAT IS THE SIGNIFICANCE OF THE STRING?
AKERY KICKING INTO HIGH GEAR
Why d'ya think they call 'em The Heartbreaker?

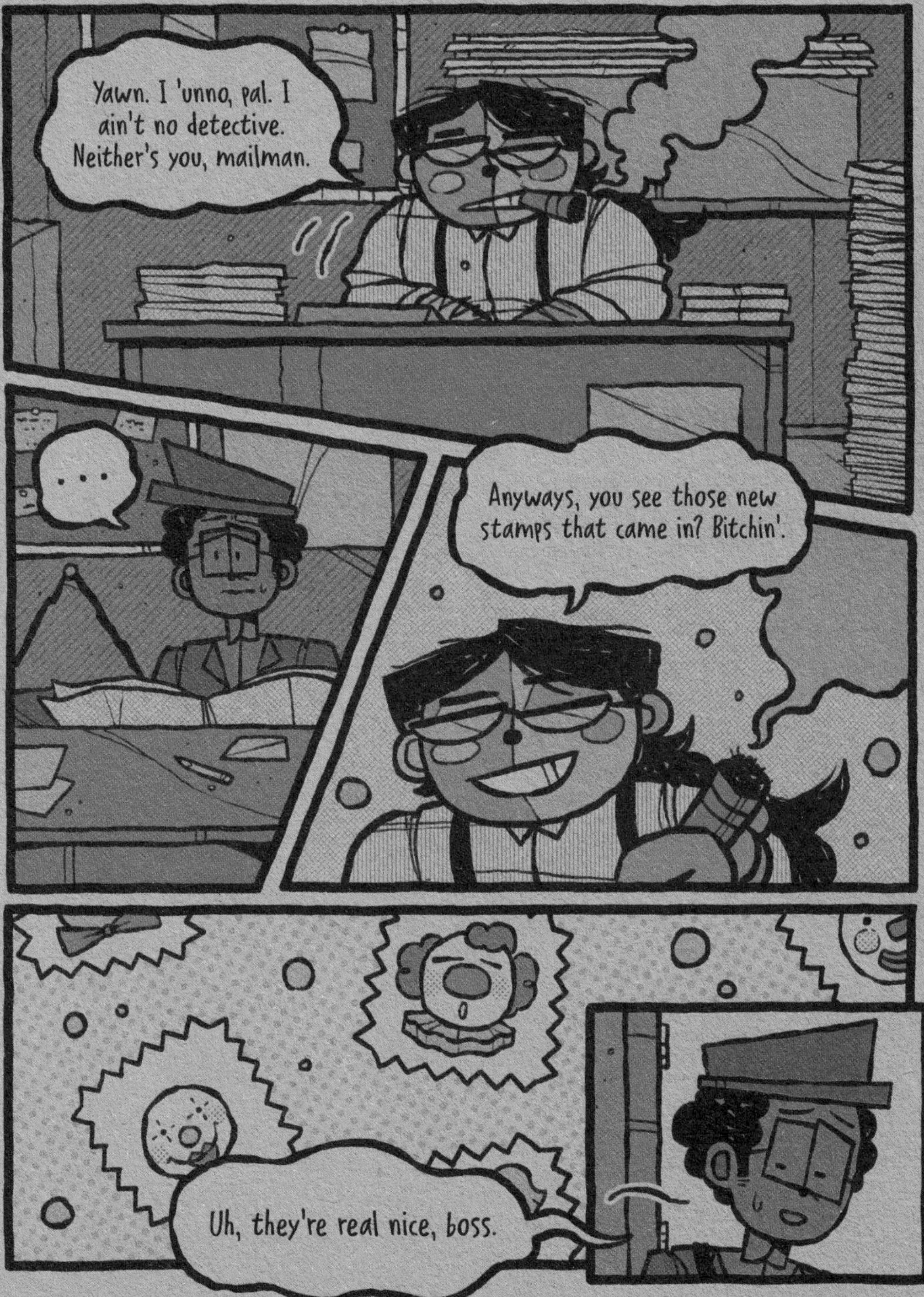
Yawn. I 'unno, pal. I ain't no detective. Neither's you, mailman.
...
Anyways, you see those new stamps that came in? Bitchin'.
Uh, they're real nice, boss.

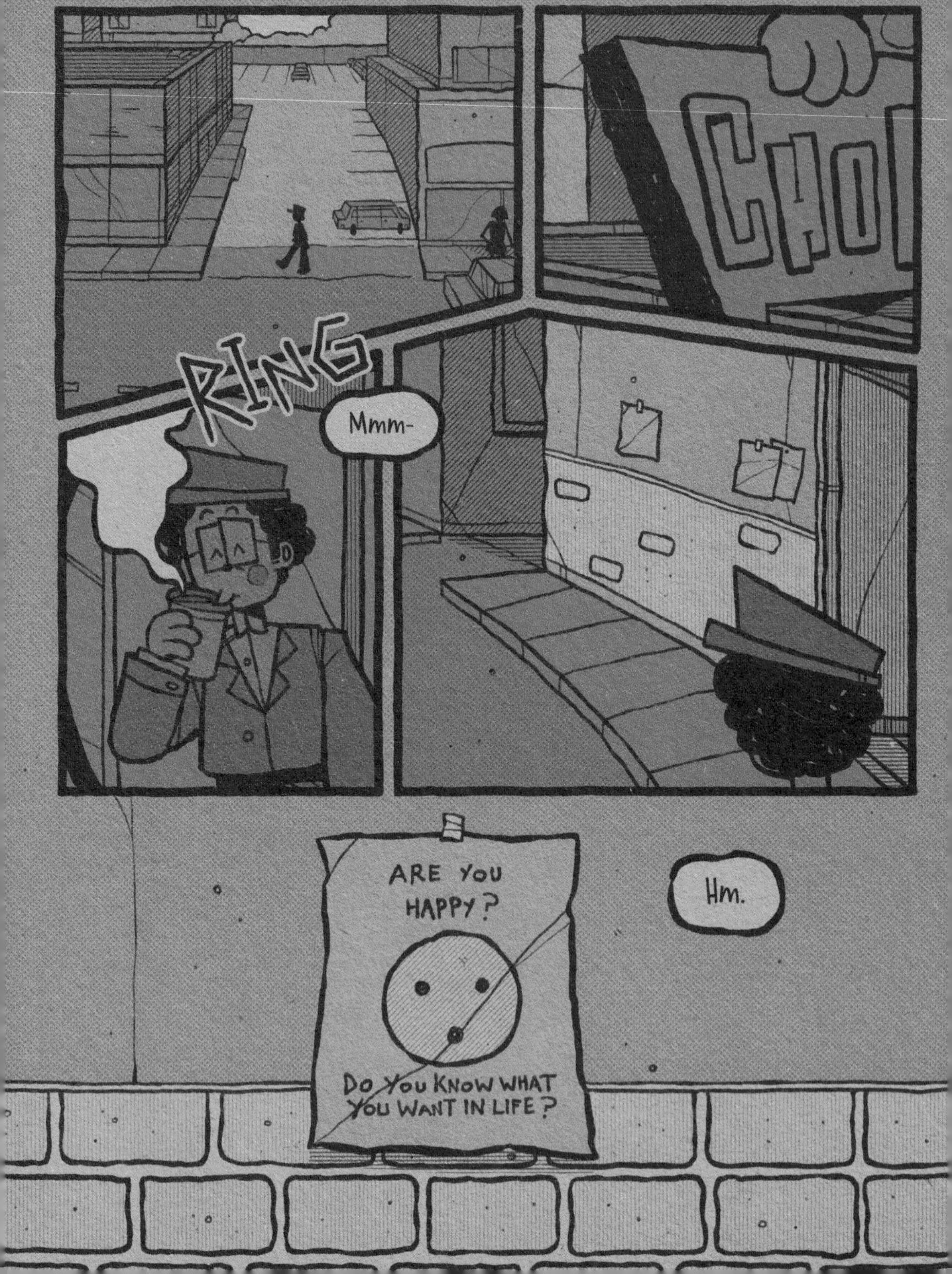
CHO
RING
Mmm-
ARE YOU HAPPY?
DO YOU KNOW WHAT YOU WANT IN LIFE?
Hm.

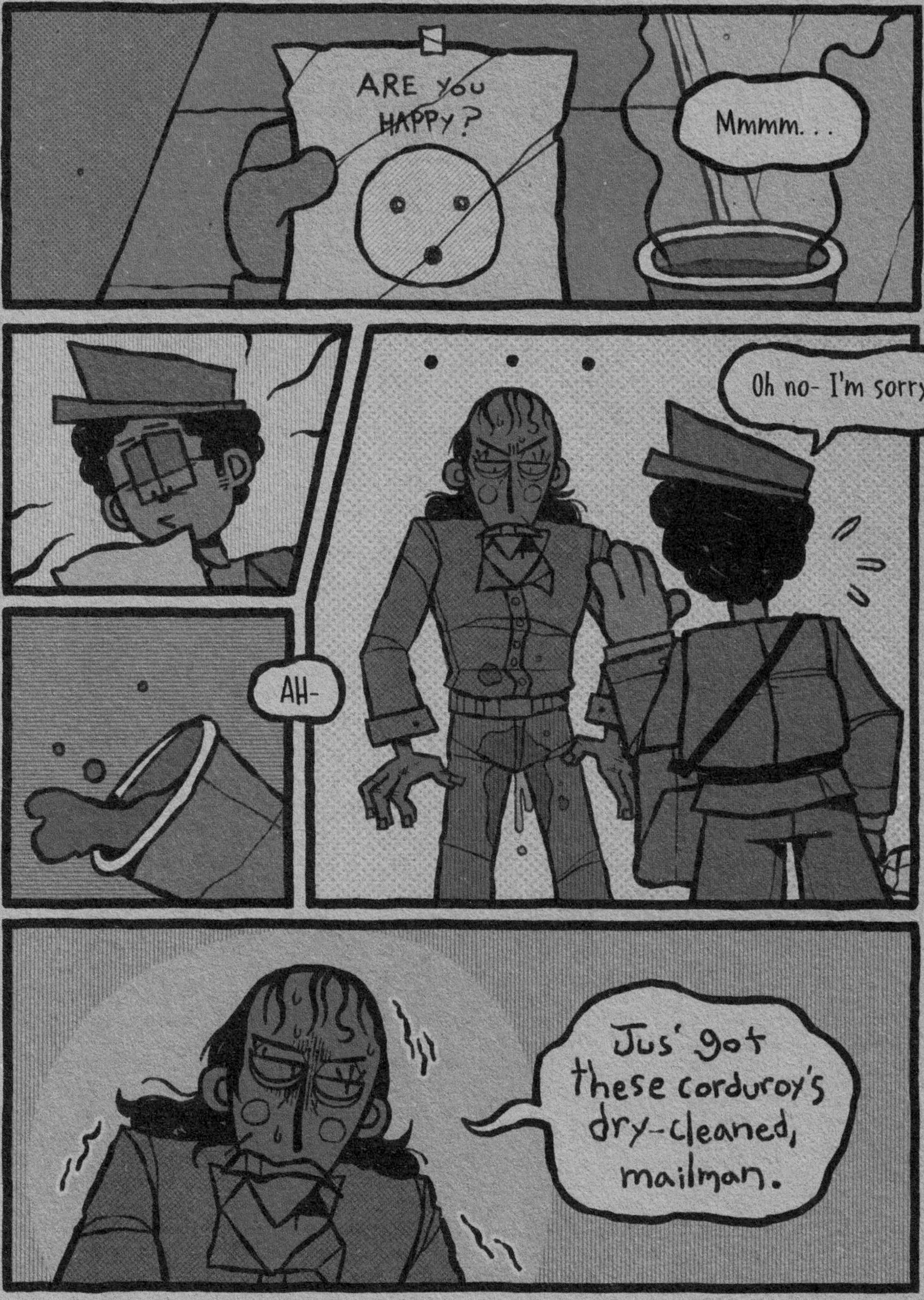
ARE you HAPPY?
Mmmm. . .
AH-
• • •
Oh no- I'm sorry!
Jus' got these corduroy's dry-cleaned, mailman.

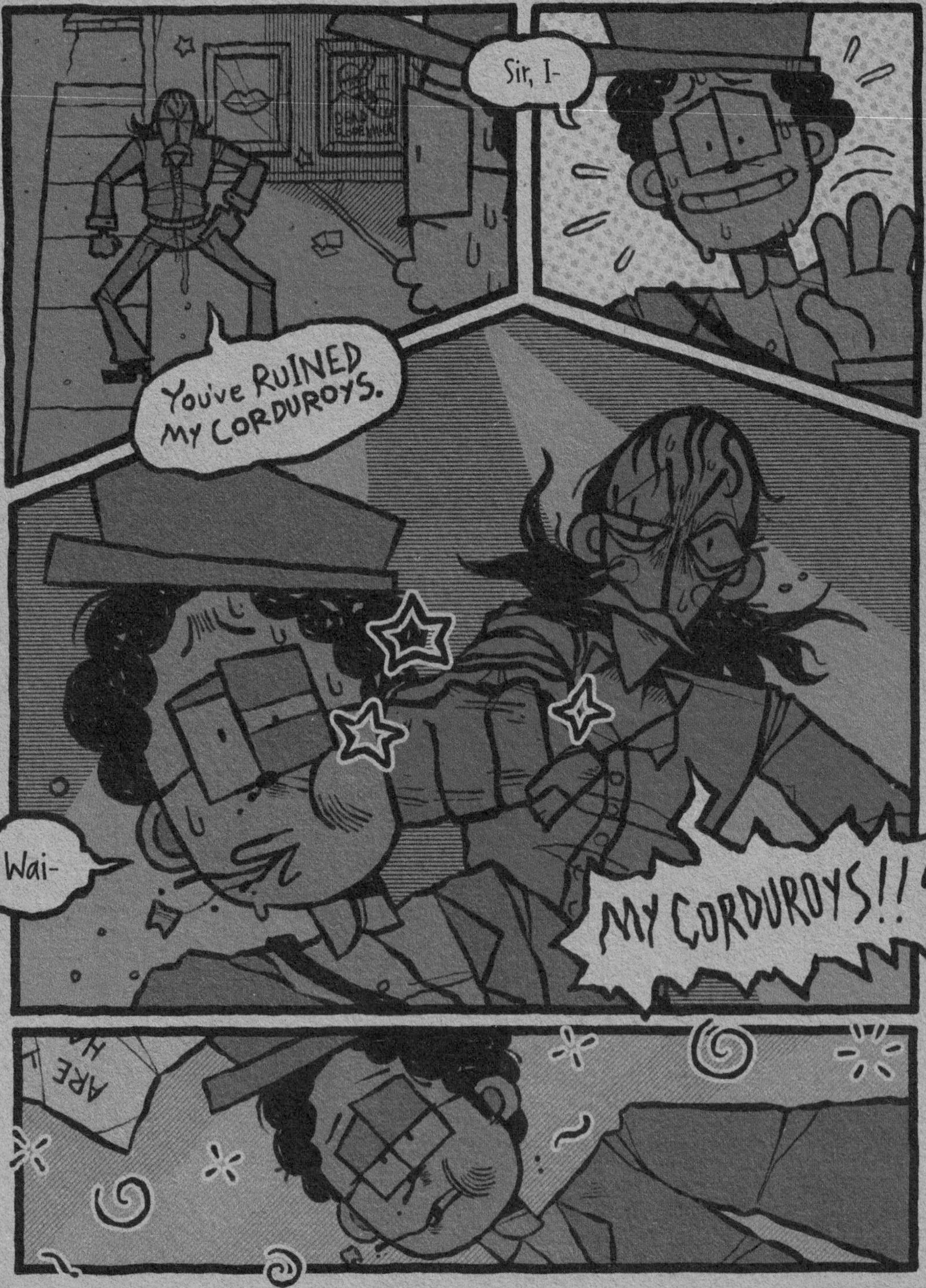
Sir, I-
You've RUINED MY CORDUROYS.
Wai-
MY CORDUROYS!!

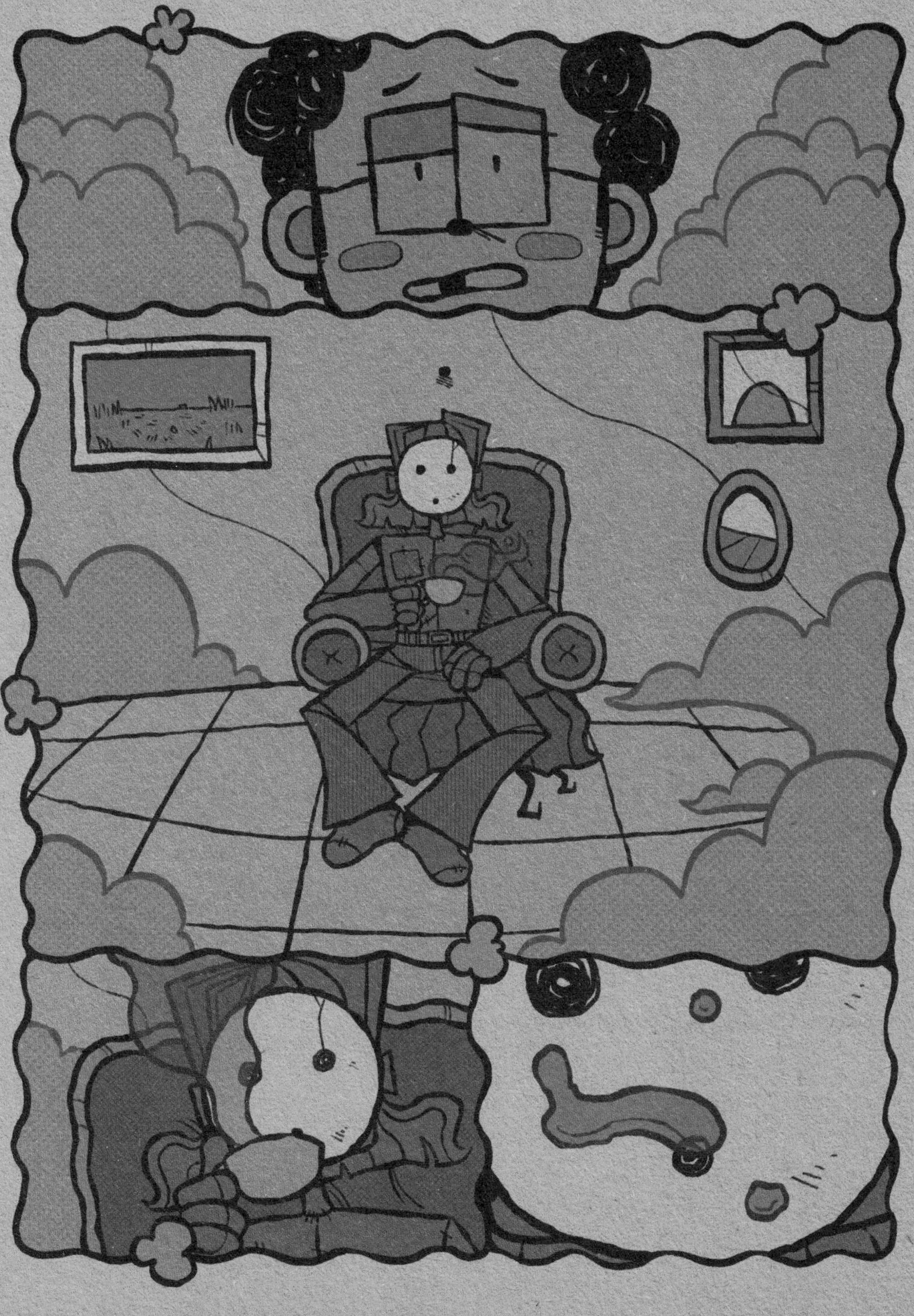

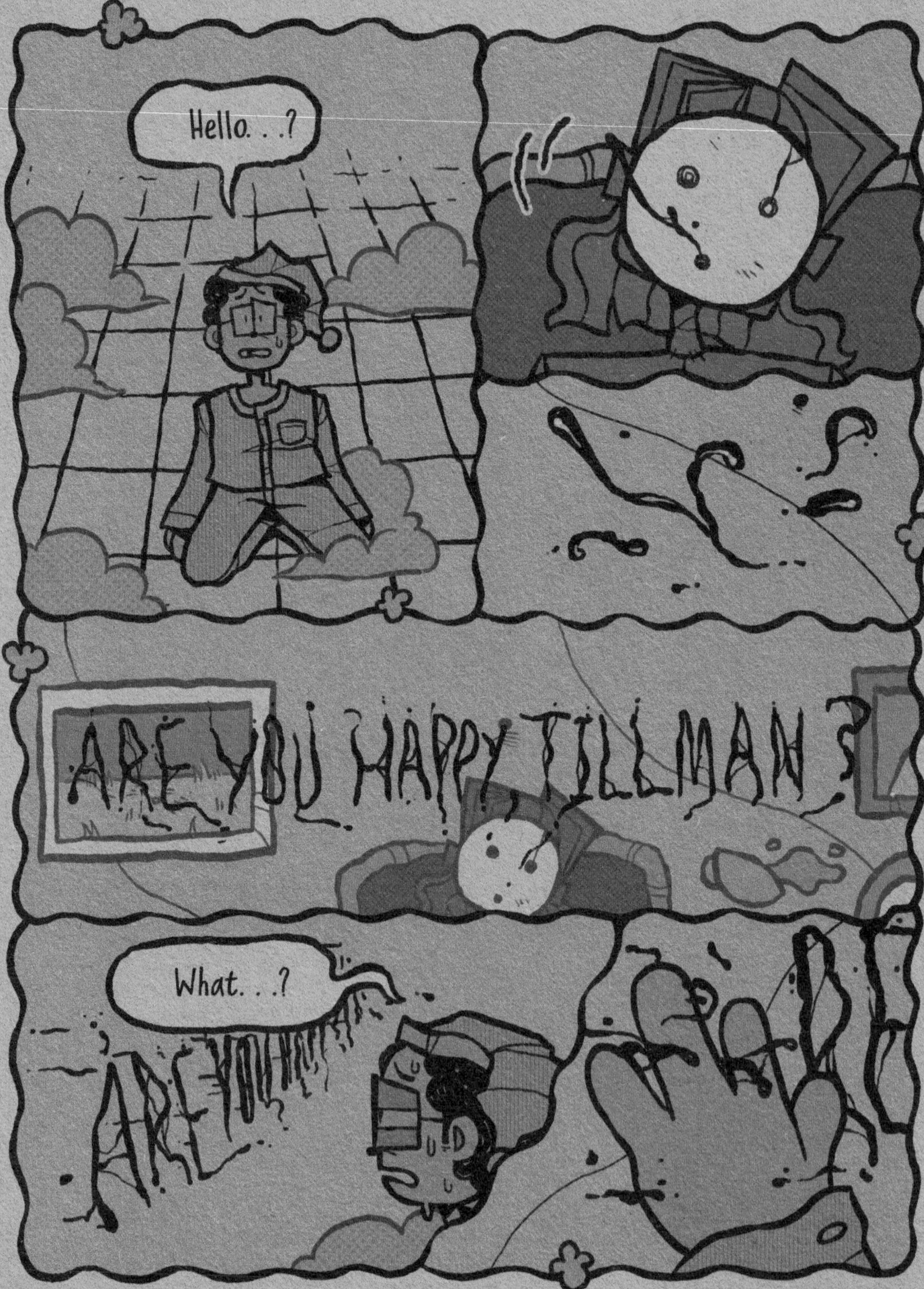
Hello. . .?
ARE YOU HAPPY TILLMAN?
What. . .?
ARE YOU

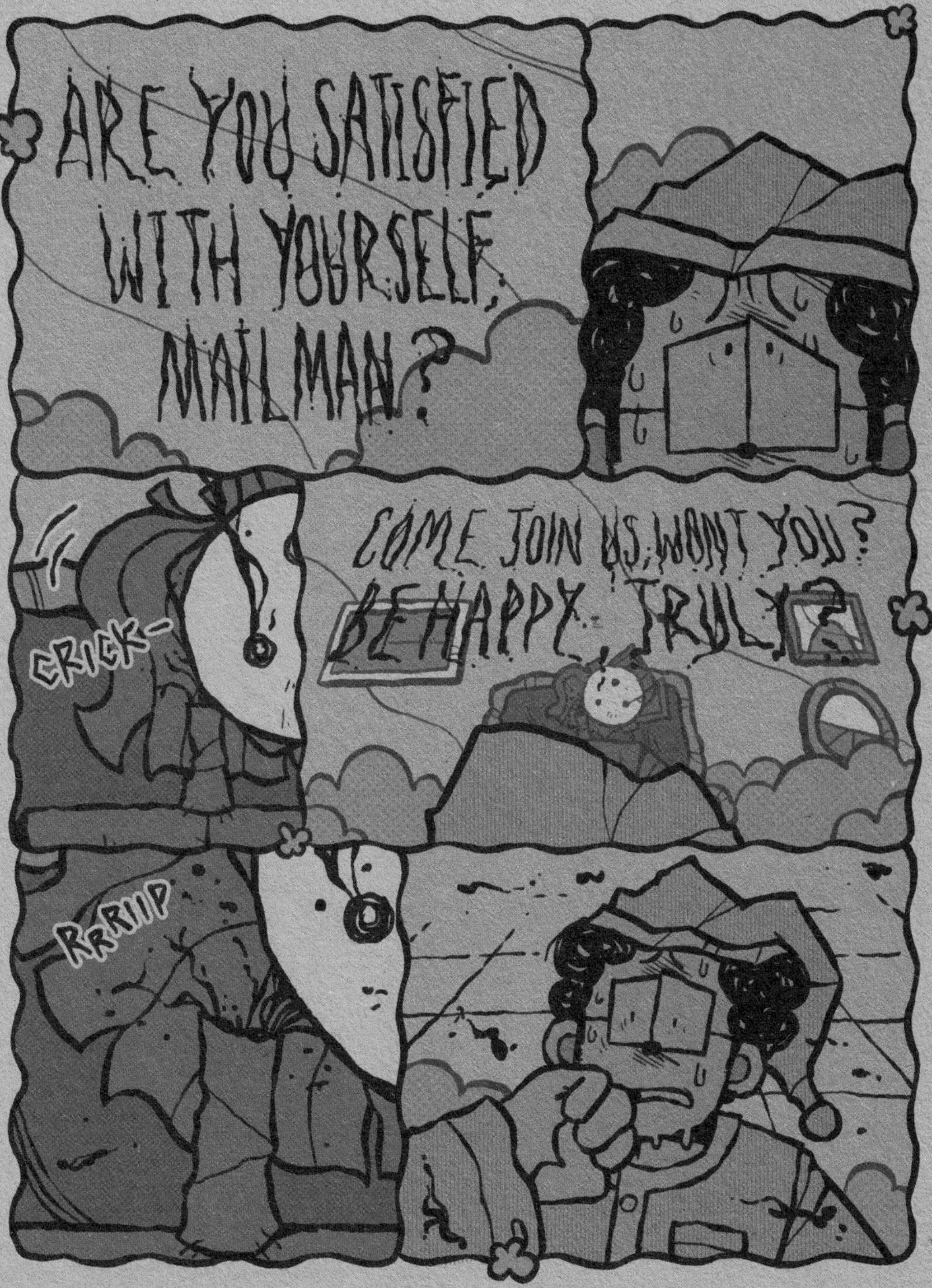
ARE YOU SATISFIED WITH YOURSELF, MAILMAN?
CRICK-
COME JOIN US, WON'T YOU?
BE HAPPY, TRULY?
RRRIIP

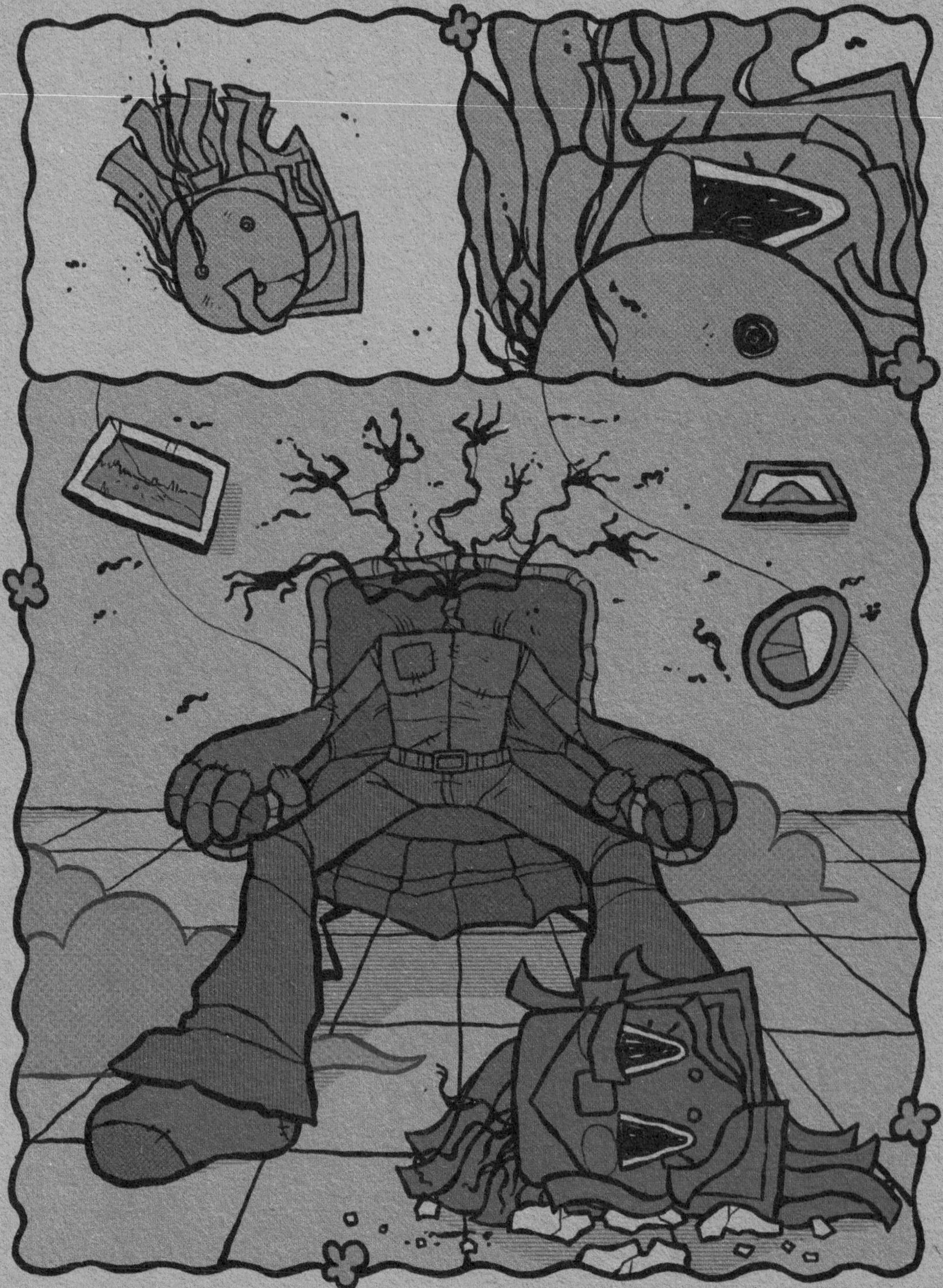

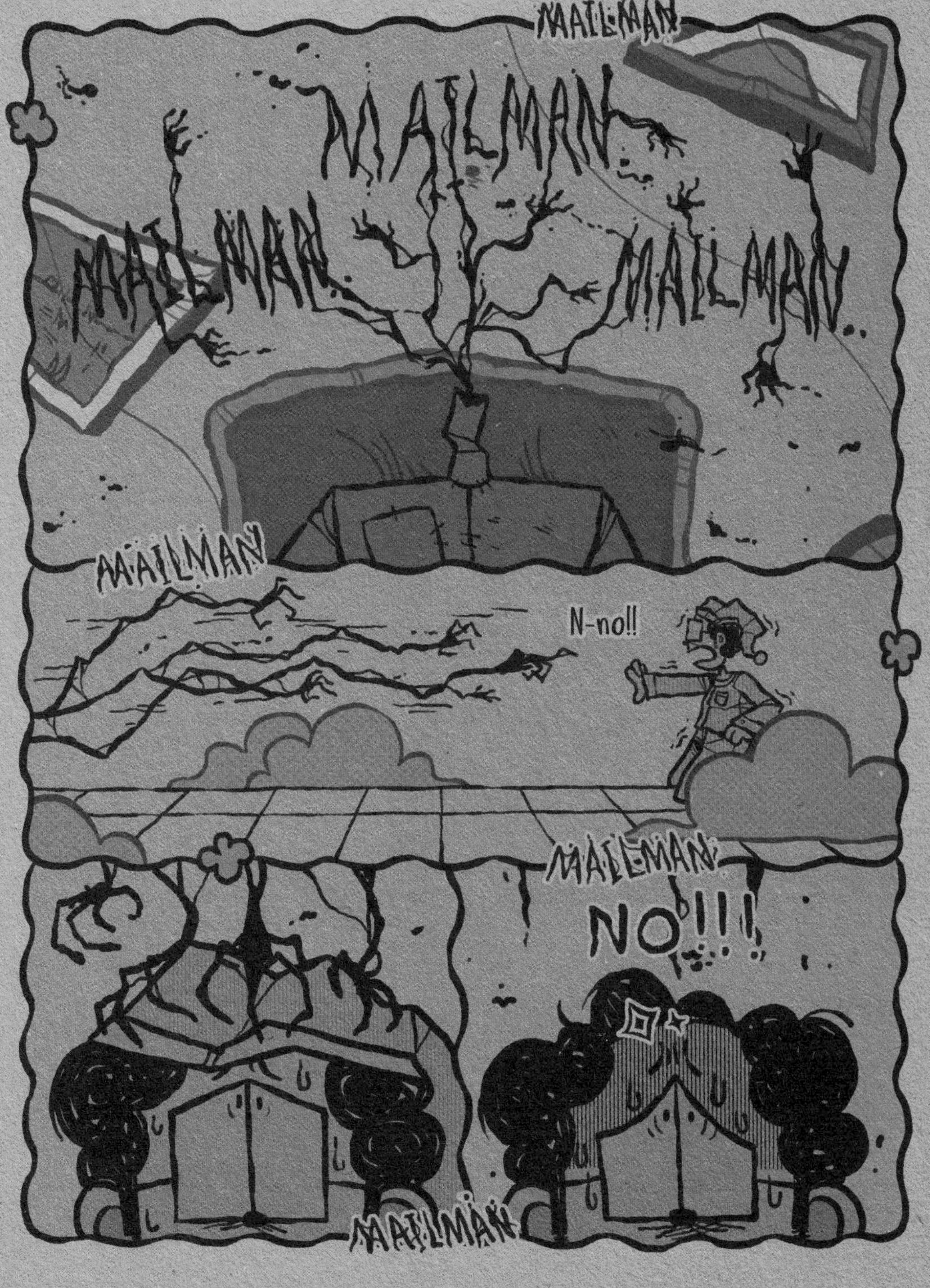
MAILMAN
MAILMAN
MAILMAN
MAILMAN
MAILMAN
N-no!!
MAILMAN
NO!!!
MAILMAN

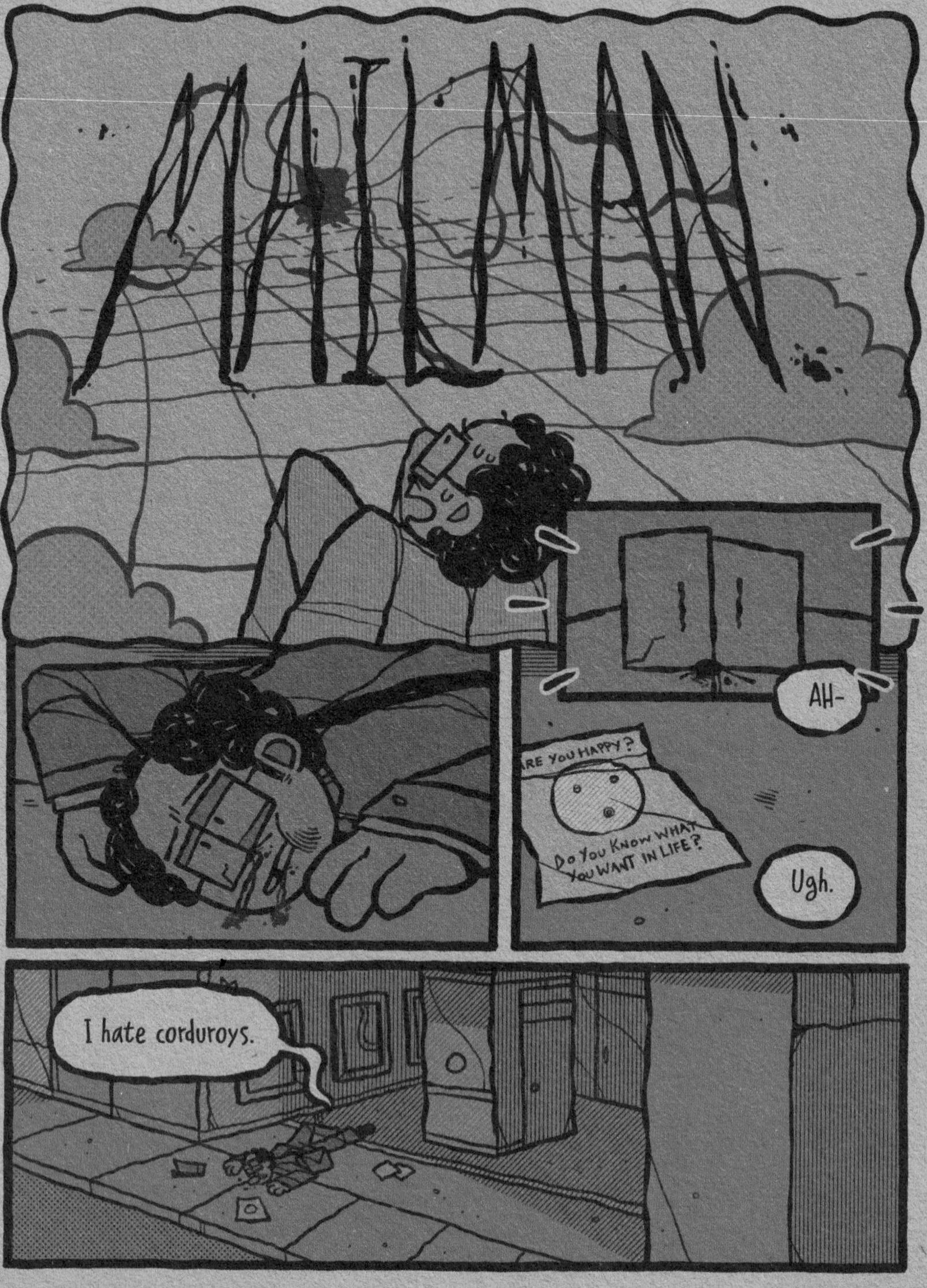
MAILMAN
AH-
ARE YOU HAPPY?
DO YOU KNOW WHAT YOU WANT IN LIFE?
Ugh.
I hate corduroys.

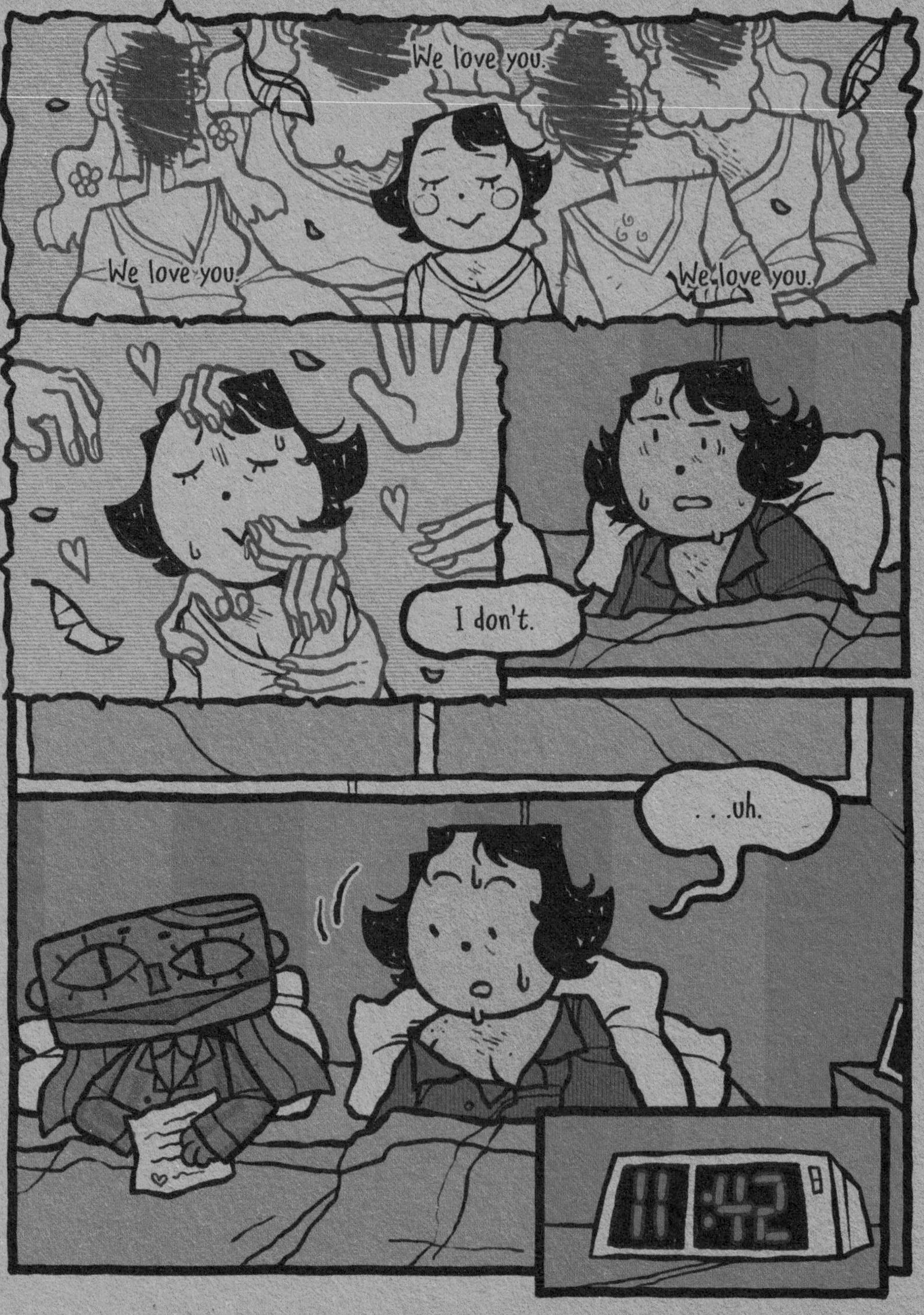
We love you.
We love you.
We love you.
I don't.
. . .uh.

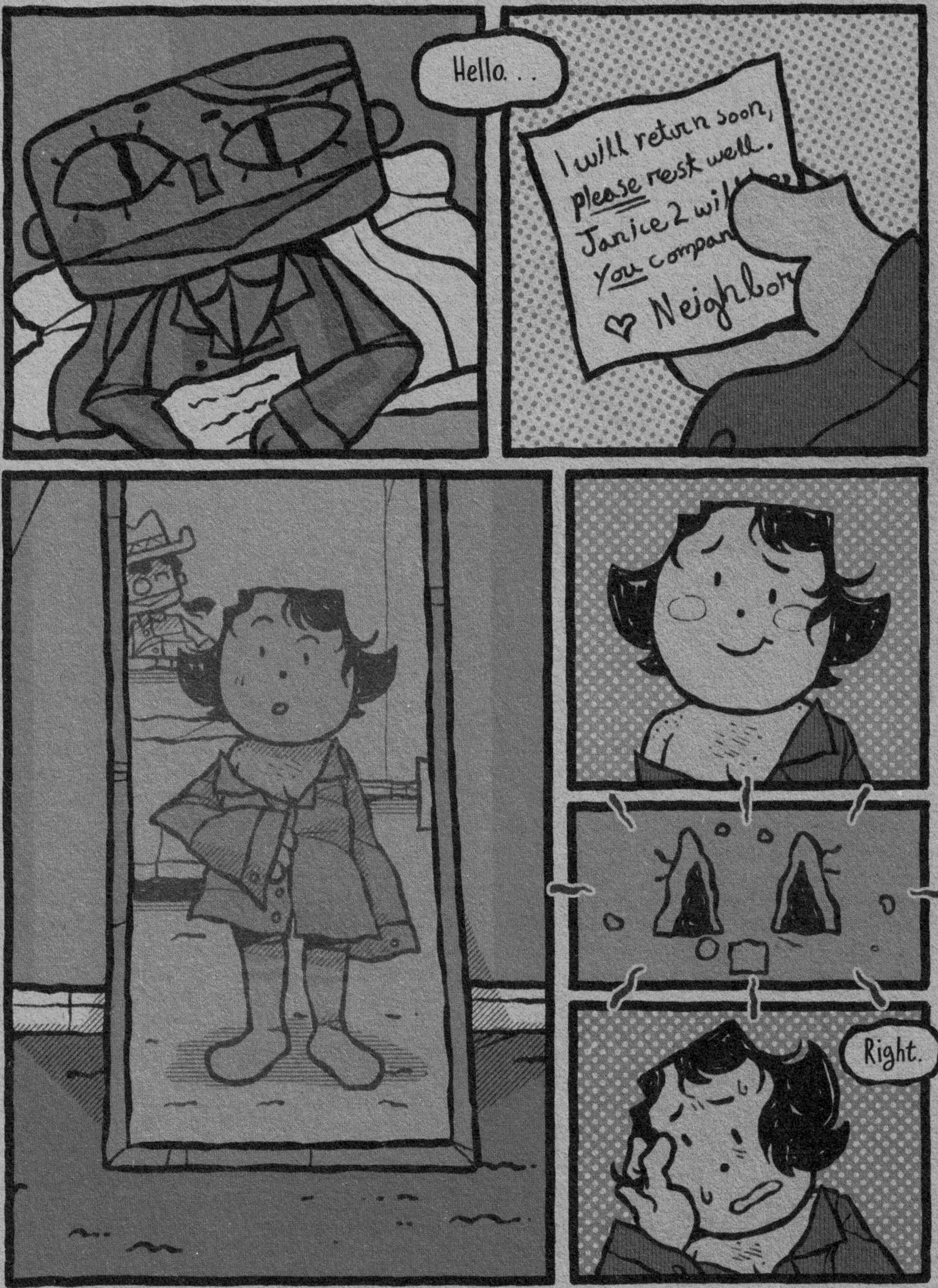
Hello. . .
I will return soon,
please rest well.
Janice 2 will
You compan
♡ Neighbor
Right.

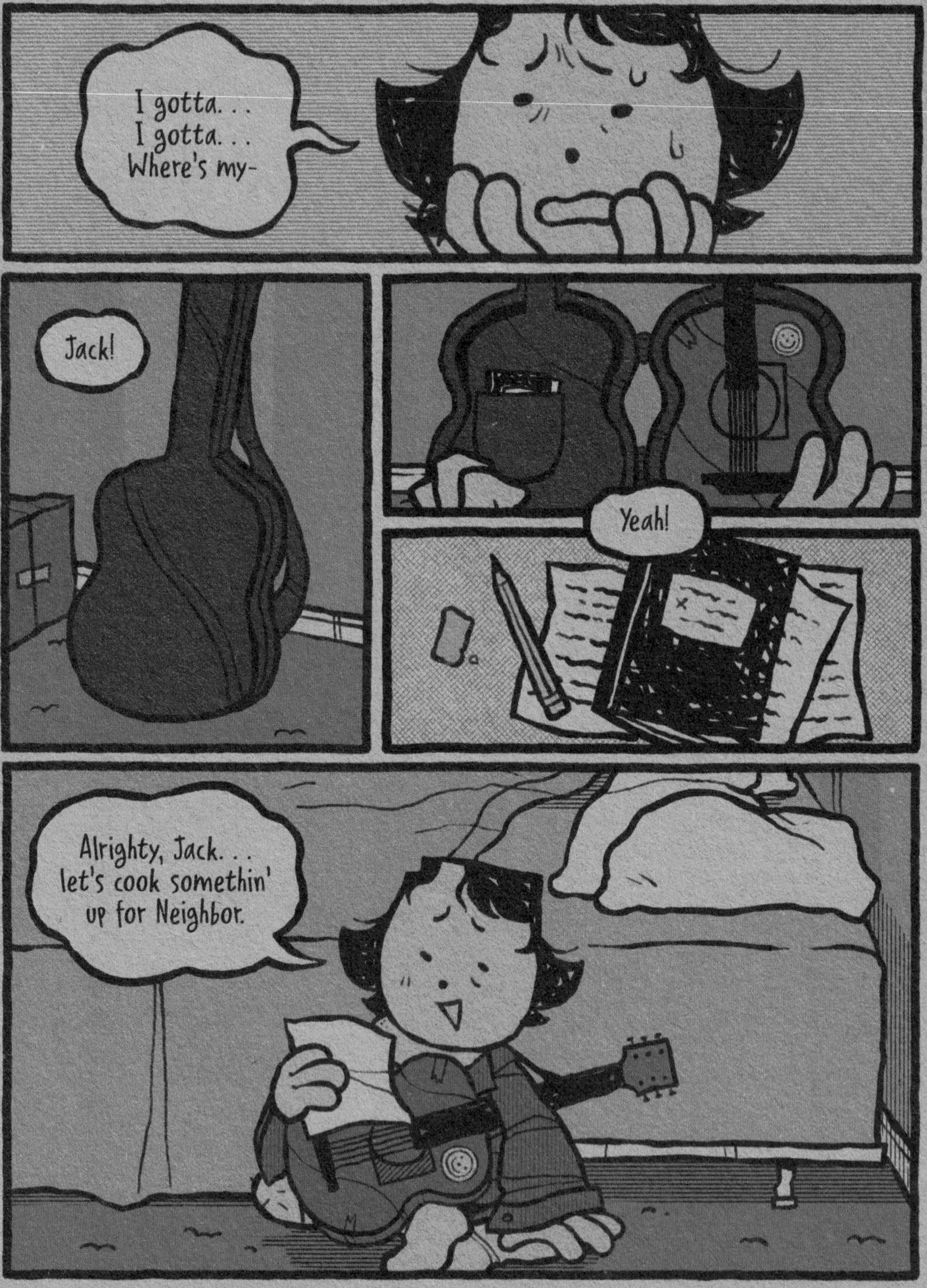
I gotta. . .
I gotta. . .
Where's my-
Jack!
Yeah!
Alrighty, Jack. . . let's cook somethin' up for Neighbor.

No, no, it sounds stupid. . .
It's silly!!
. . .you like it? Really?
N'awwwh. . . thank ya. . .

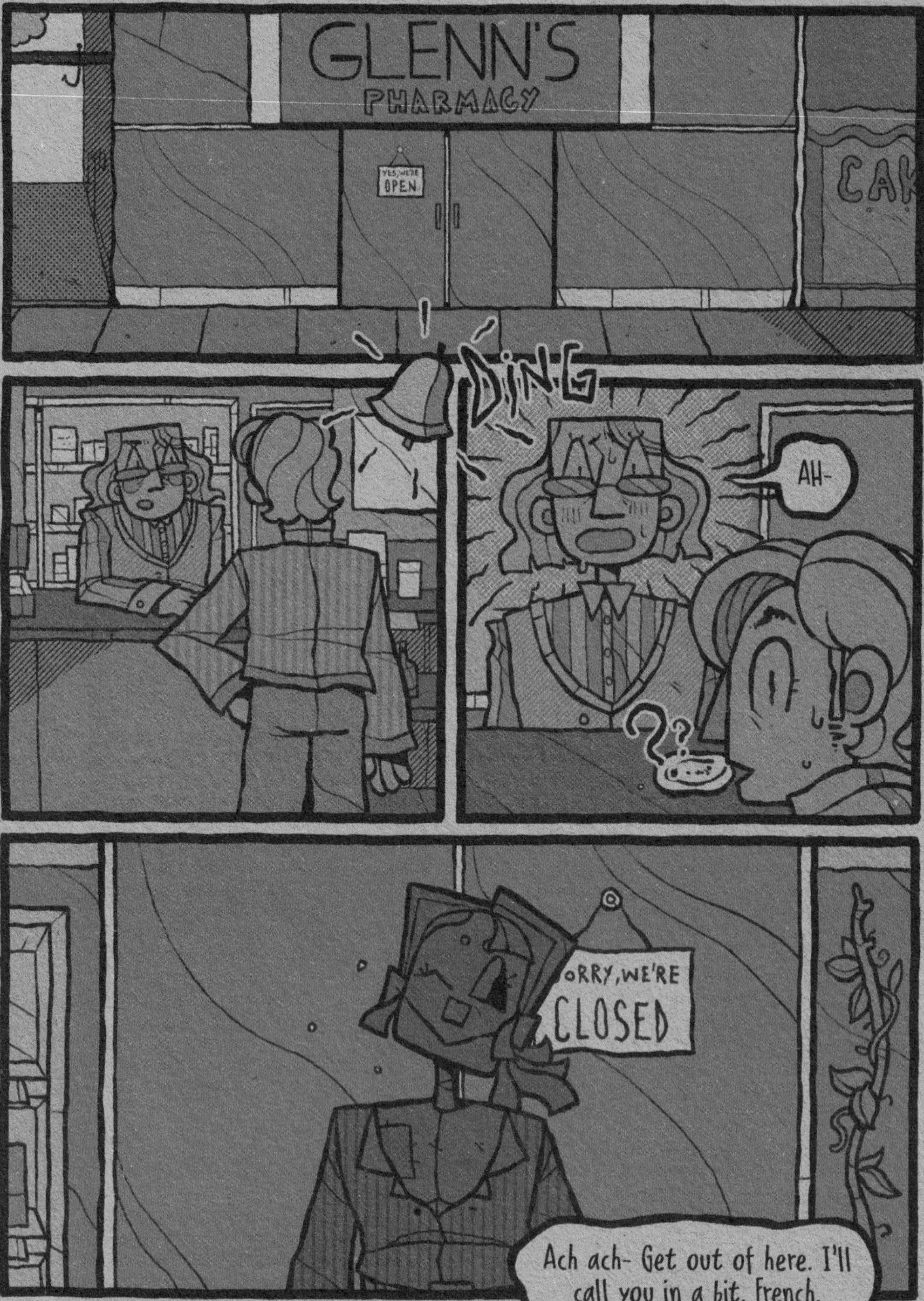
GLENN'S
PHARMACY
YES, WE'RE OPEN.
CAK
DING
AH-
ORRY, WE'RE CLOSED
Ach ach- Get out of here. I'll call you in a bit, French.

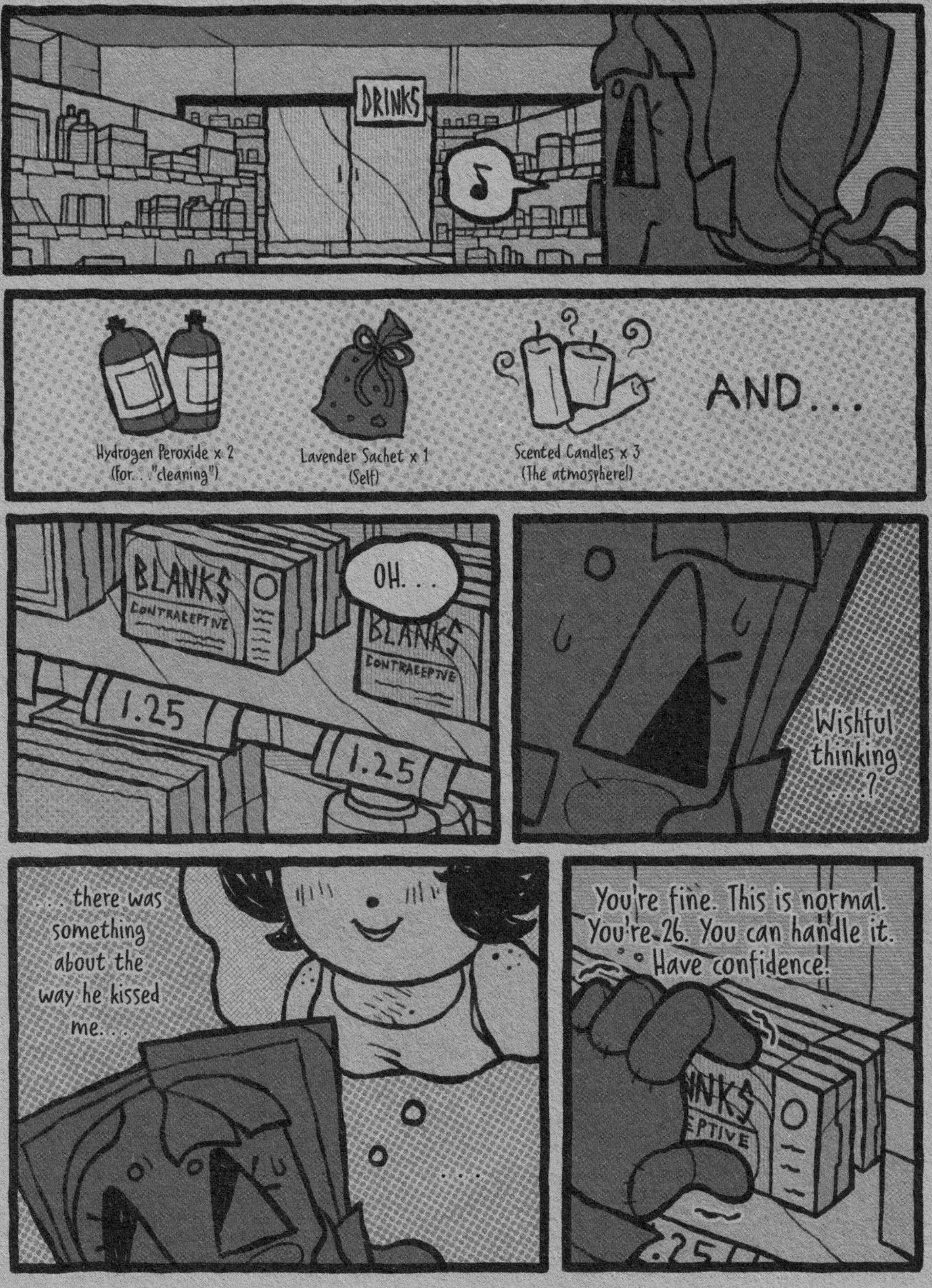
DRINKS
AND...
Hydrogen Peroxide x 2
(For..."cleaning")
Lavender Sachet x 1
(Self)
Scented Candles x 3
(The atmosphere!)
BLANKS
CONTRACEPTIVE
OH...
1.25
Wishful thinking ...?
...there was something about the way he kissed me...
You're fine. This is normal. You're 26. You can handle it. Have confidence!

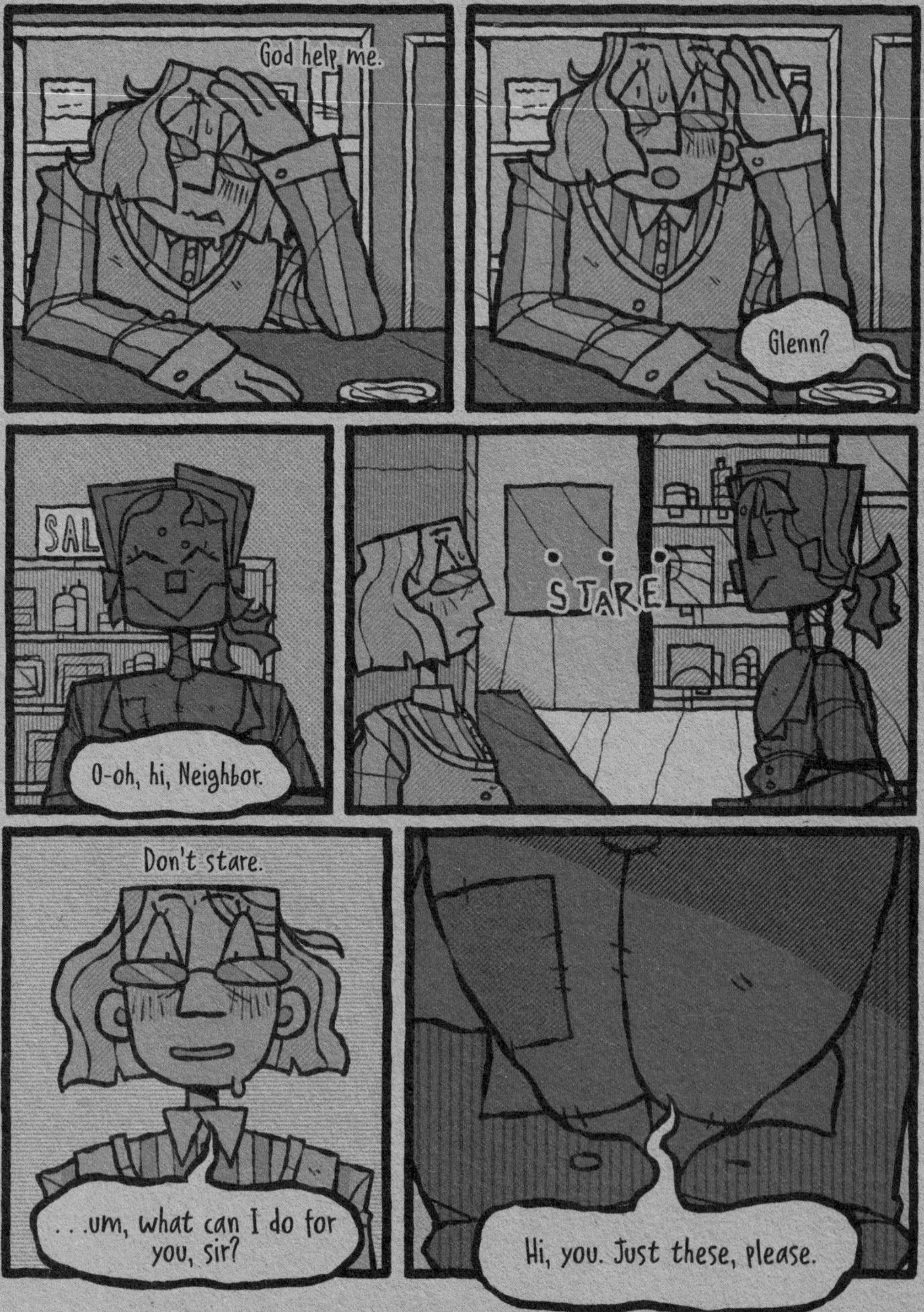
God help me.
Glenn?
O-oh, hi, Neighbor.
STARE
Don't stare.
. . .um, what can I do for you, sir?
Hi, you. Just these, please.

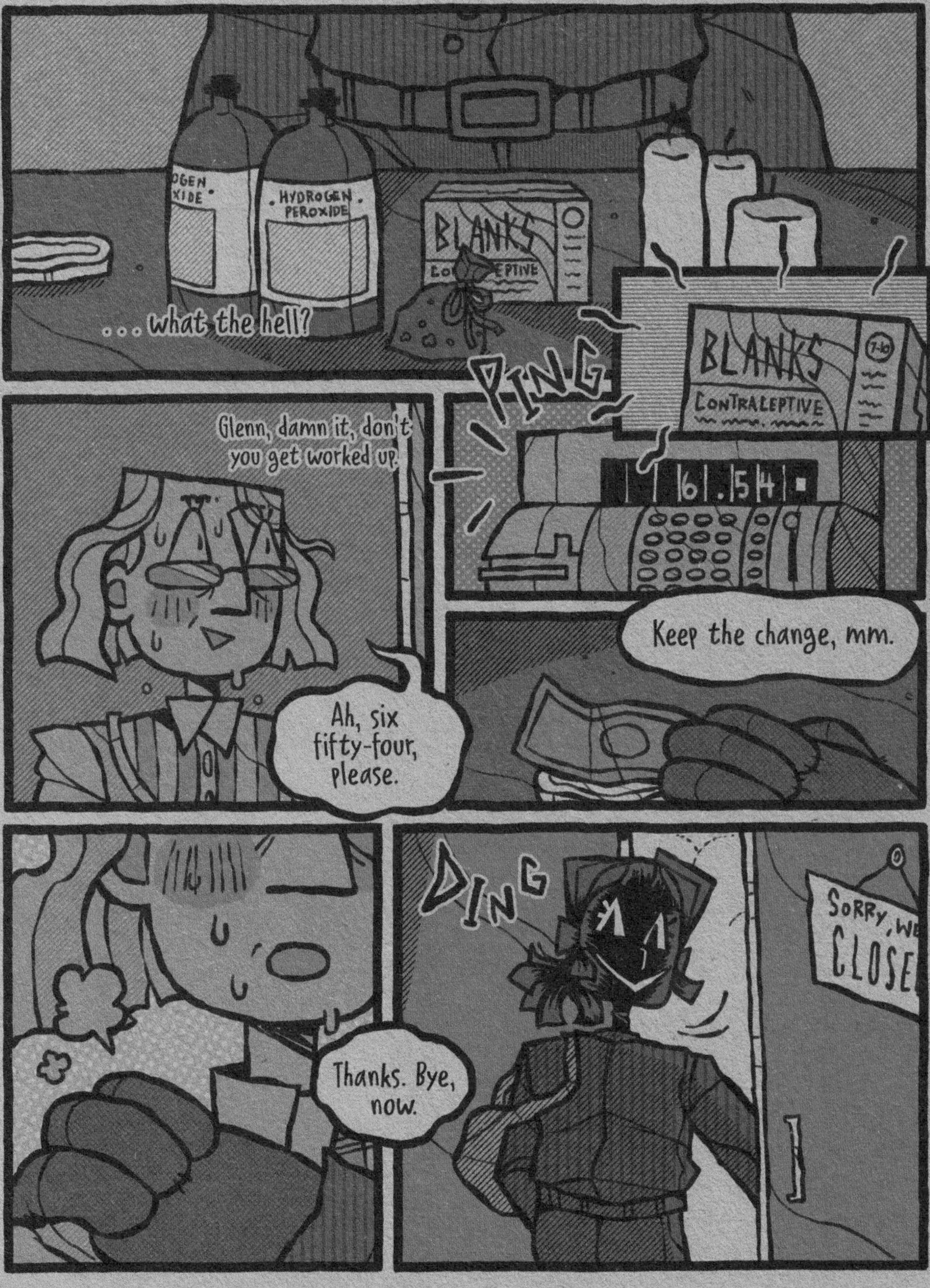
HYDROGEN PEROXIDE
BLANKS
...what the hell?
PING
BLANKS
CONTRALEPTIVE
6.54
Glenn, damn it, don't you get worked up.
Ah, six fifty-four, please.
Keep the change, mm.
Thanks. Bye, now.
DING
SORRY, WE
CLOSE

Glenn, J-C! Get a HOLD of yourself, man. You're not like that. We've already been over this. You had a WIFE. You're just uhh . . .lonely. And stressed. Confused. This guy comes by twice a week to do your housework and you're just. . . fantasizing. . . staring at his. . . uhhhhfUCK!

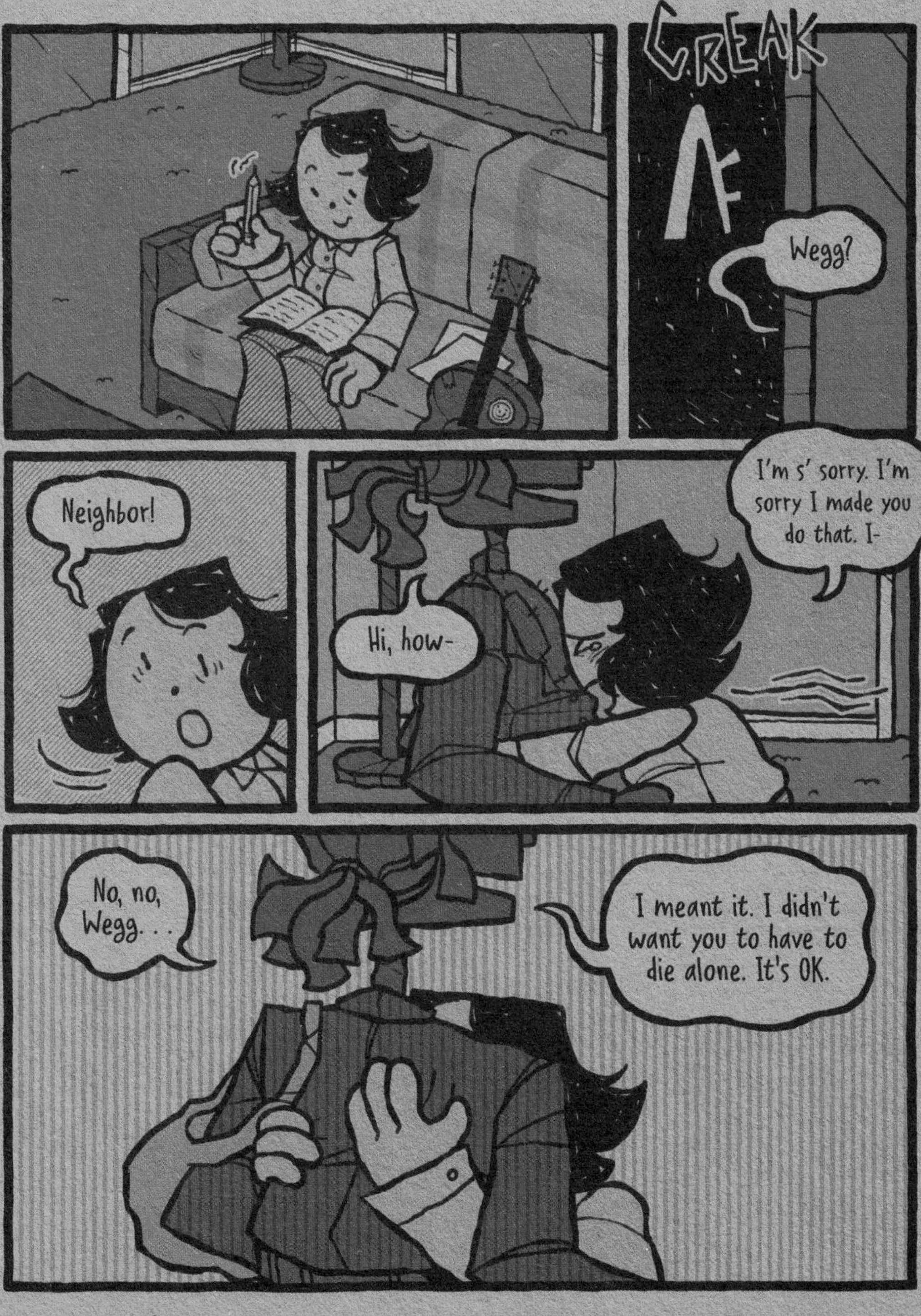
CREAK
Wegg?
Neighbor!
Hi, how-
I'm s' sorry. I'm sorry I made you do that. I-
No, no, Wegg. . .
I meant it. I didn't want you to have to die alone. It's OK.

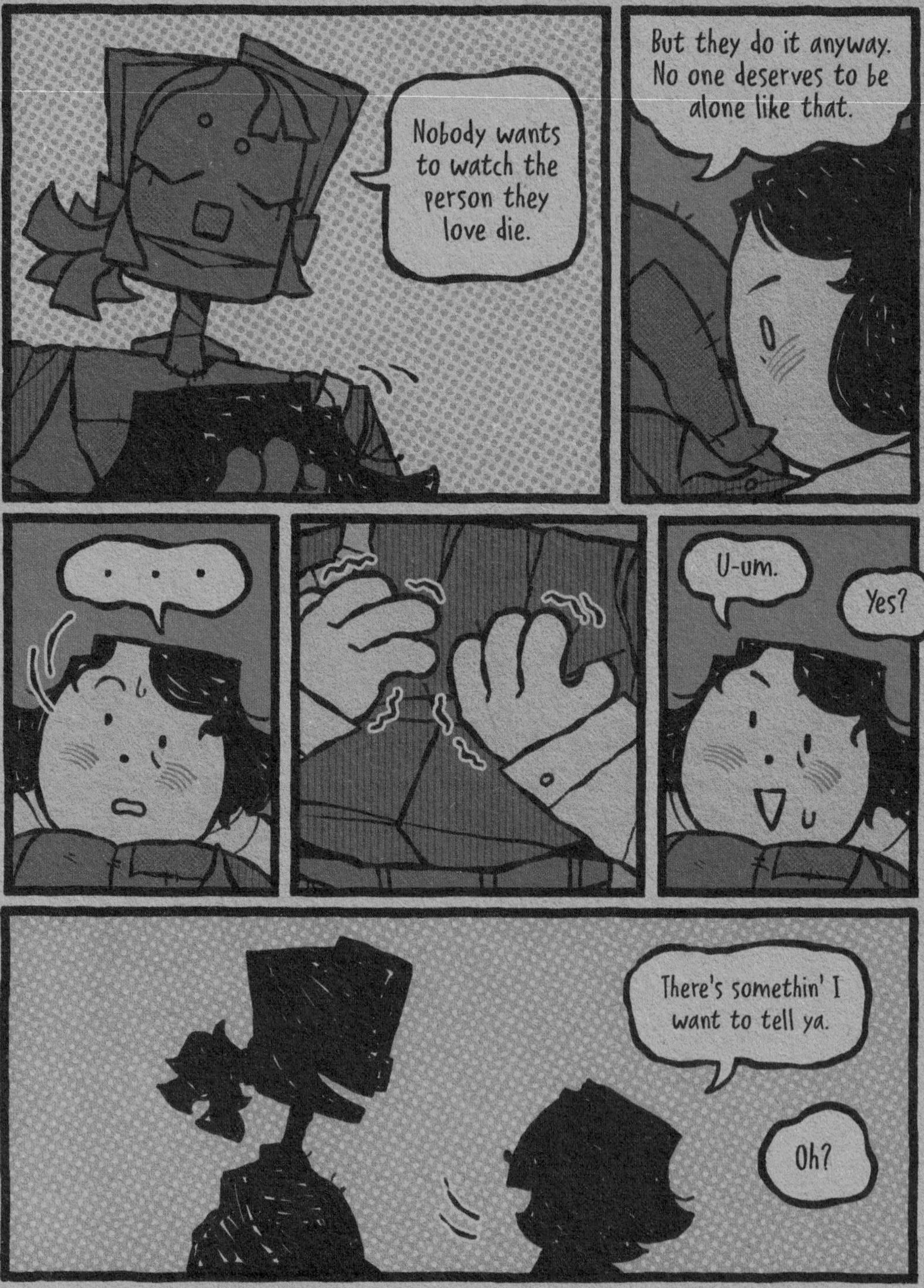
Nobody wants to watch the person they love die.
But they do it anyway. No one deserves to be alone like that.
...
U-um.
Yes?
There's somethin' I want to tell ya.
Oh?

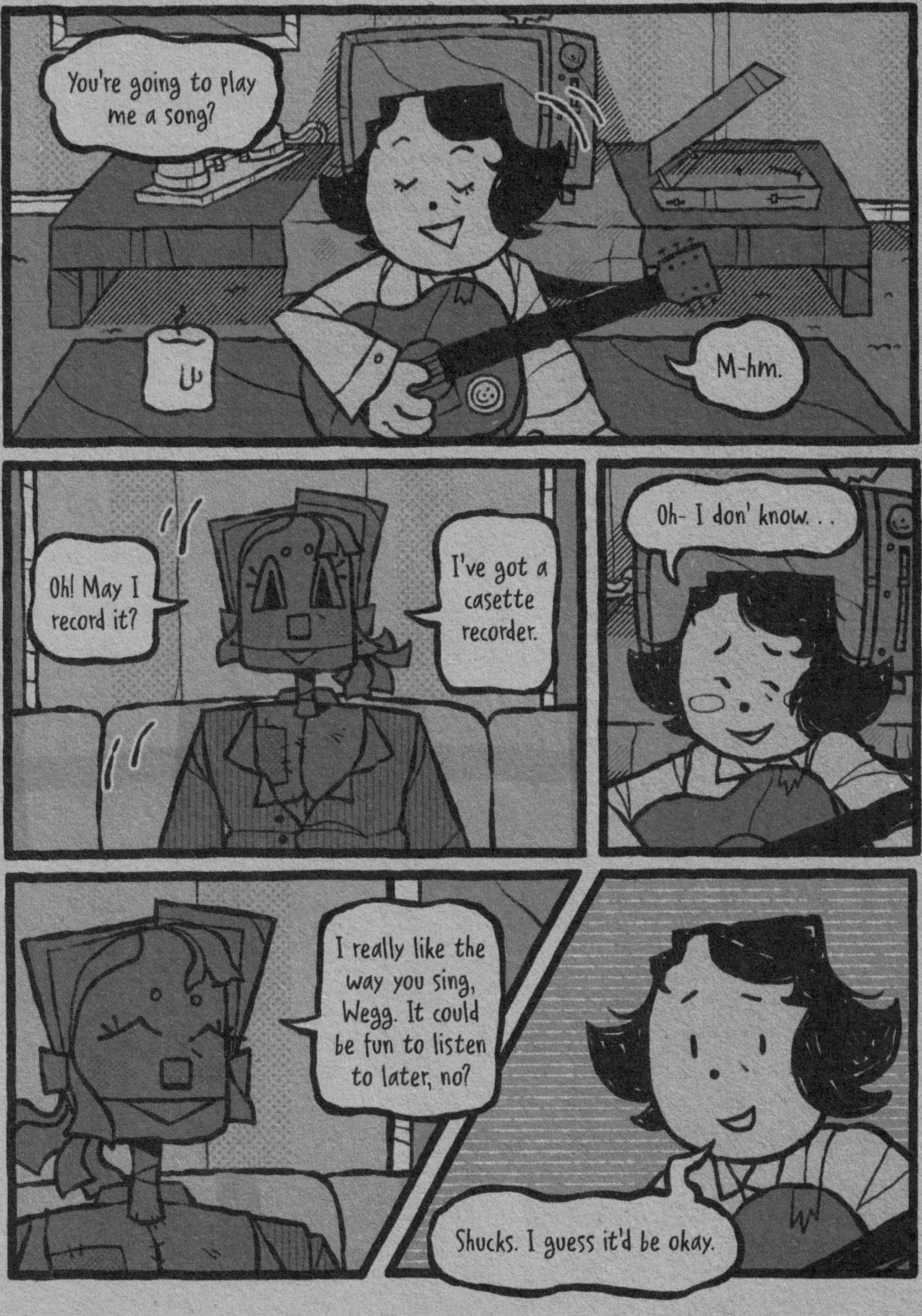
You're going to play me a song?
M-hm.
Oh! May I record it?
I've got a casette recorder.
Oh- I don' know. . .
I really like the way you sing, Wegg. It could be fun to listen to later, no?
Shucks. I guess it'd be okay.

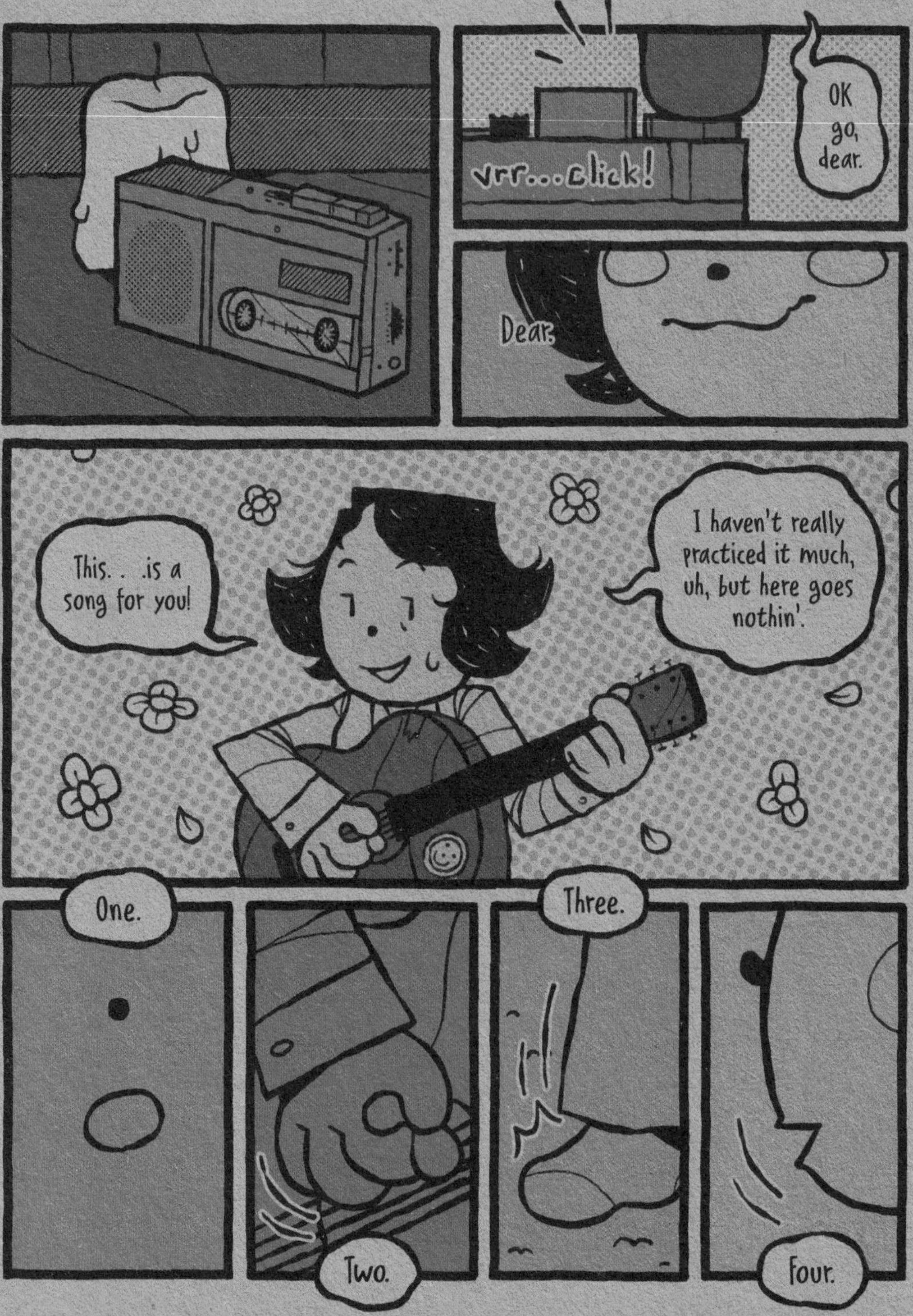
vrr...click!
OK go, dear.
Dear.
This. . .is a song for you!
I haven't really practiced it much, uh, but here goes nothin'.
One.
Two.
Three.
Four.

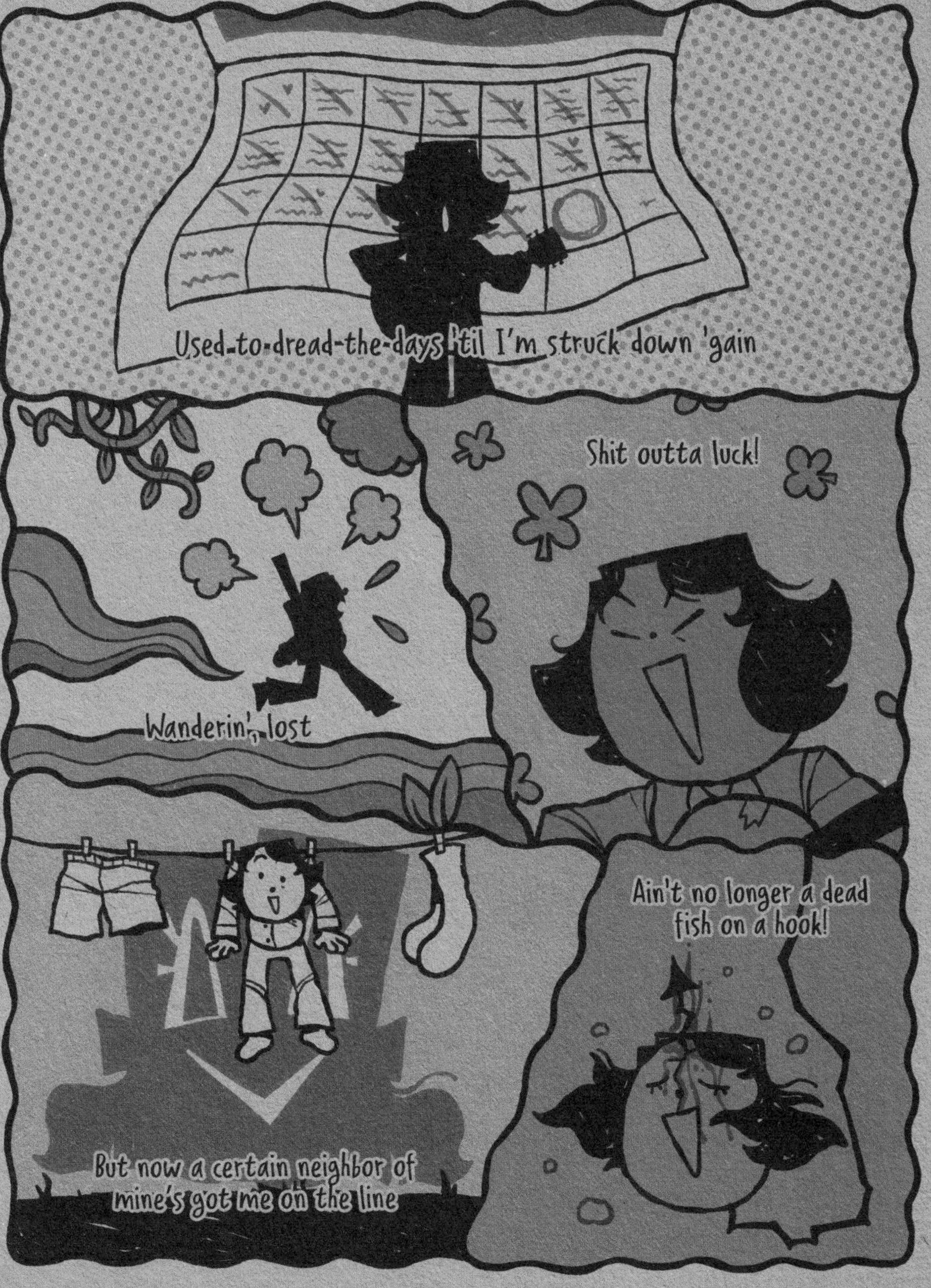
Used-to-dread-the-days 'til I'm struck down 'gain
Wanderin', lost
Shit outta luck!
But now a certain neighbor of mine's got me on the line
Ain't no longer a dead fish on a hook!

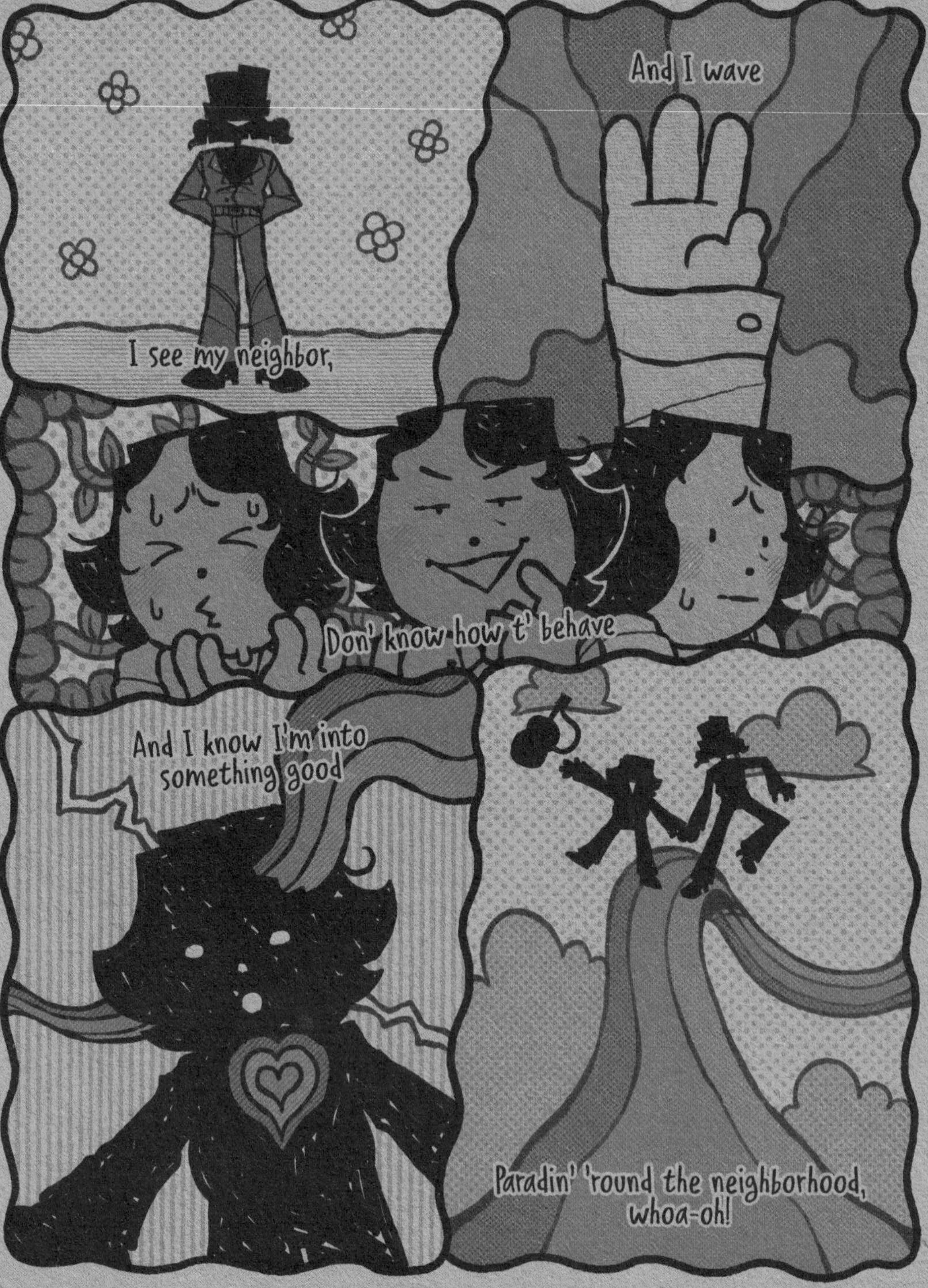
I see my neighbor,
And I wave
Don' know how t' behave
And I know I'm into something good
Paradin' 'round the neighborhood, whoa-oh!

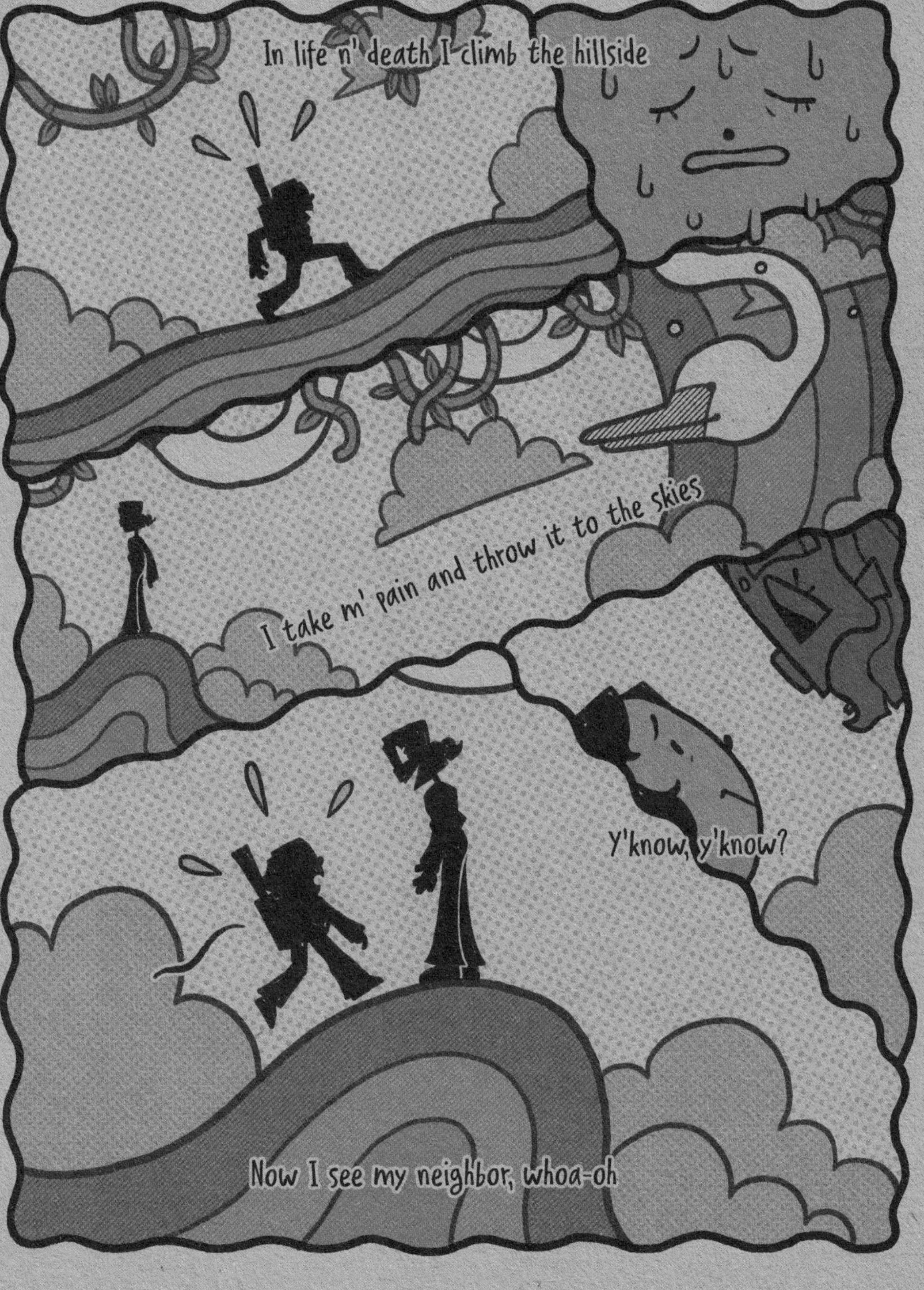
In life n' death I climb the hillside
I take m' pain and throw it to the skies
Y'know, y'know?
Now I see my neighbor, whoa-oh

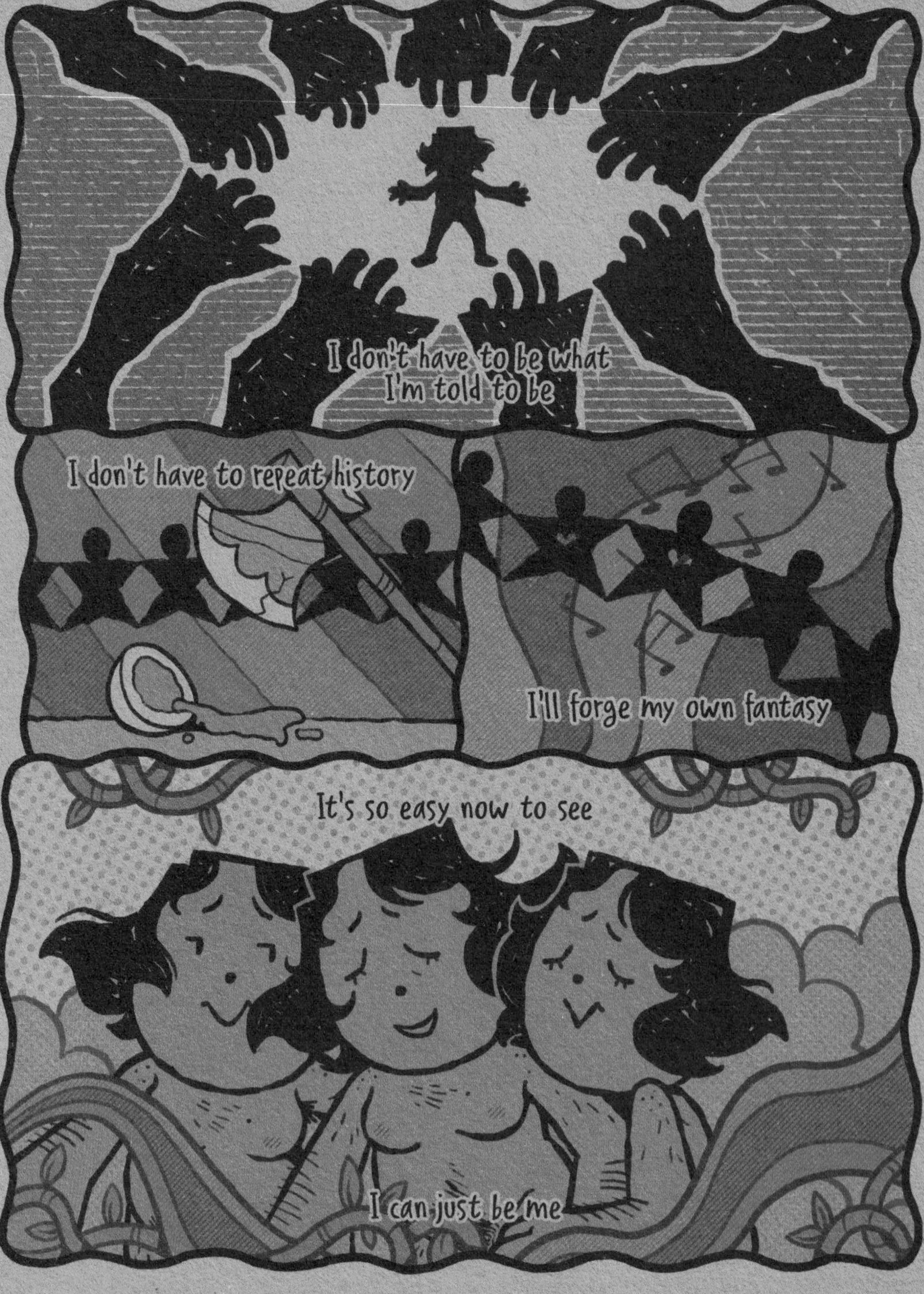
I don't have to be what
I'm told to be
I don't have to repeat history
I'll forge my own fantasy
It's so easy now to see
I can just be me

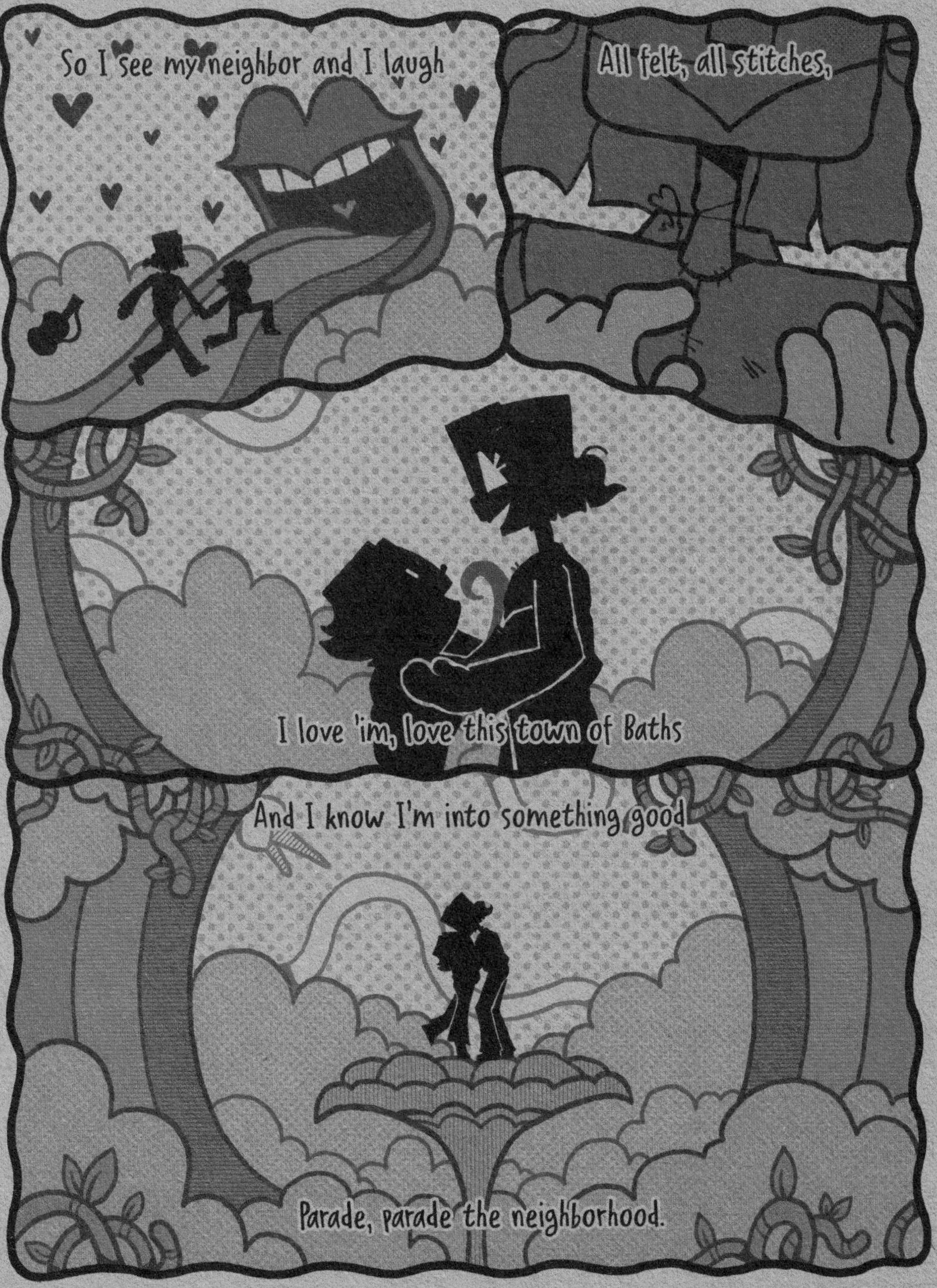
So I see my neighbor and I laugh
All felt, all stitches,
I love 'im, love this town of Baths
And I know I'm into something good
Parade, parade the neighborhood.

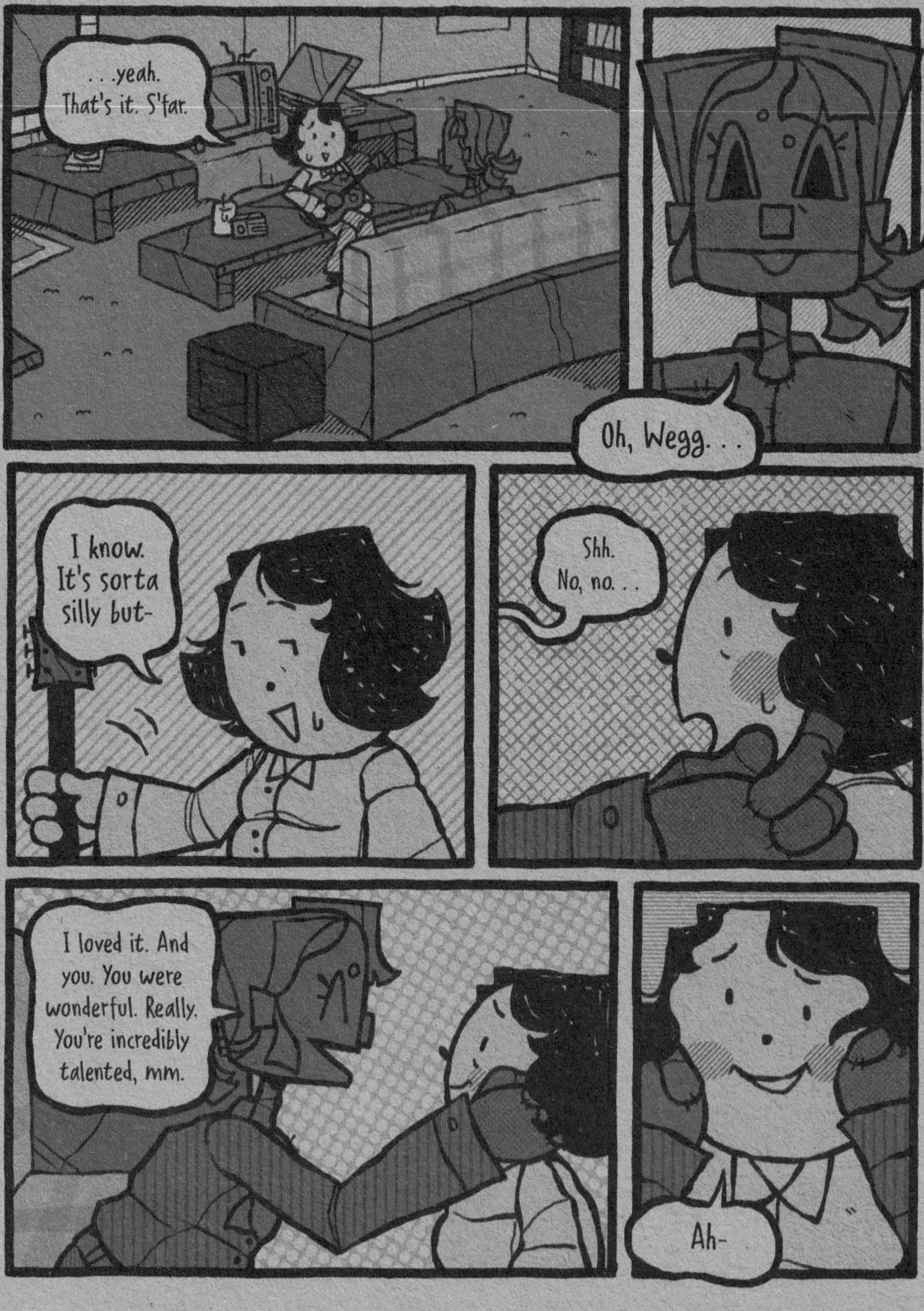
. . .yeah. That's it. S'far.
Oh, Wegg. . .
I know. It's sorta silly but-
Shh. No, no. . .
I loved it. And you. You were wonderful. Really. You're incredibly talented, mm.
Ah-

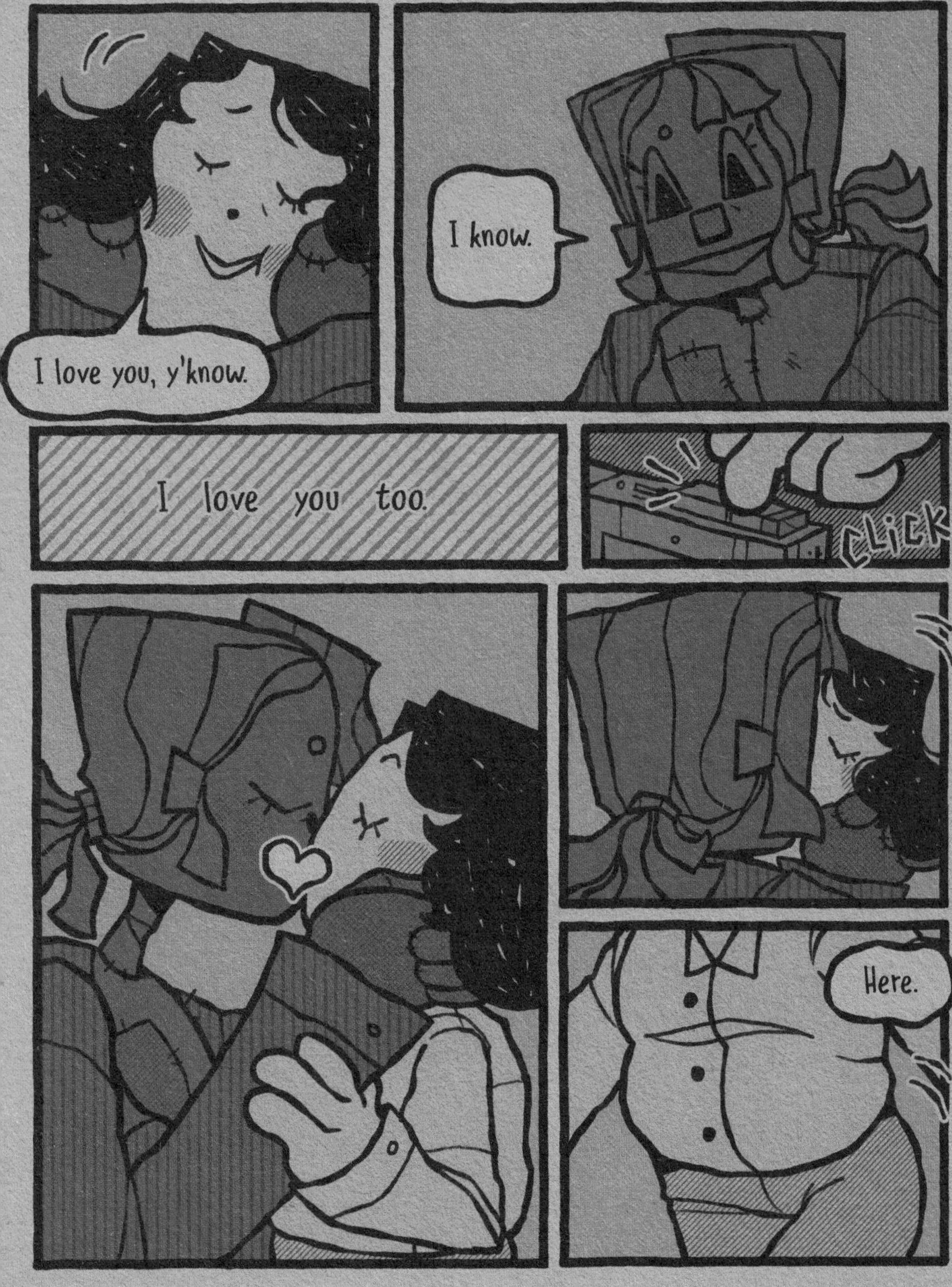
I love you, y'know.
I know.
I love you too.
CLICK
Here.

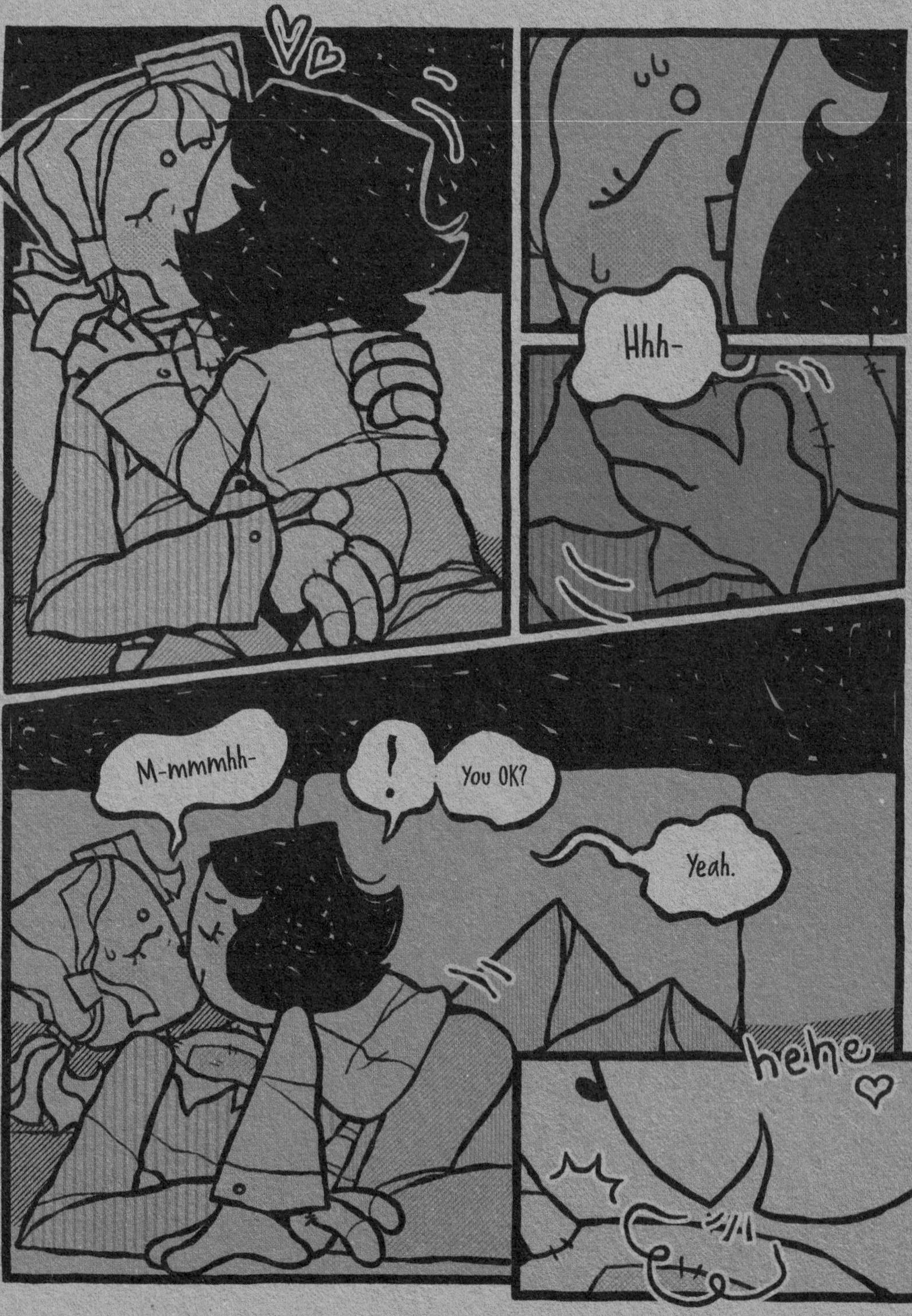
Hhh-
M-mmmhh-
!
You OK?
Yeah.
hehe

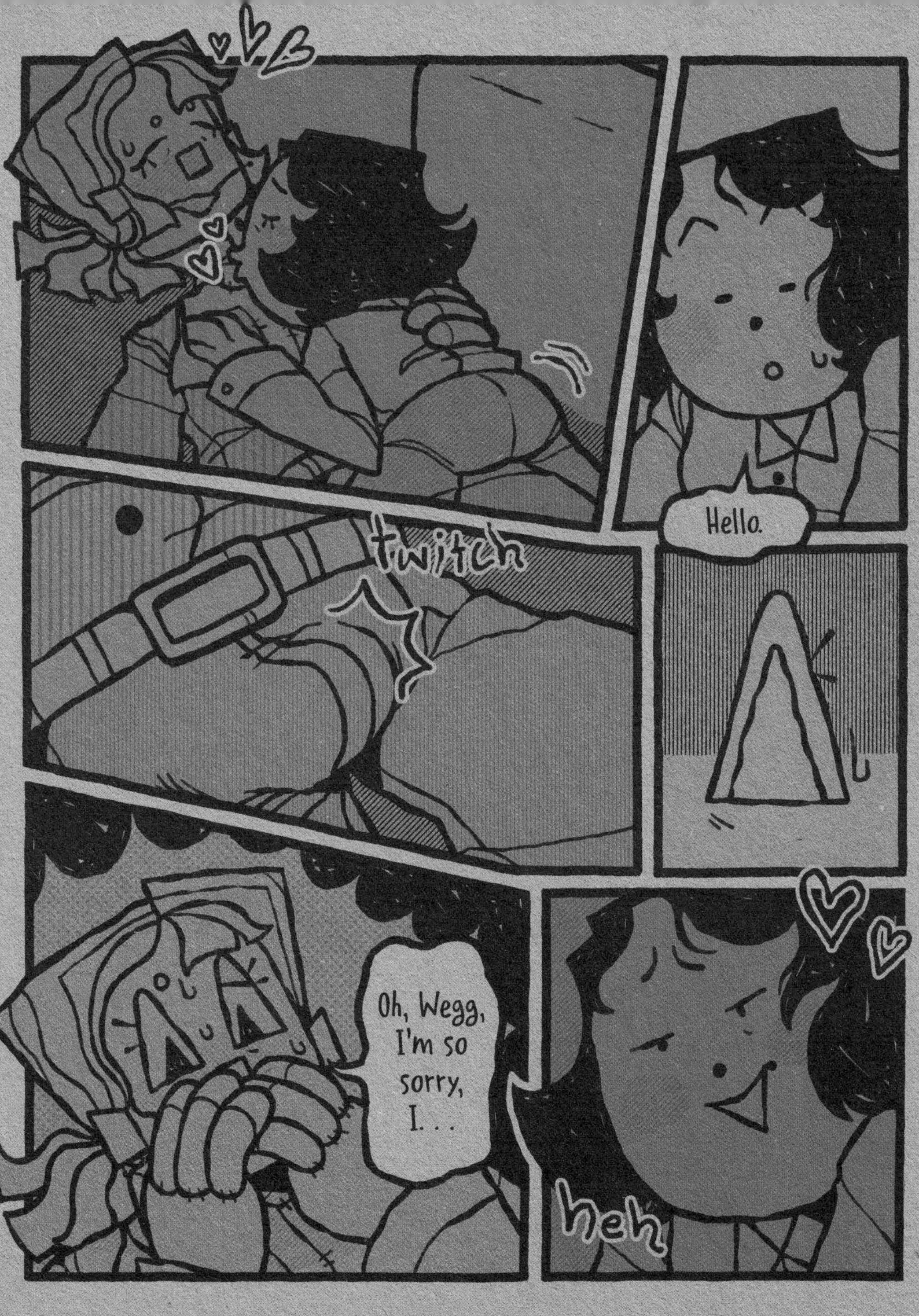
Hello.
twitch
Oh, Wegg, I'm so sorry, I. . .
heh

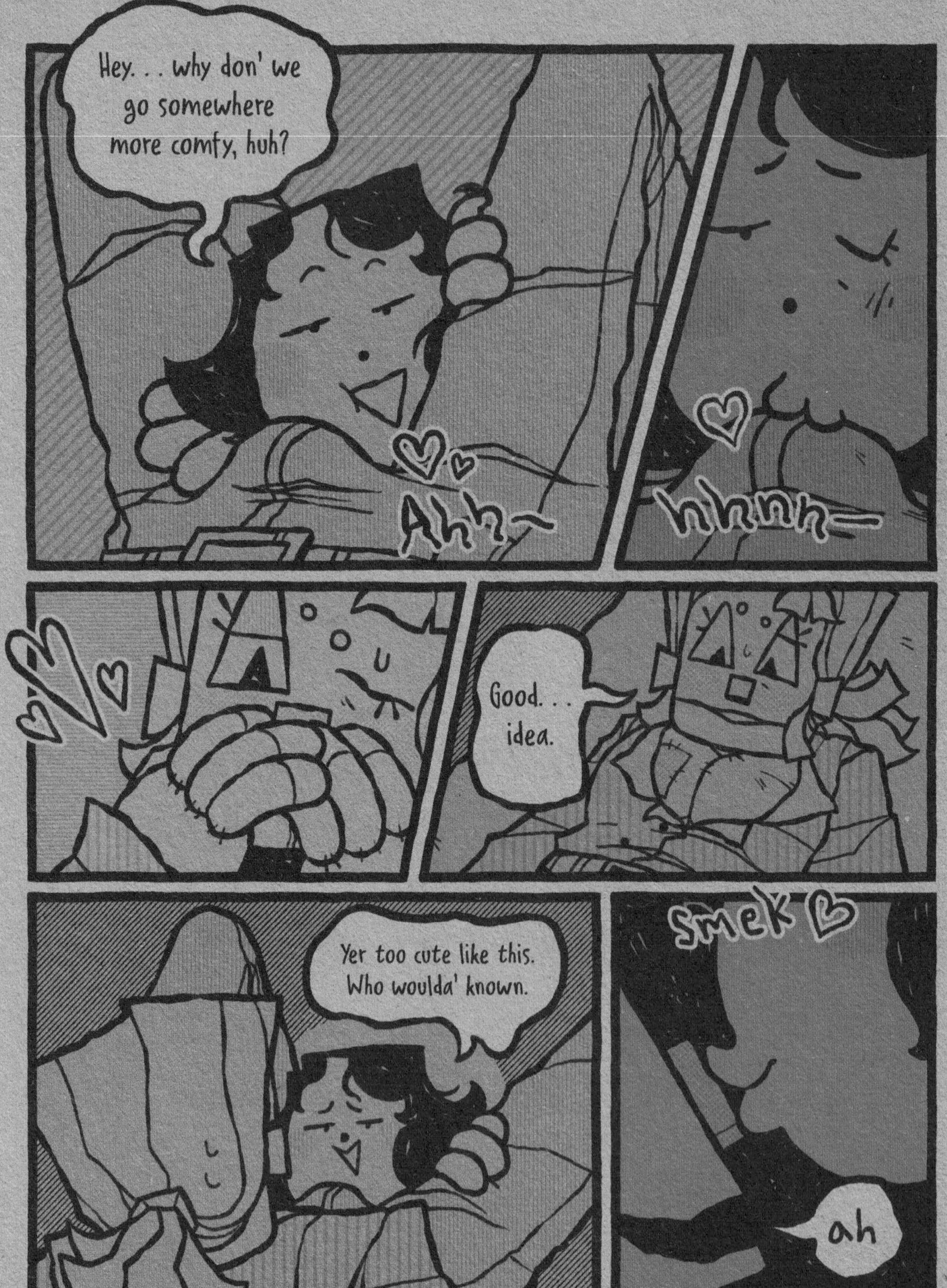
Hey. . . why don' we go somewhere more comfy, huh?
Ahh~
hhnnh—
Good. . . idea.
Yer too cute like this. Who woulda' known.
smek
ah

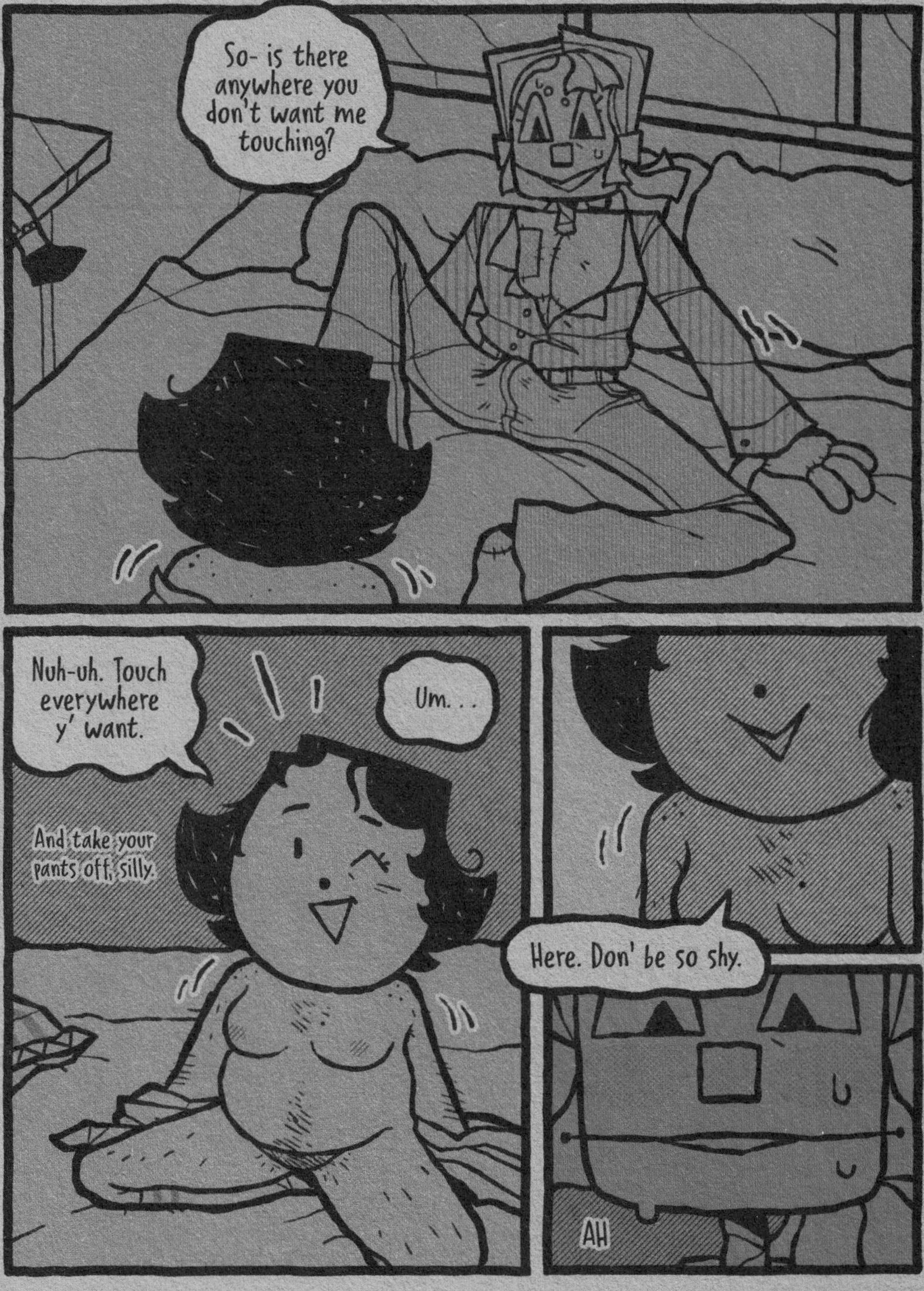
So- is there anywhere you don't want me touching?
Nuh-uh. Touch everywhere y' want.
Um. . .
And take your pants off, silly.
Here. Don' be so shy.
AH

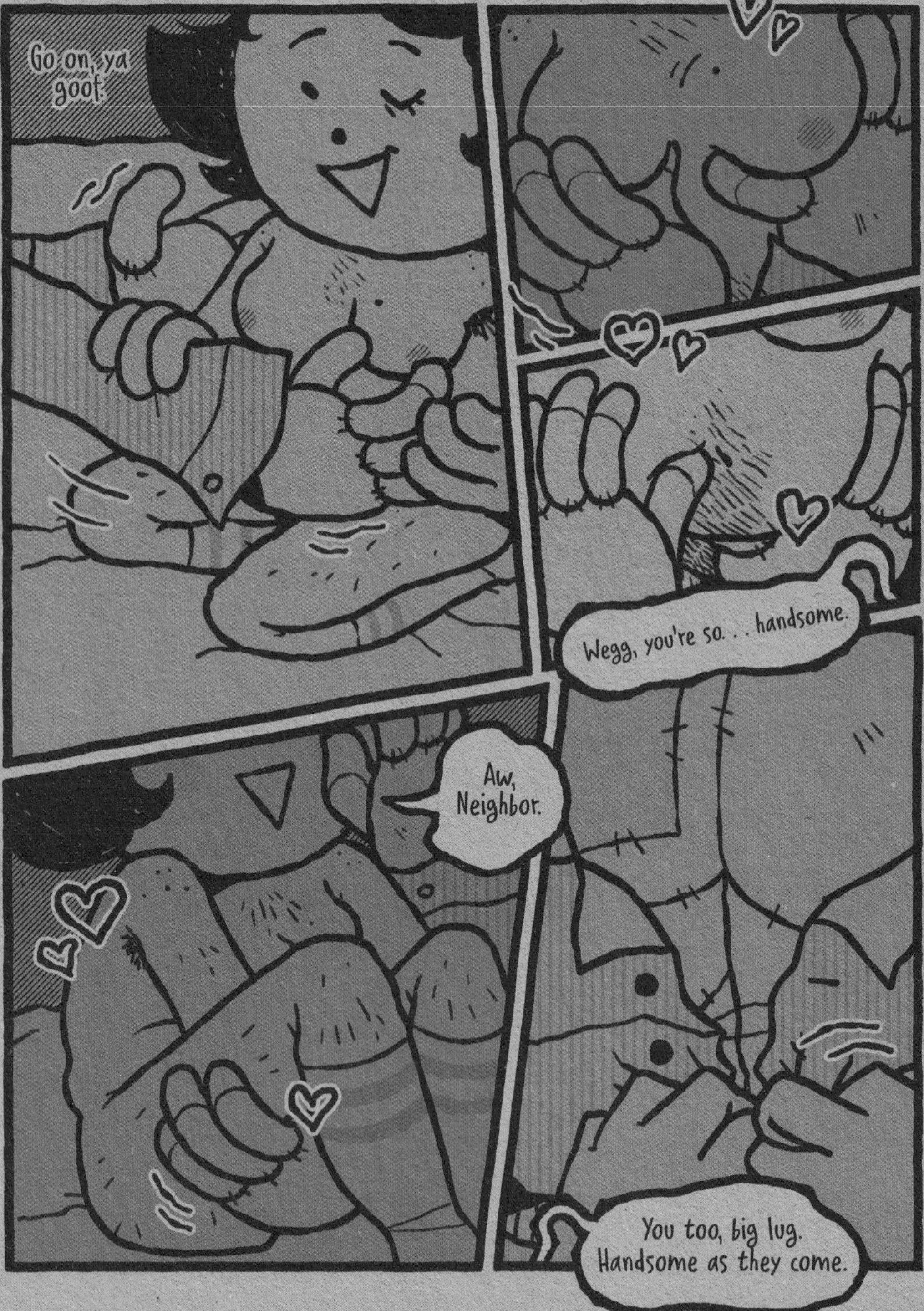
Go on, ya goof.
Wegg, you're so. . . handsome.
Aw, Neighbor.
You too, big lug. Handsome as they come.

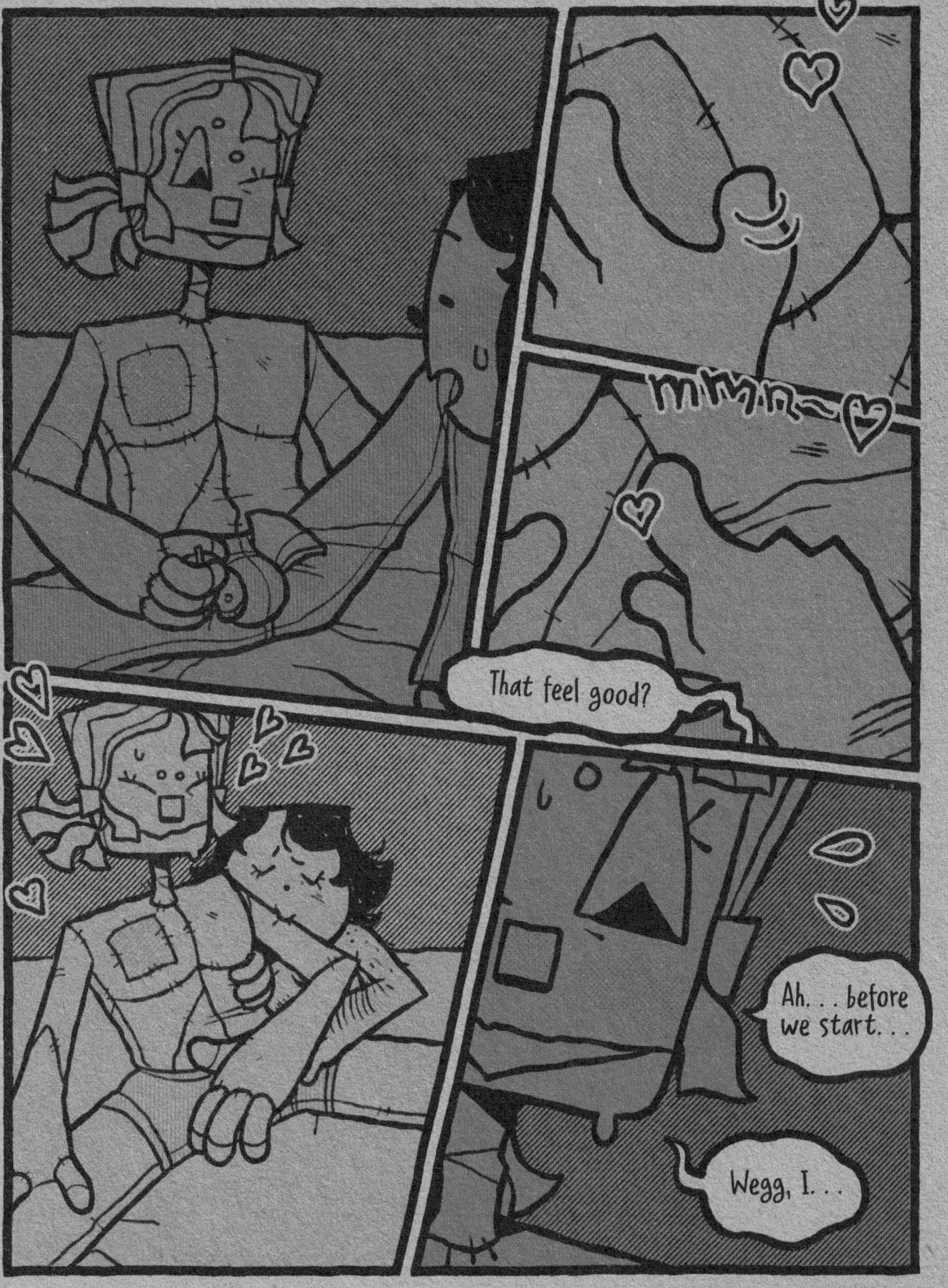
mmn~
That feel good?
Ah. . . before we start. . .
Wegg, I. . .

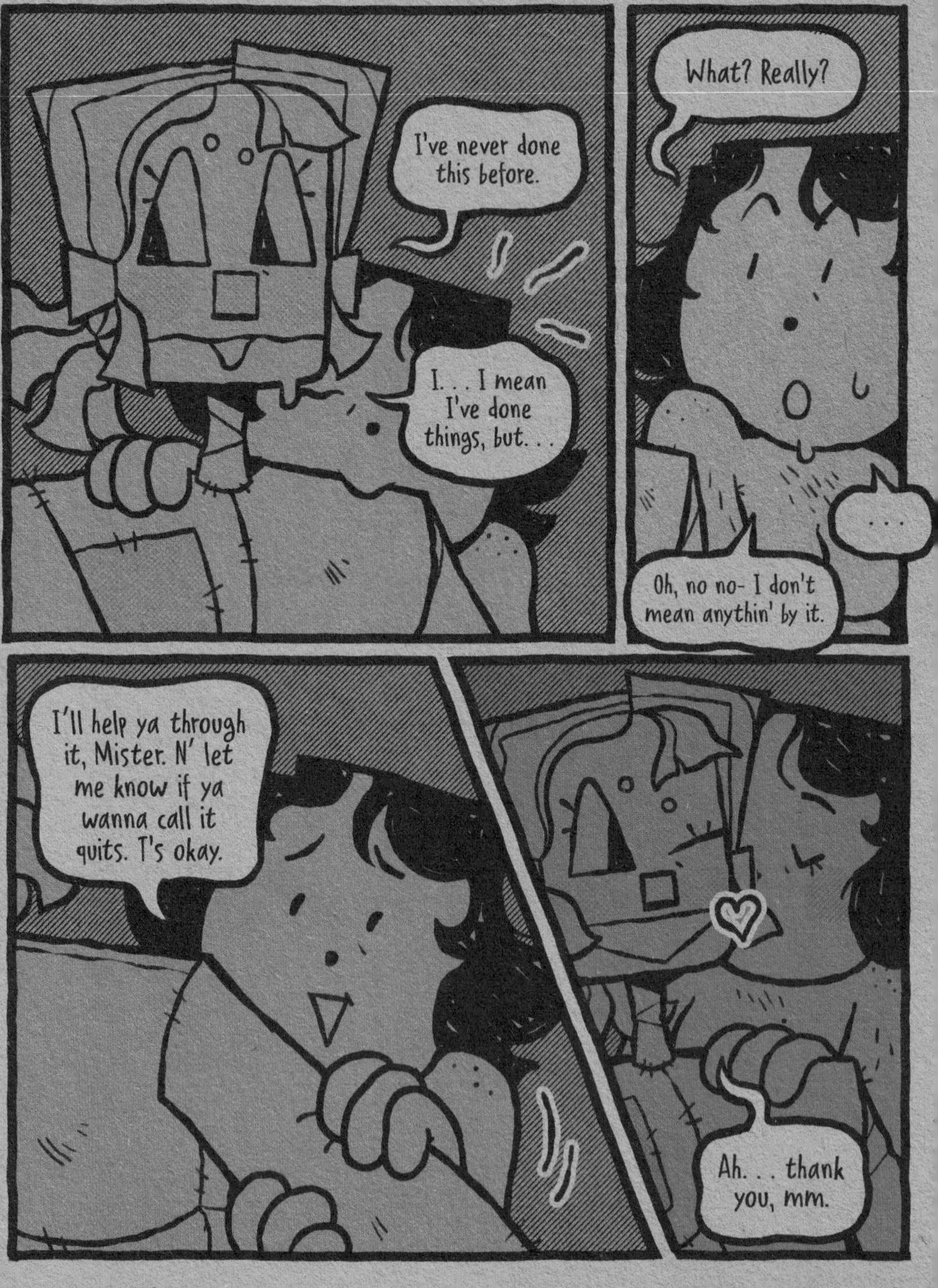
I've never done this before.
I. . . I mean I've done things, but. . .
What? Really?
. . .
Oh, no no- I don't mean anythin' by it.
I'll help ya through it, Mister. N' let me know if ya wanna call it quits. T's okay.
Ah. . . thank you, mm.

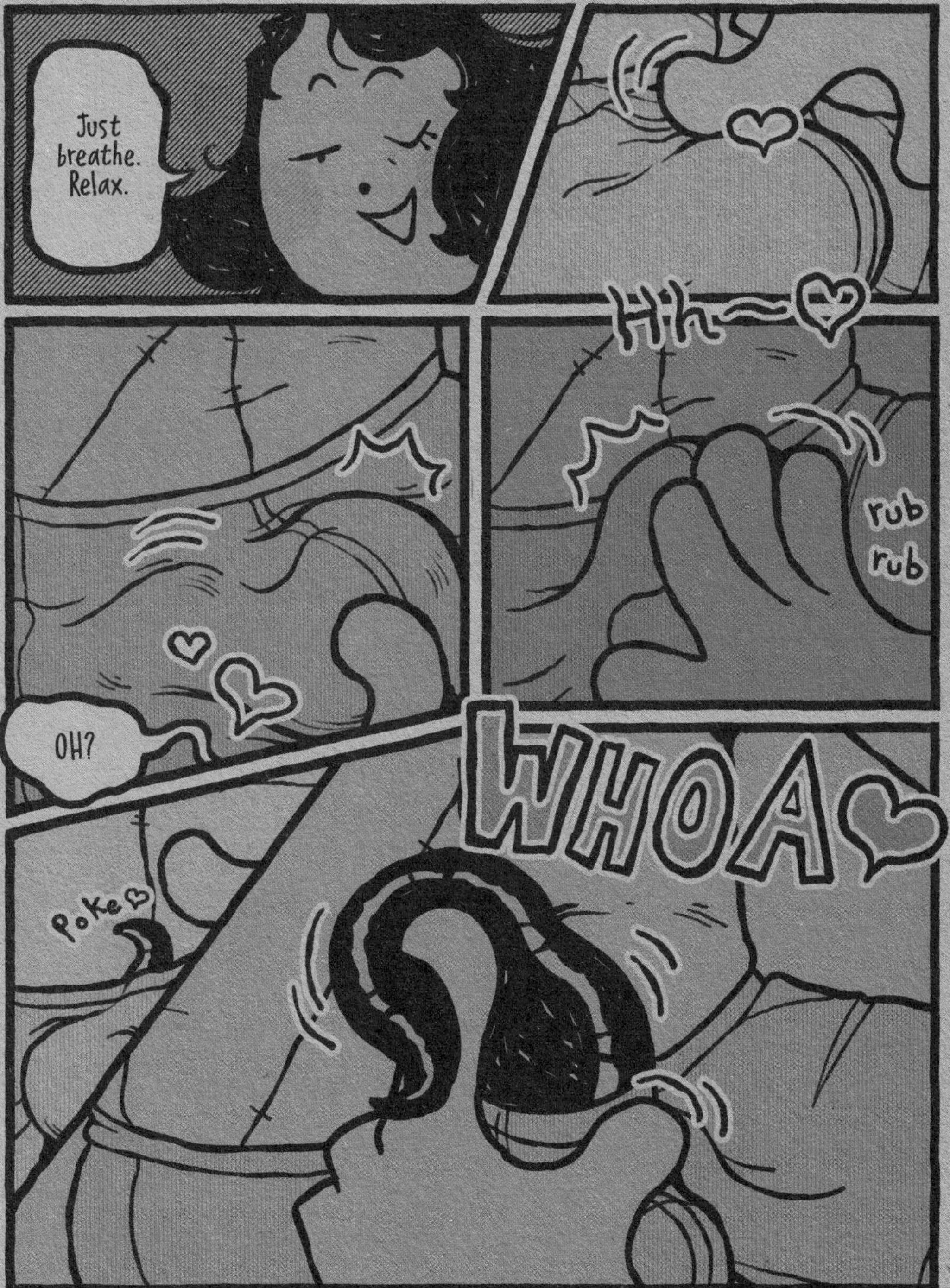
Just breathe. Relax.
Hh~
rub rub
OH?
WHOA
Poke

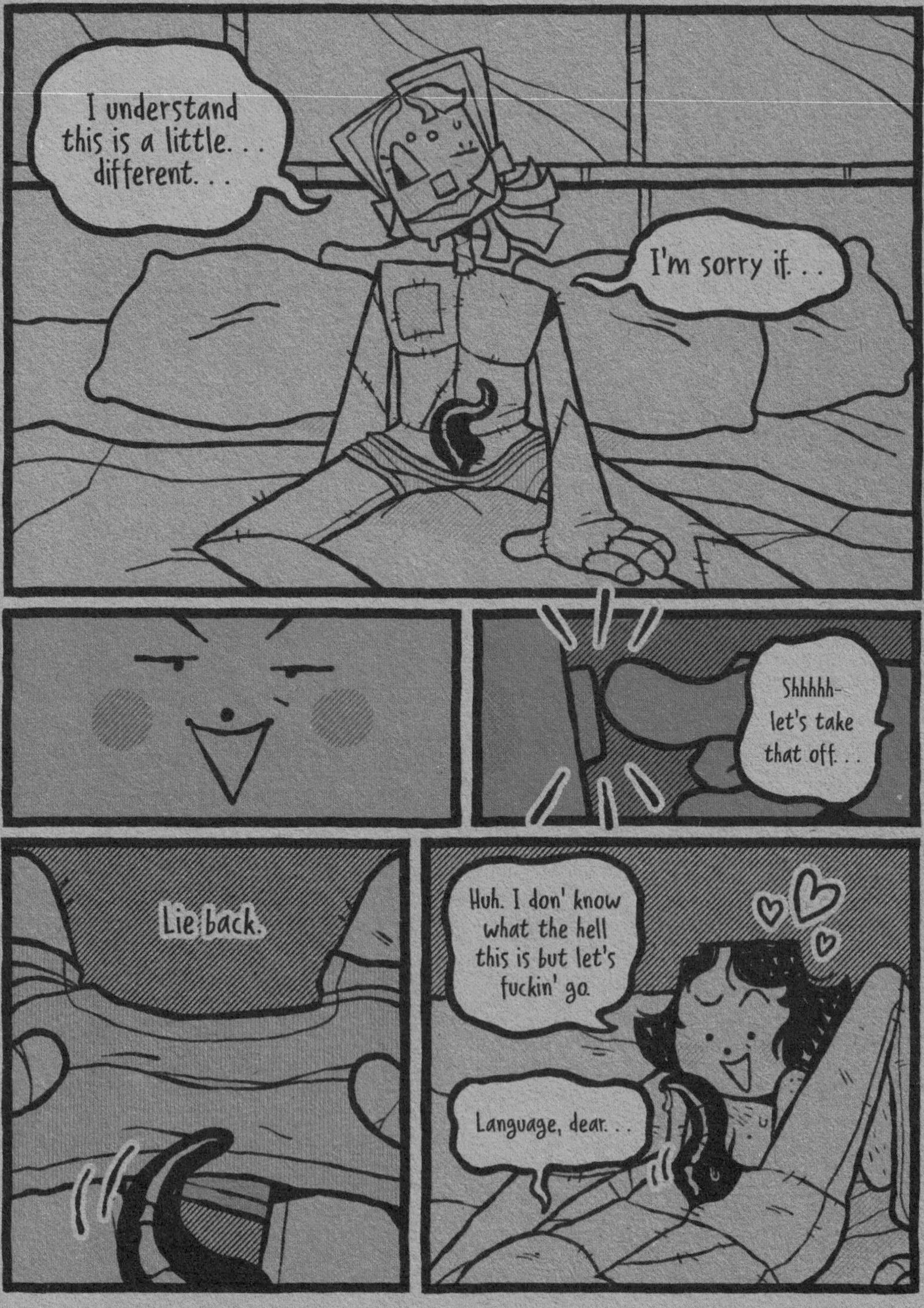
I understand this is a little... different...
I'm sorry if...
Shhhhh- let's take that off...
Lie back.
Huh. I don' know what the hell this is but let's fuckin' go.
Language, dear...

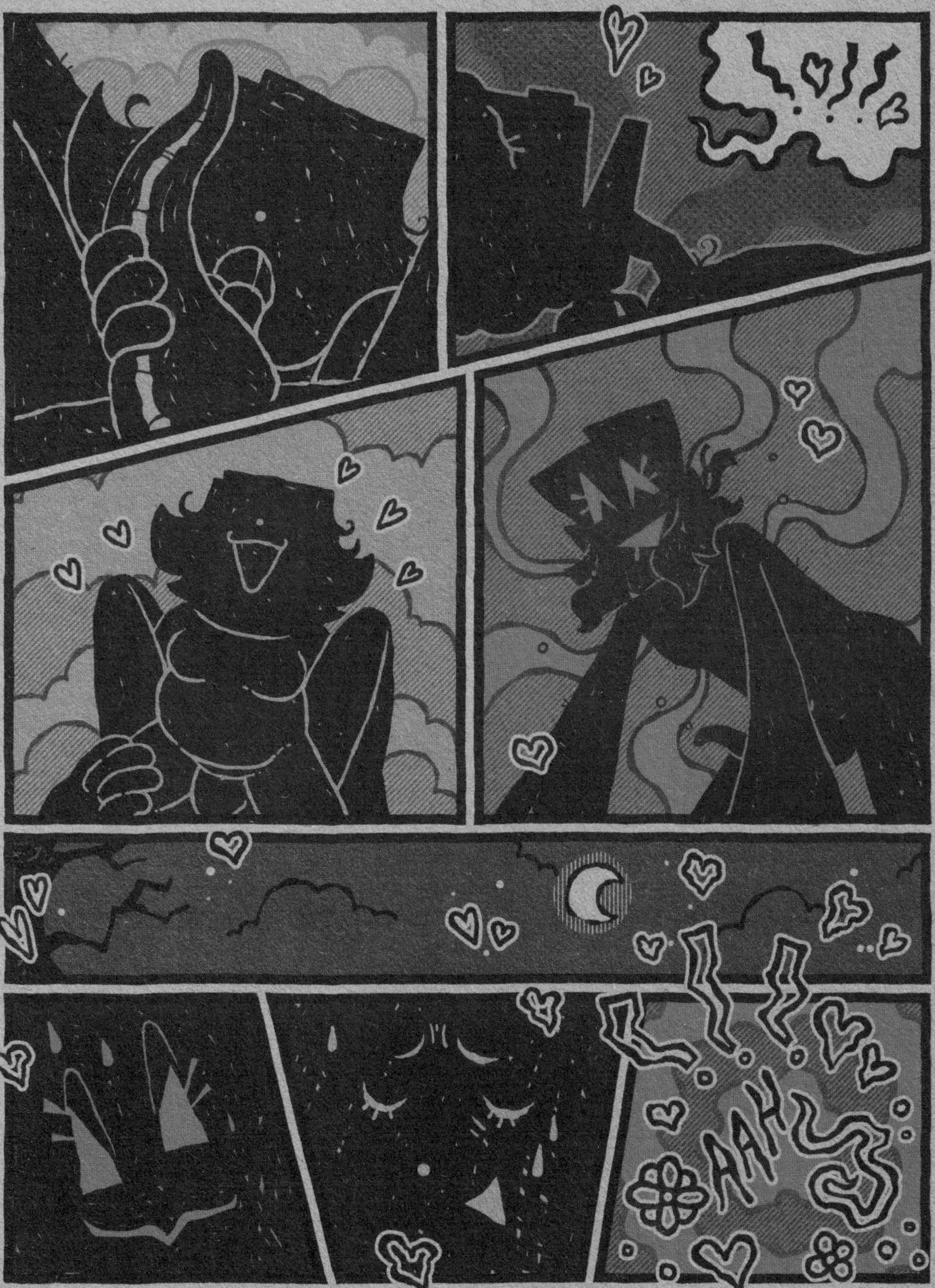
AAH

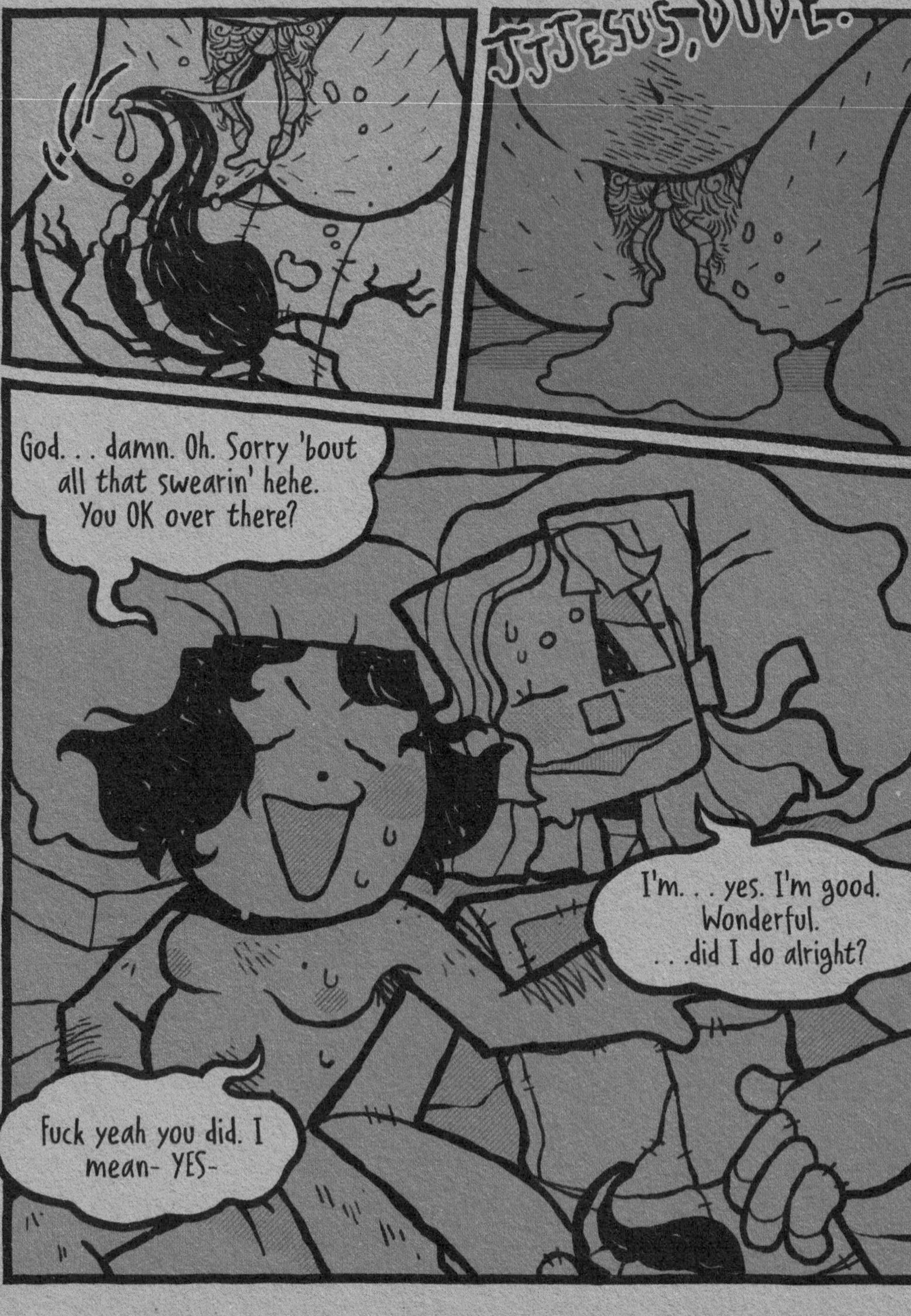
JJJESUS, DUDE.
God. . . damn. Oh. Sorry 'bout all that swearin' hehe. You OK over there?
I'm. . . yes. I'm good. Wonderful. . . .did I do alright?
Fuck yeah you did. I mean- YES-

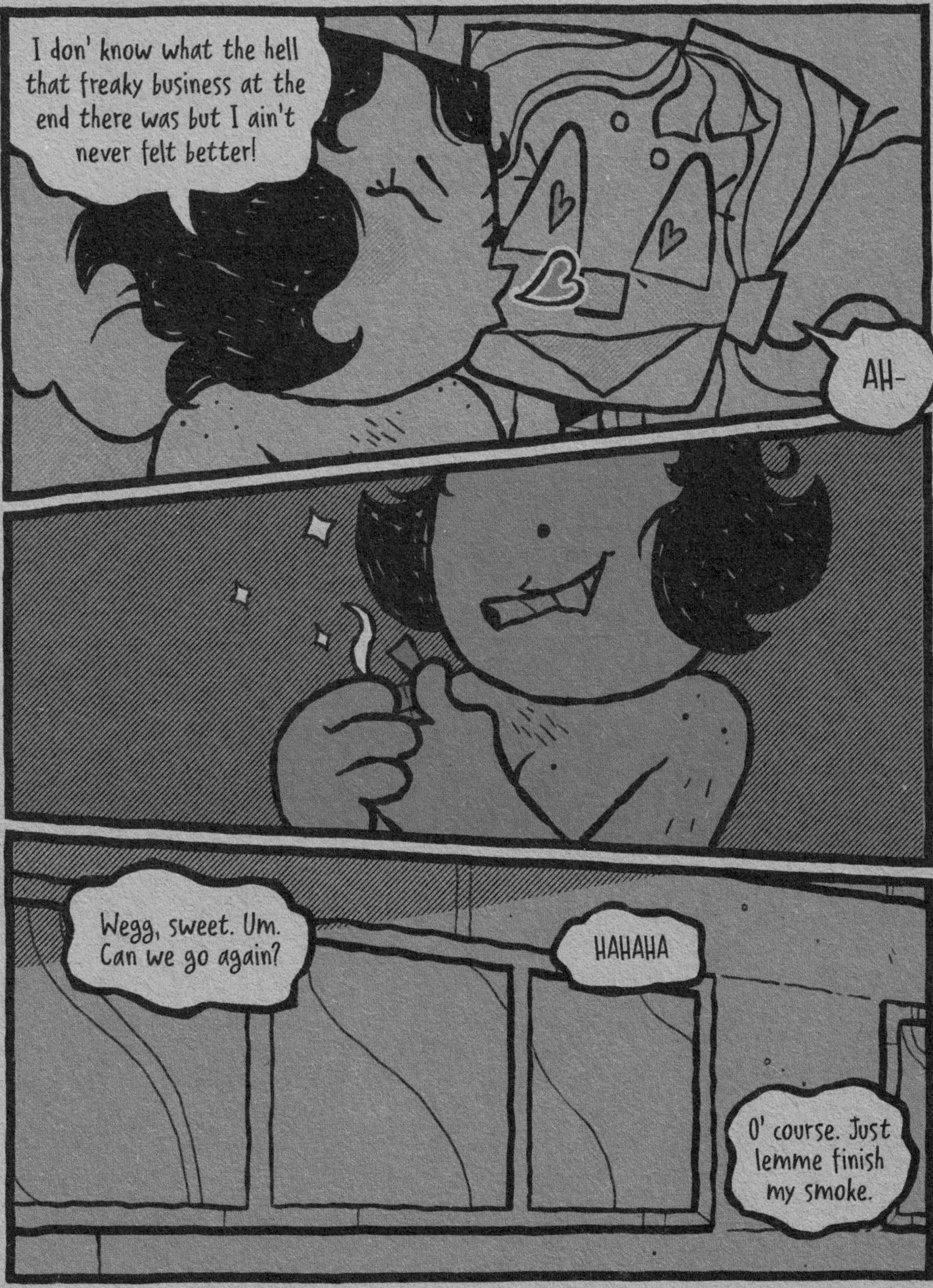
I don' know what the hell that freaky business at the end there was but I ain't never felt better!
AH-
Wegg, sweet. Um. Can we go again?
HAHAHA
O' course. Just lemme finish my smoke.

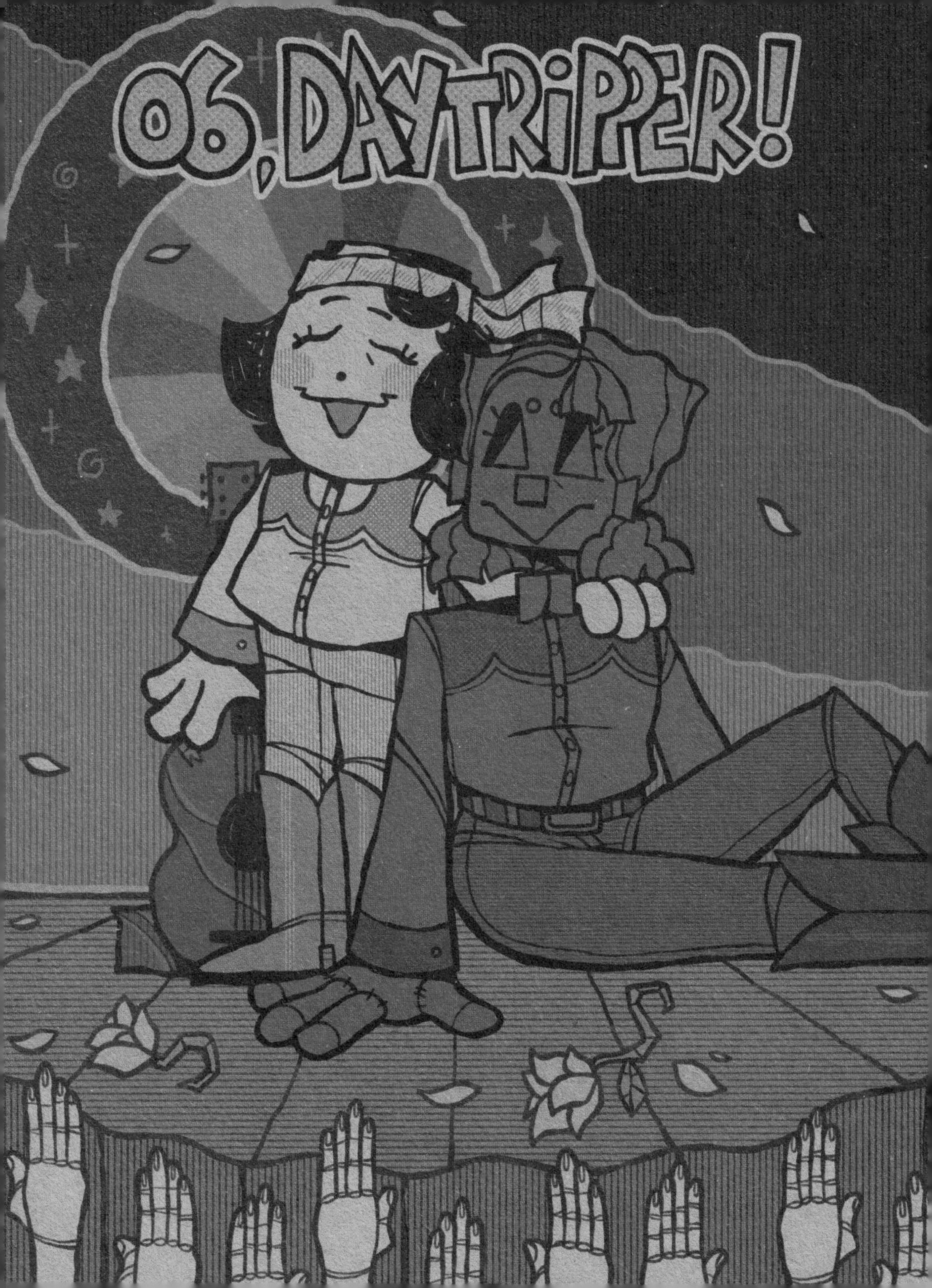
06, DAYTRIPPER!

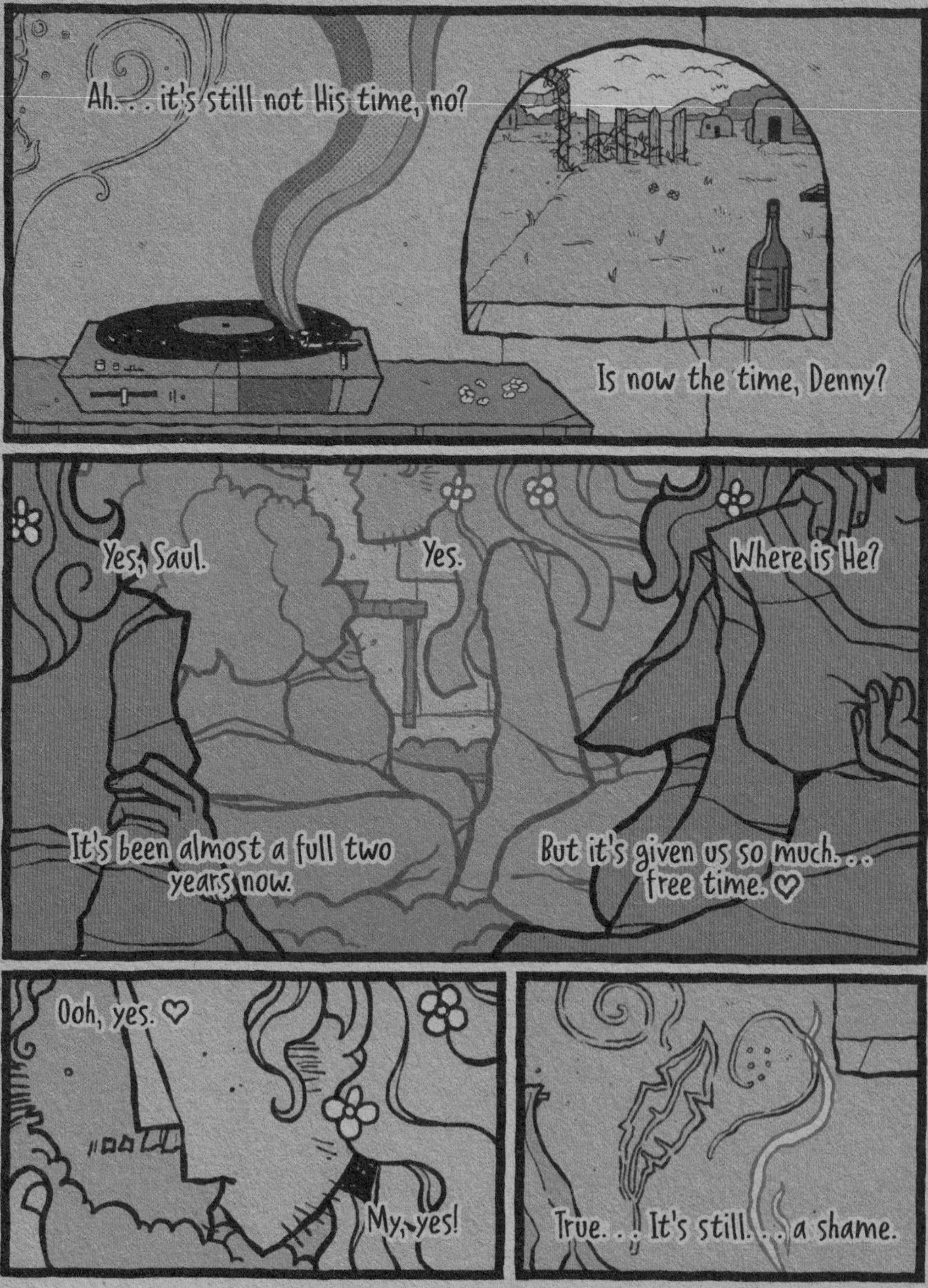
Ah. . . it's still not His time, no?
Is now the time, Denny?
Yes, Saul.
Yes.
Where is He?
It's been almost a full two years now.
But it's given us so much. . . free time. ♡
Ooh, yes. ♡
My, yes!
True. . . It's still. . . a shame.

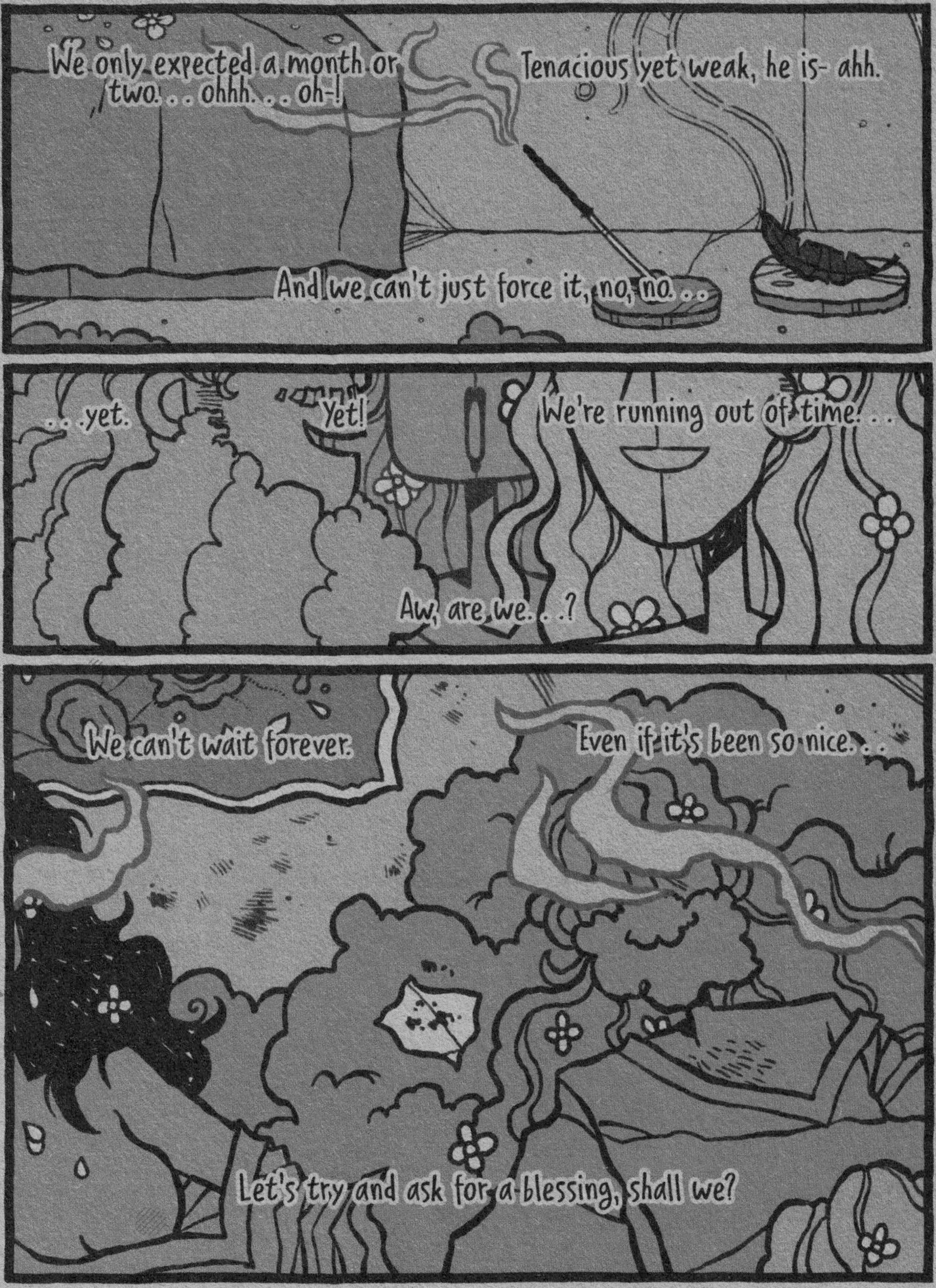
We only expected a month or two. . . ohhh. . . oh-!
Tenacious yet weak, he is- ahh.
And we can't just force it, no, no. . .
. . .yet.
Yet!
We're running out of time. . .
Aw, are we. . .?
We can't wait forever.
Even if it's been so nice. . .
Let's try and ask for a blessing, shall we?

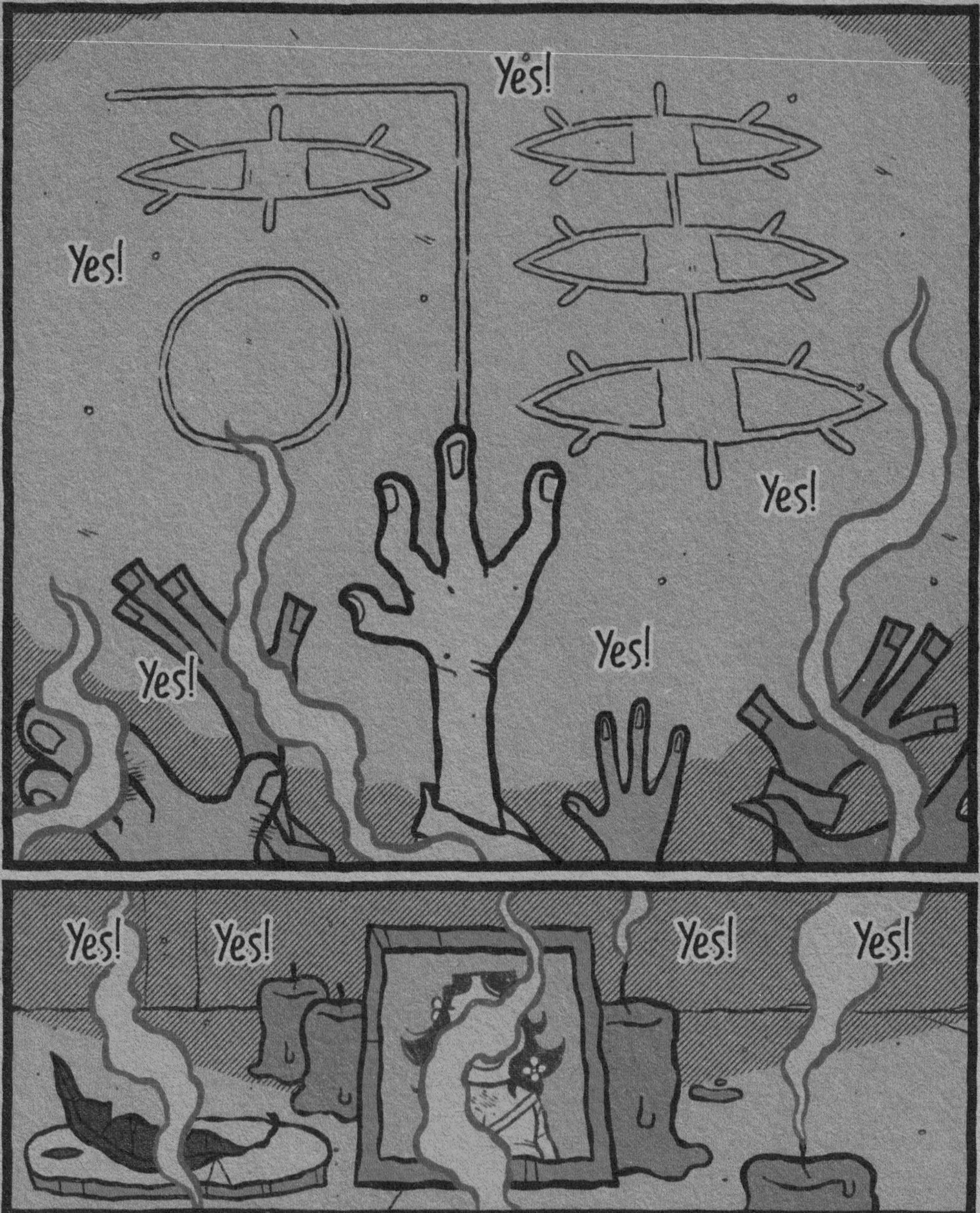
Yes!
Yes!
Yes!
Yes!
Yes!
Yes!
Yes!
Yes!
Yes!

MAY 1974

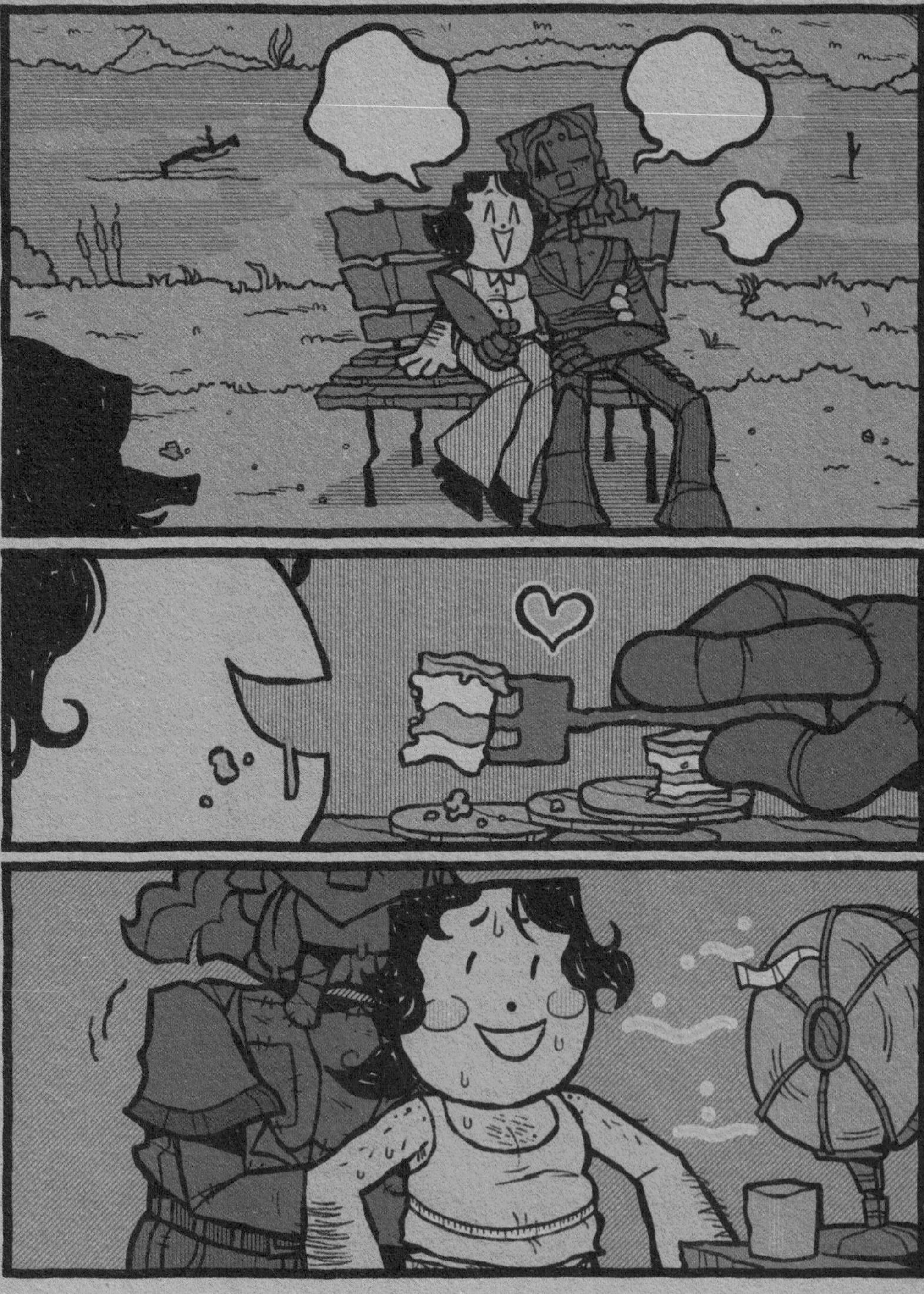

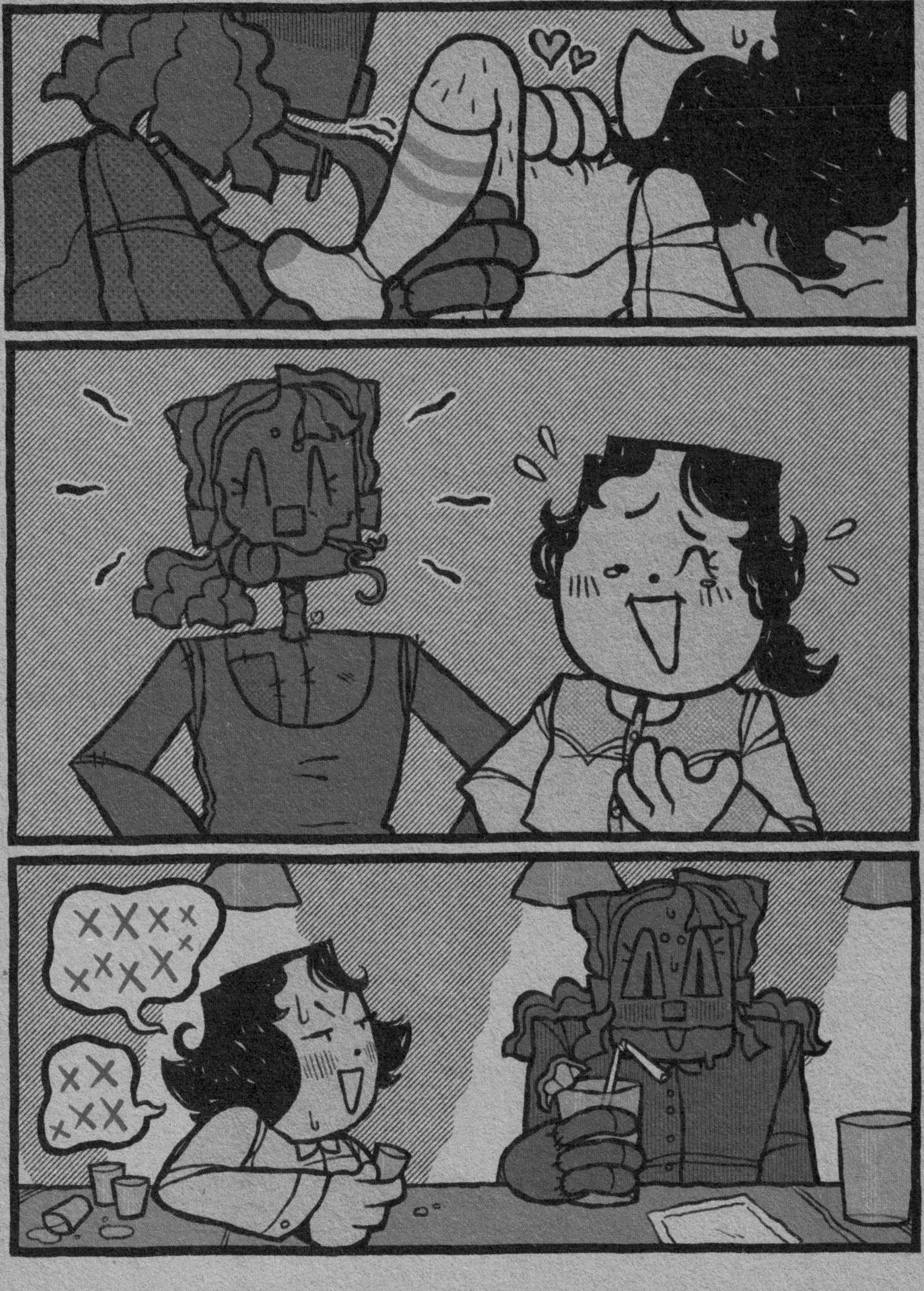

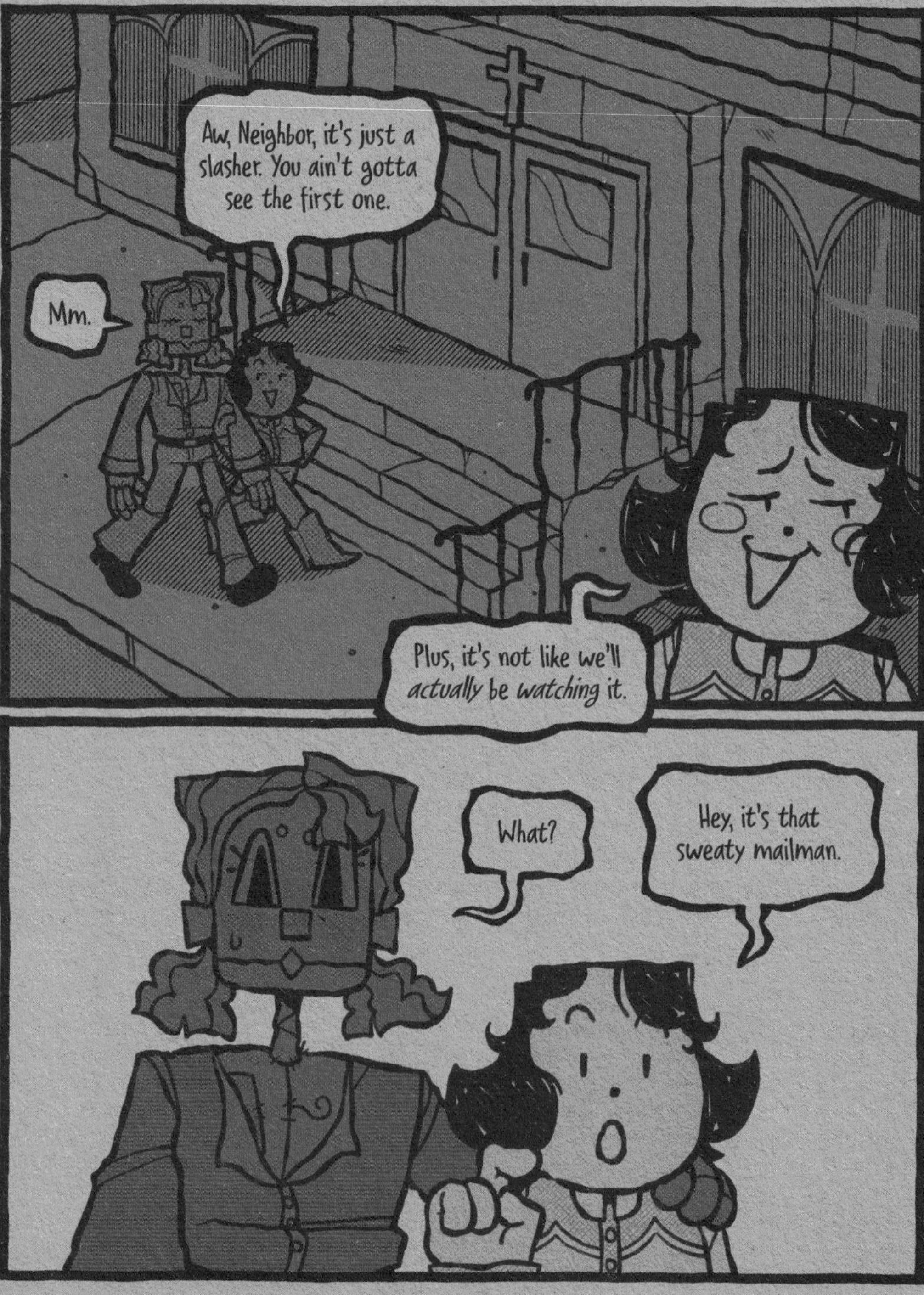
Aw, Neighbor, it's just a slasher. You ain't gotta see the first one.
Mm.
Plus, it's not like we'll *actually* be *watching* it.
Hey, it's that sweaty mailman.
What?

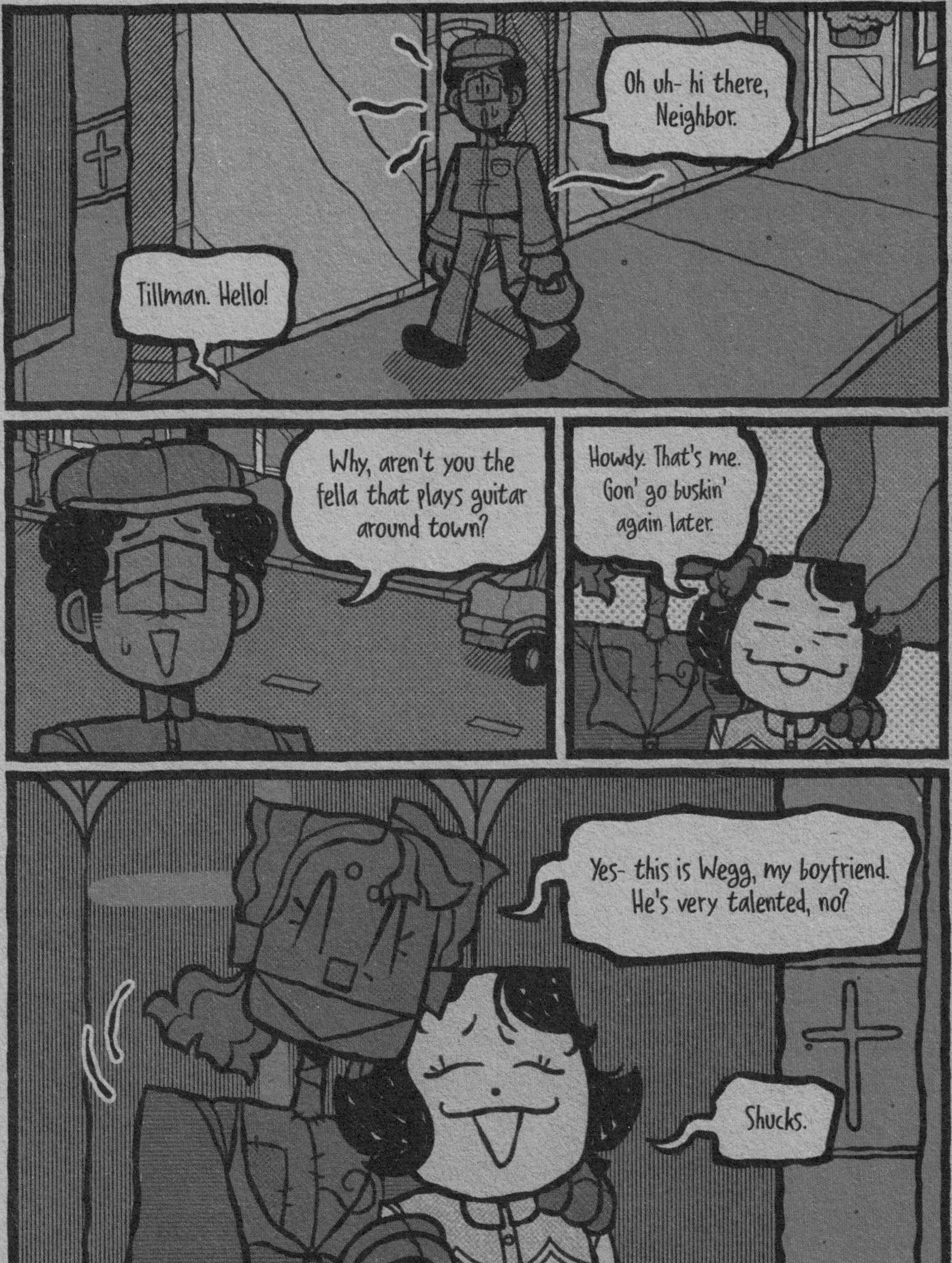
Oh uh- hi there, Neighbor.
Tillman. Hello!
Why, aren't you the fella that plays guitar around town?
Howdy. That's me. Gon' go buskin' again later.
Yes- this is Wegg, my boyfriend. He's very talented, no?
Shucks.

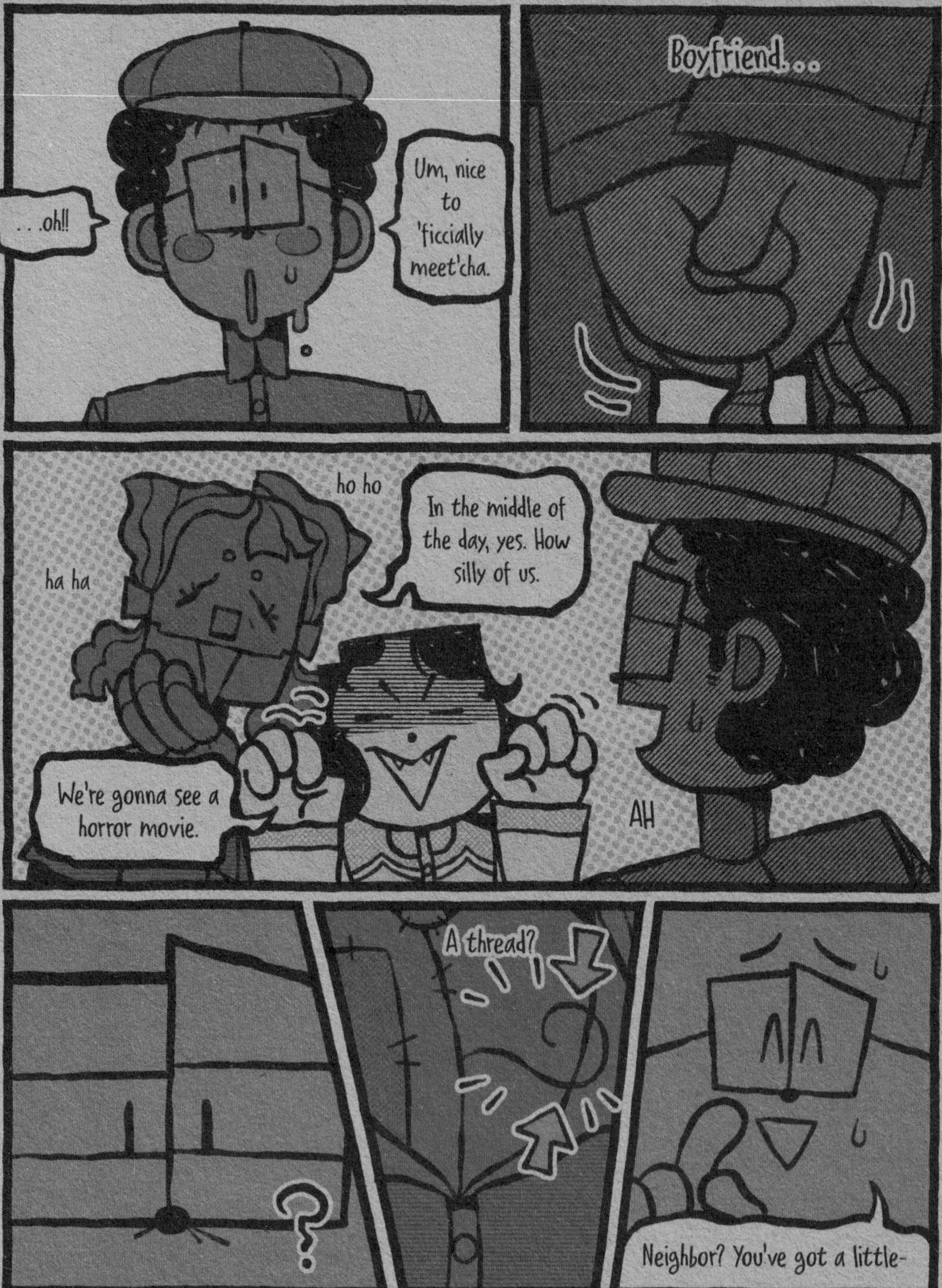

. . .oh!!
Um, nice to 'ficcially meet'cha.
Boyfriend. . .
ha ha
ho ho
In the middle of the day, yes. How silly of us.
We're gonna see a horror movie.
AH
?
A thread?
Neighbor? You've got a little-

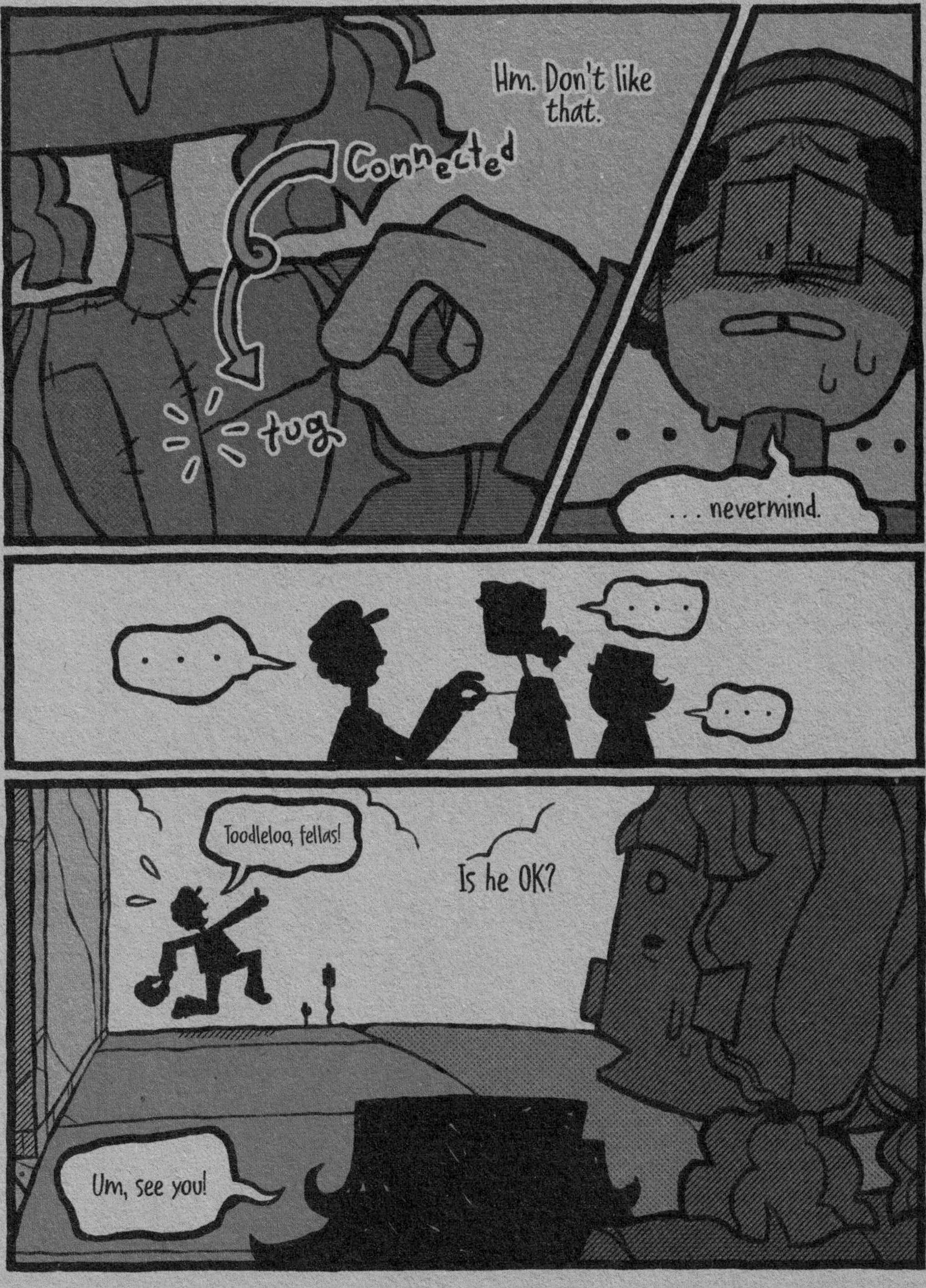
Hm. Don't like that.
Connected
tug
. . .
. . . nevermind.
. . .
. . .
. . .
Toodleloo, fellas!
Is he OK?
Um, see you!

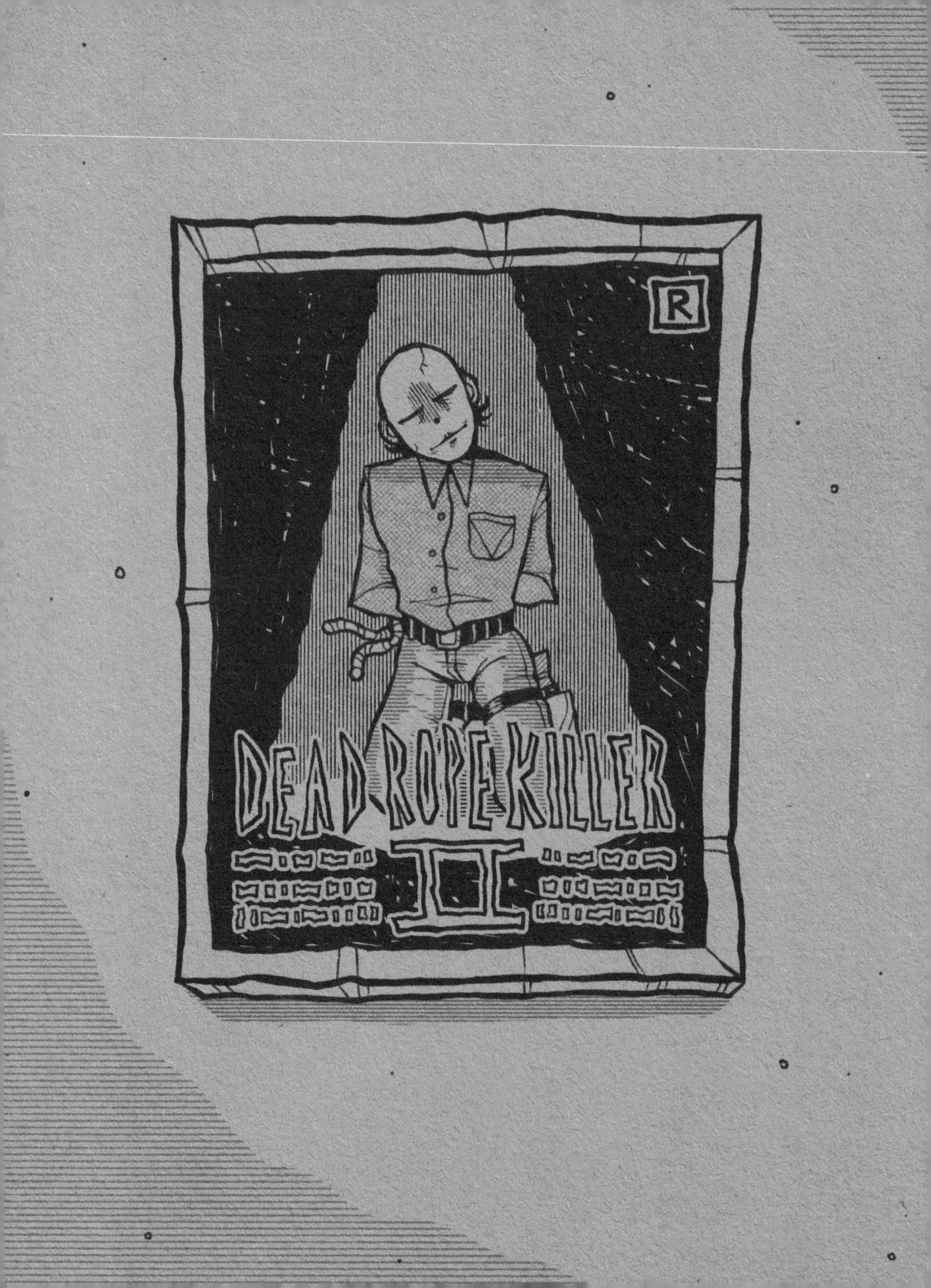
R
DEAD ROPE KILLER
II

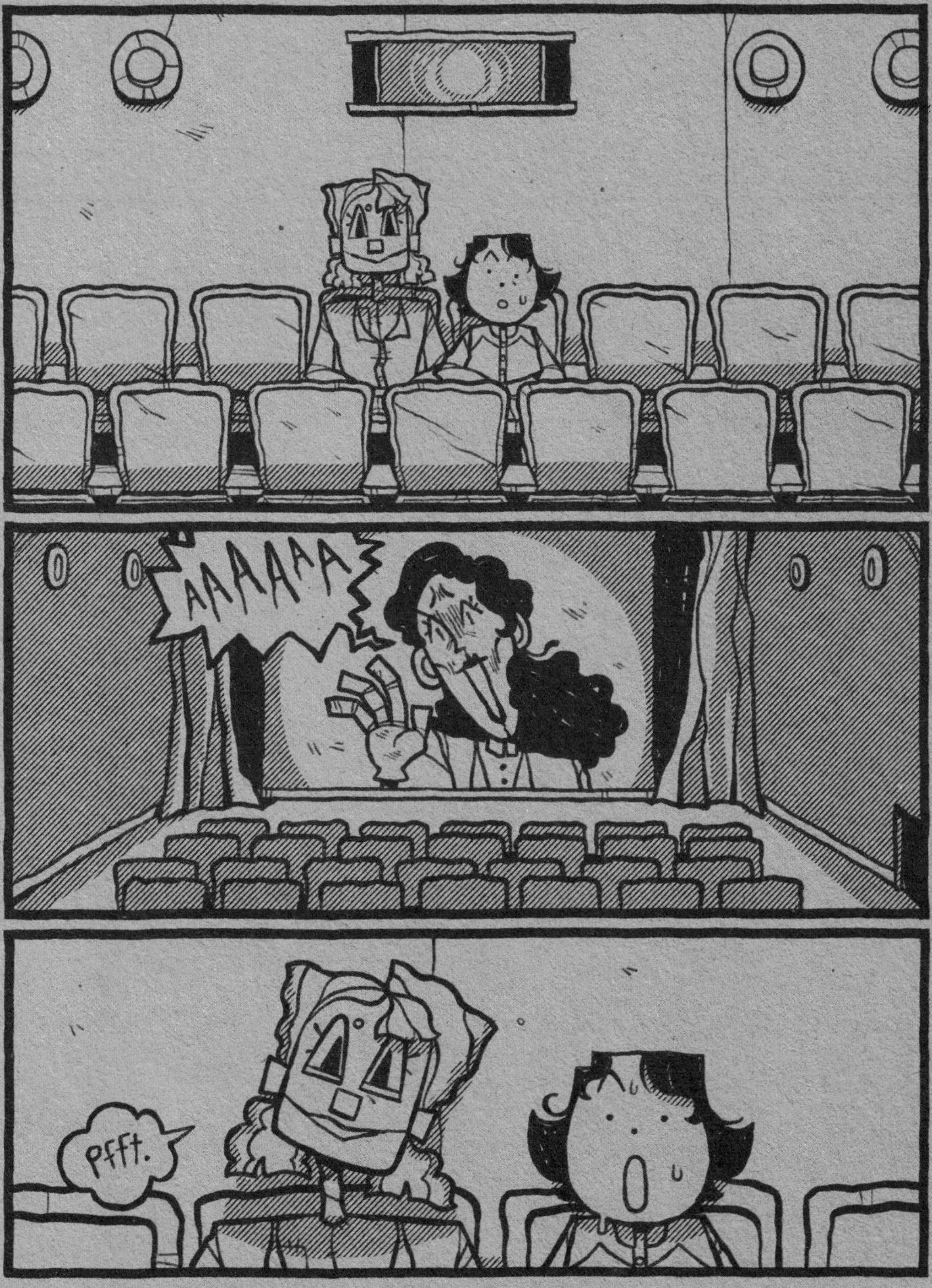
AAAAAA
pfft.

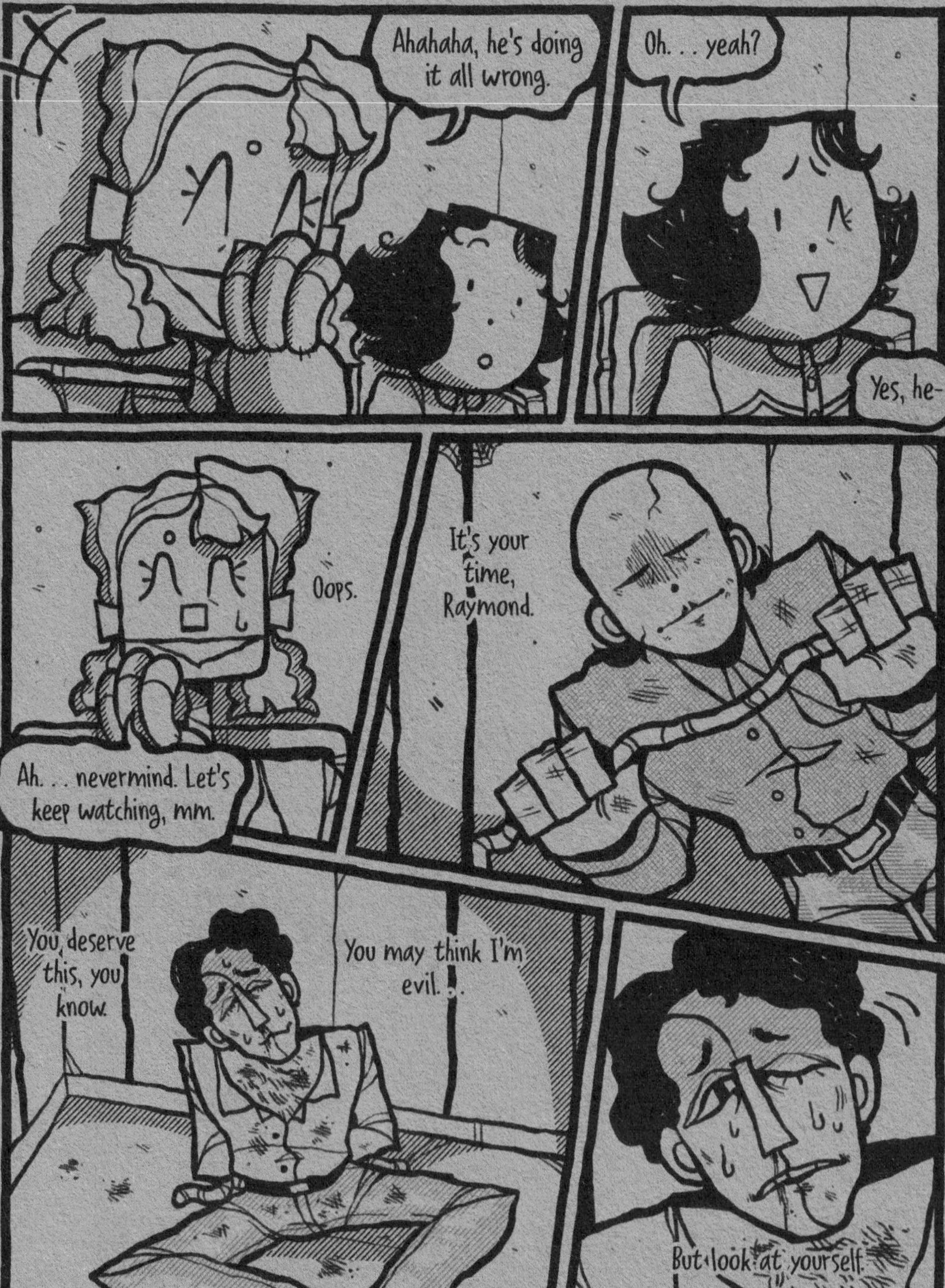

Ahahaha, he's doing it all wrong.
Oh. . . yeah?
Yes, he-
Oops.
Ah. . . nevermind. Let's keep watching, mm.
It's your time, Raymond.
You deserve this, you know.
You may think I'm evil. . .
But look at yourself.

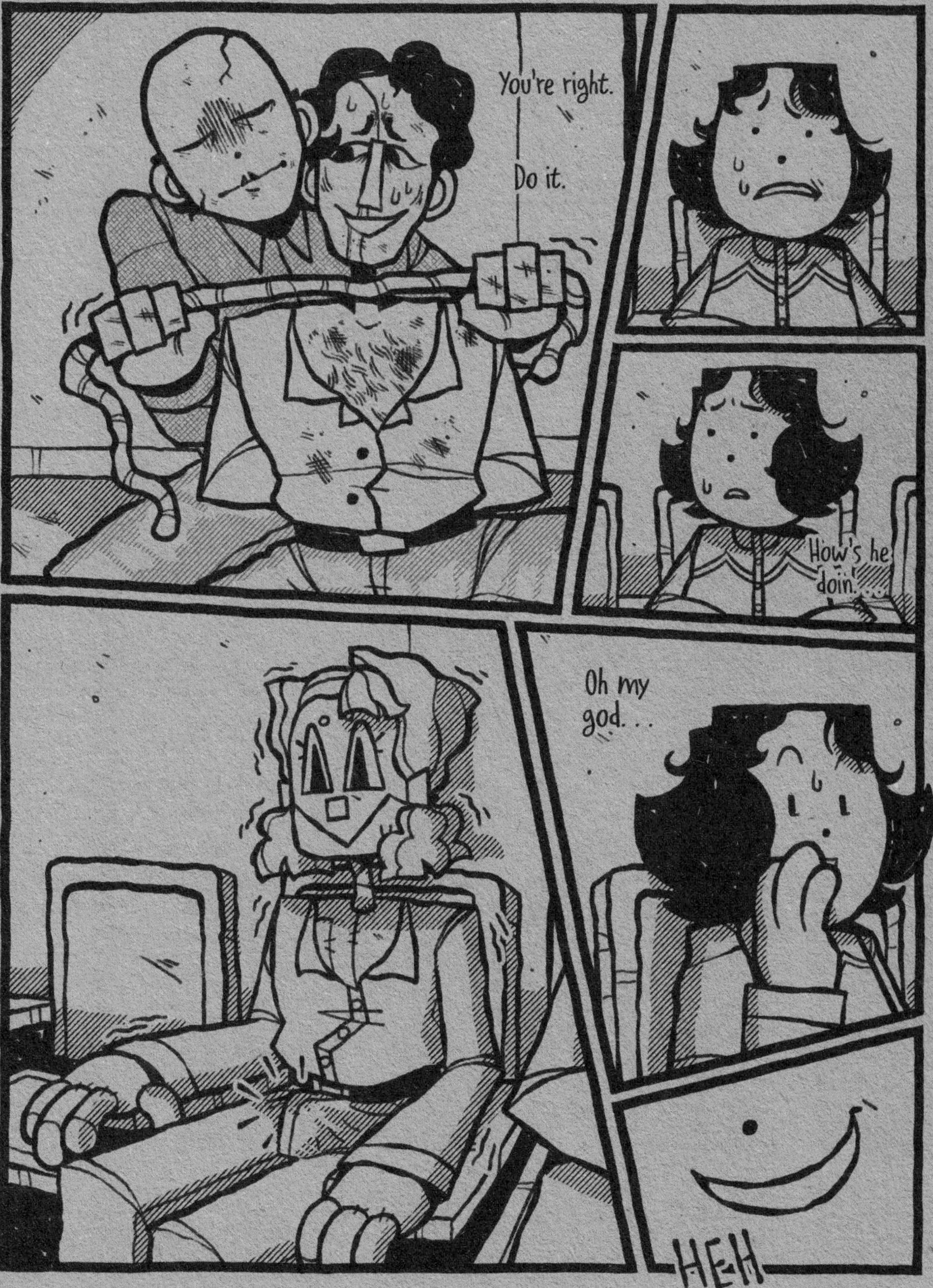
You're right.
Do it.
How's he doin'...
Oh my god...
HEH

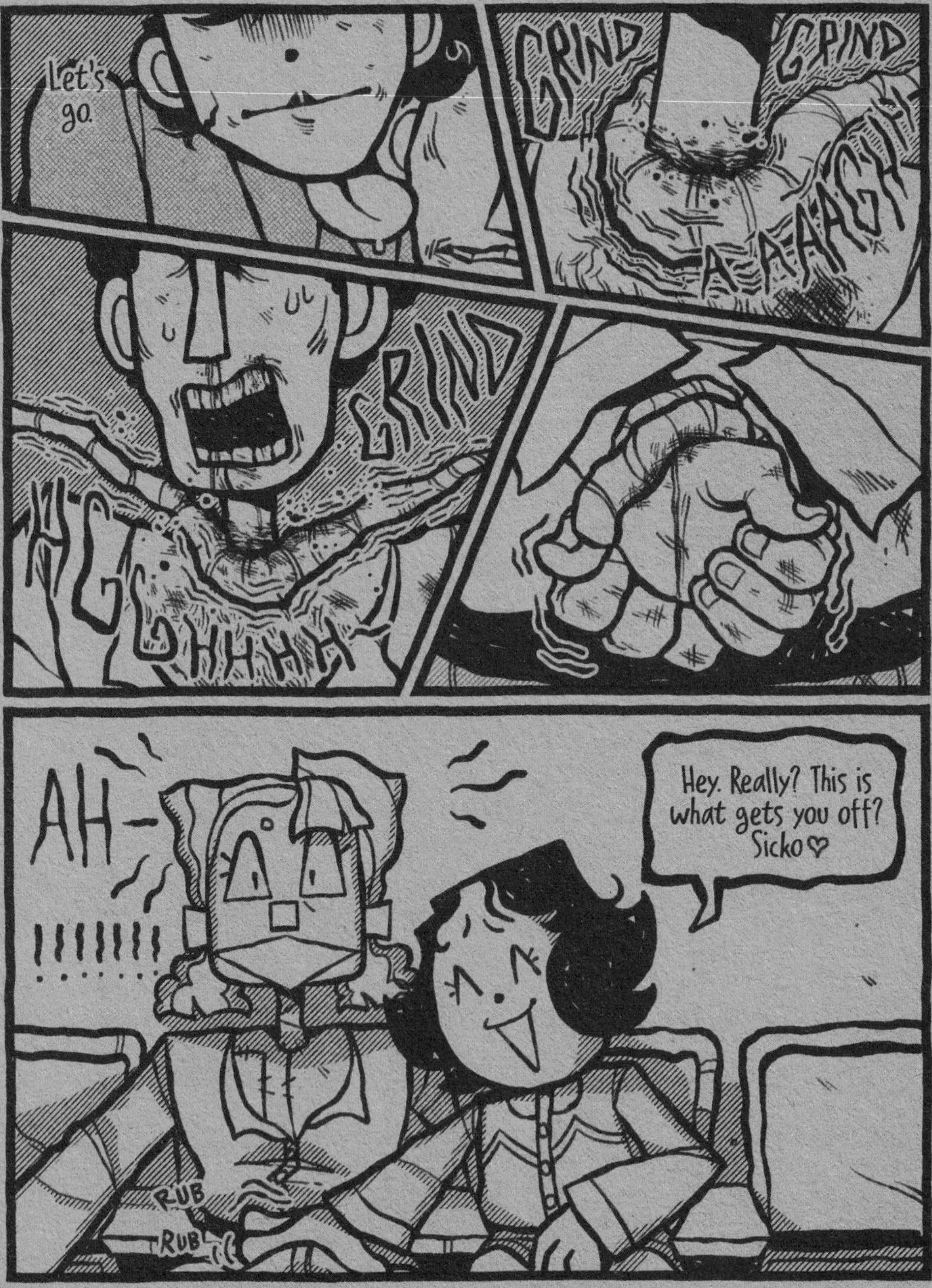
Let's go.
GRIND GRIND
AAAAGH
GRIND
HGGHHHH
AH-
!!!!!!!
Hey. Really? This is what gets you off? Sicko♡
RUB
RUB

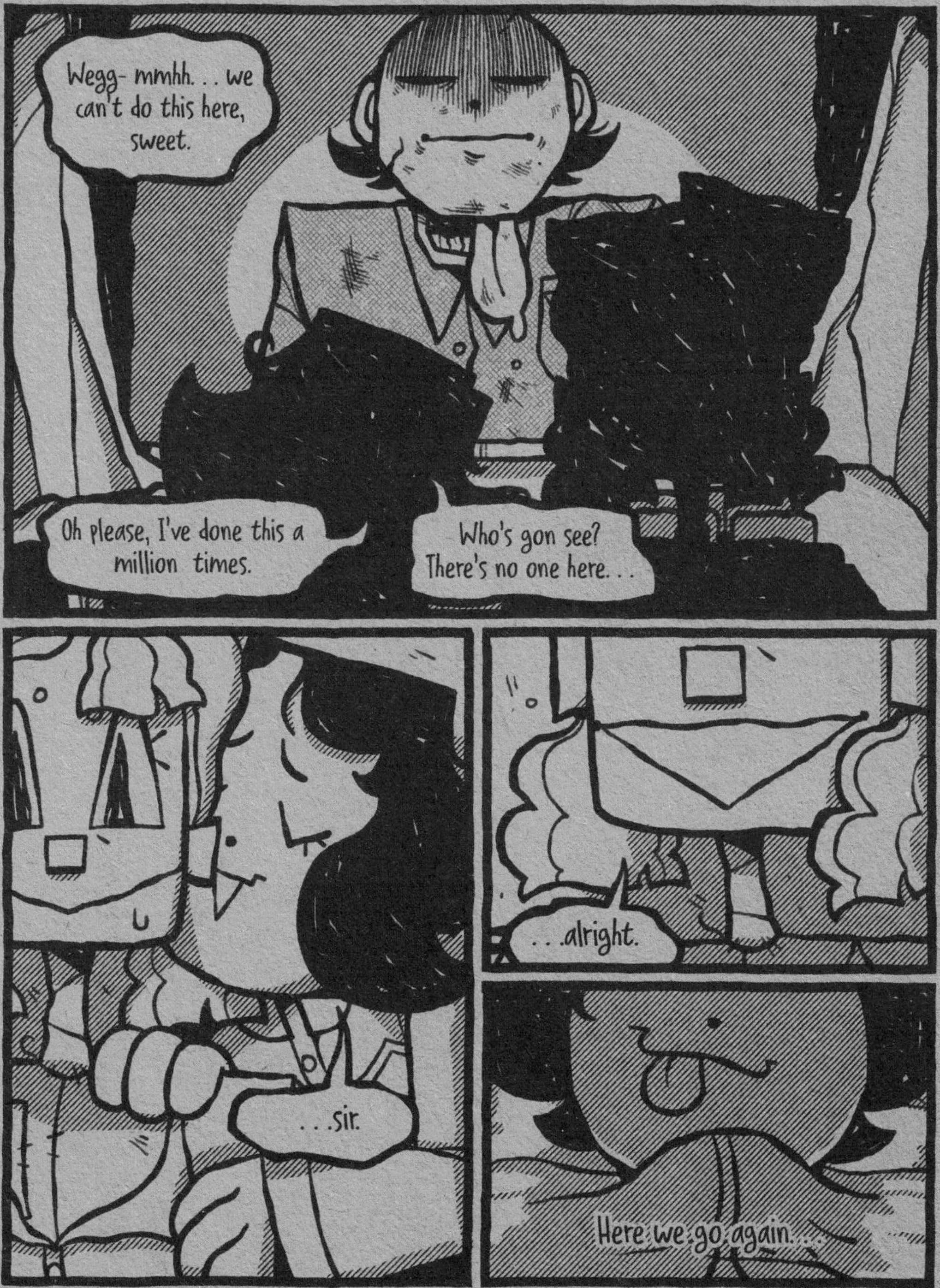
Wegg- mmhh. . . we can't do this here, sweet.
Oh please, I've done this a million times.
Who's gon see? There's no one here. . .
. . .sir.
. . .alright.
Here we go again. . .

Get outta here with that.
You know I don't wear
that shit anymore.
I don't care! I don't care!
Get out!

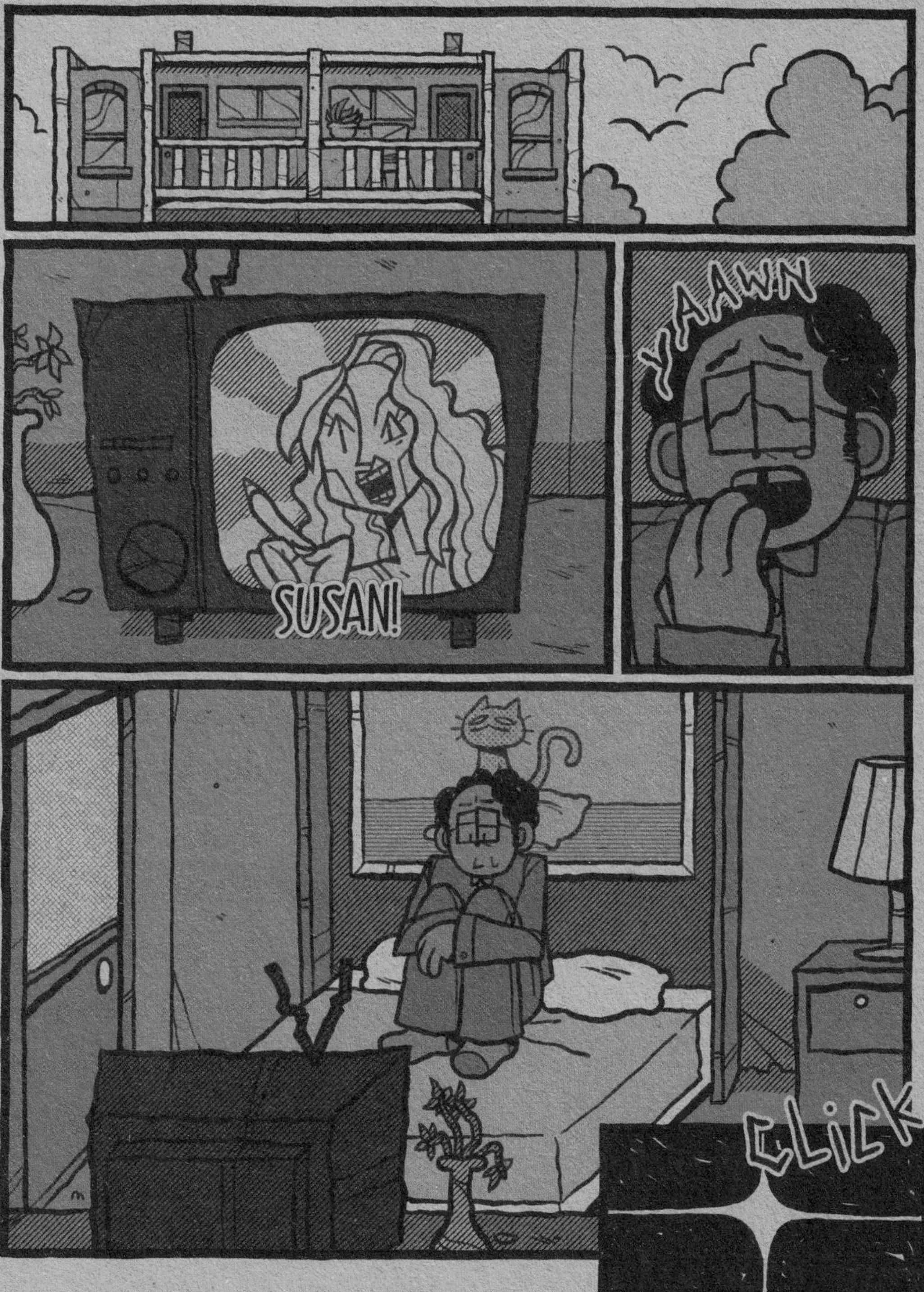
SUSAN!
YAAWN
CLICK

Can't stop thinkin' bout it.

ARE YOU HAPPY?

DO YOU KNOW WHAT YOU WANT IN LIFE?

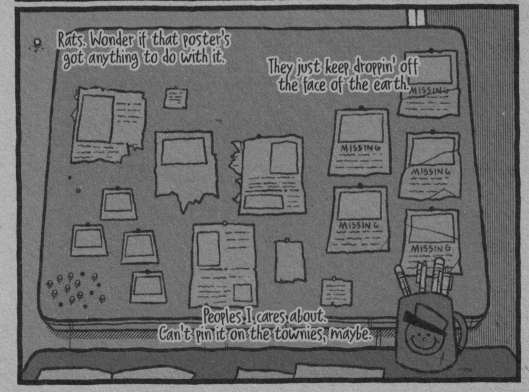

Rats. Wonder if that poster's got anything to do with it.

They just keep droppin' off the face of the earth.

MISSING

MISSING

MISSING

MISSING

MISSING

Peoples I cares about. Can't pin it on the townies, maybe.

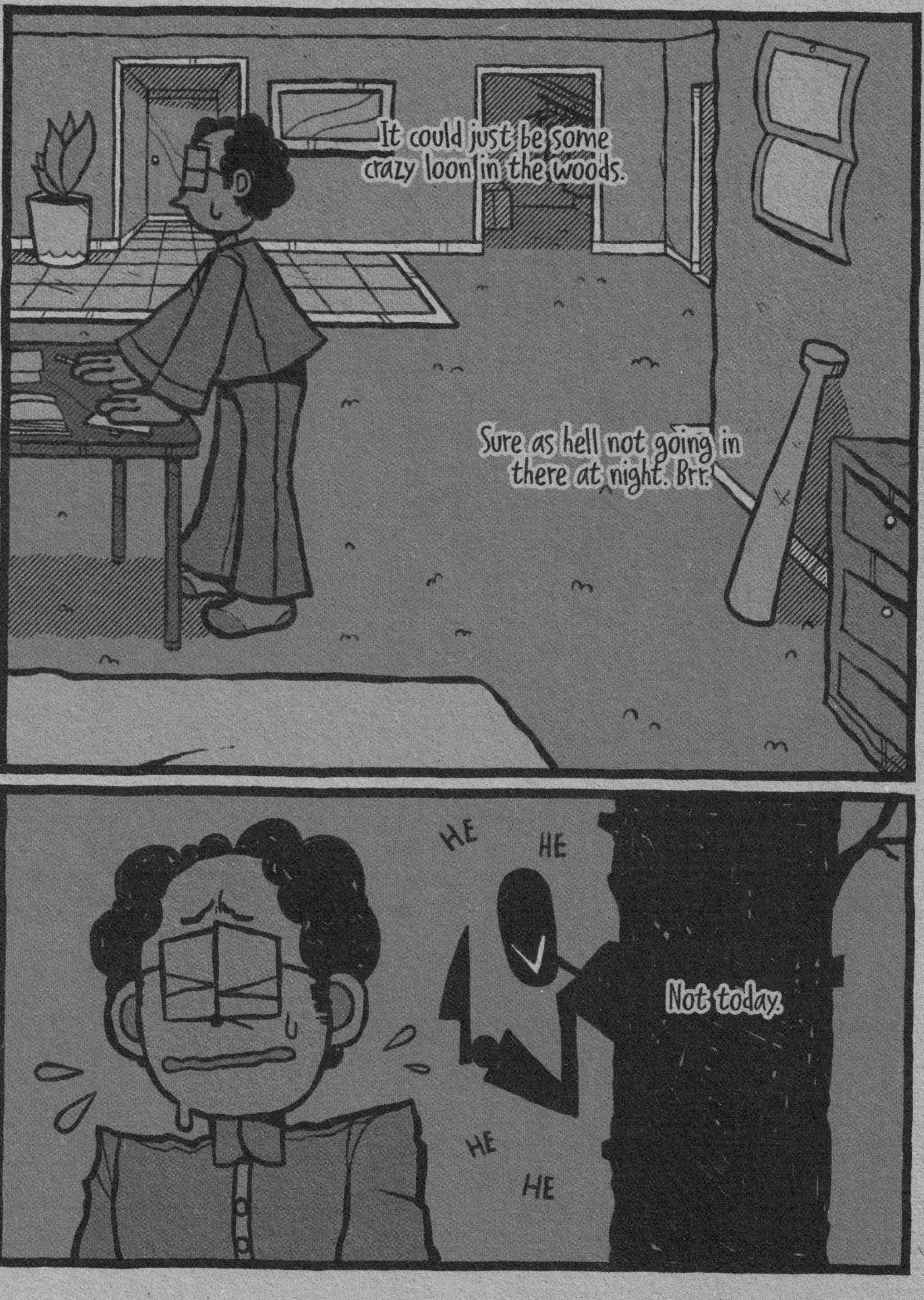
It could just be some crazy loon in the woods.
Sure as hell not going in there at night. Brr.
HE
HE
Not today.
HE
HE

What's the thread?

ER'S WIFE
SAPEARS

...barring Kevin, maybe.

Hm. Rarold is pretty. . . Rarold.

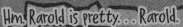

FARMER'S WIFE
DISSAPEARS

Awful in every way. Definitely Heartbreaker material.

Would that be too obvious, though?

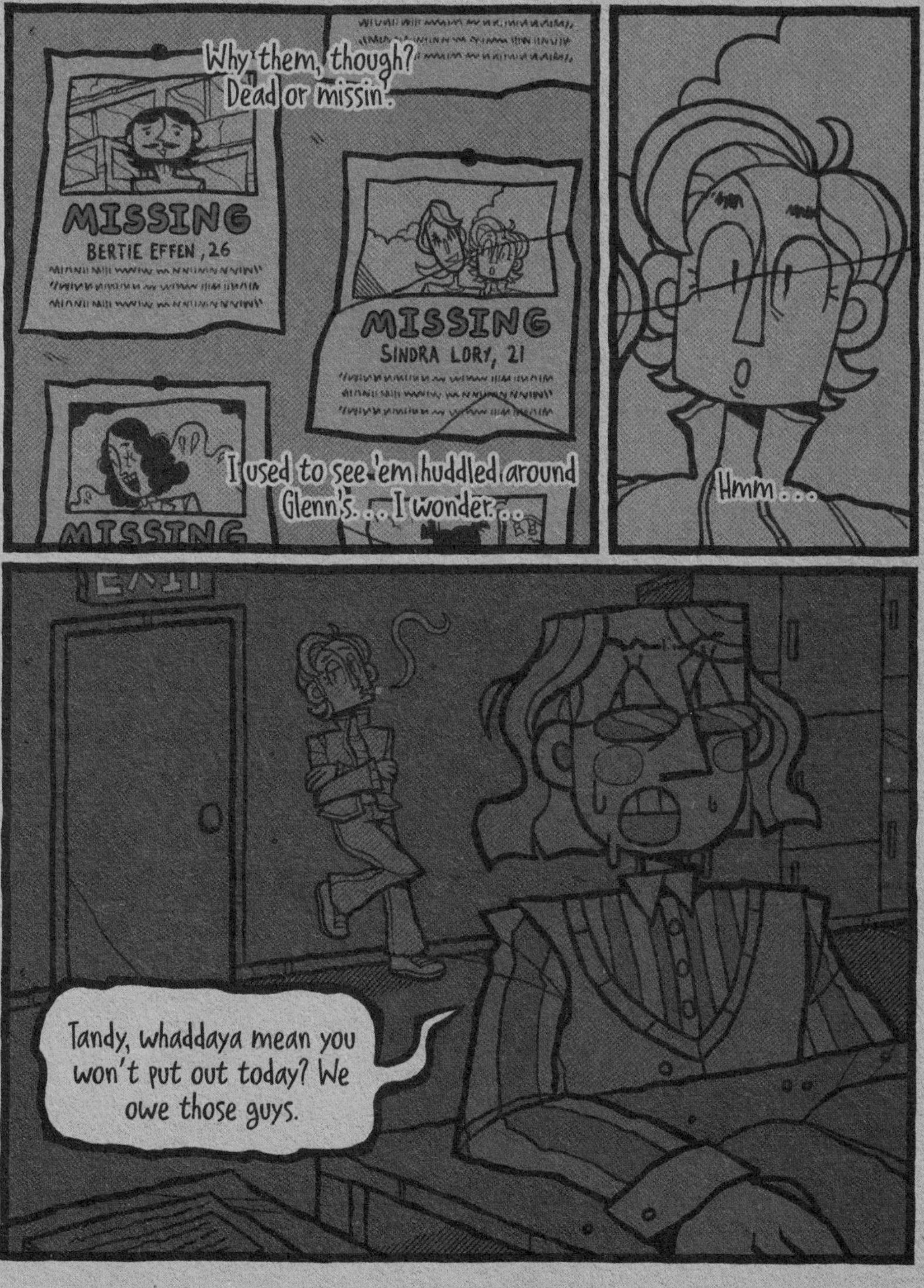
Why them, though? Dead or missin'.
MISSING
BERTIE EFFEN, 26
MISSING
SINDRA LORY, 21
I used to see 'em huddled around Glenn's. . . I wonder. . .
Hmm . . .
Tandy, whaddaya mean you won't put out today? We owe those guys.

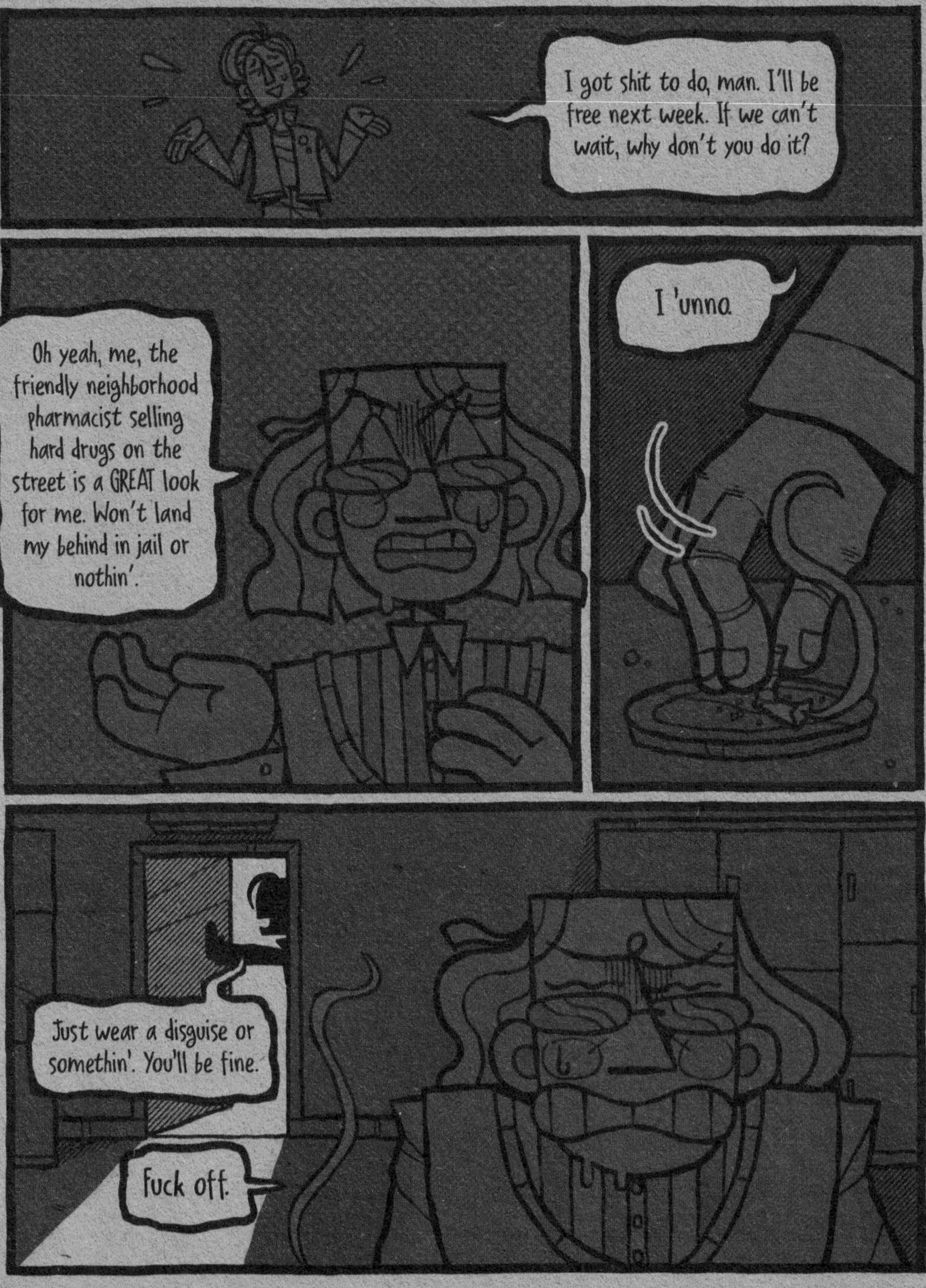
I got shit to do, man. I'll be free next week. If we can't wait, why don't you do it?
Oh yeah, me, the friendly neighborhood pharmacist selling hard drugs on the street is a GREAT look for me. Won't land my behind in jail or nothin'.
I 'unno.
Just wear a disguise or somethin'. You'll be fine.
Fuck off.

That movie wasn't very good. . .

Like you were watchin', heh.

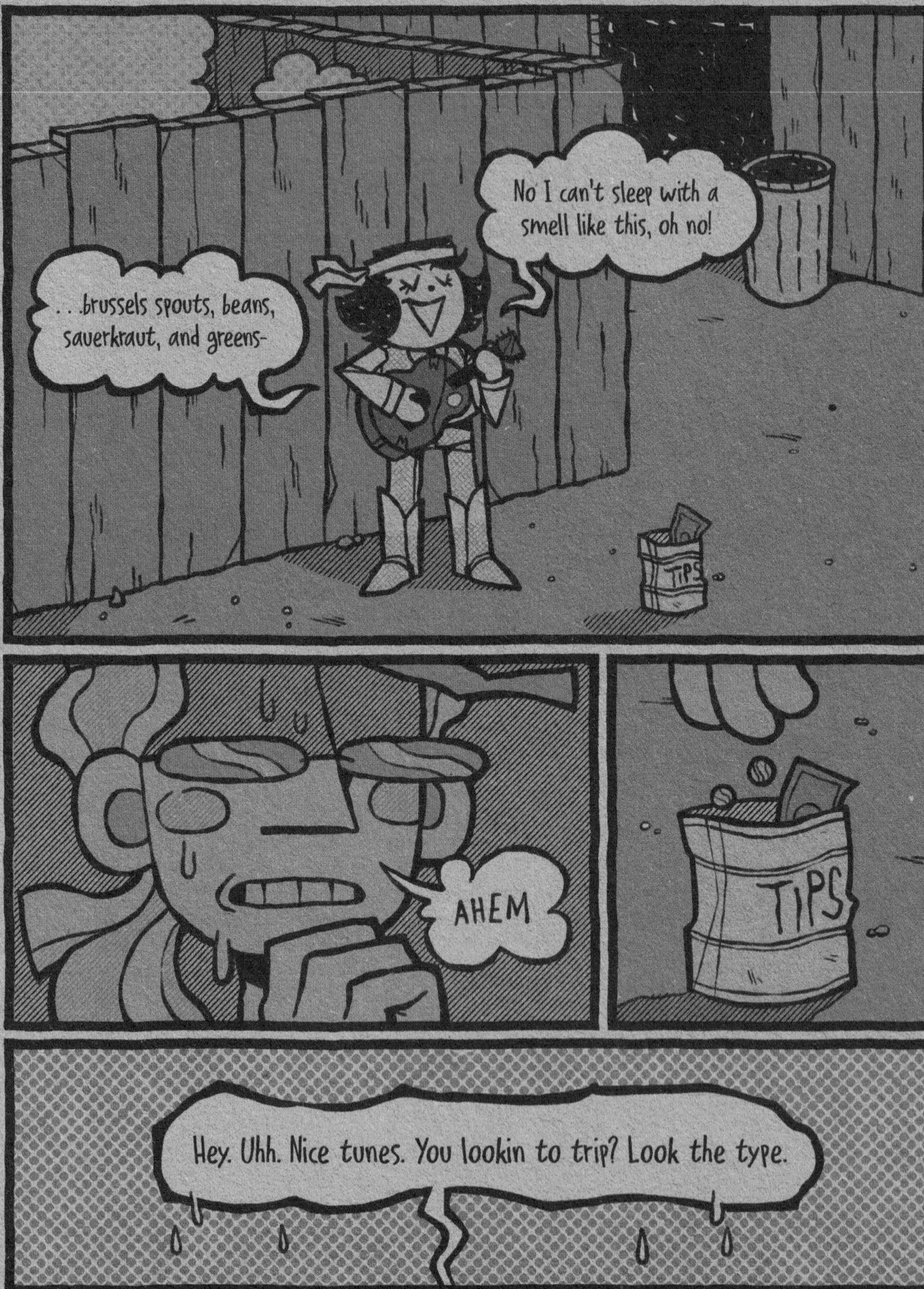
. . .brussels spouts, beans, sauerkraut, and greens-
No I can't sleep with a smell like this, oh no!
TIPS
AHEM
TIPS
Hey. Uhh. Nice tunes. You lookin to trip? Look the type.

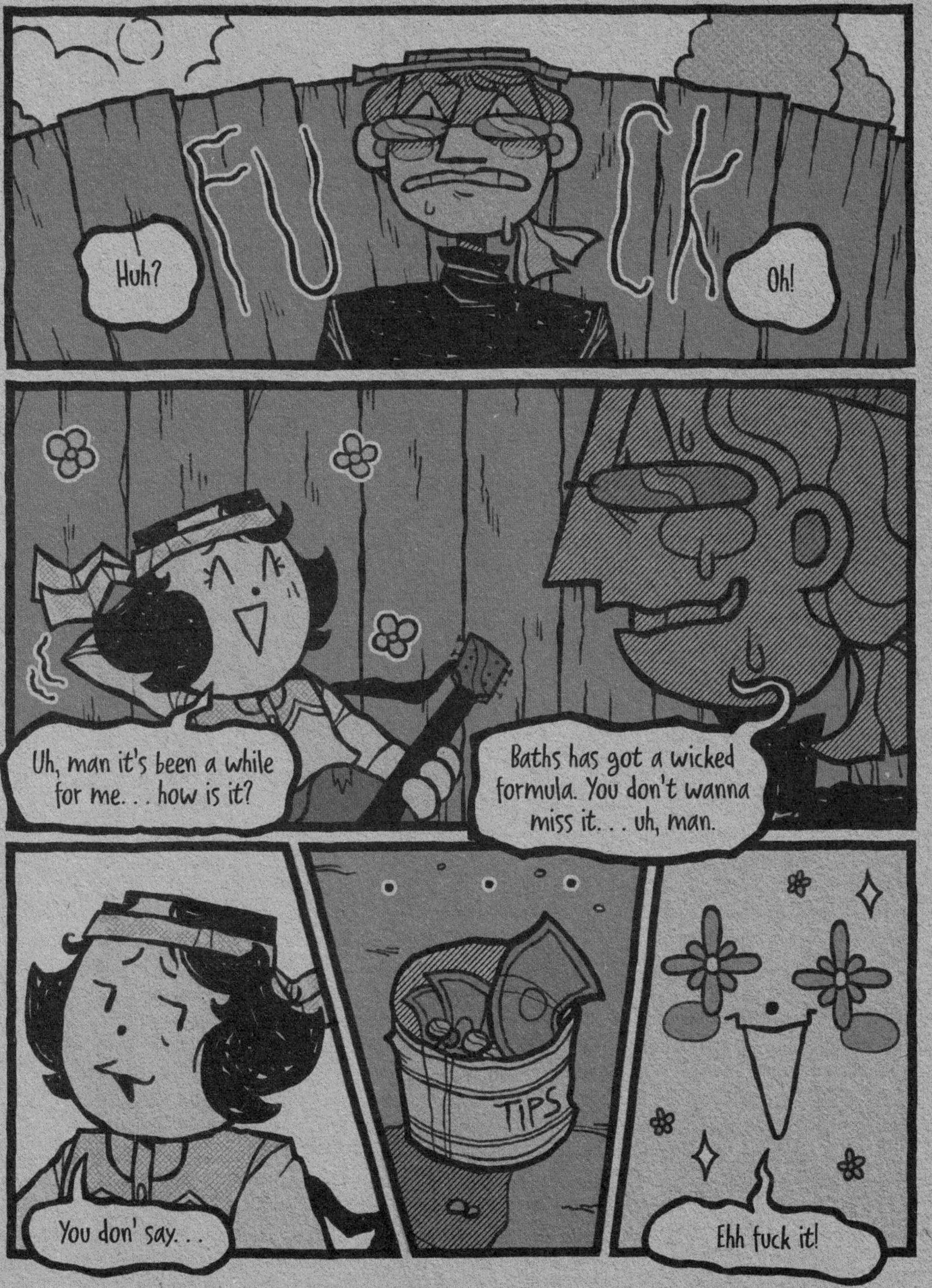
FUCK
Huh?
Oh!
Uh, man it's been a while for me. . . how is it?
Baths has got a wicked formula. You don't wanna miss it. . . uh, man.
You don' say. . .
TIPS
Ehh fuck it!

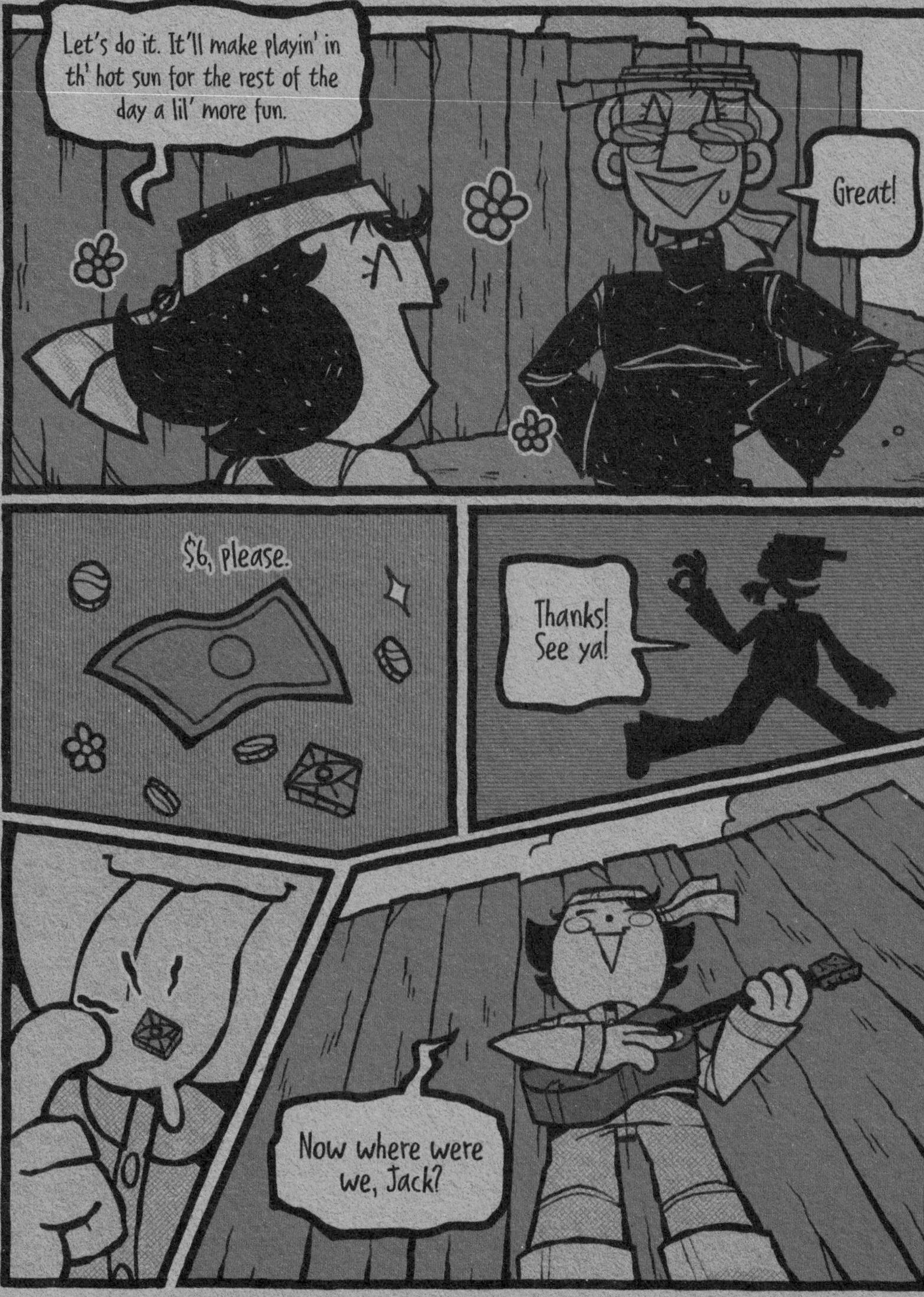

Let's do it. It'll make playin' in th' hot sun for the rest of the day a lil' more fun.
Great!
$6, please.
Thanks! See ya!
Now where were we, Jack?

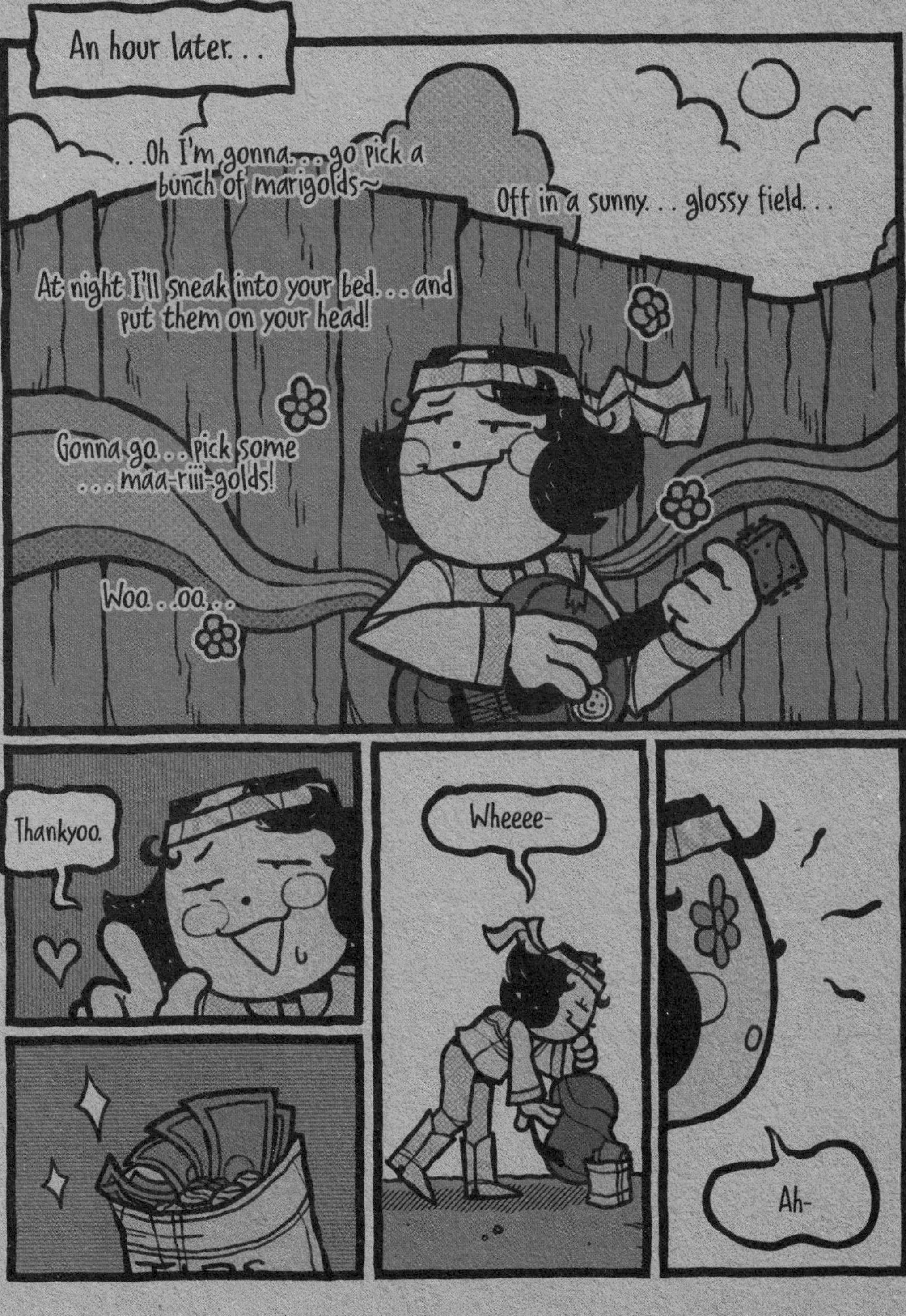

An hour later. . .
. . .Oh I'm gonna. . . go pick a bunch of marigolds~
Off in a sunny. . . glossy field. . .
At night I'll sneak into your bed. . . and put them on your head!
Gonna go. . . pick some . . . maa-riii-golds!
Woo. . .oo. . .
Thankyoo.
Wheeee-
Ah-

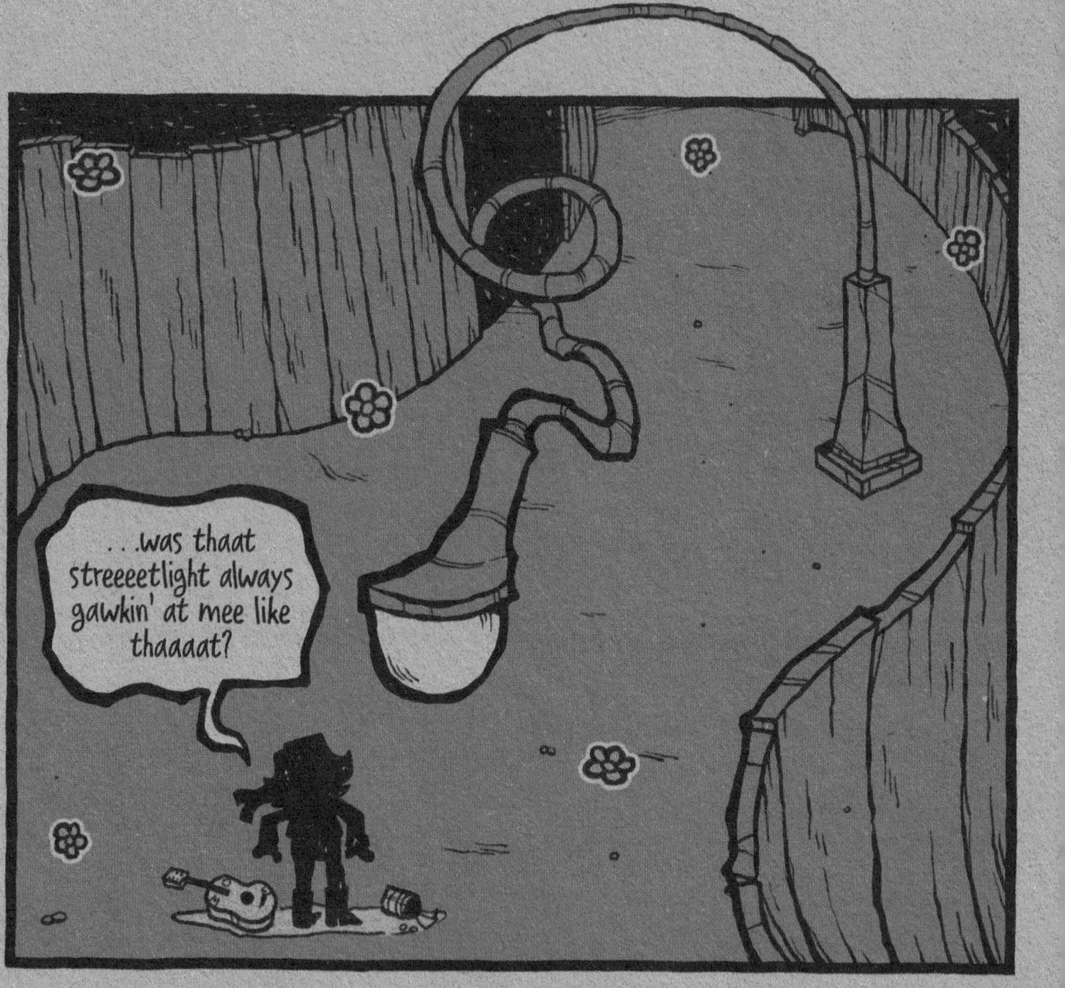
. . .was thaat streeeetlight always gawkin' at mee like thaaaat?

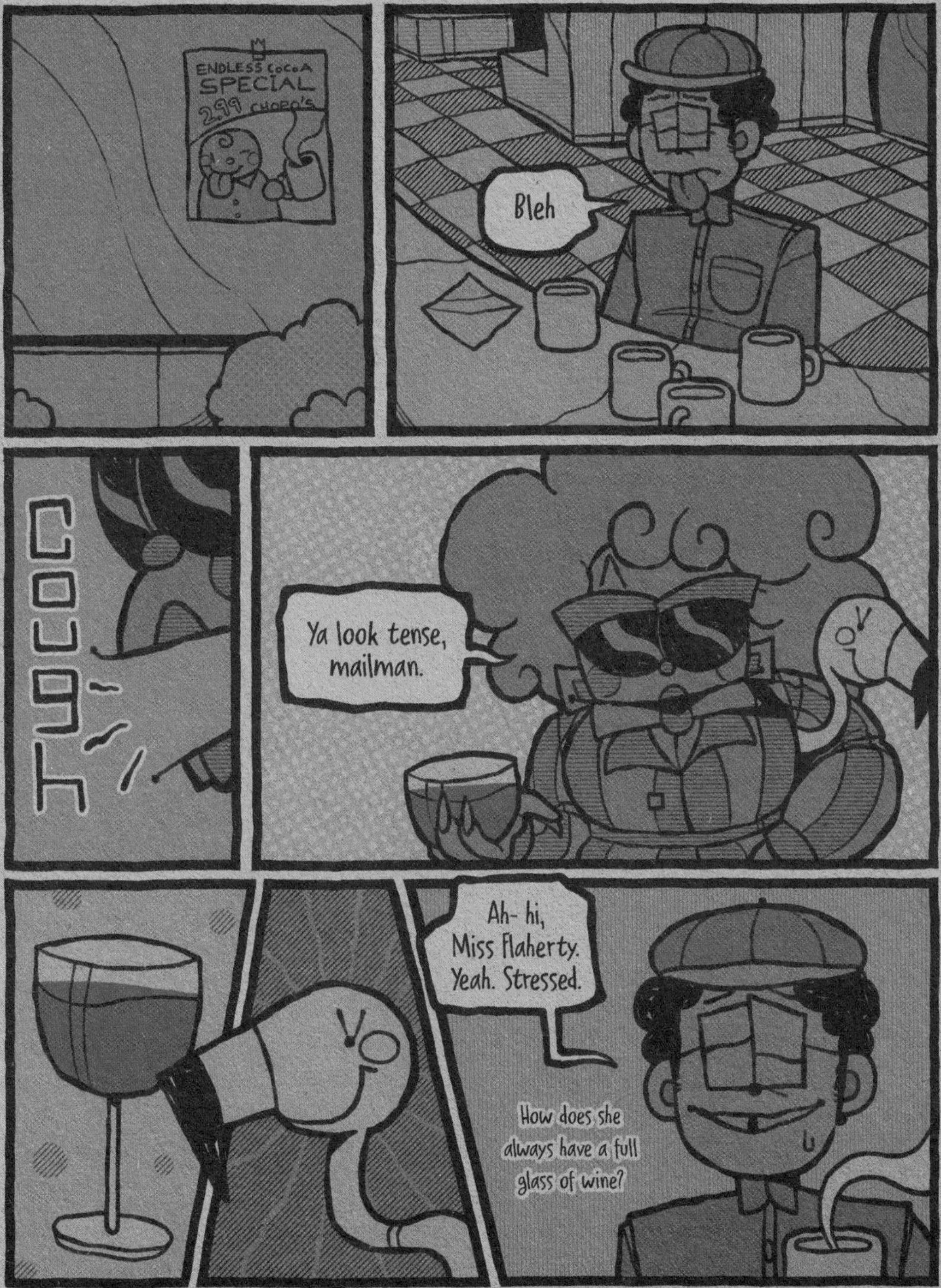
ENDLESS COCOA SPECIAL
2.99 CHOPO's
Bleh
COUGH
Ya look tense, mailman.
Ah- hi, Miss Flaherty. Yeah. Stressed.
How does she always have a full glass of wine?

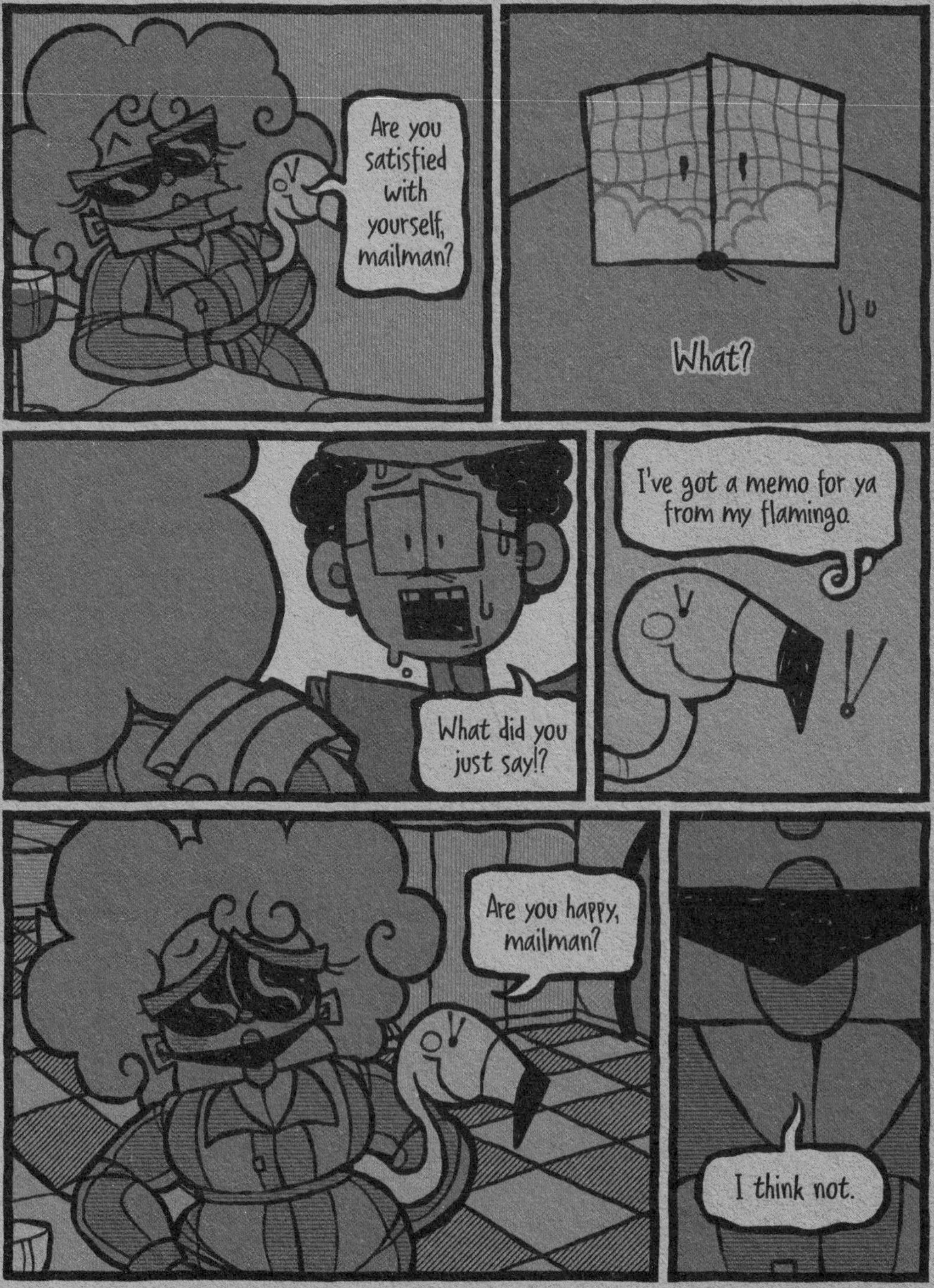
Are you satisfied with yourself, mailman?
What?
What did you just say!?
I've got a memo for ya from my flamingo.
Are you happy, mailman?
I think not.

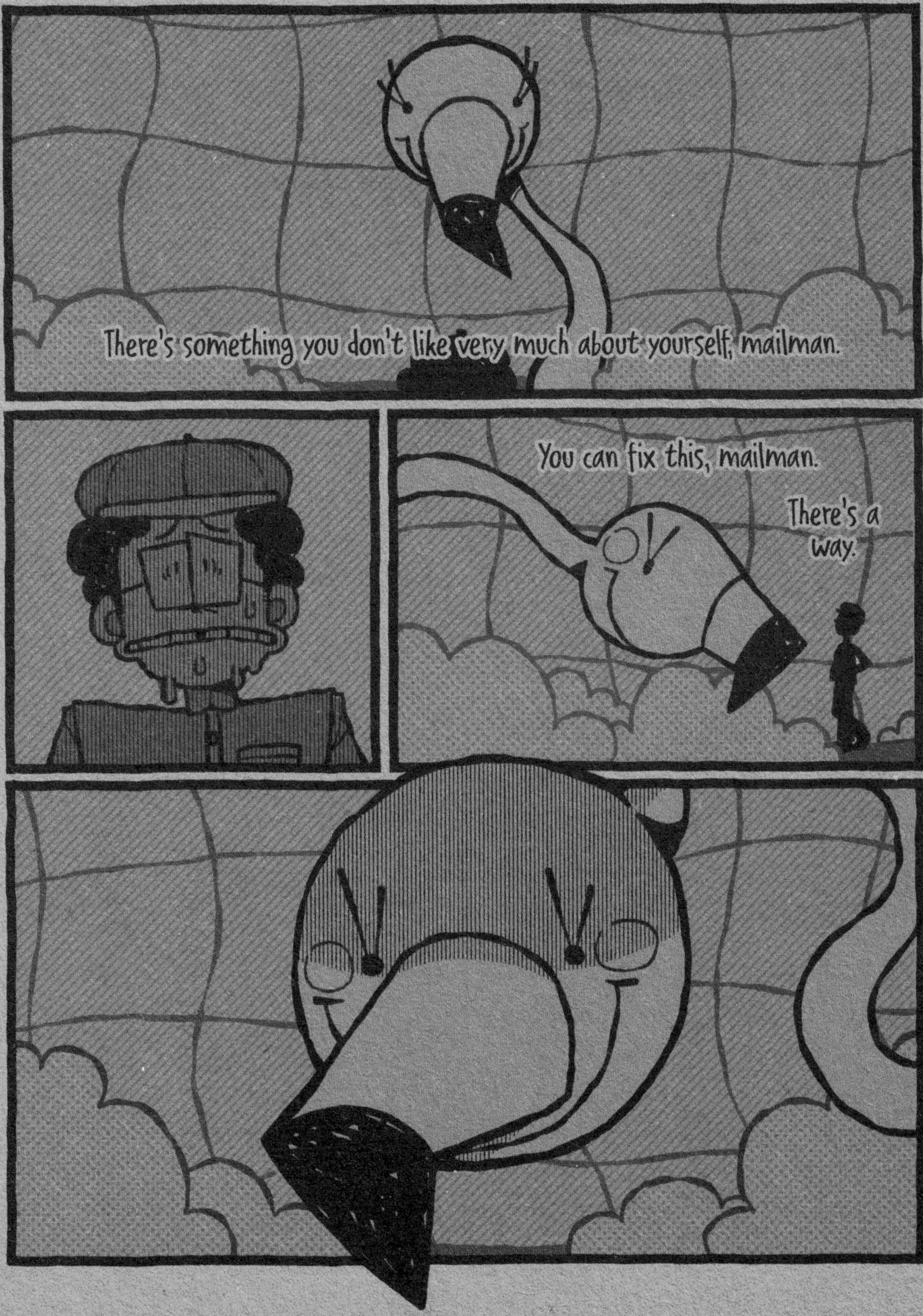
There's something you don't like very much about yourself, mailman.
You can fix this, mailman.
There's a way.

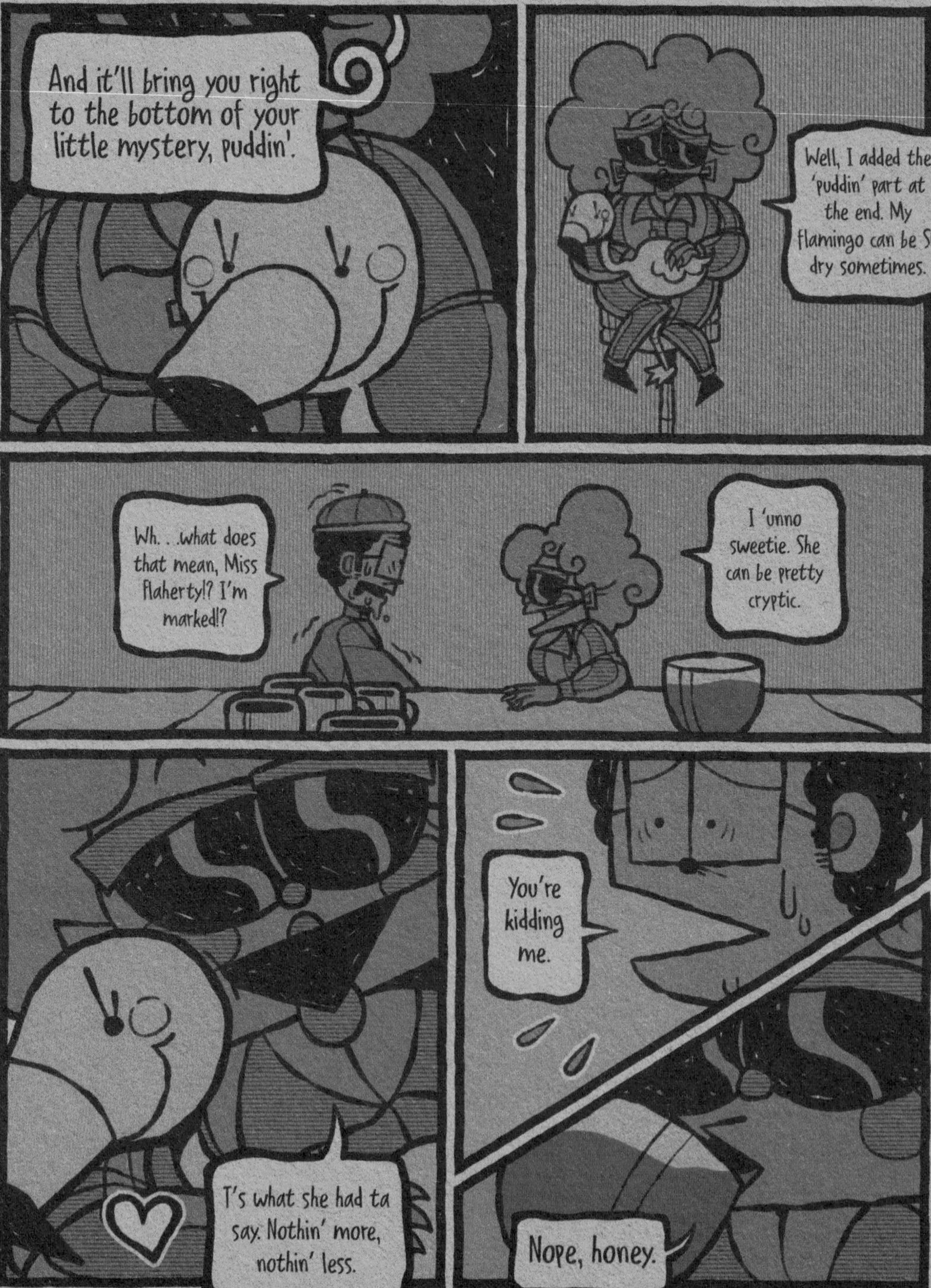
And it'll bring you right to the bottom of your little mystery, puddin'.
Well, I added the 'puddin' part at the end. My flamingo can be SO dry sometimes.
Wh. . .what does that mean, Miss Flaherty!? I'm marked!?
I 'unno sweetie. She can be pretty cryptic.
T's what she had ta say. Nothin' more, nothin' less.
You're kidding me.
Nope, honey.

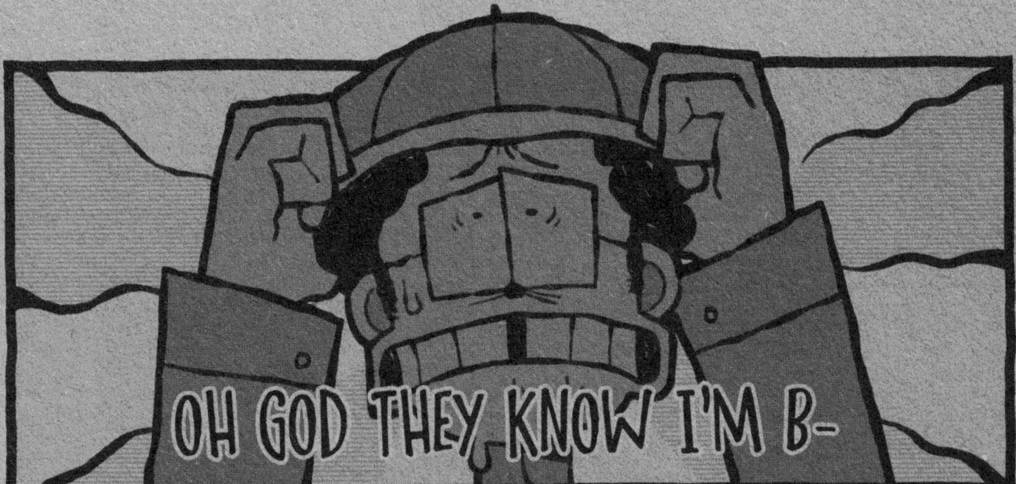
OH GOD THEY KNOW I'M B-

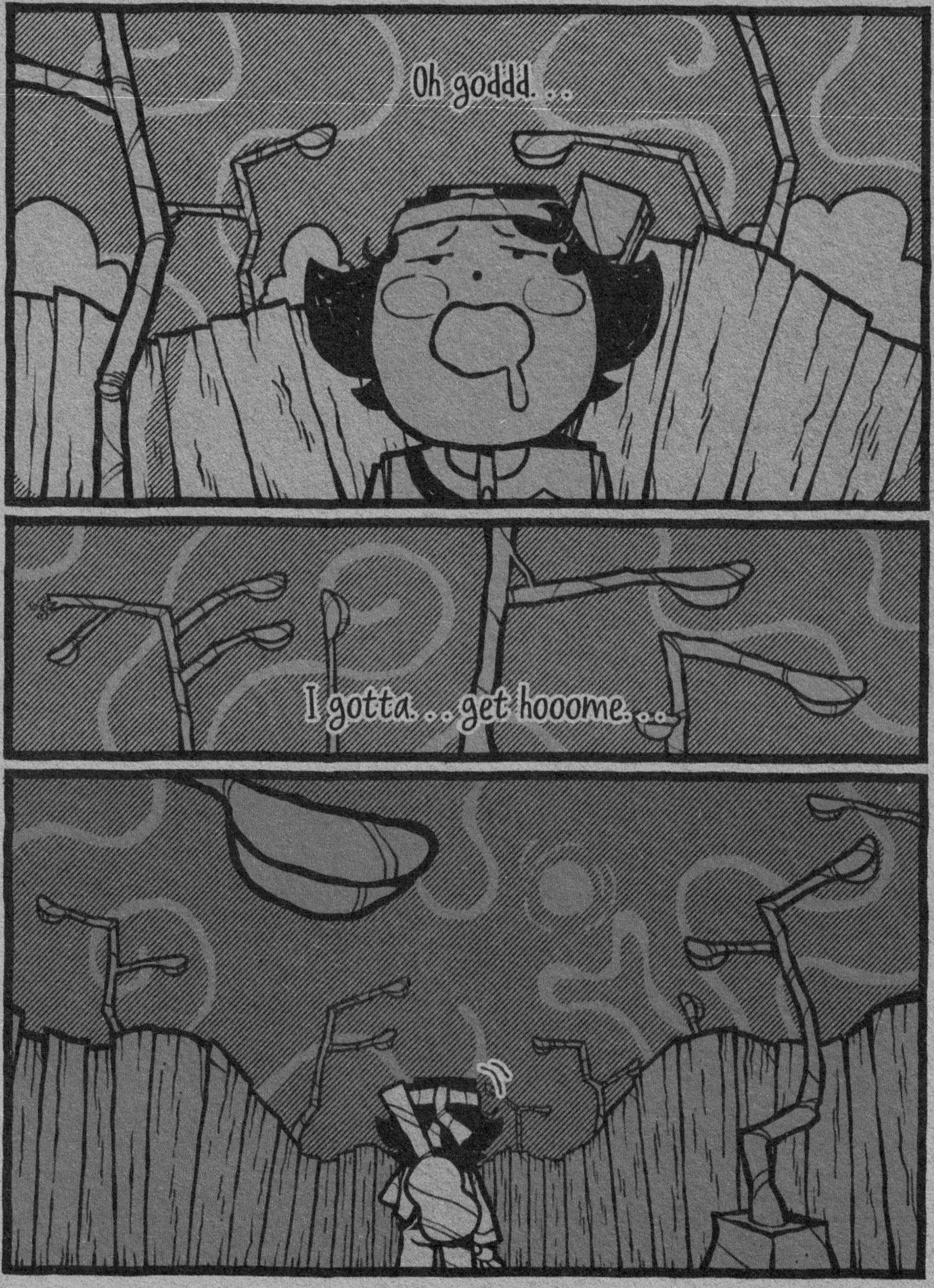
Oh goddd. . .
I gotta. . . get hooome. . .

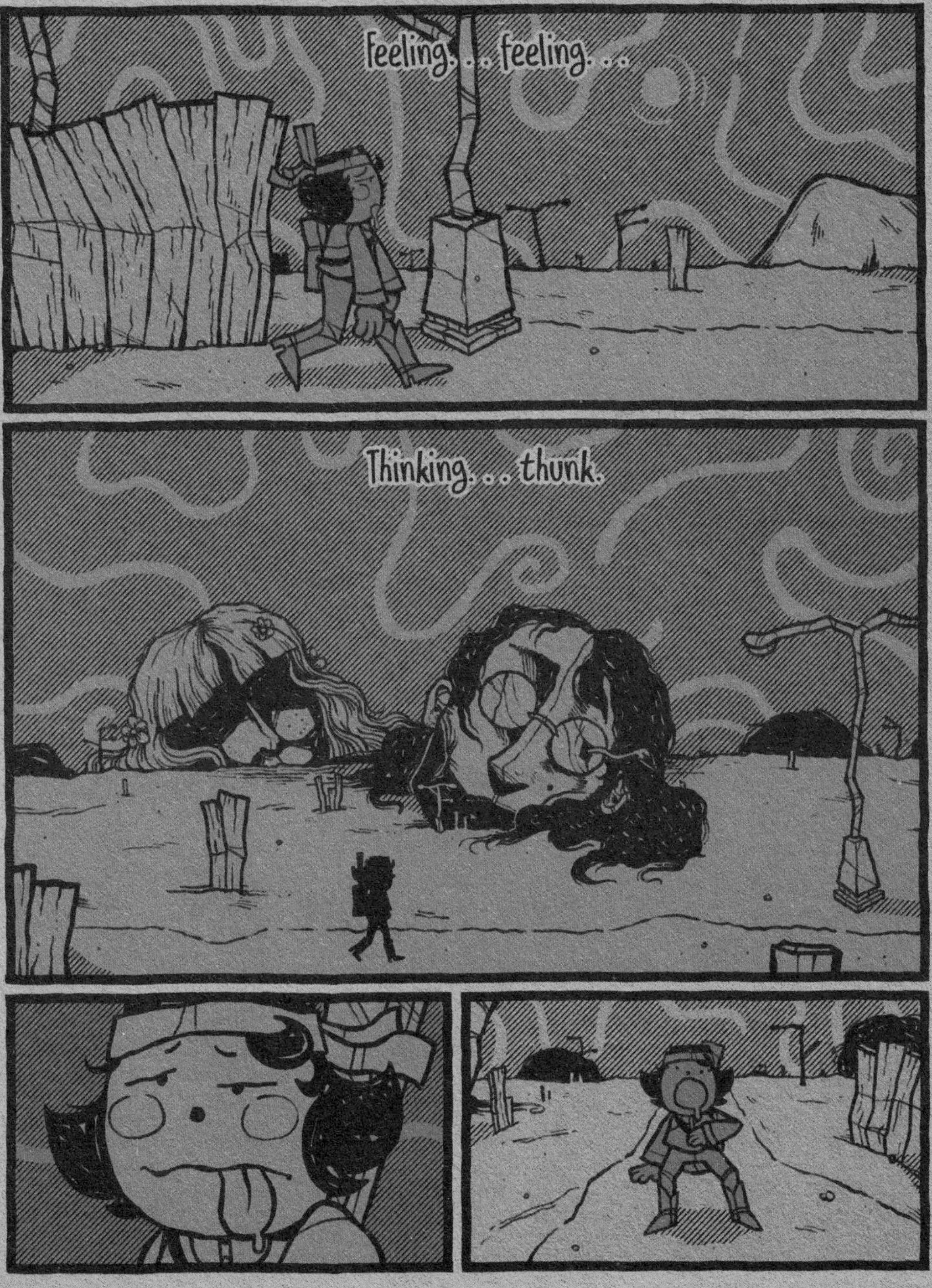
feeling. . . feeling. . .
Thinking. . . thunk.

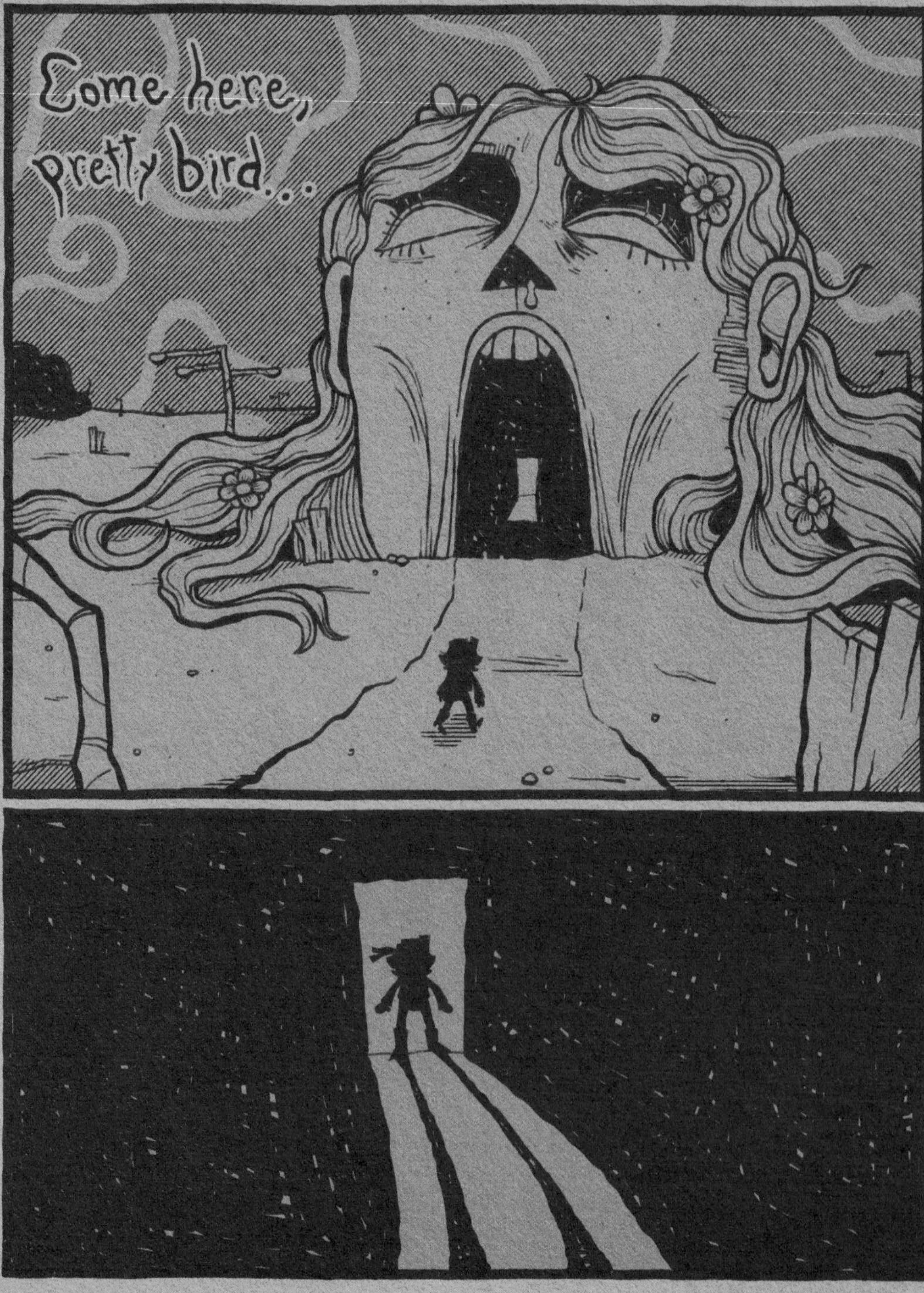
Come here, pretty bird...

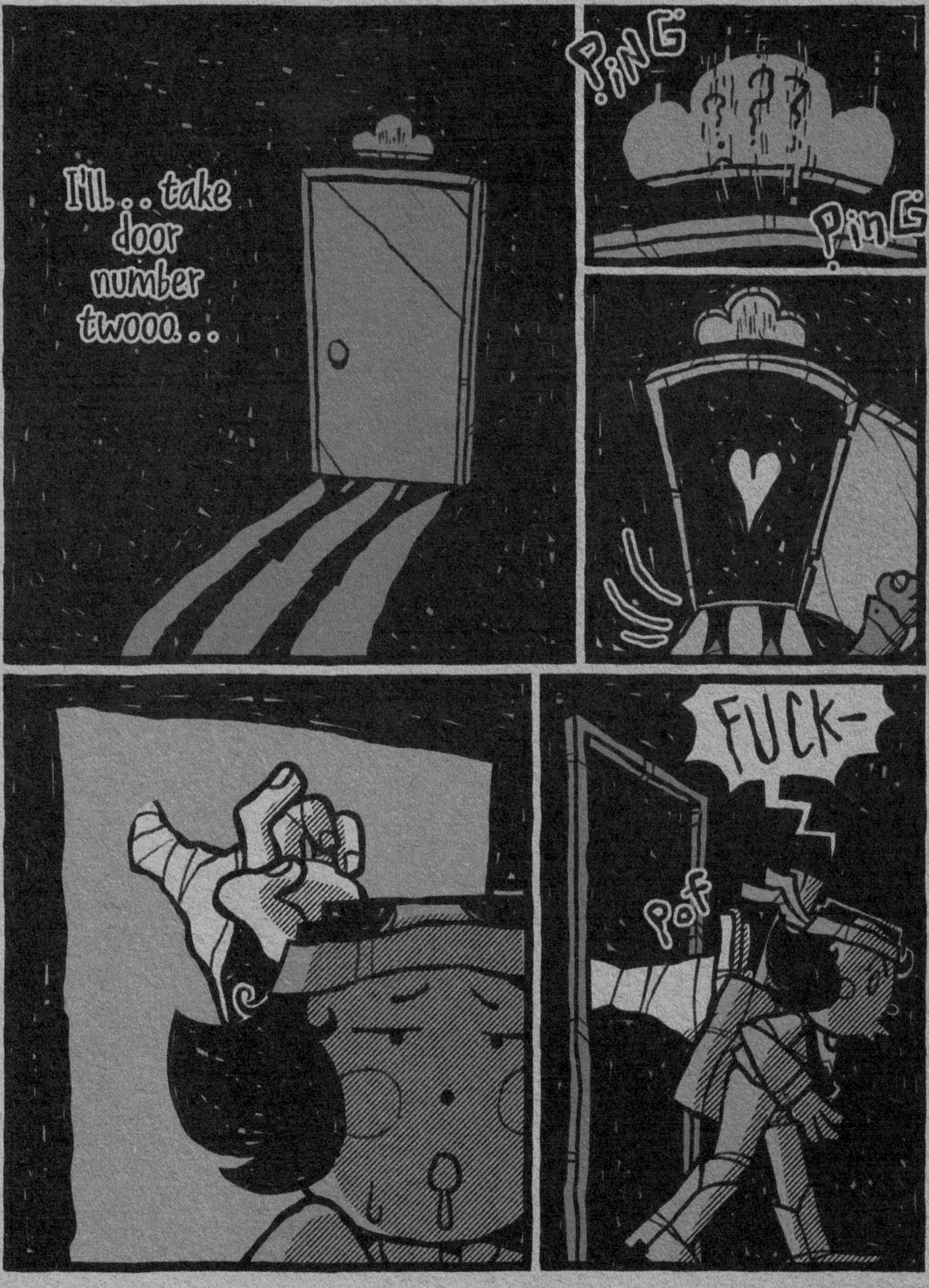
I'll . . take door number twooo. . .
PiNG
PiNG
FUCK-
Pof

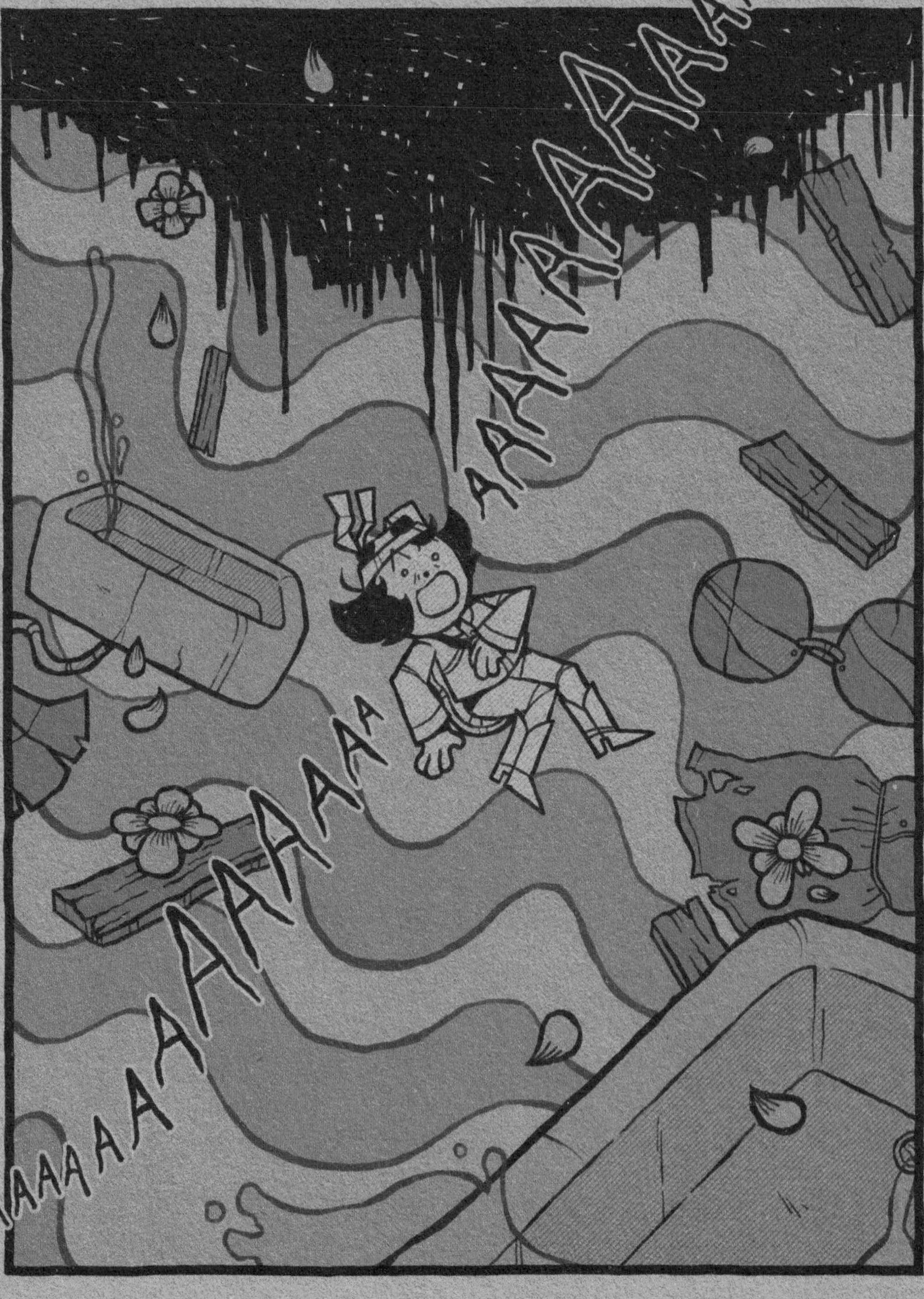
AAAAAAAAAAAAAAAAAAAAAAAAA

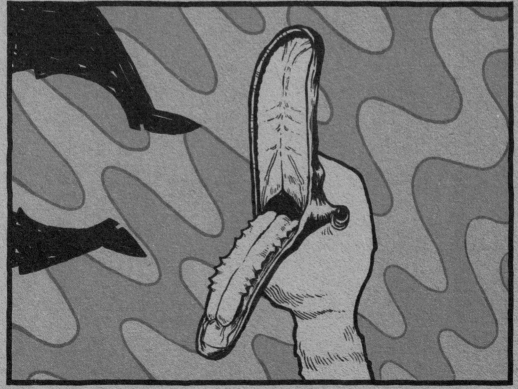

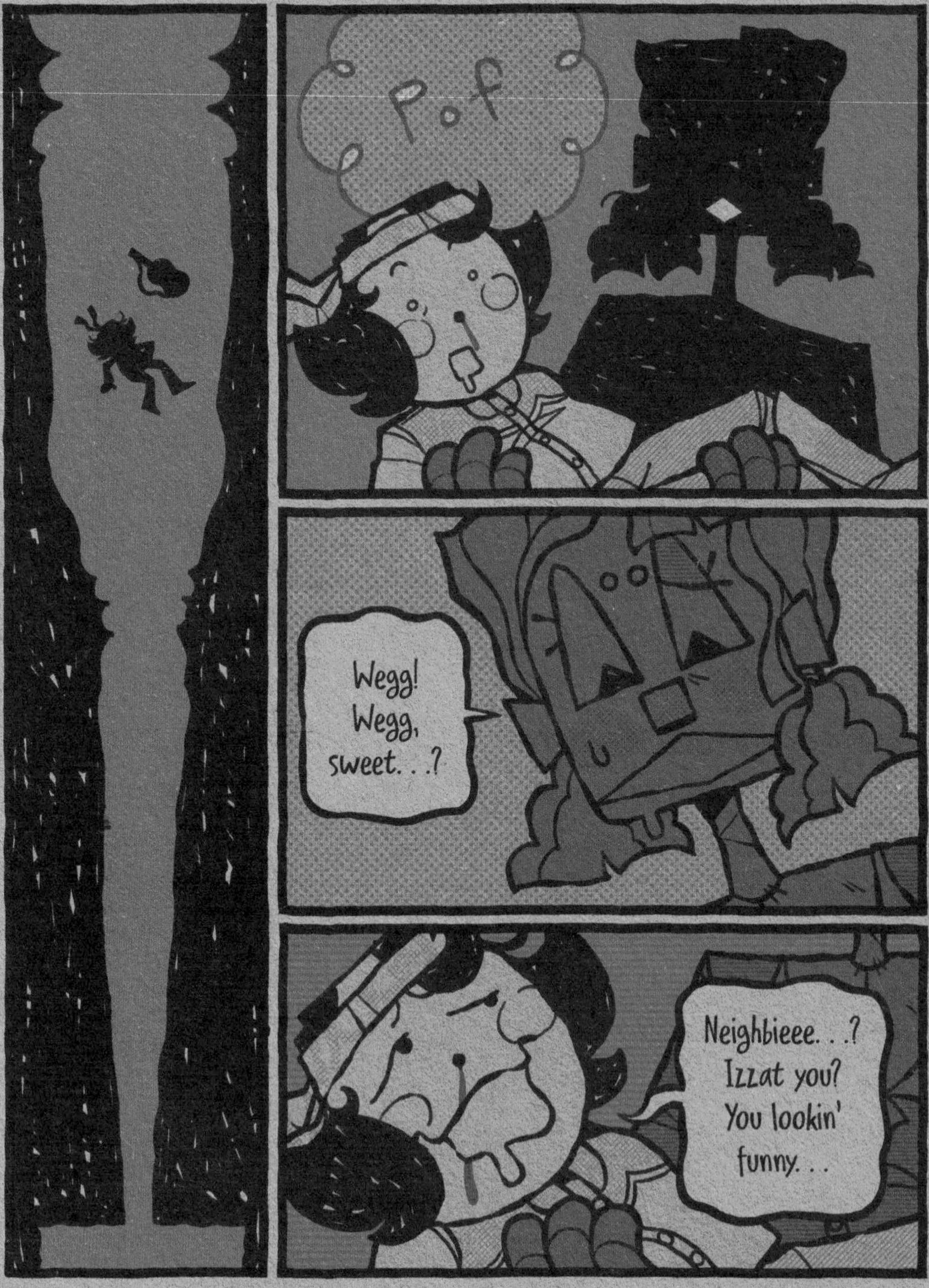
Pof
Wegg! Wegg, sweet. . .?
Neighbieee. . .? Izzat you? You lookin' funny. . .

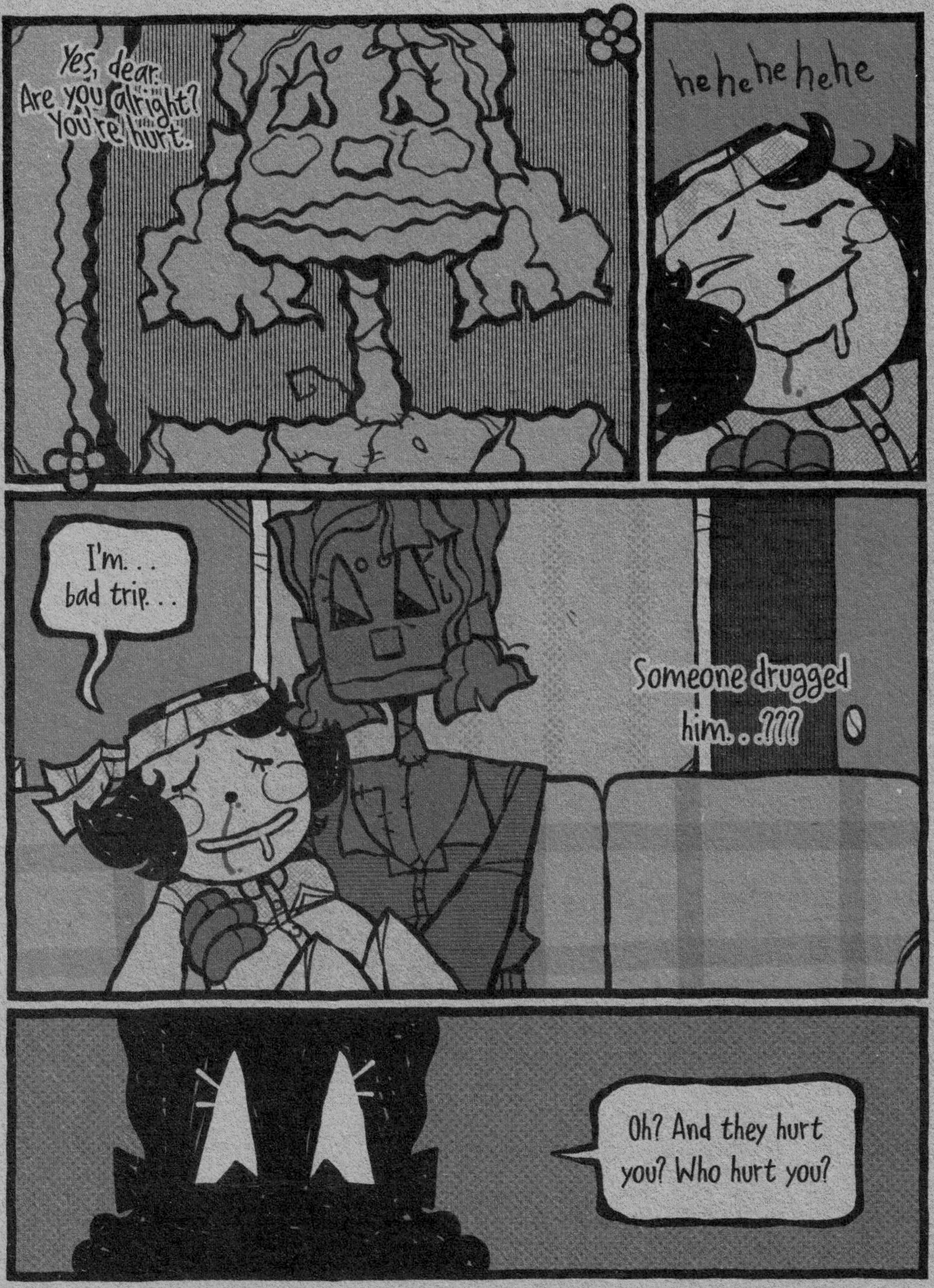
Yes, dear. Are you alright? You're hurt.
hehehehehehe
I'm. . . bad trip. . .
Someone drugged him. . .???
Oh? And they hurt you? Who hurt you?

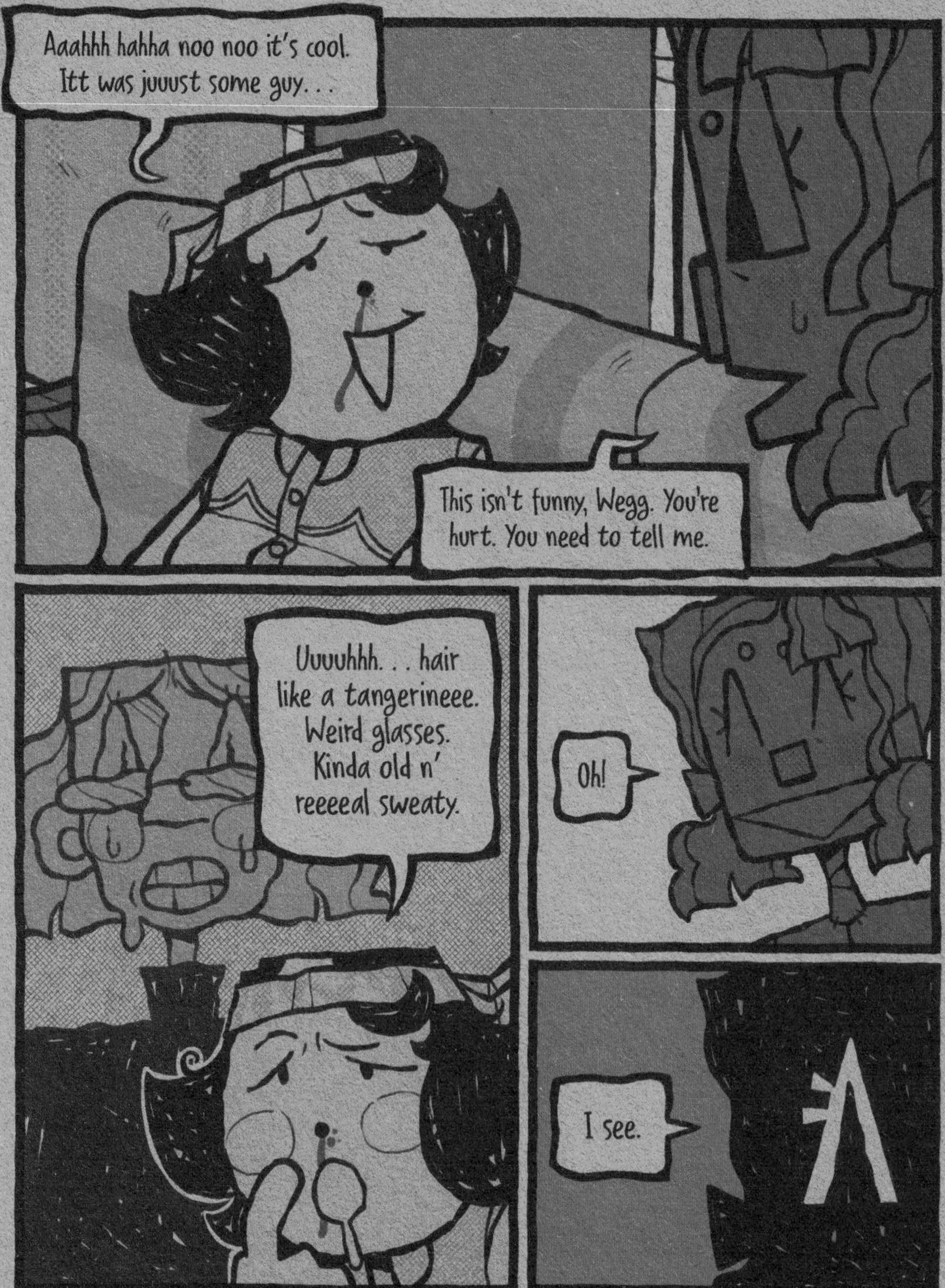
Aaahhh hahha noo noo it's cool. Itt was juuust some guy. . .
This isn't funny, Wegg. You're hurt. You need to tell me.
Uuuuhhh. . . hair like a tangerineee. Weird glasses. Kinda old n' reeeeal sweaty.
Oh!
I see.

I might know the guy.

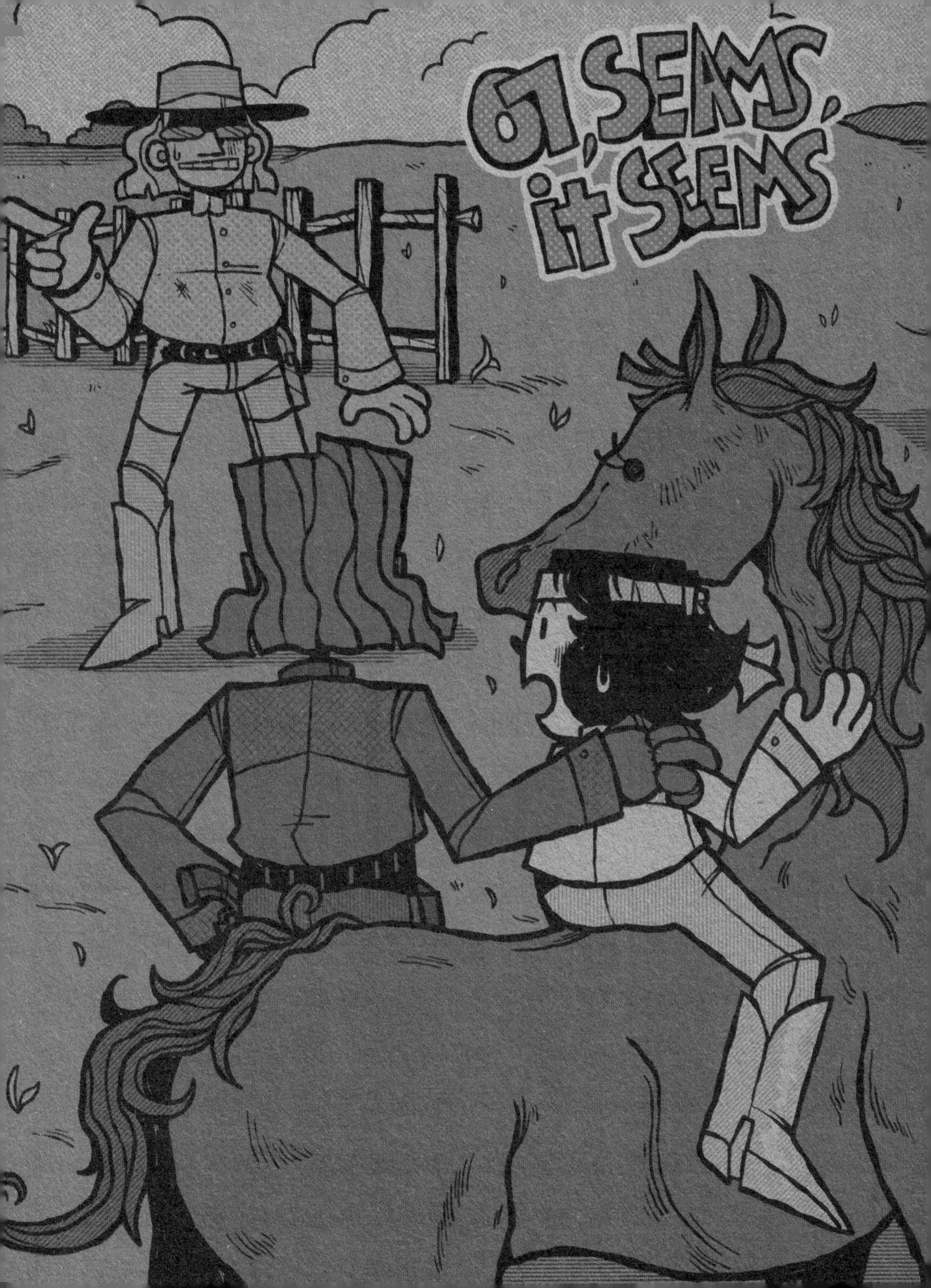
67, SEAMS, it SEEMS

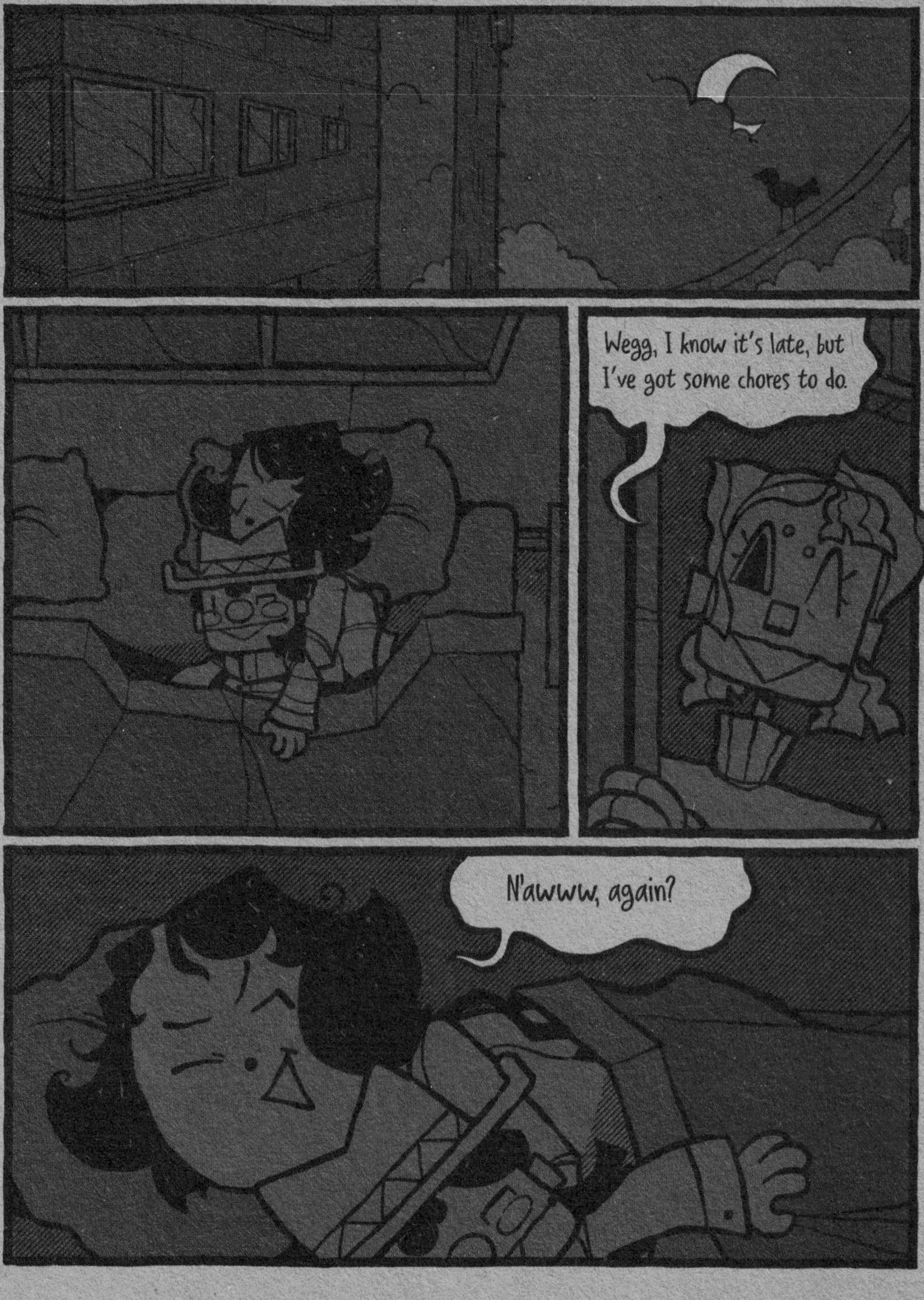
Wegg, I know it's late, but I've got some chores to do.
N'awww, again?

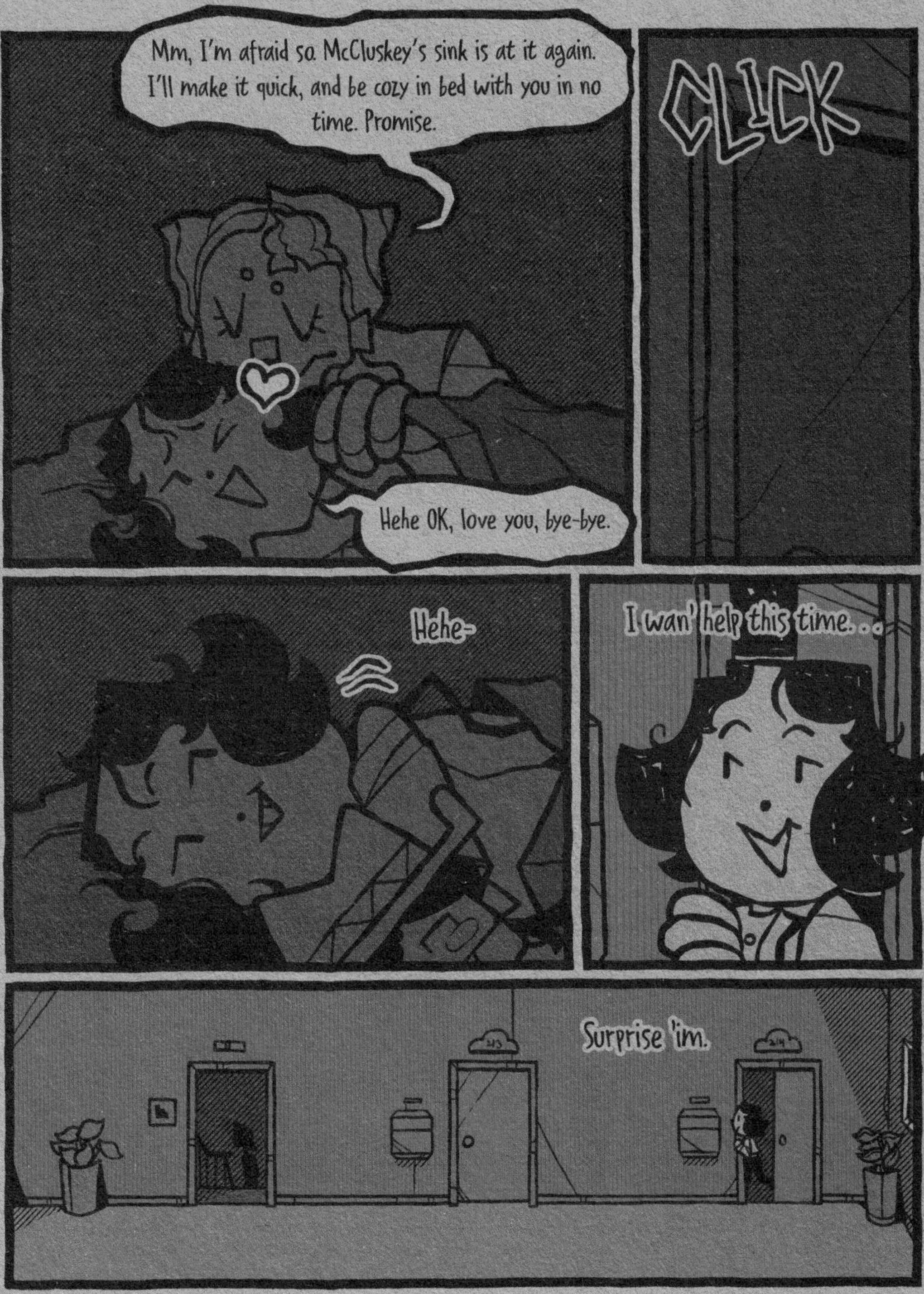
Mm, I'm afraid so. McCluskey's sink is at it again. I'll make it quick, and be cozy in bed with you in no time. Promise.
Hehe OK, love you, bye-bye.
CLICK
Hehe-
I wan' help this time. . .
Surprise 'im.

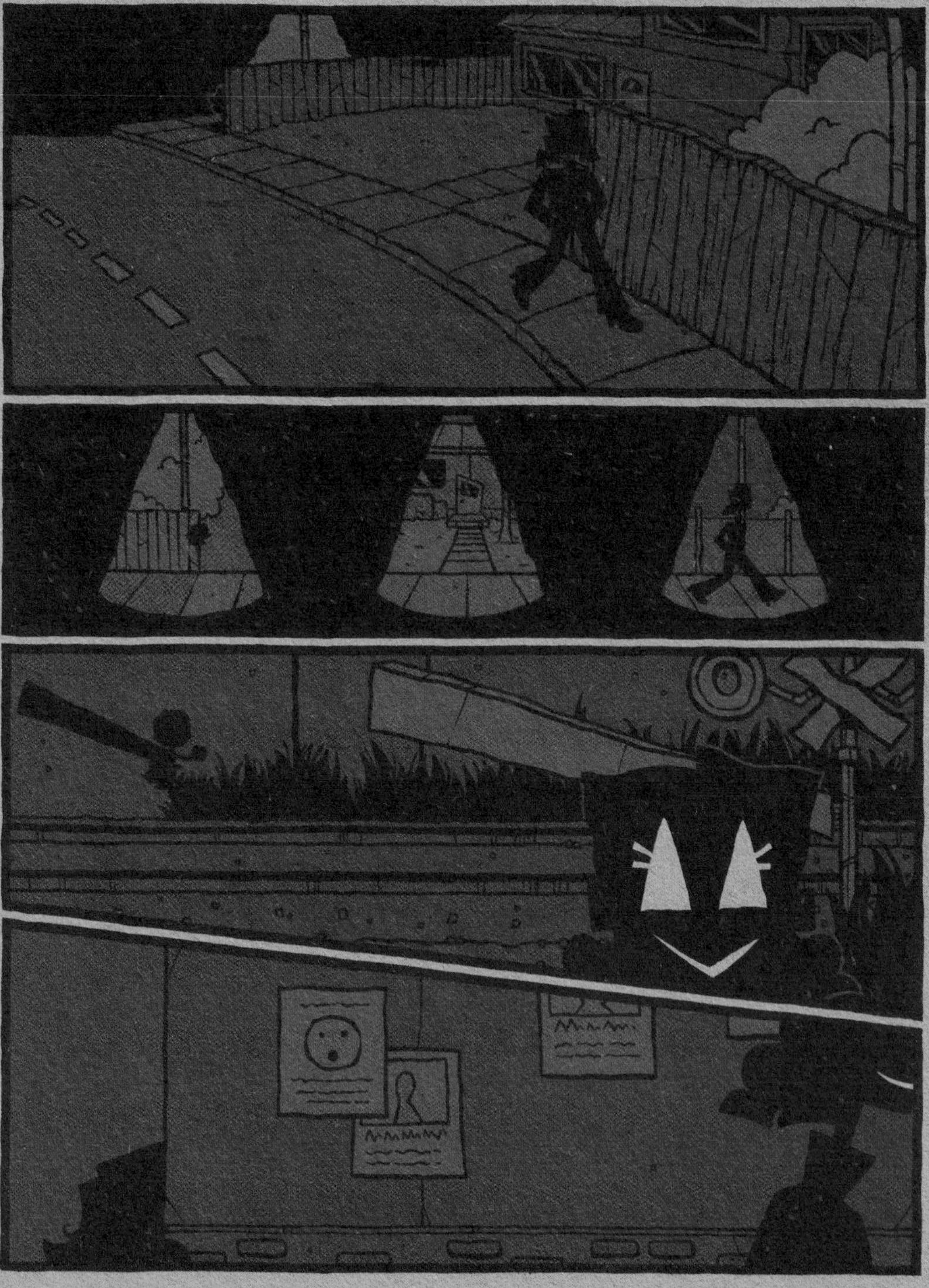

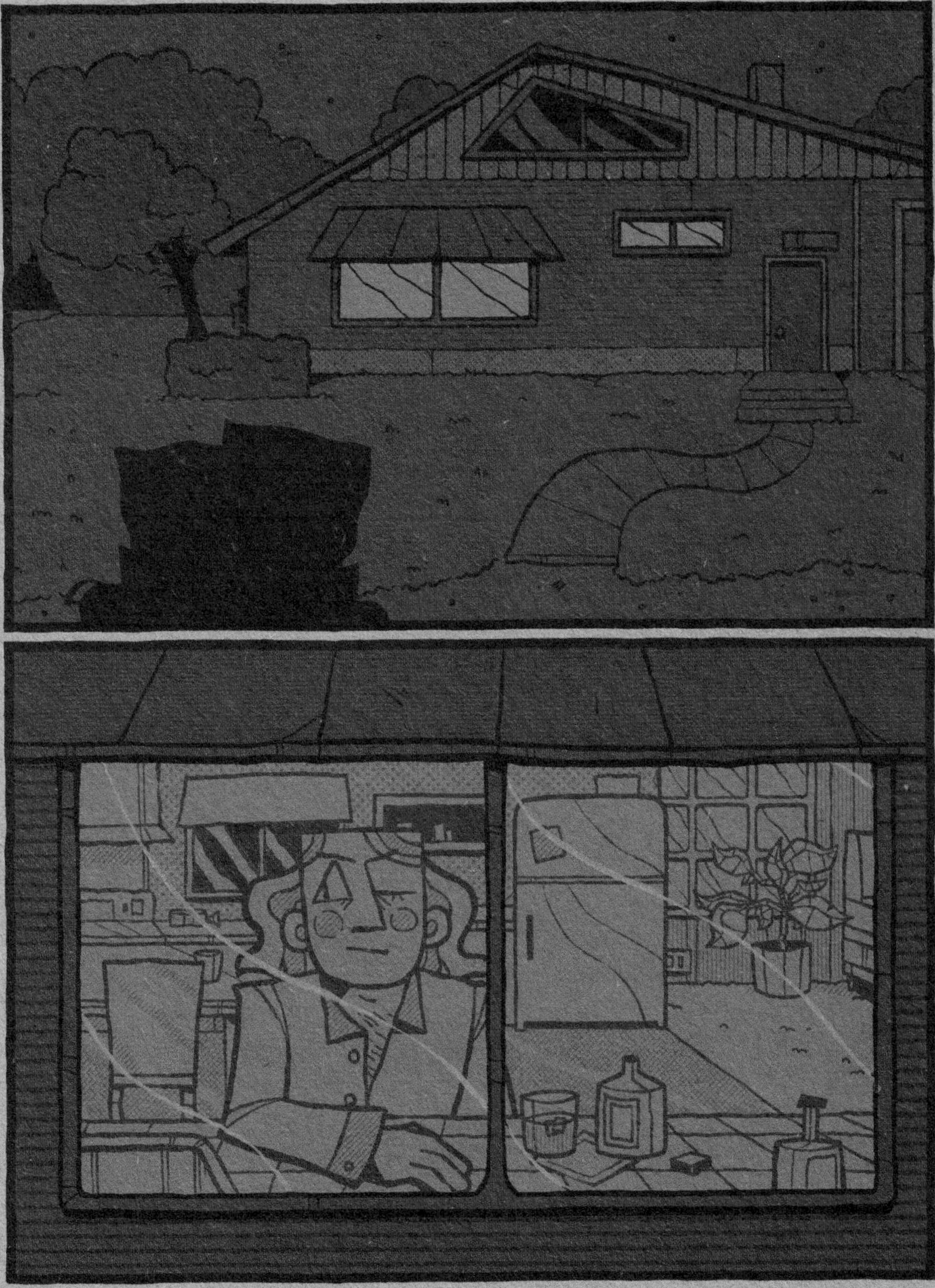

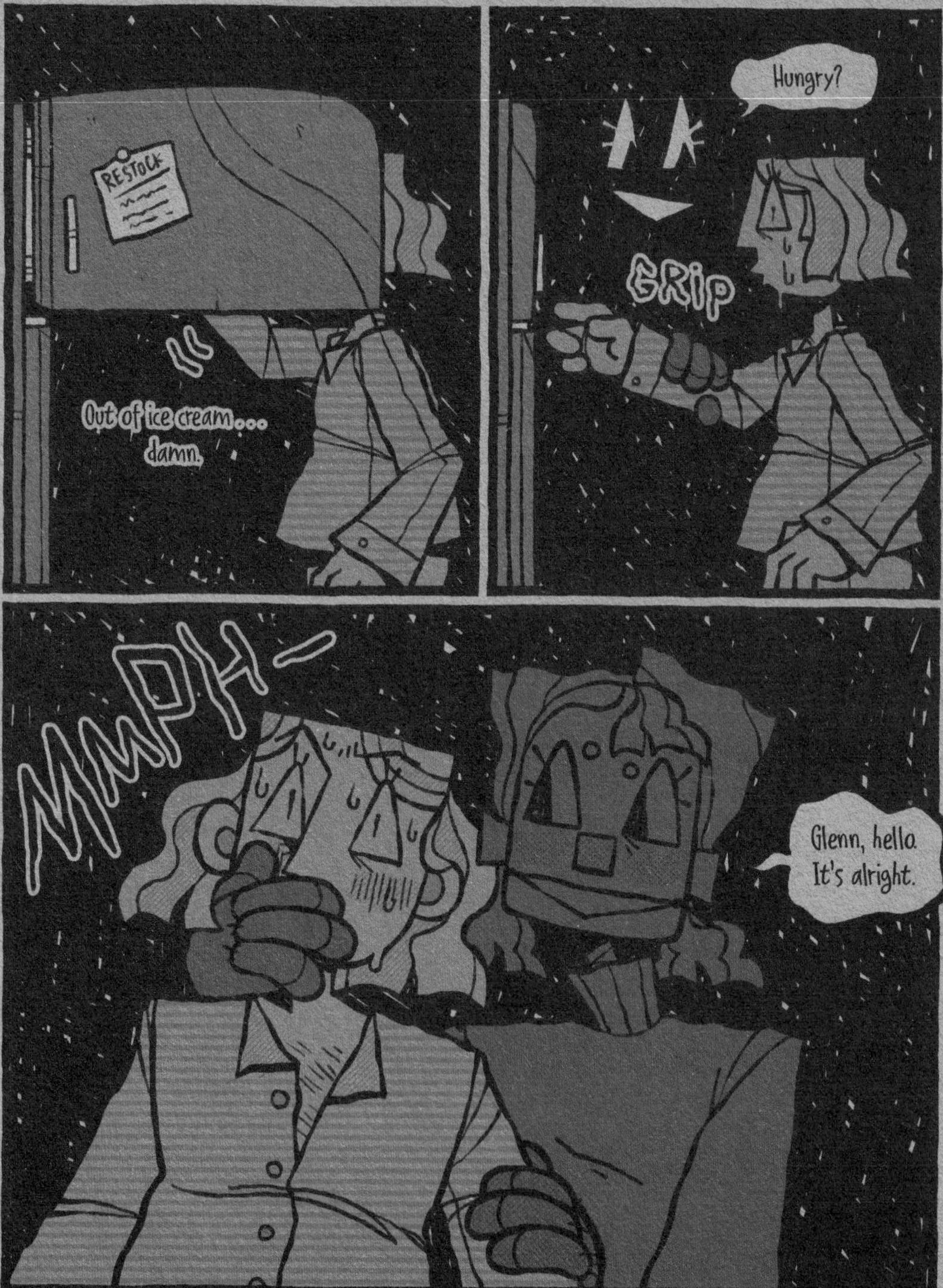
RESTOCK
Out of ice cream...
damn.
Hungry?
GRip
MMPH-
Glenn, hello.
It's alright.

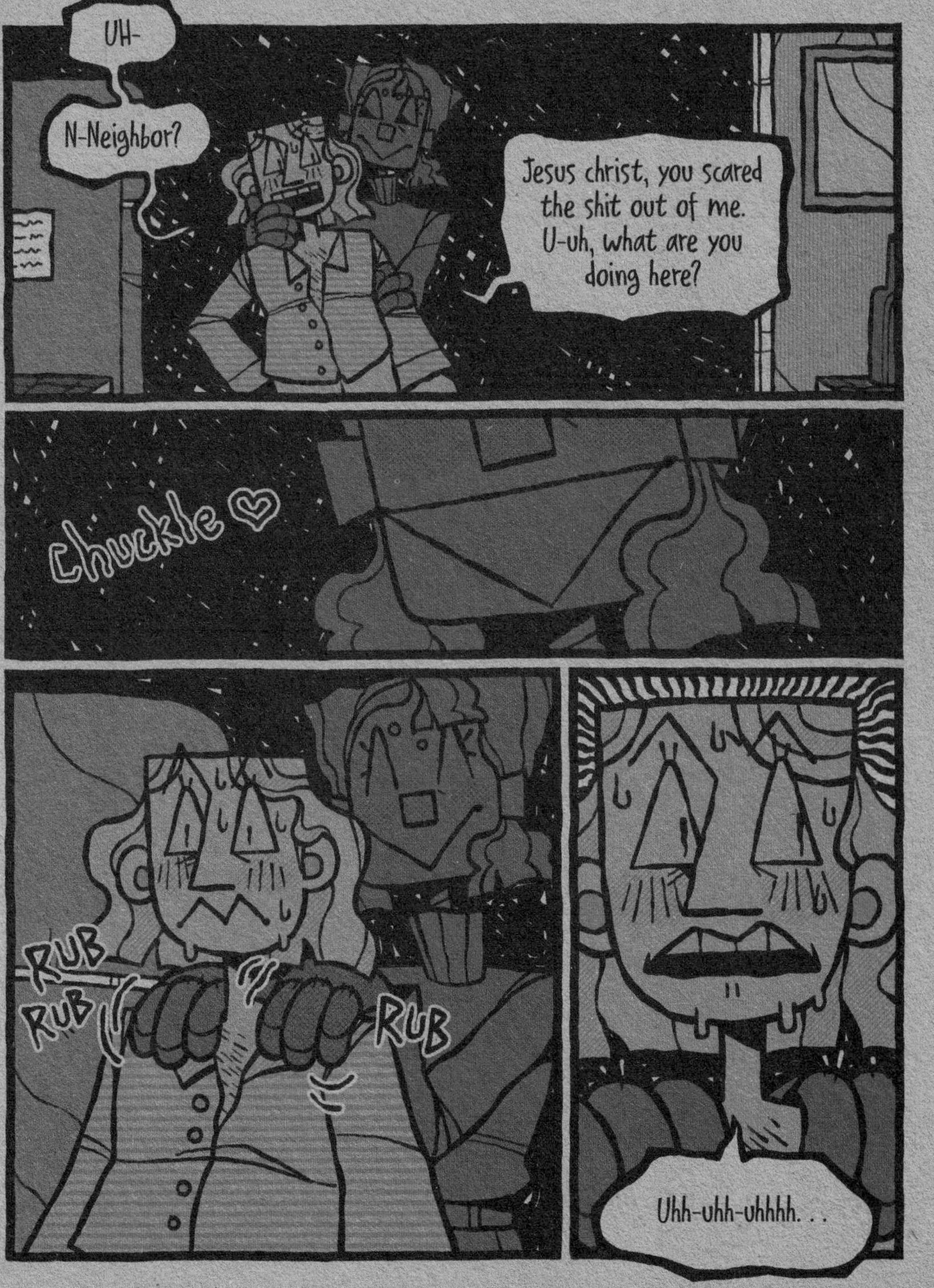
UH-
N-Neighbor?
Jesus christ, you scared the shit out of me. U-uh, what are you doing here?
chuckle ♡
RUB RUB
RUB
Uhh-uhh-uhhhh. . .

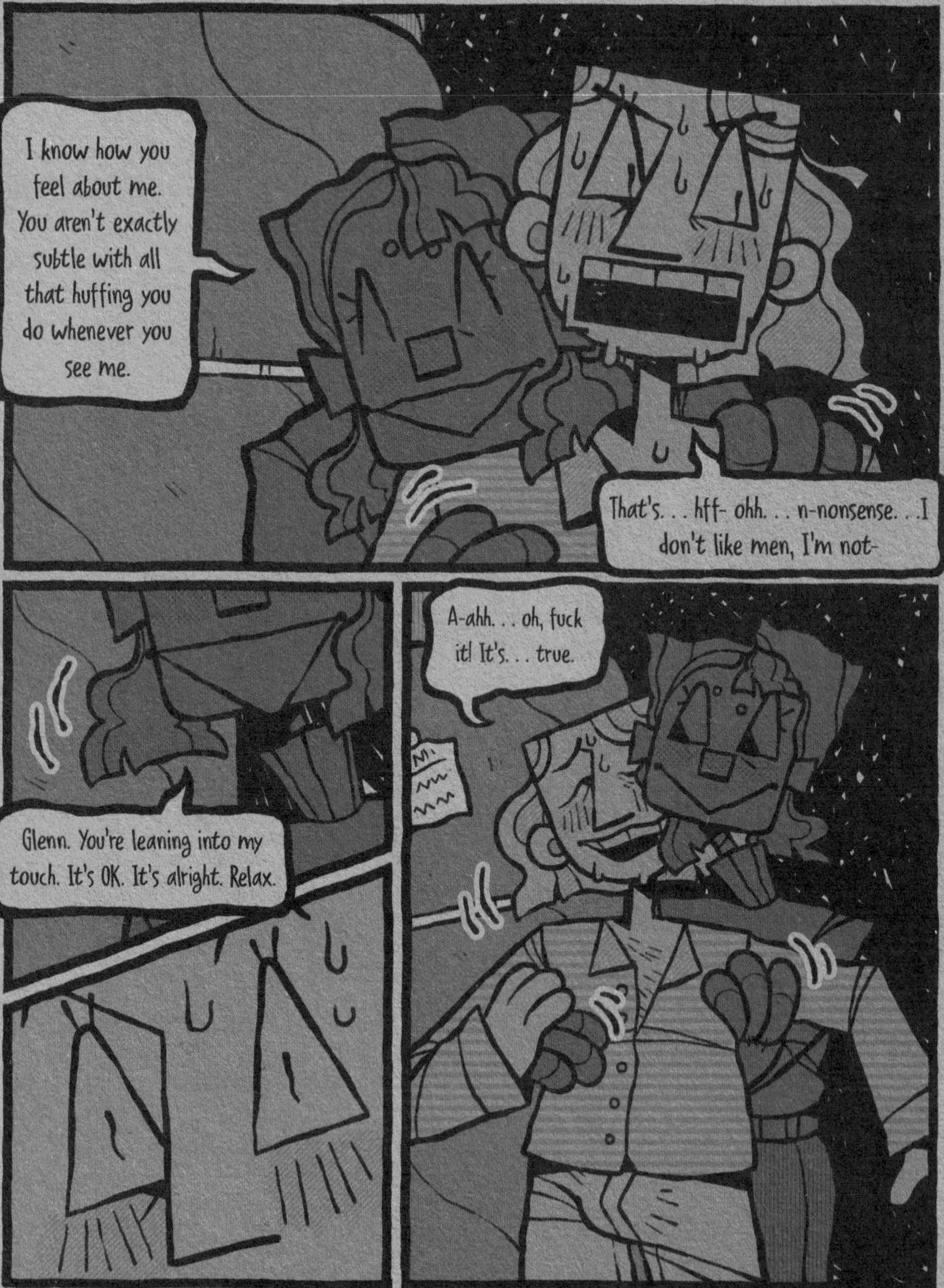
I know how you feel about me. You aren't exactly subtle with all that huffing you do whenever you see me.
That's. . . hff- ohh. . . n-nonsense. . .I don't like men, I'm not-
Glenn. You're leaning into my touch. It's OK. It's alright. Relax.
A-ahh. . . oh, fuck it! It's. . . true.

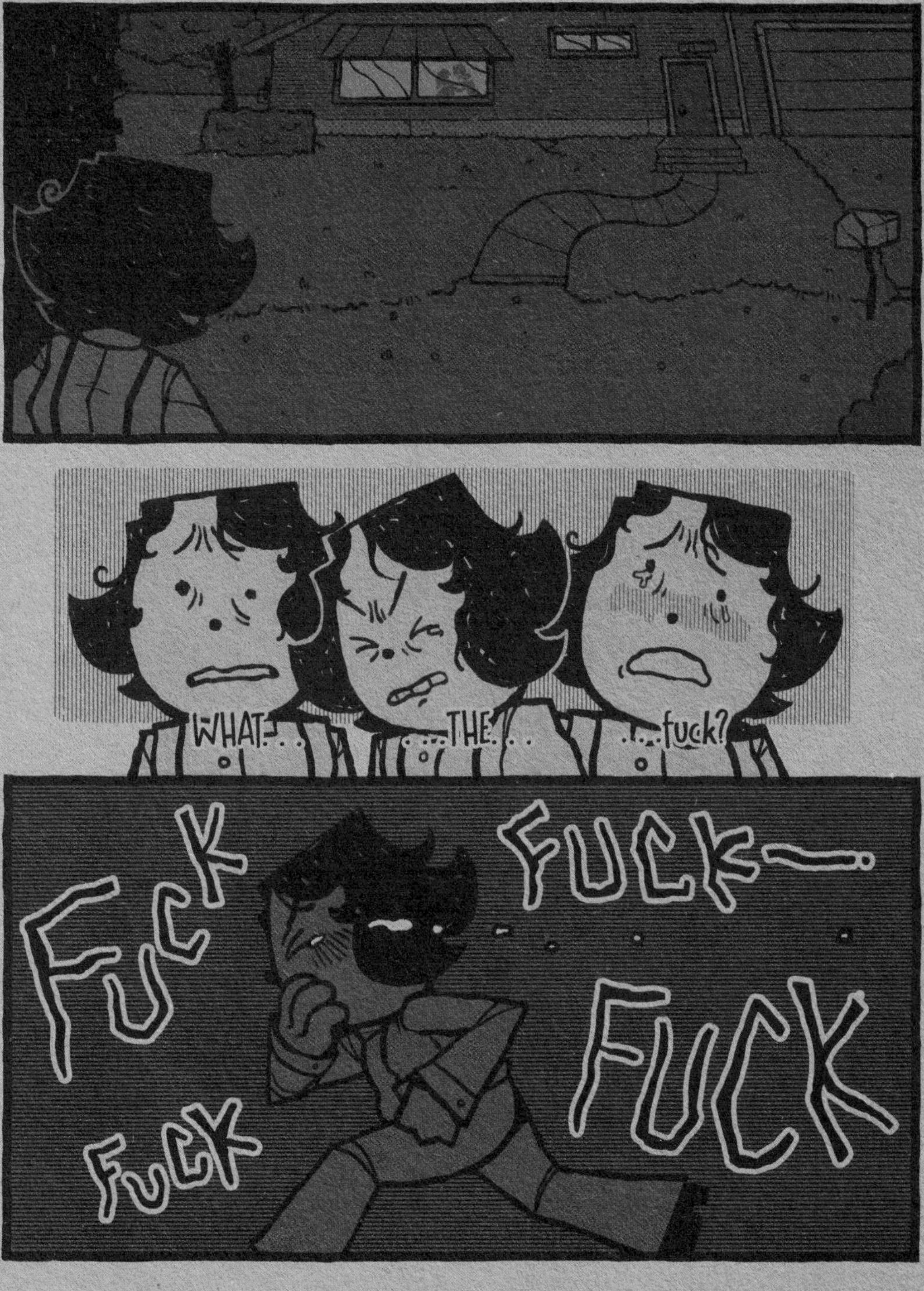
WHAT. . .
. . .THE. . .
. . .fuck?
FUCK
FUCK—. . . .
FUCK
FUCK

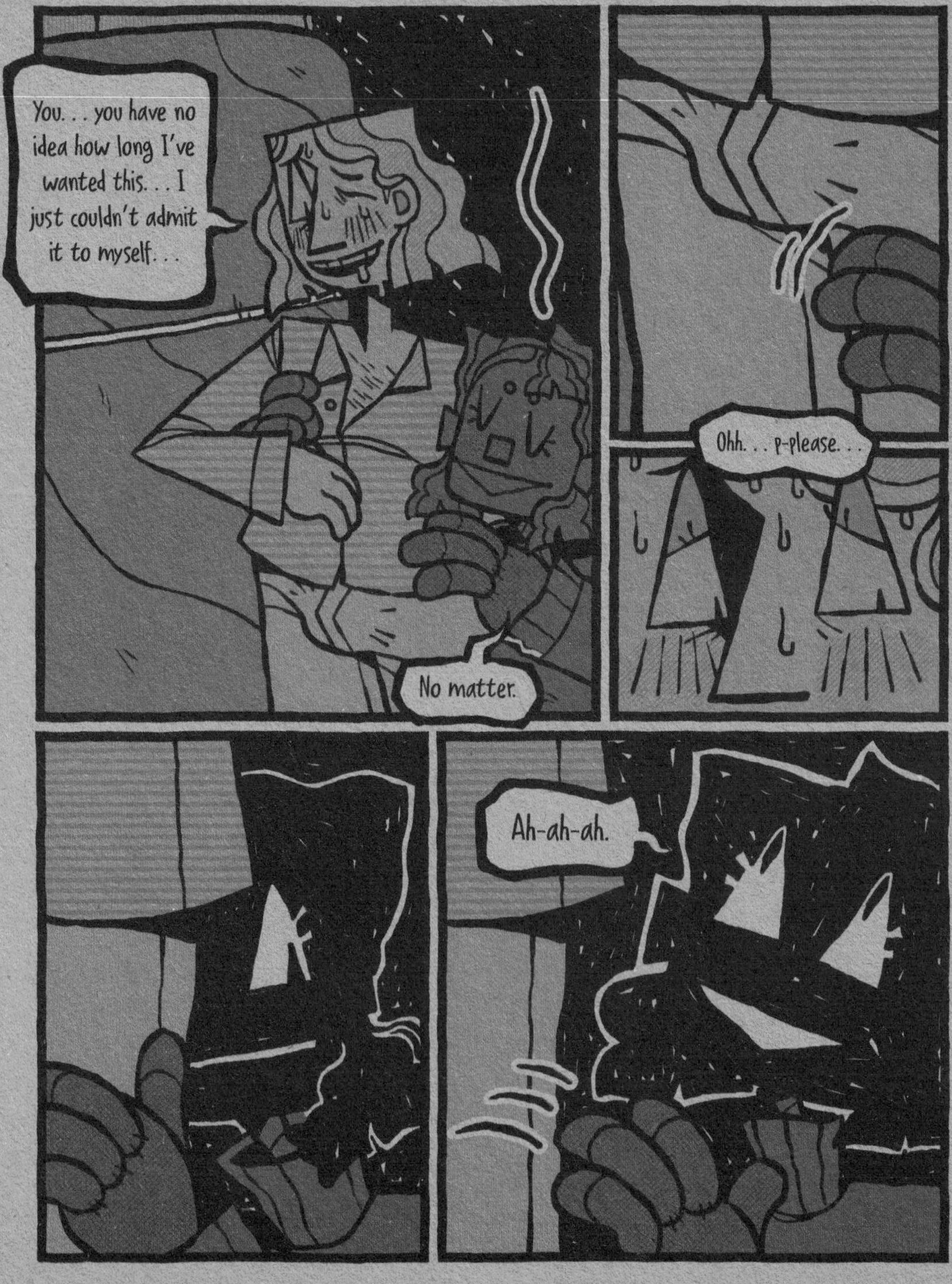
You. . . you have no idea how long I've wanted this. . . I just couldn't admit it to myself. . .
No matter.
Ohh. . . p-please. . .
Ah-ah-ah.

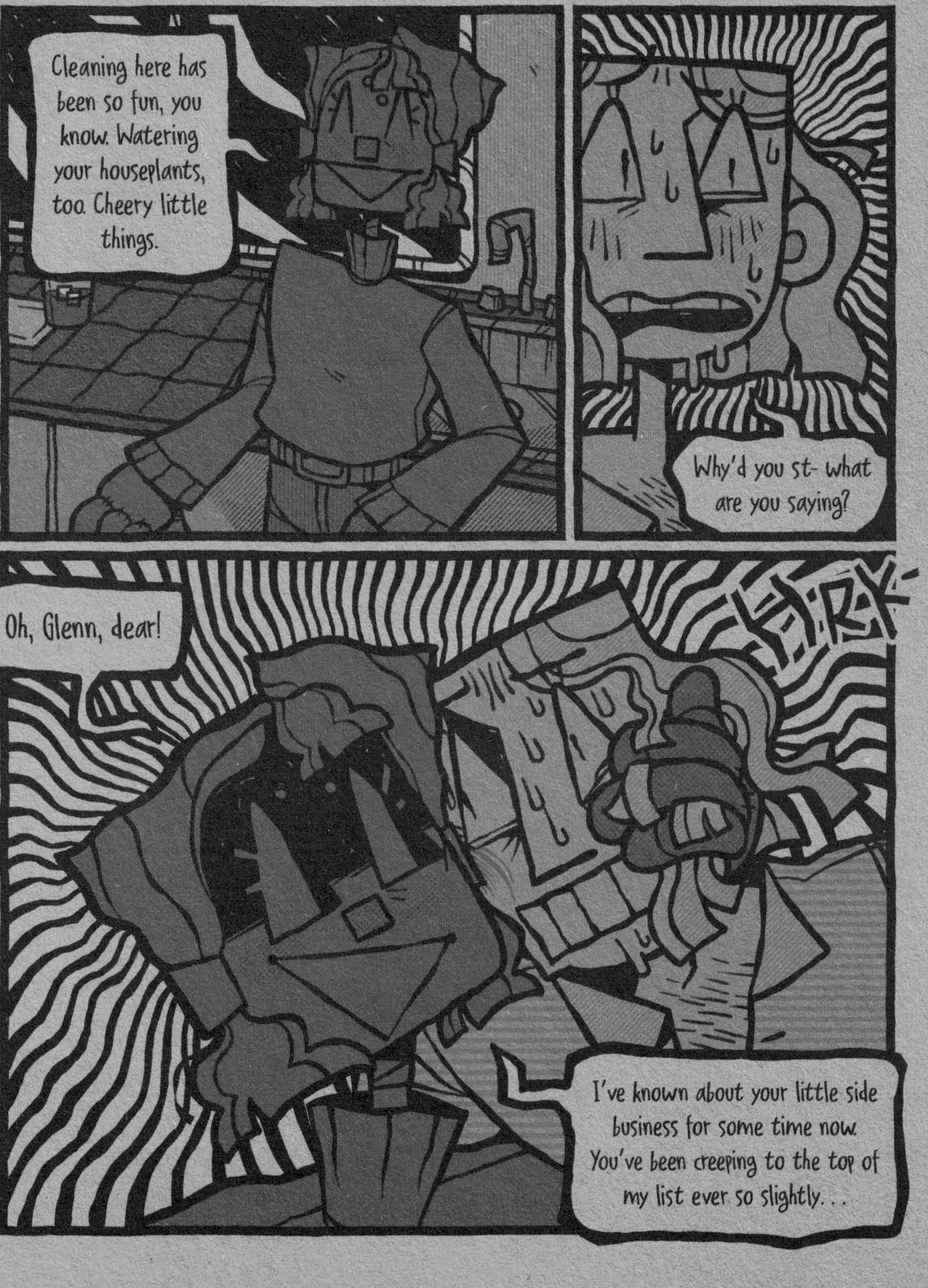
Cleaning here has been so fun, you know. Watering your houseplants, too. Cheery little things.
Why'd you st- what are you saying?
Oh, Glenn, dear!
HURK
I've known about your little side business for some time now. You've been creeping to the top of my list ever so slightly. . .

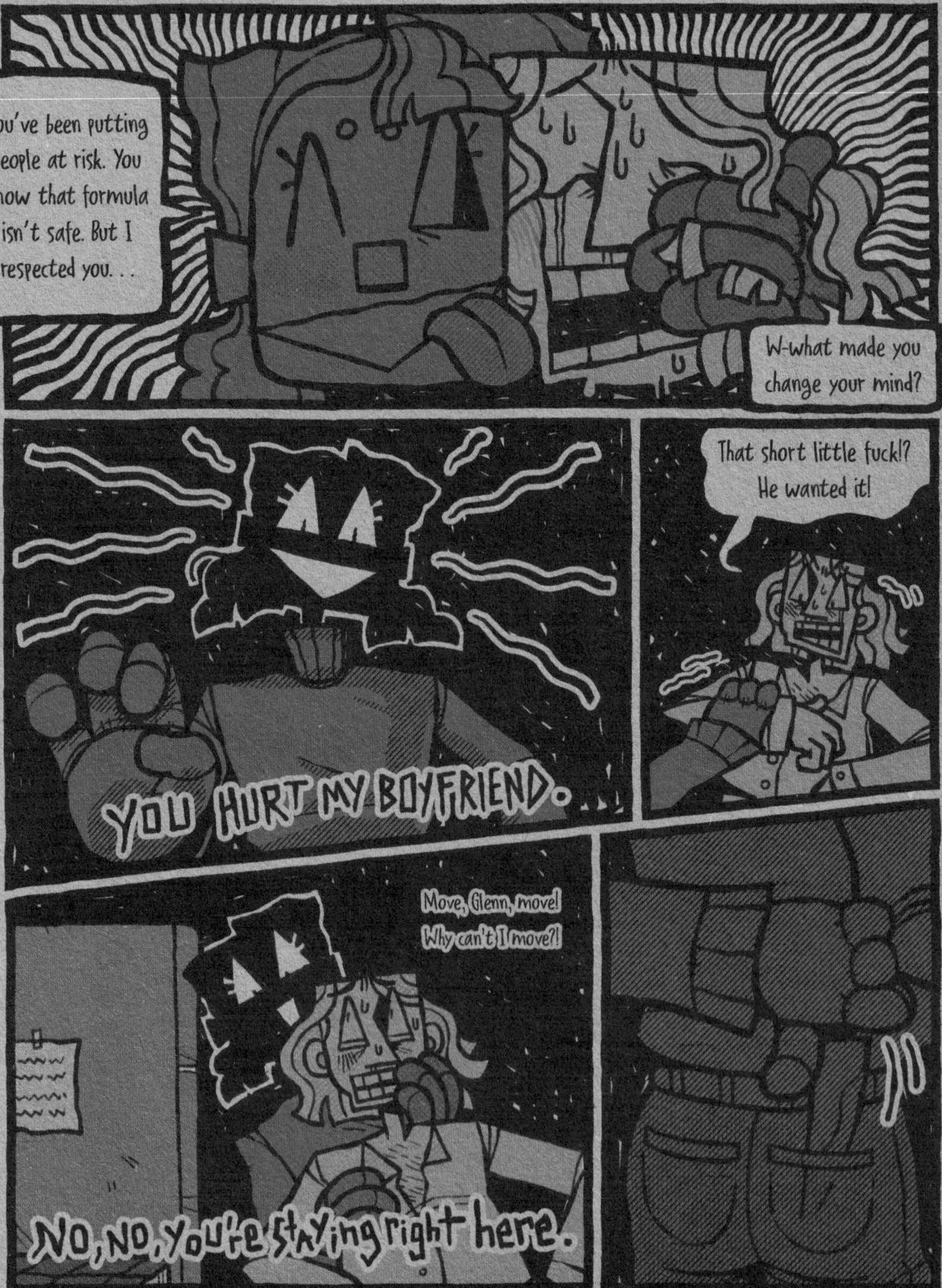
You've been putting people at risk. You know that formula isn't safe. But I respected you. . .
W-what made you change your mind?
YOU HURT MY BOYFRIEND.
That short little fuck!? He wanted it!
Move, Glenn, move!
Why can't I move?!
NO, NO, YOU'RE STAYING RIGHT HERE.

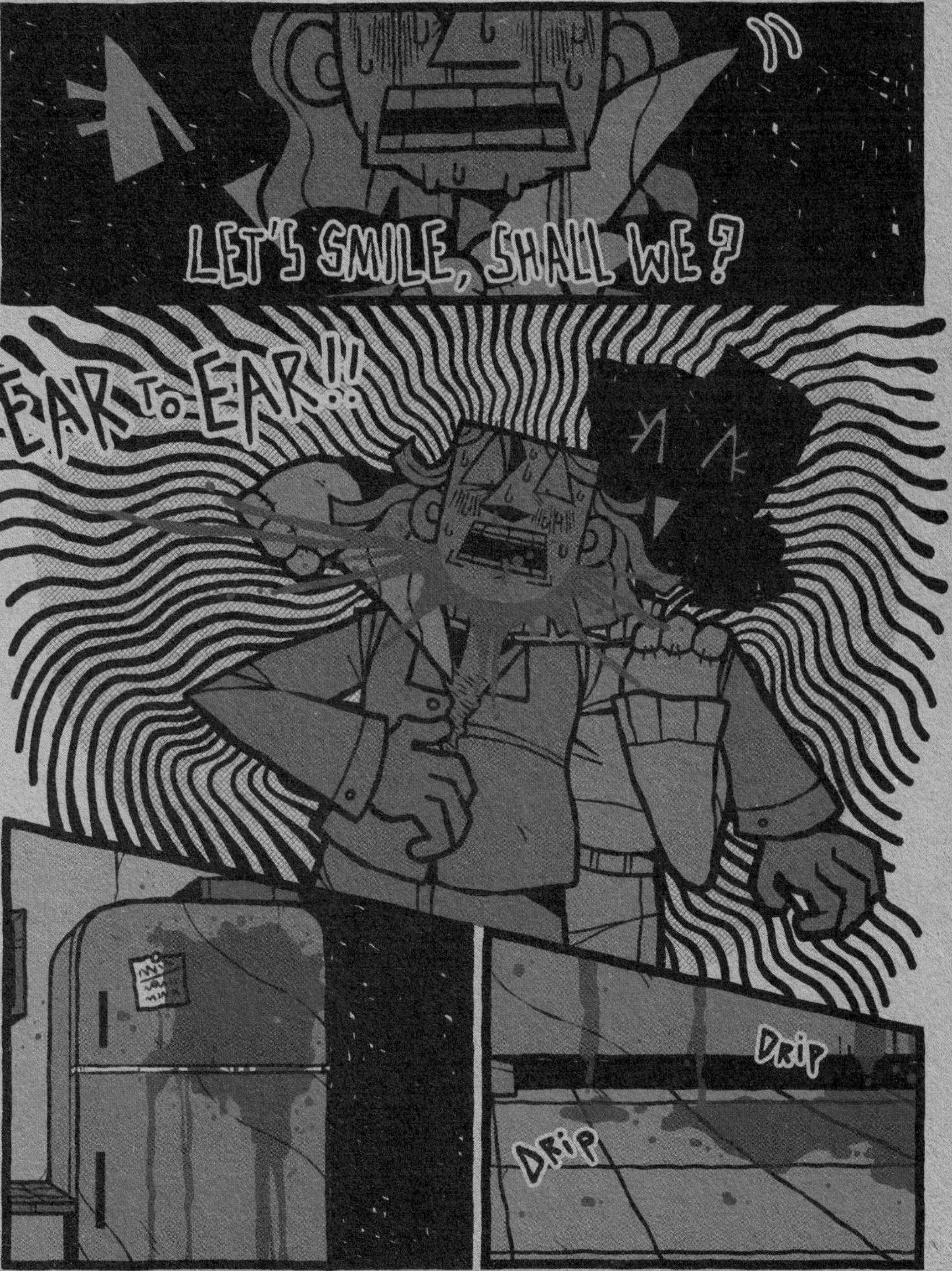
LET'S SMILE, SHALL WE?
EAR TO EAR!!
DRIP
DRIP

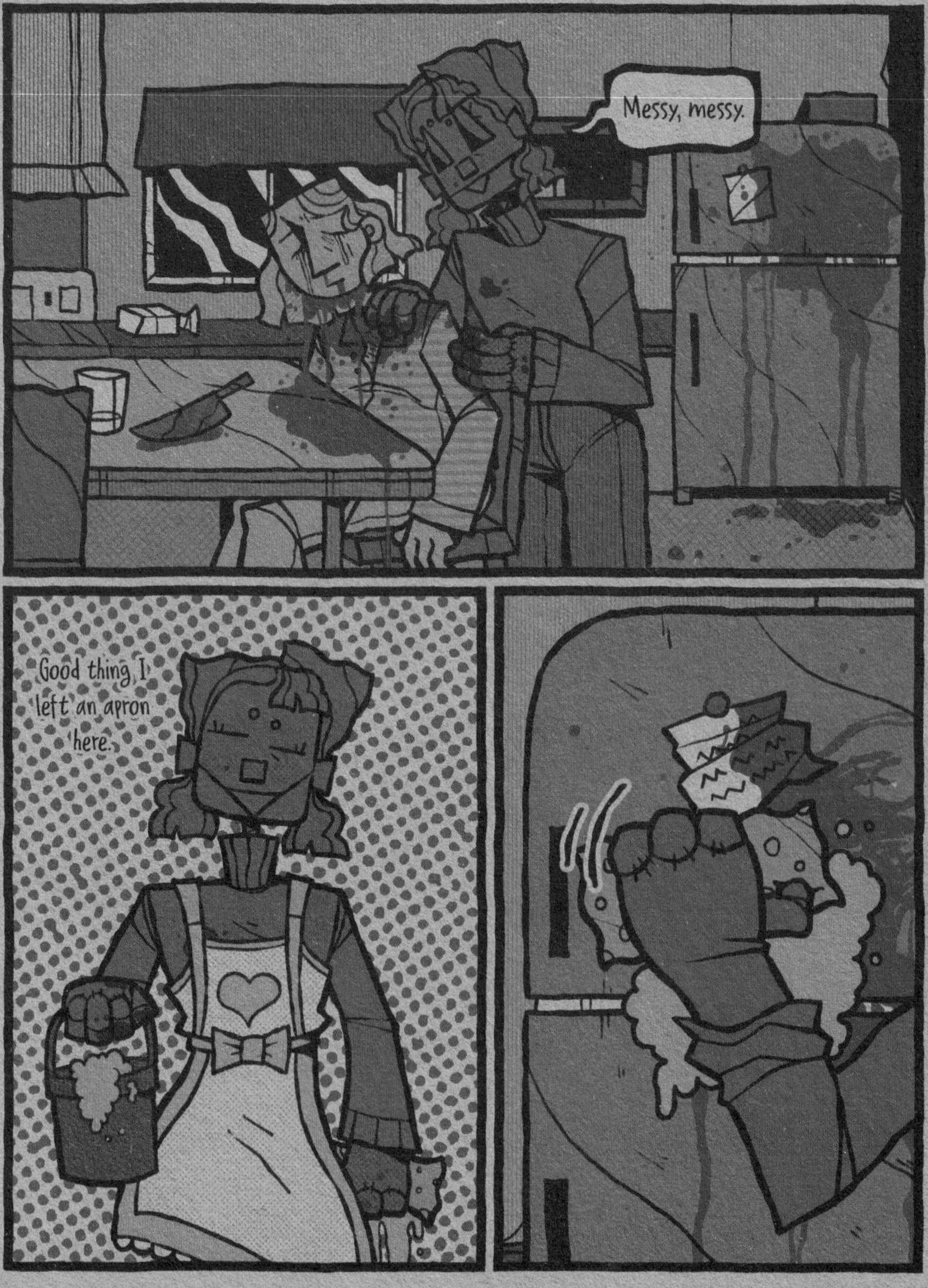
Messy, messy.
Good thing I left an apron here.

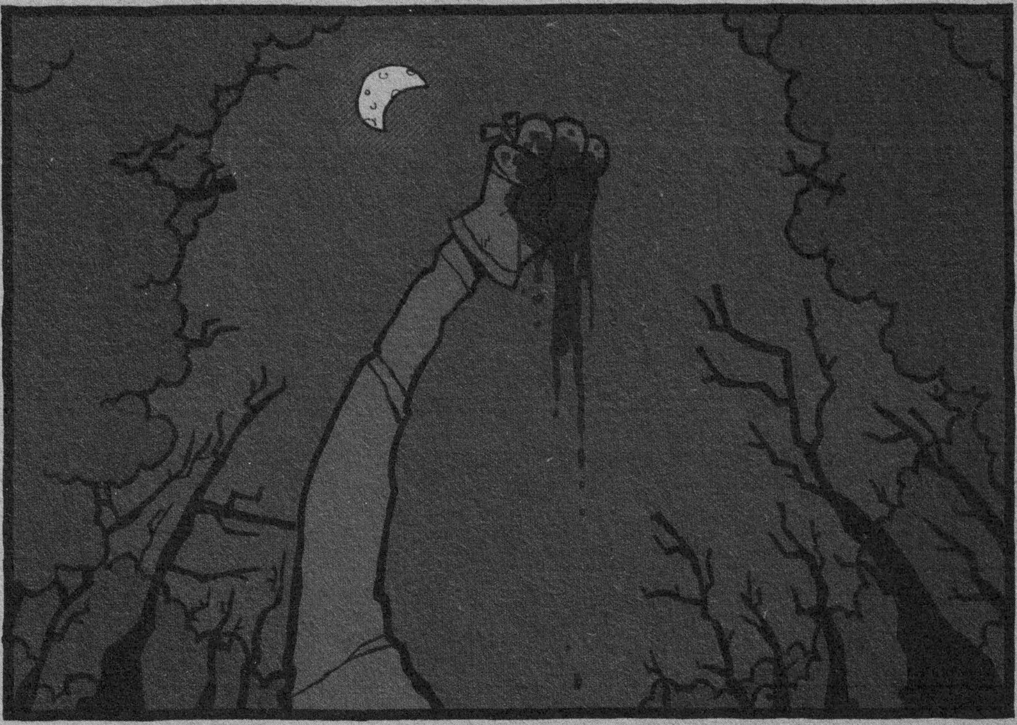

AM I OK?

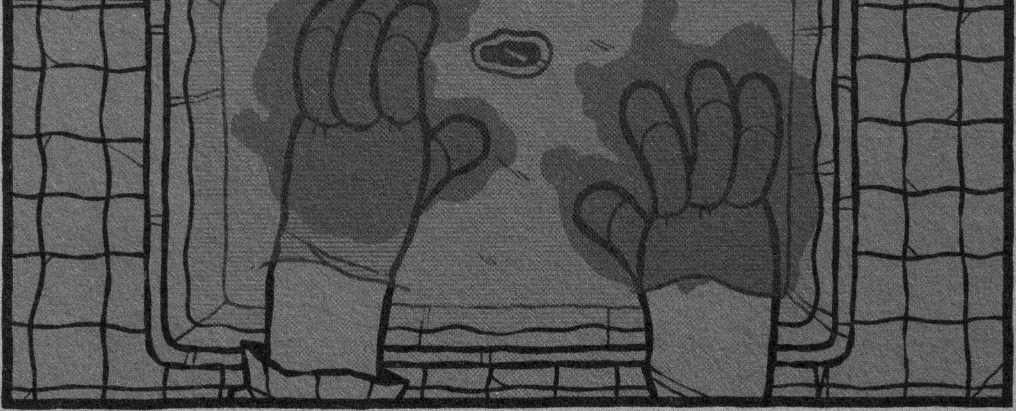

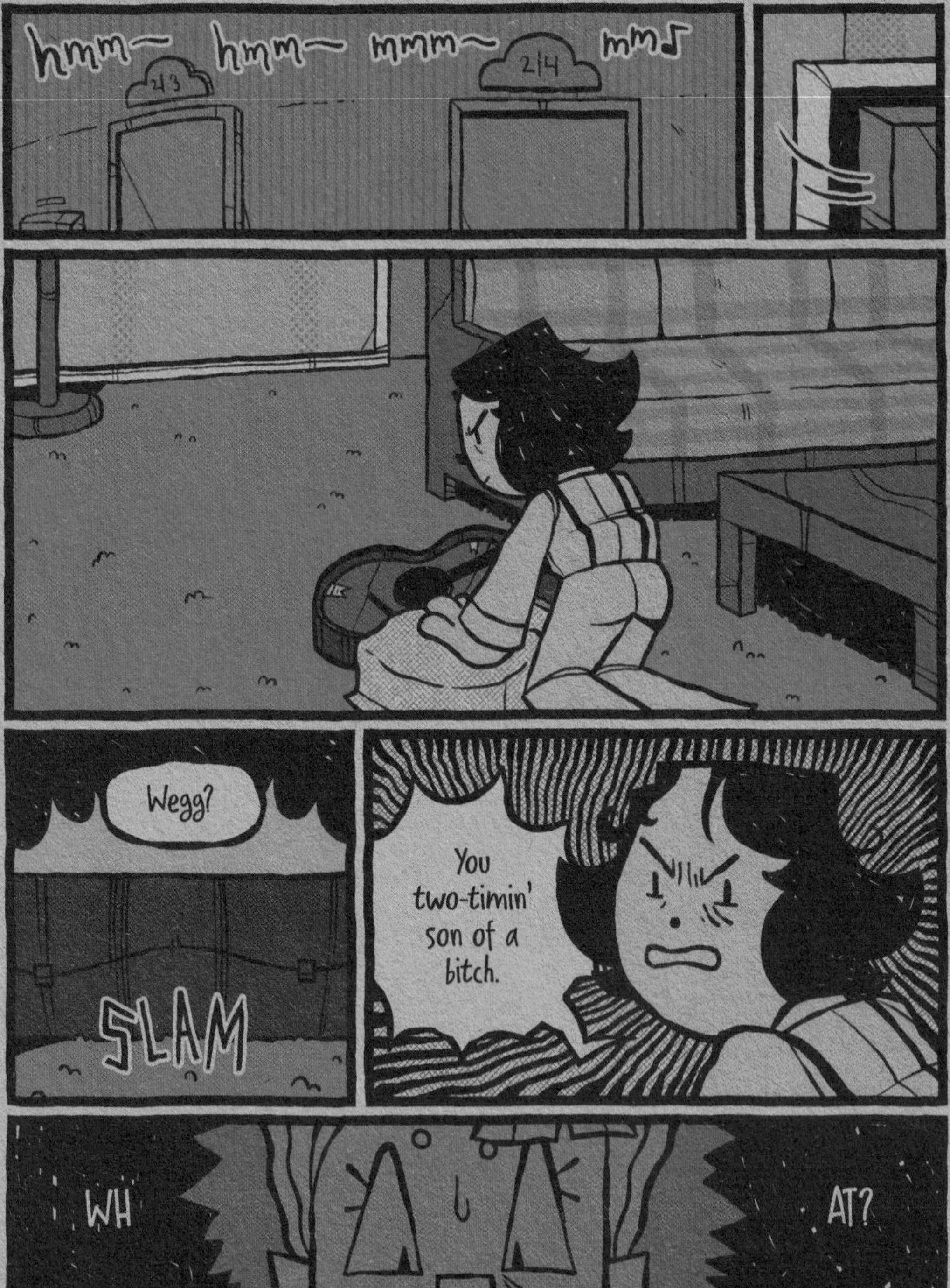
hmm~ hmm~ mmm~ mm♪
213
214
Wegg?
SLAM
You two-timin' son of a bitch.
WH AT?

Followed ya earlier. Saw ya fuckin' with the tangerine guy.

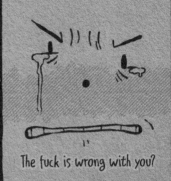

The fuck is wrong with you?

Oh. Oh, no no no. Wegg, that wasn't—

WASN'T WHAT!?

I take it you...

...missed the part where I slit his throat...

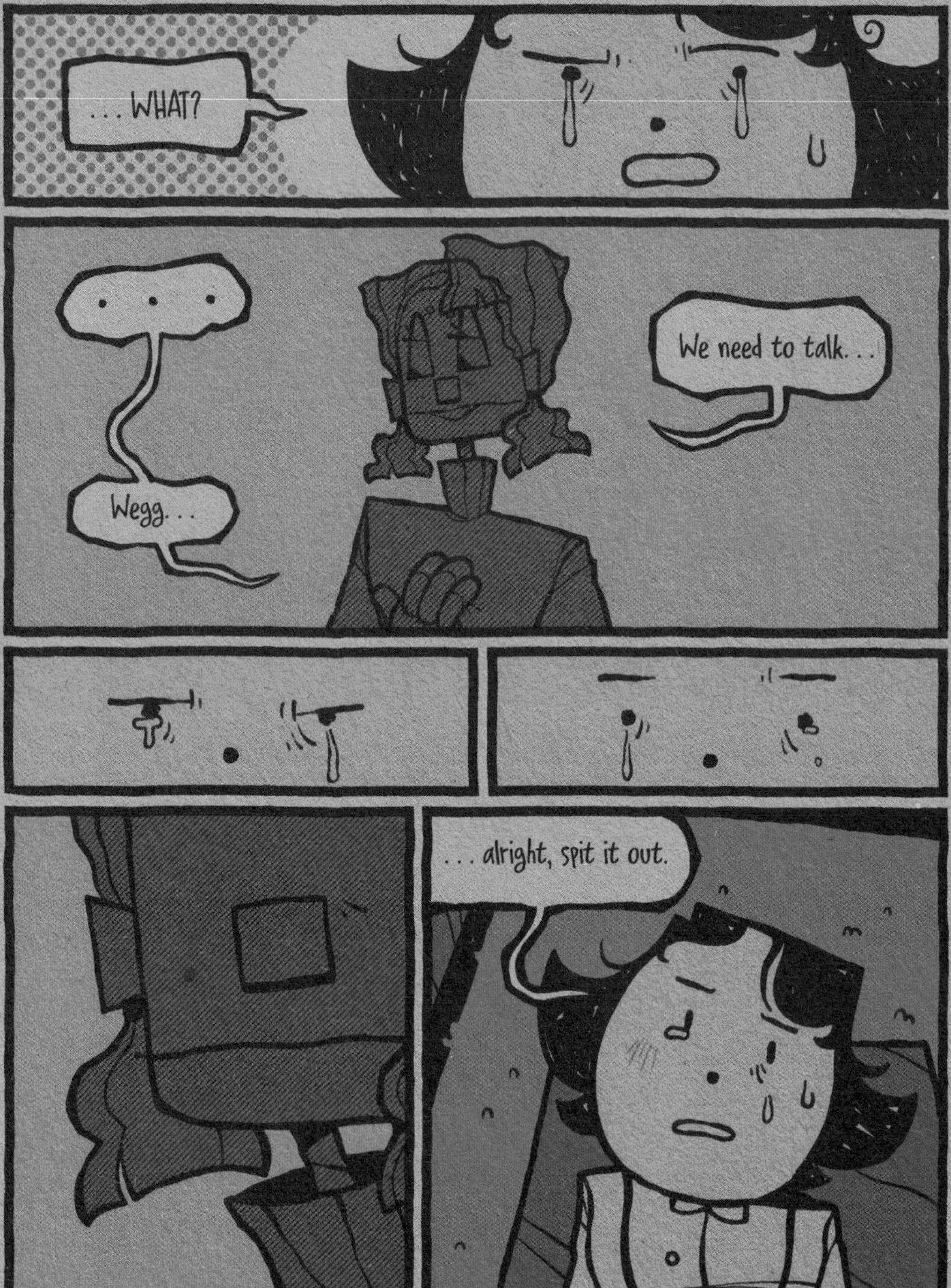
. . . WHAT?
. . .
Wegg. . .
We need to talk. . .
. . . alright, spit it out.

Wegg, just like you need to die to live, I need to kill.

I have a penance to pay. If I fail, I cannot keep my body.

I'm happy now. This is how I want to be.

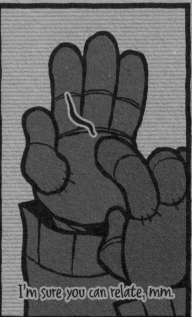

I'm sure you can relate, mm.

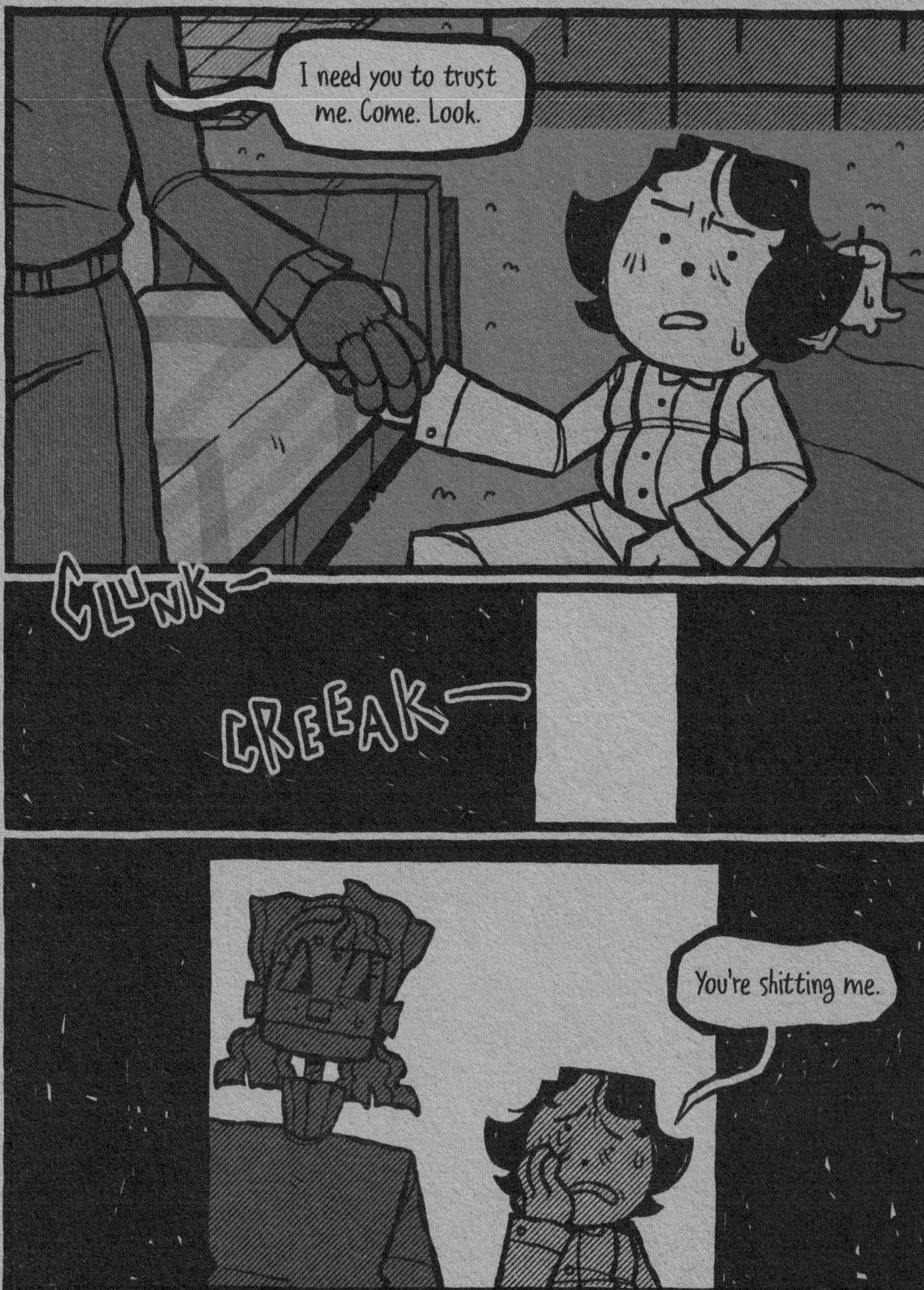
I need you to trust me. Come. Look.
CLUNK—
CREEAK—
You're shitting me.

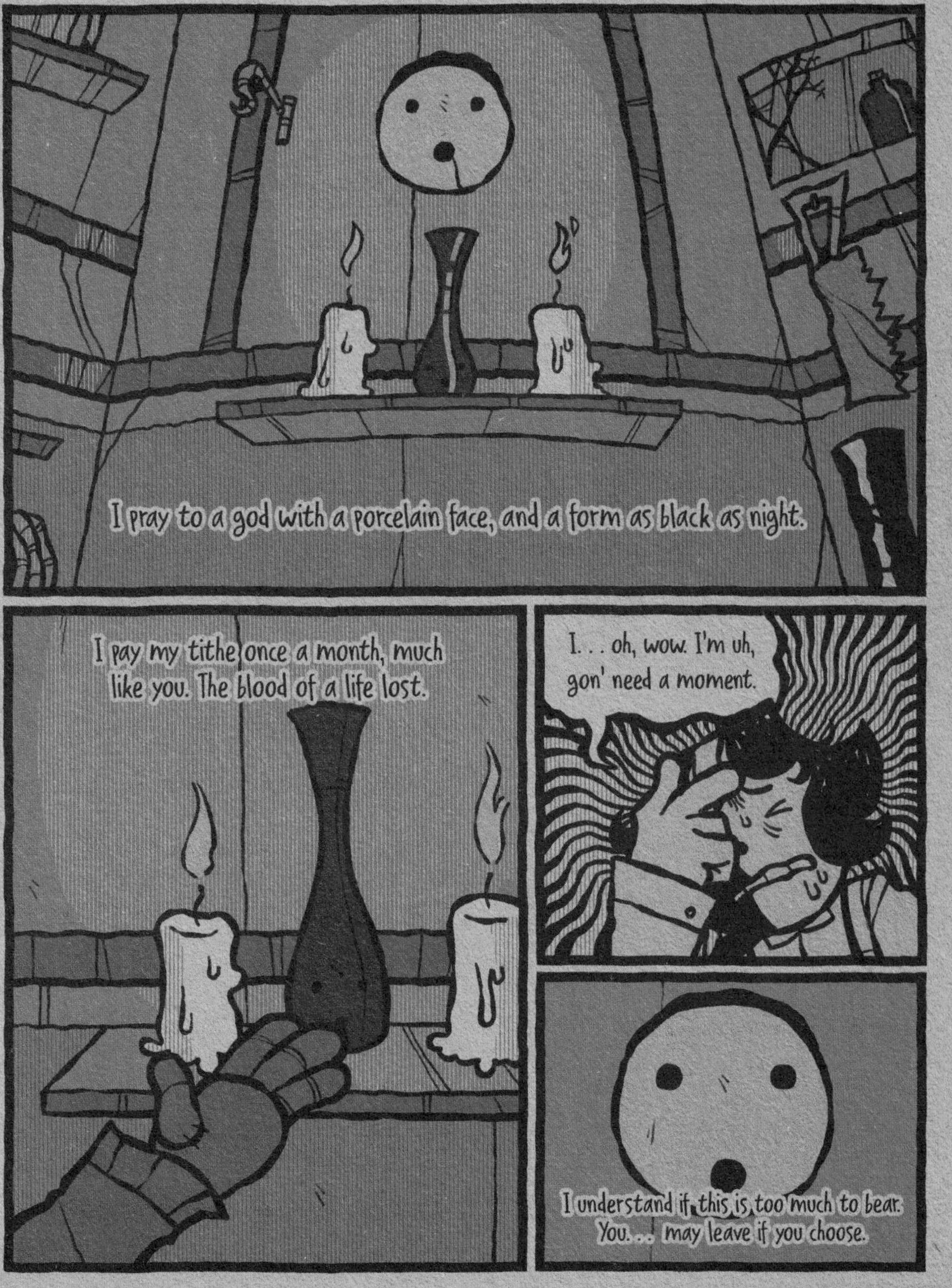
I pray to a god with a porcelain face, and a form as black as night.
I pay my tithe once a month, much like you. The blood of a life lost.
I. . . oh, wow. I'm uh, gon' need a moment.
I understand if this is too much to bear. You. . . may leave if you choose.

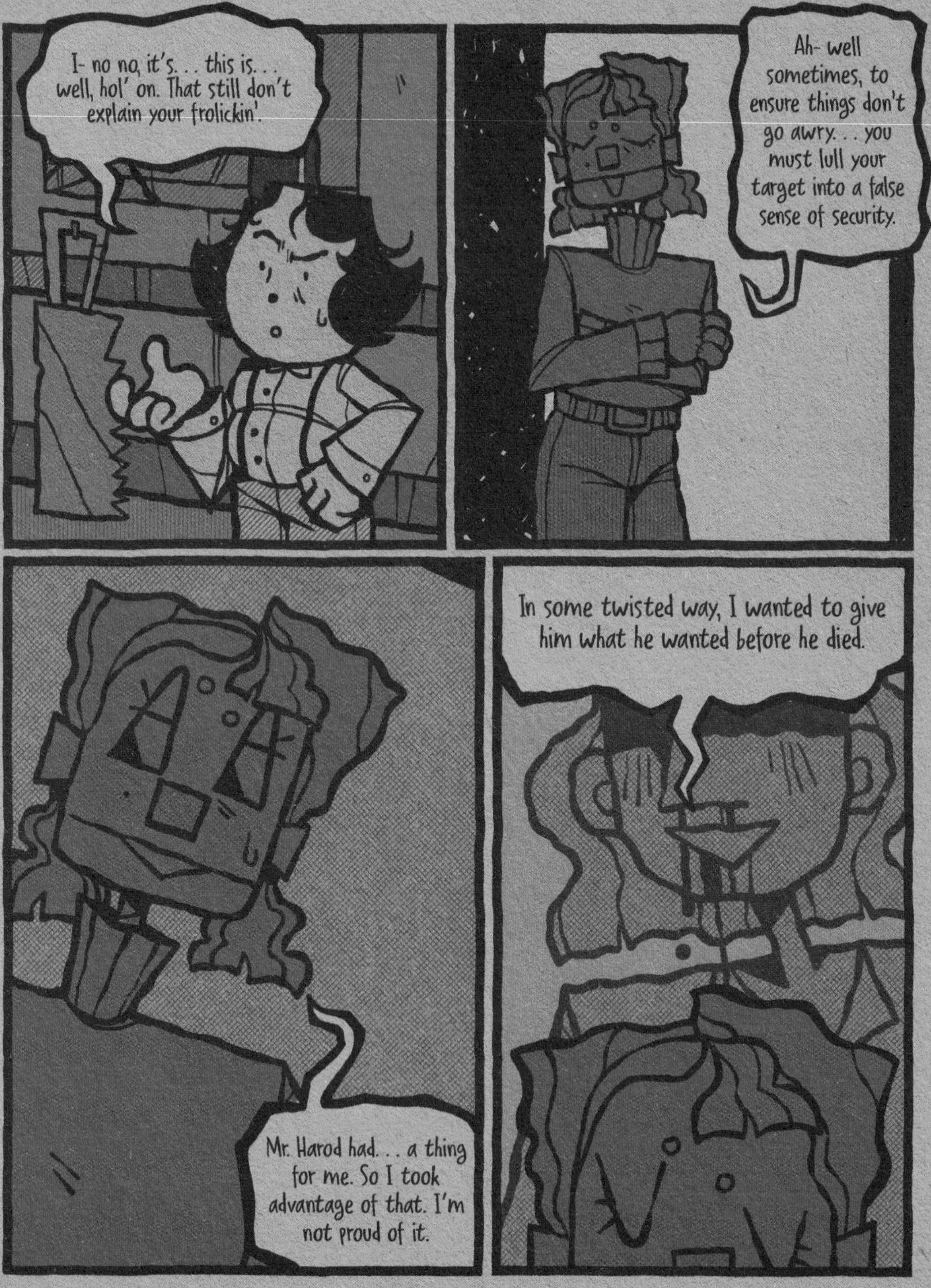
I- no no, it's. . . this is. . . well, hol' on. That still don't explain your frolickin'.
Ah- well sometimes, to ensure things don't go awry. . . you must lull your target into a false sense of security.
Mr. Harod had. . . a thing for me. So I took advantage of that. I'm not proud of it.
In some twisted way, I wanted to give him what he wanted before he died.

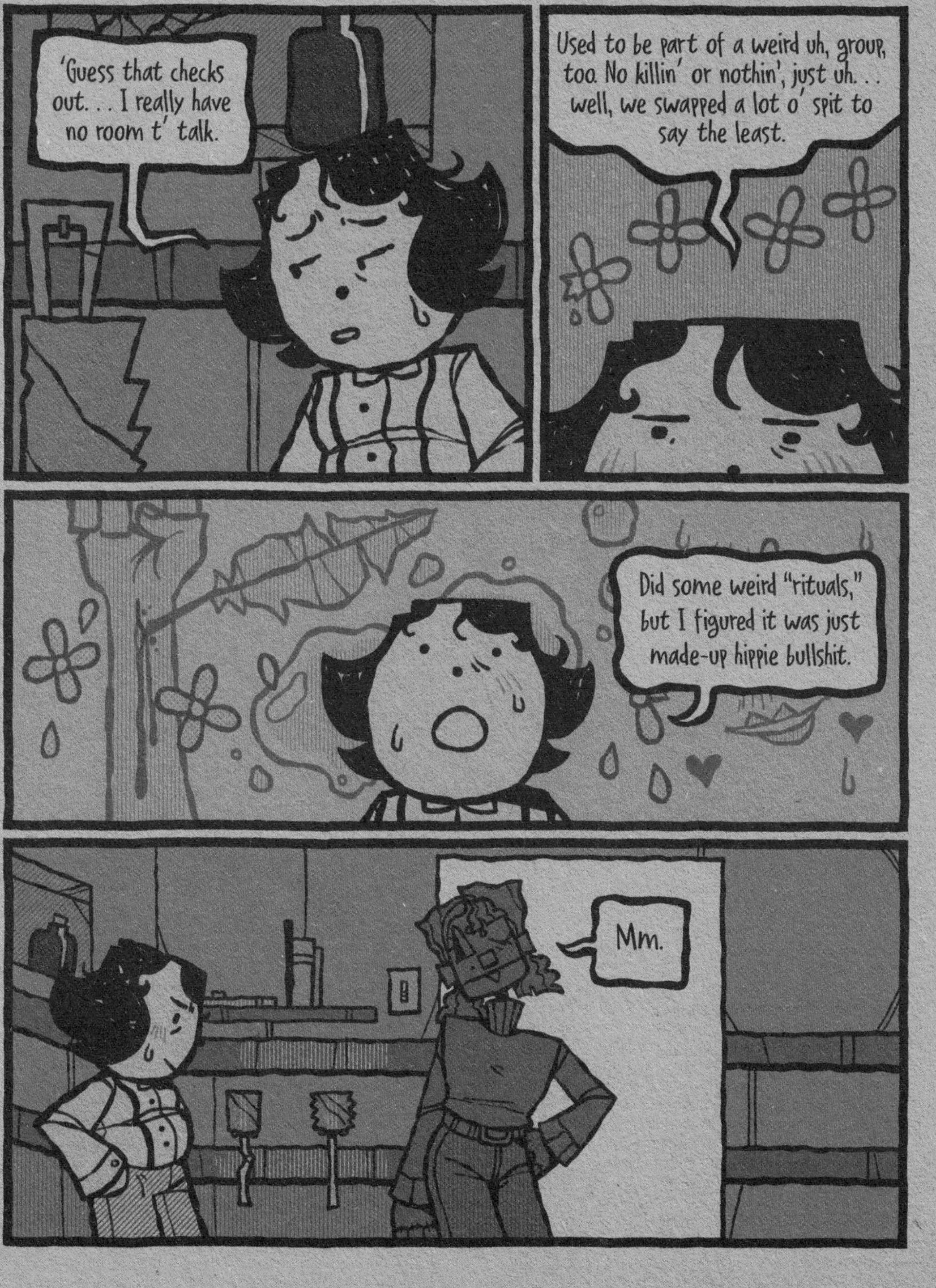
'Guess that checks out. . . I really have no room t' talk.
Used to be part of a weird uh, group, too. No killin' or nothin', just uh. . . well, we swapped a lot o' spit to say the least.
Did some weird "rituals," but I figured it was just made-up hippie bullshit.
Mm.

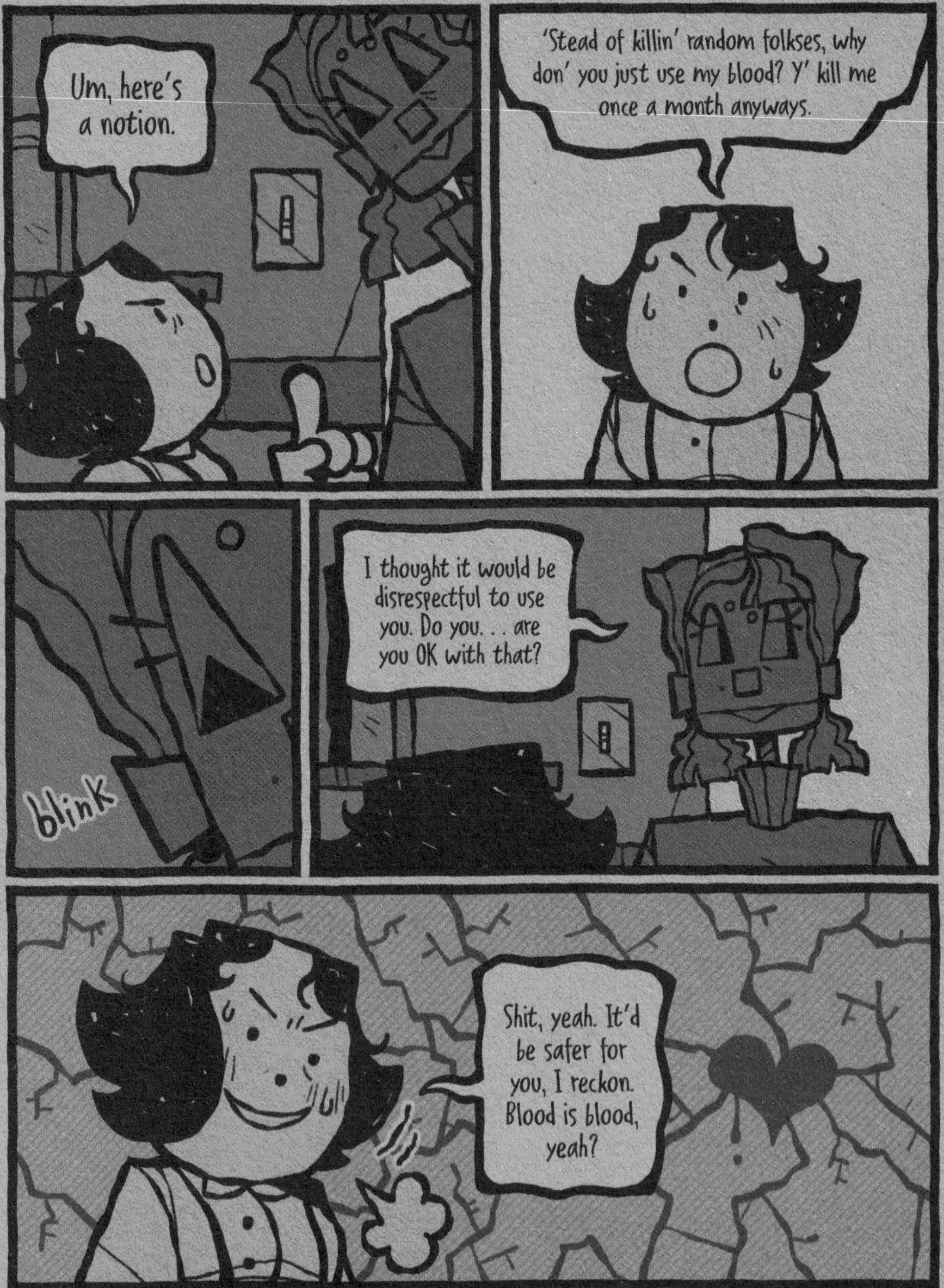
Um, here's a notion.
'Stead of killin' random folkses, why don' you just use my blood? Y' kill me once a month anyways.
blink
I thought it would be disrespectful to use you. Do you. . . are you OK with that?
Shit, yeah. It'd be safer for you, I reckon. Blood is blood, yeah?

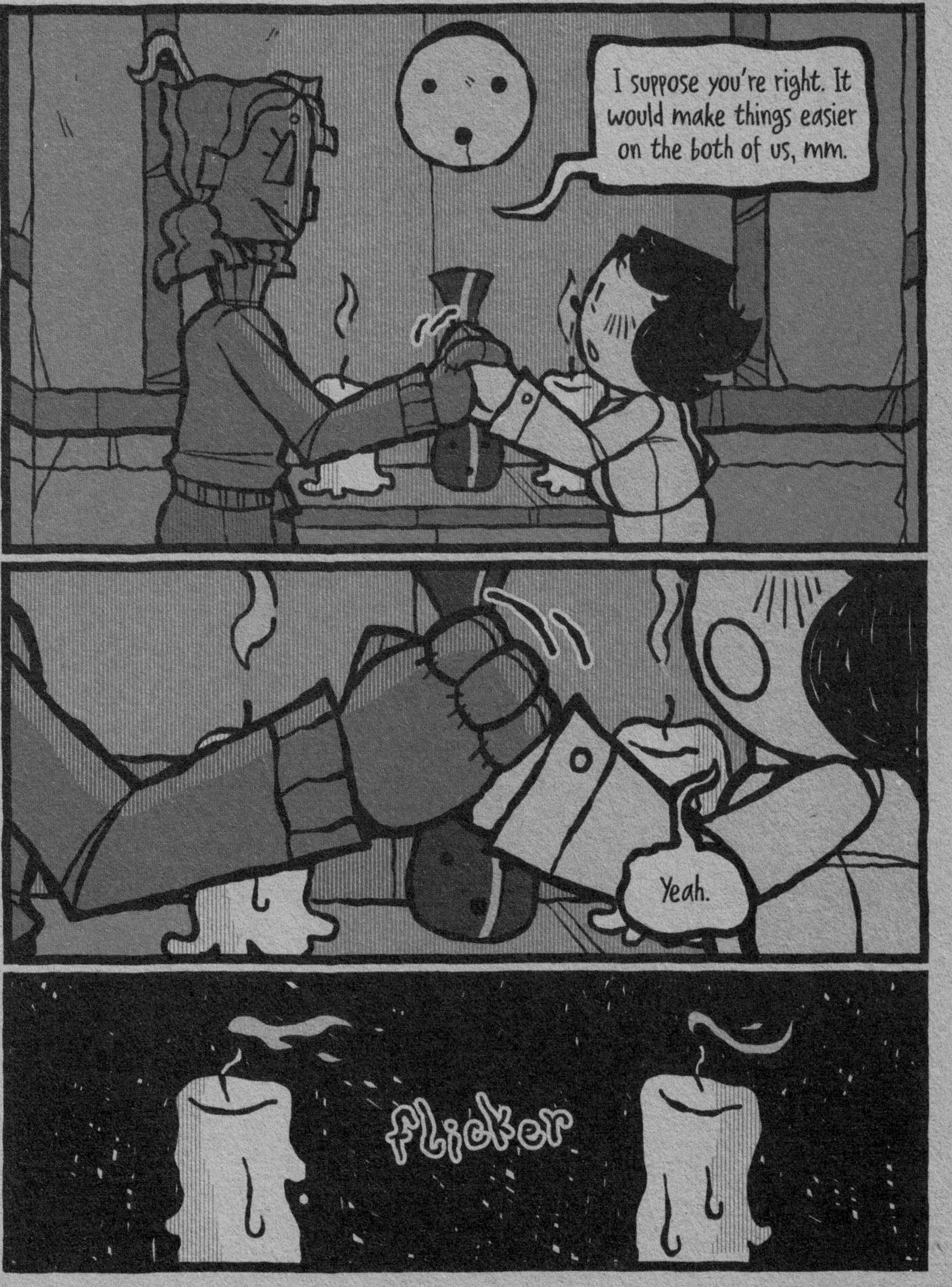
I suppose you're right. It would make things easier on the both of us, mm.
Yeah.
flicker

Love yer new lil' uh, beauty mark thing.

It's blood.

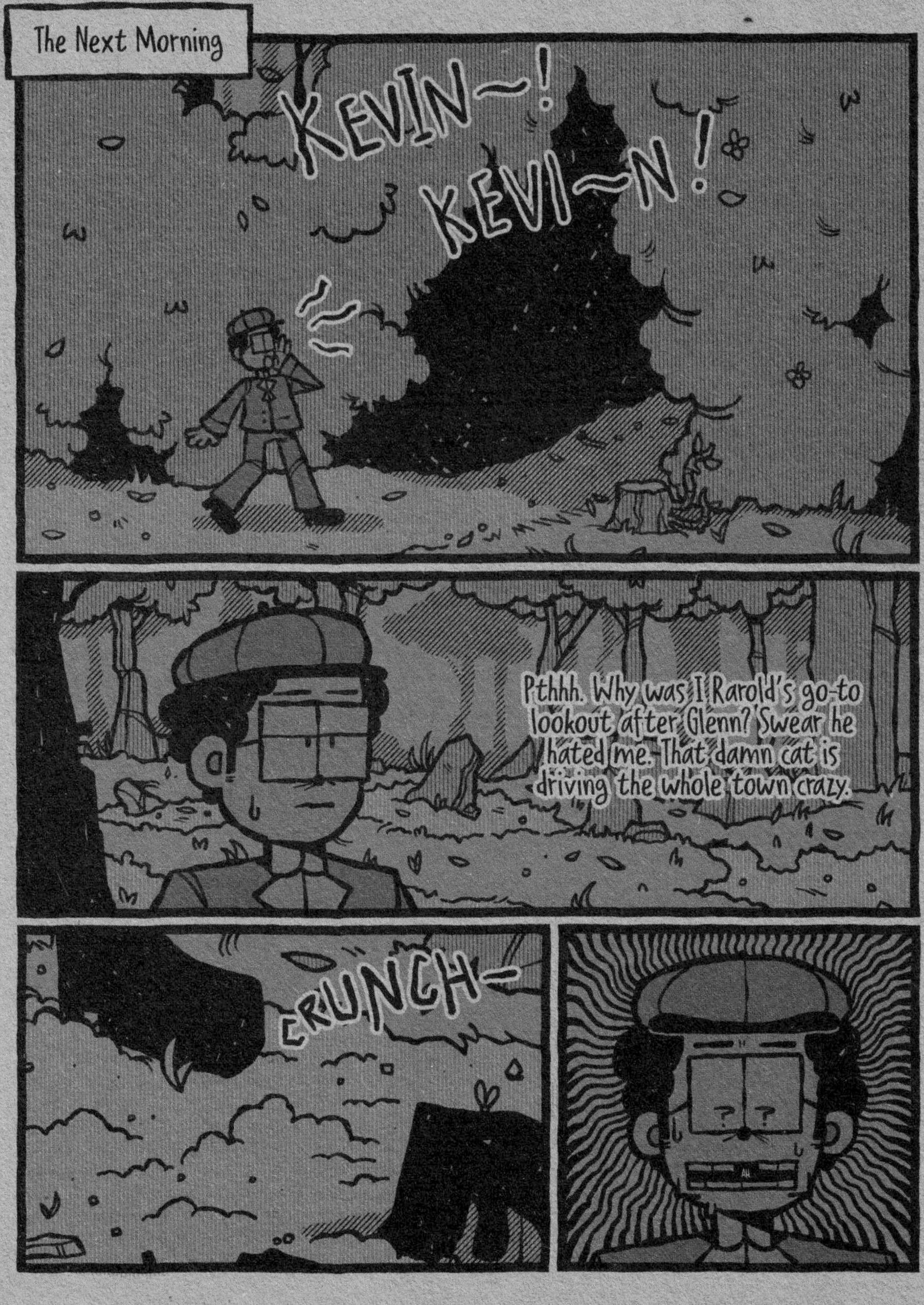
The Next Morning
KEVIN~!
KEVI~N!
Pthhh. Why was I Rarold's go-to lookout after Glenn? Swear he hated me. That damn cat is driving the whole town crazy.
CRUNCH-

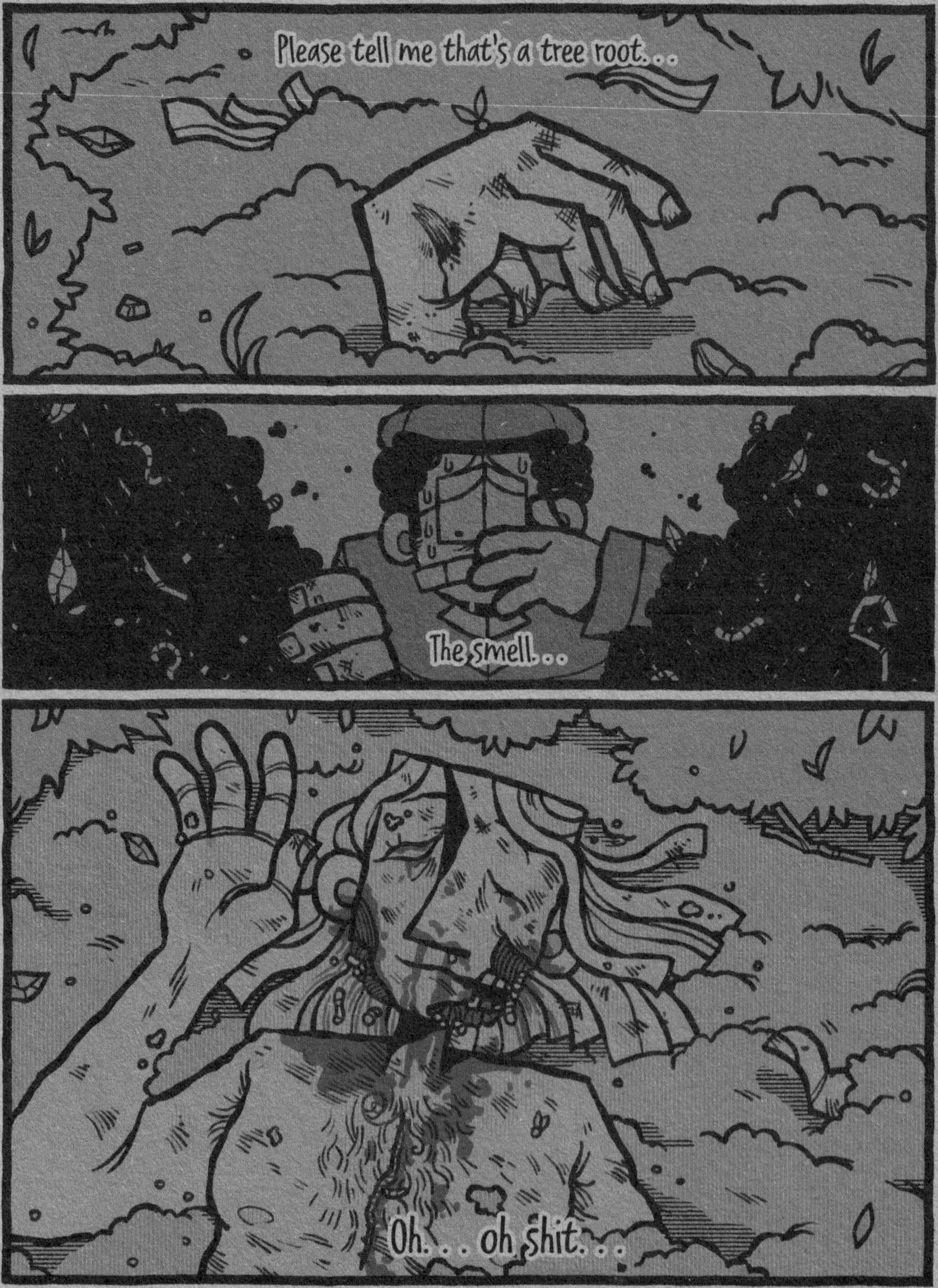
Please tell me that's a tree root. . .
The smell. . .
Oh. . . oh shit. . .

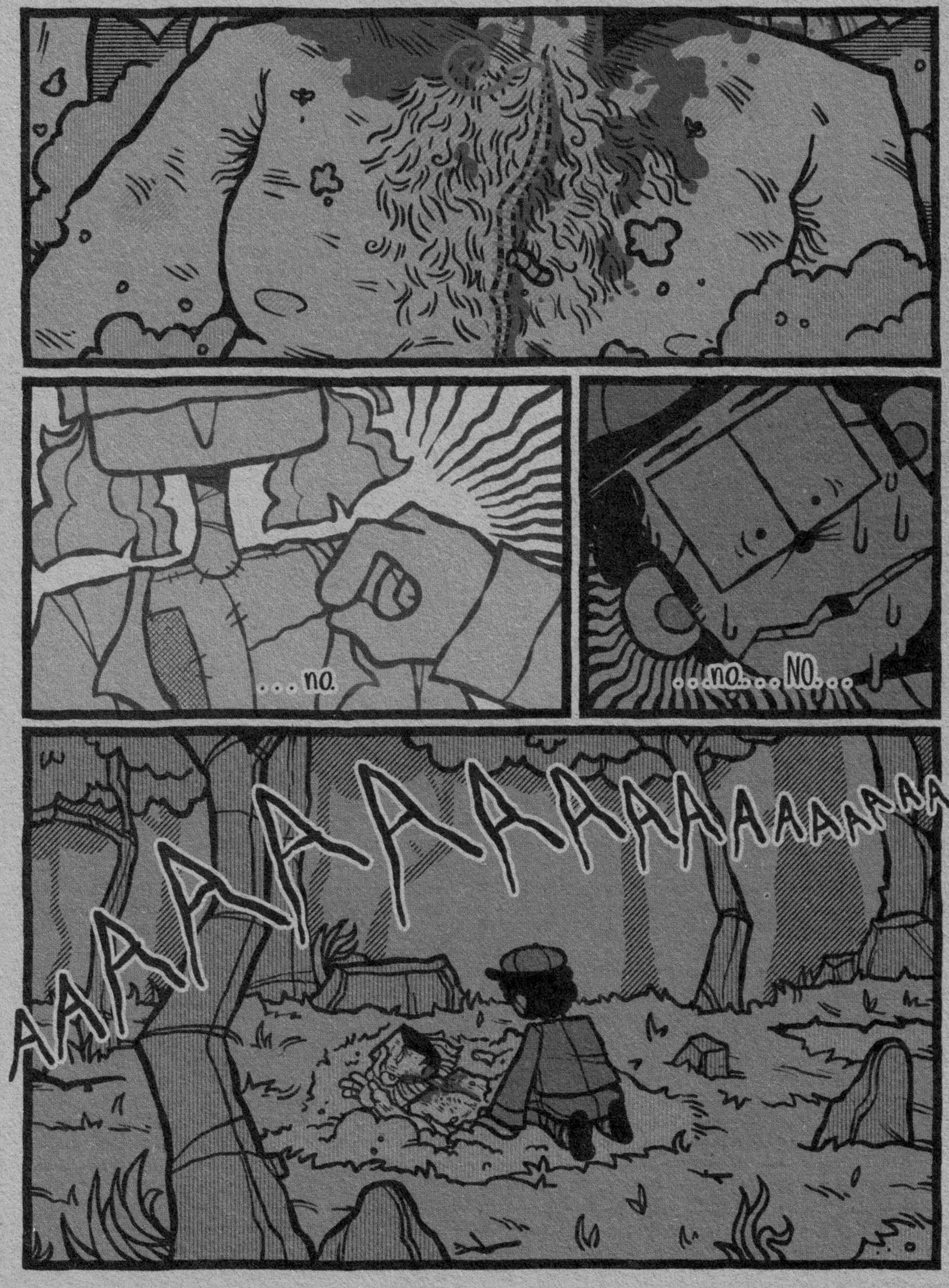
...no.
...no....NO....
AAAAAAAAAAAAAAAA

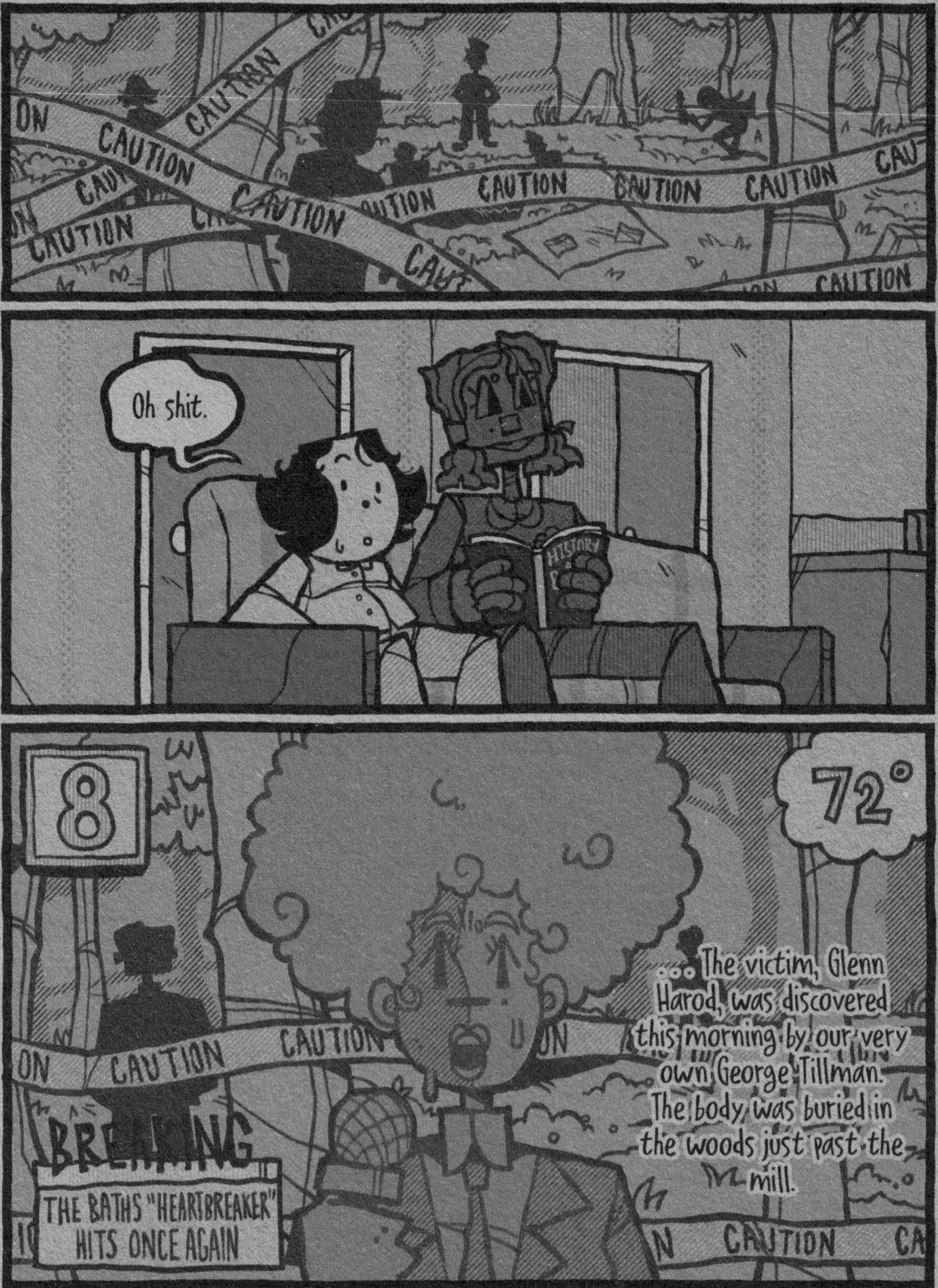
CAUTION
Oh shit.
HISTORY
8
72°
...The victim, Glenn Harod, was discovered this morning by our very own George Tillman. The body was buried in the woods just past the mill.
THE BATHS "HEARTBREAKER" HITS ONCE AGAIN

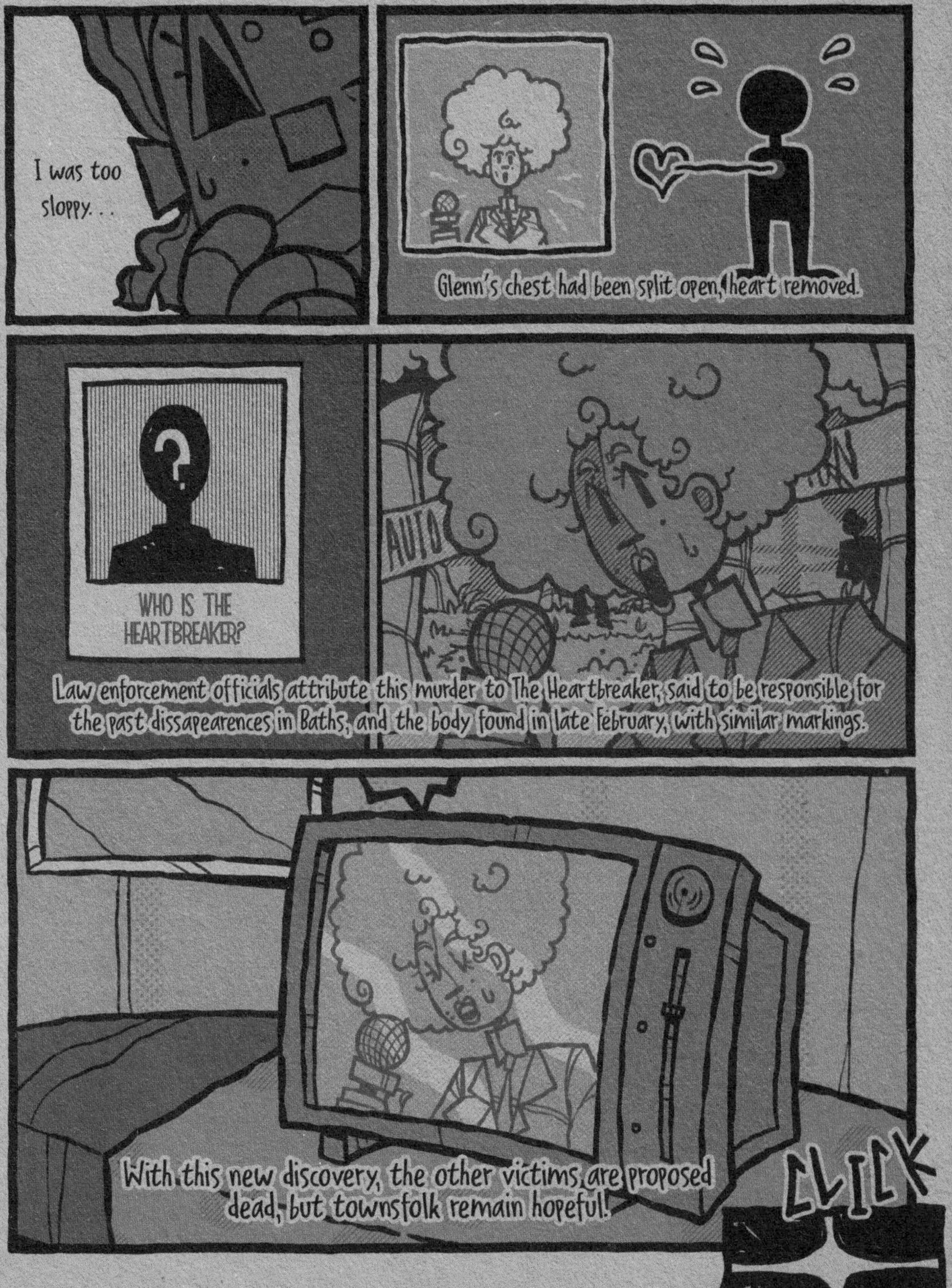
I was too sloppy. . .
Glenn's chest had been split open, heart removed.
WHO IS THE HEARTBREAKER?
AUTO
Law enforcement officials attribute this murder to The Heartbreaker, said to be responsible for the past dissapearences in Baths, and the body found in late february, with similar markings.
With this new discovery, the other victims are proposed dead, but townsfolk remain hopeful!
CLICK

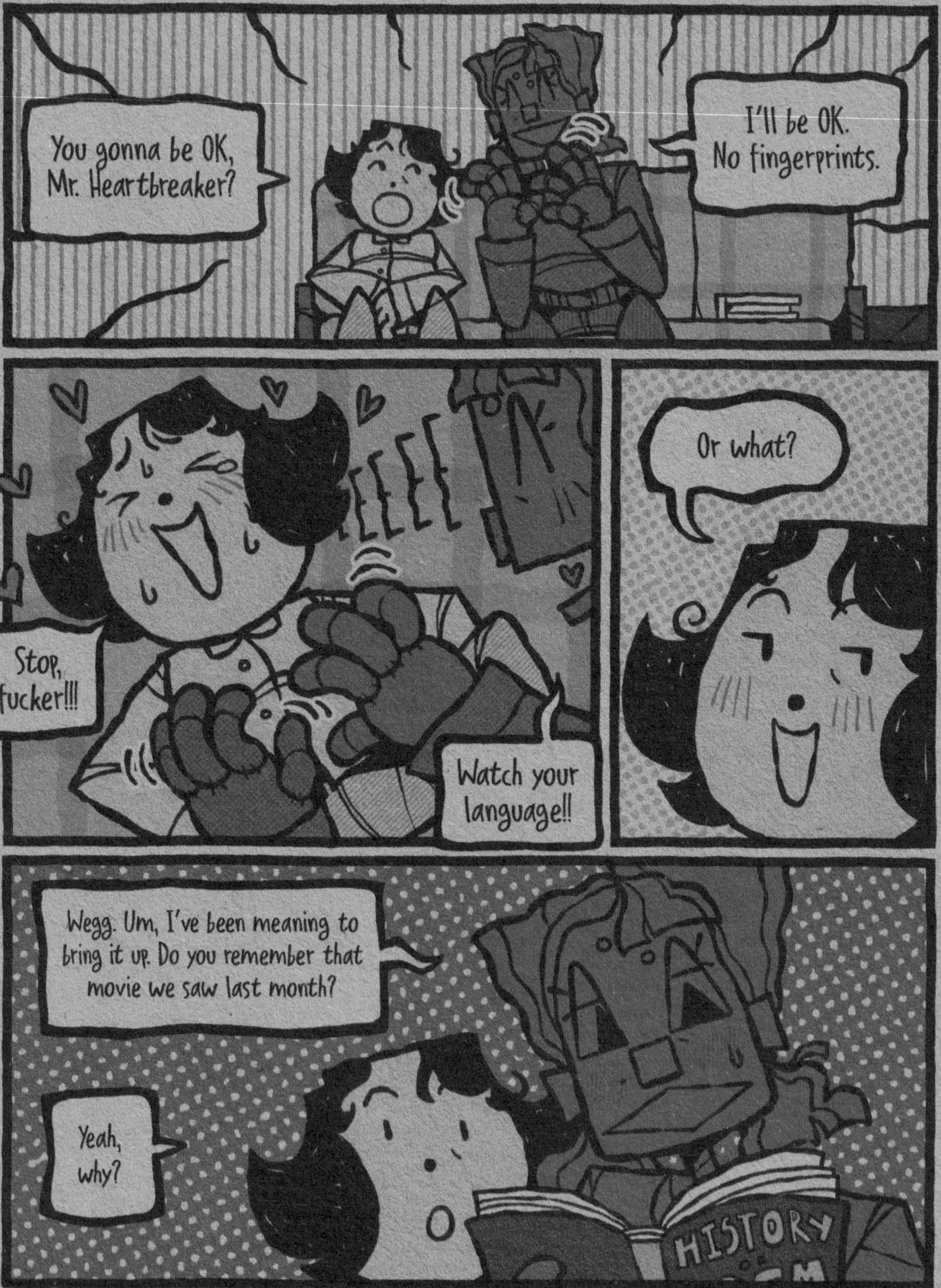
You gonna be OK, Mr. Heartbreaker?
I'll be OK. No fingerprints.
Stop, fucker!!!
EEEEE
Watch your language!!
Or what?
Wegg. Um, I've been meaning to bring it up. Do you remember that movie we saw last month?
Yeah, why?
HISTORY

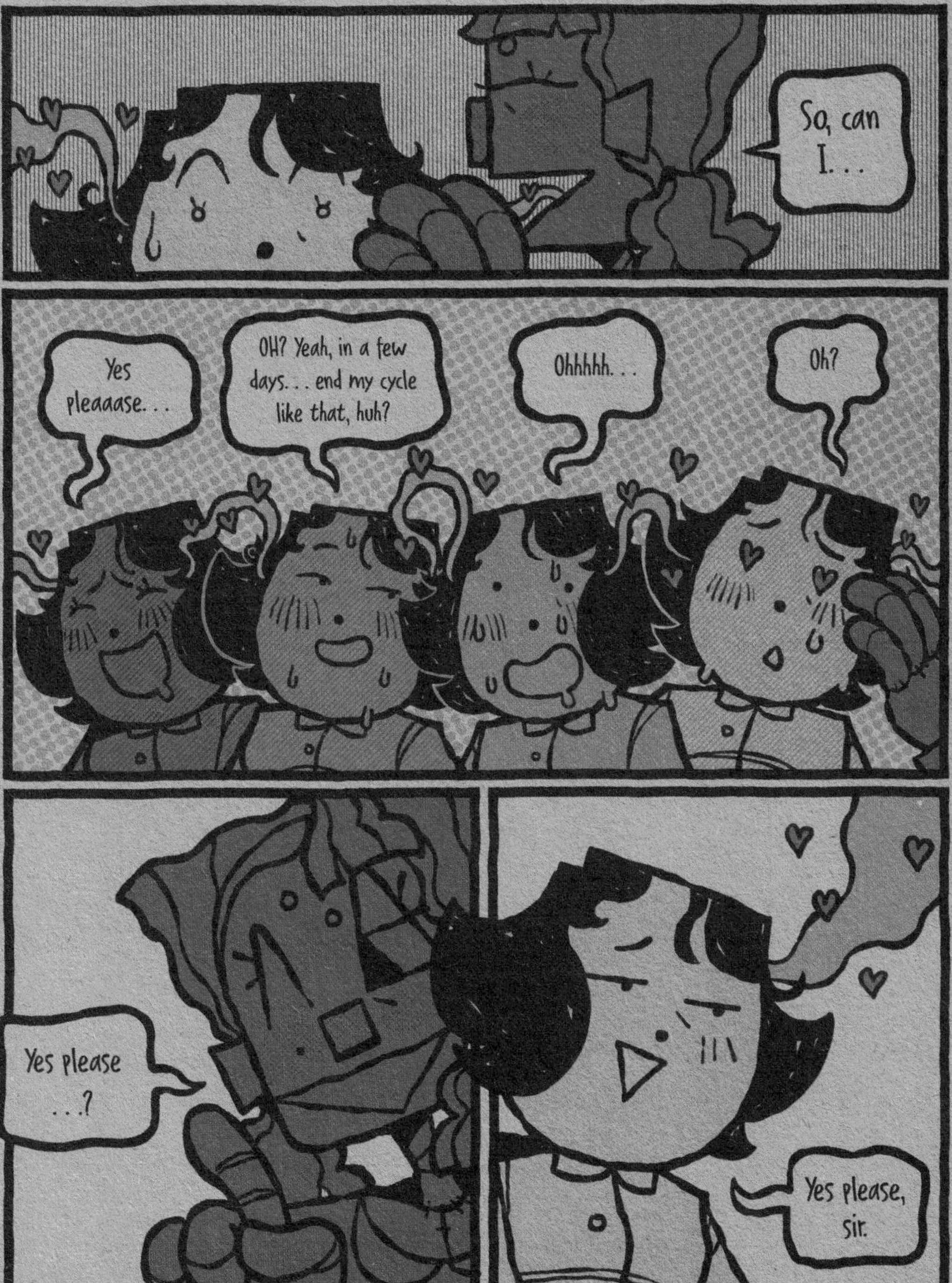
So, can I. . .
Yes pleaaase. . .
OH? Yeah, in a few days. . . end my cycle like that, huh?
Ohhhhh. . .
Oh?
Yes please . . .?
Yes please, sir.

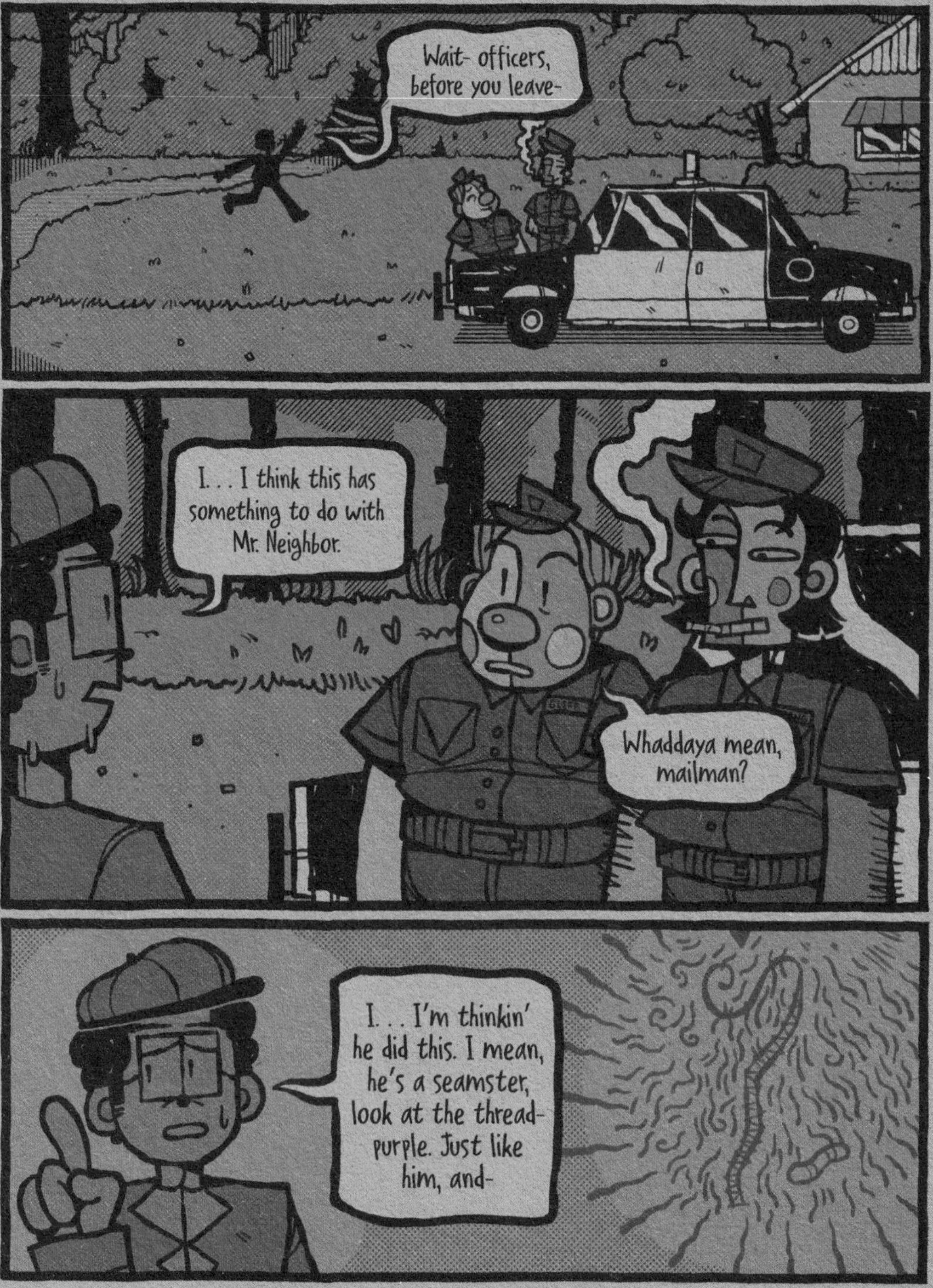
Wait- officers, before you leave-
I. . . I think this has something to do with Mr. Neighbor.
Whaddaya mean, mailman?
I. . . I'm thinkin' he did this. I mean, he's a seamster, look at the thread- purple. Just like him, and-

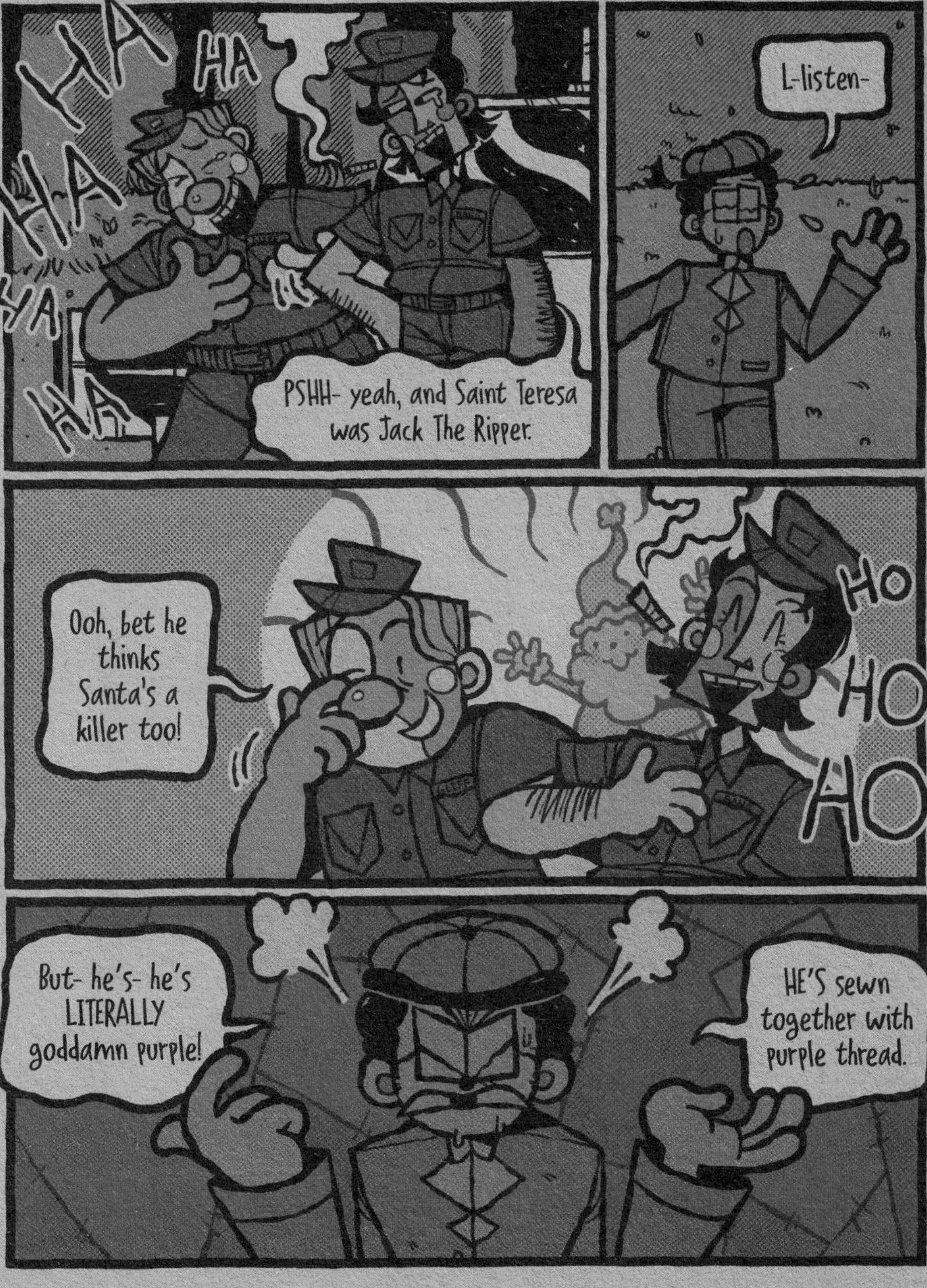
HA HA HA HA HA HA
PSHH- yeah, and Saint Teresa was Jack The Ripper.
L-listen-
Ooh, bet he thinks Santa's a killer too!
HO HO HO
But- he's- he's LITERALLY goddamn purple!
HE'S sewn together with purple thread.

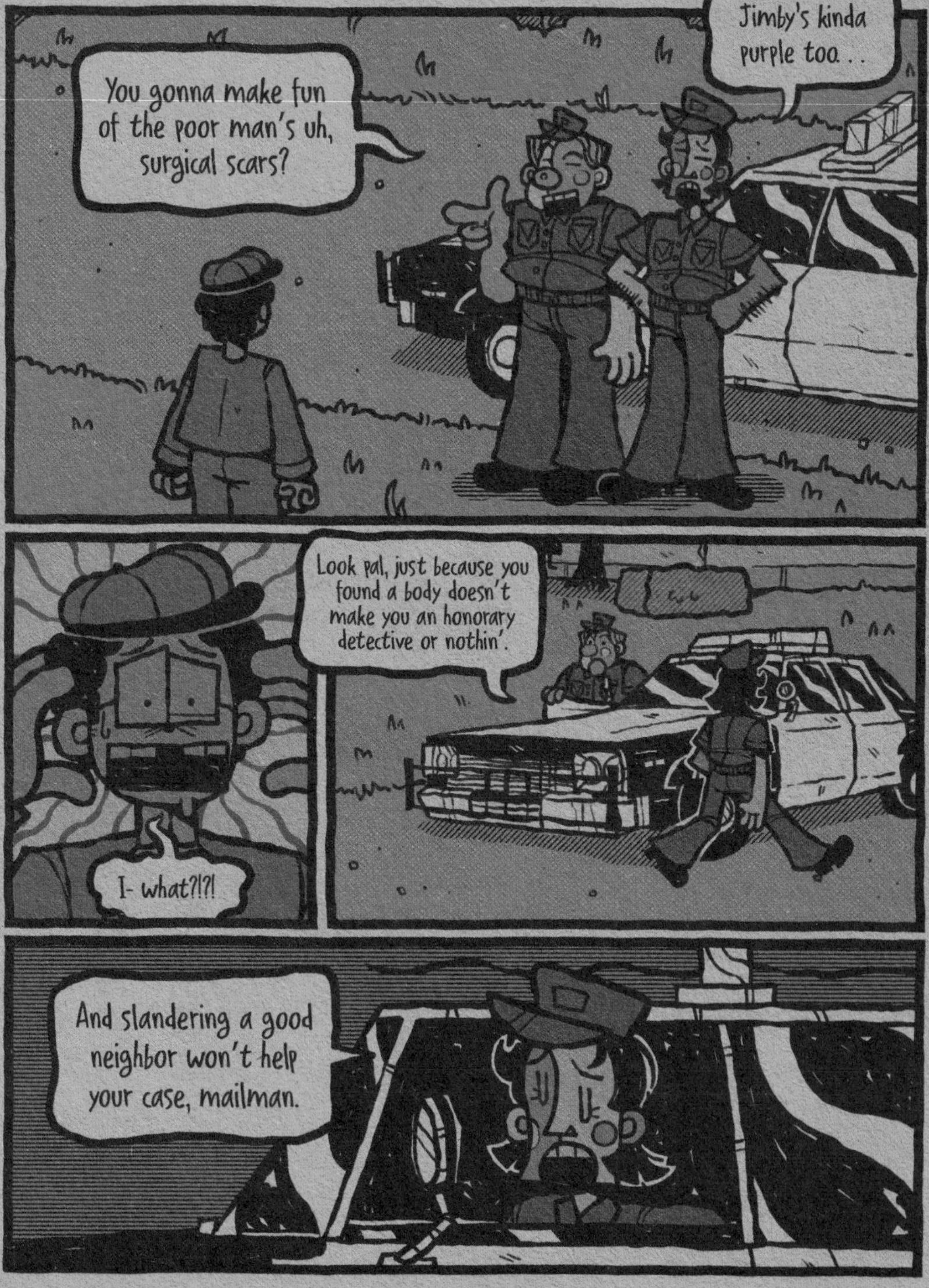
You gonna make fun of the poor man's uh, surgical scars?
Jimby's kinda purple too. . .
I- what?!?!
Look pal, just because you found a body doesn't make you an honorary detective or nothin'.
And slandering a good neighbor won't help your case, mailman.

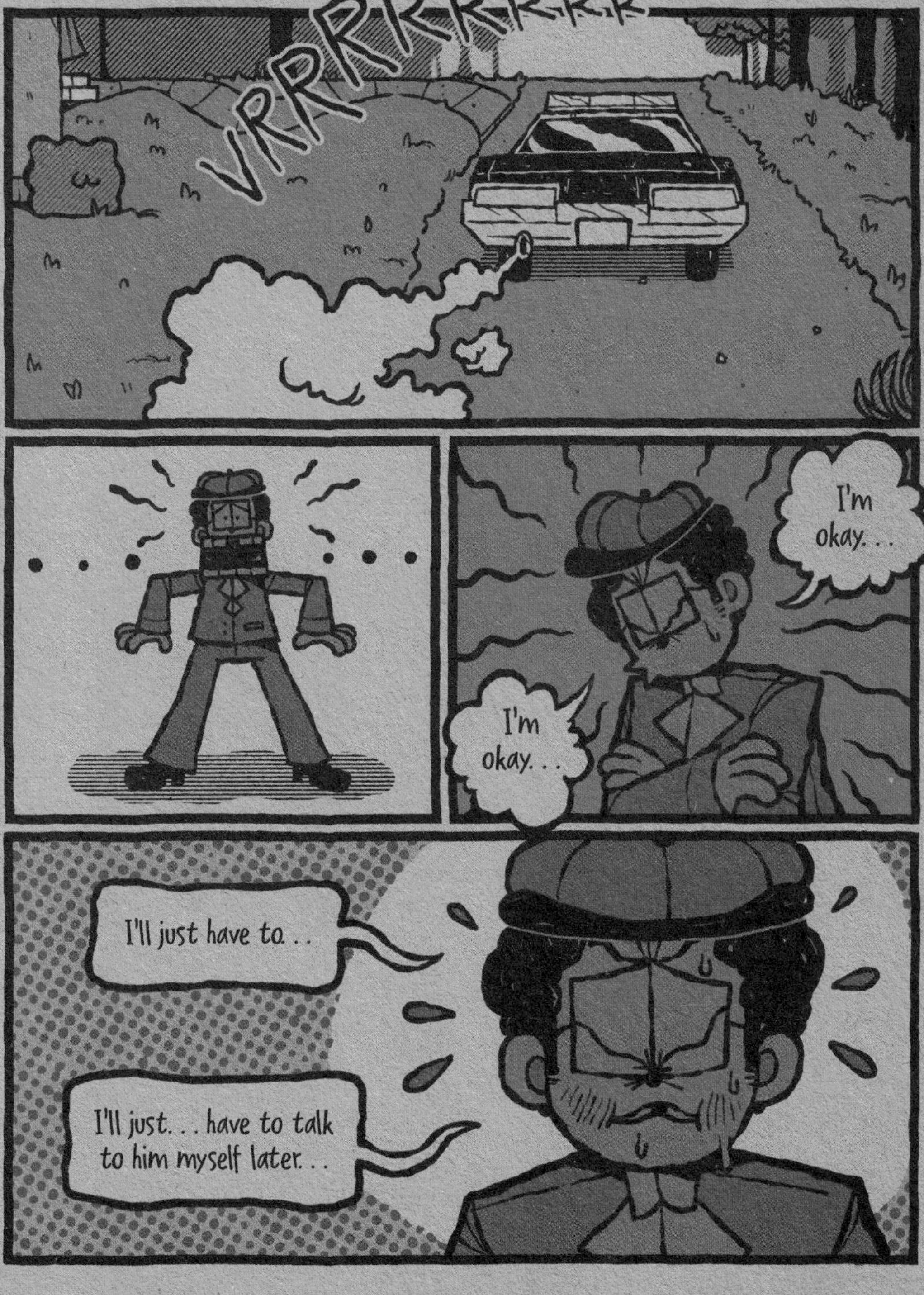
VRRRRRRRRR
I'm okay. . .
I'm okay. . .
I'll just have to. . .
I'll just. . . have to talk to him myself later. . .

What are those funny
carvin's you made, Lew?
Looks like a big ol' swan.
. . . a god, huh?
Well, they're real pretty.
. . . you see Him in me?
Aw, shucks.

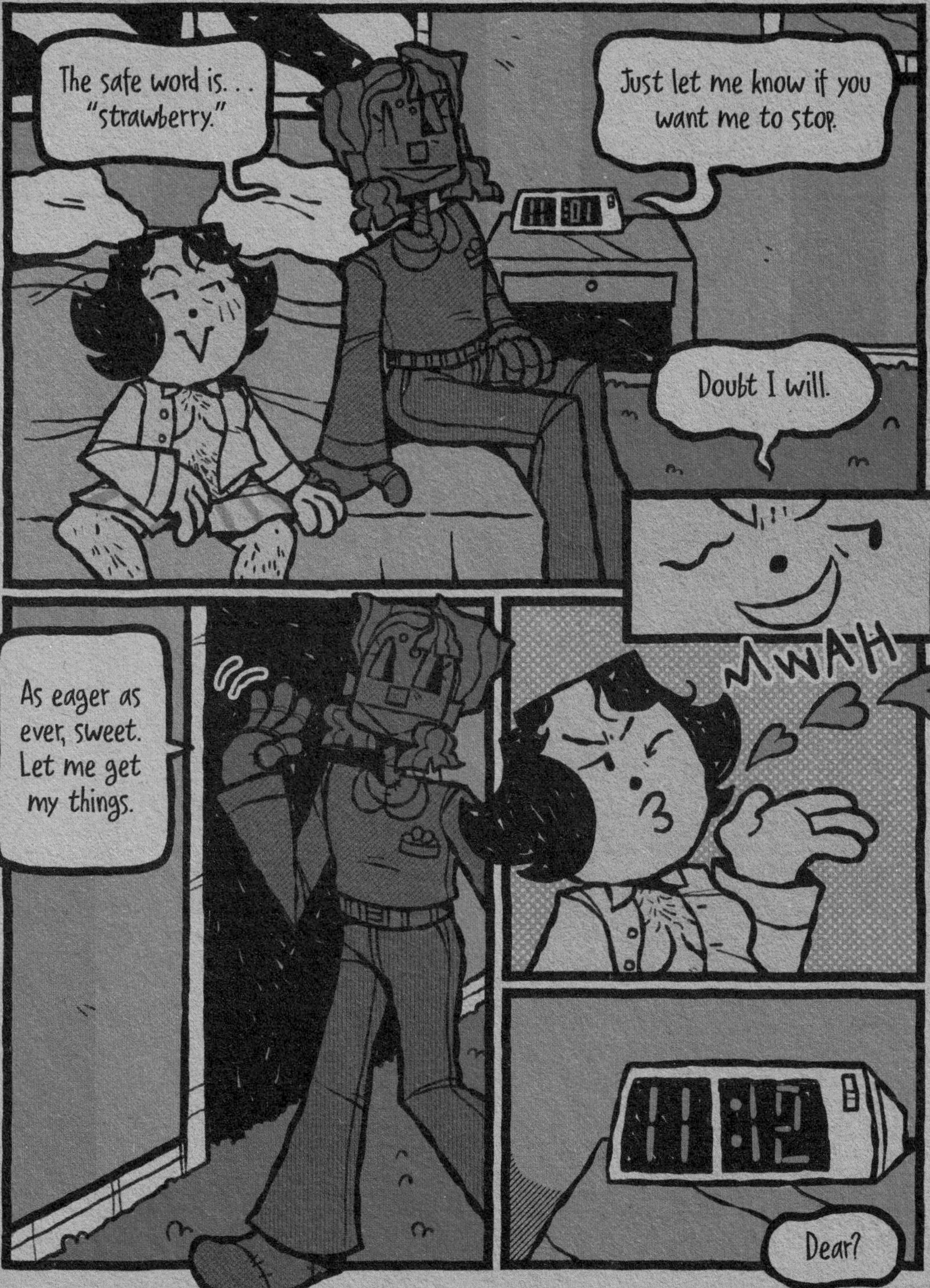
The safe word is. . . "strawberry."
Just let me know if you want me to stop.
Doubt I will.
MWAH
As eager as ever, sweet. Let me get my things.
Dear?

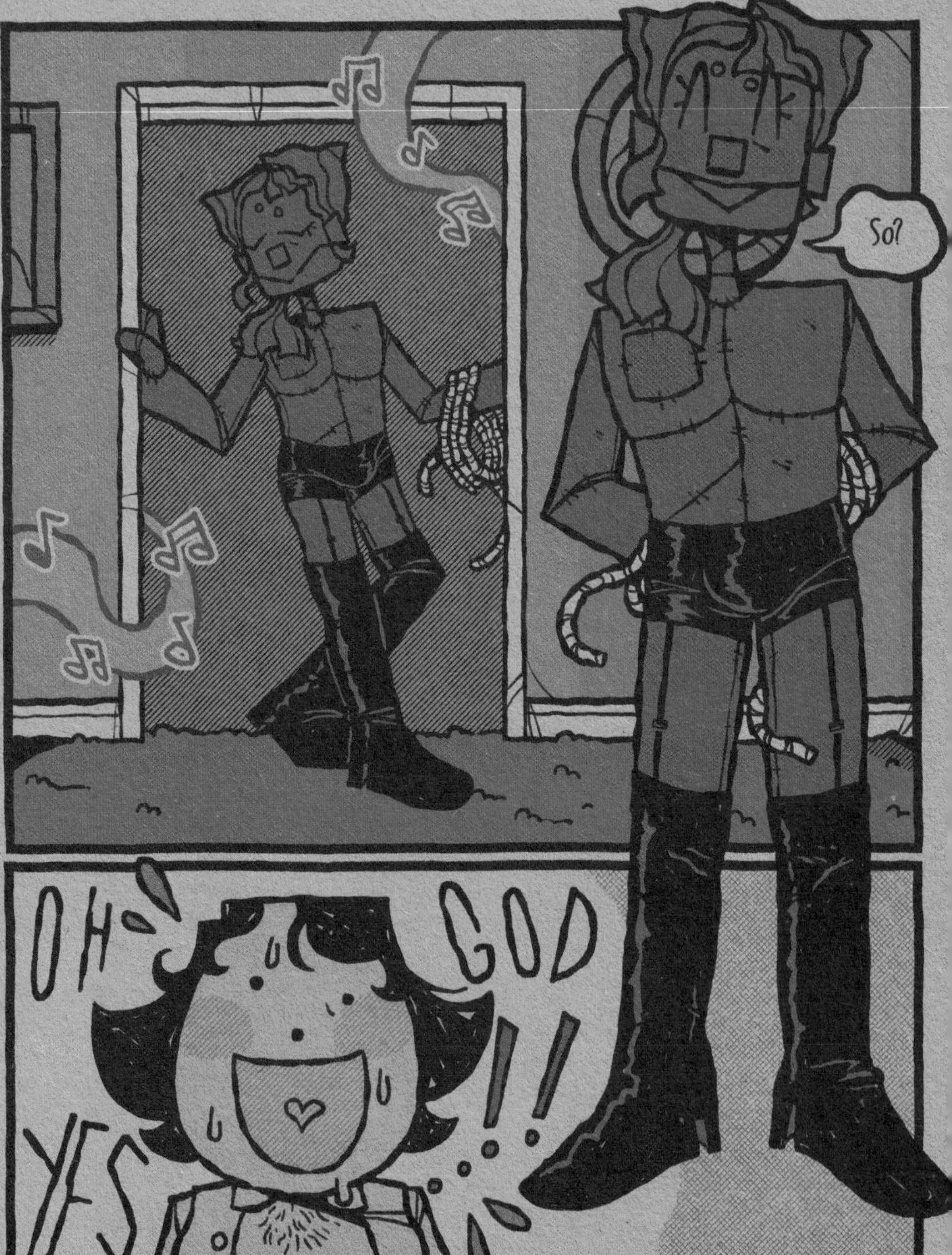
So?
OH GOD YES!!

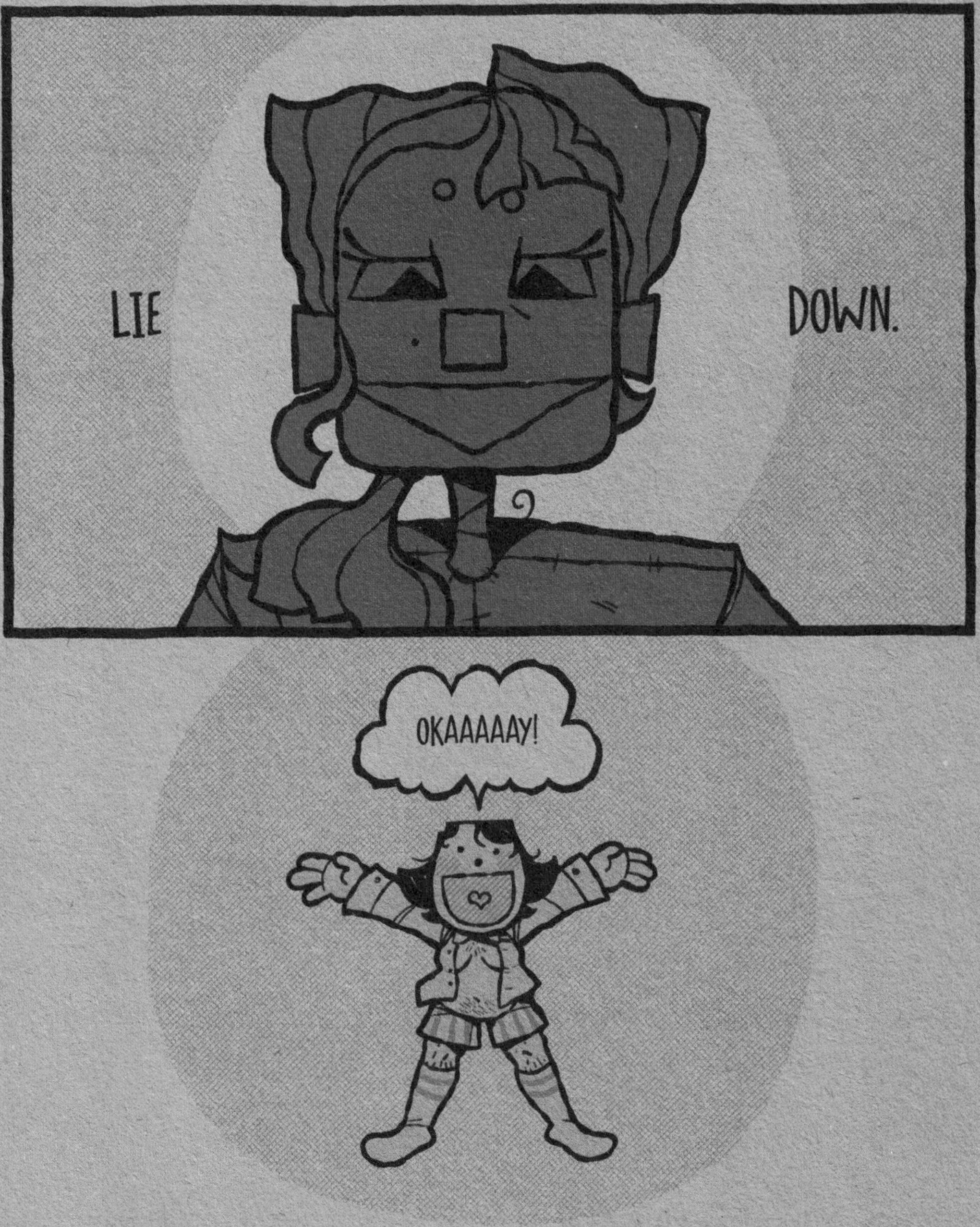
LIE
DOWN.
OKAAAAAY!

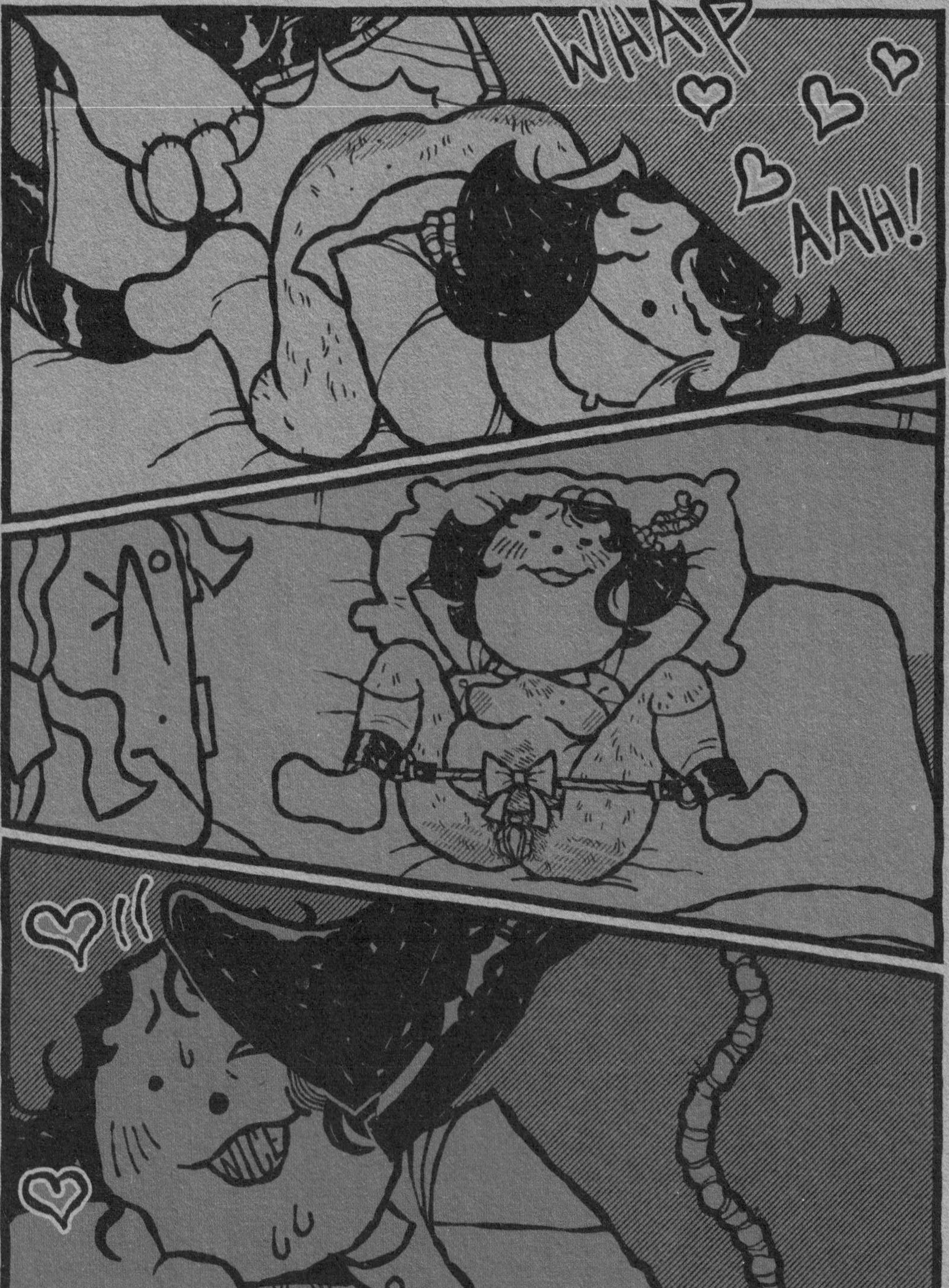
WHAP
AAH!

...alright, let's see what Neighbor's dealio is.

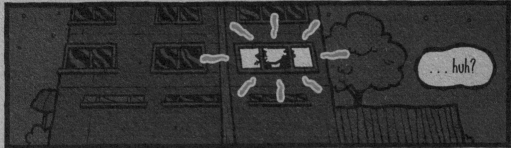

...huh?

AH!!?!? AH SHIT-

UH   UH   UH

P-PAYPHONE !!!

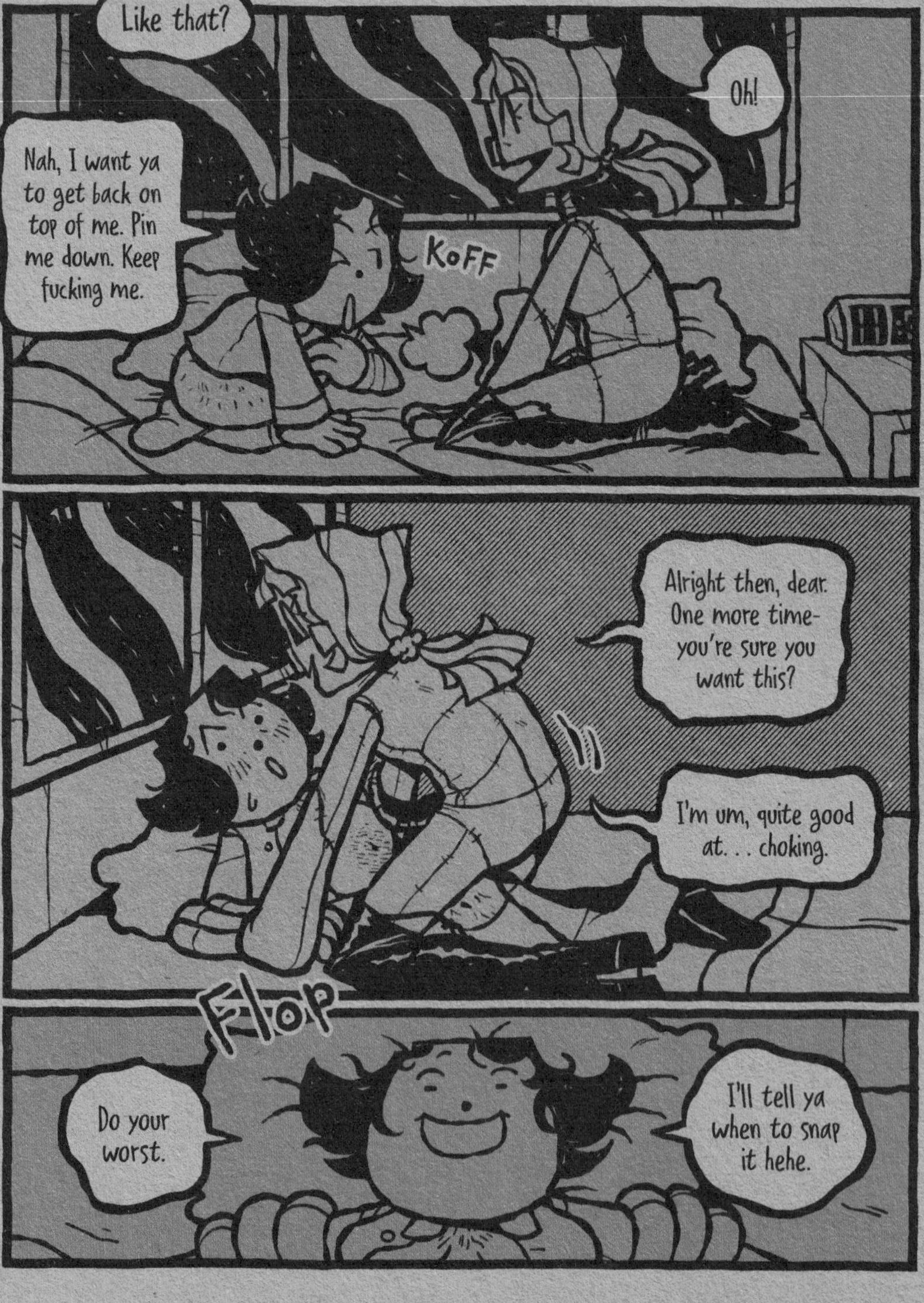
Like that?
Oh!
Nah, I want ya to get back on top of me. Pin me down. Keep fucking me.
KoFF
Alright then, dear. One more time- you're sure you want this?
I'm um, quite good at. . . choking.
Flop
Do your worst.
I'll tell ya when to snap it hehe.

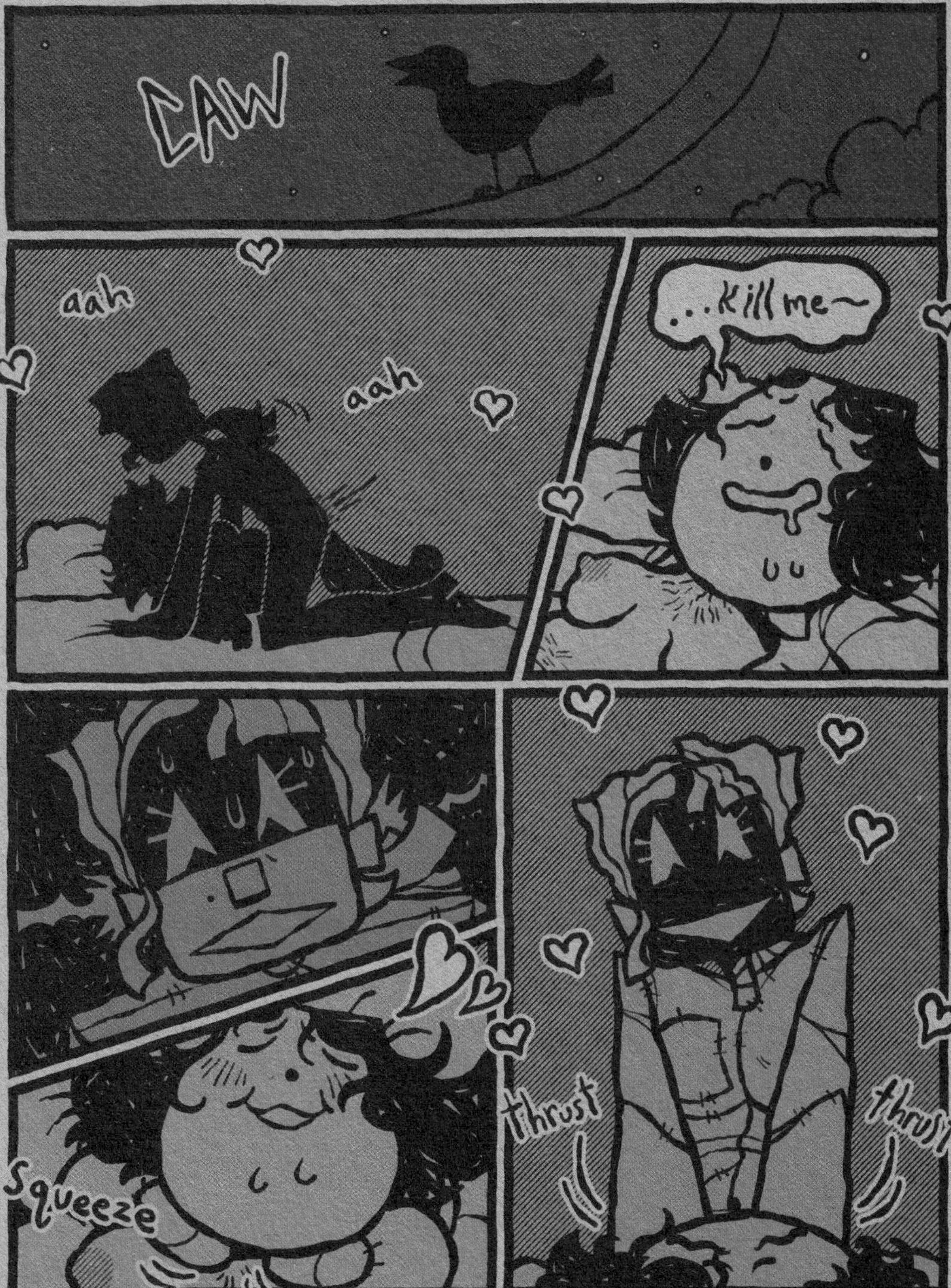
CAW
aah
aah
...Kill me~
squeeze
thrust
thrust

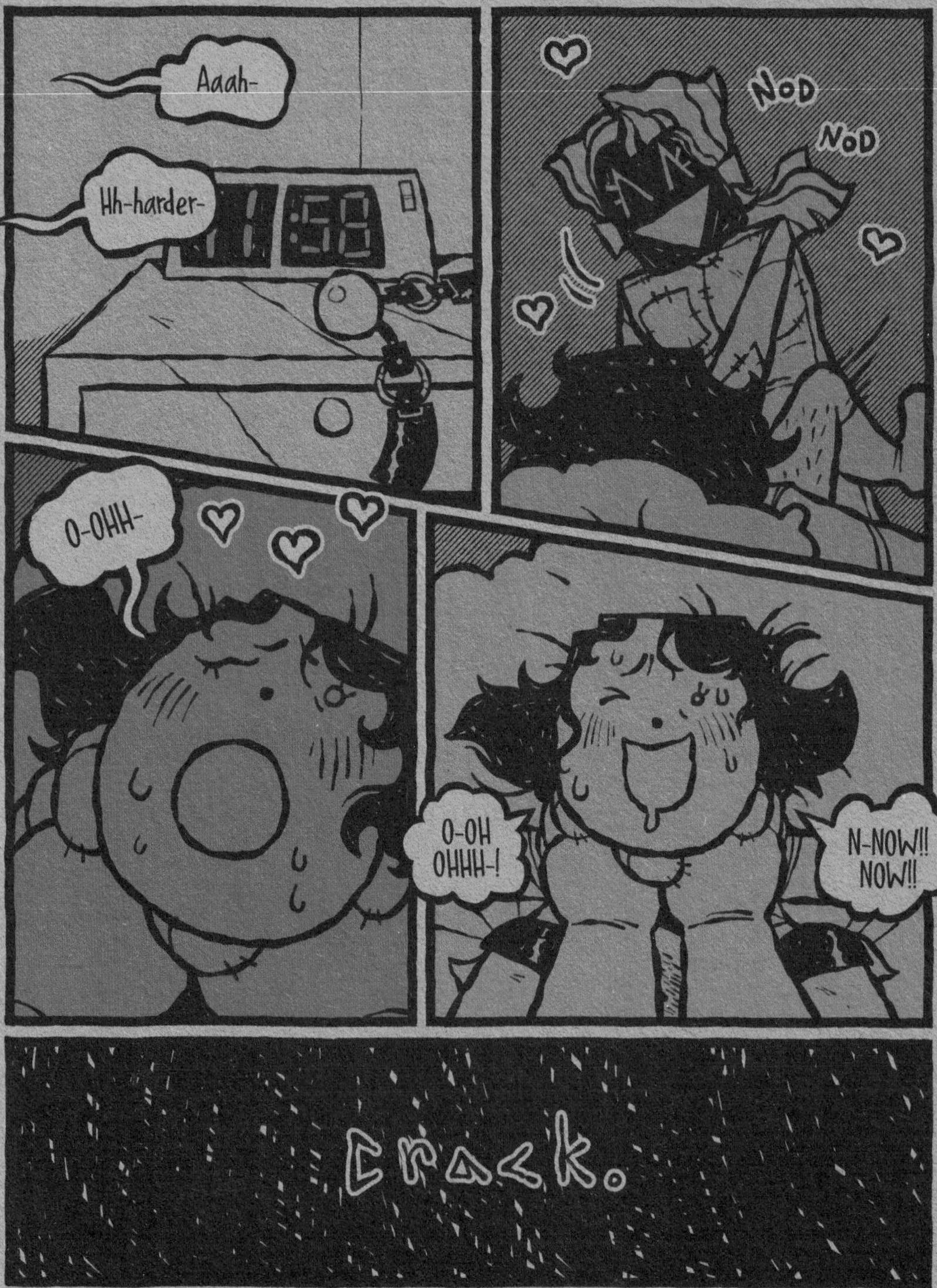
Aaah-
Hh-harder-
NOD
NOD
O-OHH-
O-OH
OHHH-!
N-NOW!!
NOW!!
crack.

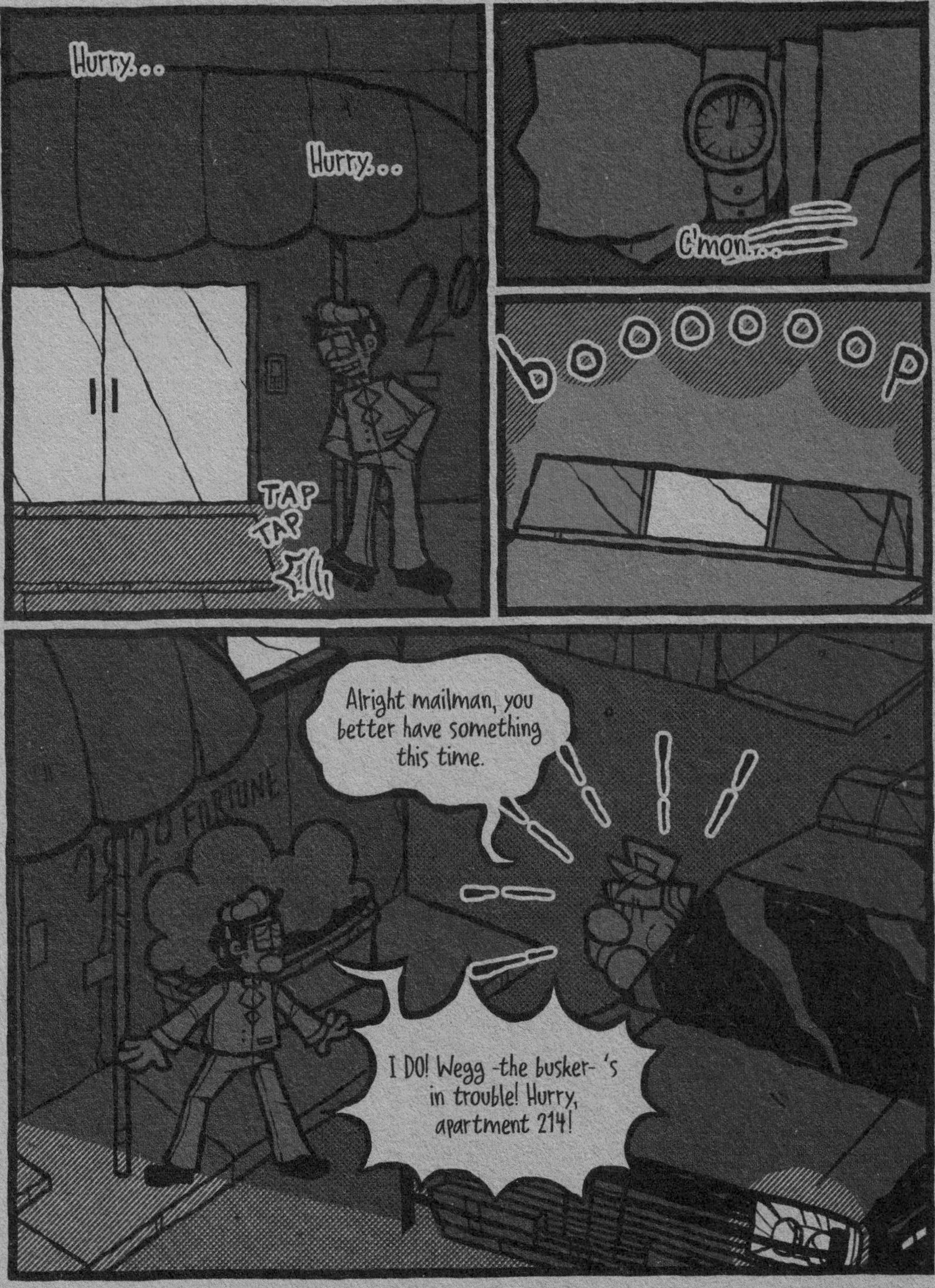
Hurry...
Hurry...
TAP
TAP
C'mon...
booooooop
Alright mailman, you better have something this time.
I DO! Wegg -the busker- 's in trouble! Hurry, apartment 214!

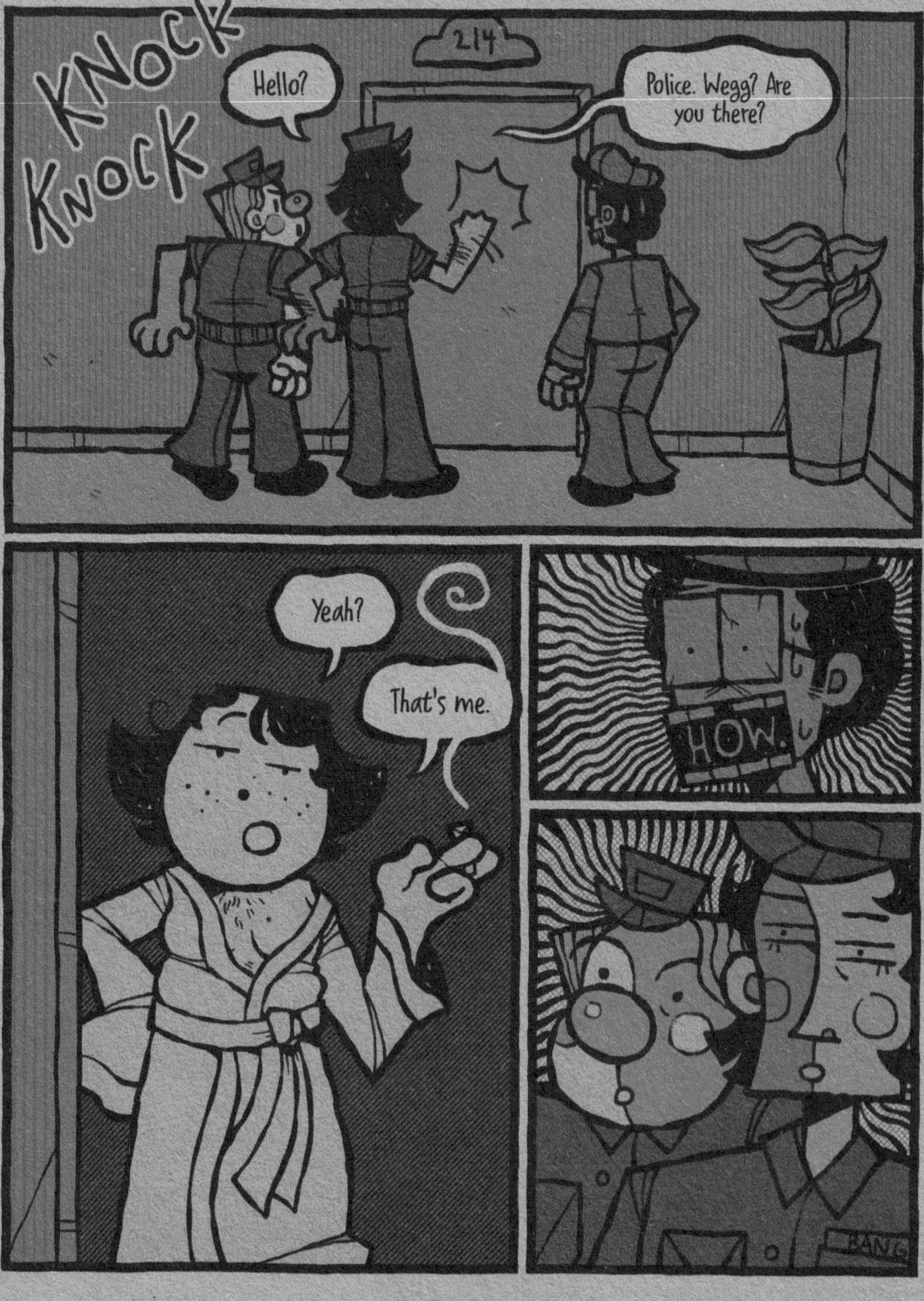
KNOCK KNOCK
Hello?
214
Police. Wegg? Are you there?
Yeah?
That's me.
HOW.
BANG

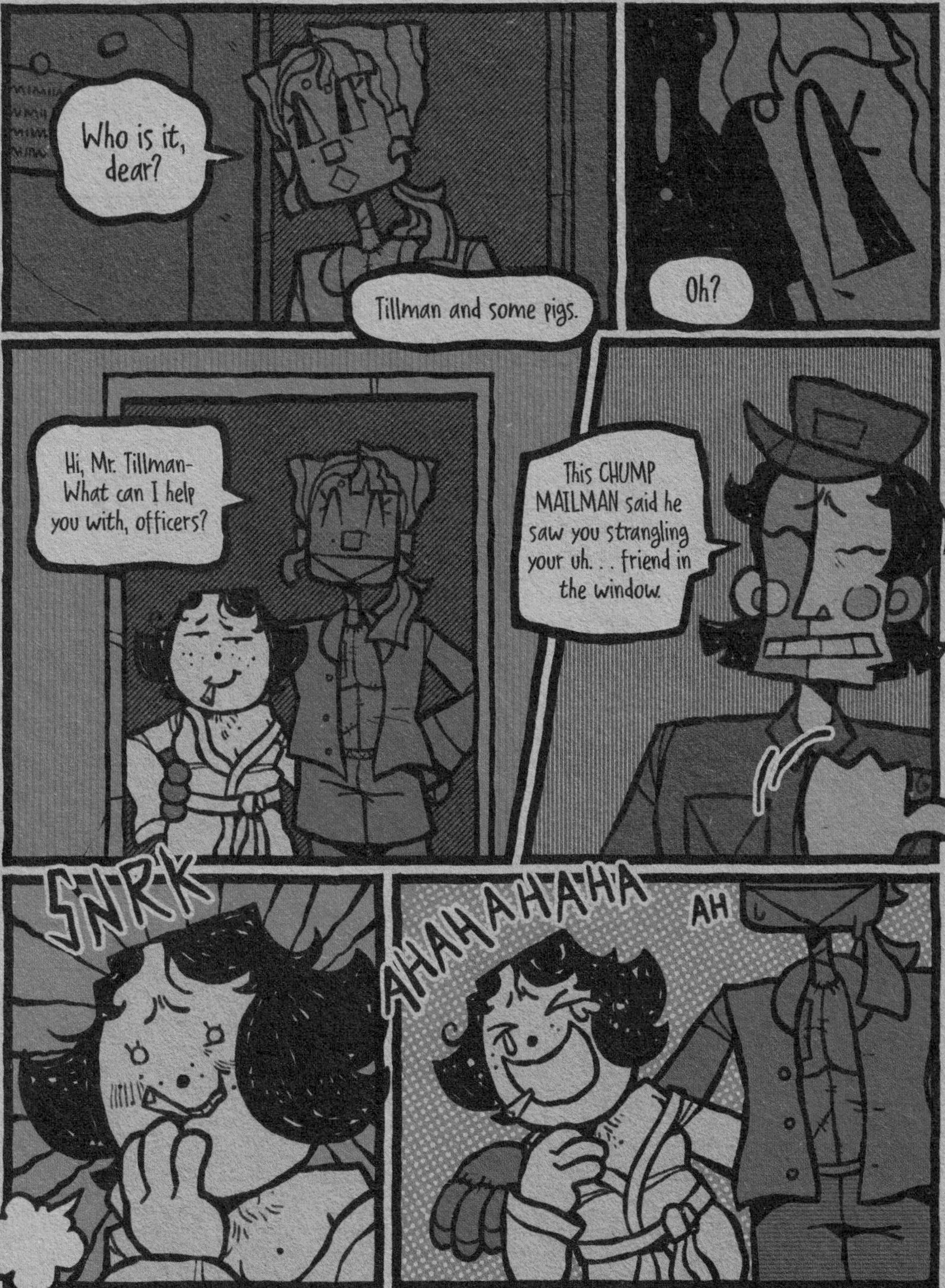
Who is it, dear?
Tillman and some pigs.
Oh?
Hi, Mr. Tillman- What can I help you with, officers?
This CHUMP MAILMAN said he saw you strangling your uh. . . friend in the window.
SNRK
AHAHAHAHAHA
AH

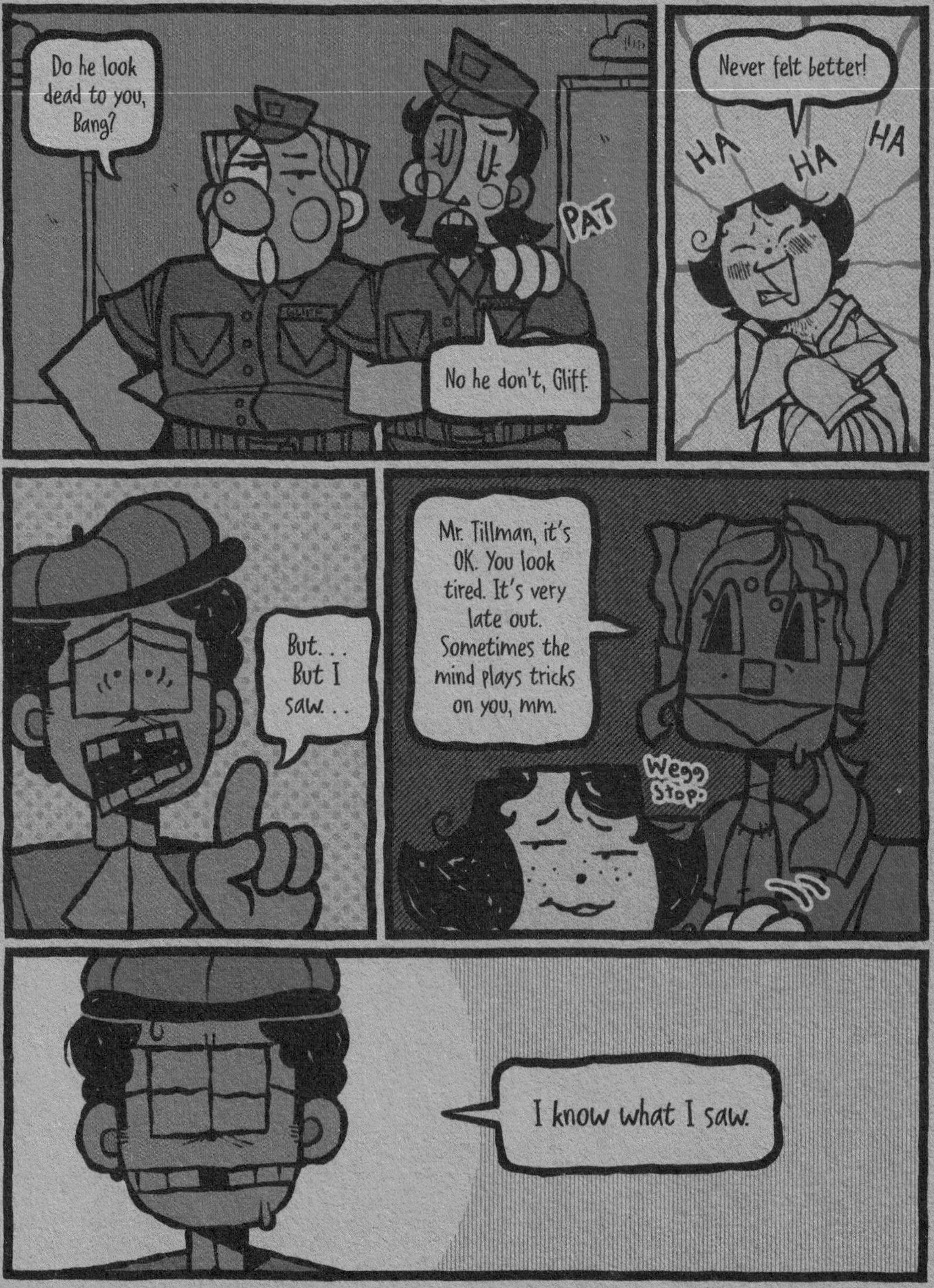
Do he look dead to you, Bang?
PAT
No he don't, Gliff.
Never felt better!
HA HA HA
But... But I saw...
Mr. Tillman, it's OK. You look tired. It's very late out. Sometimes the mind plays tricks on you, mm.
Wegg Stop.
I know what I saw.

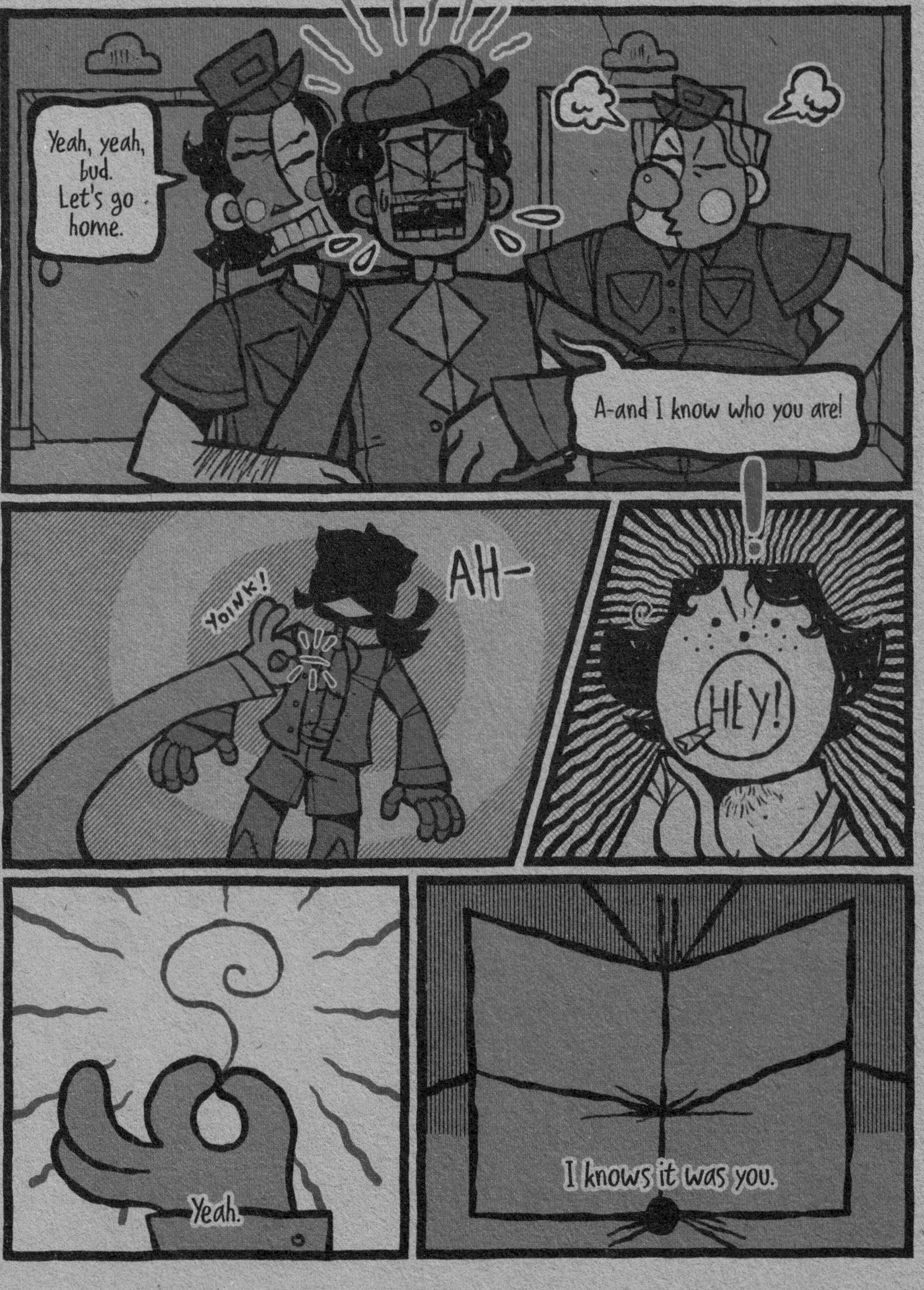
Yeah, yeah, bud. Let's go home.
A-and I know who you are!
!
YOINK!
AH-
HEY!
Yeah.
I knows it was you.

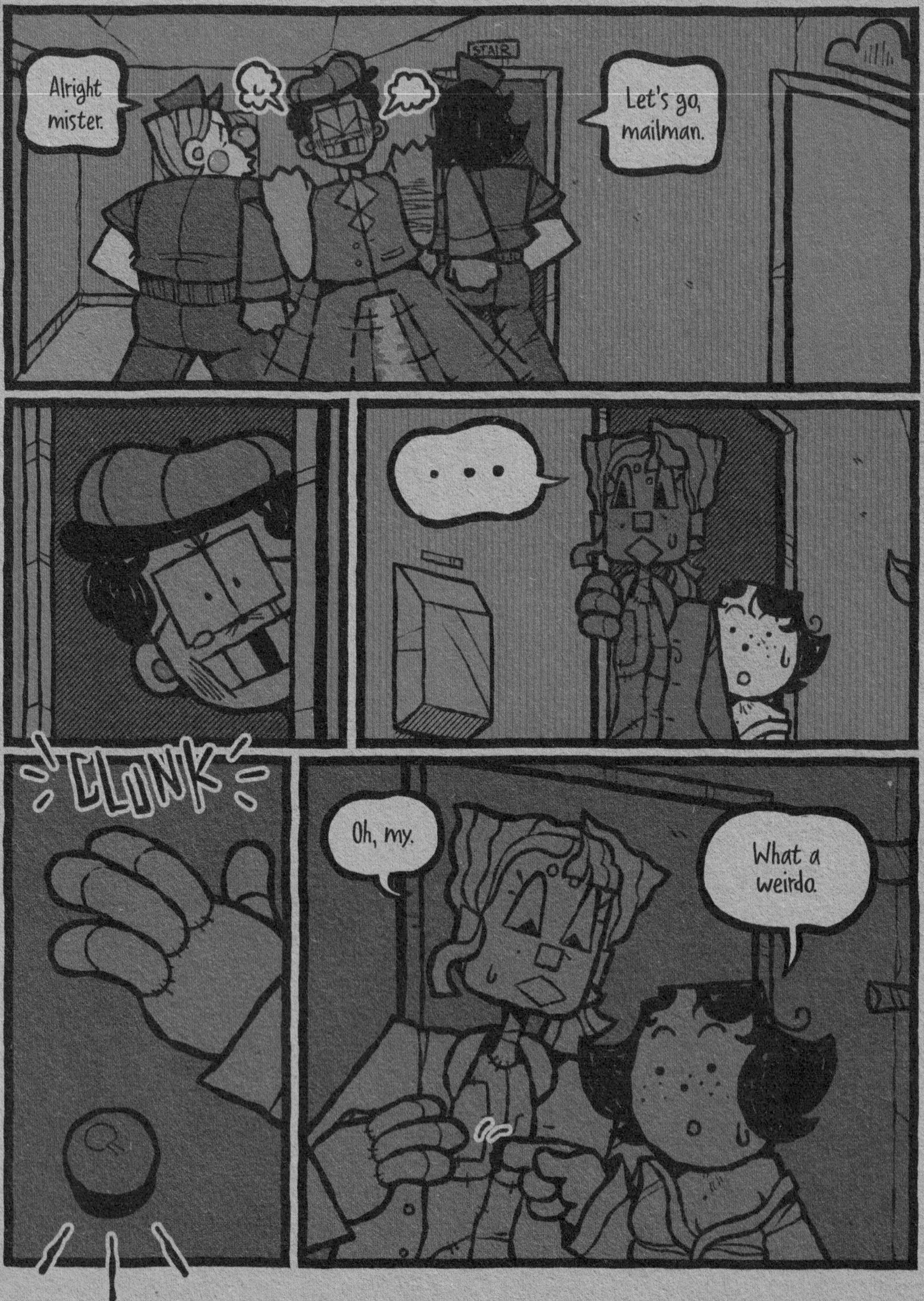
STAIR
Alright mister.
Let's go, mailman.
...
CLONK
Oh, my.
What a weirdo.

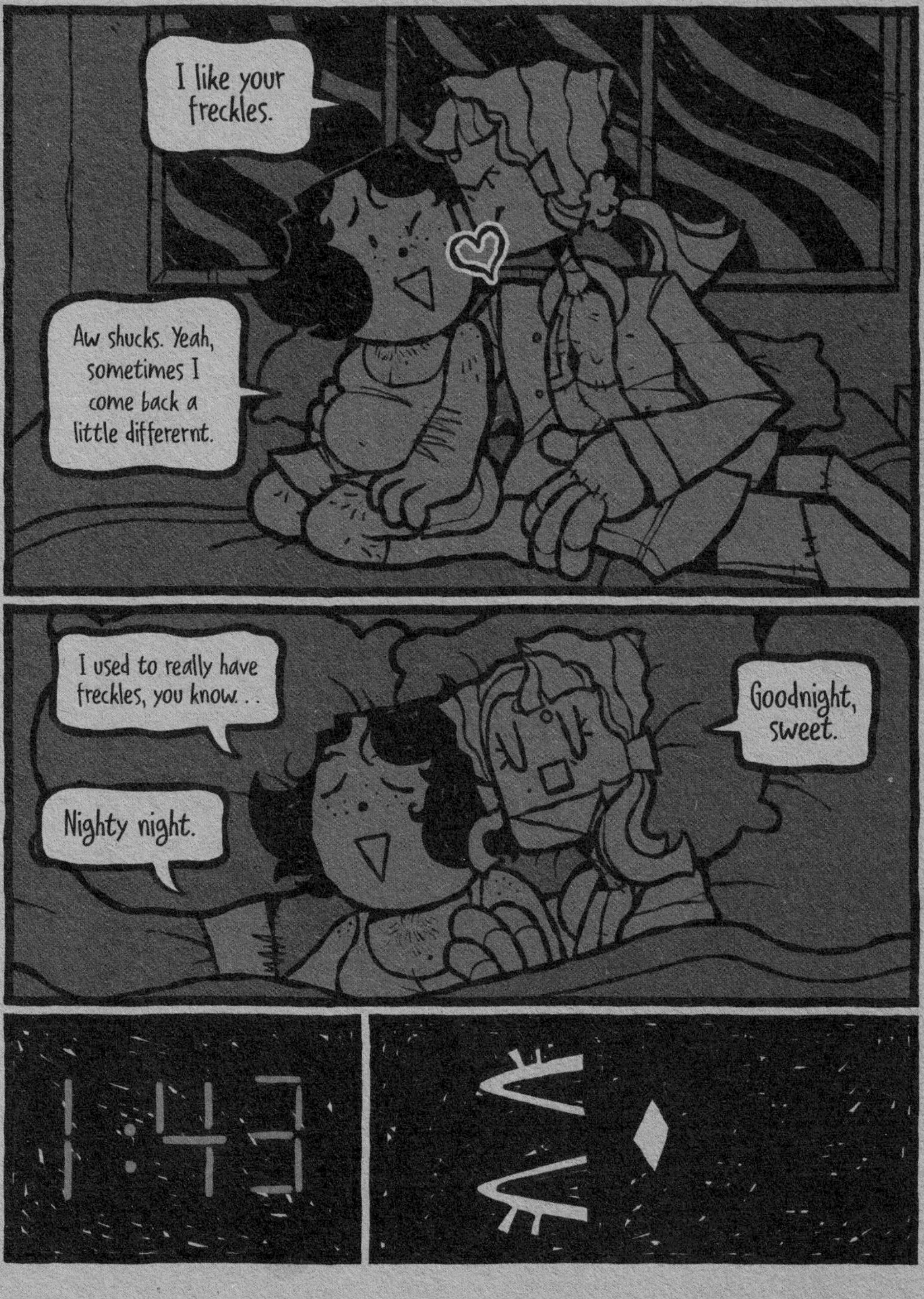
I like your freckles.
Aw shucks. Yeah, sometimes I come back a little differernt.
I used to really have freckles, you know. . .
Goodnight, sweet.
Nighty night.
1:43

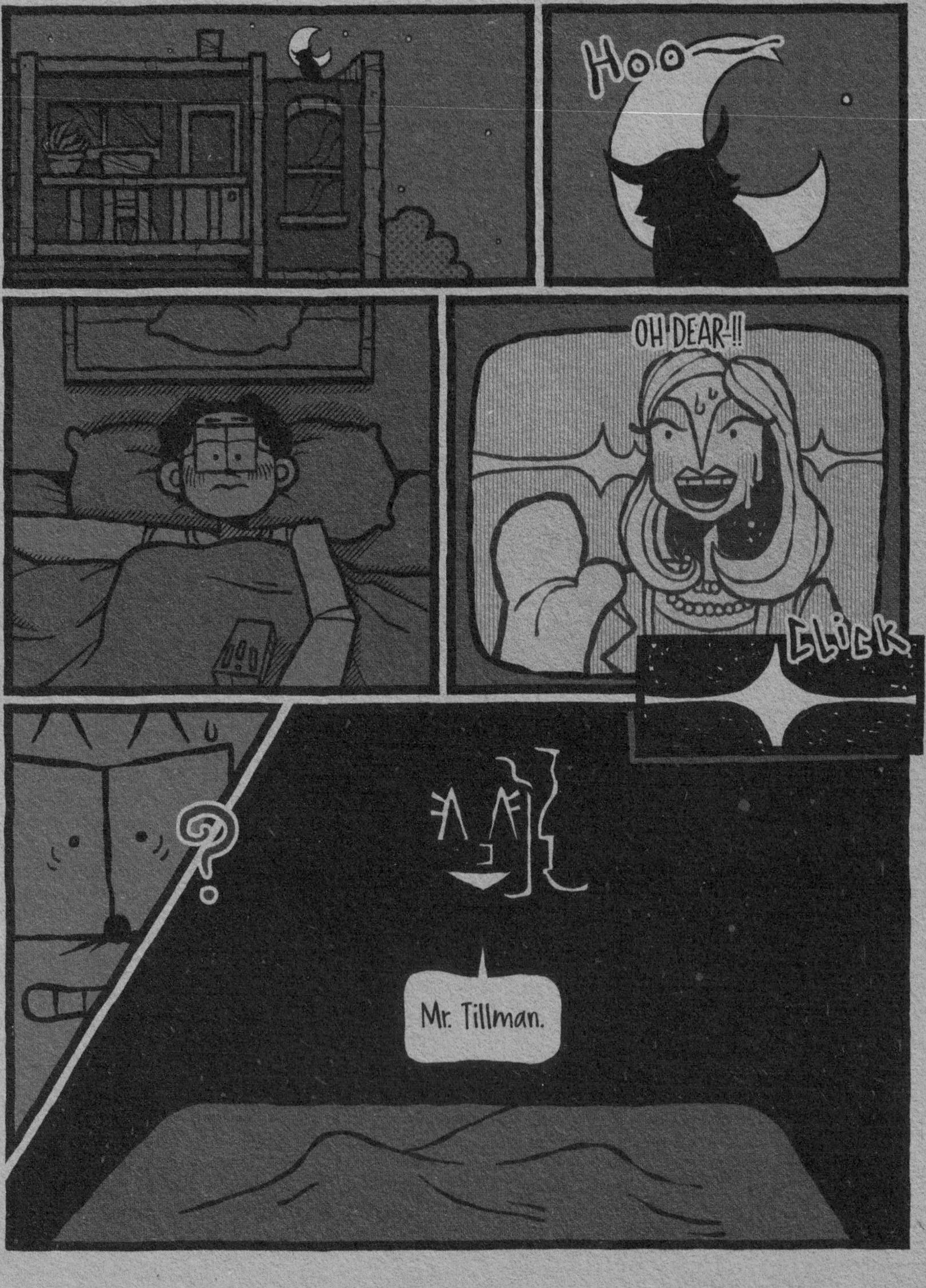

Hoo
OH DEAR-!!
CLICK
Mr. Tillman.

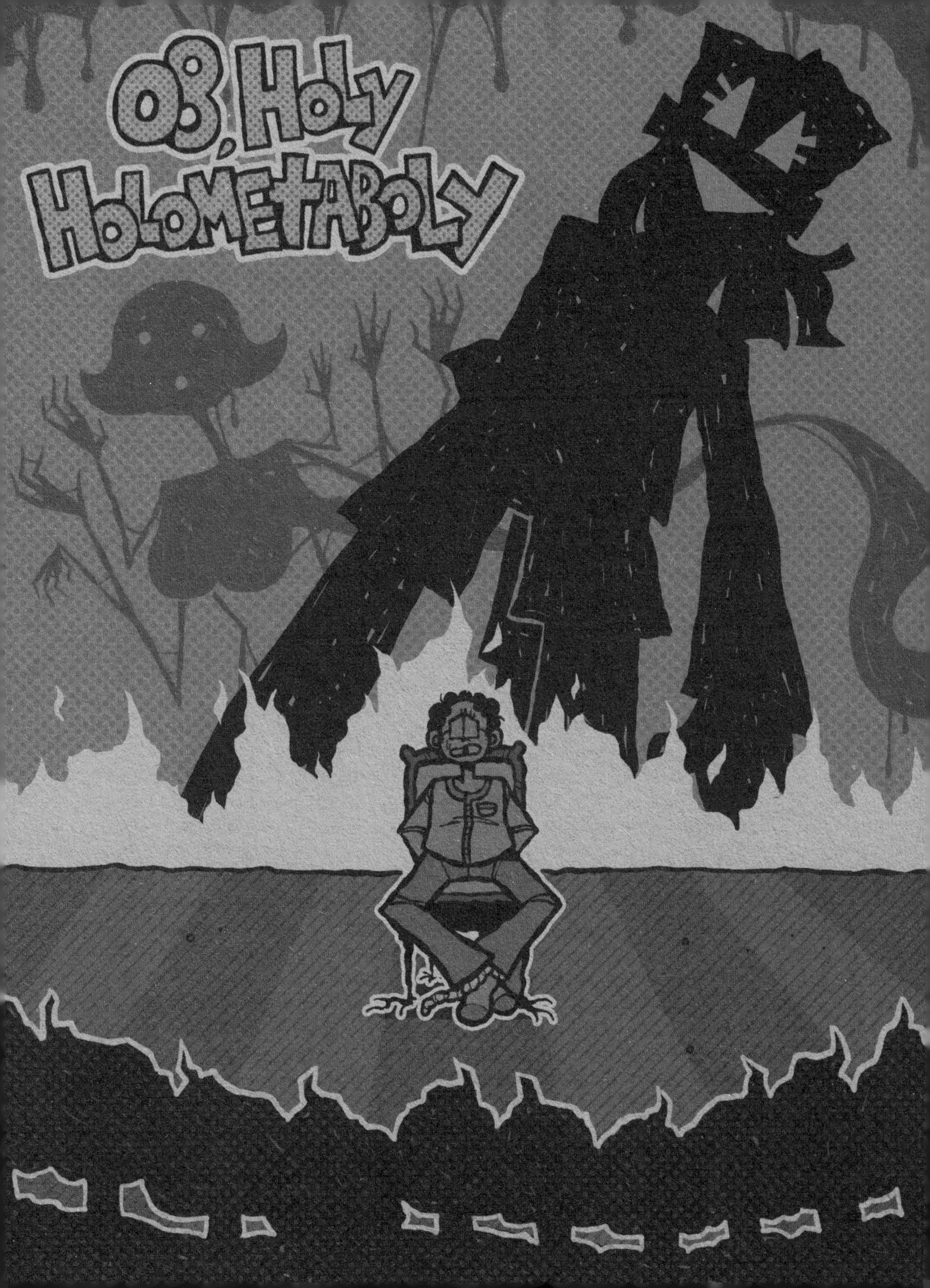
08, Holy
Holometaboly

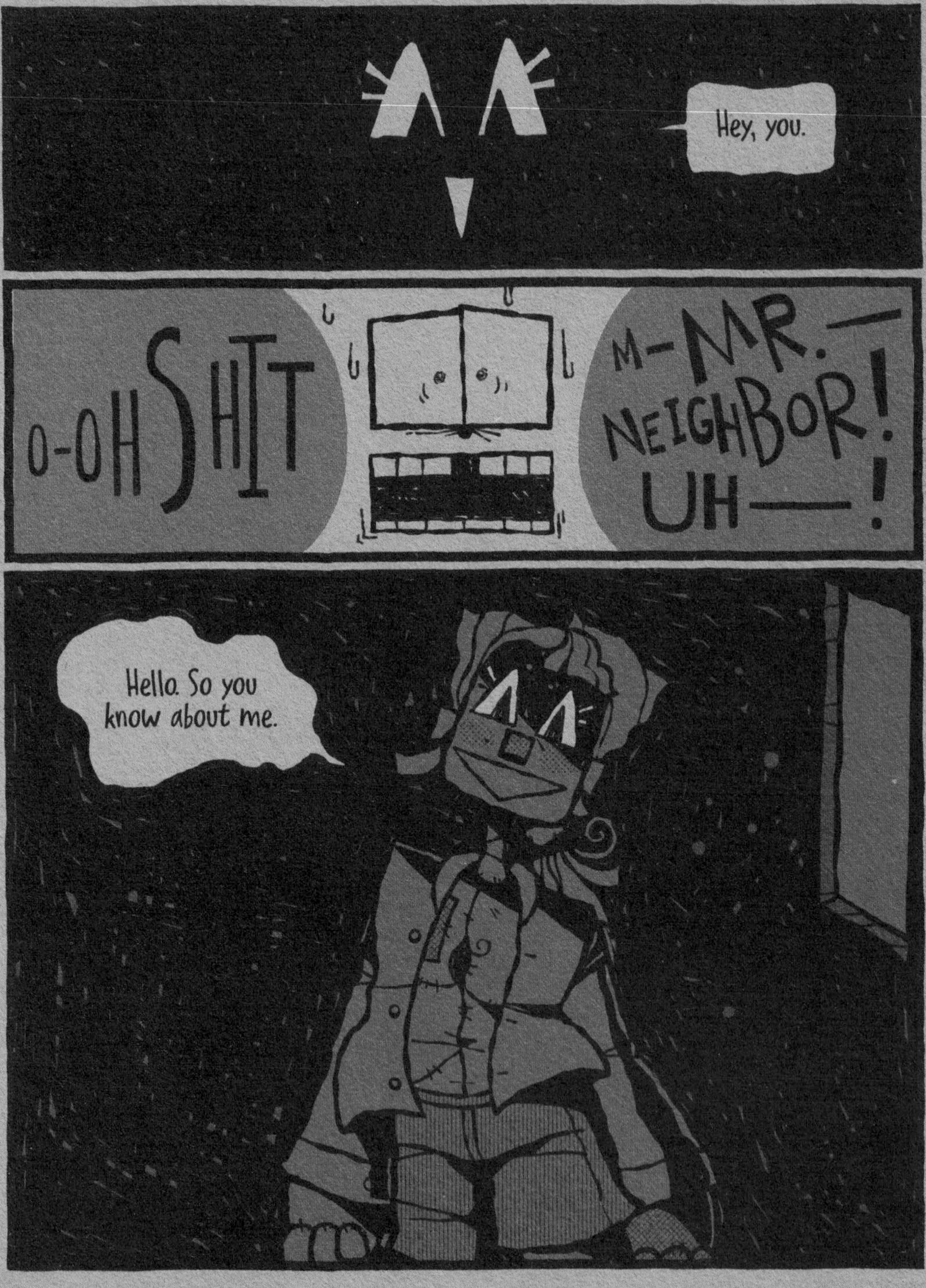
Hey, you.
O-OH SHIT
M-MR.— NEIGHBOR! UH—!
Hello. So you know about me.

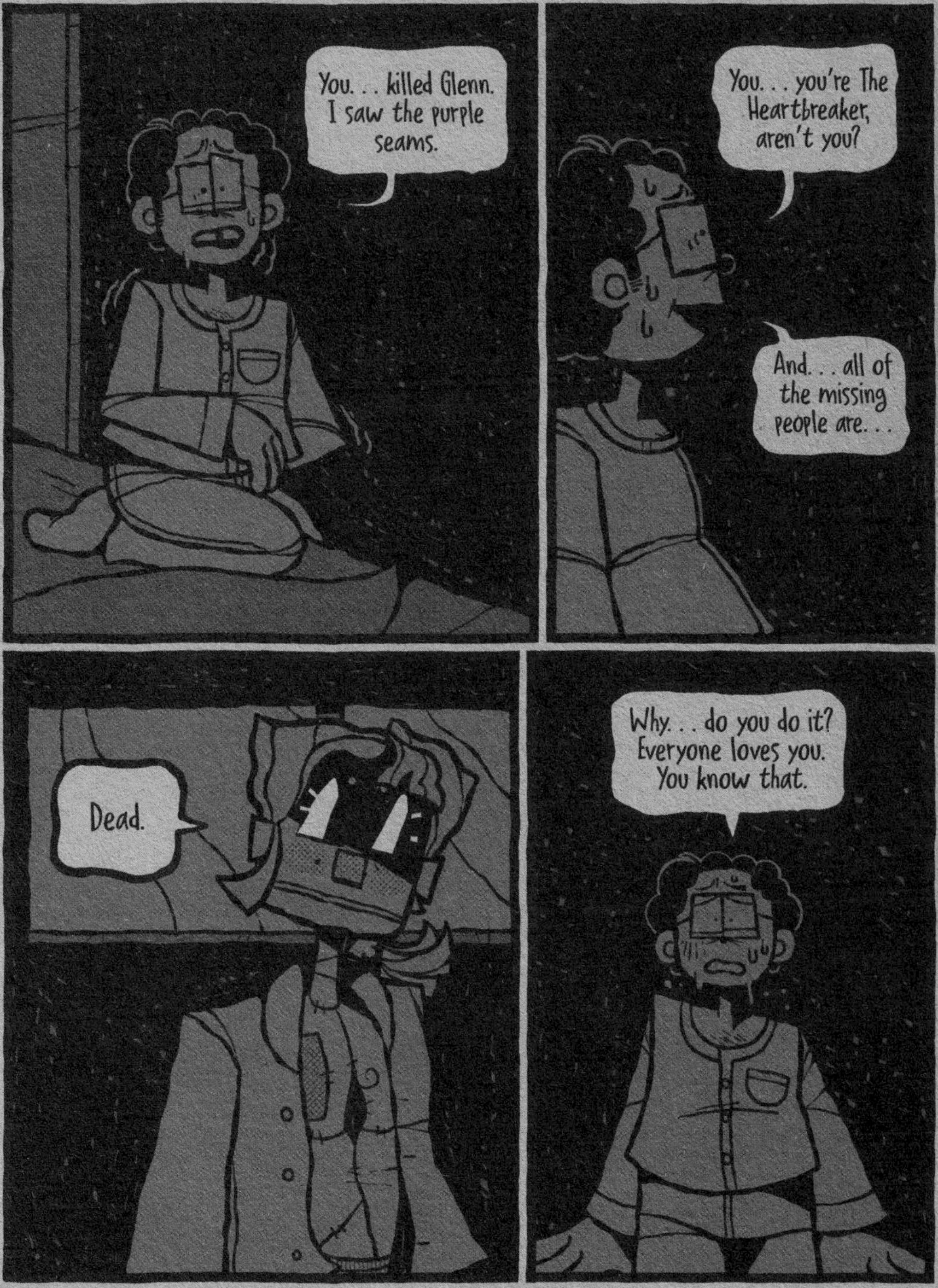
You. . . killed Glenn. I saw the purple seams.
You. . . you're The Heartbreaker, aren't you?
And. . . all of the missing people are. . .
Dead.
Why. . . do you do it? Everyone loves you. You know that.

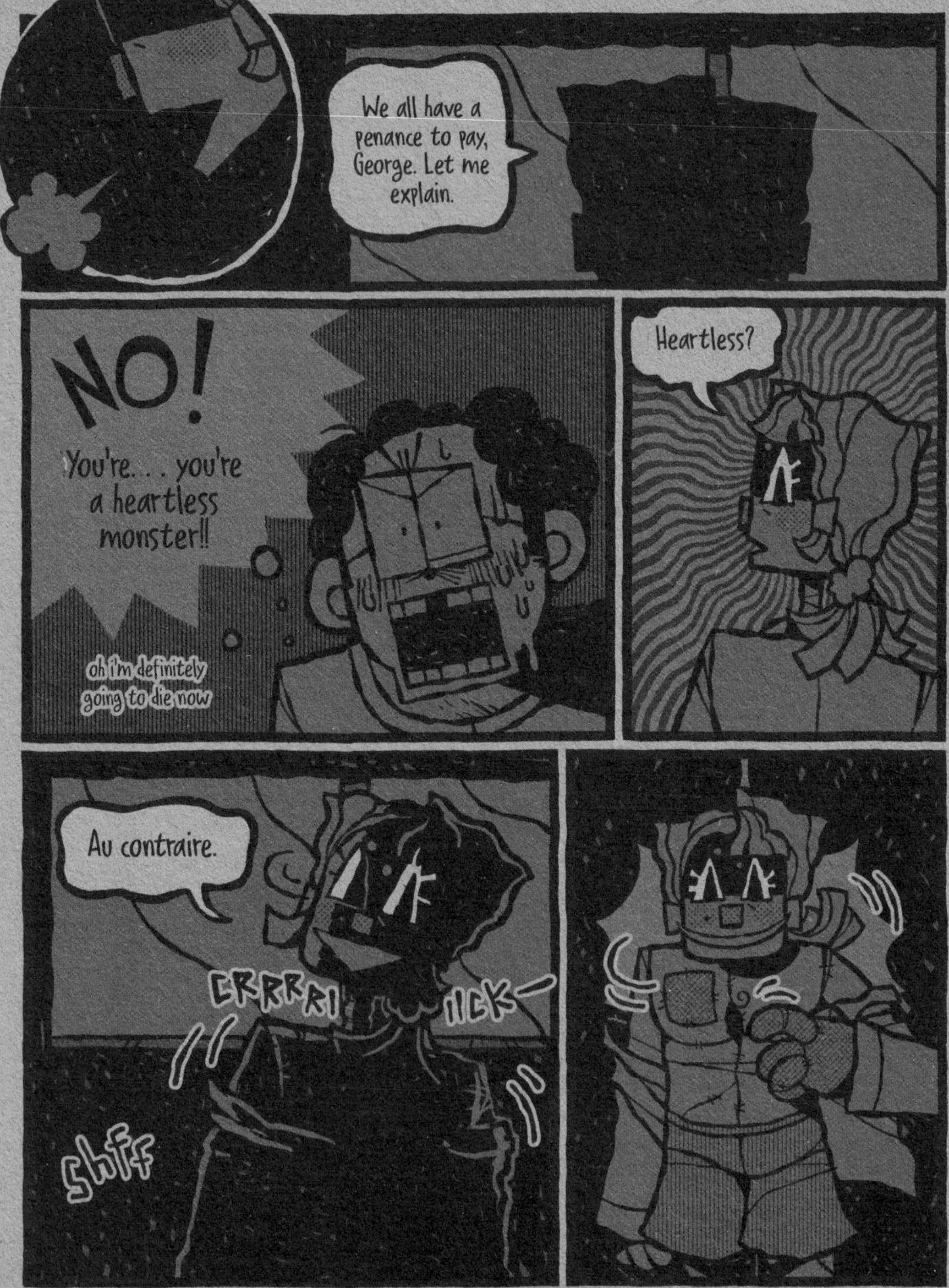
We all have a penance to pay, George. Let me explain.
NO!
You're. . . . you're a heartless monster!!
oh i'm definitely going to die now
Heartless?
Au contraire.
CRRRRI
ICK—
shff

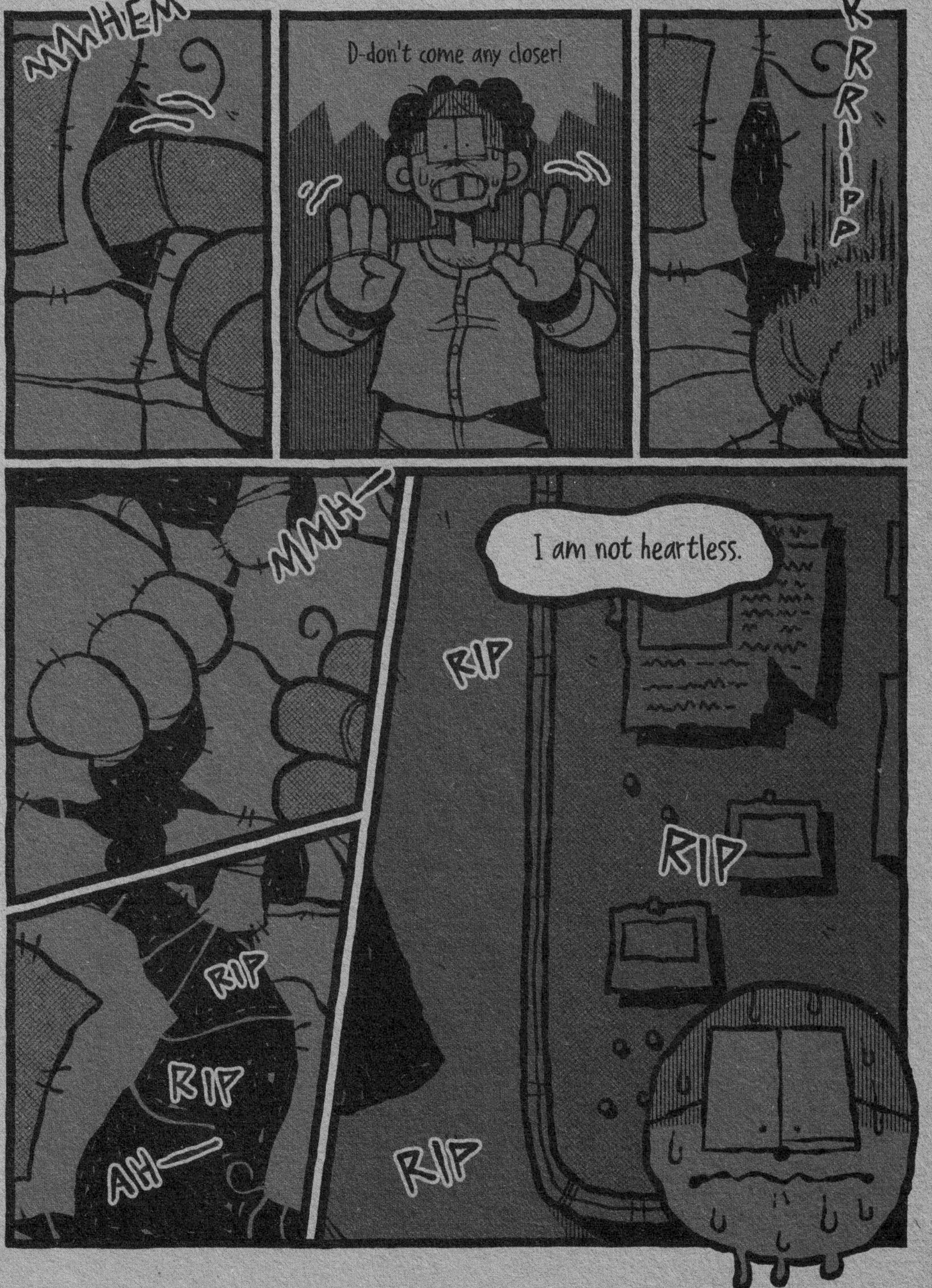
MMHEM
D-don't come any closer!
RRRIIPP
MMH—
I am not heartless.
RIP
RIP
RIP
RIP
RIP
AH—

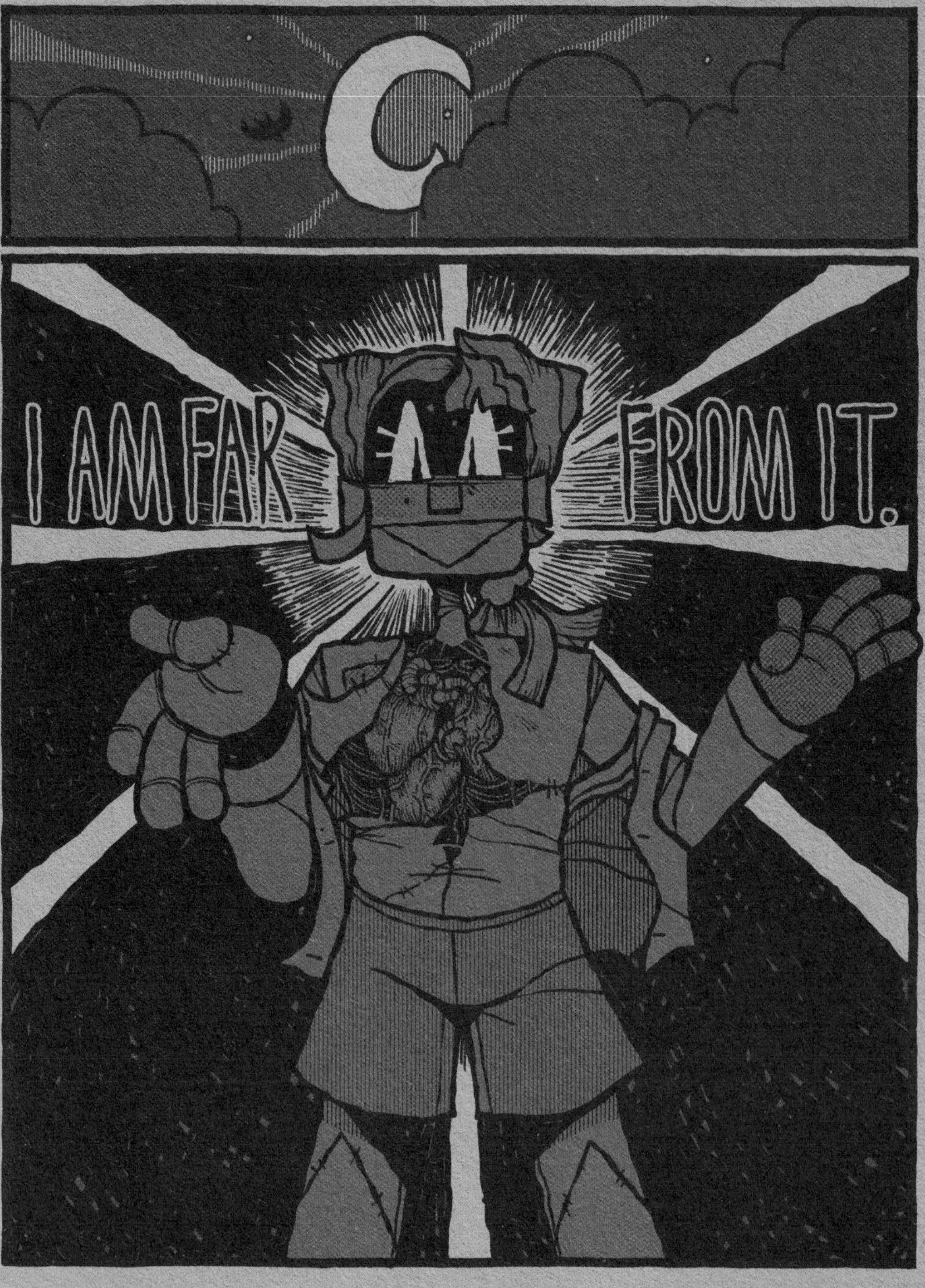
I AM FAR
FROM IT.

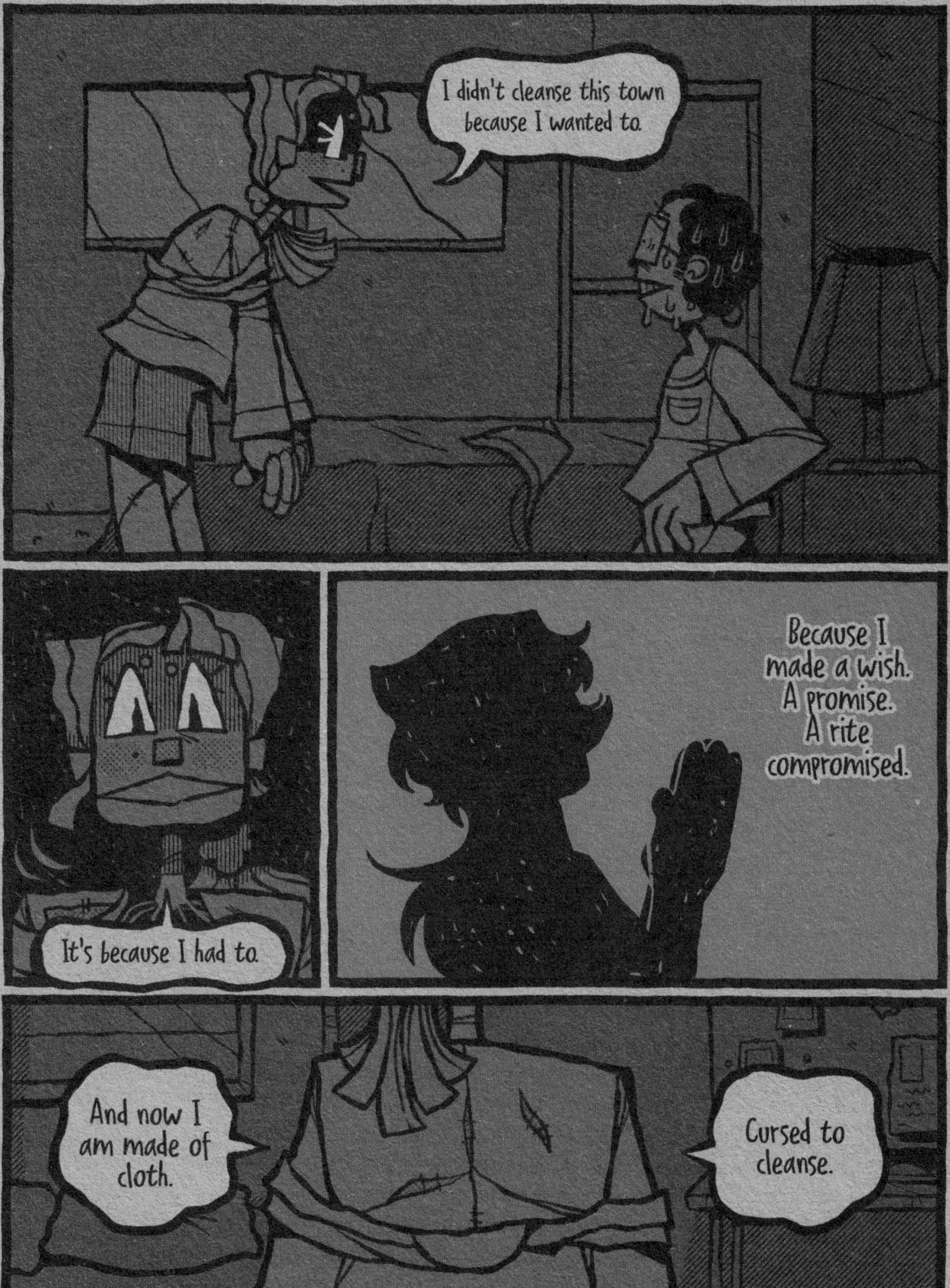
I didn't cleanse this town because I wanted to.
It's because I had to.
Because I made a wish. A promise. A rite compromised.
And now I am made of cloth.
Cursed to cleanse.

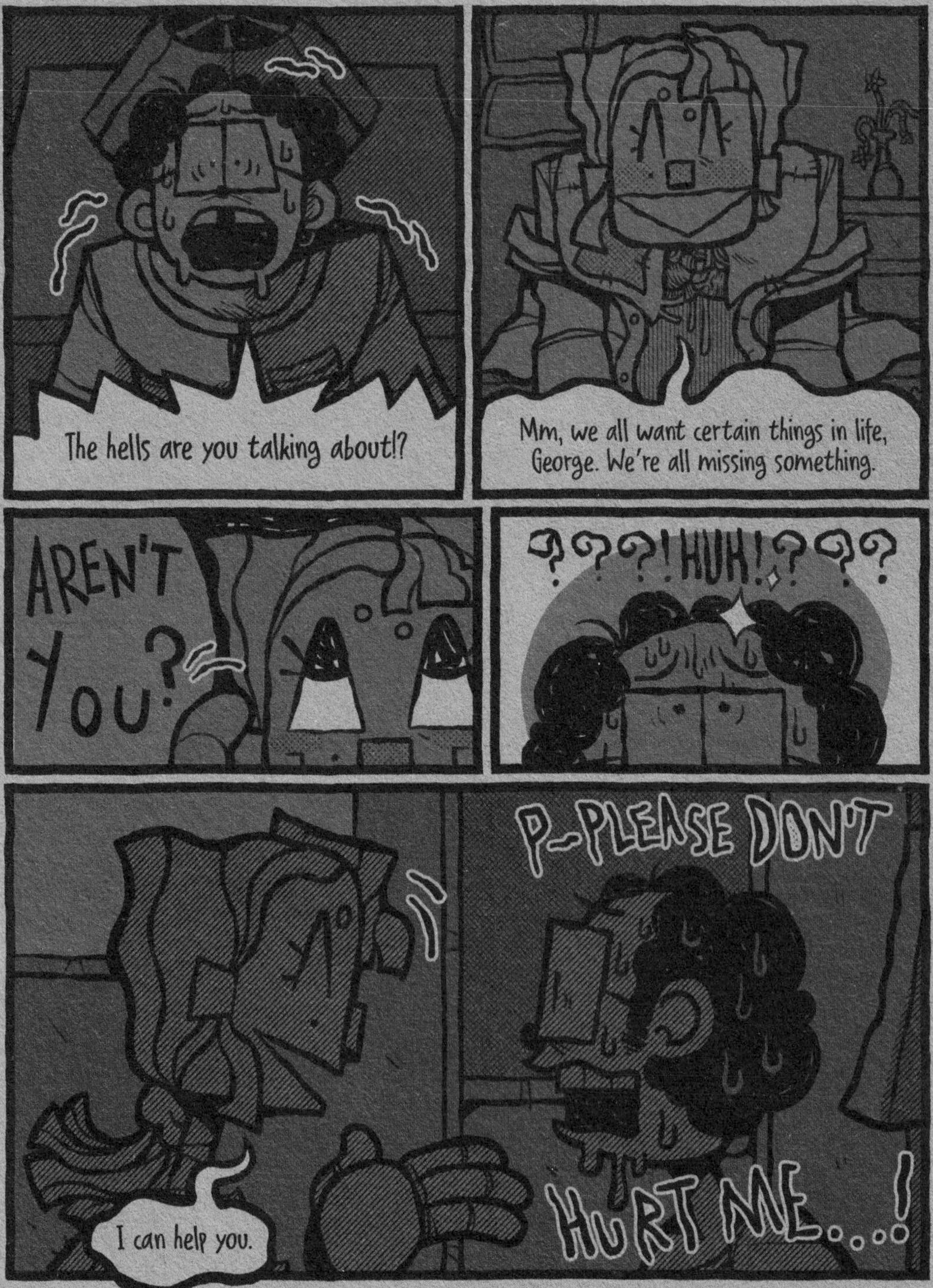
The hells are you talking about!?
Mm, we all want certain things in life, George. We're all missing something.
AREN'T YOU?
???!HUH!???
P-PLEASE DON'T
I can help you.
HURT ME...!

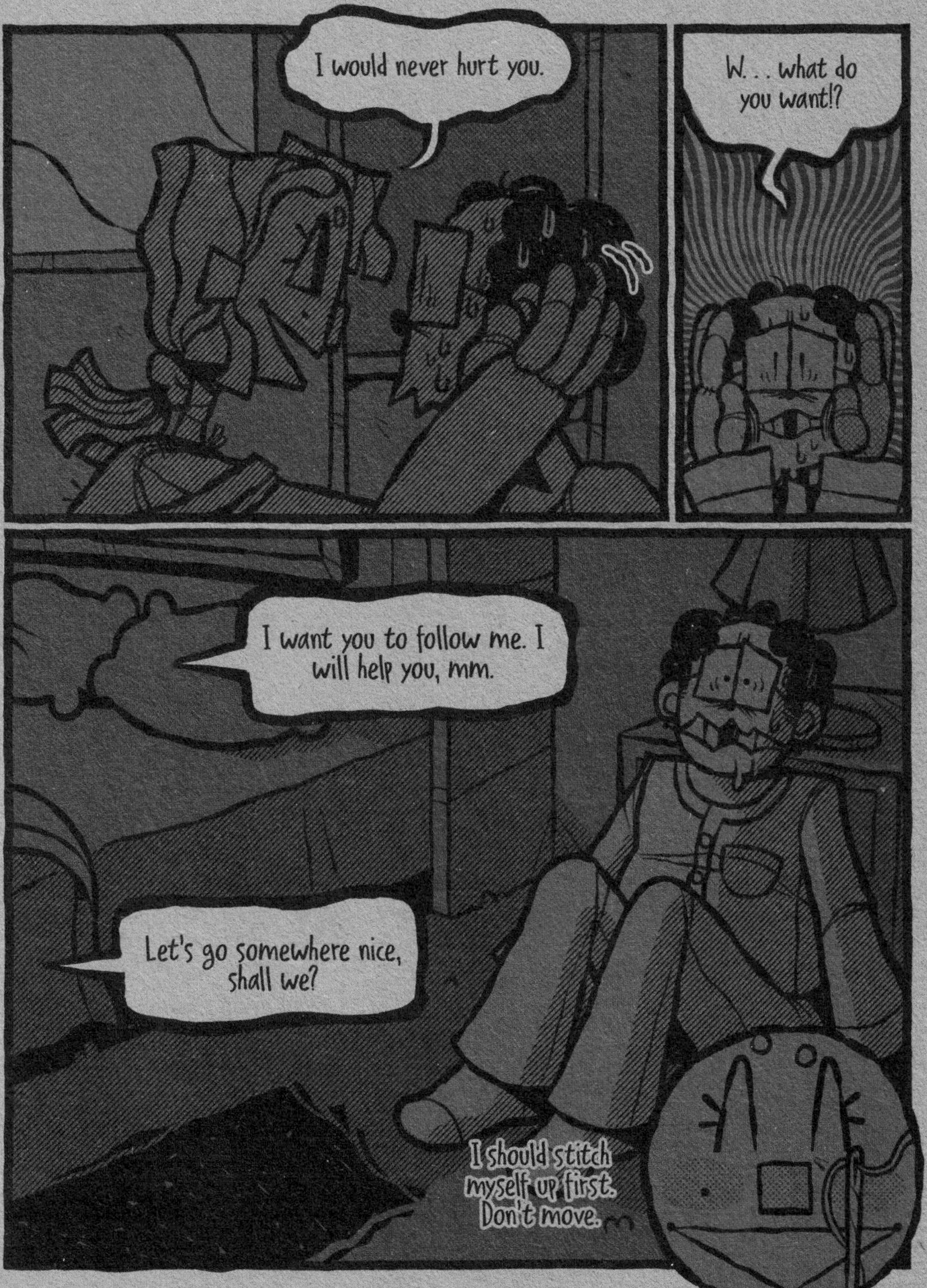
I would never hurt you.
W. . . what do you want!?
I want you to follow me. I will help you, mm.
Let's go somewhere nice, shall we?
I should stitch myself up first. Don't move.

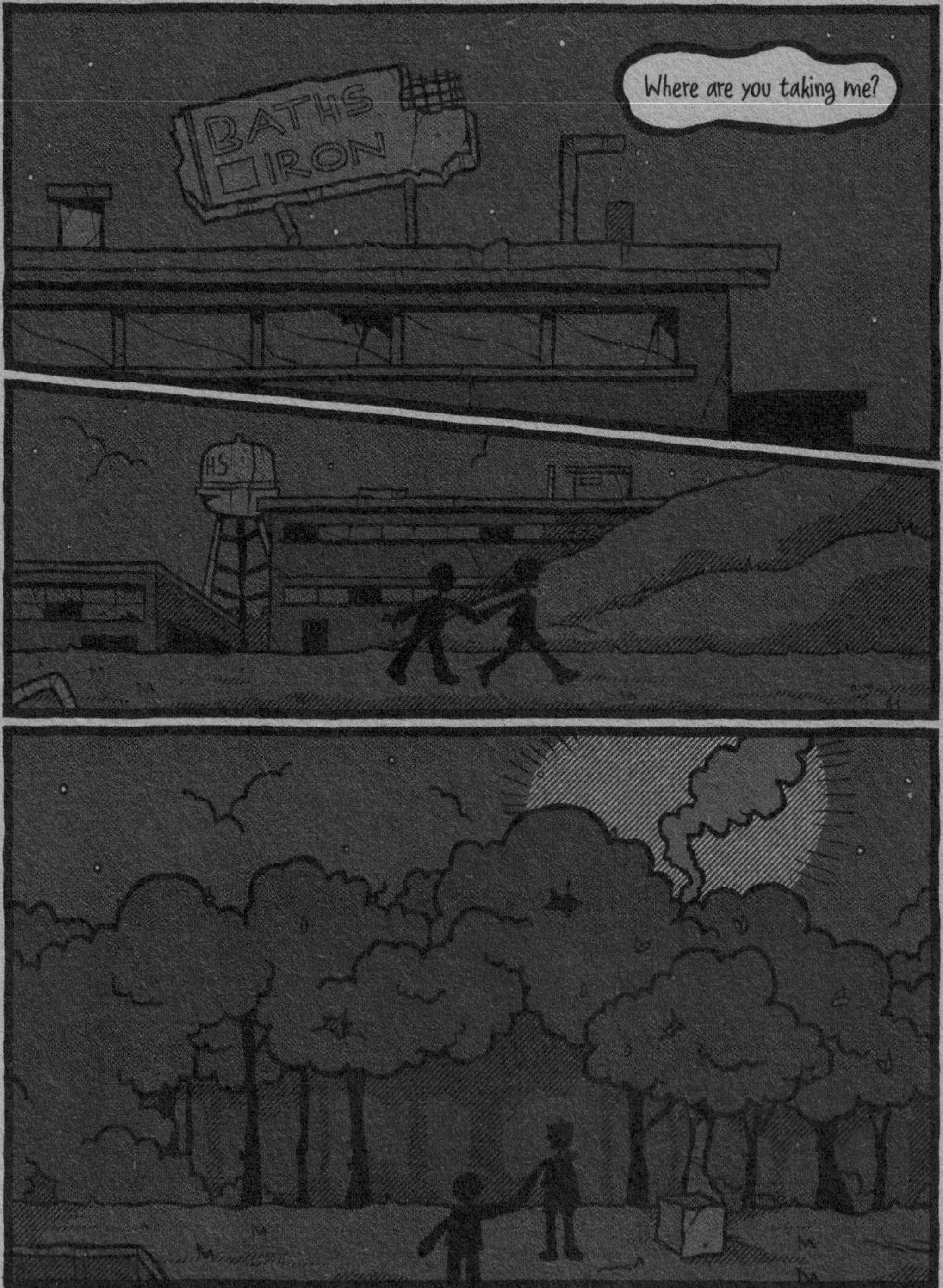
Where are you taking me?
BATHS
IRON
HS

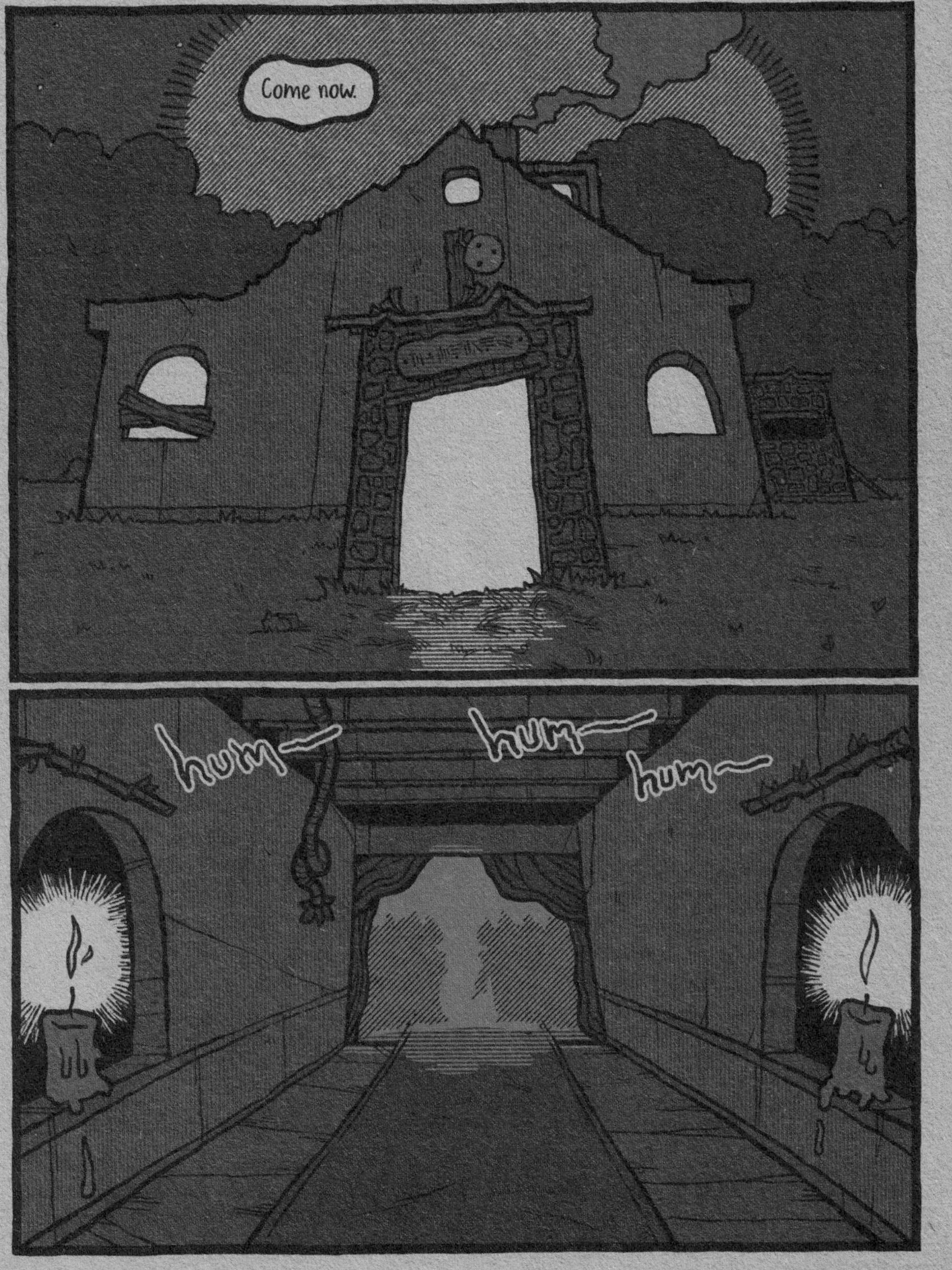
Come now.
hum~
hum~
hum~

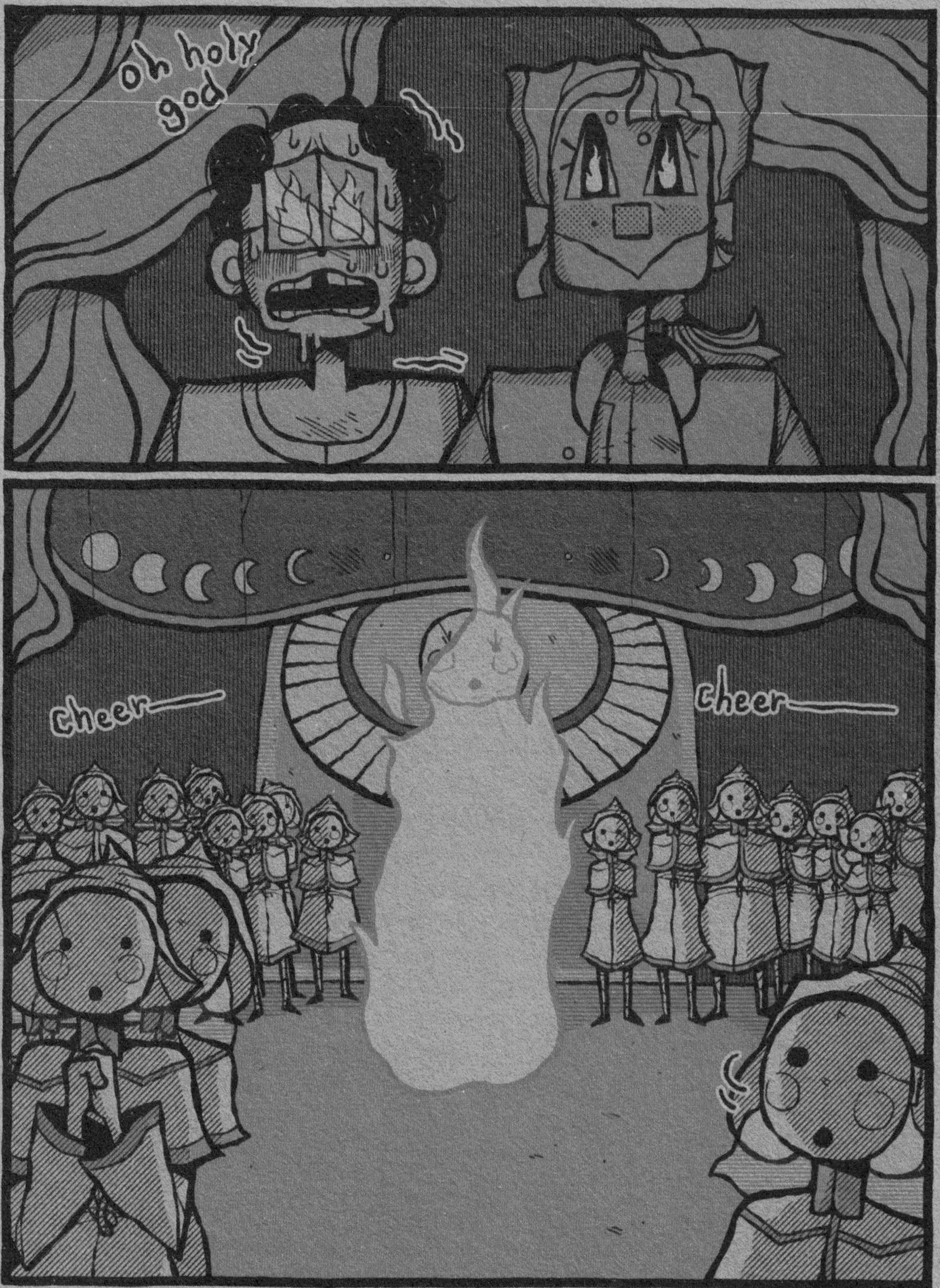
oh holy god
cheer——
cheer——

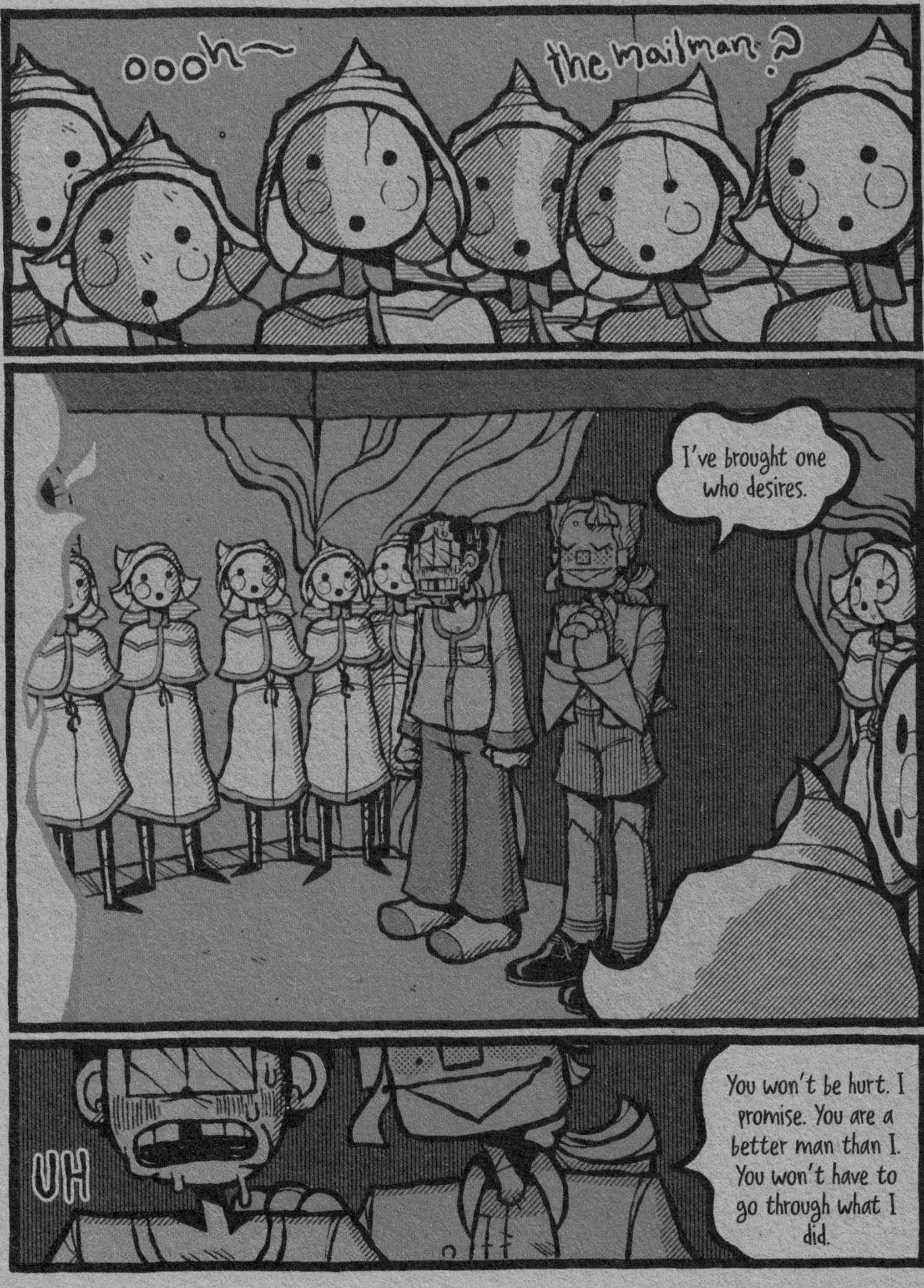
oooh~
the mailman?
I've brought one who desires.
UH
You won't be hurt. I promise. You are a better man than I. You won't have to go through what I did.

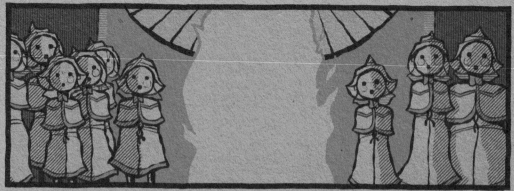

He desires?

He desires.

Do you desire?

Say yes. You'll get what you want.

Y-yes.

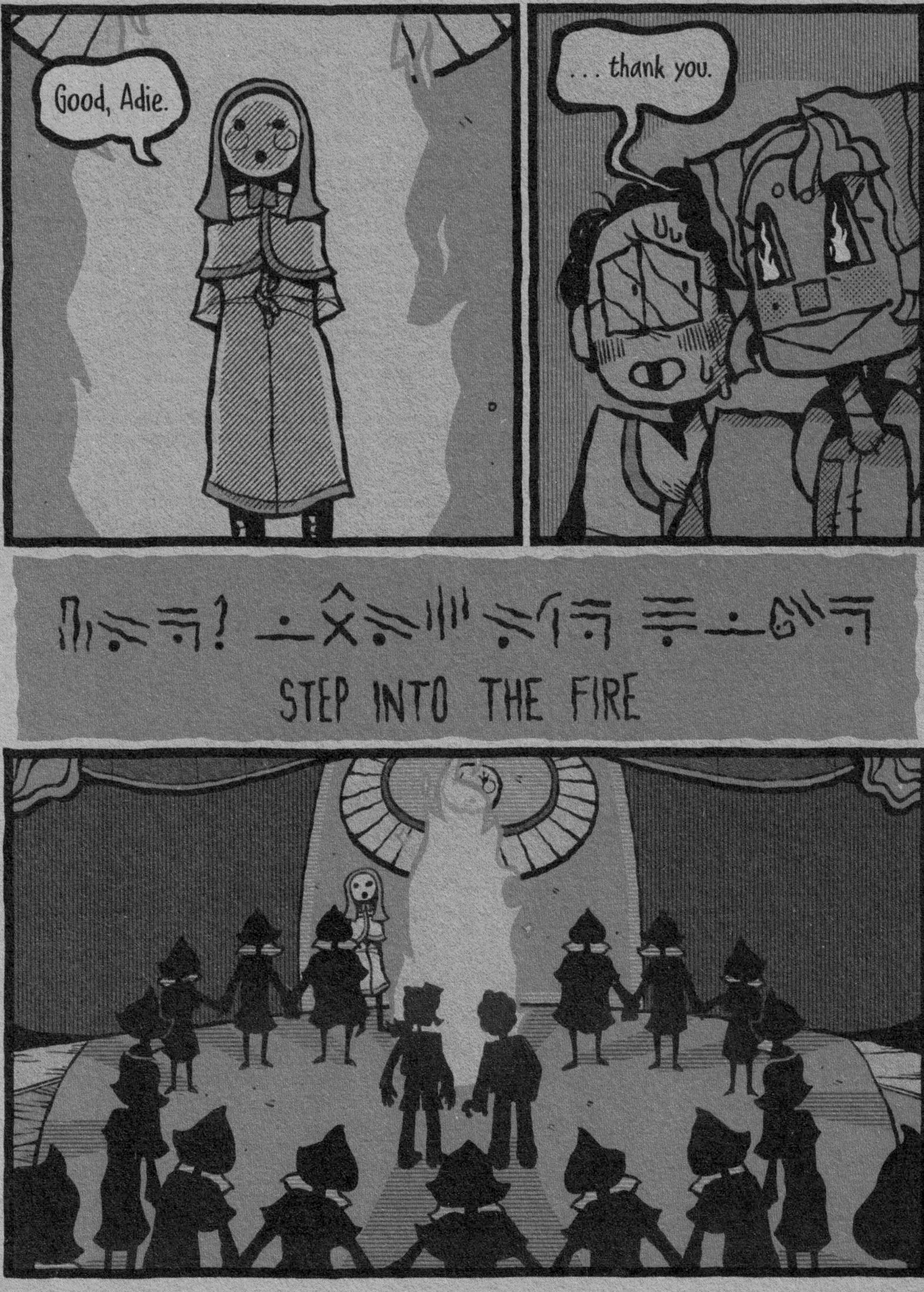
Good, Adie.
. . . thank you.
STEP INTO THE FIRE

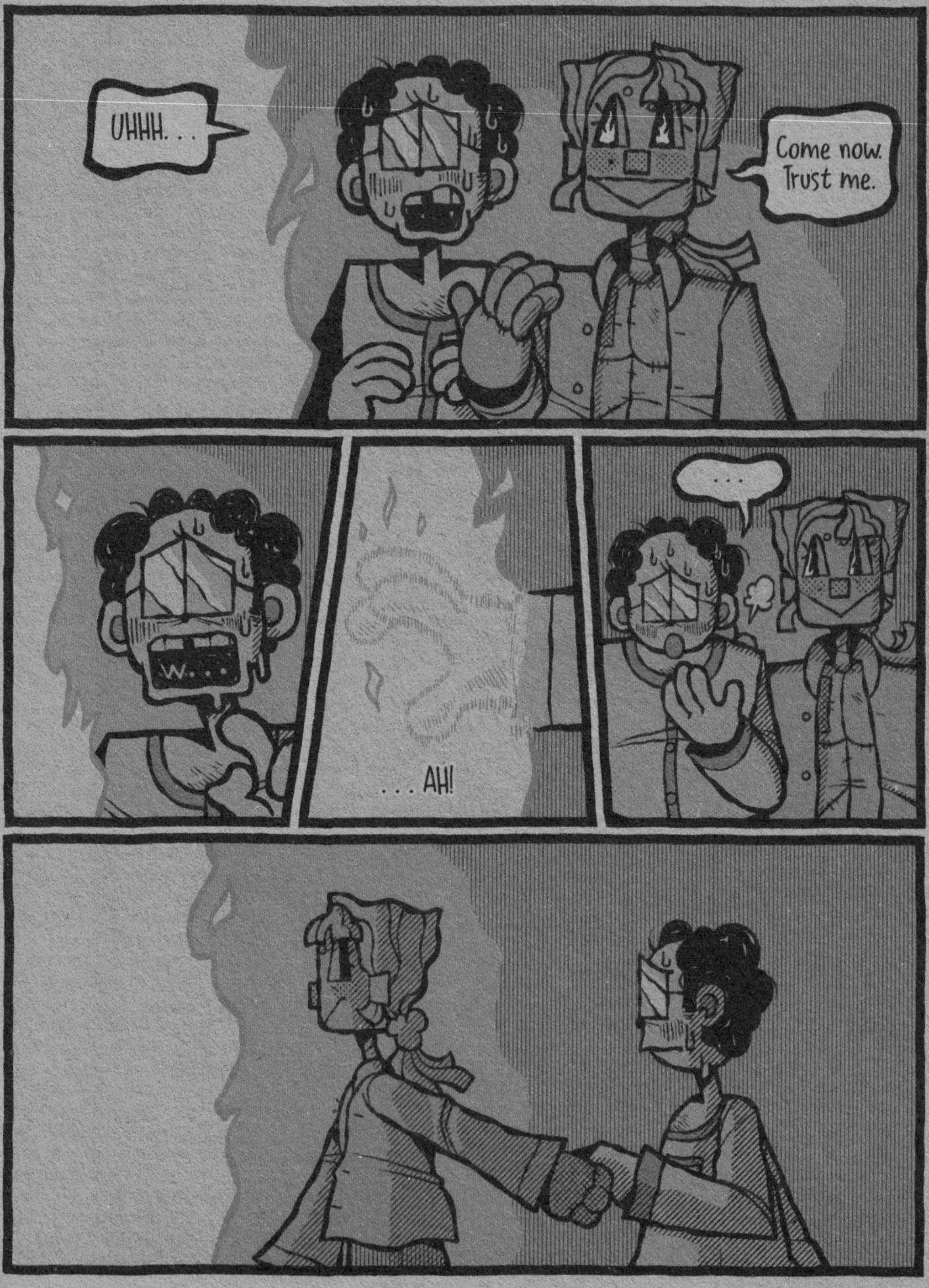
UHHH. . .
Come now. Trust me.
W. . .
. . . AH!
. . .

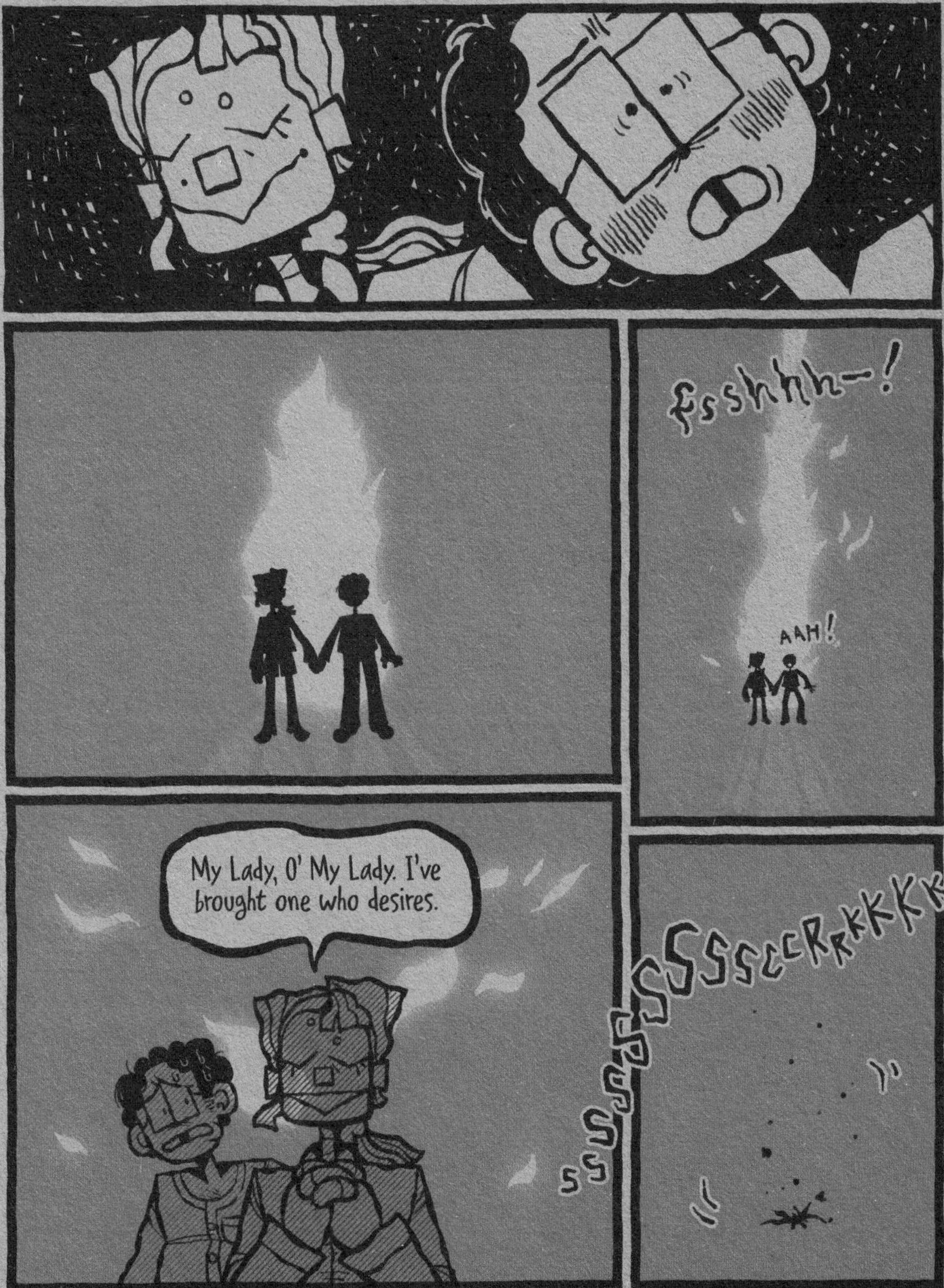
fsshhh—!
AAH!
My Lady, O' My Lady. I've brought one who desires.
SSSSSSSSSSSSSCCRRKKKK

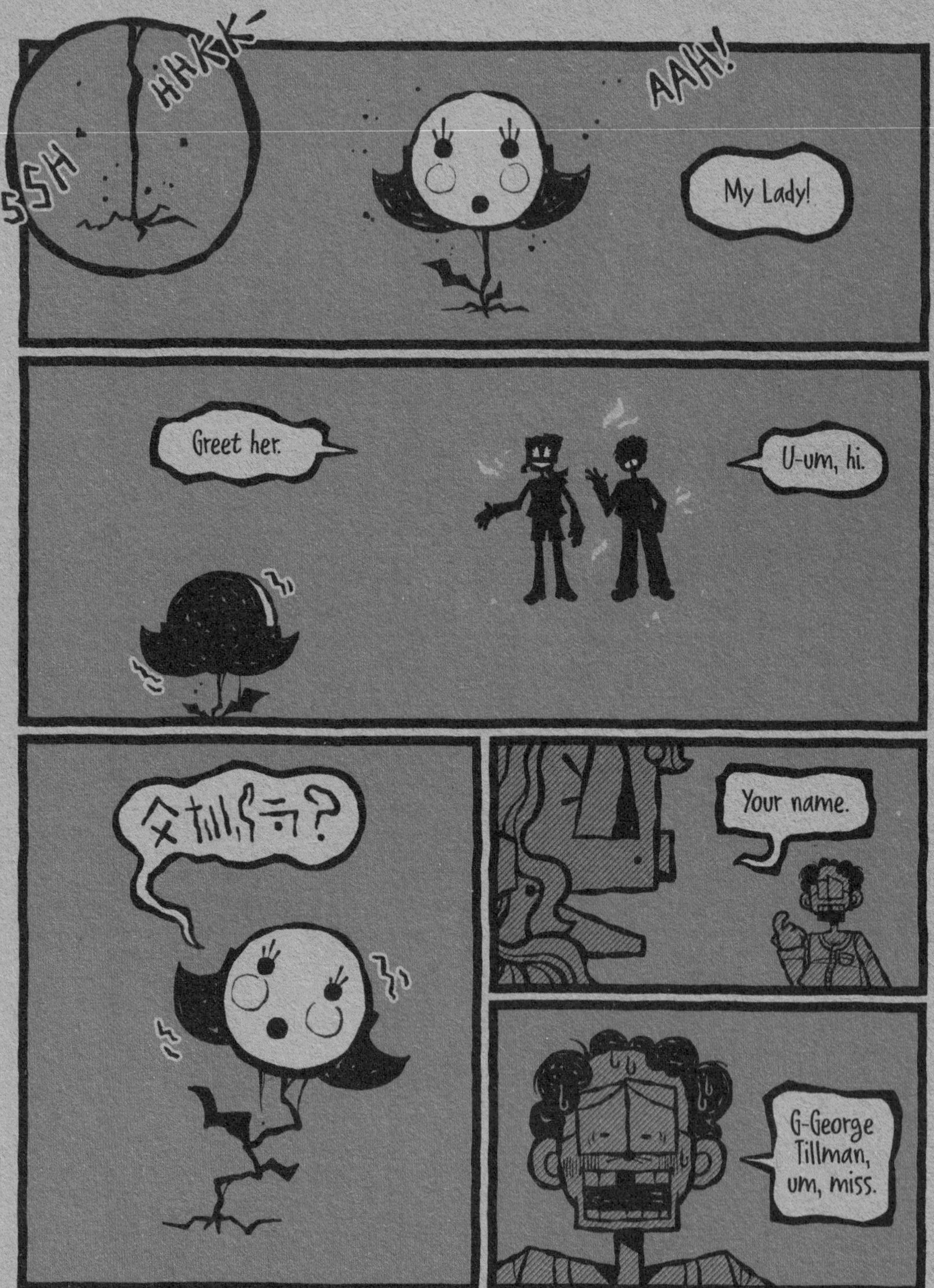
SSHHAKK!
AAH!
My Lady!
Greet her.
U-um, hi.
Your name.
G-George Tillman, um, miss.

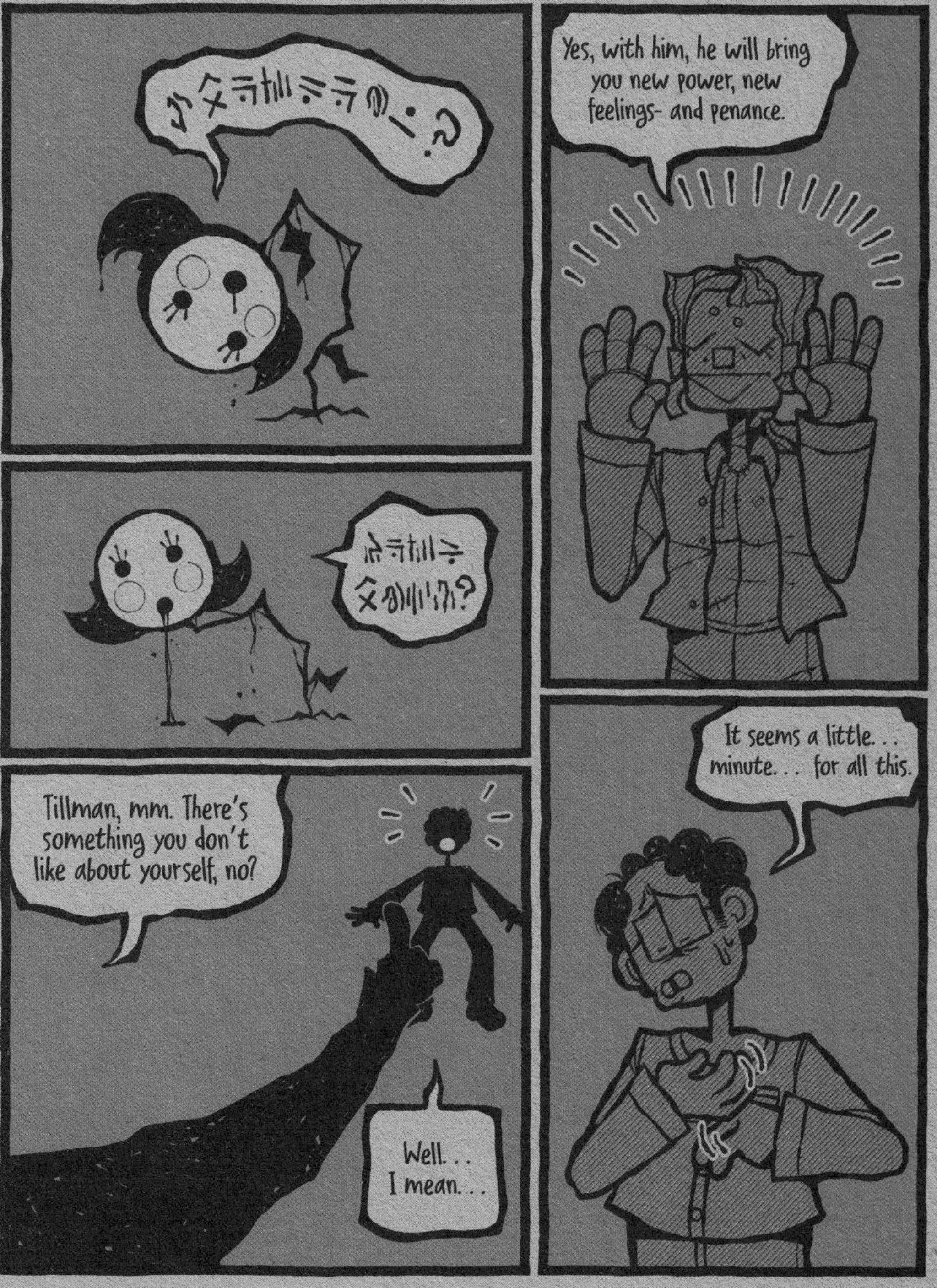
Yes, with him, he will bring you new power, new feelings- and penance.
Tillman, mm. There's something you don't like about yourself, no?
Well. . . I mean. . .
It seems a little. . . minute. . . for all this.

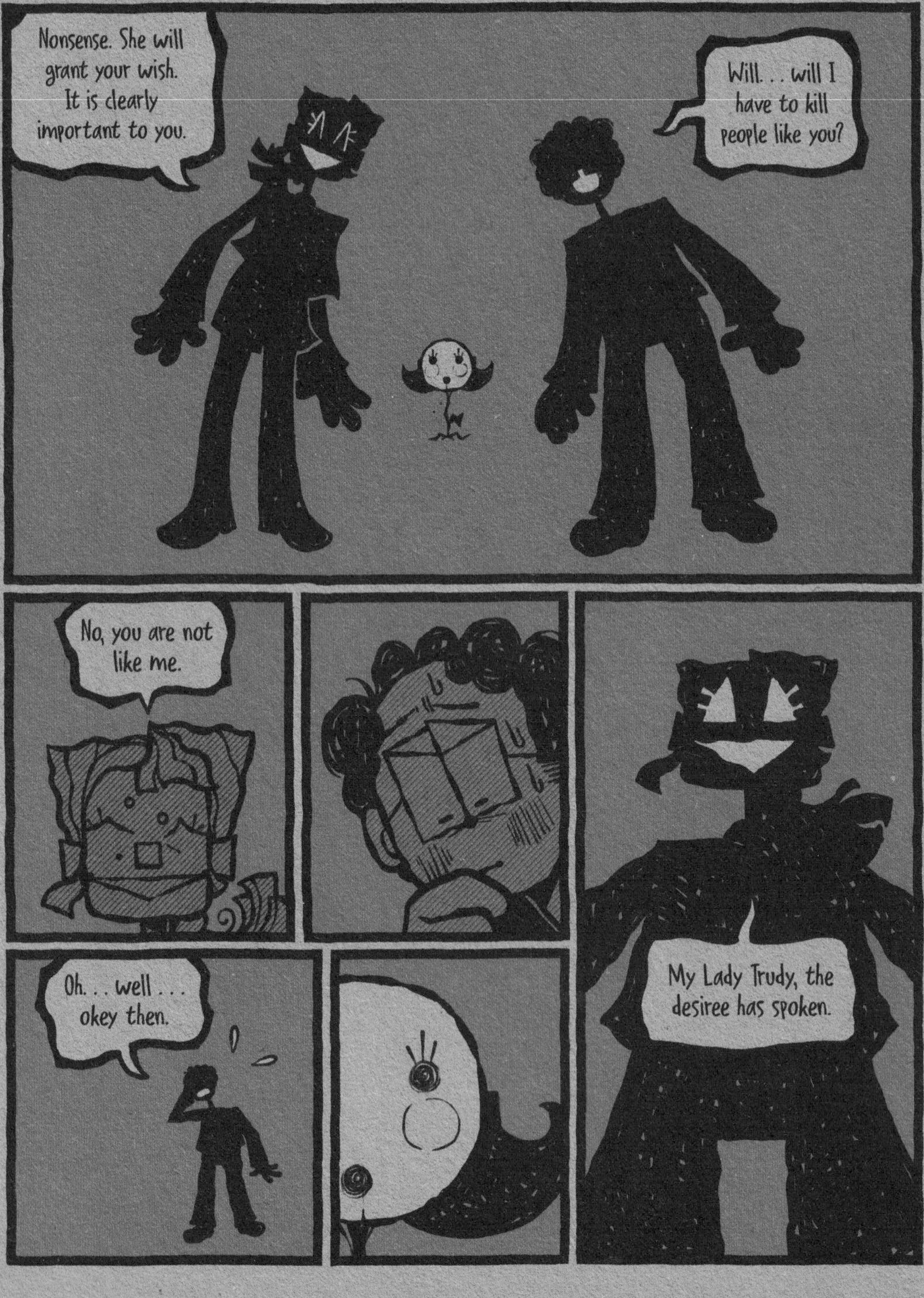

Nonsense. She will grant your wish. It is clearly important to you.
Will. . . will I have to kill people like you?
No, you are not like me.
My Lady Trudy, the desiree has spoken.
Oh. . . well . . . okey then.

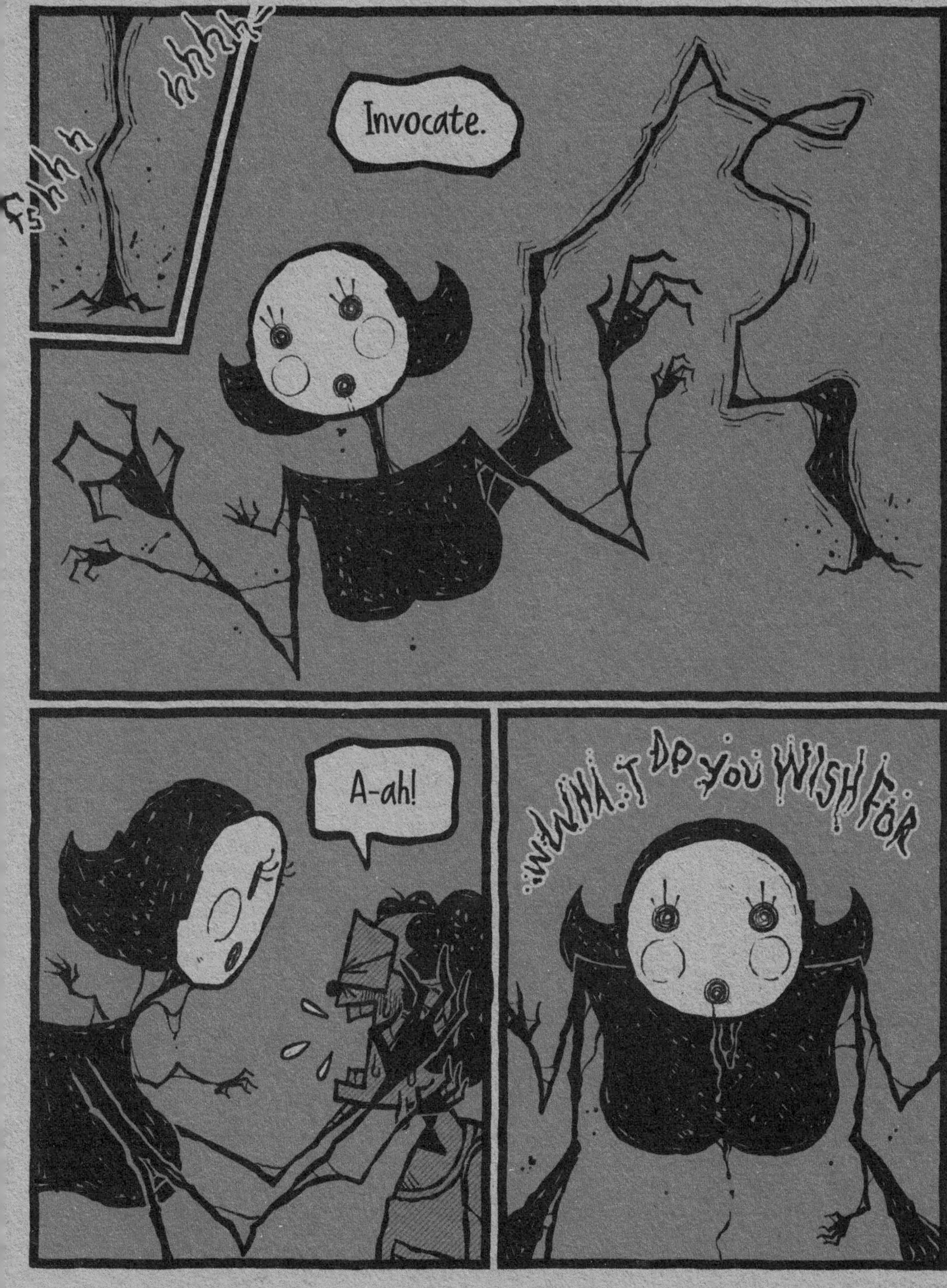

Fshhh hhhhk
Invocate.
A-ah!
WHA.T DO you WISH FOR

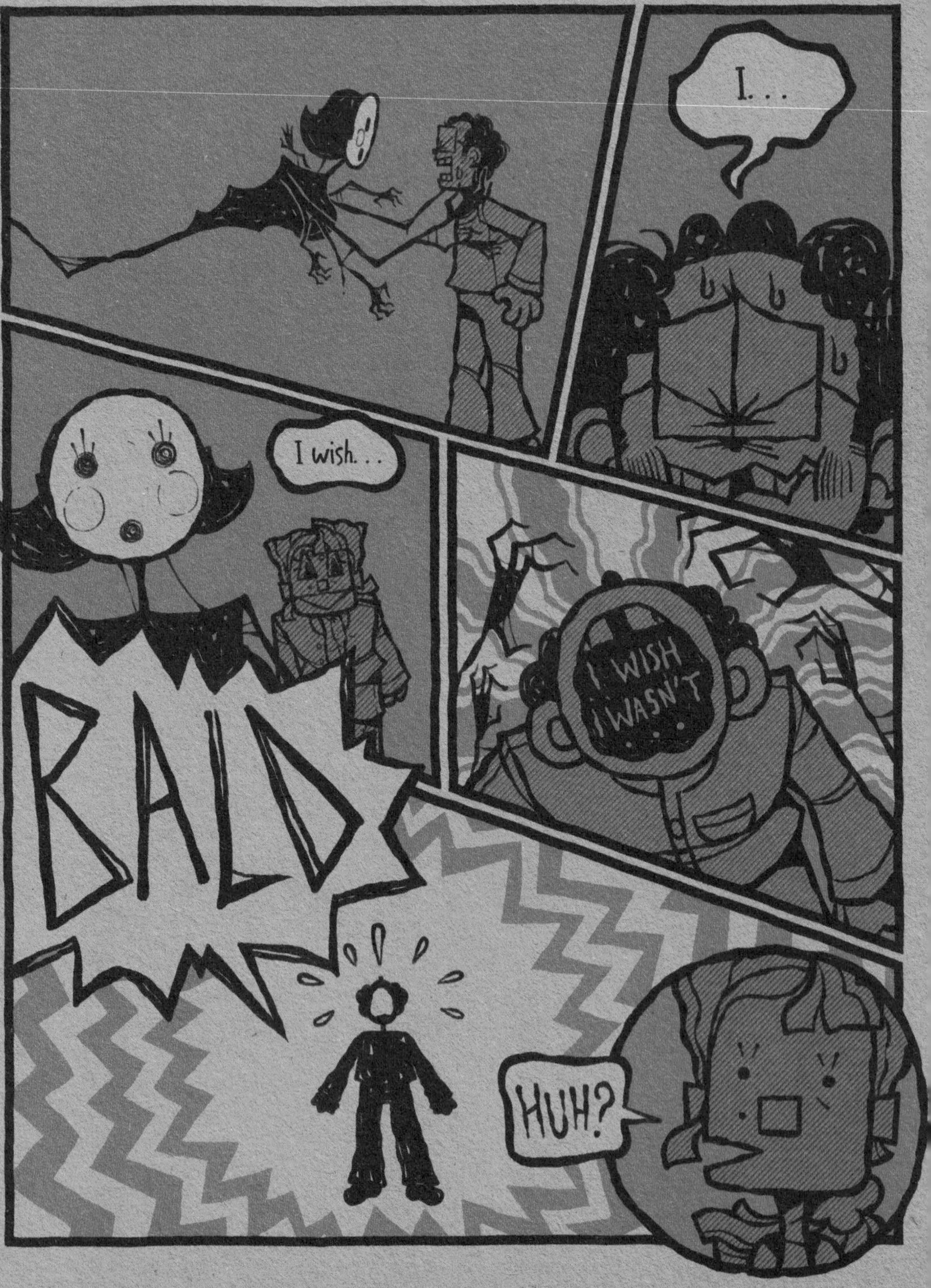
I...
I wish...
BALD
I WISH I WASN'T...
HUH?

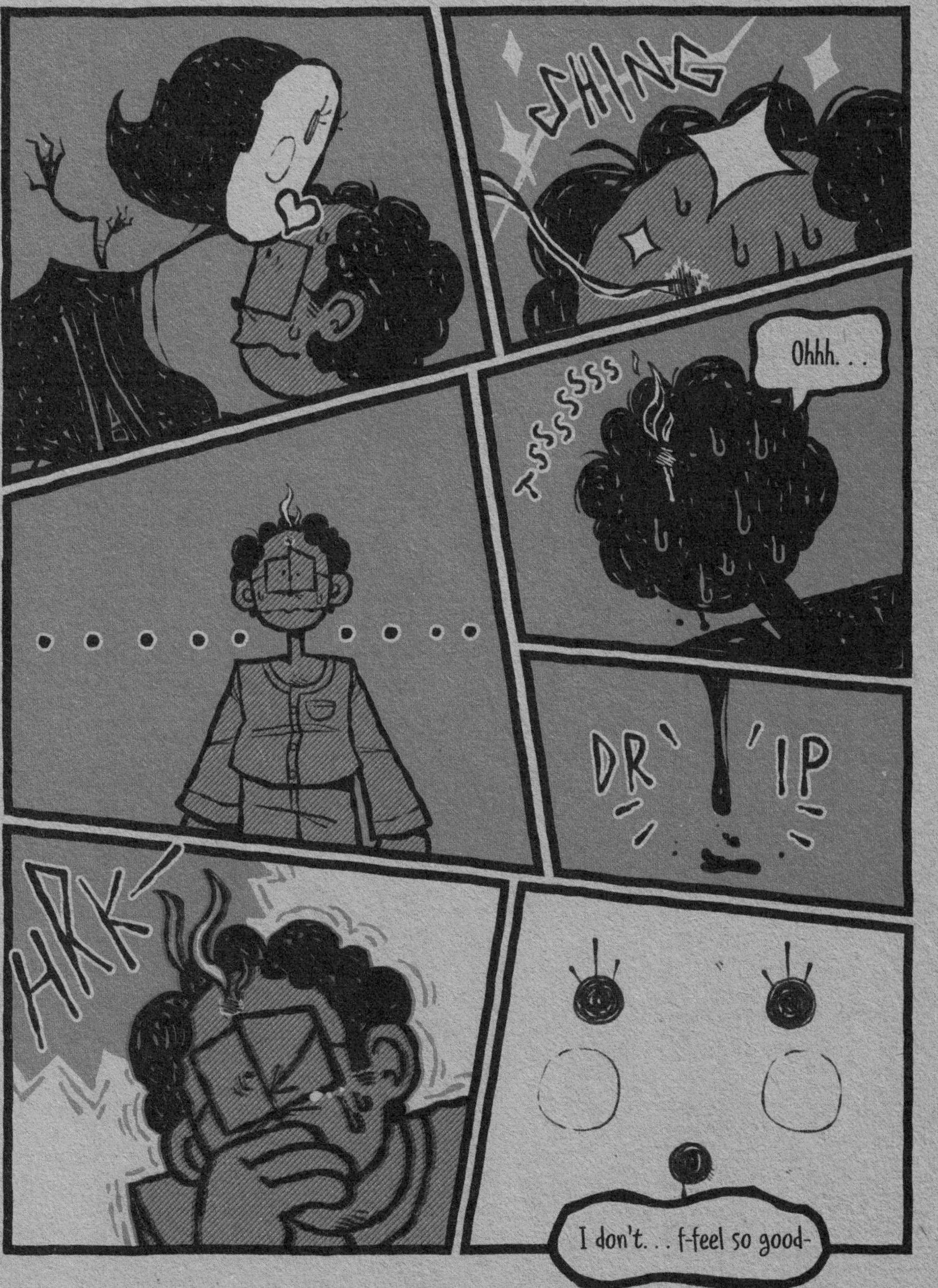
SHING
Ohhh. . .
TSSSSSSS
. . . .
DR IP
HRK
I don't. . . f-feel so good-

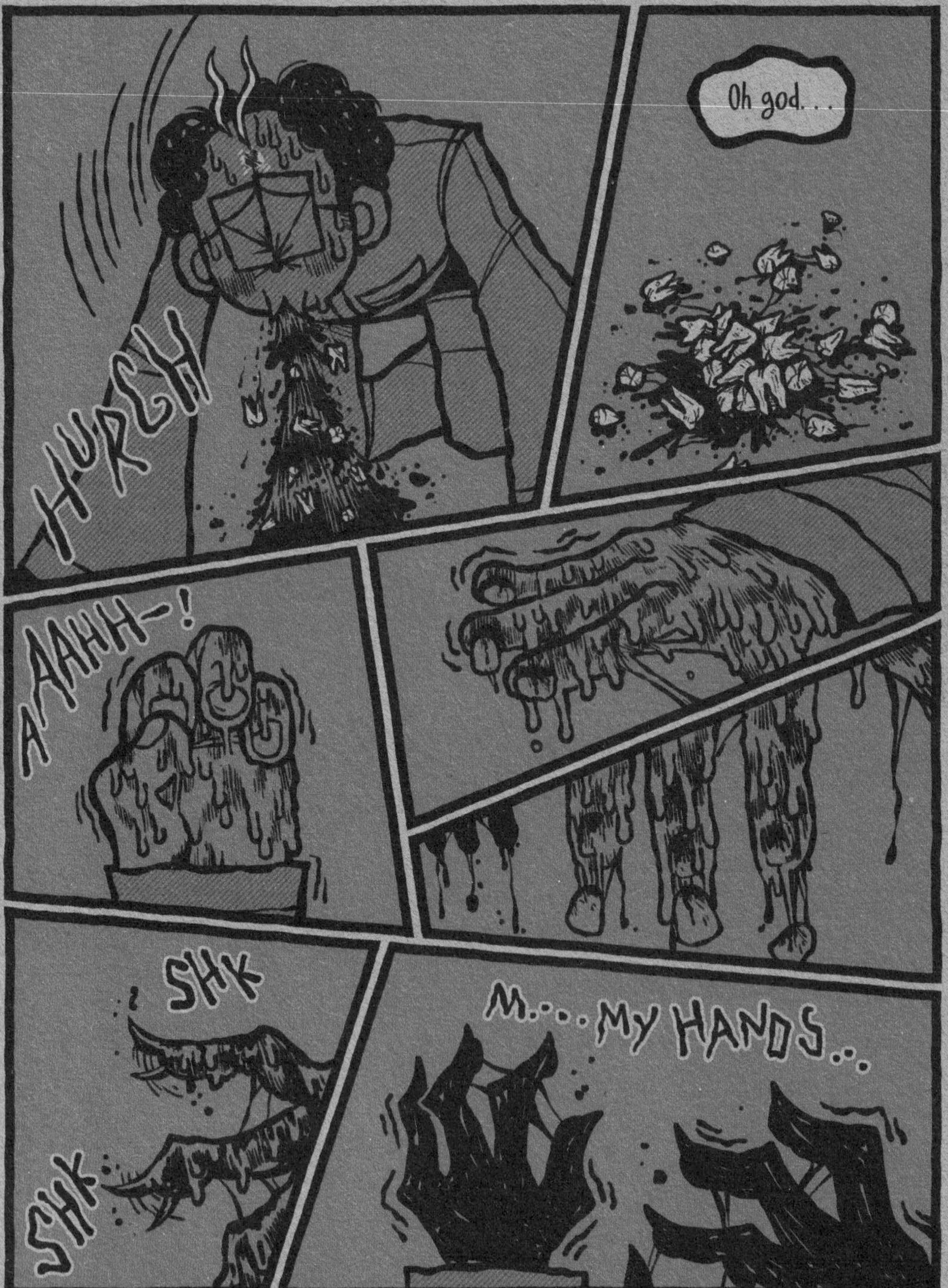
HURGH
Oh god. . .
AAAHH-!
SHK
SHK
M. . . MY HANDS. . .

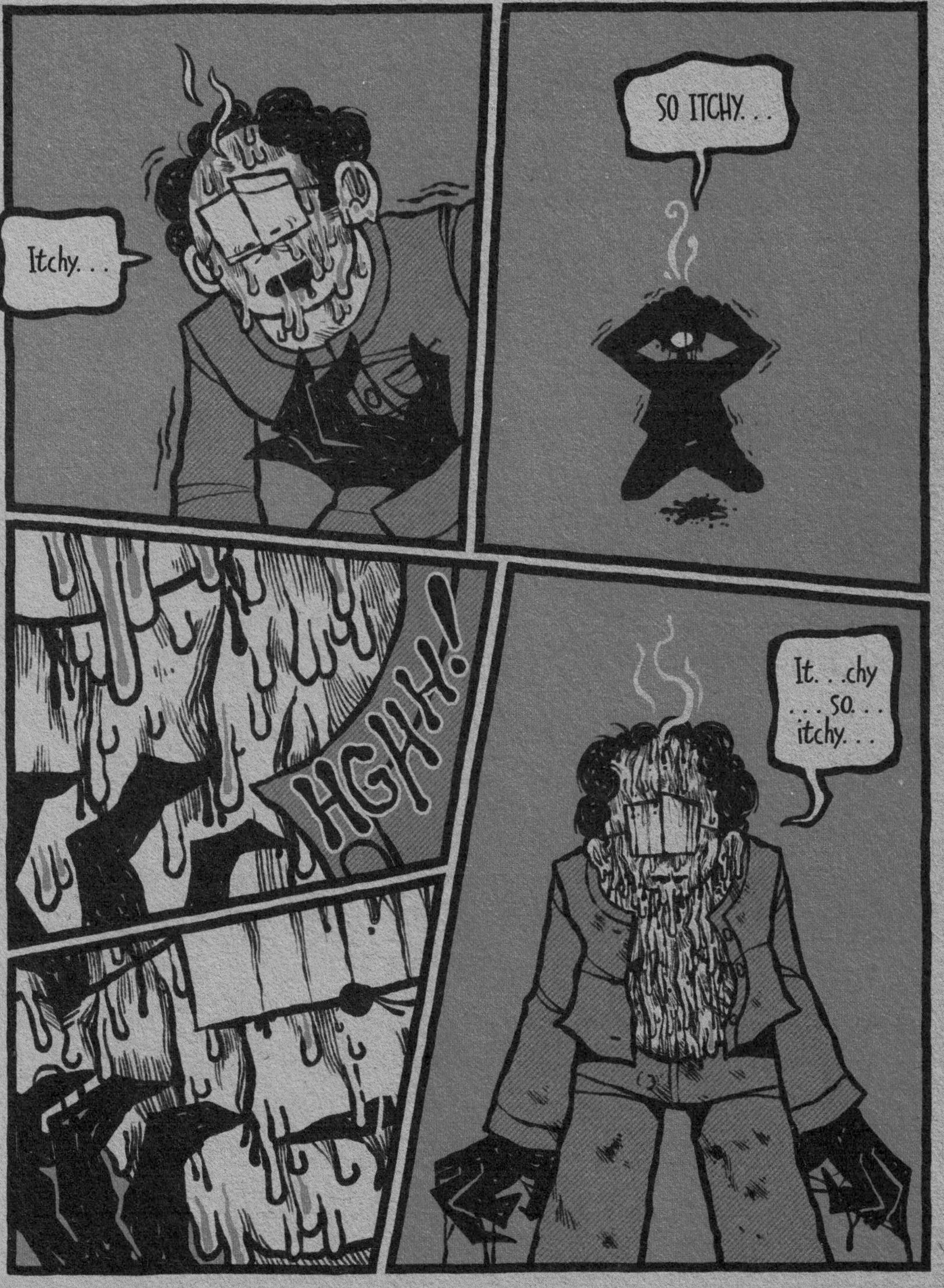
Itchy. . .
SO ITCHY. . .
HGHH!
It. . .chy . . . so. . . itchy. . .

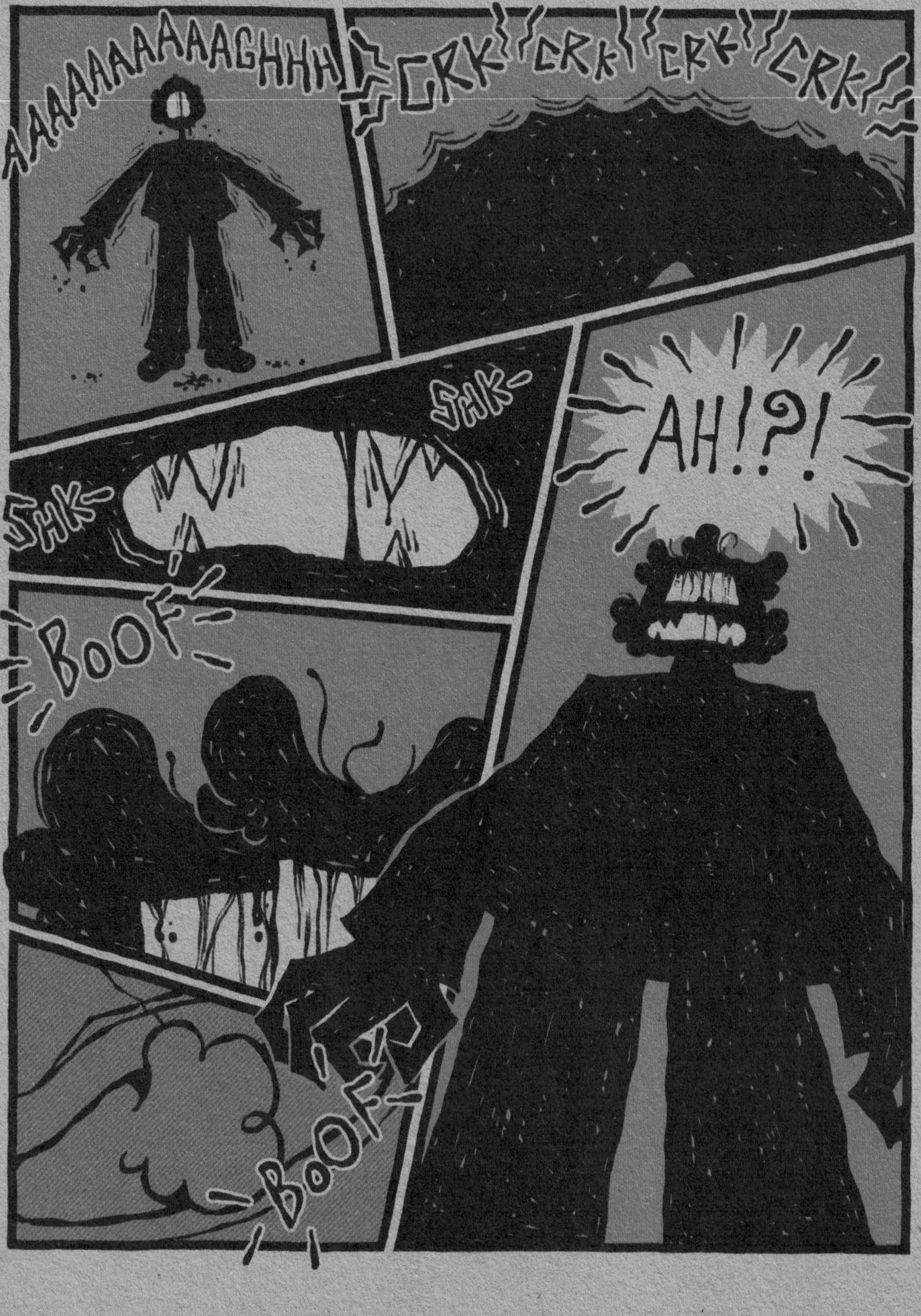
AAAAAAAAAAGHHH
CRK CRK CRK CRK
SHK-
SHK-
AH!?!
BOOF
BOOF

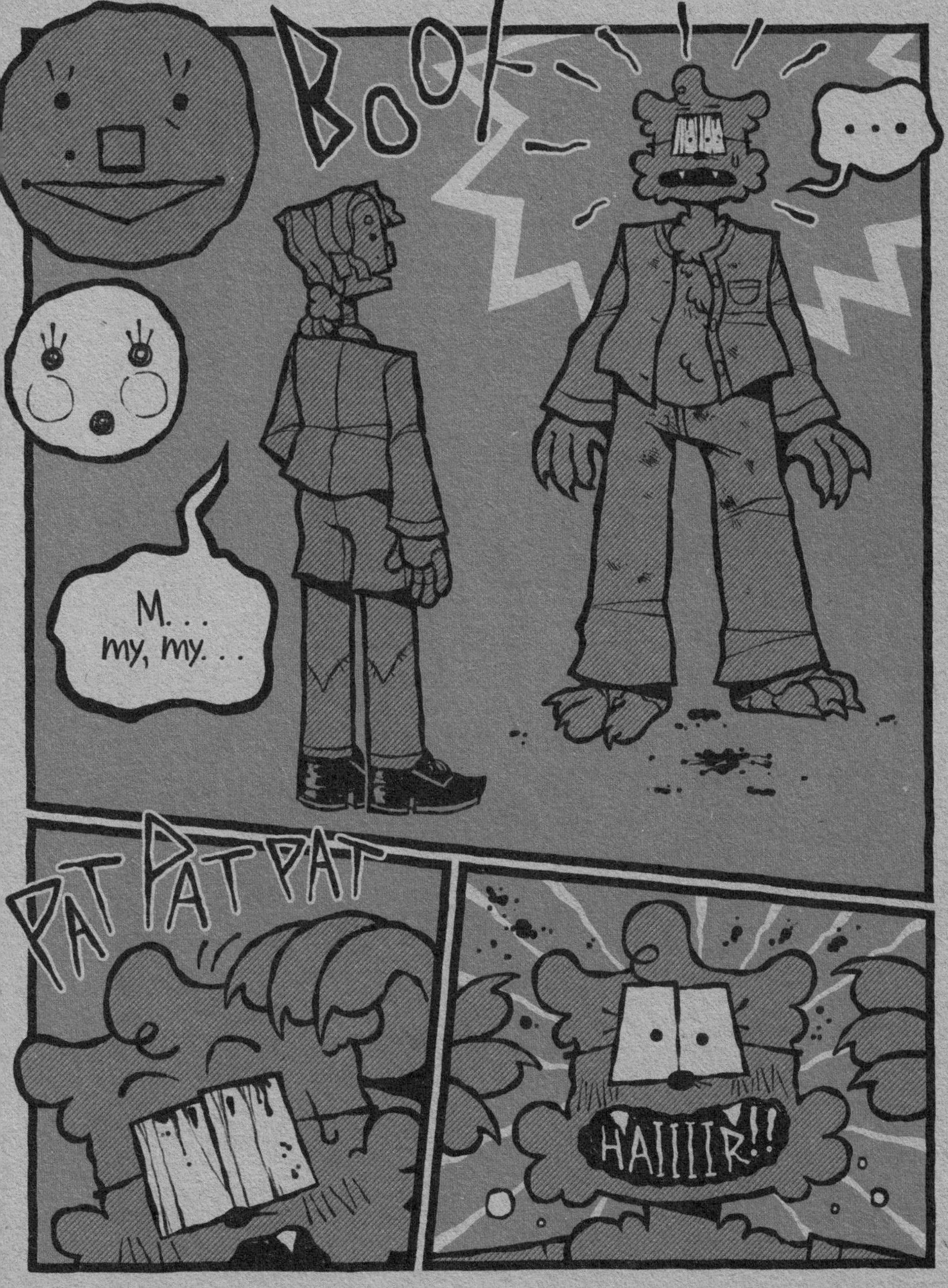
BOOF
M. . .
my, my. . .
. . .
PAT PAT PAT
HAIIIR!!

O-oh, yes, I can hear ya now, uh, Trudy, miss.

6 teeth!?!? In the mailbox every month!?

I . . .

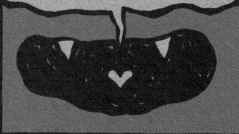

They regrow? Oh. That's not s' bad.

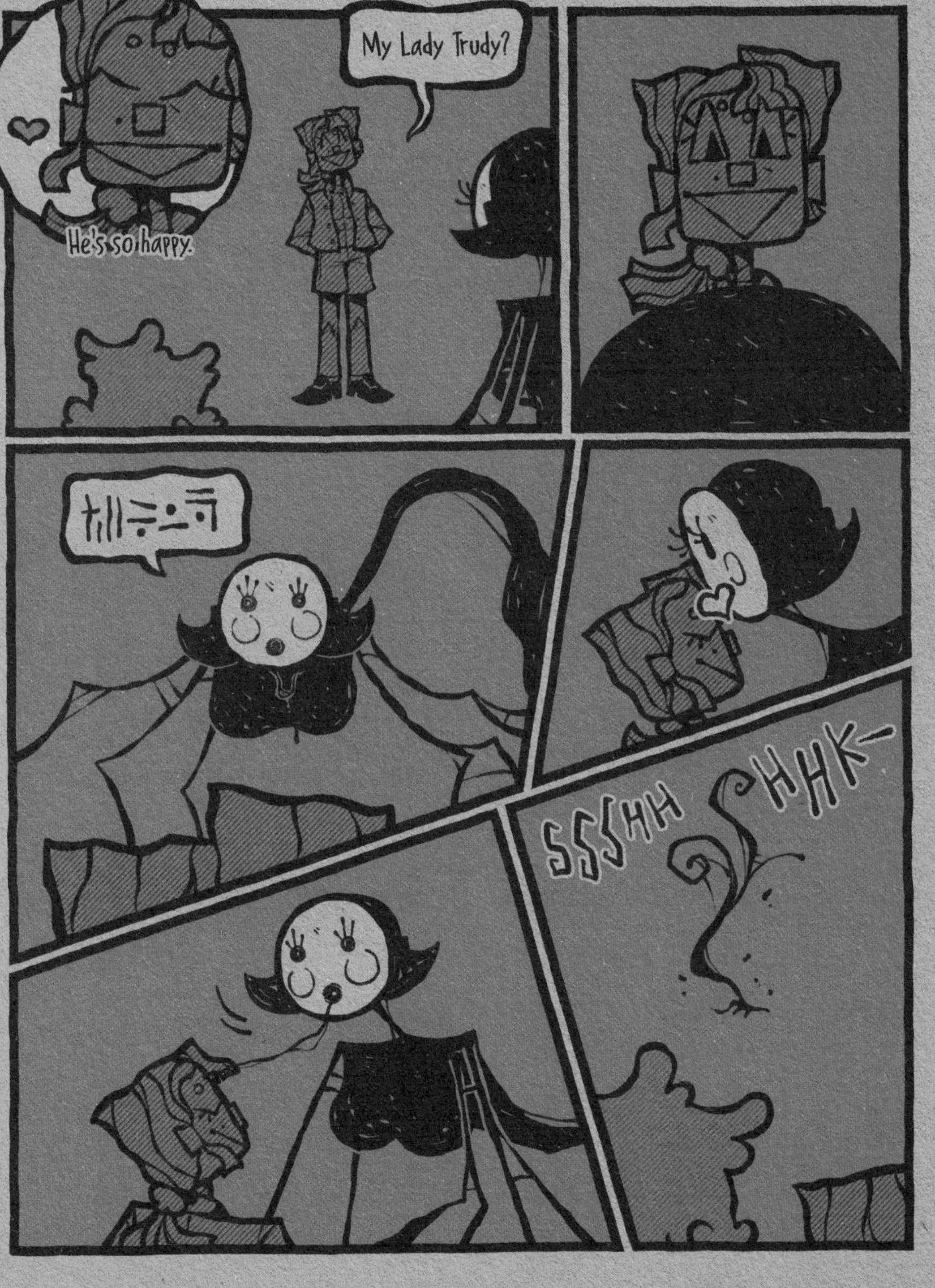
He's so happy.
My Lady Trudy?
SSSHH HHK-

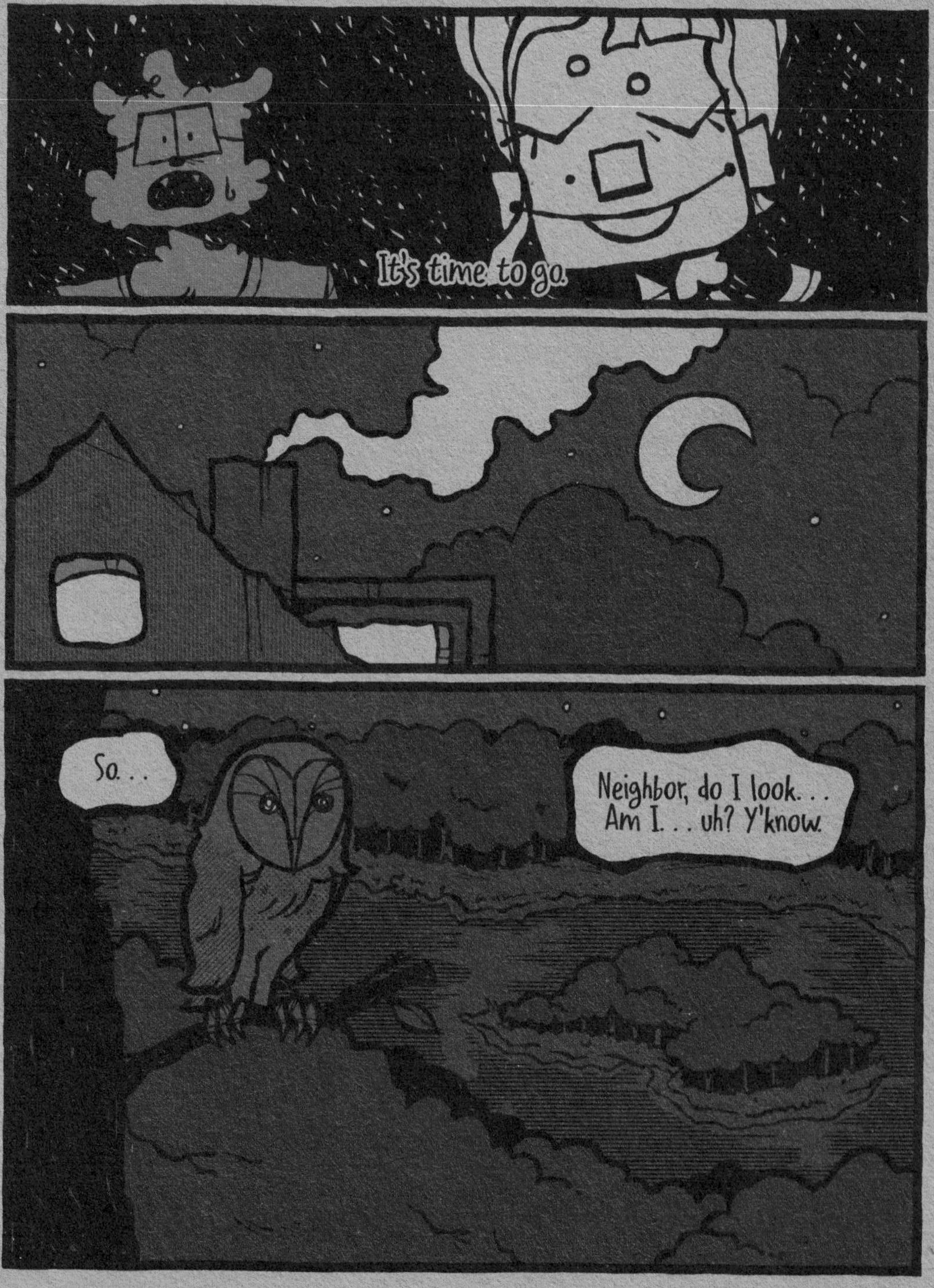
It's time to go.
So. . .
Neighbor, do I look. . . Am I. . . uh? Y'know.

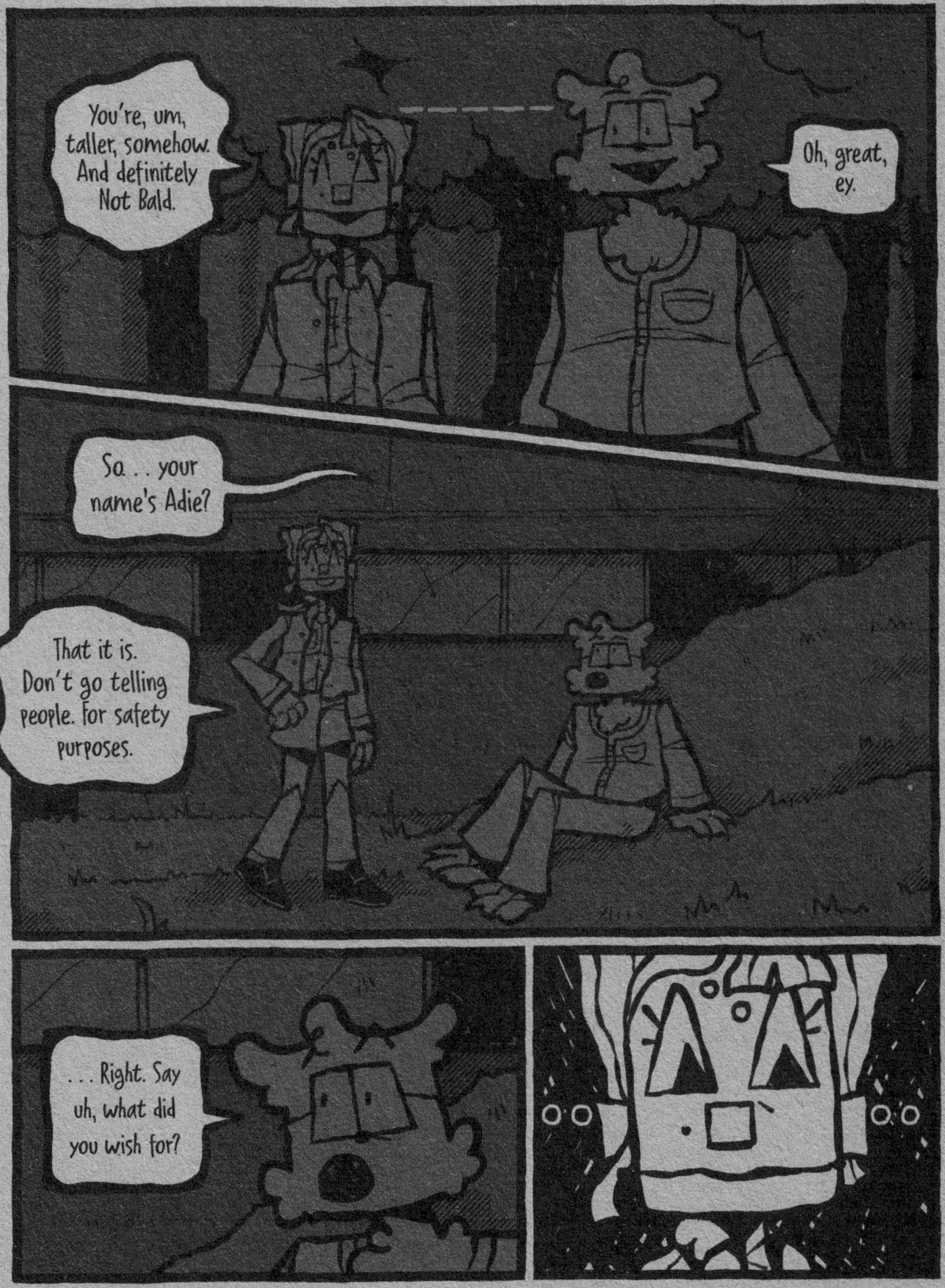
You're, um, taller, somehow. And definitely Not Bald.
Oh, great, ey.
So. . . your name's Adie?
That it is. Don't go telling people. For safety purposes.
. . . Right. Say uh, what did you wish for?

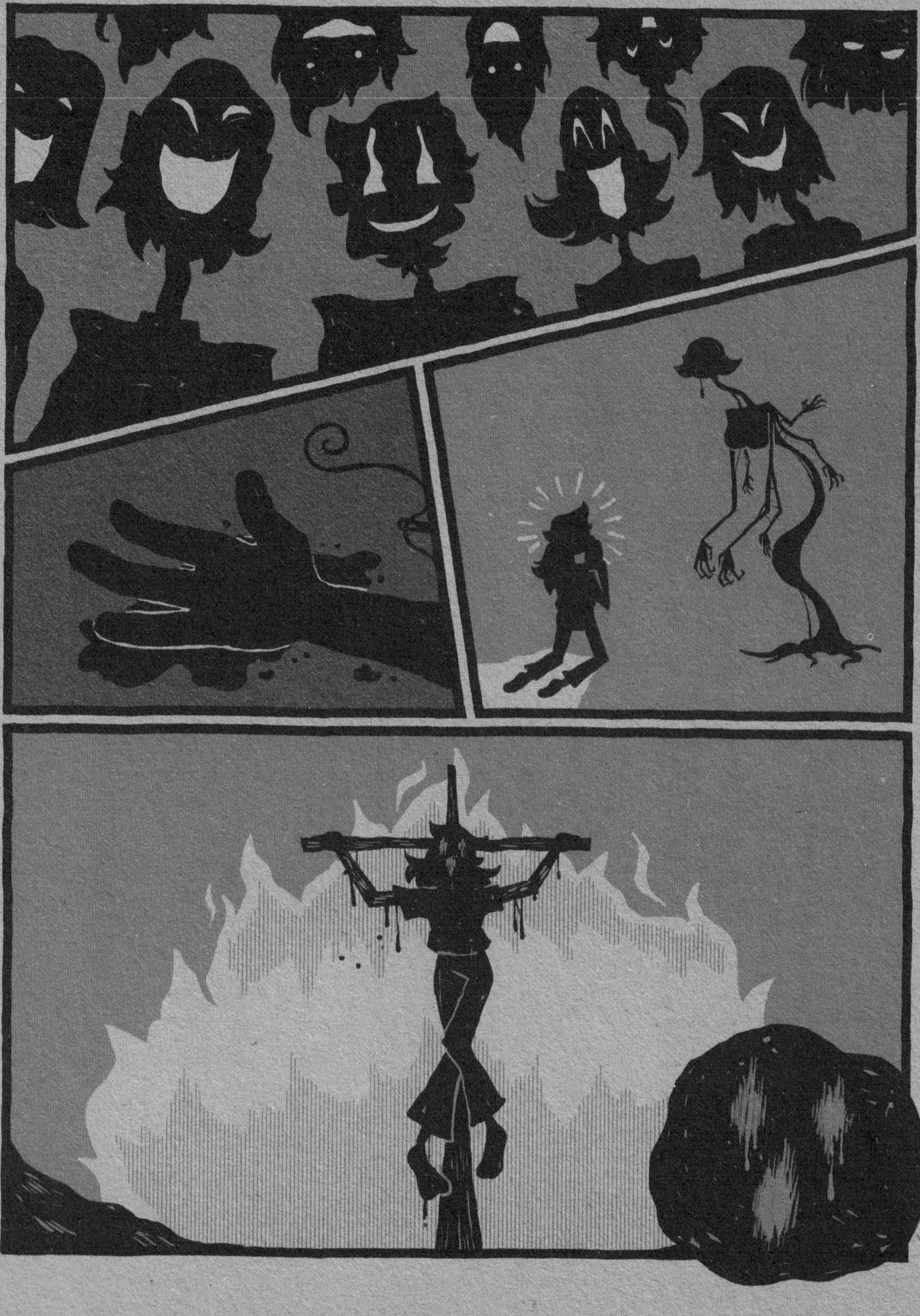

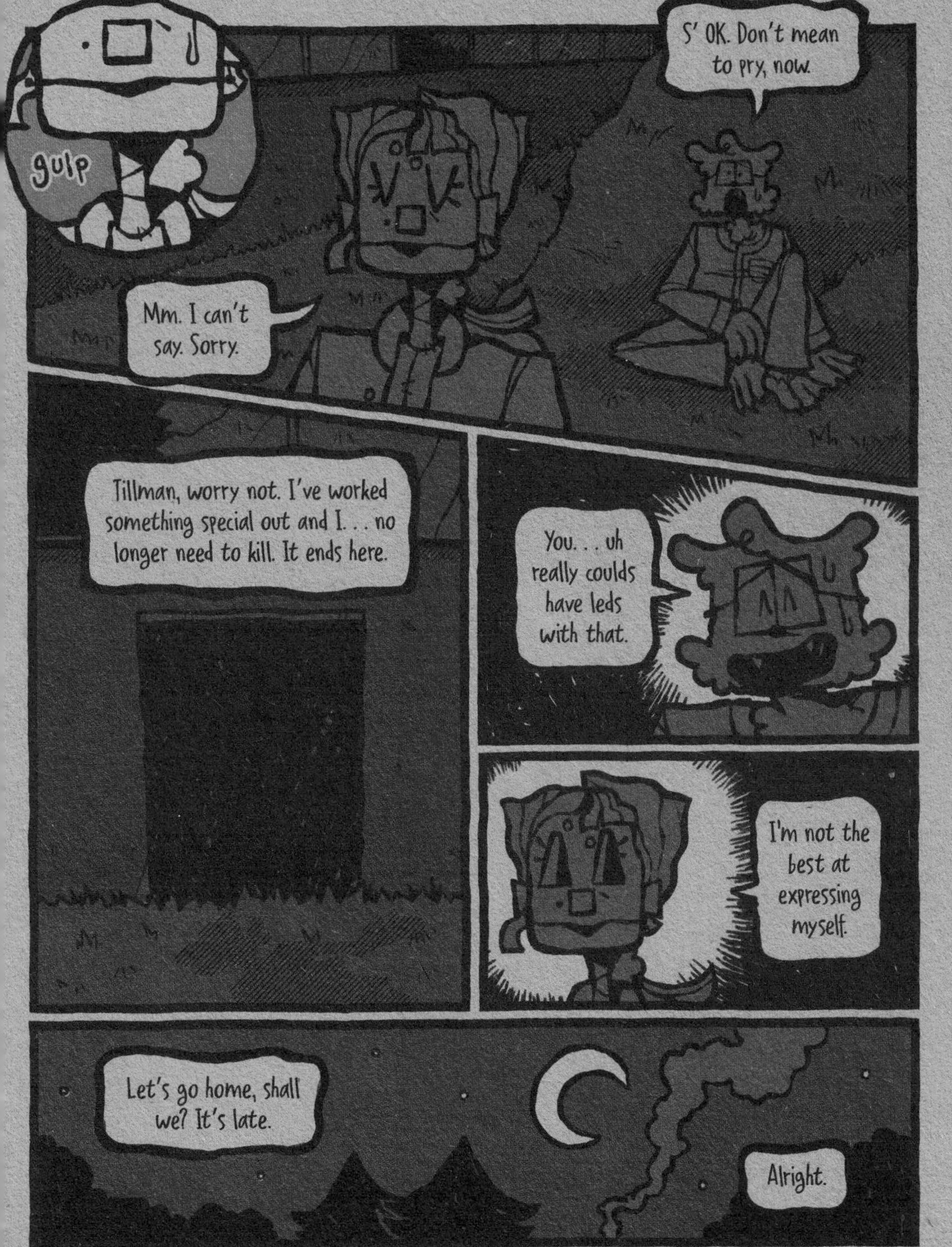
gulp
S' OK. Don't mean to pry, now.
Mm. I can't say. Sorry.
Tillman, worry not. I've worked something special out and I. . . no longer need to kill. It ends here.
You. . . uh really coulds have leds with that.
I'm not the best at expressing myself.
Let's go home, shall we? It's late.
Alright.

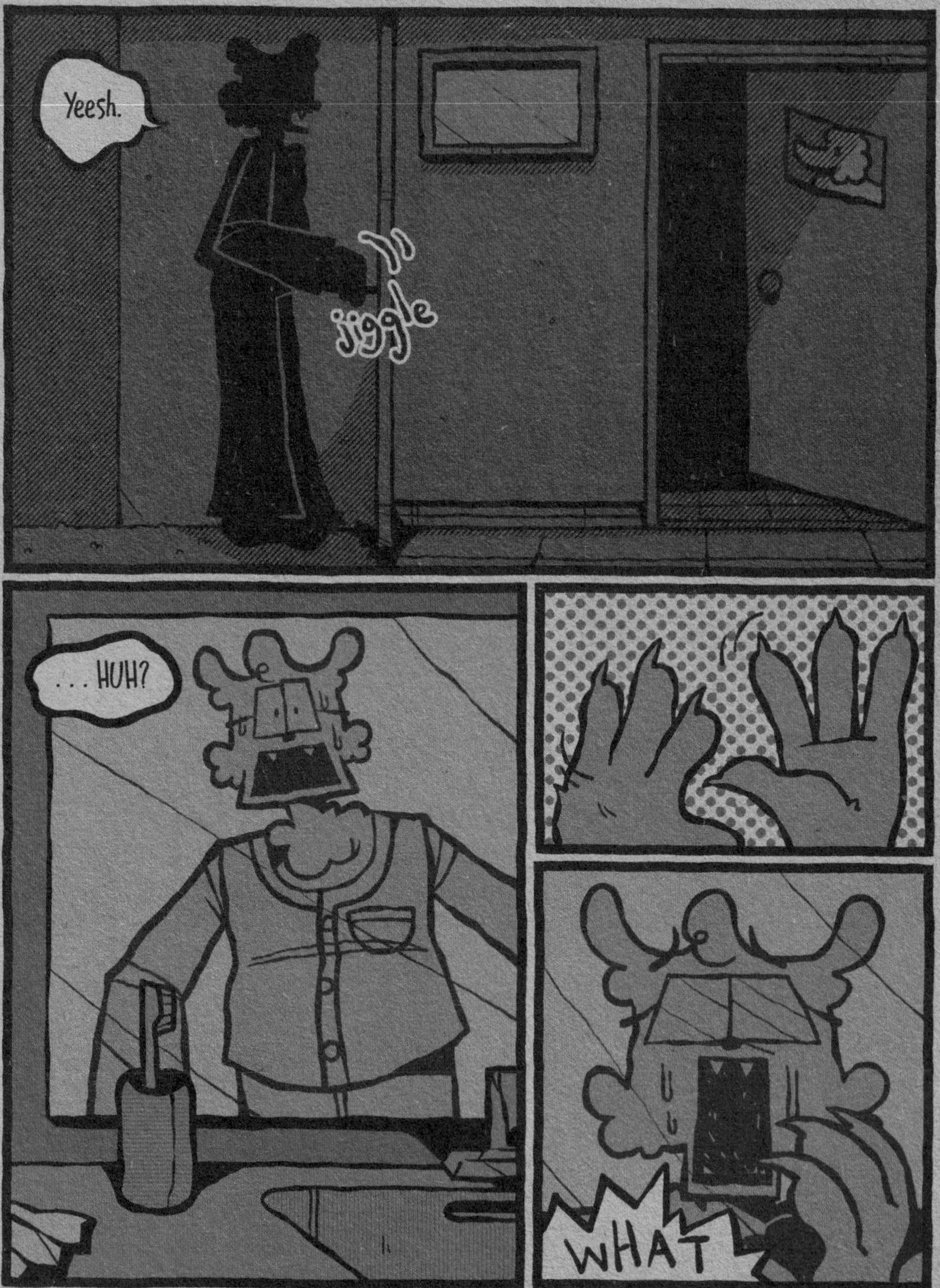
Yeesh.
jiggle
...HUH?
WHAT

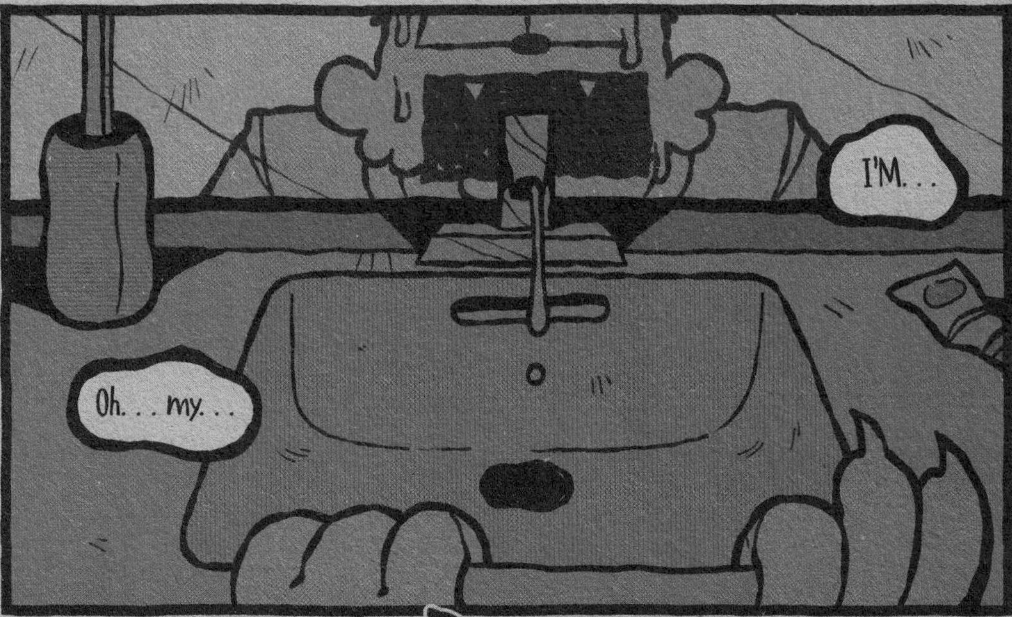
I'M. . .
Oh. . . my. . .

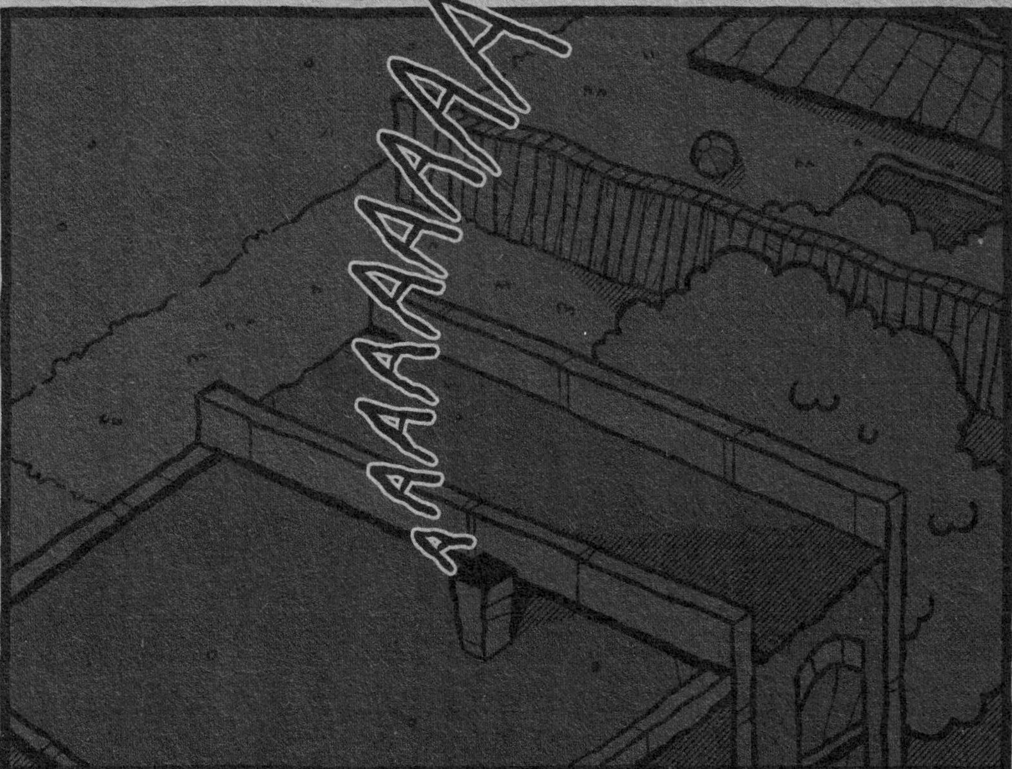
AAAAAAAAA

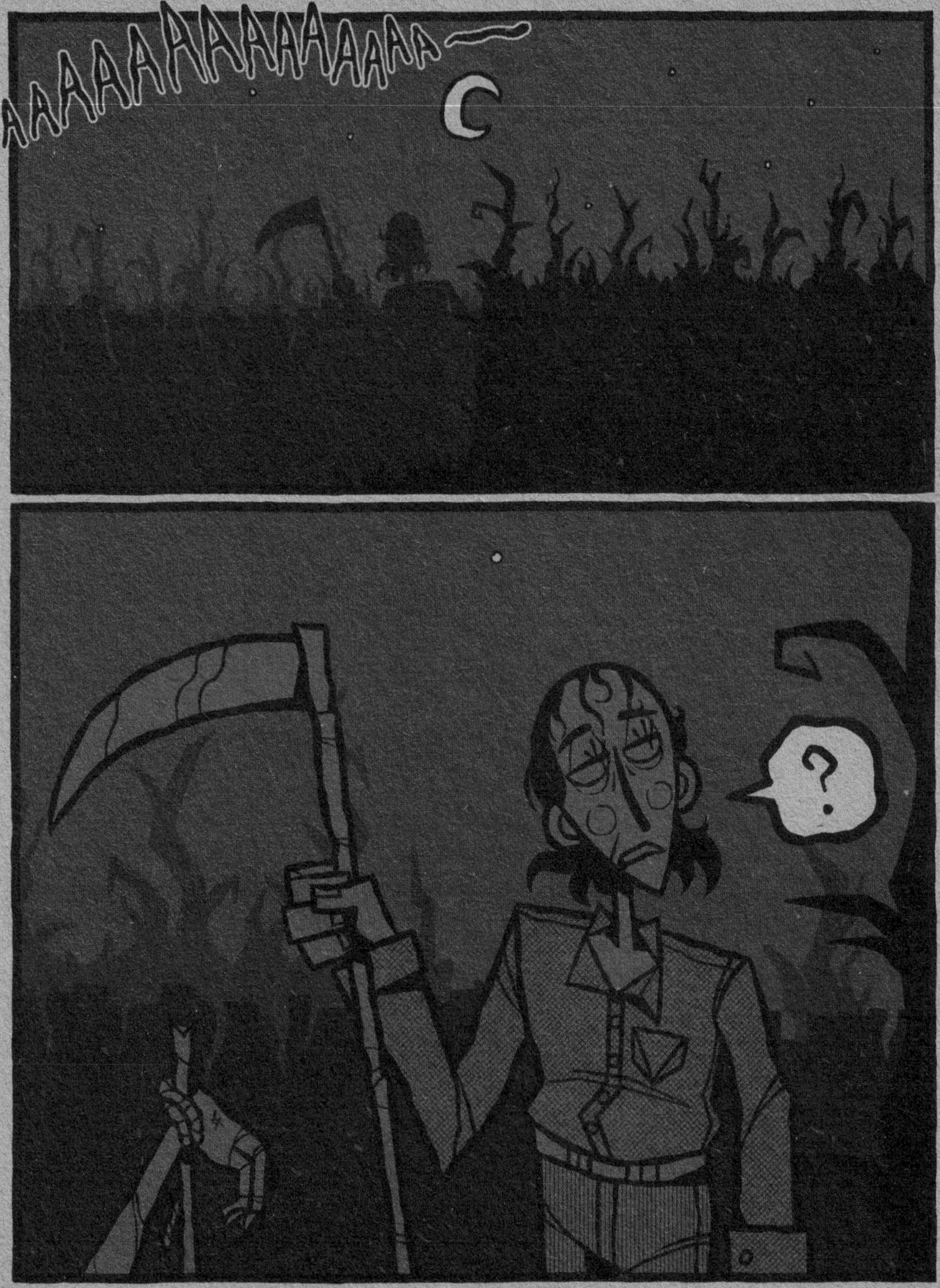
AAAAAAAAAAAAAA—
?

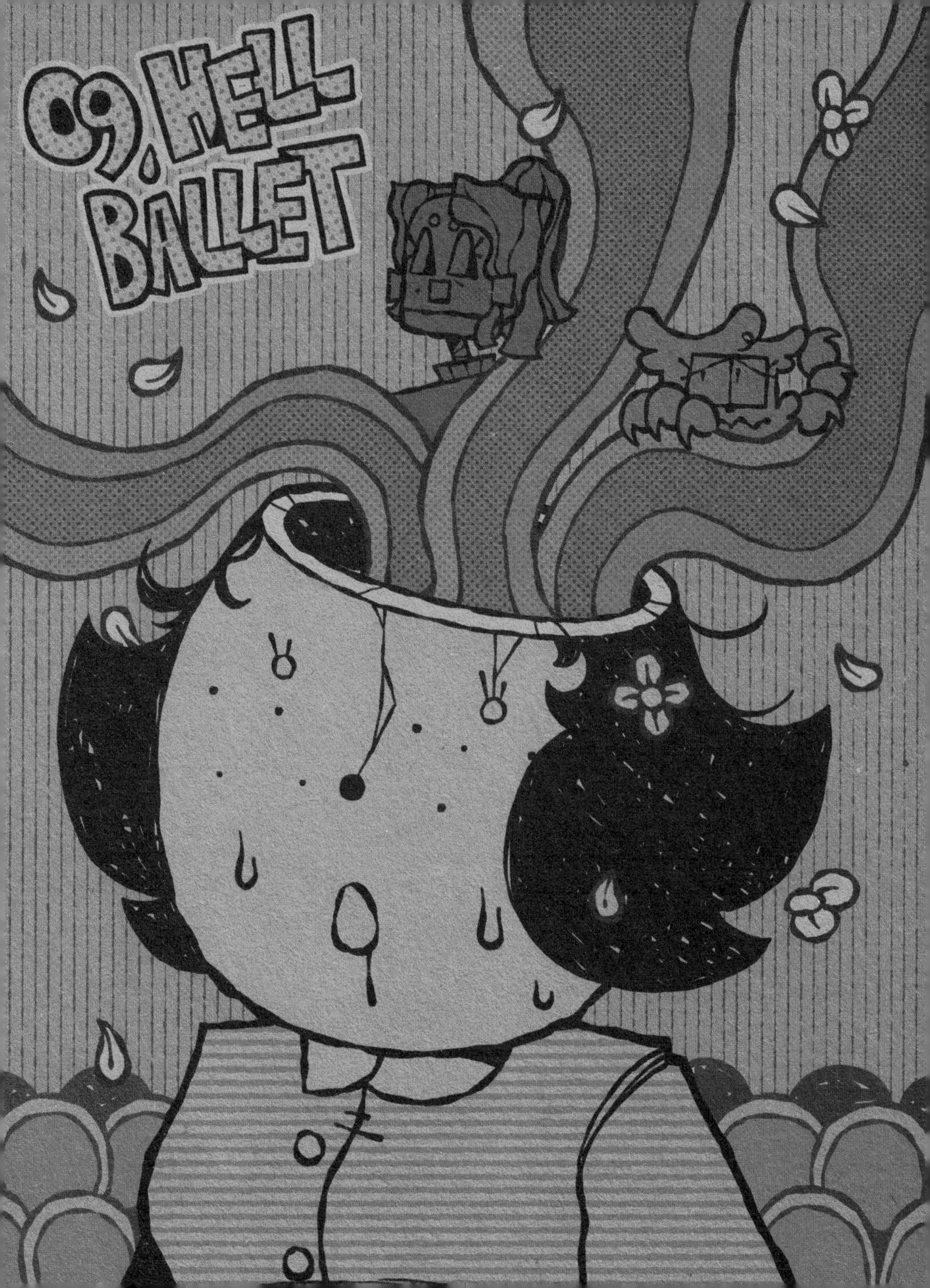
09. HELL BALLET

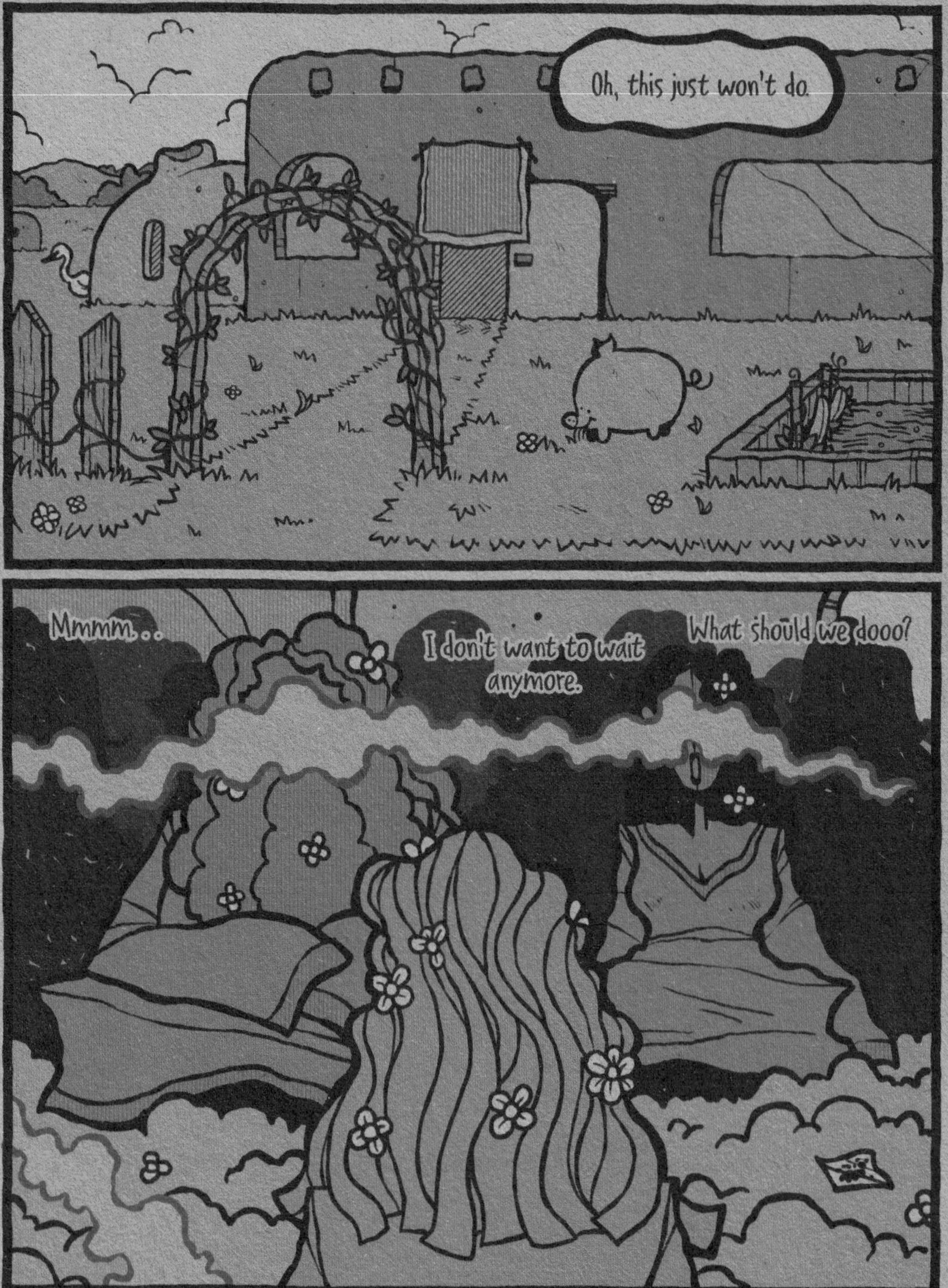
Oh, this just won't do.
Mmmm. . .
I don't want to wait anymore.
What should we dooo?

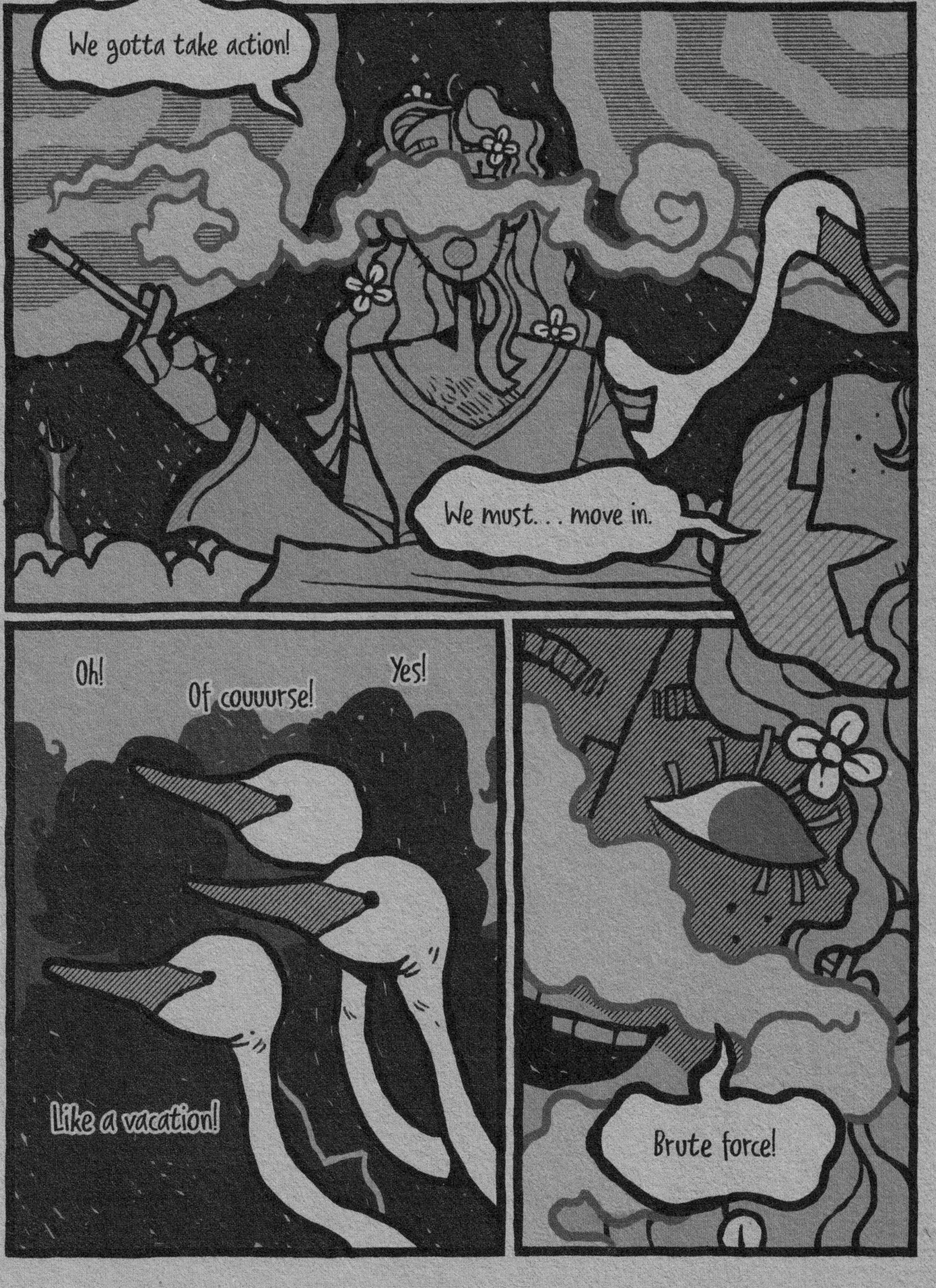
We gotta take action!
We must. . . move in.
Oh!
Of couuurse!
Yes!
Like a vacation!
Brute force!

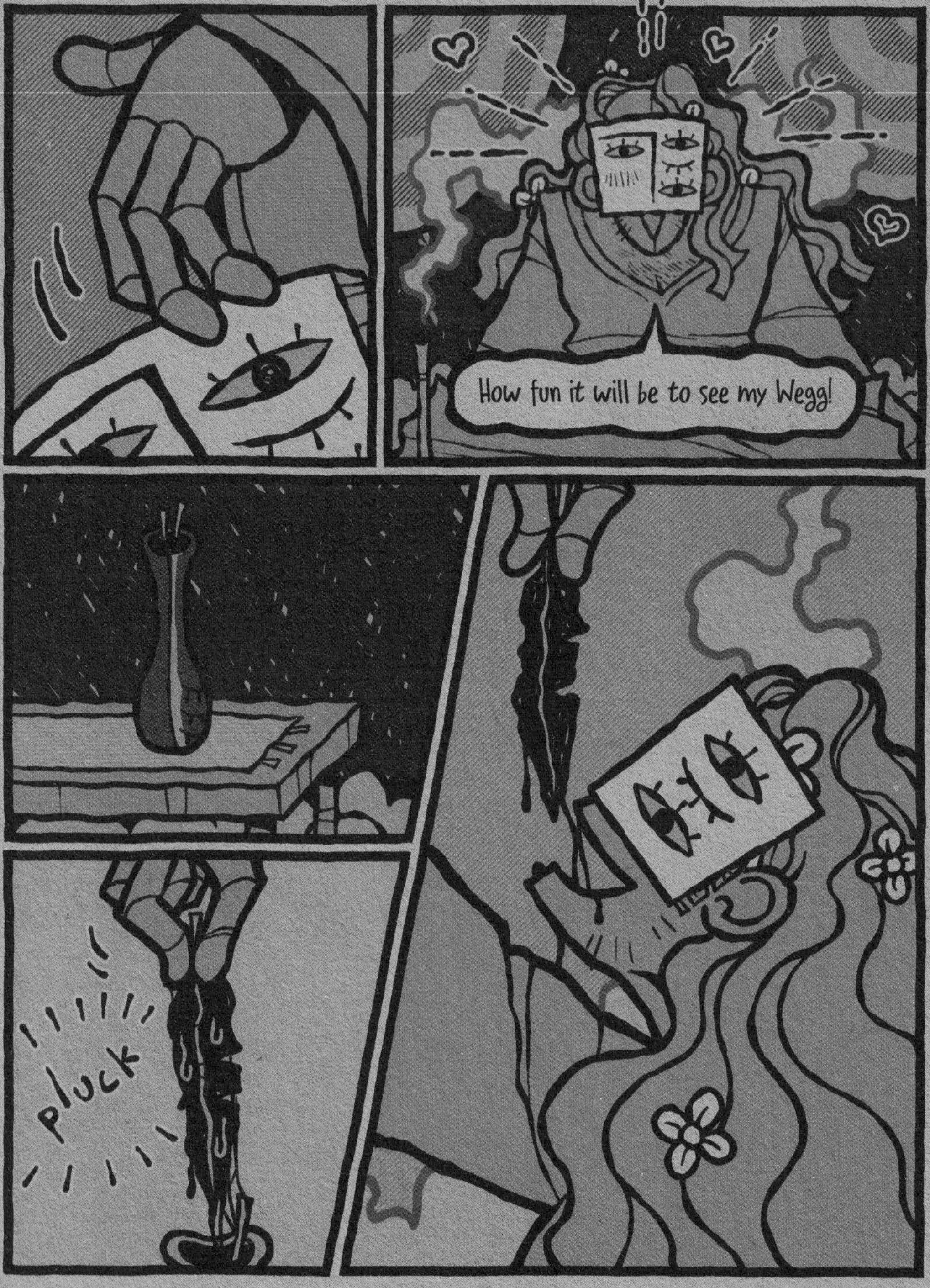
How fun it will be to see my Wegg!
pluck

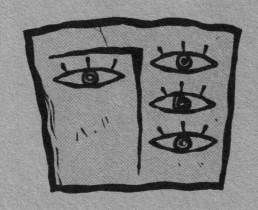

PLEASE COME HOME, WEGG

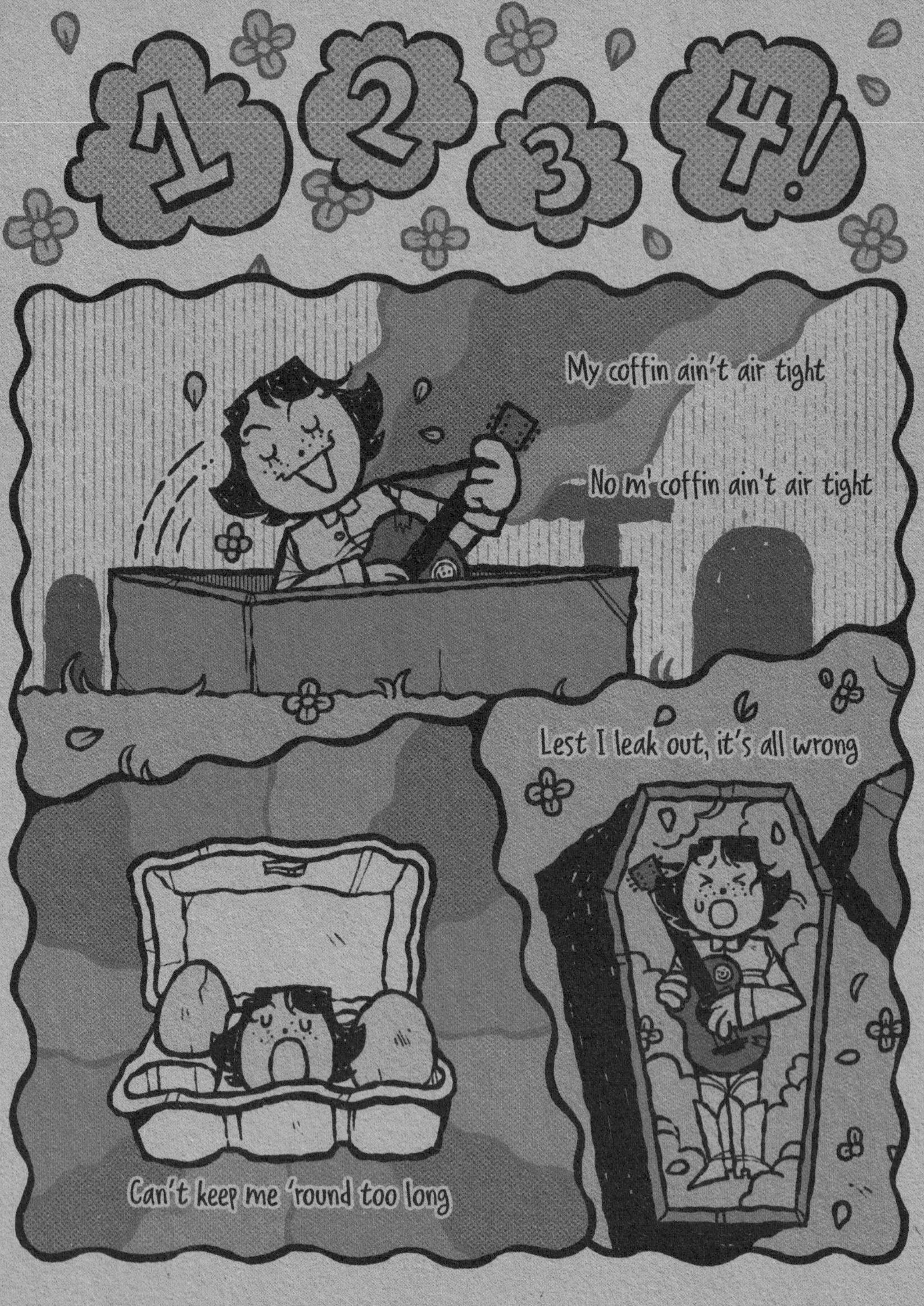
1 2 3 4!
My coffin ain't air tight
No m' coffin ain't air tight
Lest I leak out, it's all wrong
Can't keep me 'round too long

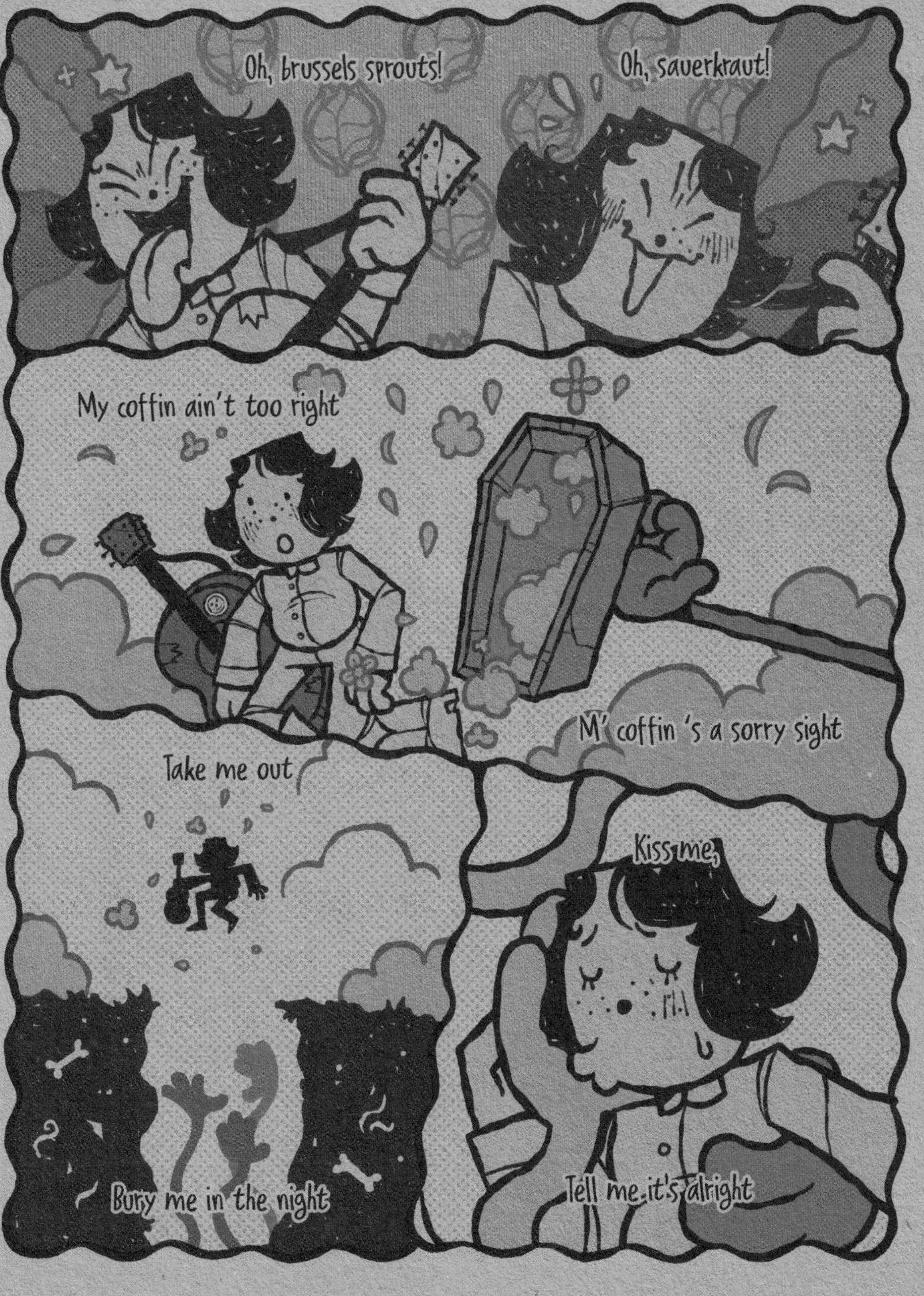
Oh, brussels sprouts!
Oh, sauerkraut!
My coffin ain't too right
M' coffin 's a sorry sight
Take me out
Bury me in the night
Kiss me,
Tell me it's alright

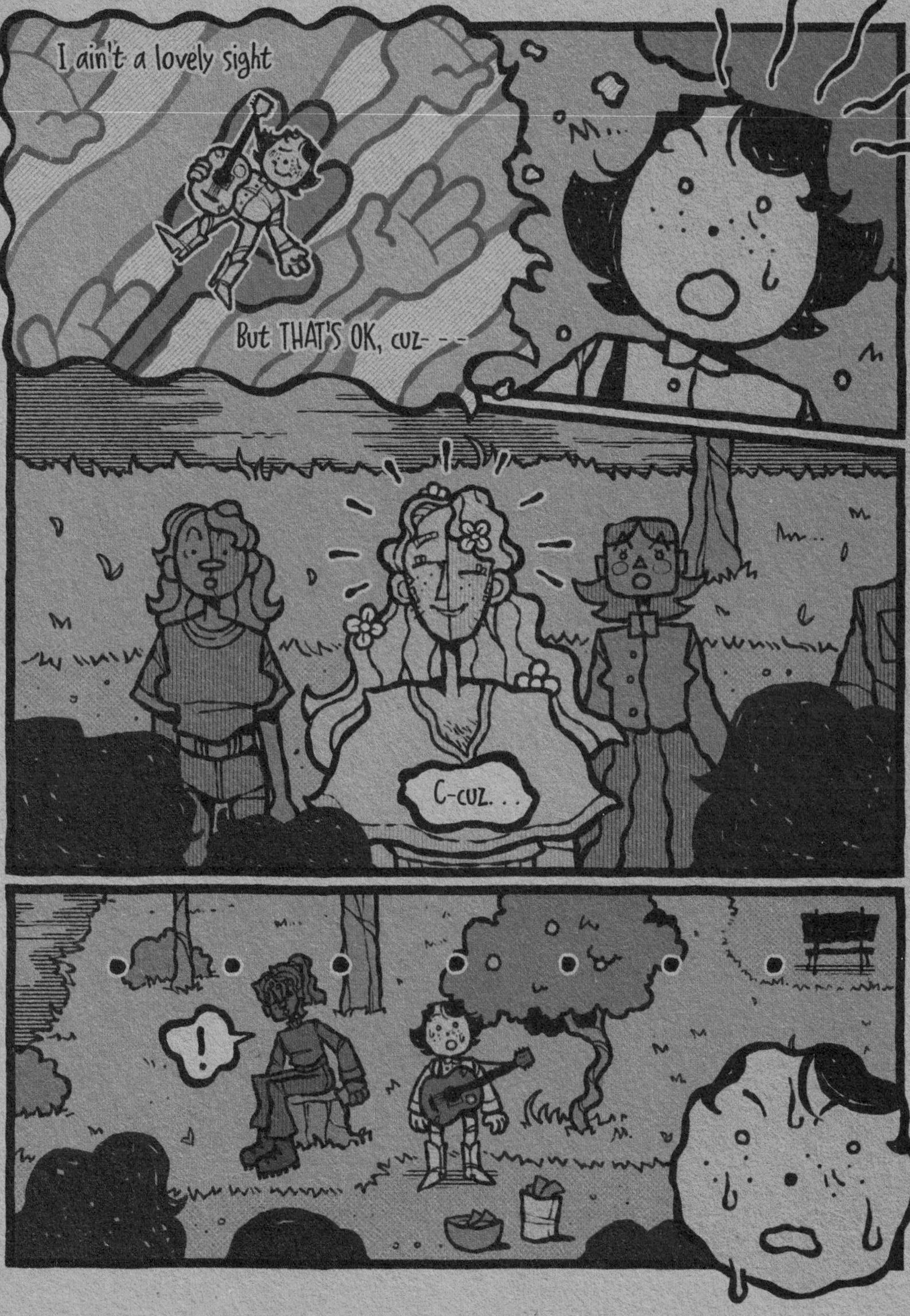

I ain't a lovely sight
But THAT'S OK, CUZ- - -
M...
C-CUZ. . .
!

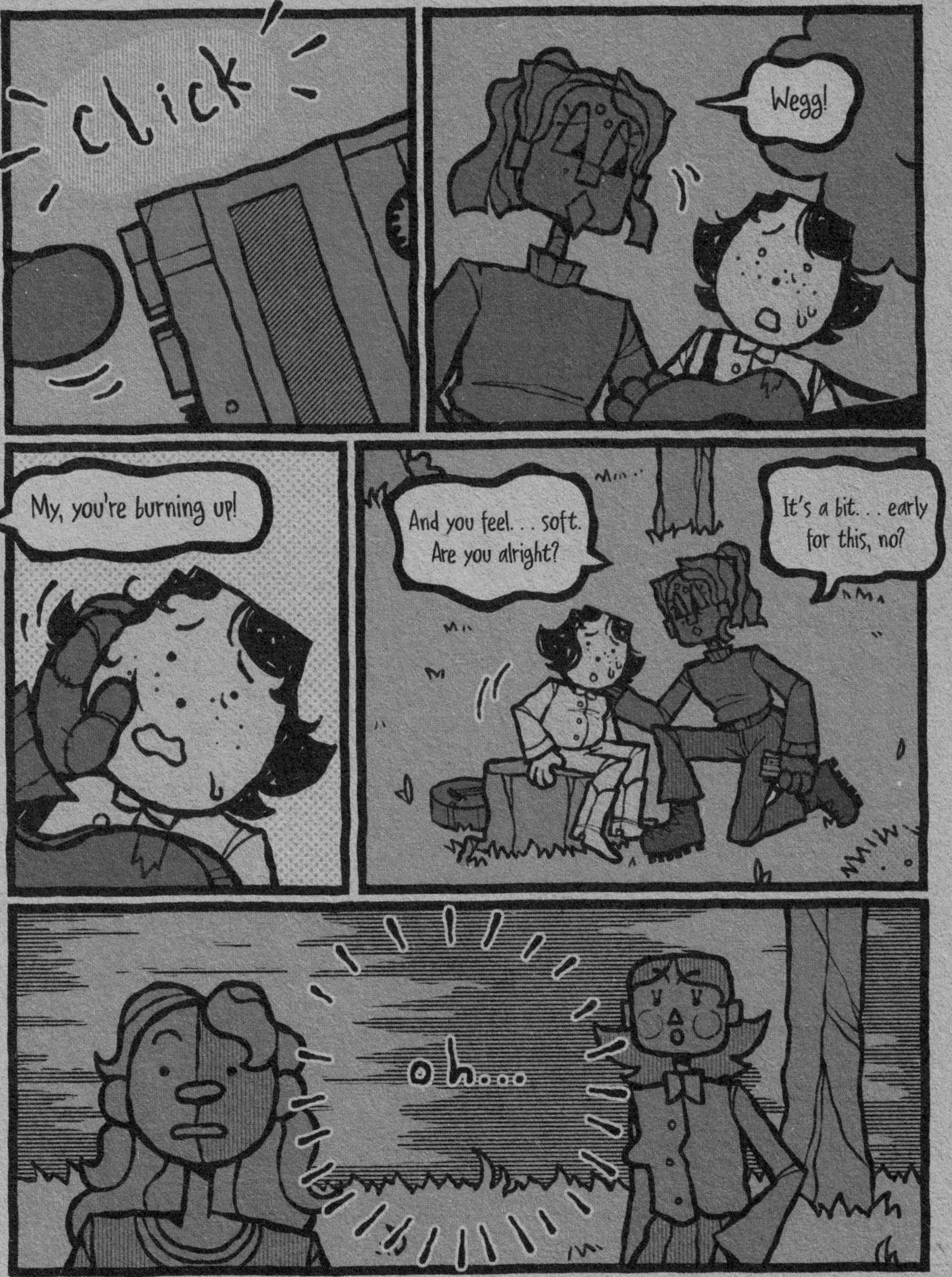
CLICK
Wegg!
My, you're burning up!
And you feel. . . soft.
Are you alright?
It's a bit. . . early
for this, no?
oh...

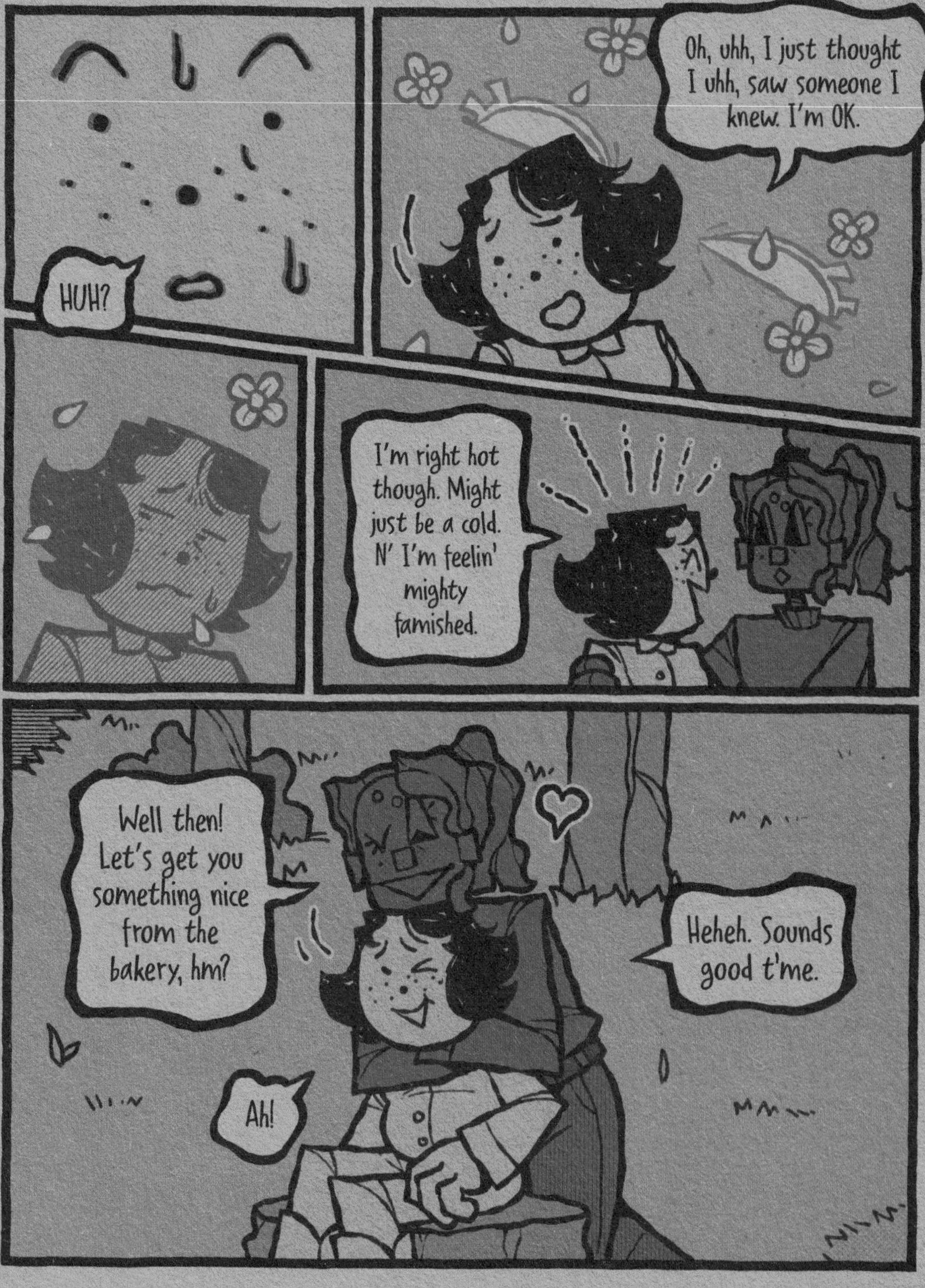
HUH?
Oh, uhh, I just thought I uhh, saw someone I knew. I'm OK.
I'm right hot though. Might just be a cold. N' I'm feelin' mighty famished.
Well then! Let's get you something nice from the bakery, hm?
Heheh. Sounds good t'me.
Ah!

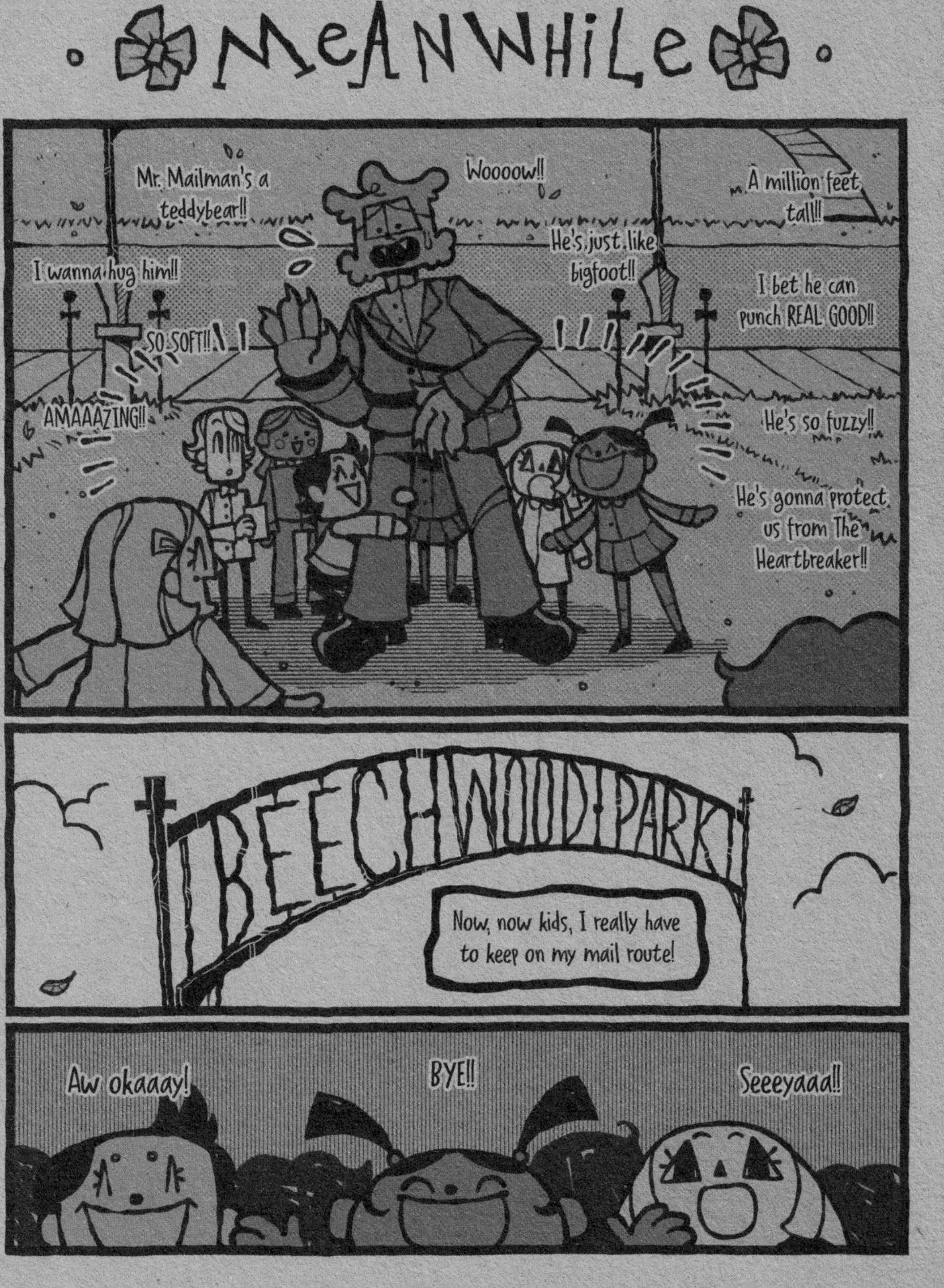
MEANWHILE
Mr. Mailman's a teddybear!!
Wooooow!!
A million feet tall!!
I wanna hug him!!
He's just like bigfoot!!
I bet he can punch REAL GOOD!!
SO SOFT!!
AMAAAZING!!
He's so fuzzy!!
He's gonna protect us from The Heartbreaker!!
BEECHWOOD PARK
Now, now kids, I really have to keep on my mail route!
Aw okaaay!
BYE!!
Seeeyaaa!!

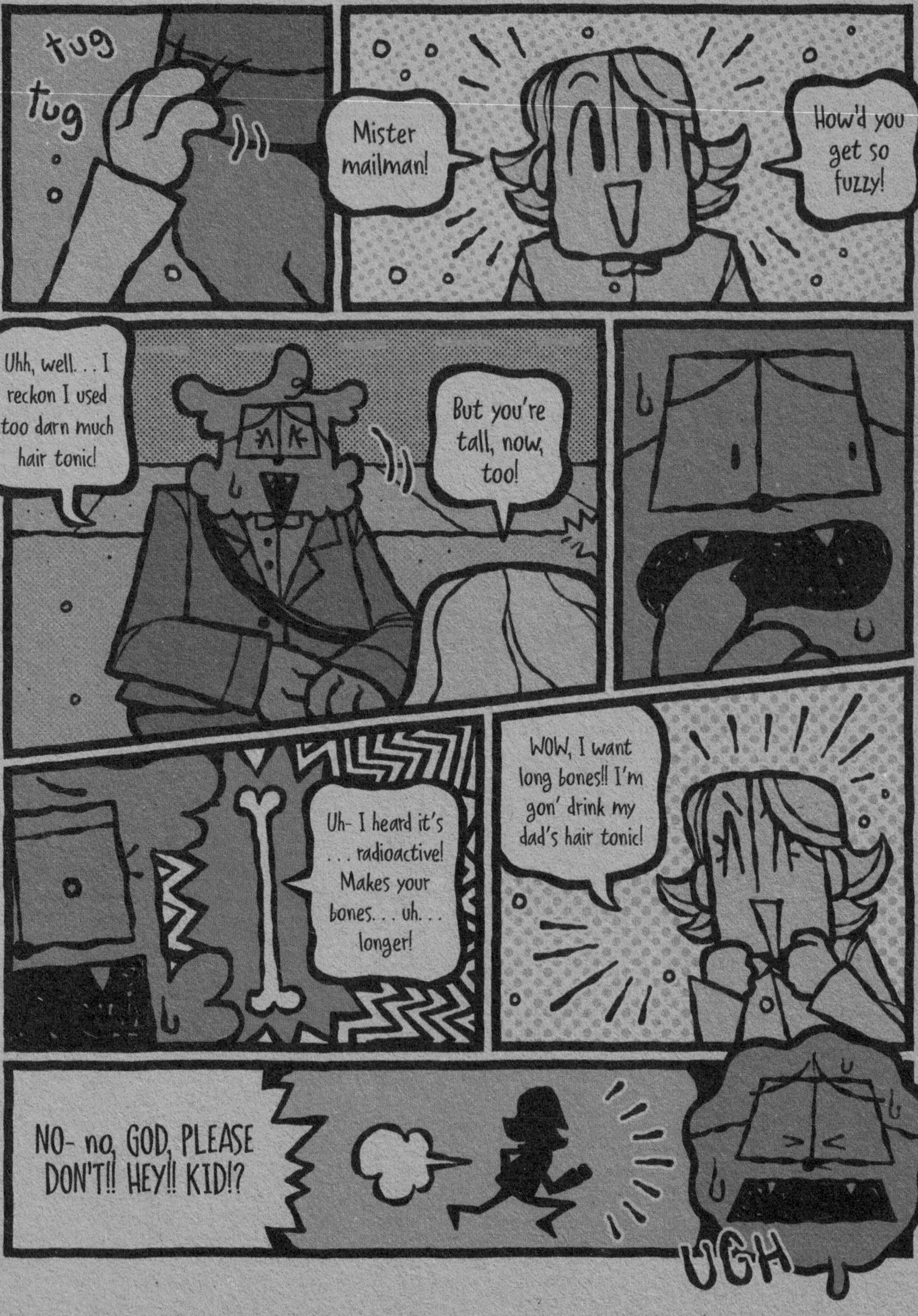
tug tug
Mister mailman!
How'd you get so fuzzy!
Uhh, well. . . I reckon I used too darn much hair tonic!
But you're tall, now, too!
Uh- I heard it's . . . radioactive! Makes your bones. . . uh. . . longer!
WOW, I want long bones!! I'm gon' drink my dad's hair tonic!
NO- no, GOD, PLEASE DON'T!! HEY!! KID!?
UGH

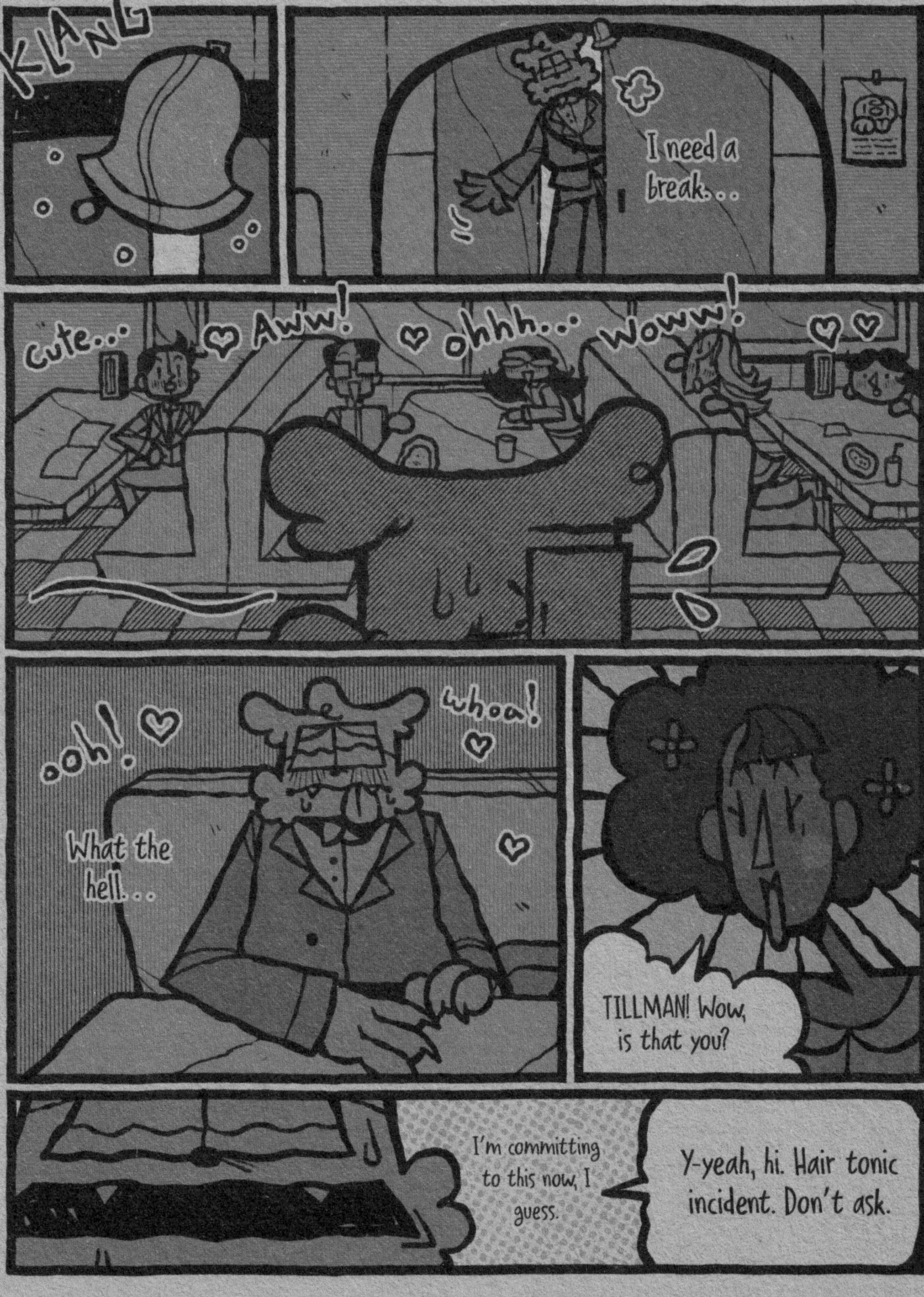
KLANG
I need a break...
cute...
Aww!
ohhh...
Woww!
ooh!
whoa!
What the hell...
TILLMAN! Wow, is that you?
I'm committing to this now, I guess.
Y-yeah, hi. Hair tonic incident. Don't ask.

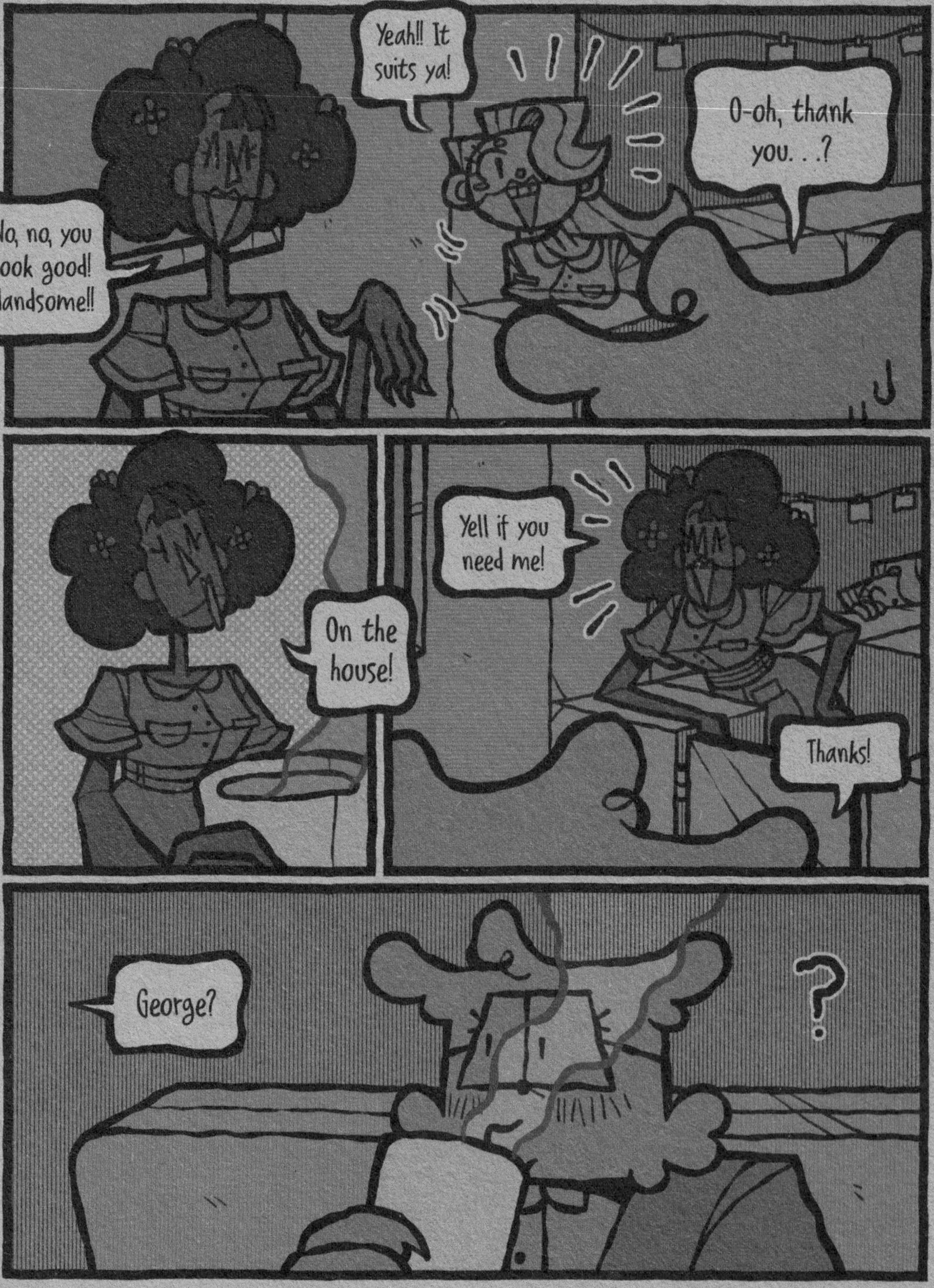
Yeah!! It suits ya!
O-oh, thank you. . .?
No, no, you look good! Handsome!!
On the house!
Yell if you need me!
Thanks!
George?
?

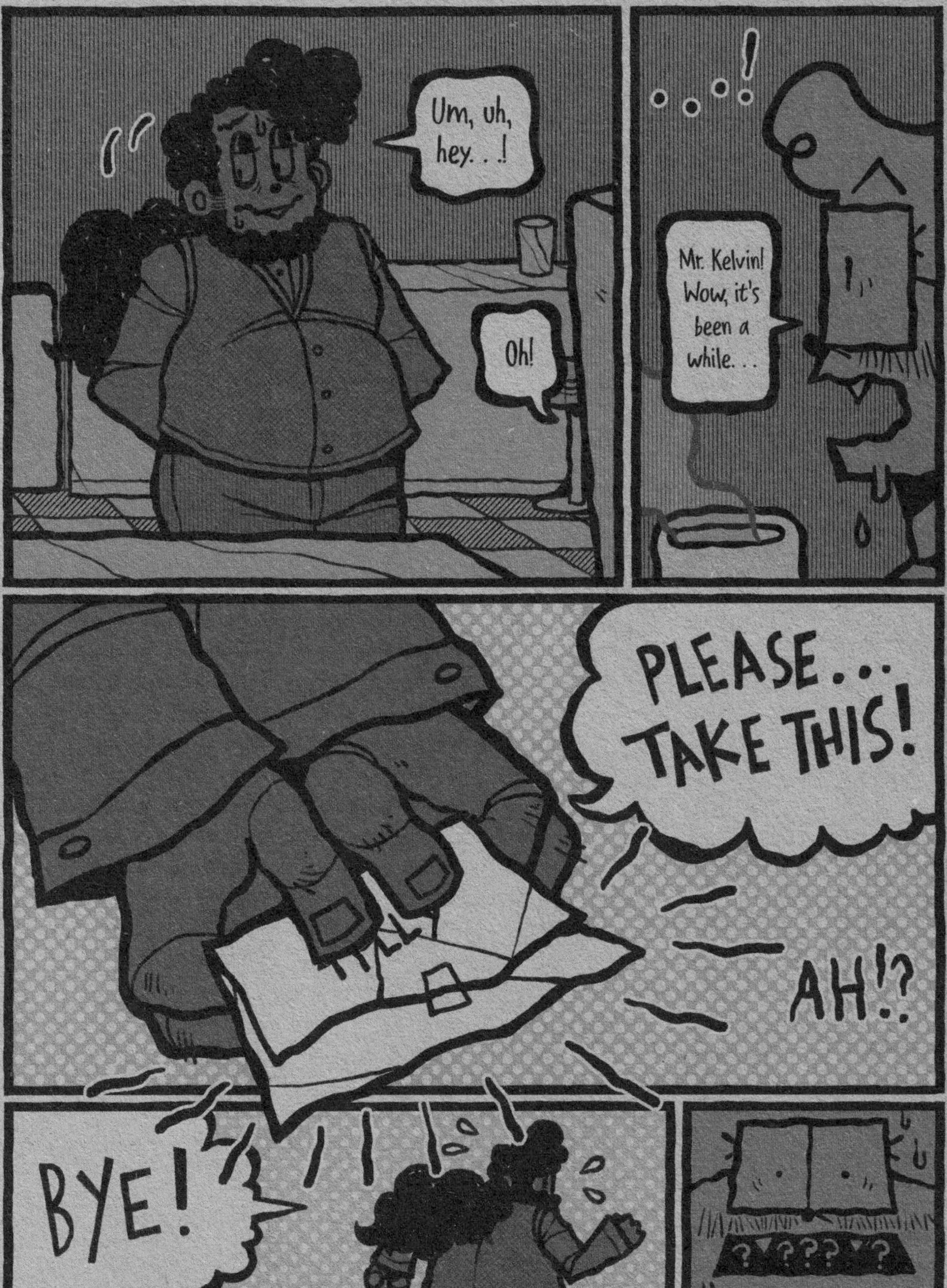
Um, uh, hey. . .!
Oh!
Mr. Kelvin! Wow, it's been a while. . .
PLEASE... TAKE THIS!
AH!?
BYE!
? ??? ?

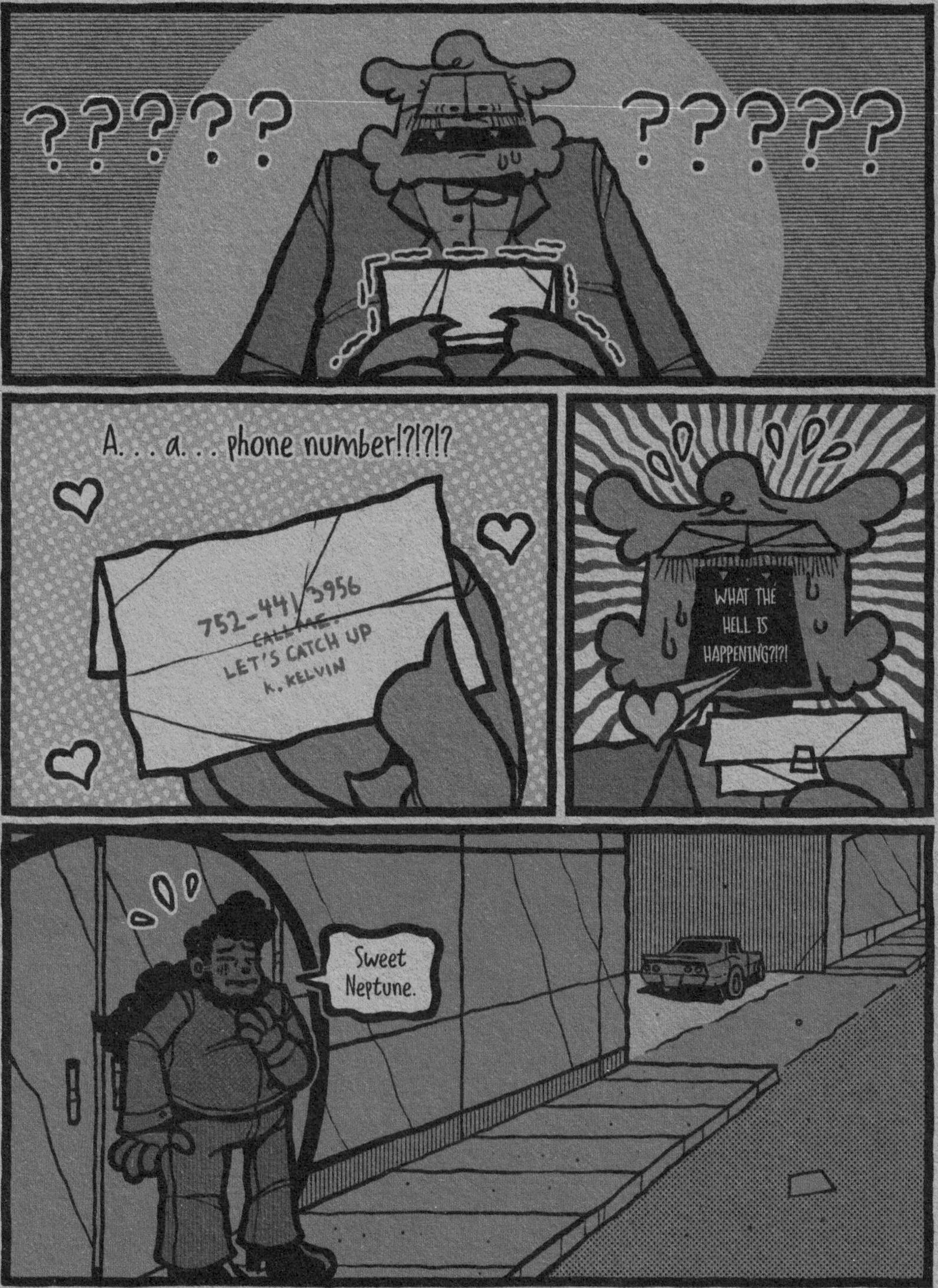
?????
?????
A. . . a. . . phone number!?!?!?
752-441 3956
CALL ME.
LET'S CATCH UP
K. KELVIN
WHAT THE HELL IS HAPPENING?!?!
Sweet Neptune.

A love ritual? Isn't that just
what we do every day?
. . . so this is really somethin'
special, huh Lew.
Well, count me in!
I really do love you. . .

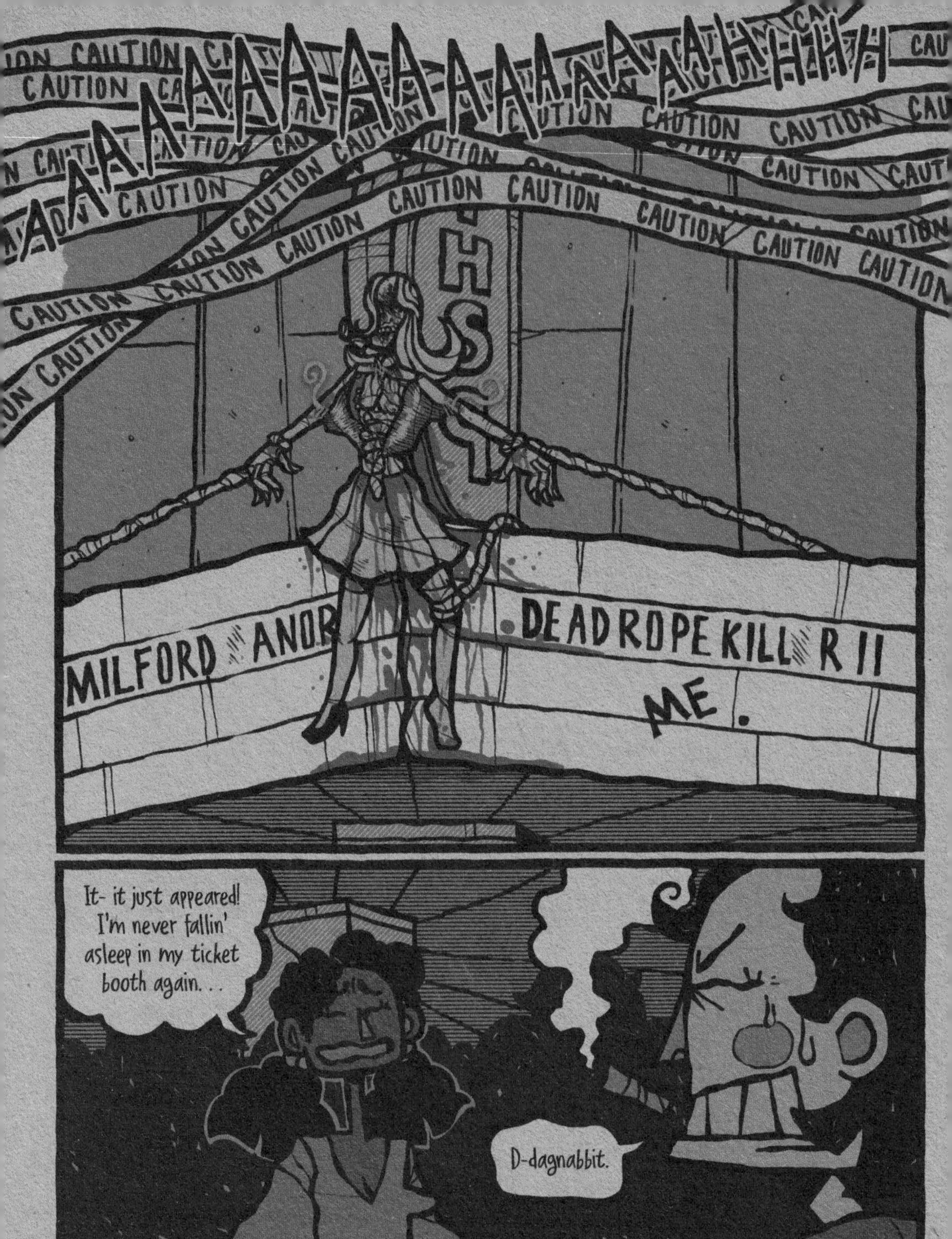
AAAAAAAAAAAAAAAAAHHHH
CAUTION
MILFORD ANOR
DEADROPEKILL R II
ME.
It- it just appeared! I'm never fallin' asleep in my ticket booth again. . .
D-dagnabbit.

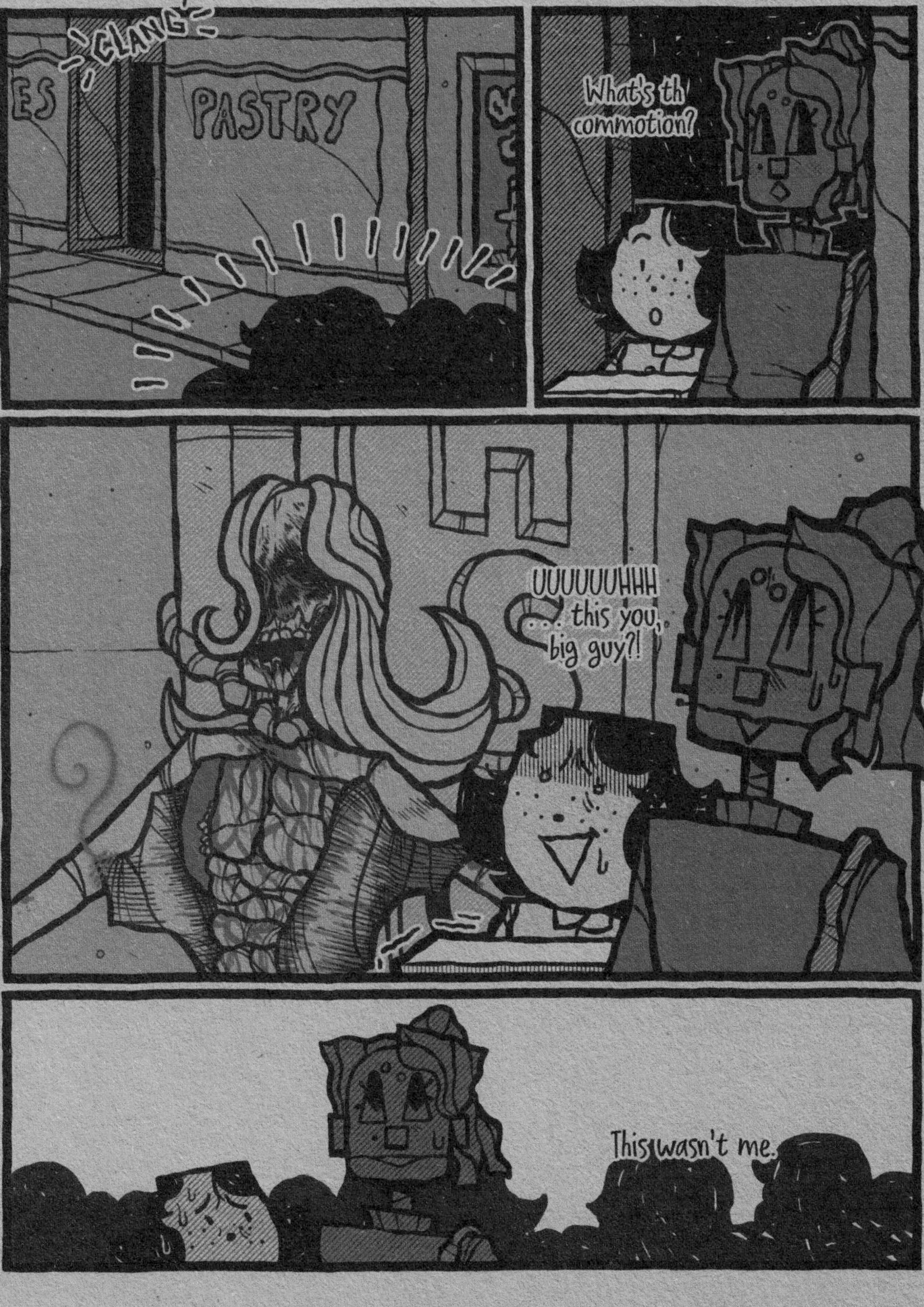
CLANG
PASTRY
What's th commotion?
UUUUUUHHH . . . this you, big guy?!
This wasn't me.

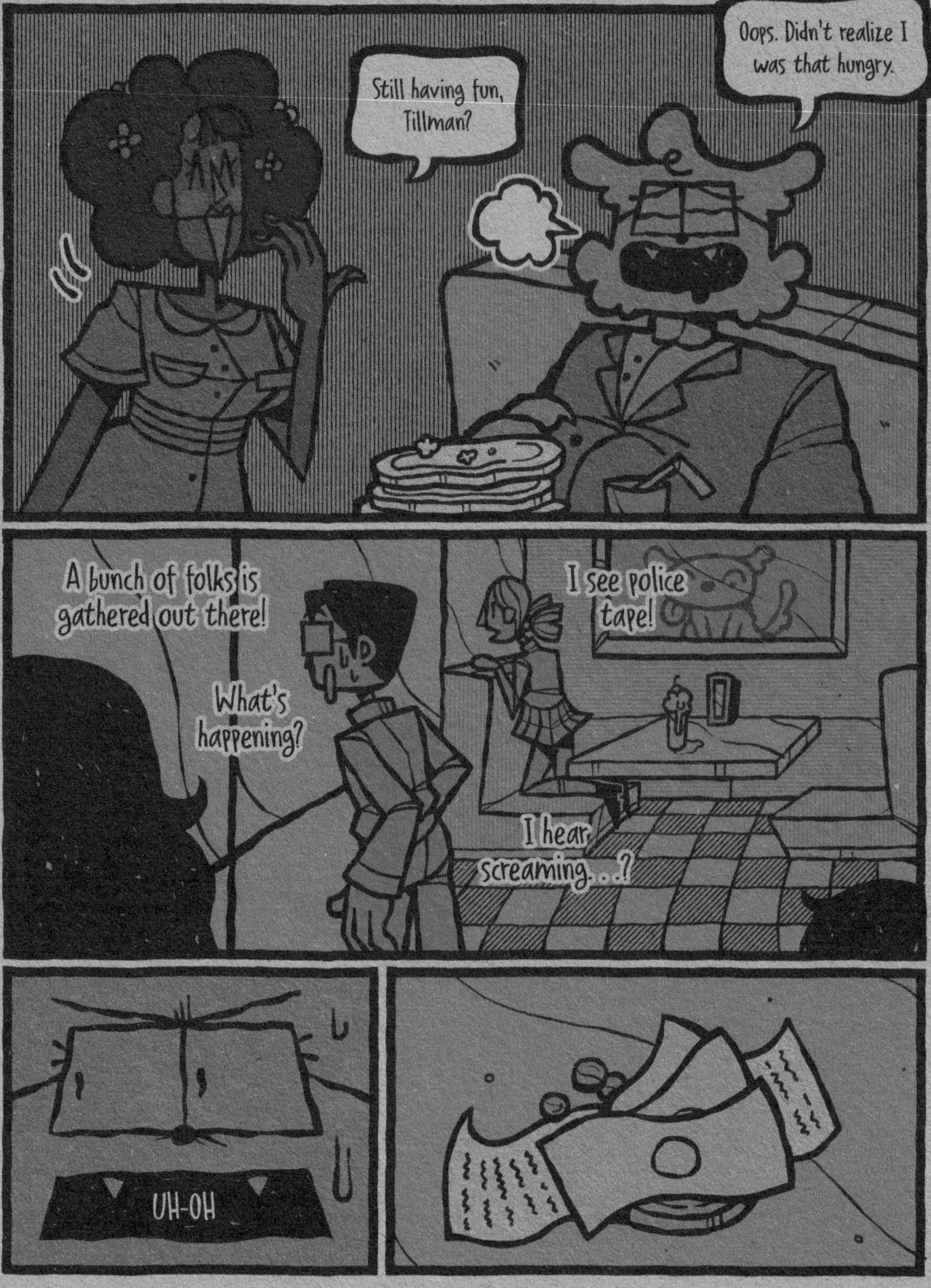
Still having fun, Tillman?
Oops. Didn't realize I was that hungry.
A bunch of folks is gathered out there!
What's happening?
I see police tape!
I hear screaming. . .?
UH-OH

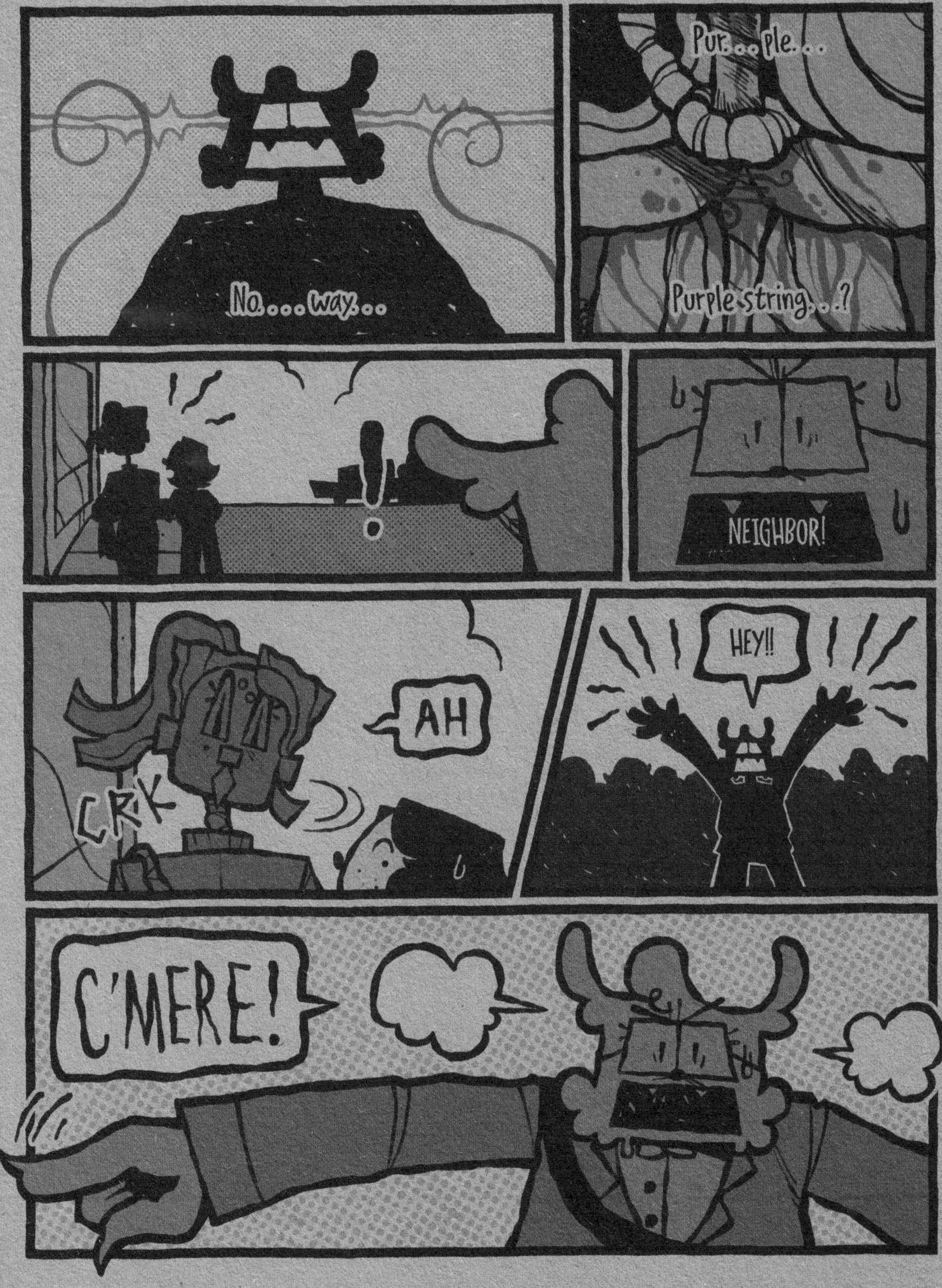
No... way...
Pur... ple...
Purple string...?
NEIGHBOR!
CRK
AH
HEY!!
C'MERE!

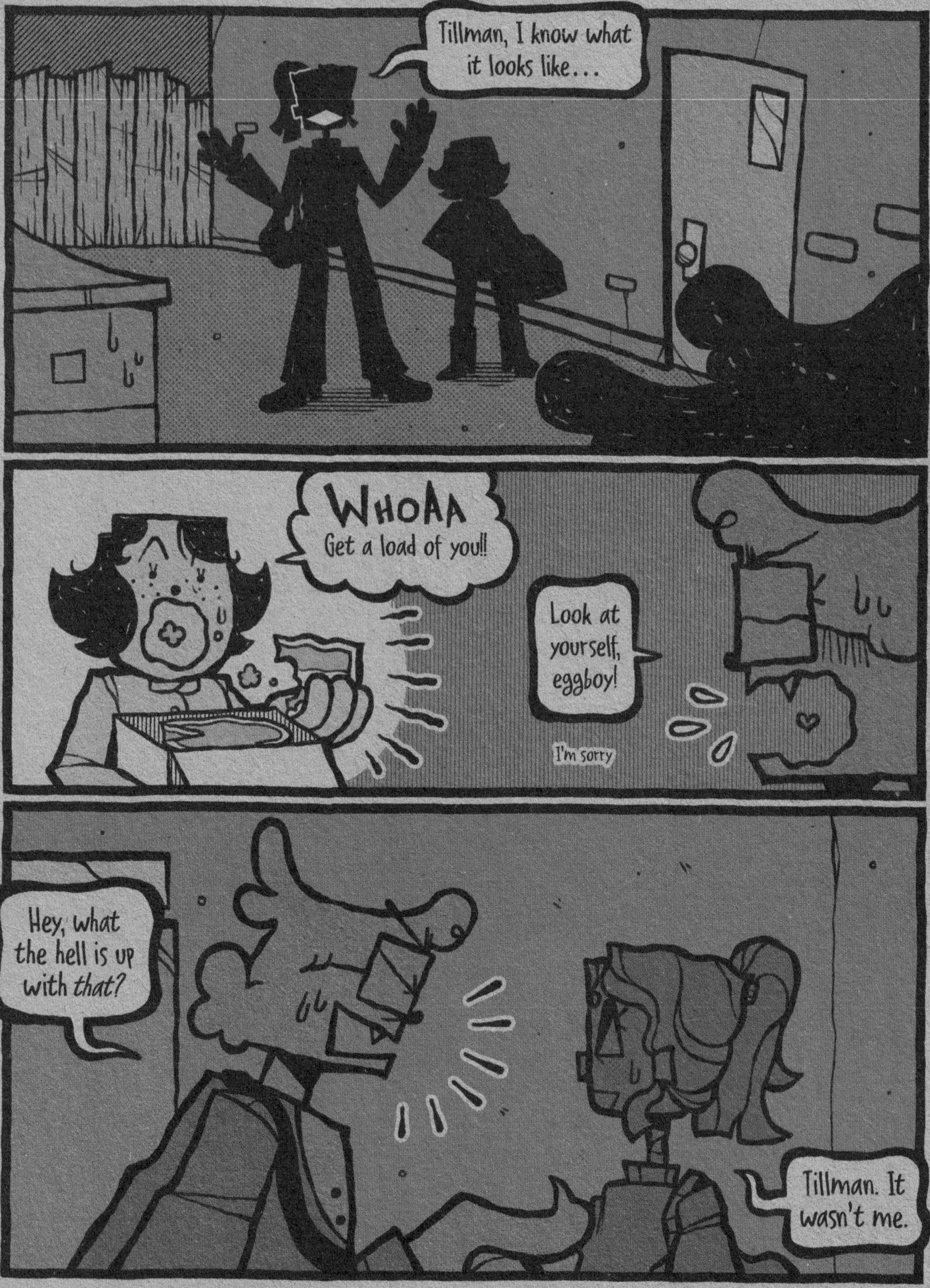
Tillman, I know what it looks like...
WHOAA
Get a load of you!!
Look at yourself, eggboy!
I'm sorry
Hey, what the hell is up with *that*?
Tillman. It wasn't me.

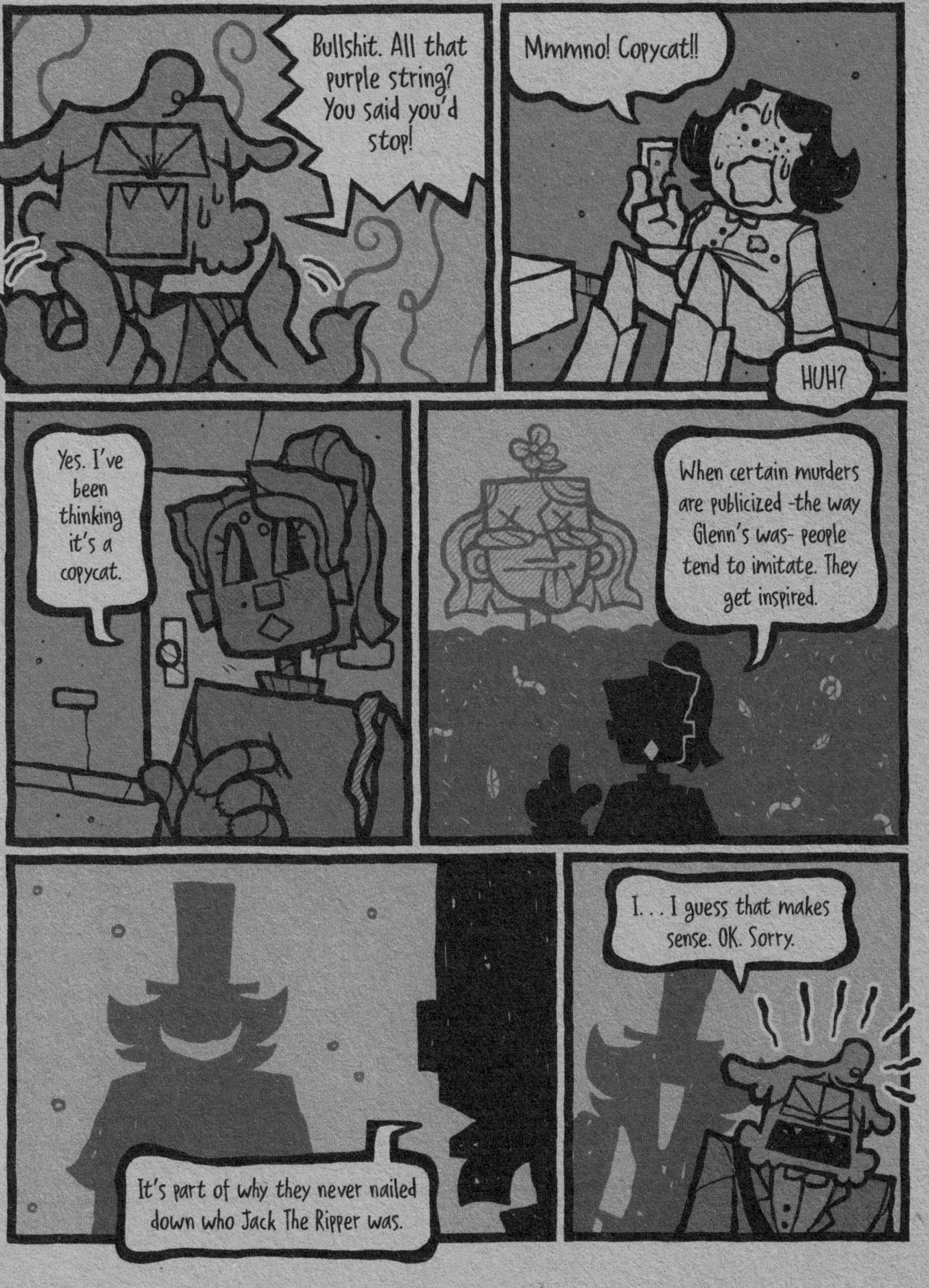
Bullshit. All that purple string? You said you'd stop!
Mmmno! Copycat!!
HUH?
Yes. I've been thinking it's a copycat.
When certain murders are publicized -the way Glenn's was- people tend to imitate. They get inspired.
It's part of why they never nailed down who Jack The Ripper was.
I... I guess that makes sense. OK. Sorry.

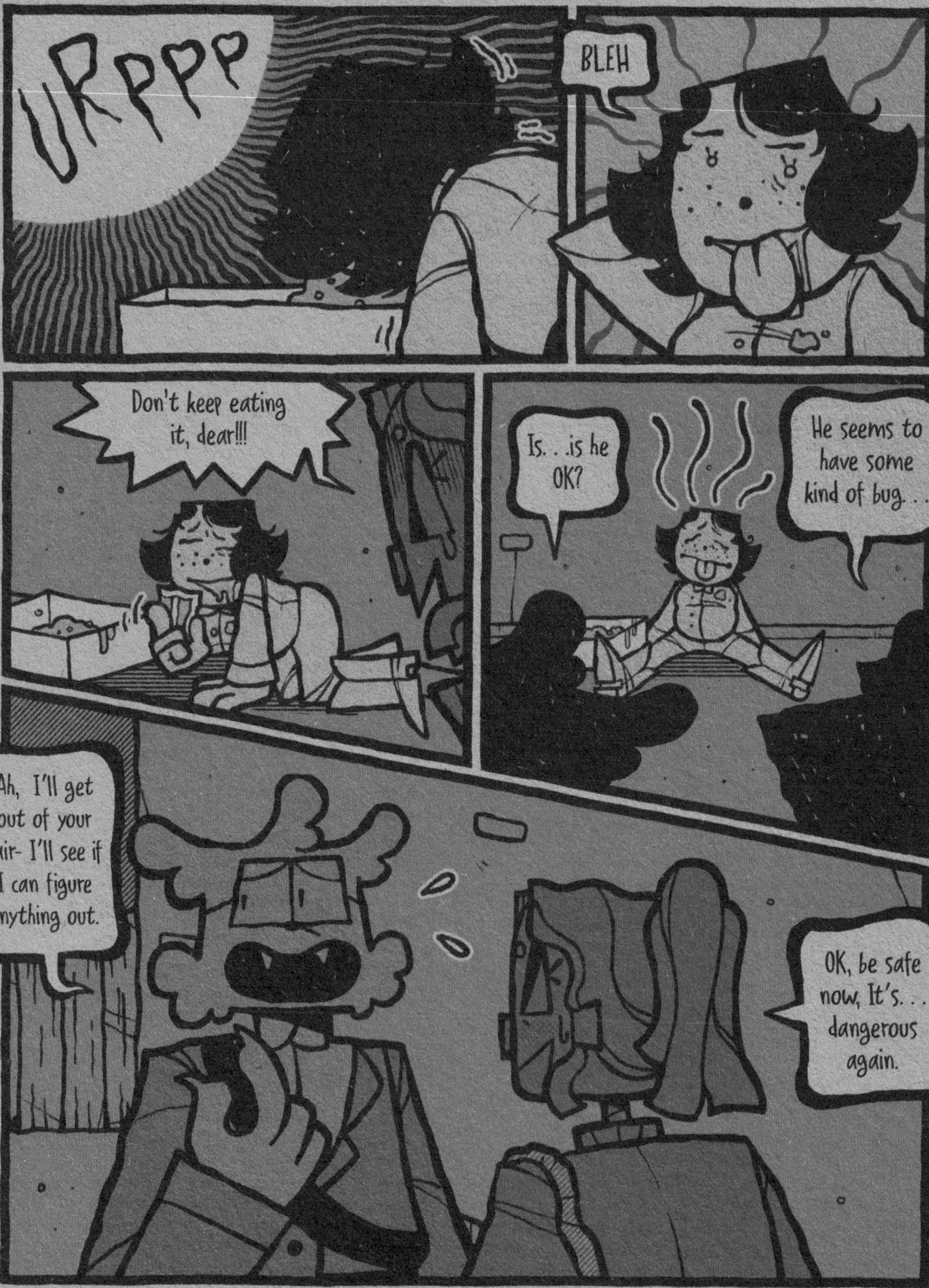
URPPP
BLEH
Don't keep eating it, dear!!!
Is. . .is he OK?
He seems to have some kind of bug. . .
Ah, I'll get out of your hair- I'll see if I can figure anything out.
OK, be safe now, It's. . . dangerous again.

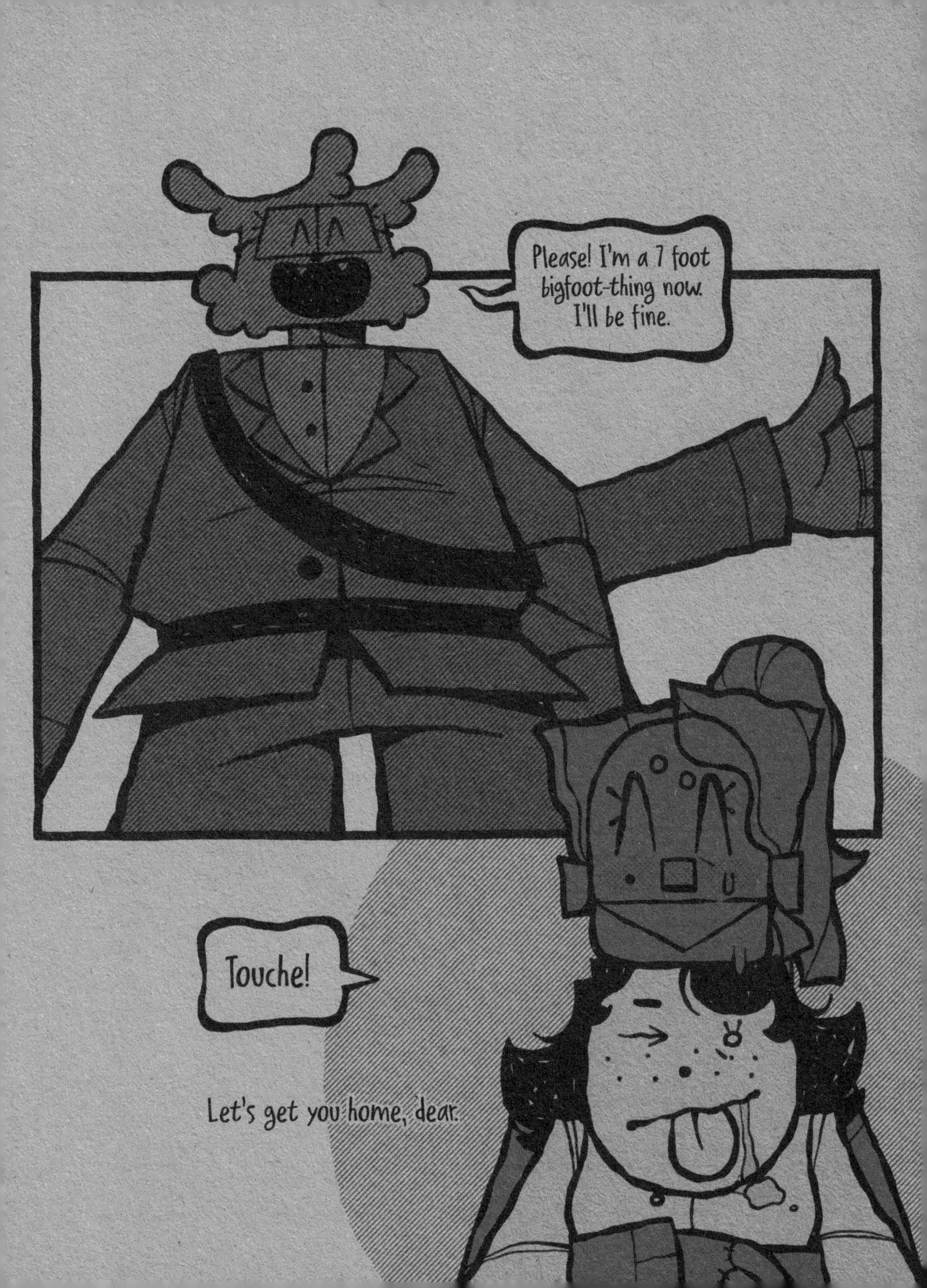
Please! I'm a 7 foot bigfoot-thing now. I'll be fine.
Touche!
Let's get you home, dear.

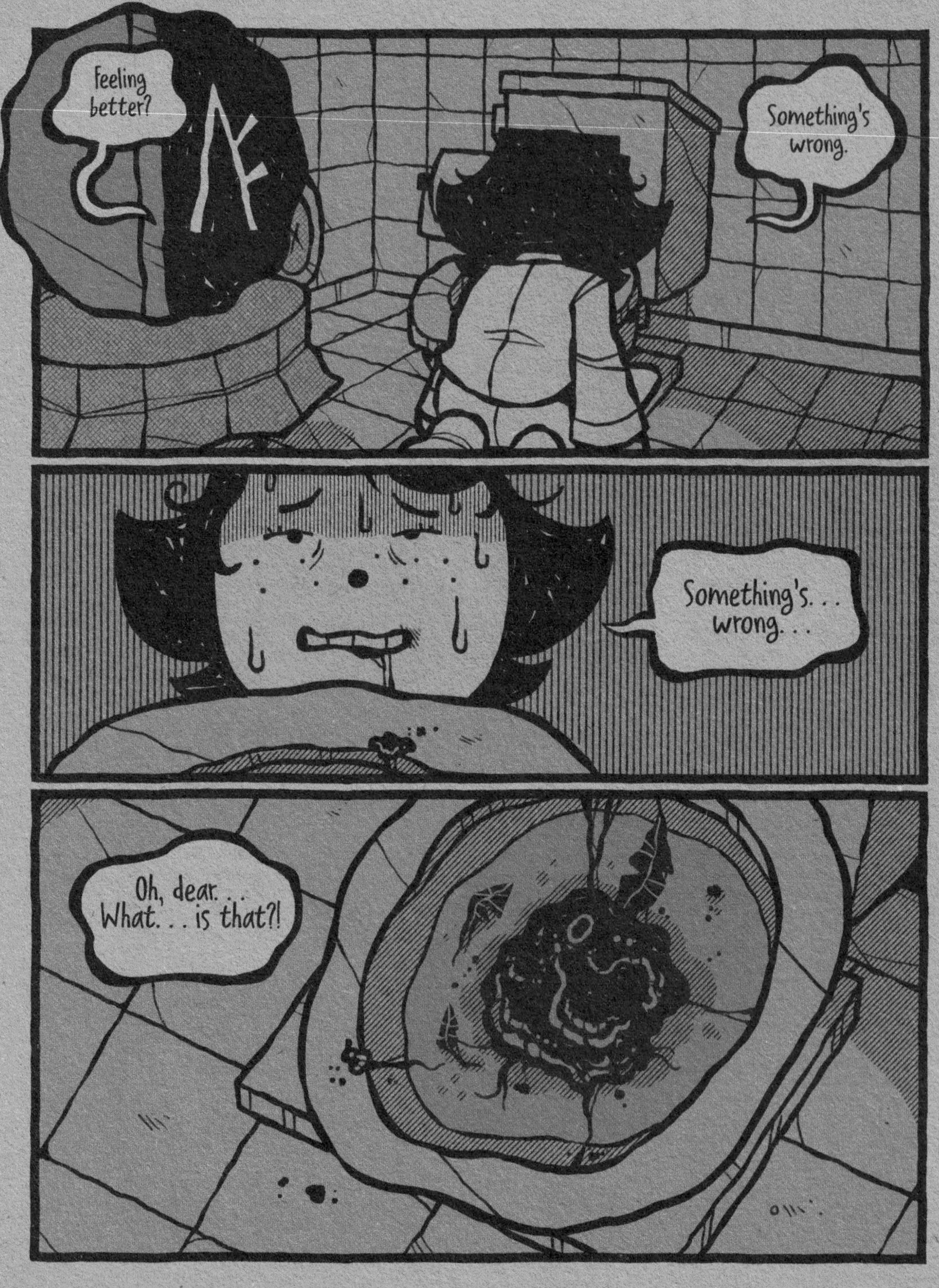
Feeling better?
Something's wrong.
Something's. . . wrong. . .
Oh, dear. . . What. . . is that?!

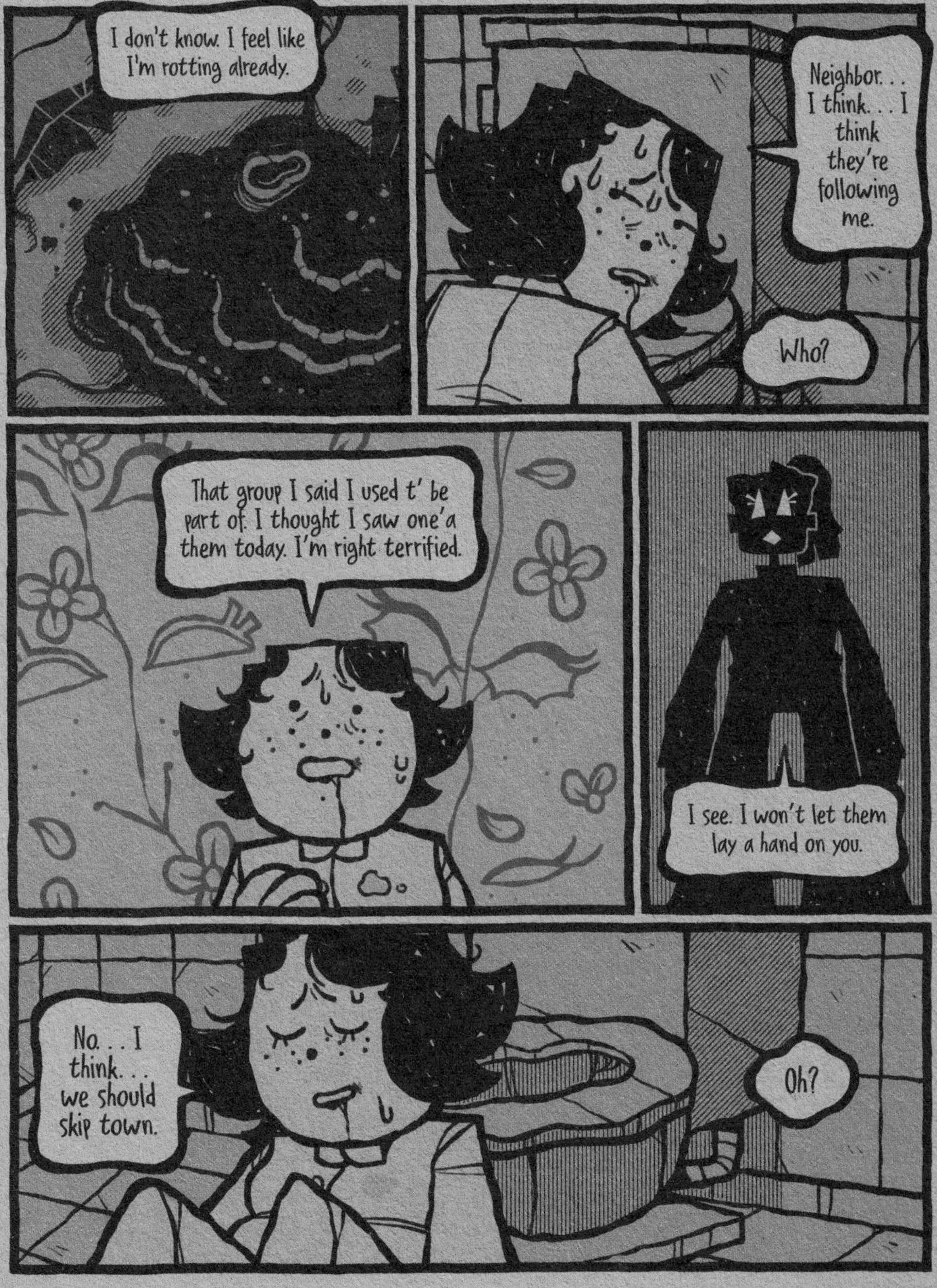
I don't know. I feel like I'm rotting already.
Neighbor. . . I think. . . I think they're following me.
Who?
That group I said I used t' be part of. I thought I saw one'a them today. I'm right terrified.
I see. I won't let them lay a hand on you.
No. . . I think. . . we should skip town.
Oh?

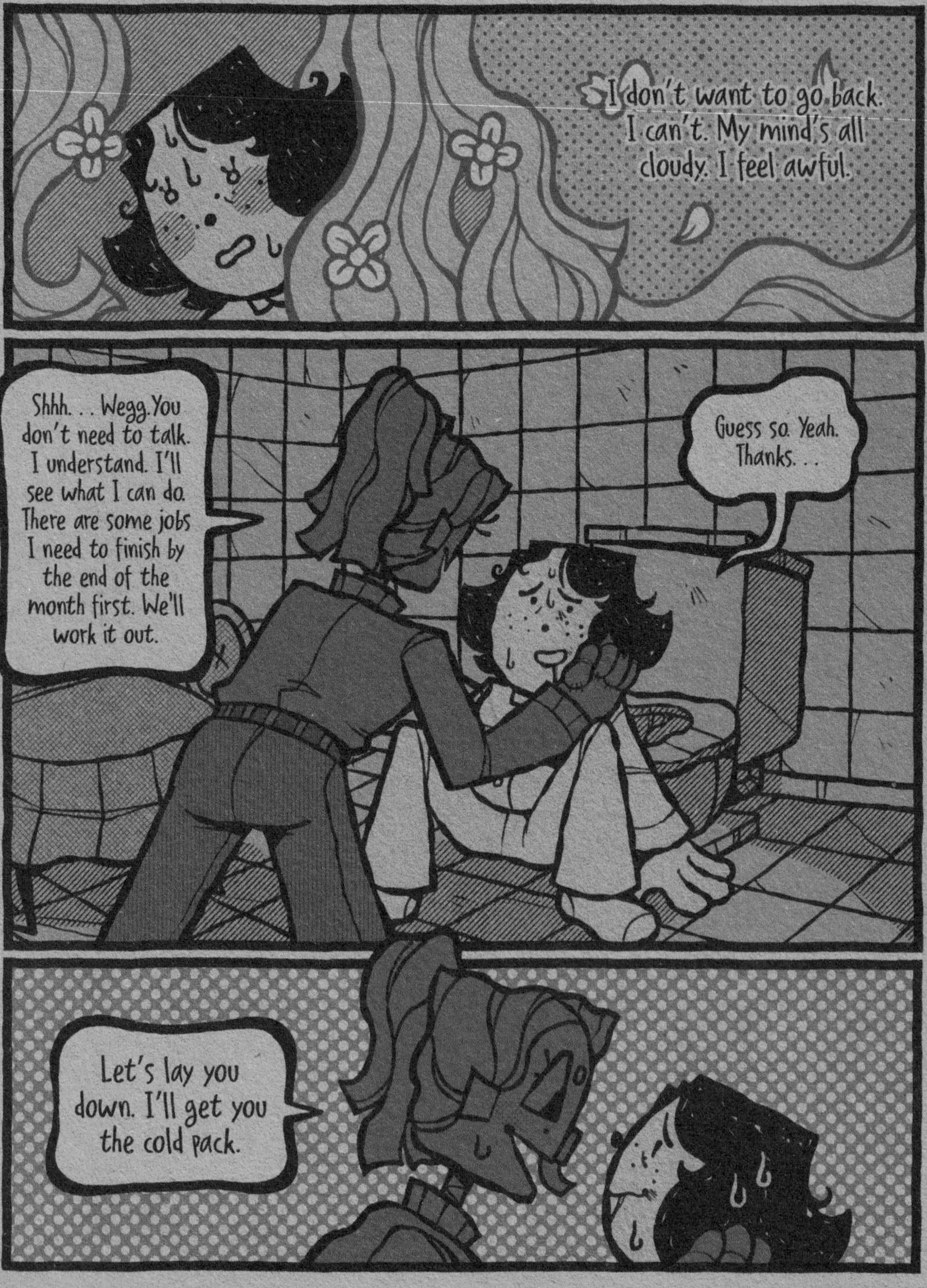
I don't want to go back. I can't. My mind's all cloudy. I feel awful.
Shhh. . . Wegg. You don't need to talk. I understand. I'll see what I can do. There are some jobs I need to finish by the end of the month first. We'll work it out.
Guess so. Yeah. Thanks. . .
Let's lay you down. I'll get you the cold pack.

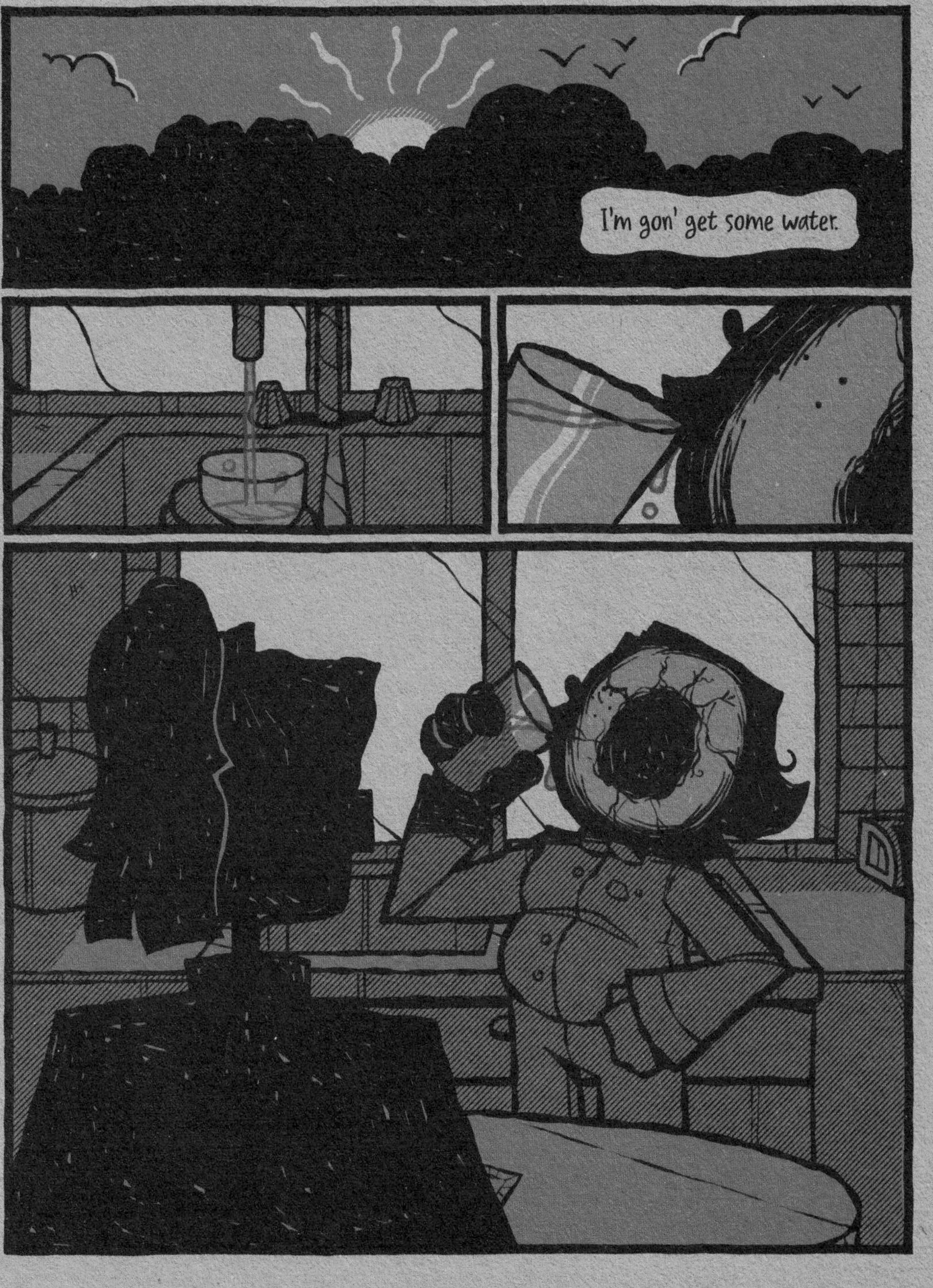
I'm gon' get some water.

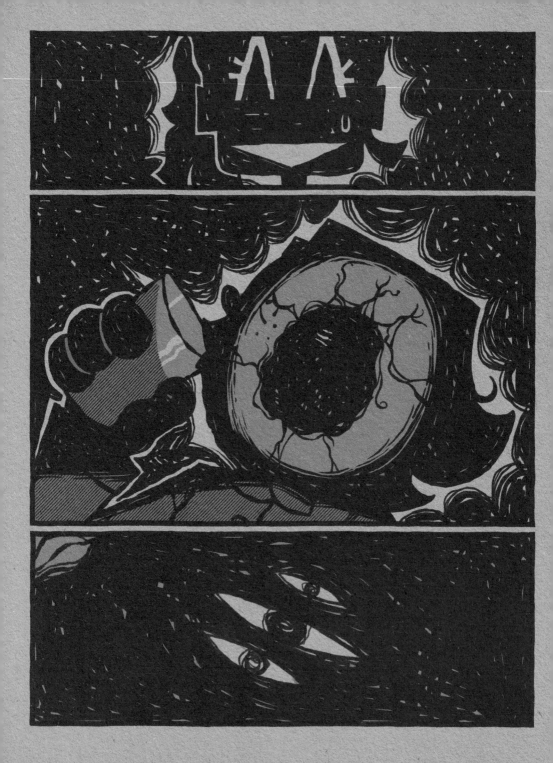

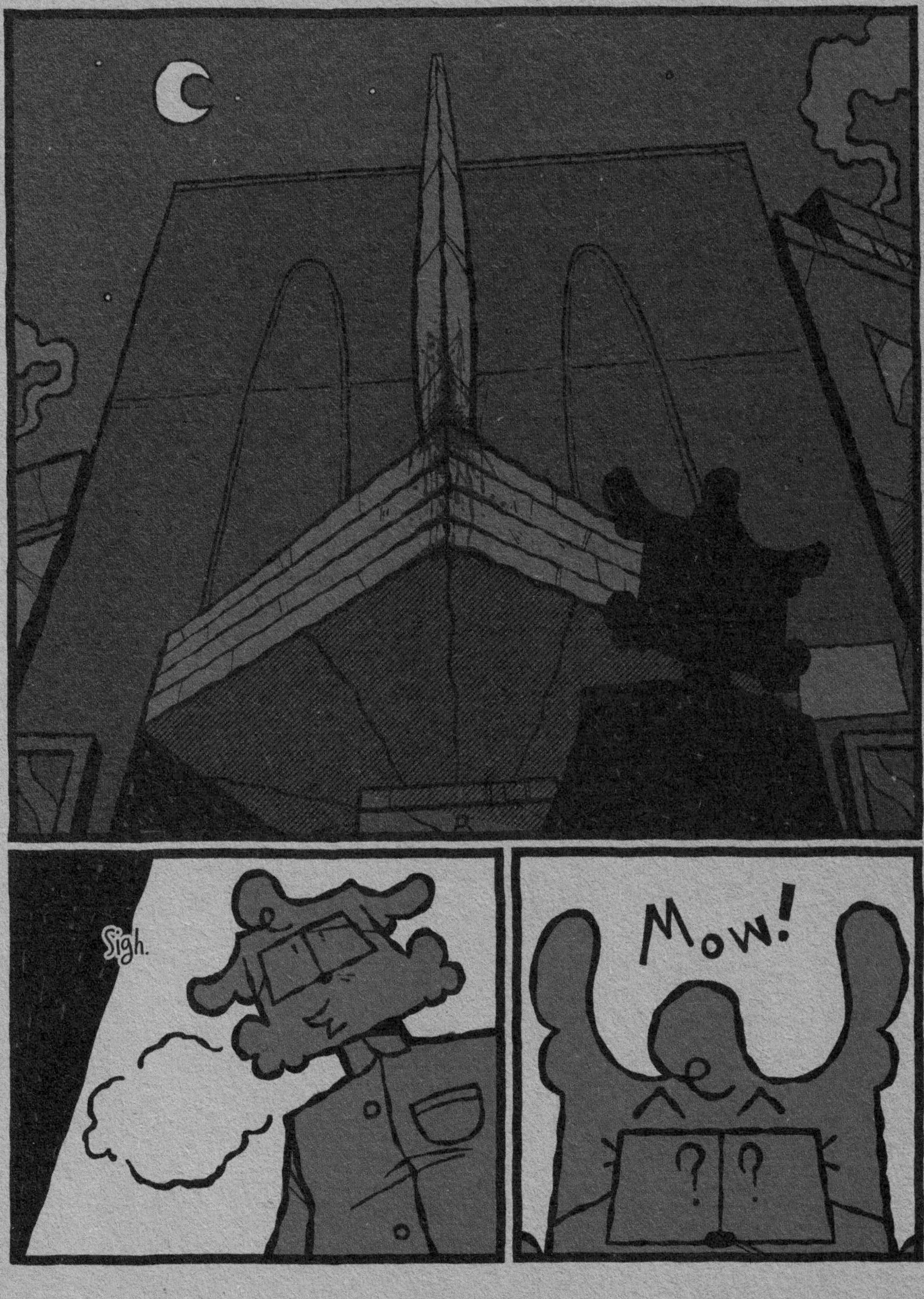
Sigh.
Mow!

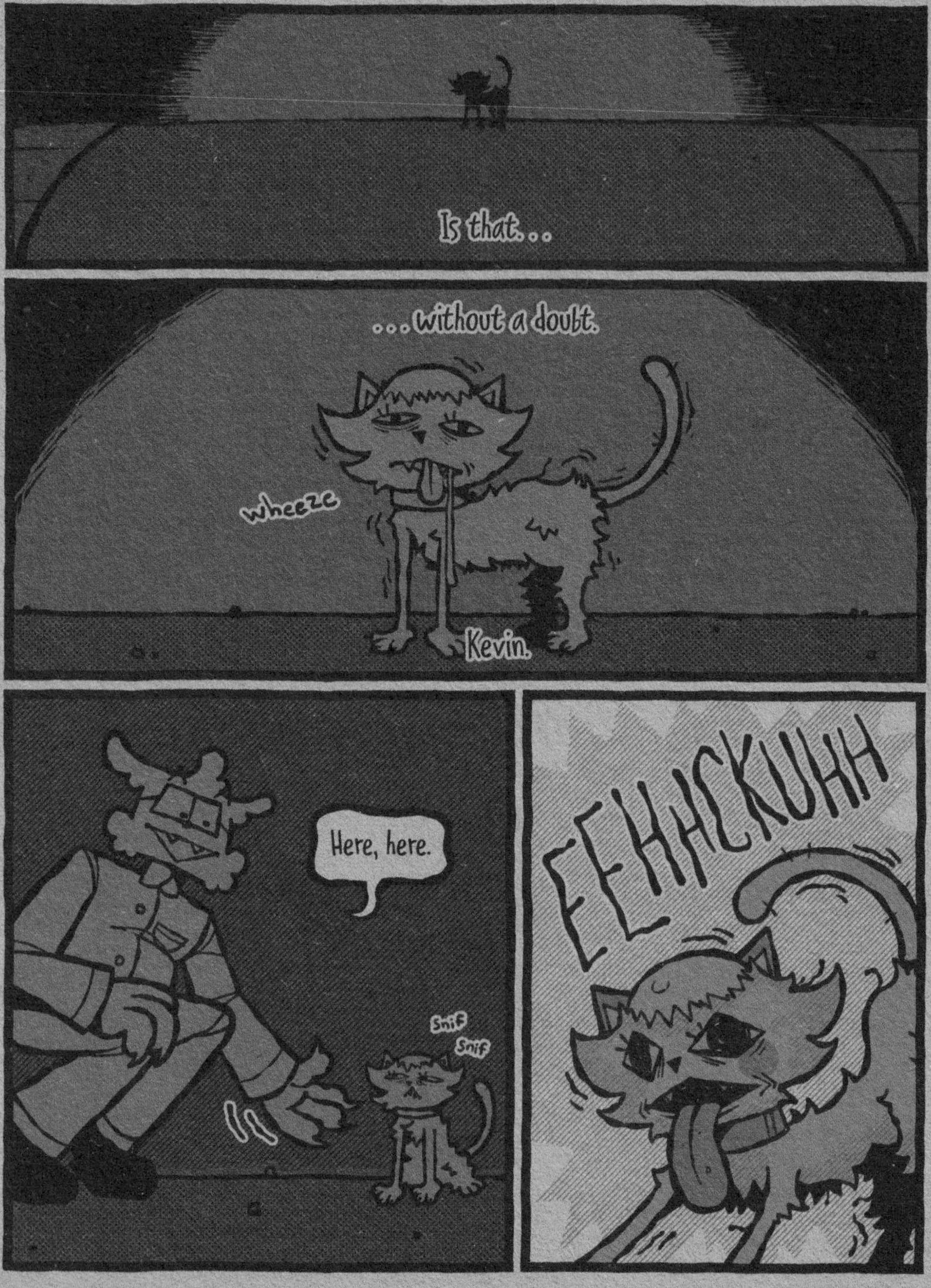
Is that...
...without a doubt.
wheeze
Kevin.
Here, here.
Snif
Snif
EEHHCKUHH

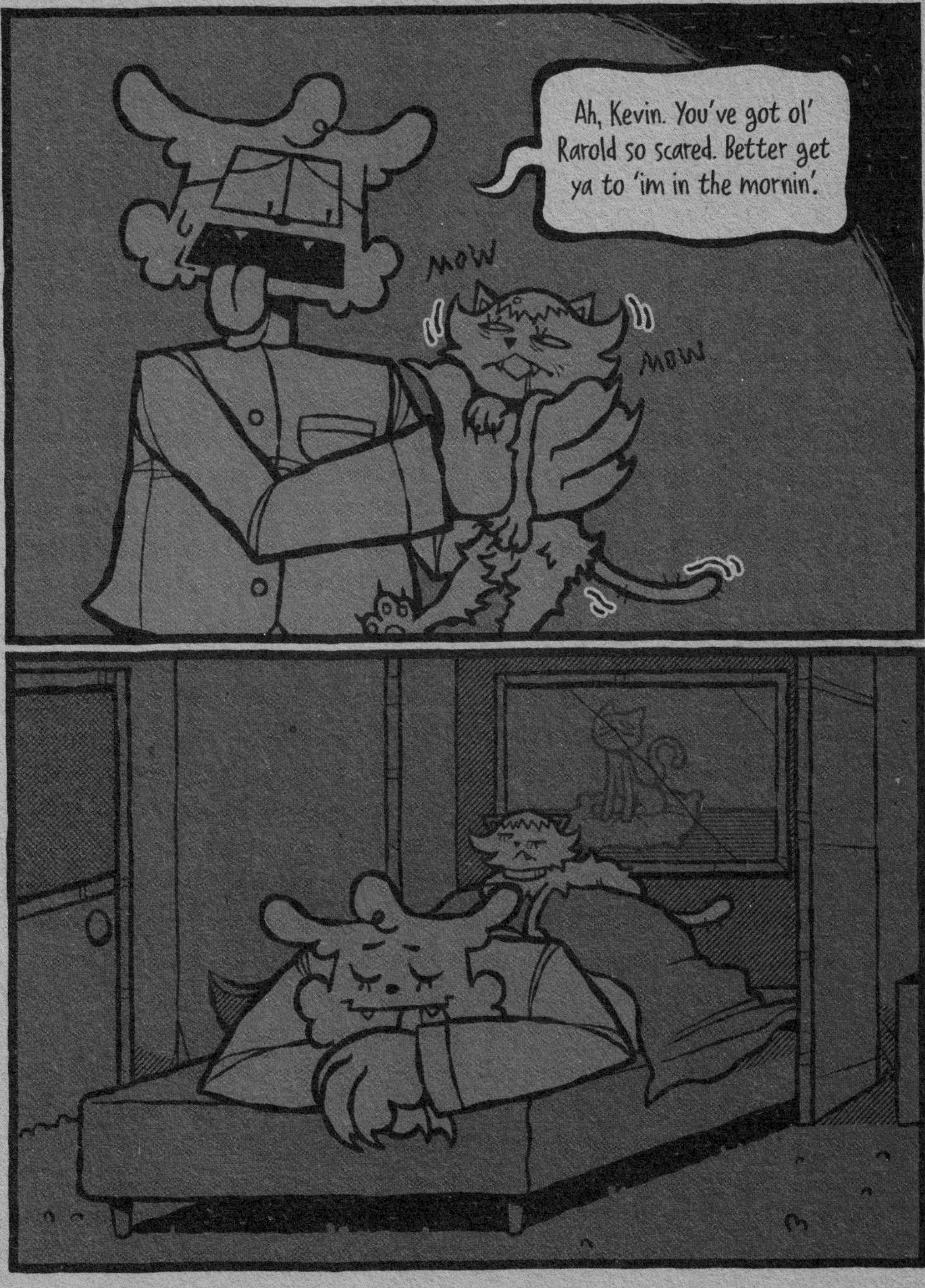
Ah, Kevin. You've got ol' Rarold so scared. Better get ya to 'im in the mornin'.
MOW
MOW

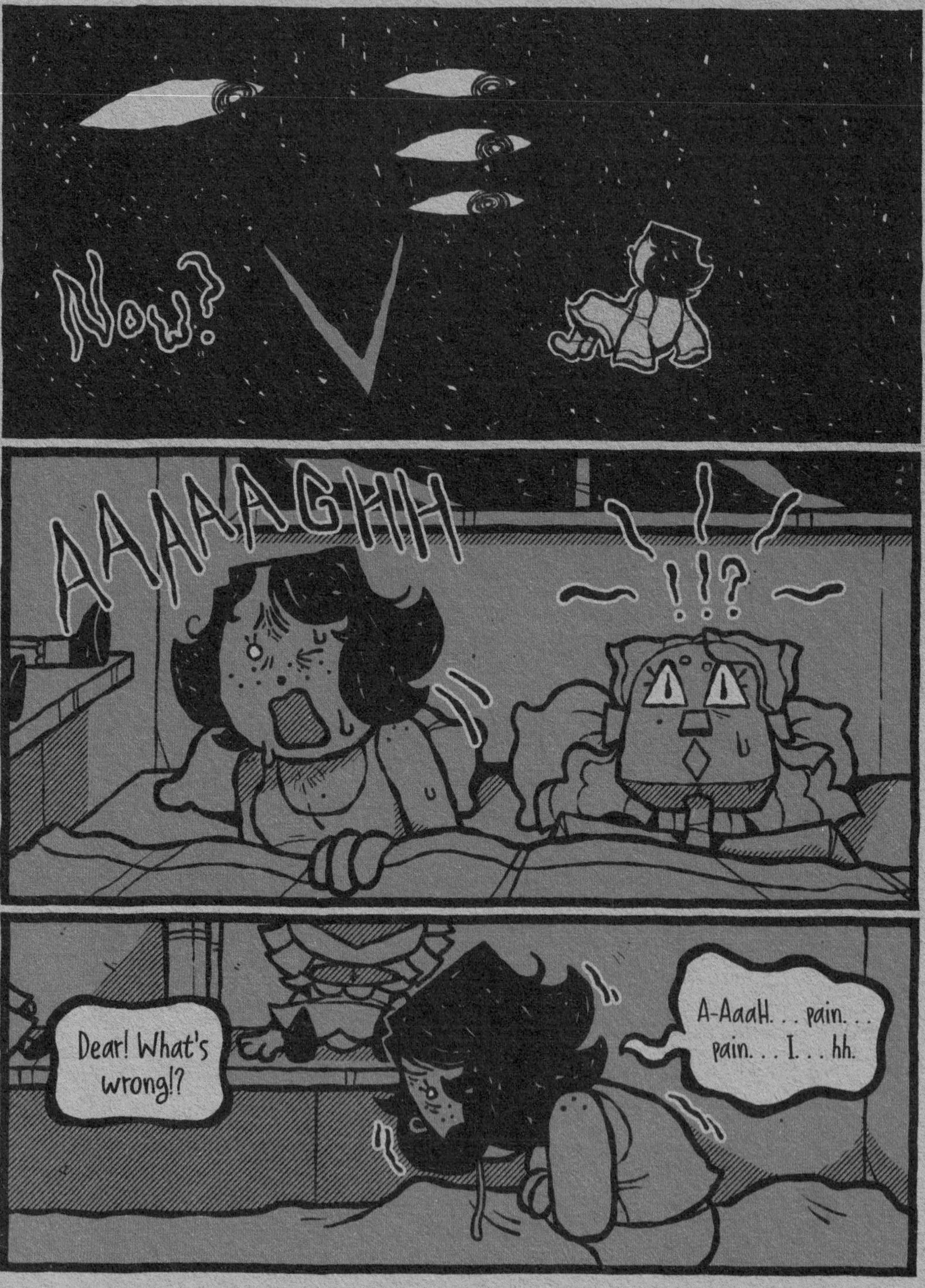
Now?
AAAAAGHH
!!?
Dear! What's wrong!?
A-AaaH. . . pain. . . pain. . . I. . . hh.

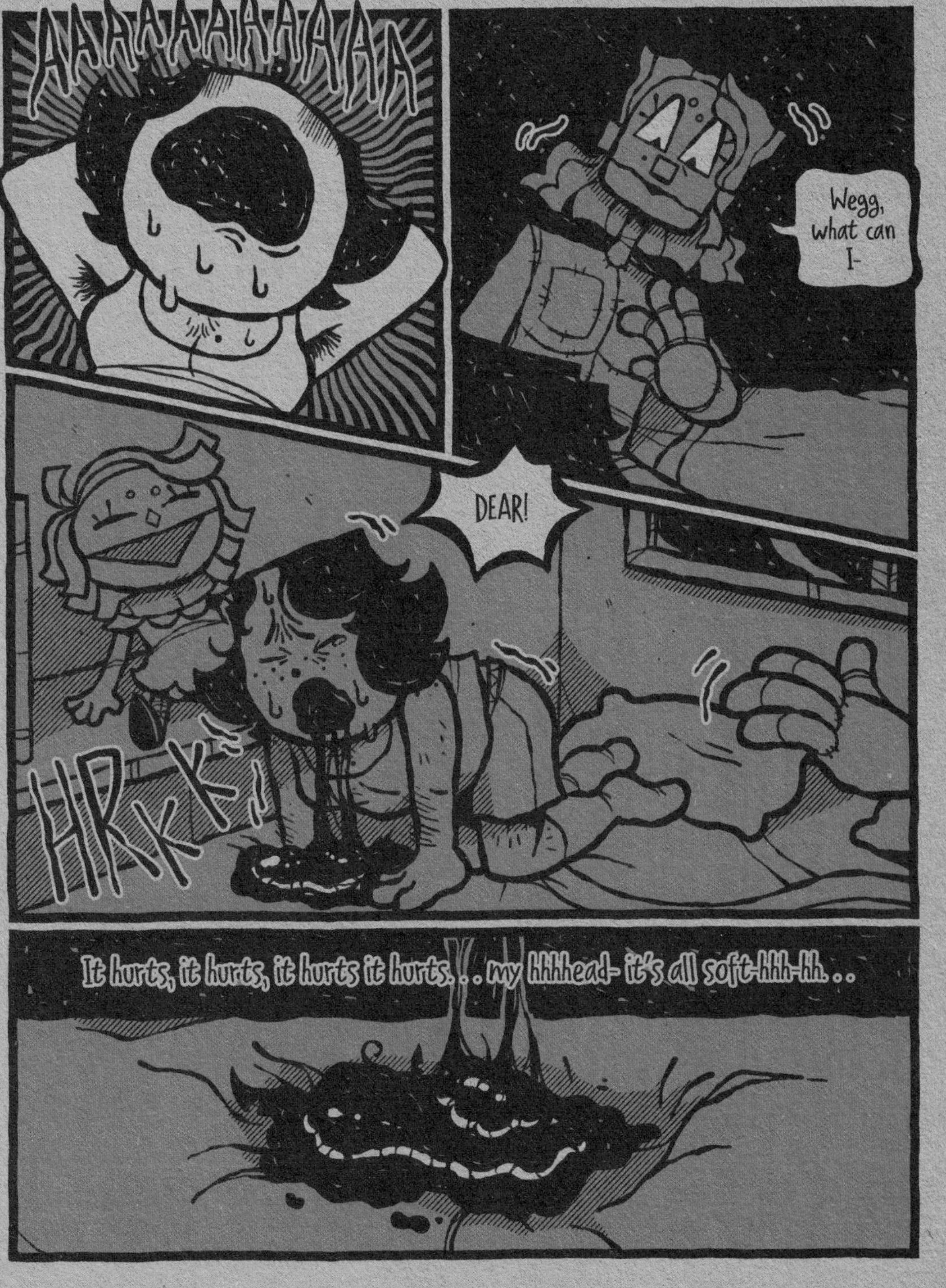
AAAAAAAAAAAA
Wegg, what can I-
DEAR!
HRKK
It hurts, it hurts, it hurts it hurts. . . my hhhhead- it's all soft-hhh-hh. . .

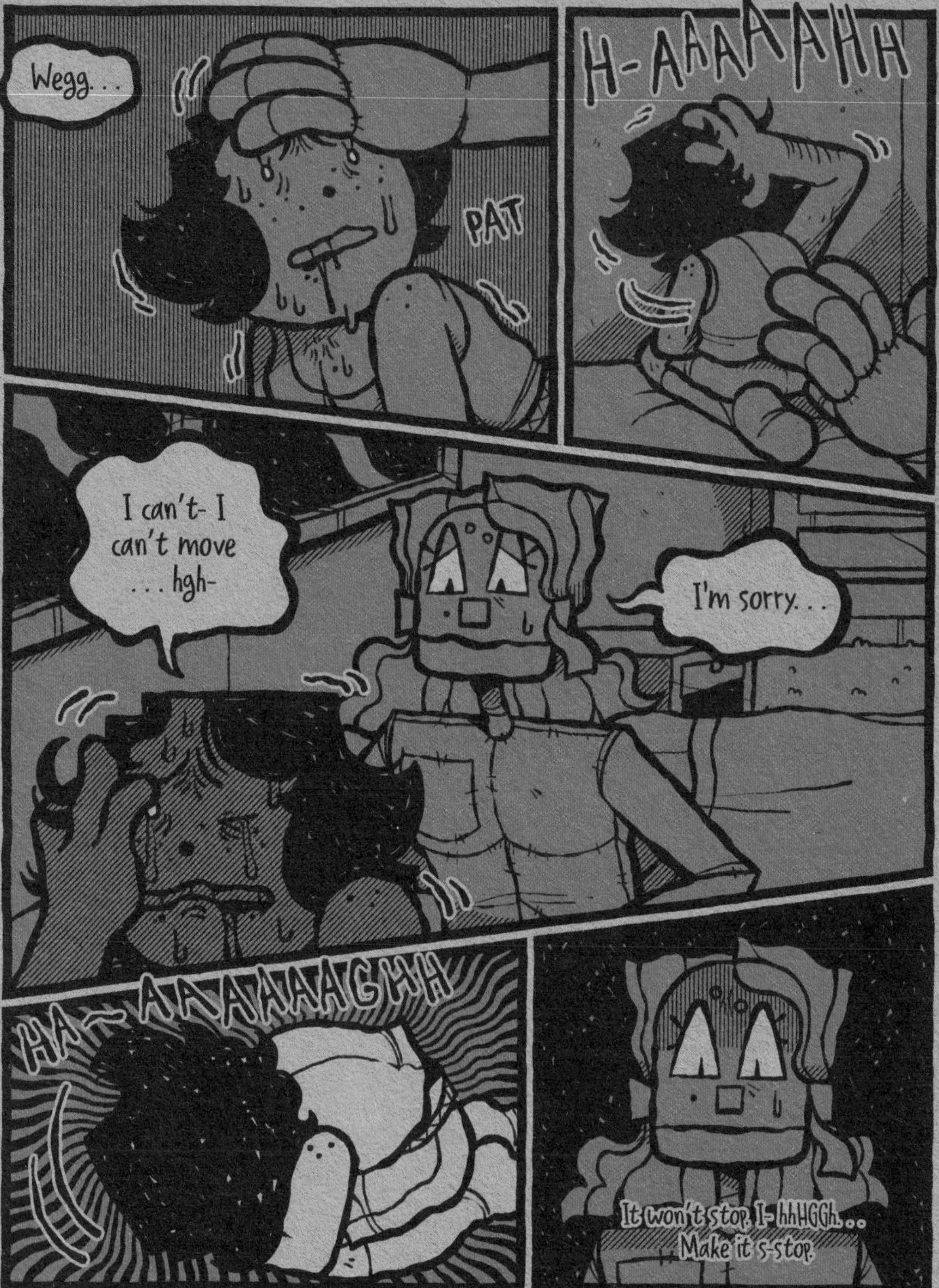
Wegg...
PAT
H-AAAAAHH
I can't- I can't move ...hgh-
I'm sorry...
HA-AAAAAAGHH
It won't stop. I- hhHGGh...
Make it s-stop.

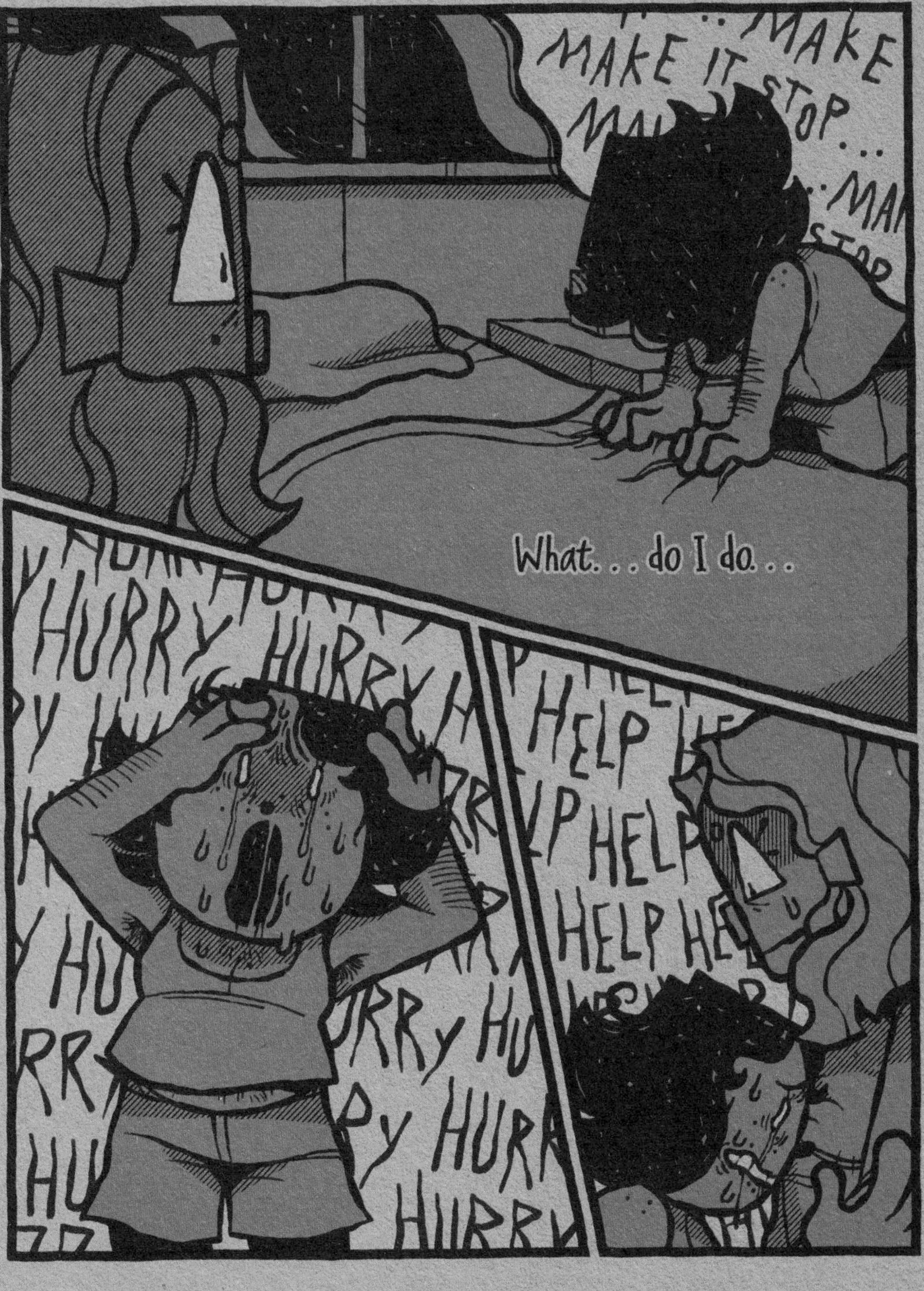
MAKE
MAKE IT STOP...
What... do I do...
HURRY HURRY
HURRY
HELP
HELP
HELP

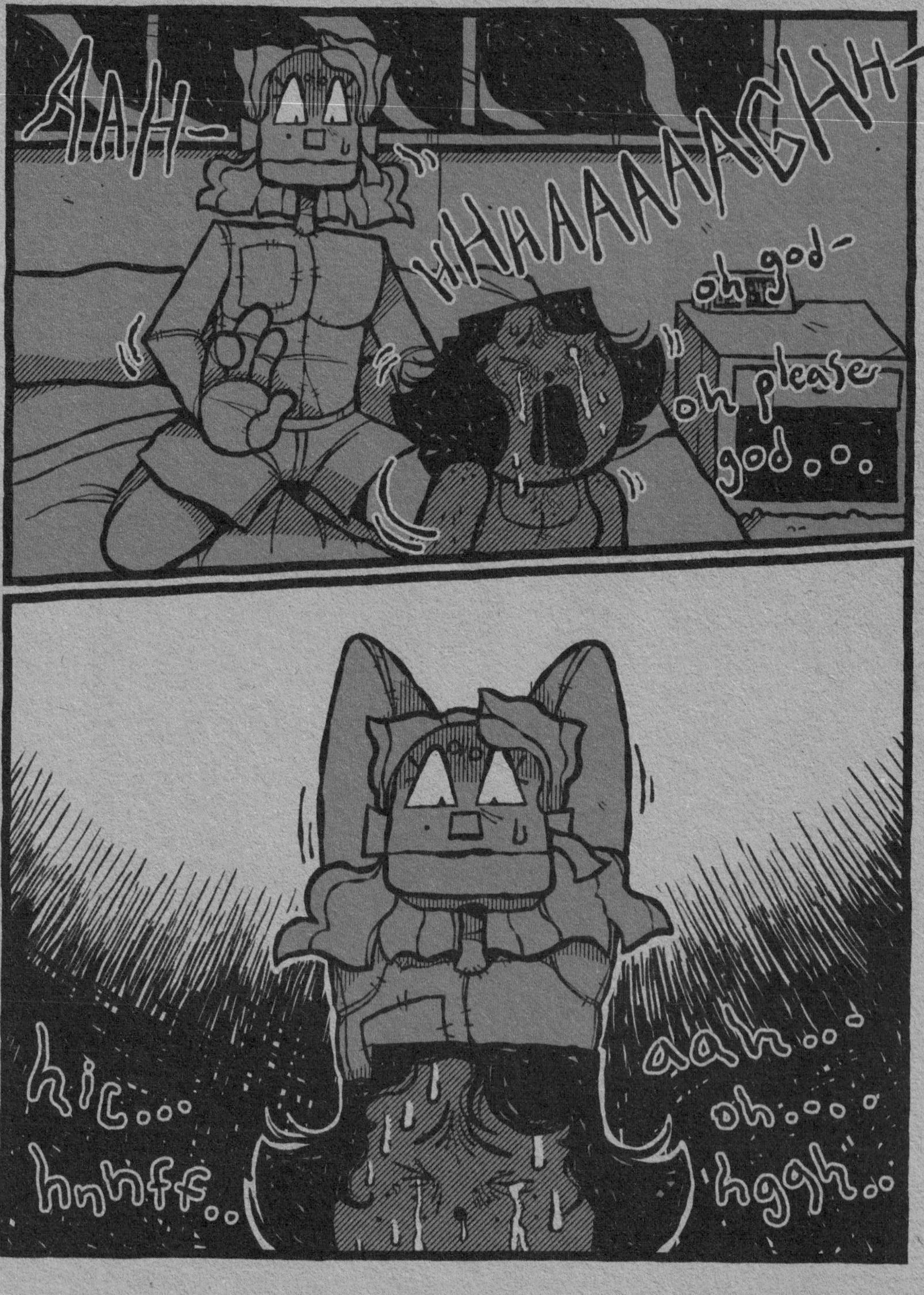
AAH-
HHHAAAAAAAGHH-
oh god-
oh please
god...
hic...
hnhff..
aah...
oh....
hggh..

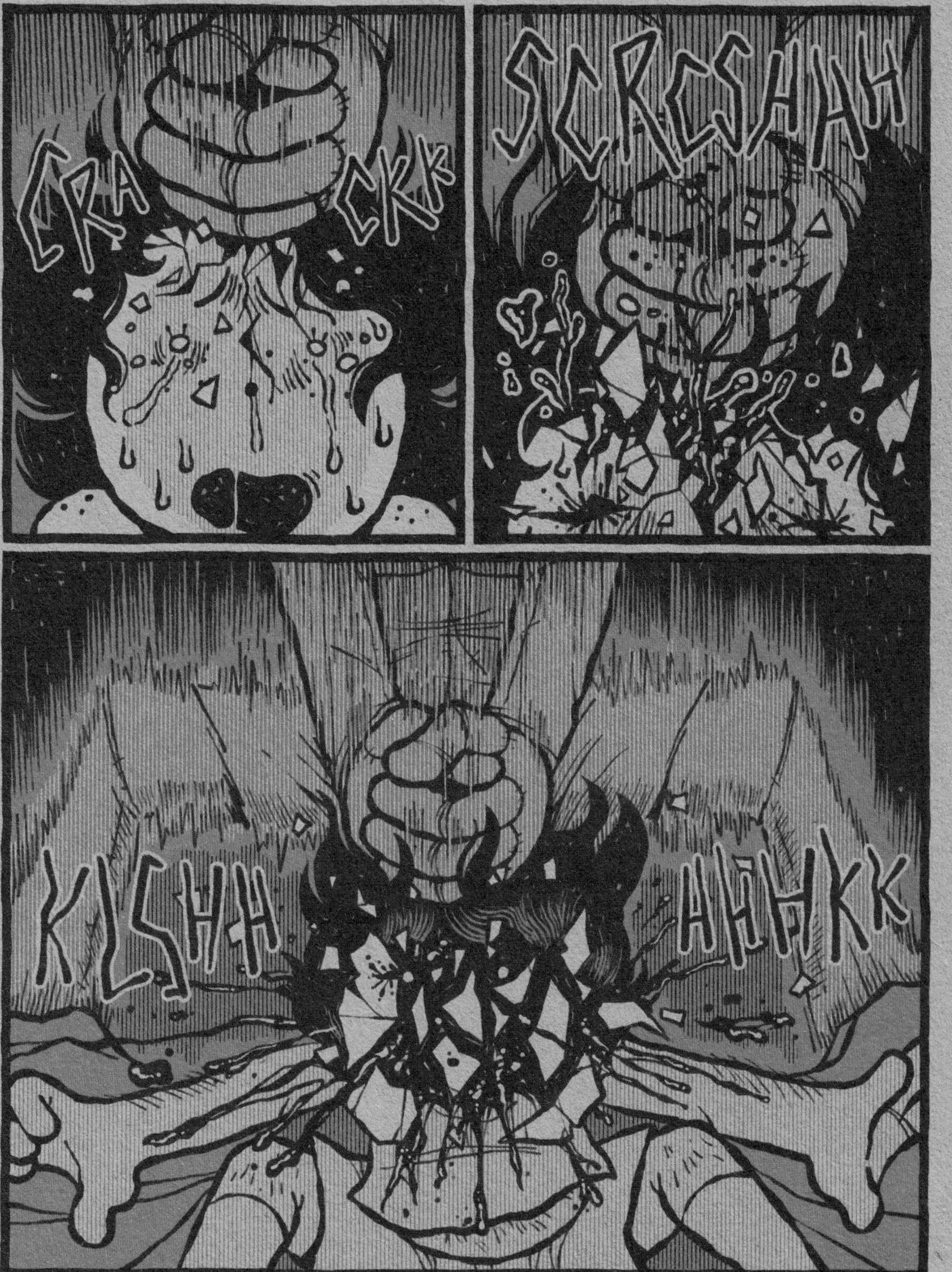
CRACKK
SCRCSHAH
KLSHH
AHHKK

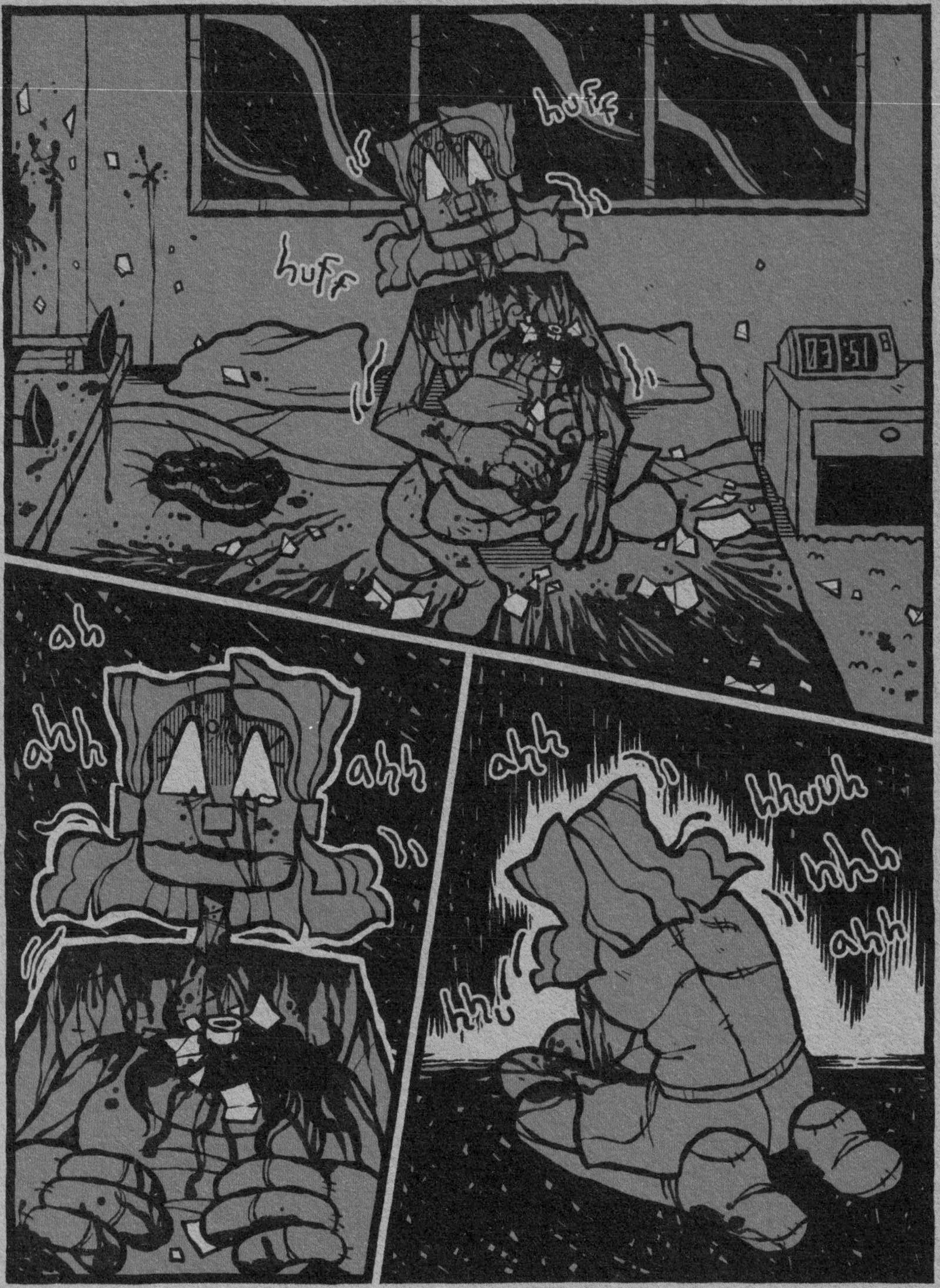
huff
huff
03:51
ah
ahh
ahh
ahh
hhuuh
hhh
ahh
hh

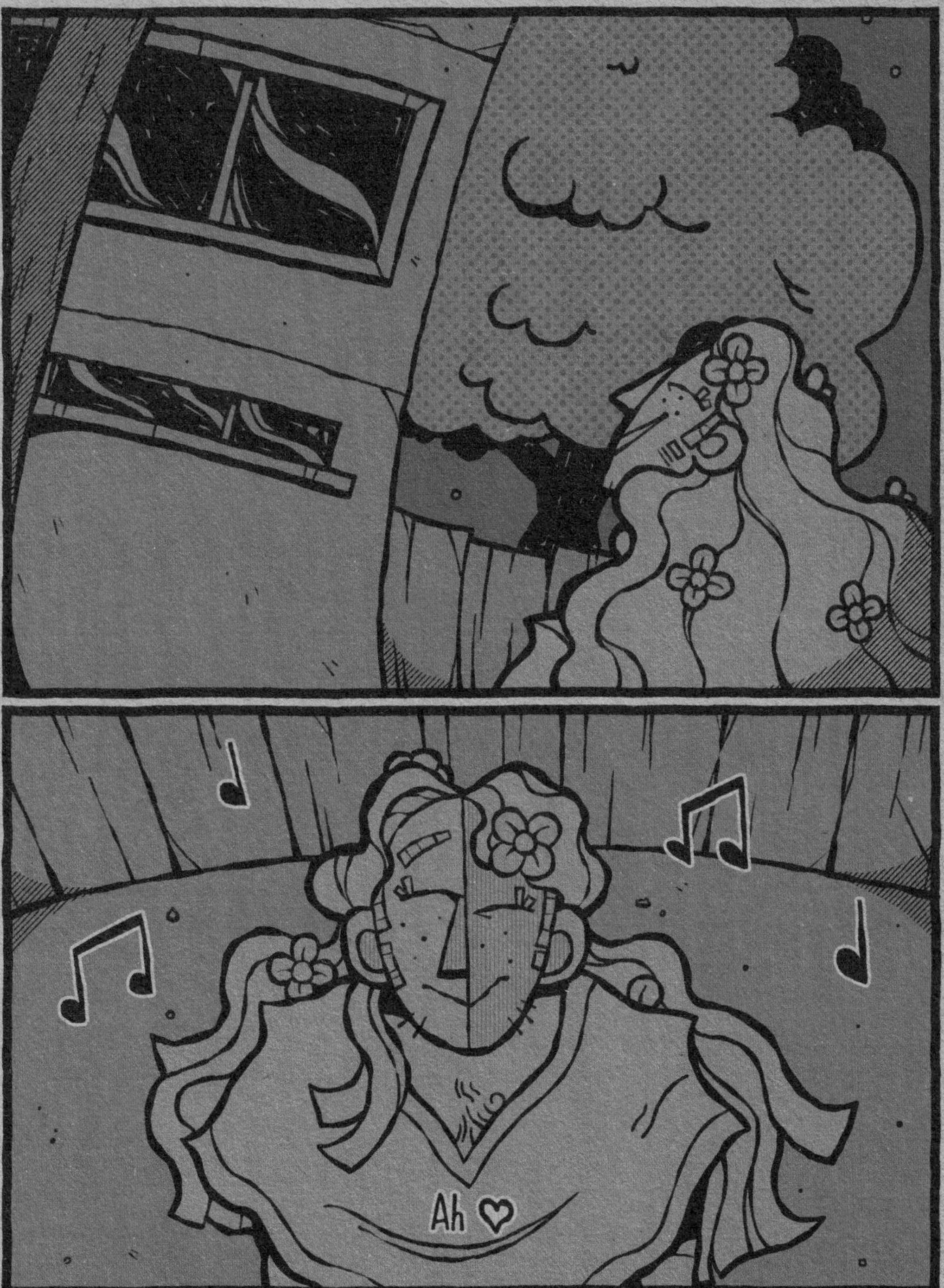
Ah ♡

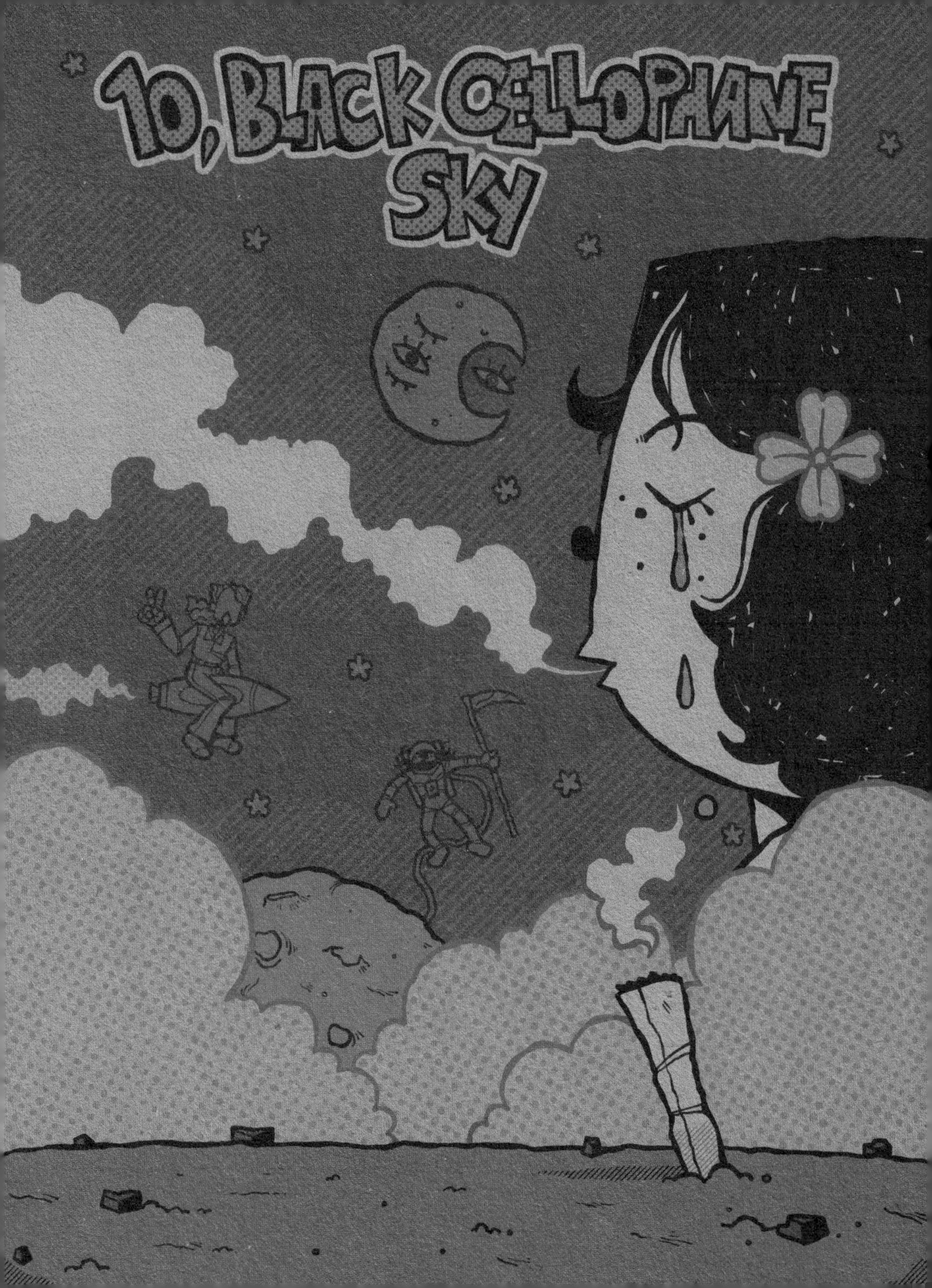
10, BLACK CELLOPHANE SKY

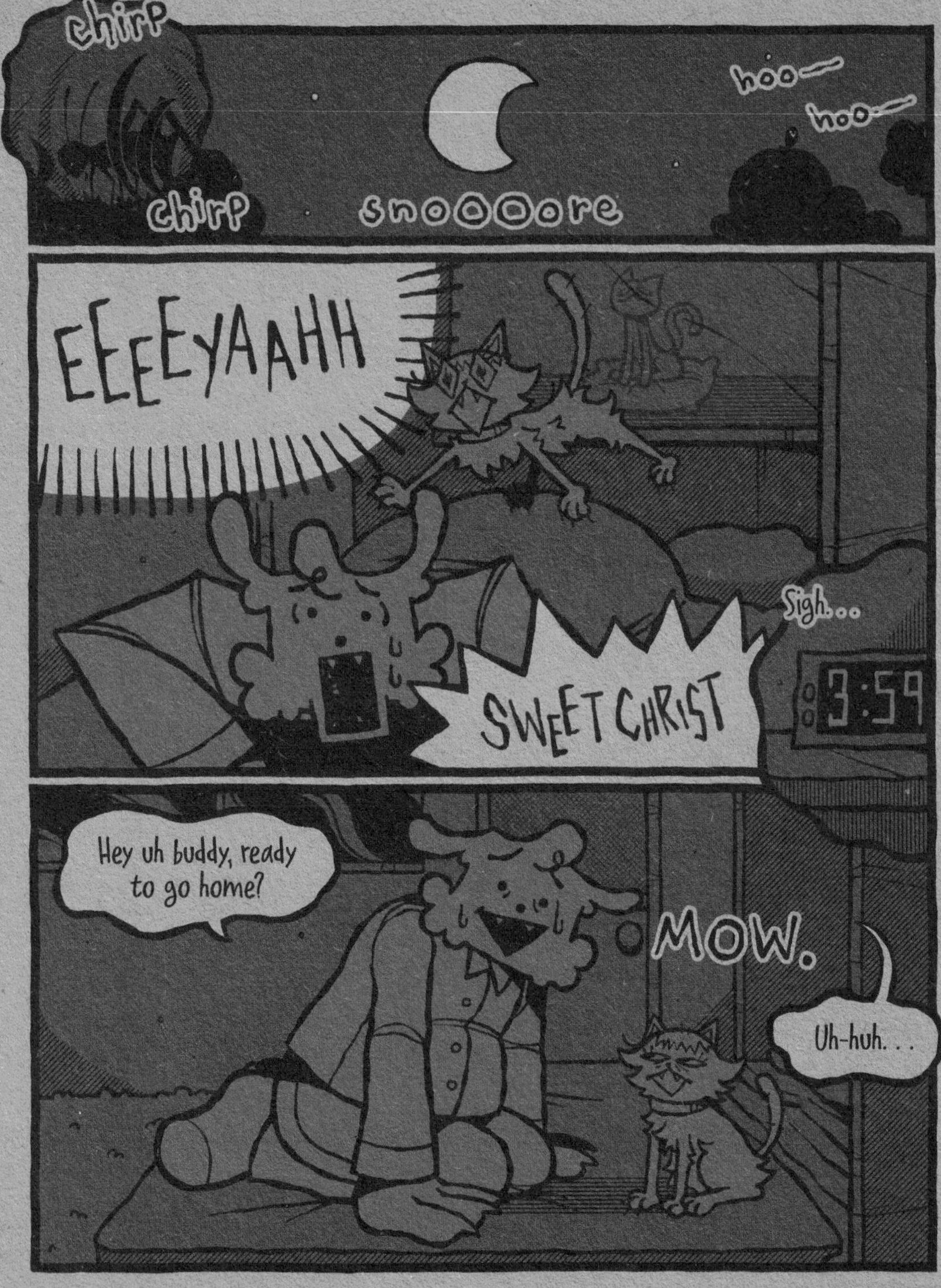
chirp
hoo—
hoo—
chirp
snoOOOore
EEEEYAAHH
Sigh...
SWEET CHRIST
3:59
Hey uh buddy, ready to go home?
MOW.
Uh-huh. . .

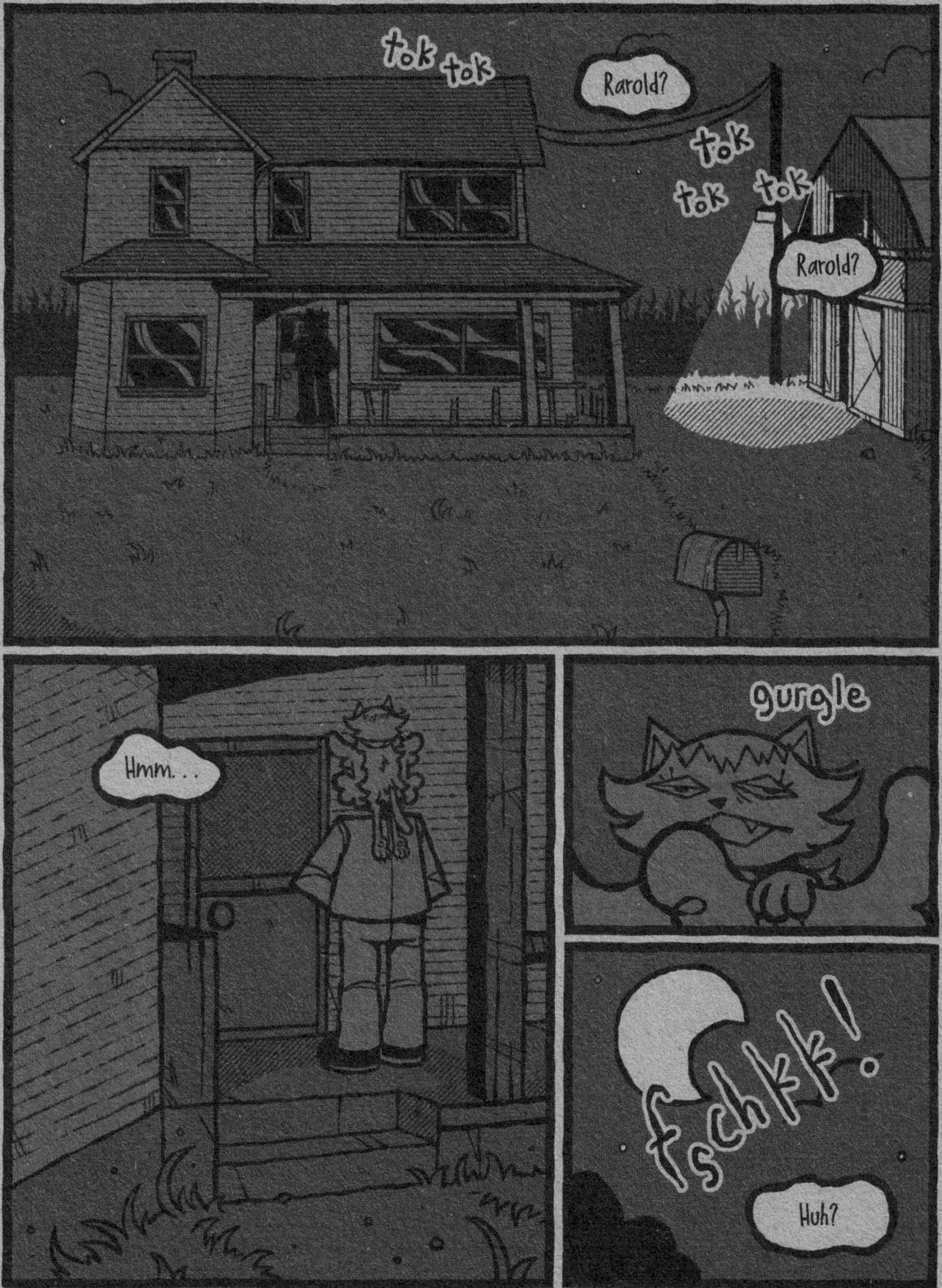
tok tok
Rarold?
tok
tok tok
Rarold?
Hmm...
gurgle
fschkk!
Huh?

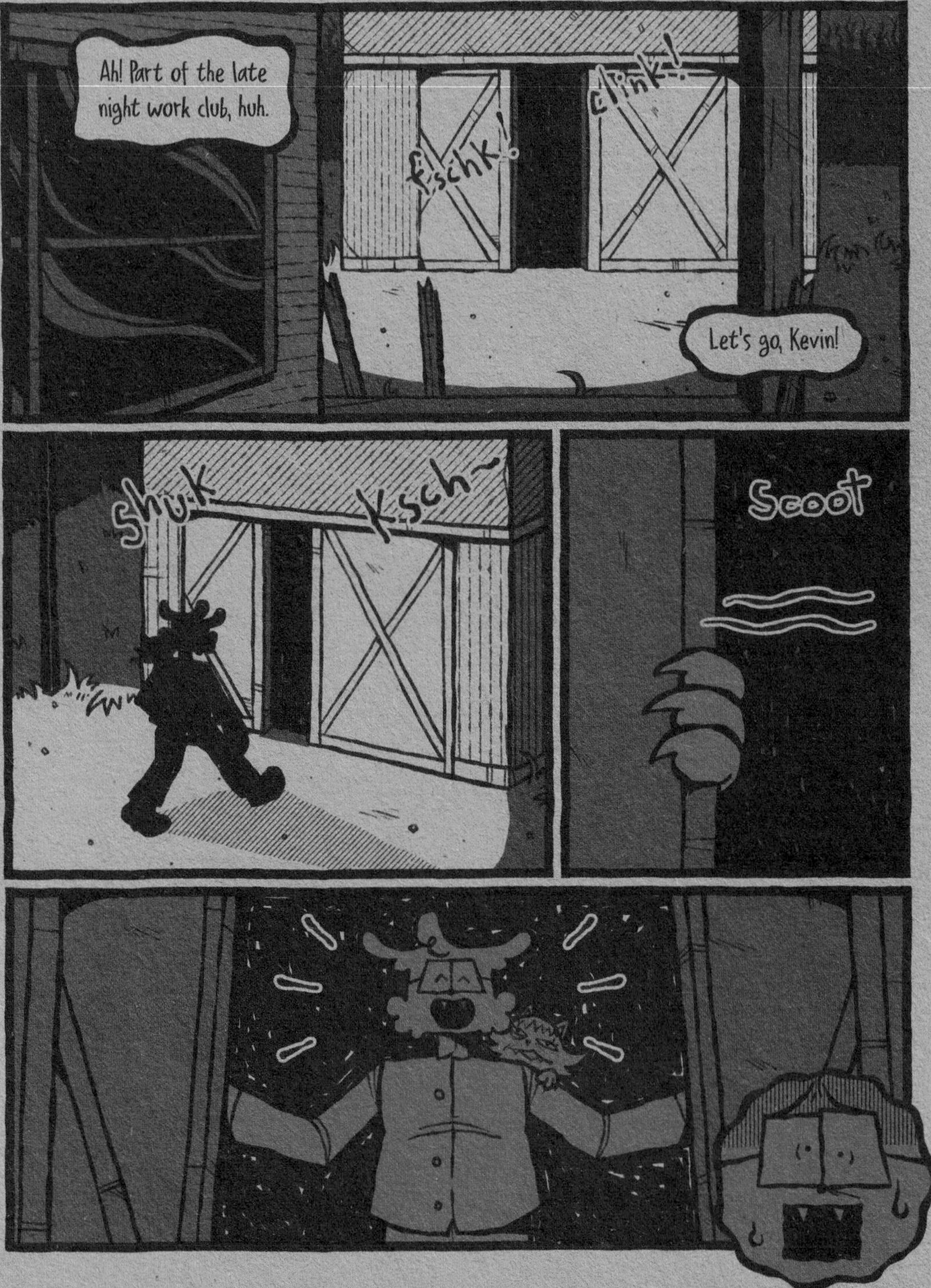
Ah! Part of the late night work club, huh.
clink!
fschk!
Let's go, Kevin!
Shuk
Ksch~
Scoot

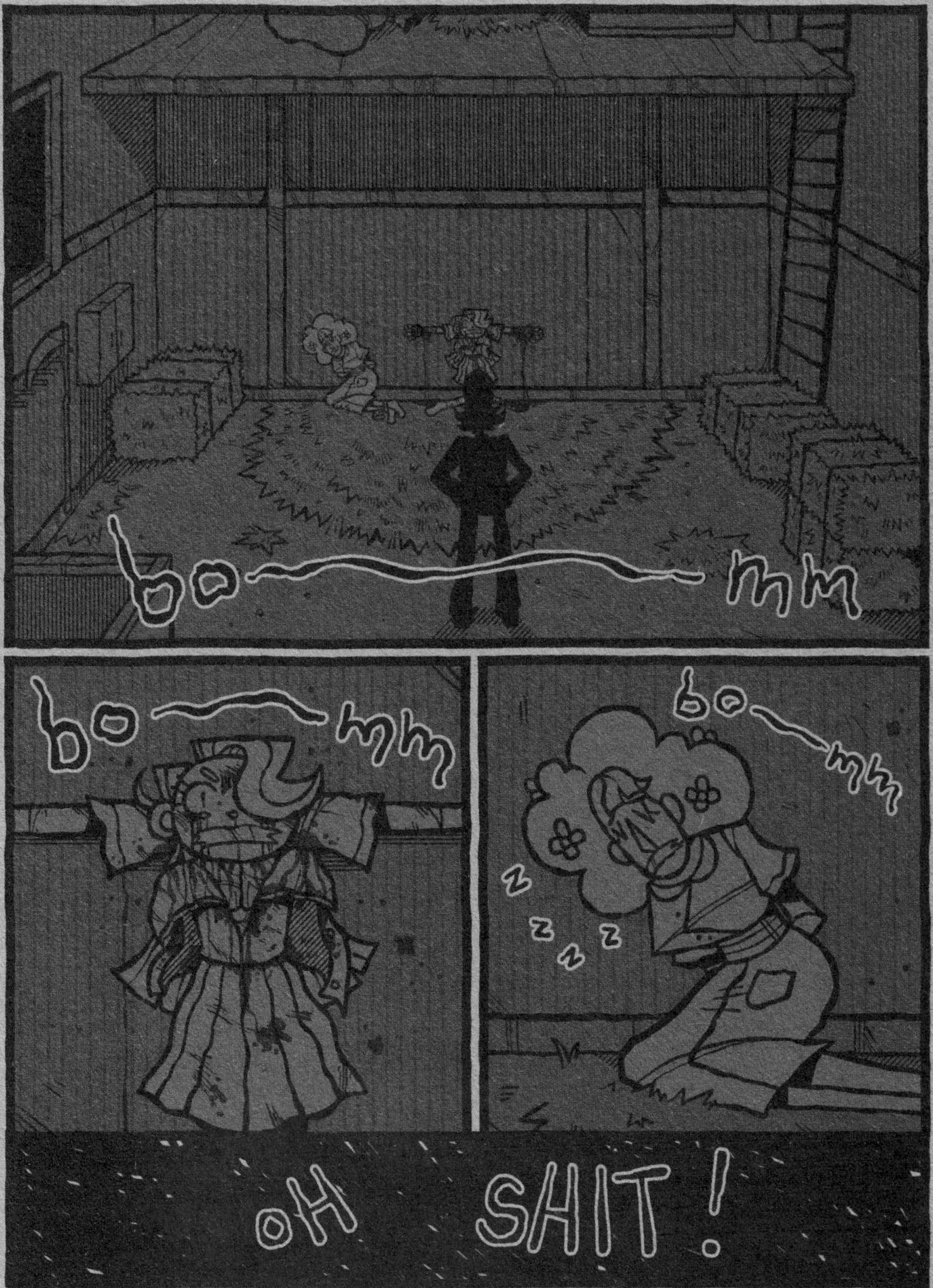
bo——mm
bo——mm
bo——mm
z z z z
oH SHIT!

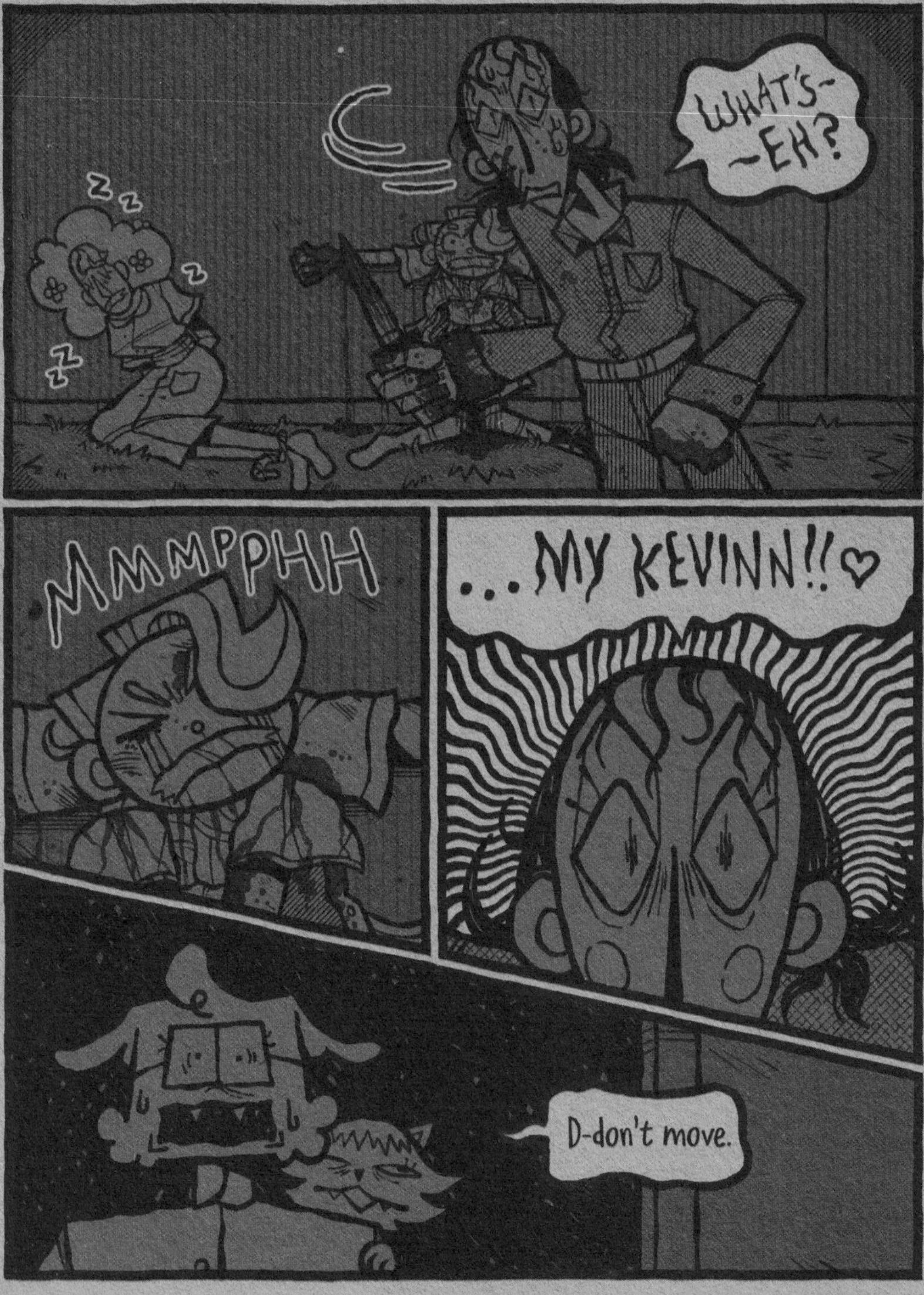
WHAT'S-
-EH?
MMMPPHH
...MY KEVINN!!♡
D-don't move.

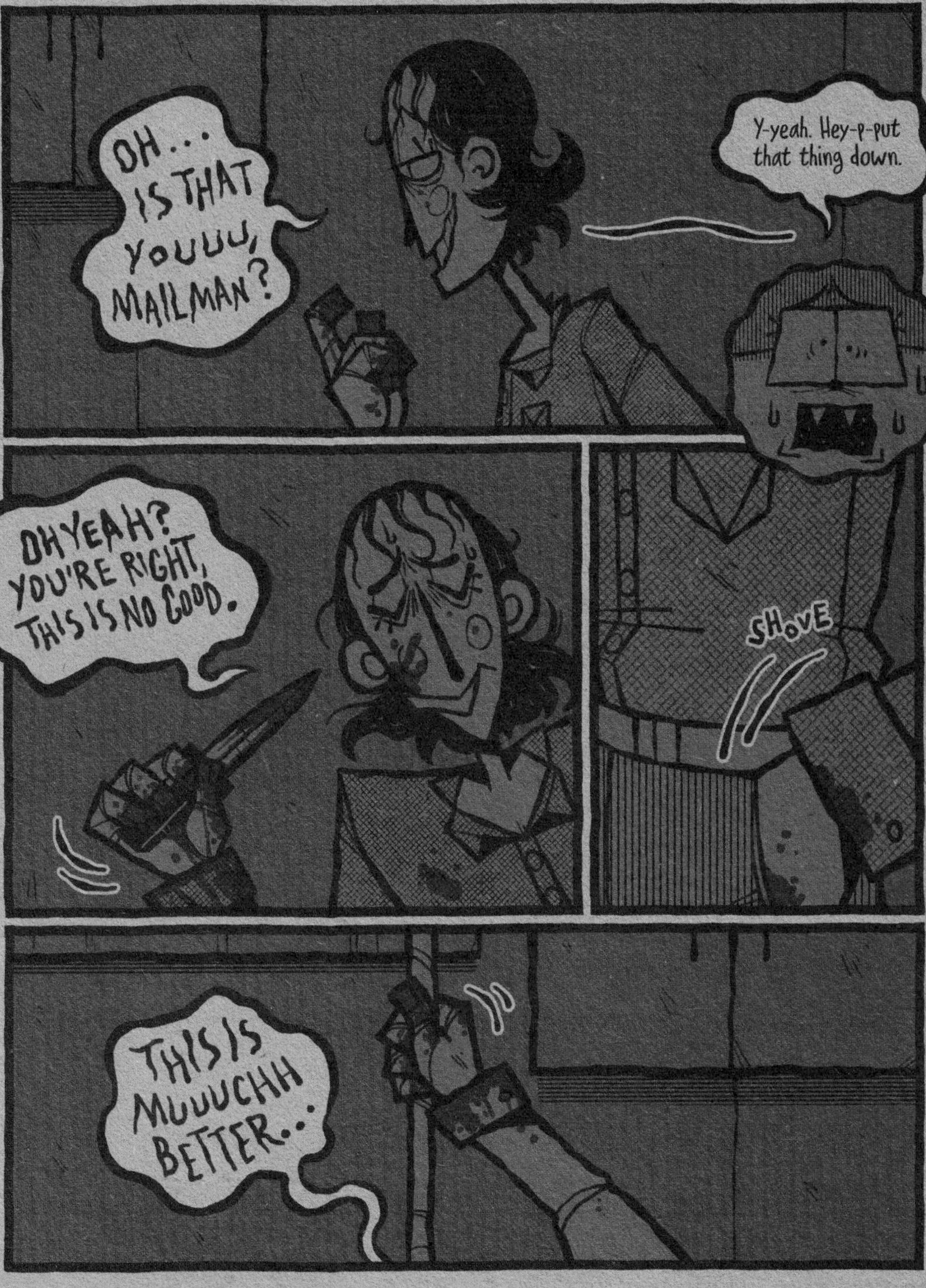
OH... IS THAT YOUUU, MAILMAN?
Y-yeah. Hey-p-put that thing down.
OH YEAH? YOU'RE RIGHT, THIS IS NO GOOD.
SHOVE
THIS IS MUUUCHH BETTER...

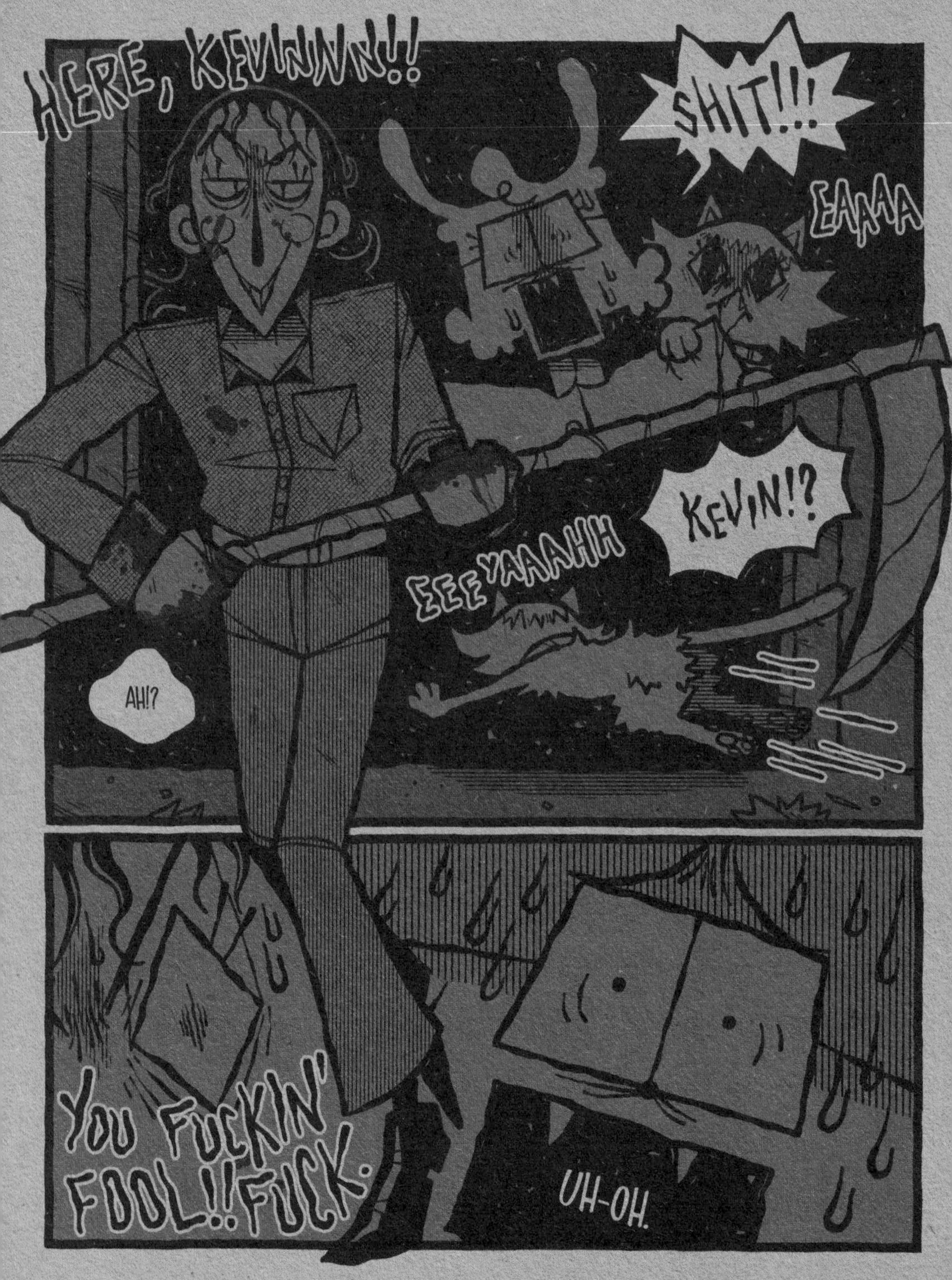
HERE, KEVINNN!!
SHIT!!!
EAAAA
KEVIN!?
EEEYAAAHH
AH!?
YOU FUCKIN' FOOL!! FUCK.
UH-OH.

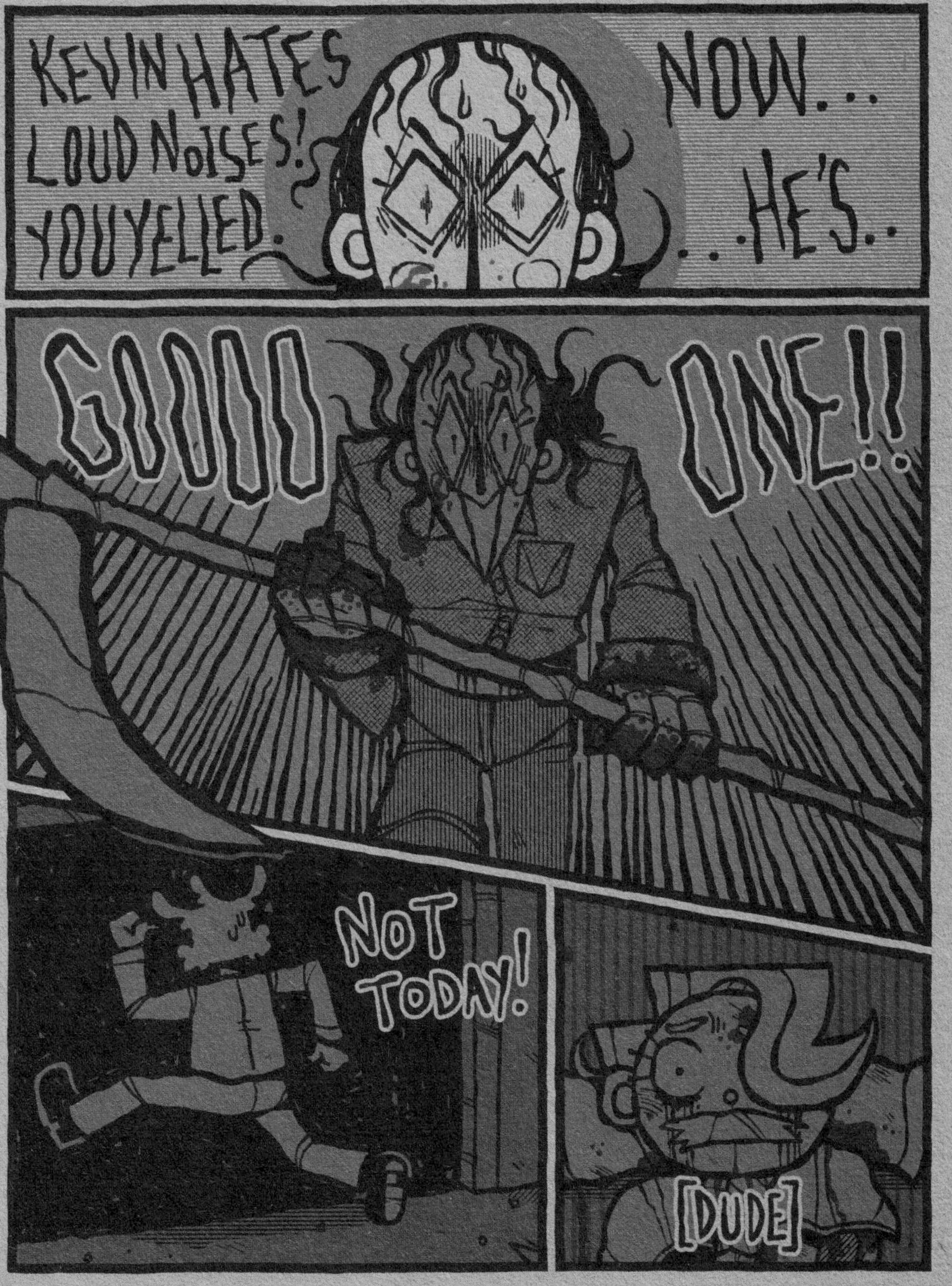
KEVIN HATES LOUD NOISES!
YOU YELLED.
NOW...
...HE'S...
GOOOO
ONE!!
NOT TODAY!
[DUDE]

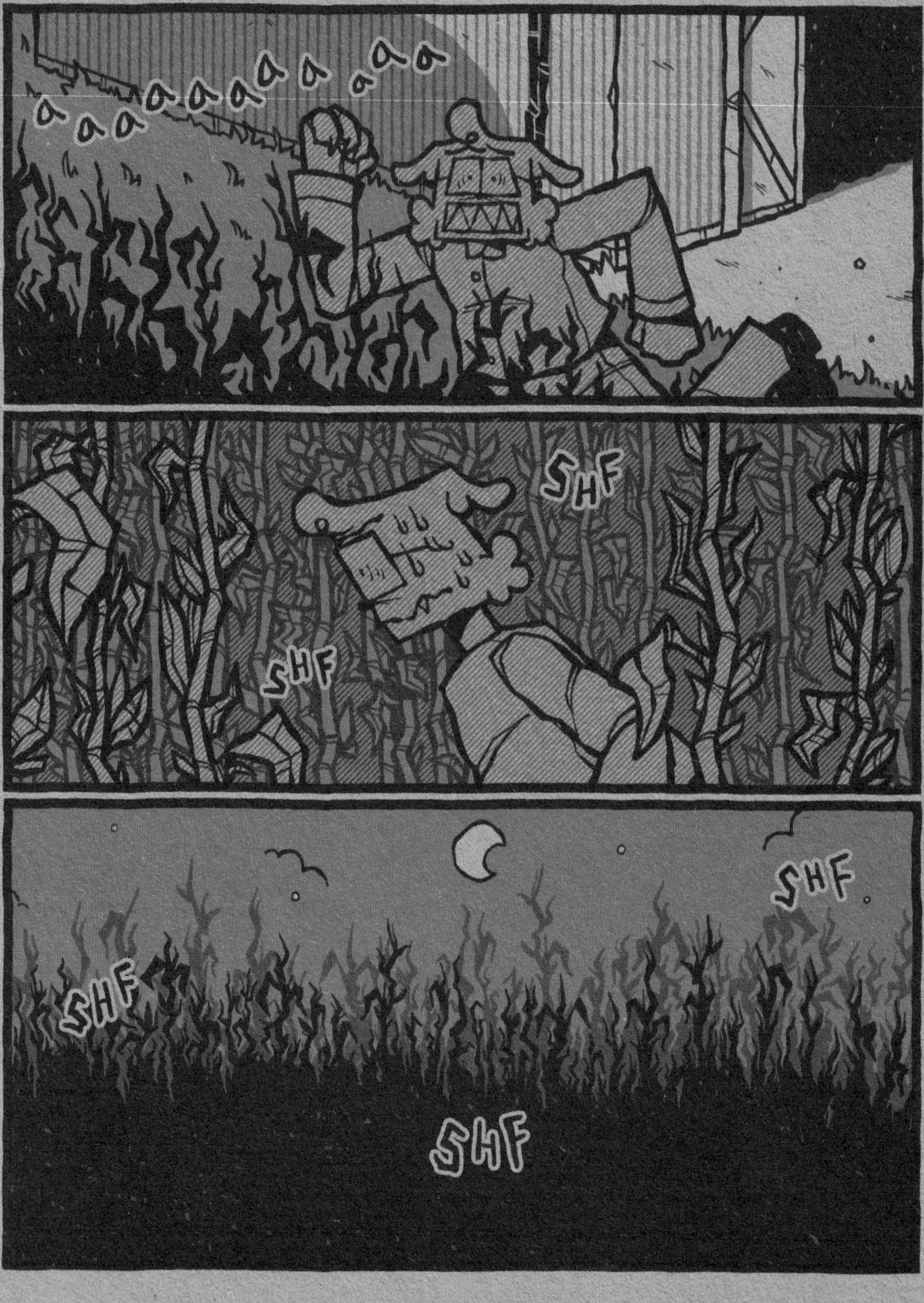
aaaaaaaaaaaaaa
SHF
SHF
SHF
SHF
SHF

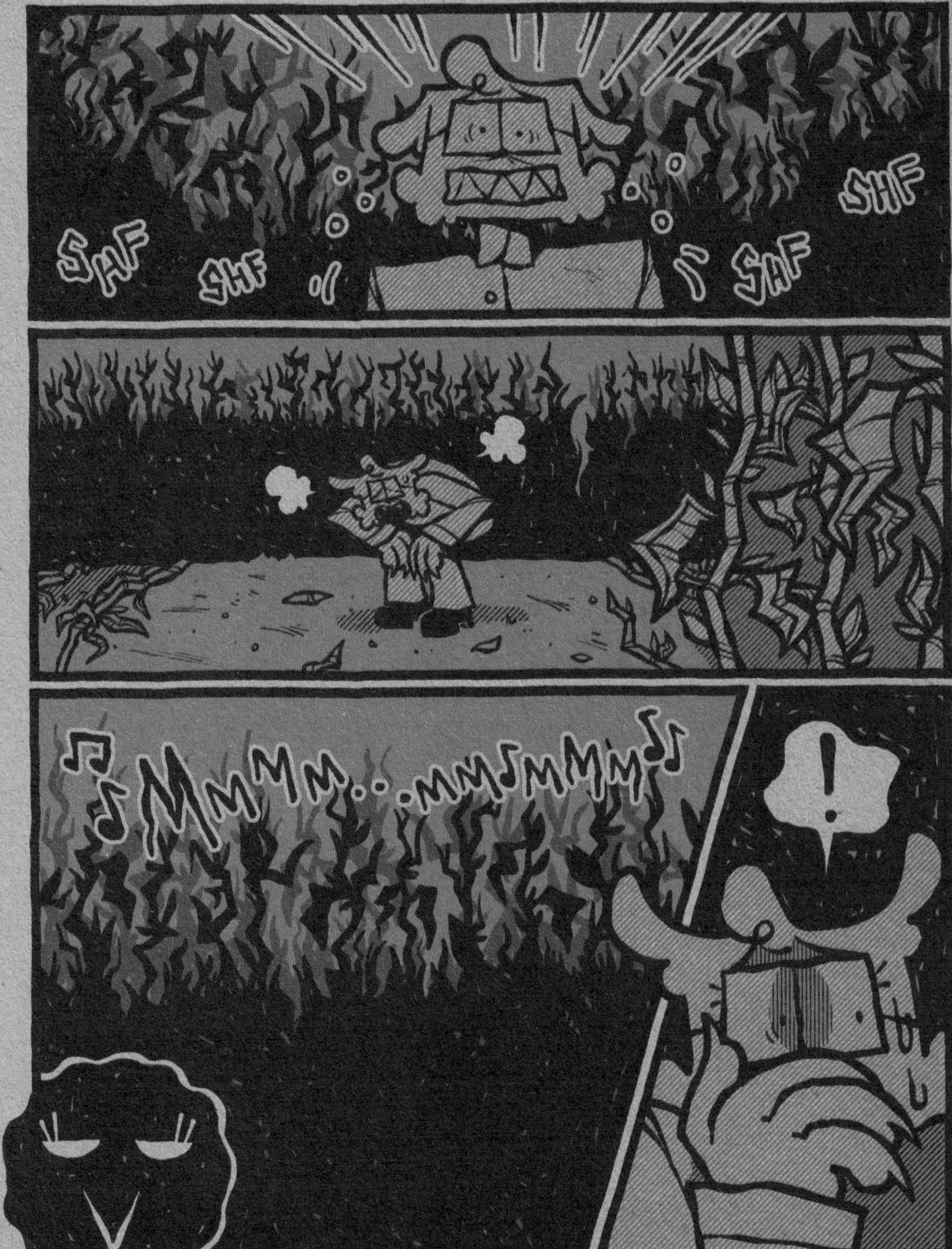
SHF
SHF
SHF
SHF
MMMM...MMMMMM
!

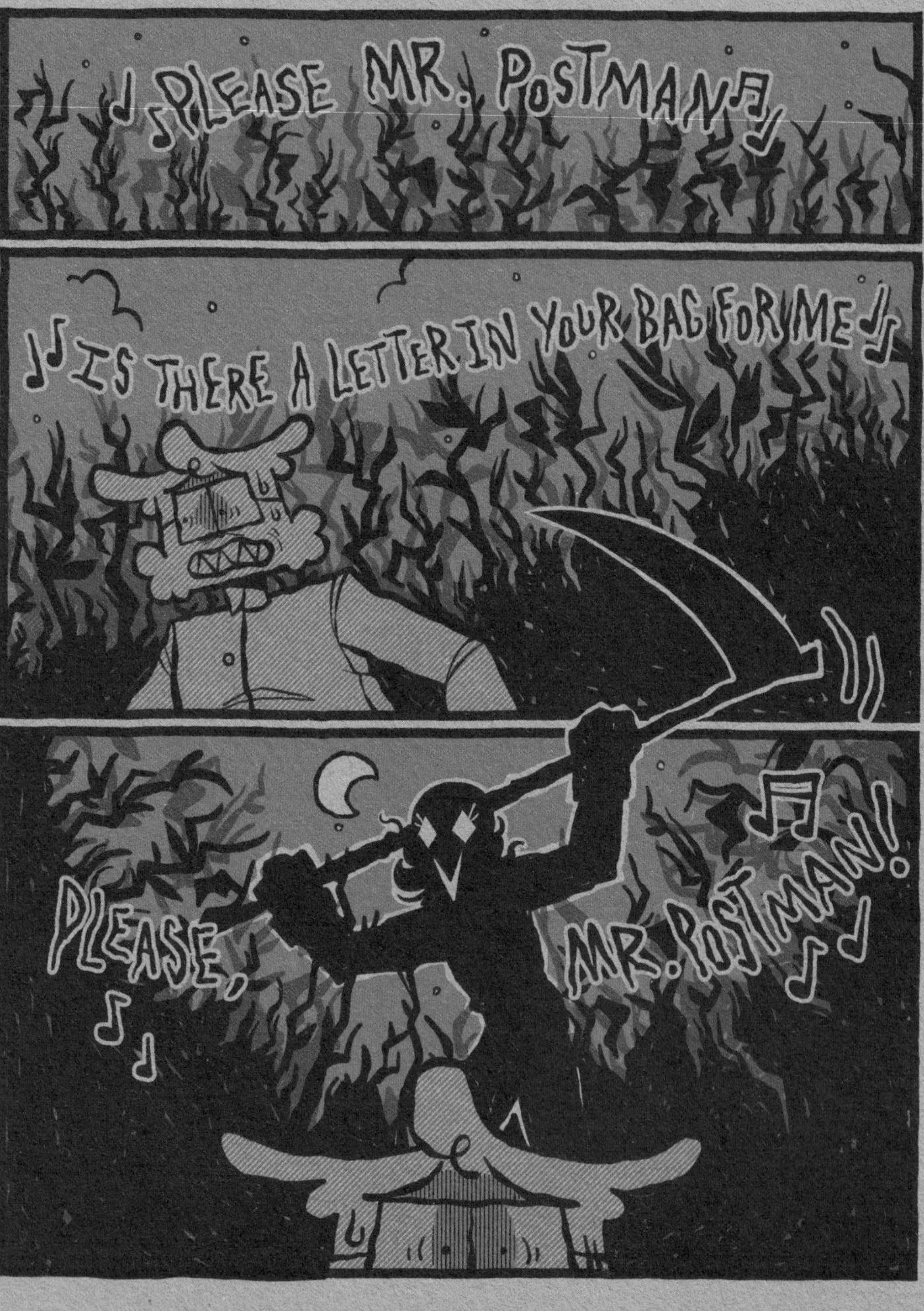
PLEASE MR. POSTMAN
IS THERE A LETTER IN YOUR BAG FOR ME
PLEASE,
MR. POSTMAN!

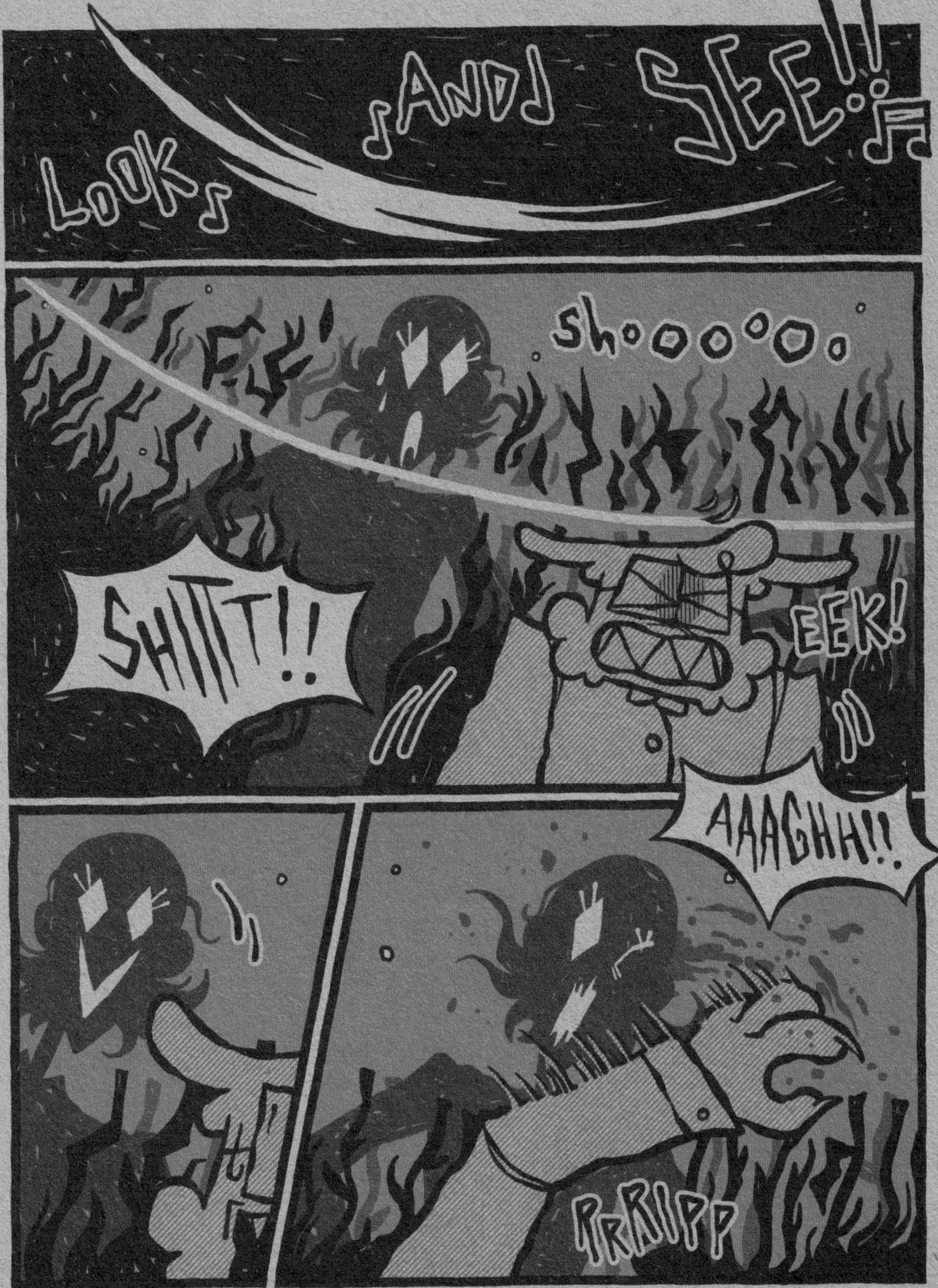
LOOK AND SEE!!
Shooooo.
SHIIIT!!
EEK!
AAAGHH!!
RRRIPP

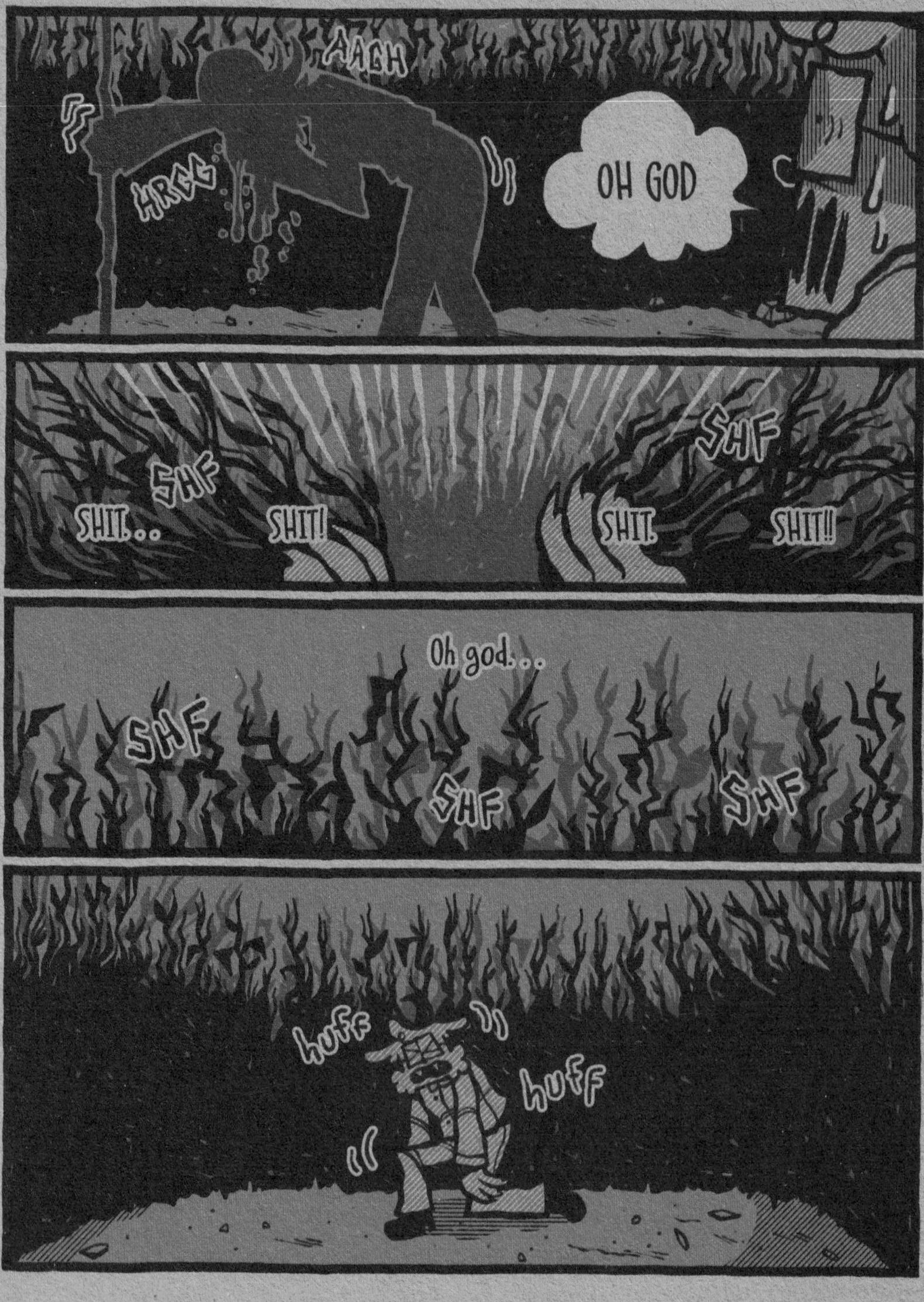
AAGH
HREG
OH GOD
SHF
SHIT...
SHIT!
SHF
SHIT.
SHIT!!
Oh god...
SHF
SHF
SHF
huff
huff

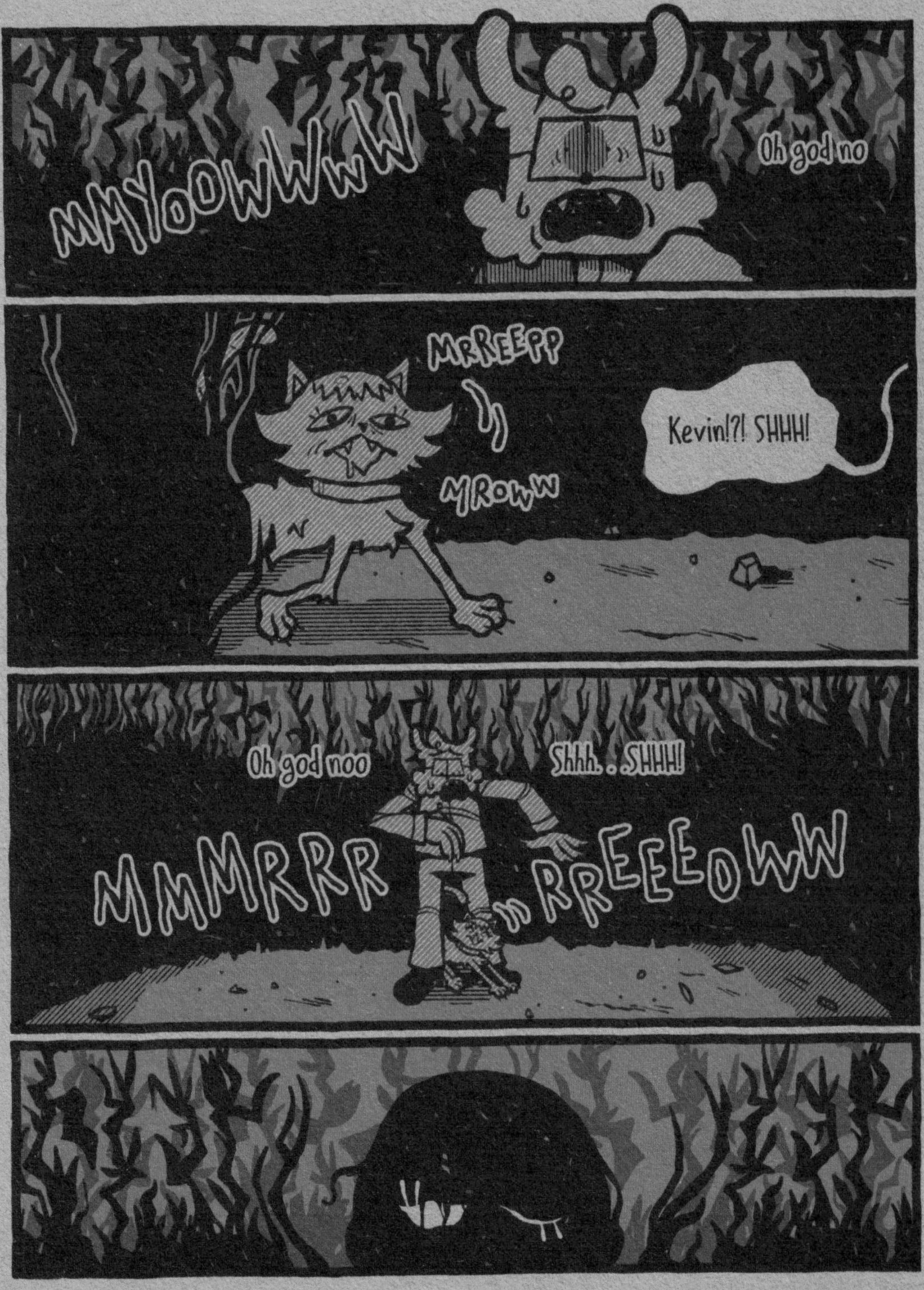
MMYOOWWWWW
Oh god no
MRREEPP
MROWW
Kevin!?! SHHH!
Oh god noo
Shhh. . SHHH!
MMMRRR
RREEEOWW

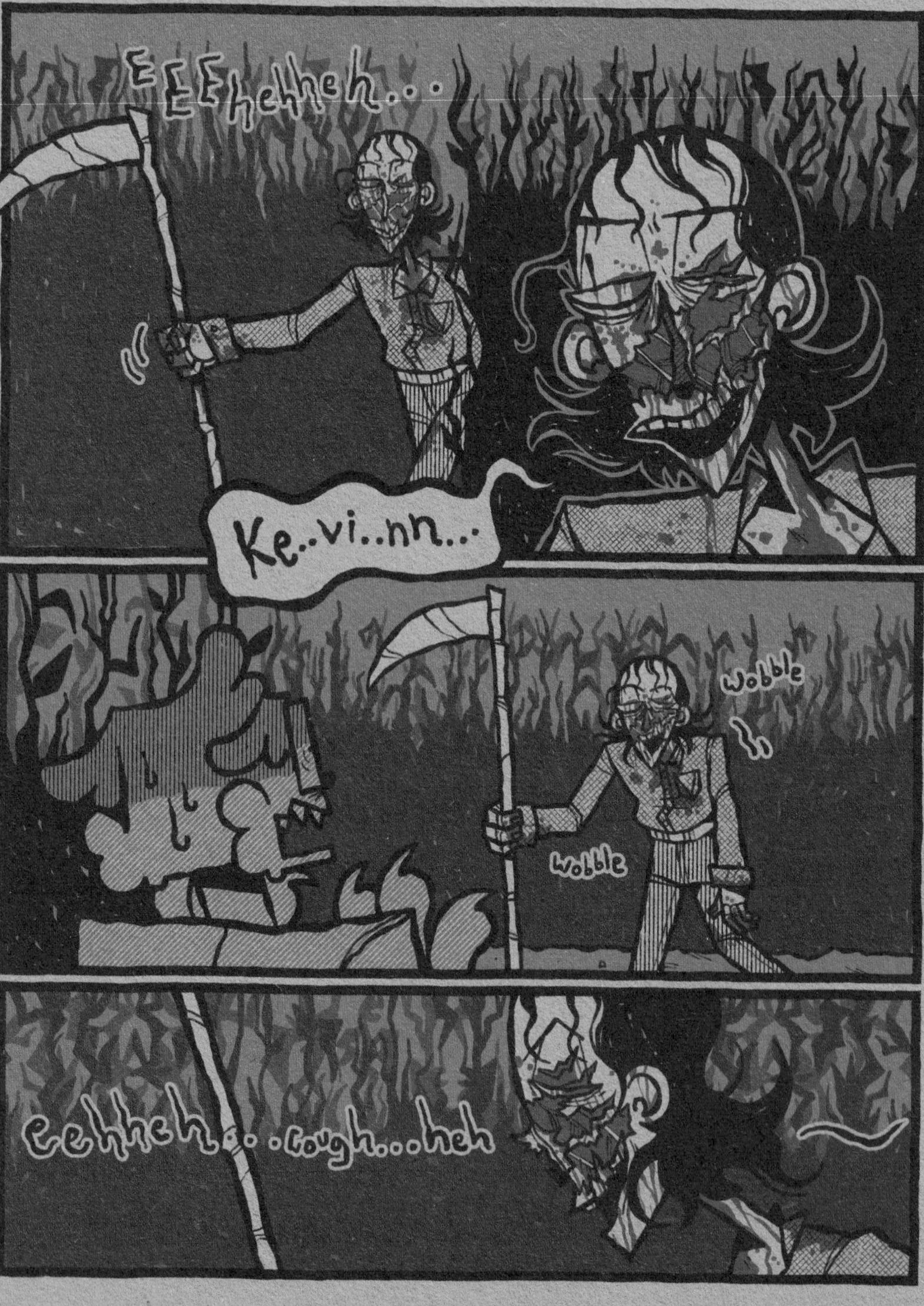
EEEhehheh...
Ke..vi..nn...
wobble
wobble
eehheh...cough...heh

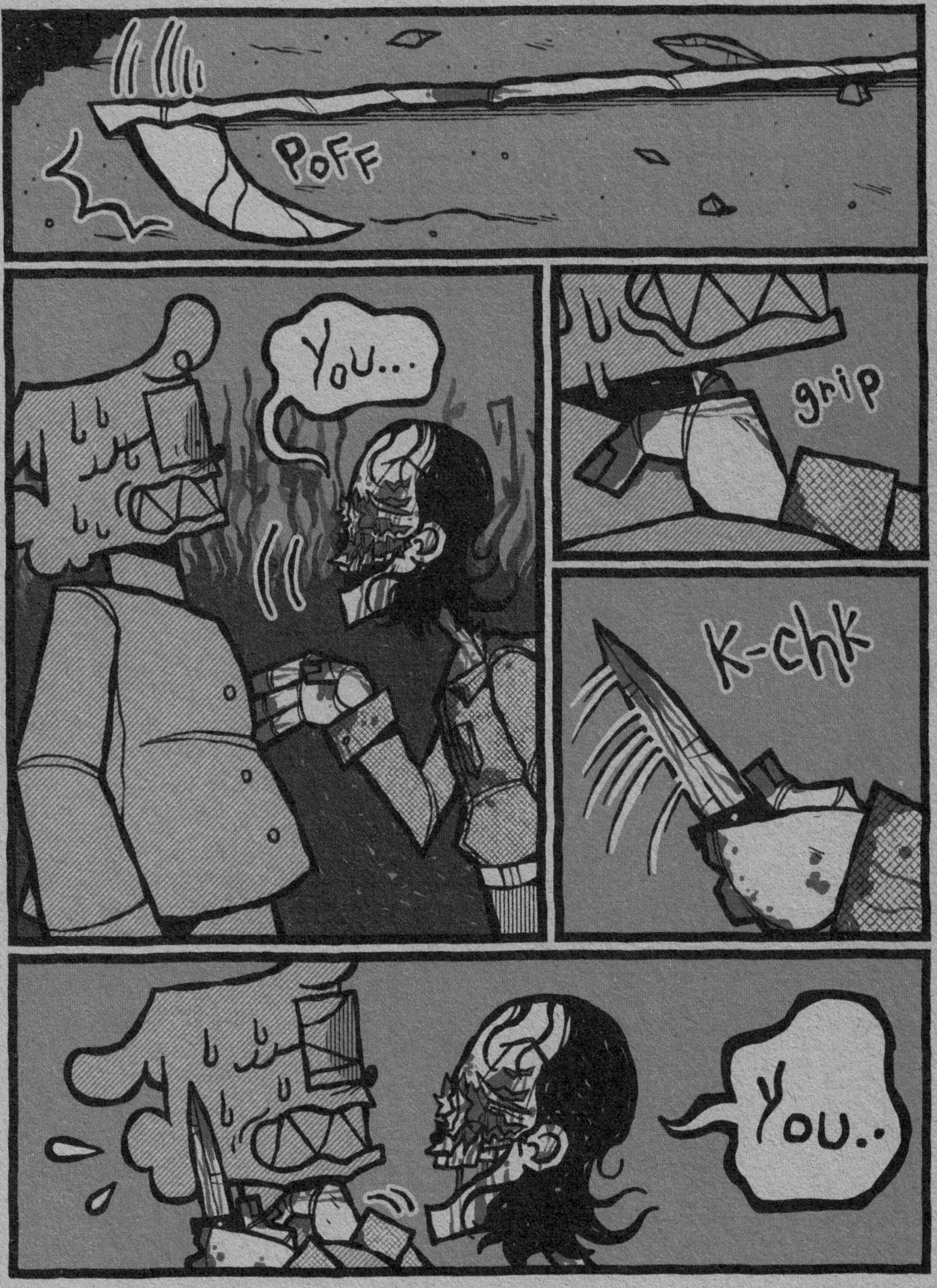
POFF
You...
grip
K-CHK
You..

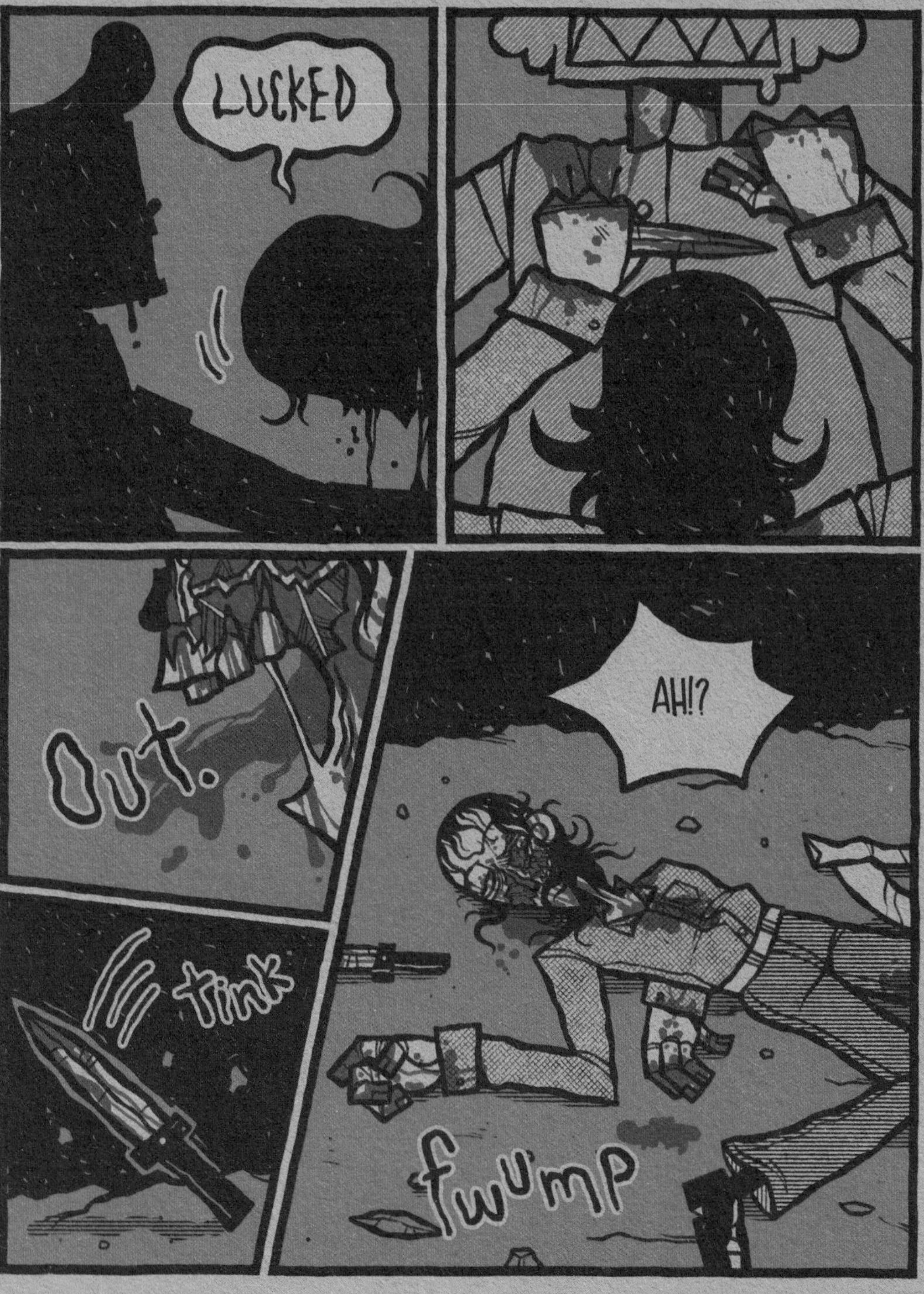
LUCKED
Out.
tink
AH!?
fwump

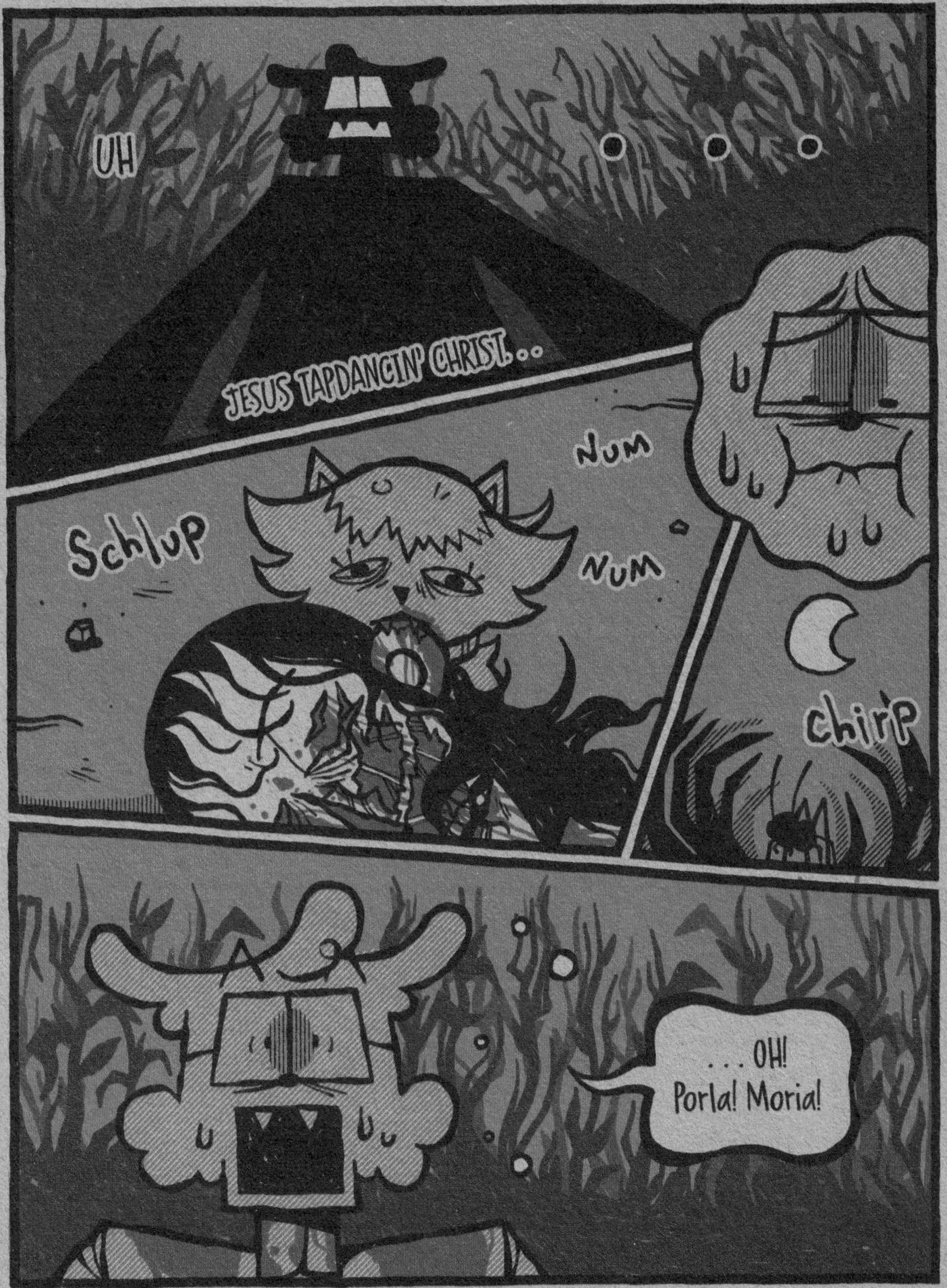
UH
. . .
JESUS TAPDANCIN' CHRIST. . .
Schlup
NUM
NUM
chirp
. . . OH!
Porla! Moria!

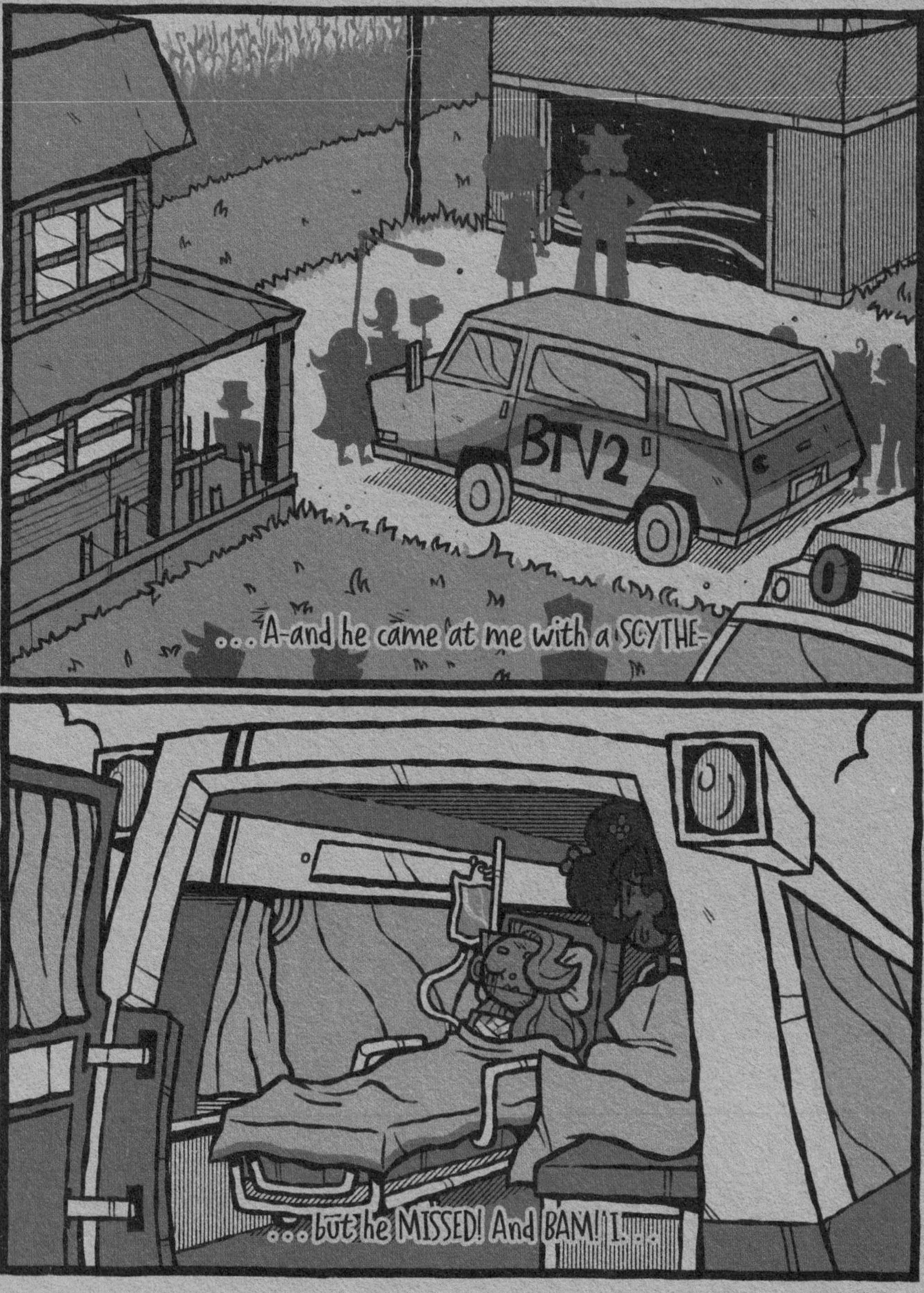

. . . A-and he came at me with a SCYTHE-
BTV2
. . . but he MISSED! And BAM! I. . .

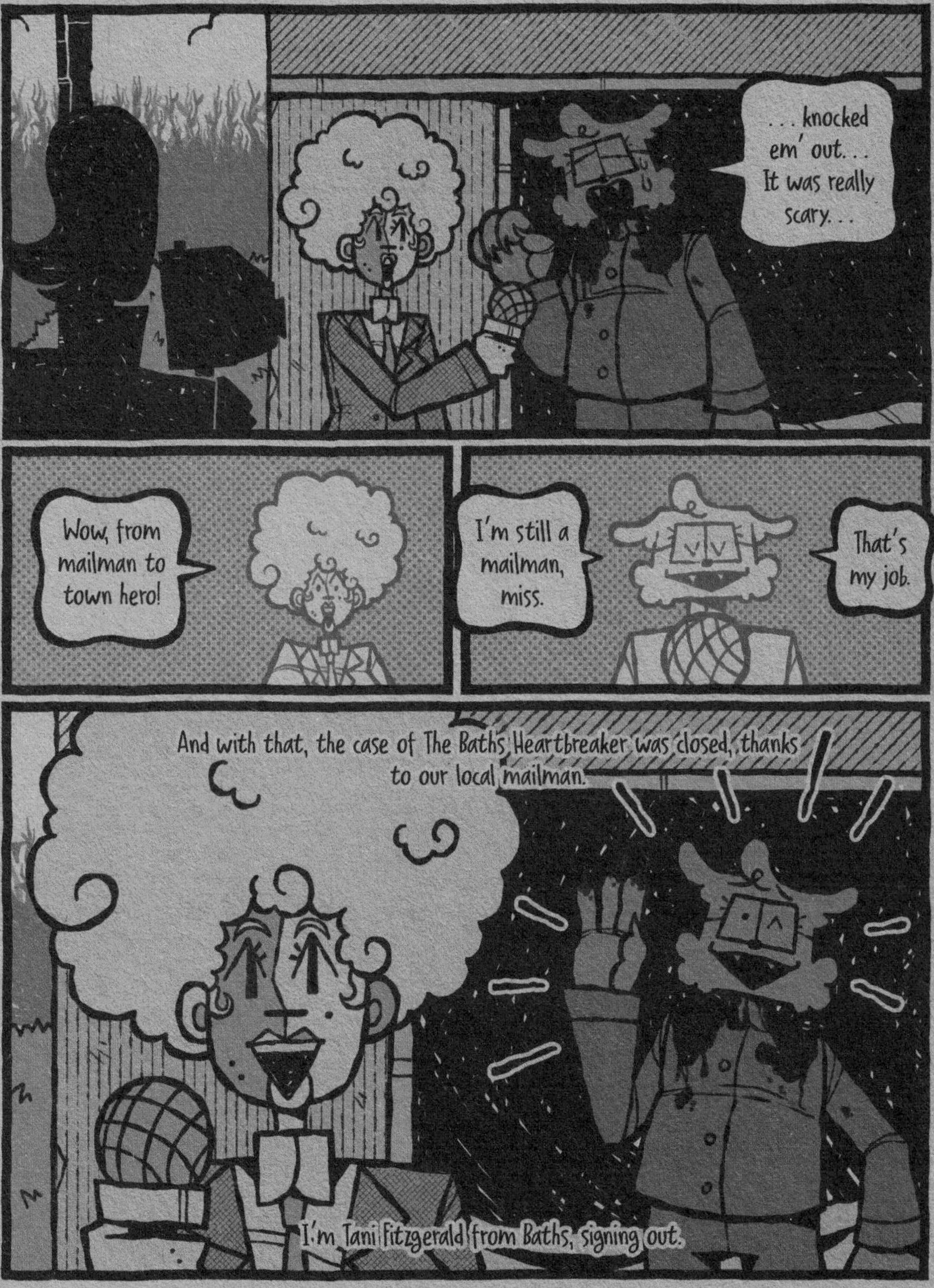

. . . knocked em' out. . . It was really scary. . .
Wow, from mailman to town hero!
I'm still a mailman, miss.
That's my job.
And with that, the case of The Baths Heartbreaker was closed, thanks to our local mailman.
I'm Tani Fitzgerald from Baths, signing out.

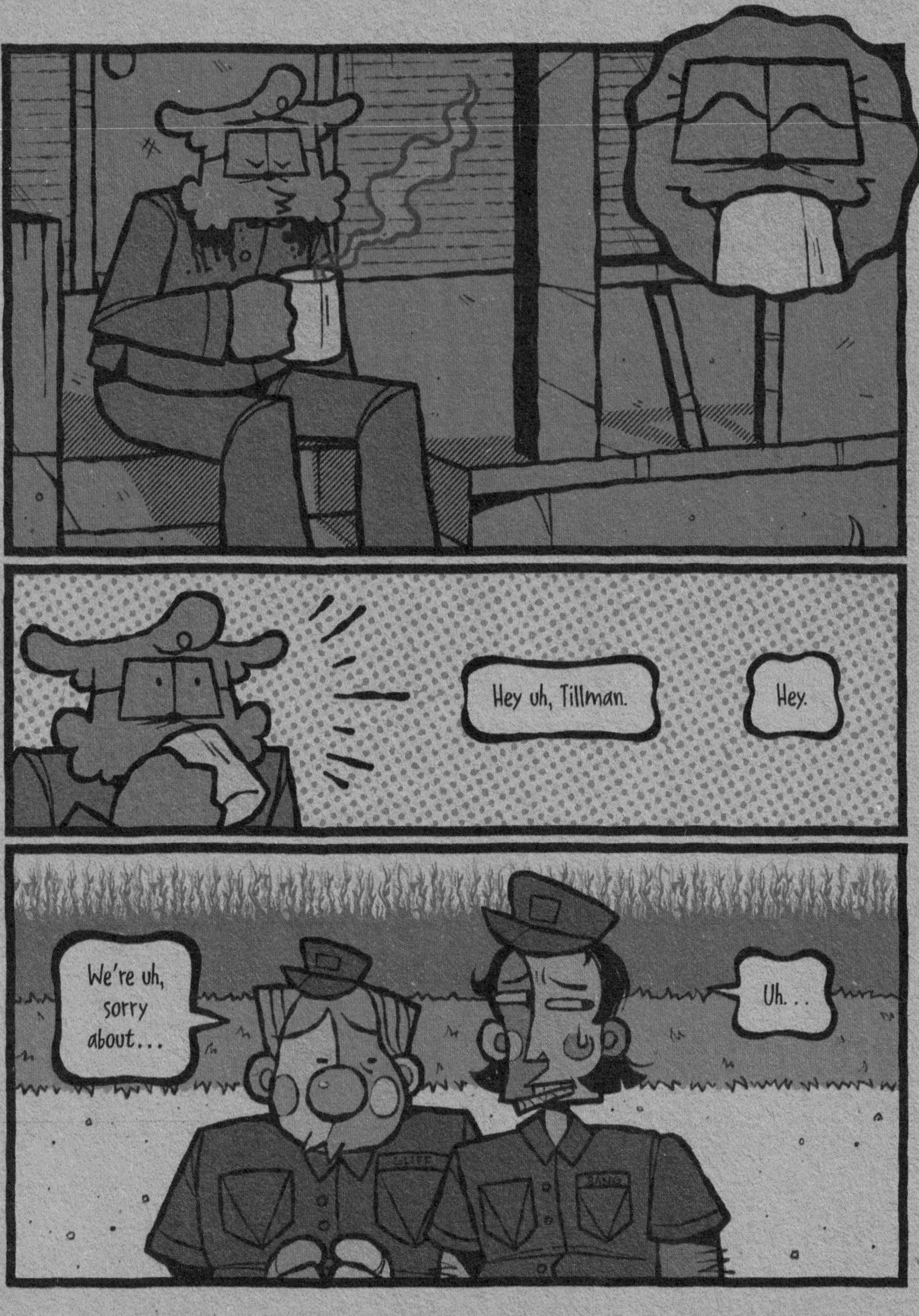
Hey uh, Tillman.
Hey.
We're uh, sorry about...
Uh...

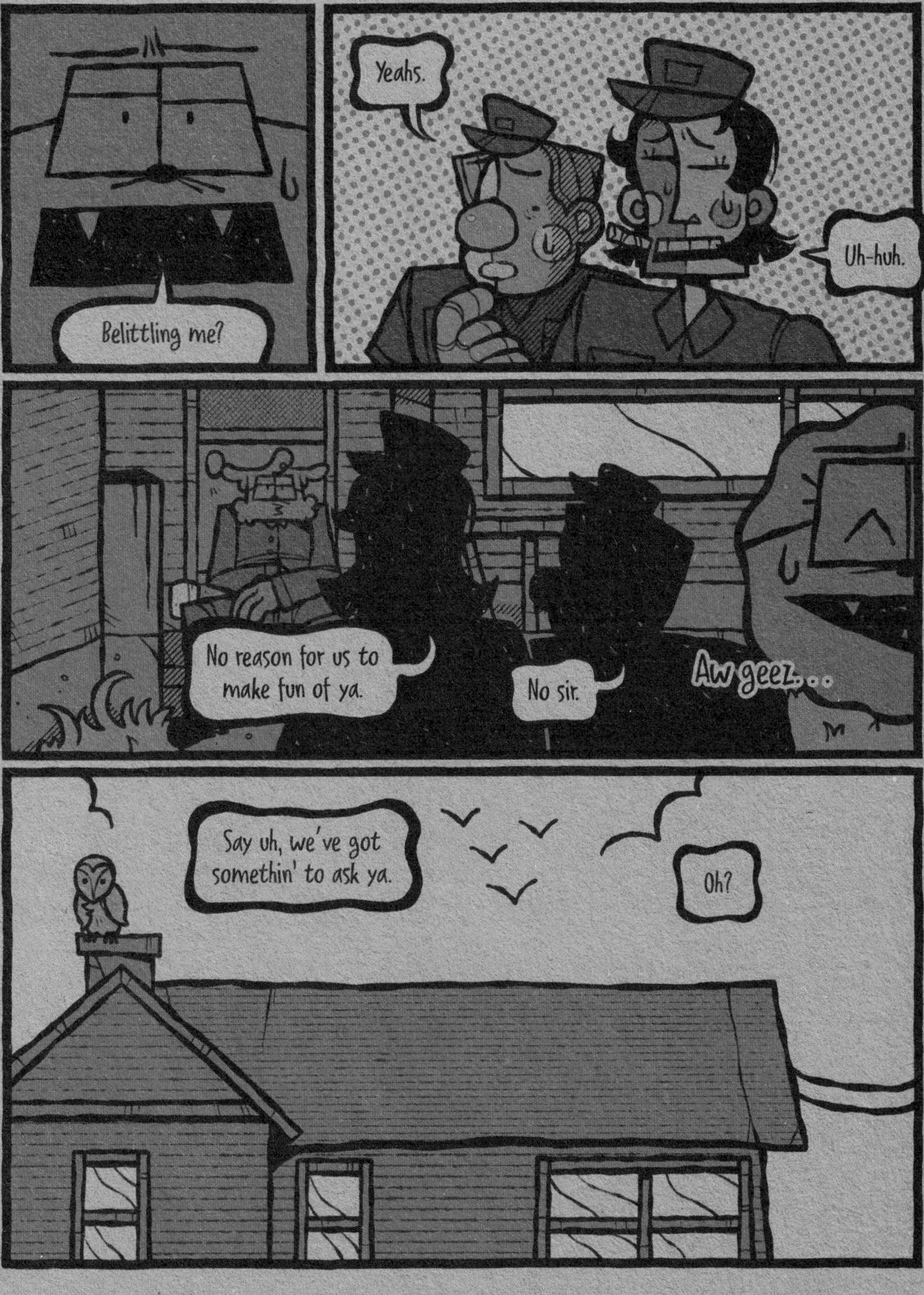
Belittling me?
Yeahs.
Uh-huh.
No reason for us to make fun of ya.
No sir.
Aw geez...
Say uh, we've got somethin' to ask ya.
Oh?

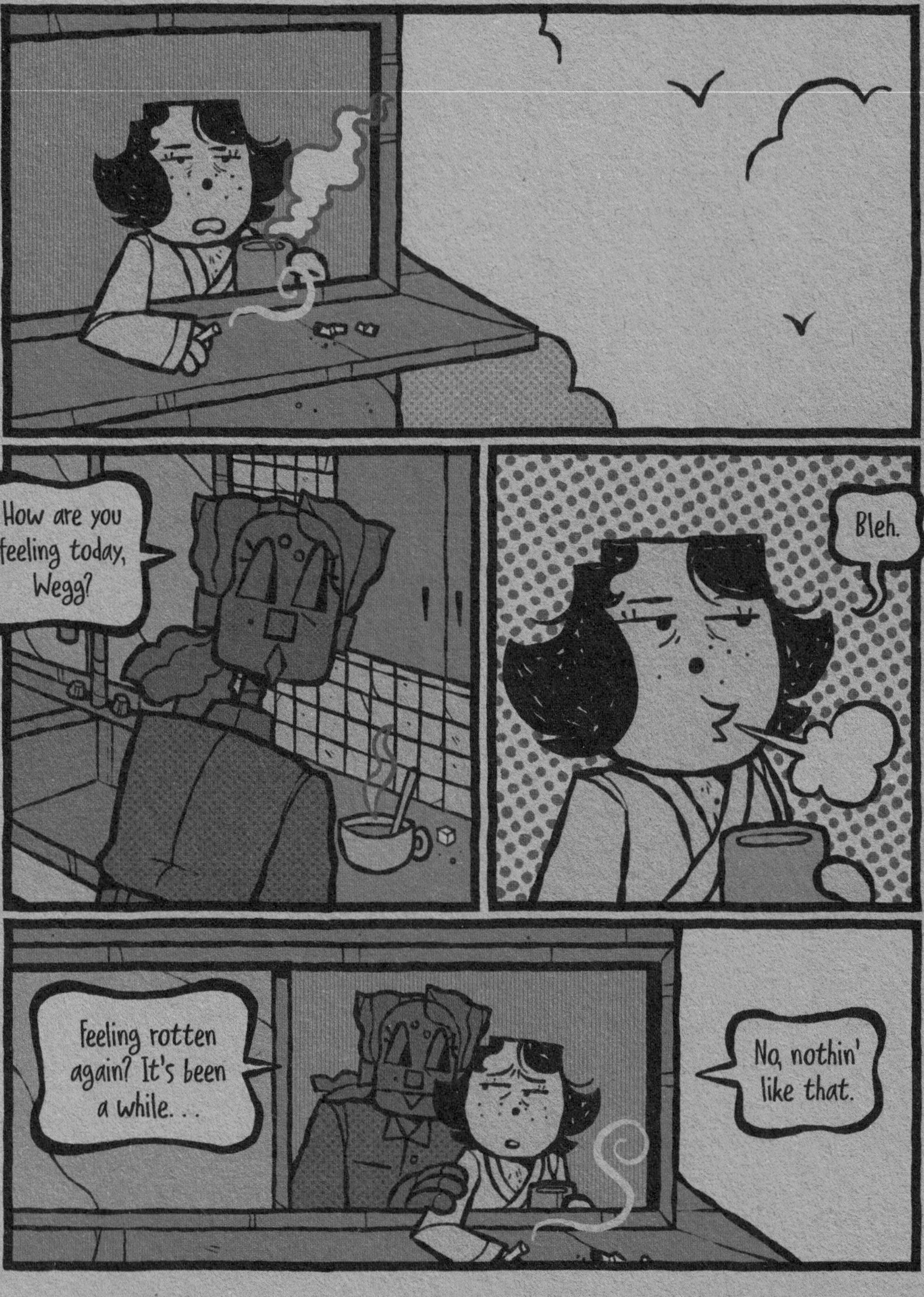
How are you feeling today, Wegg?
Bleh.
Feeling rotten again? It's been a while. . .
No, nothin' like that.

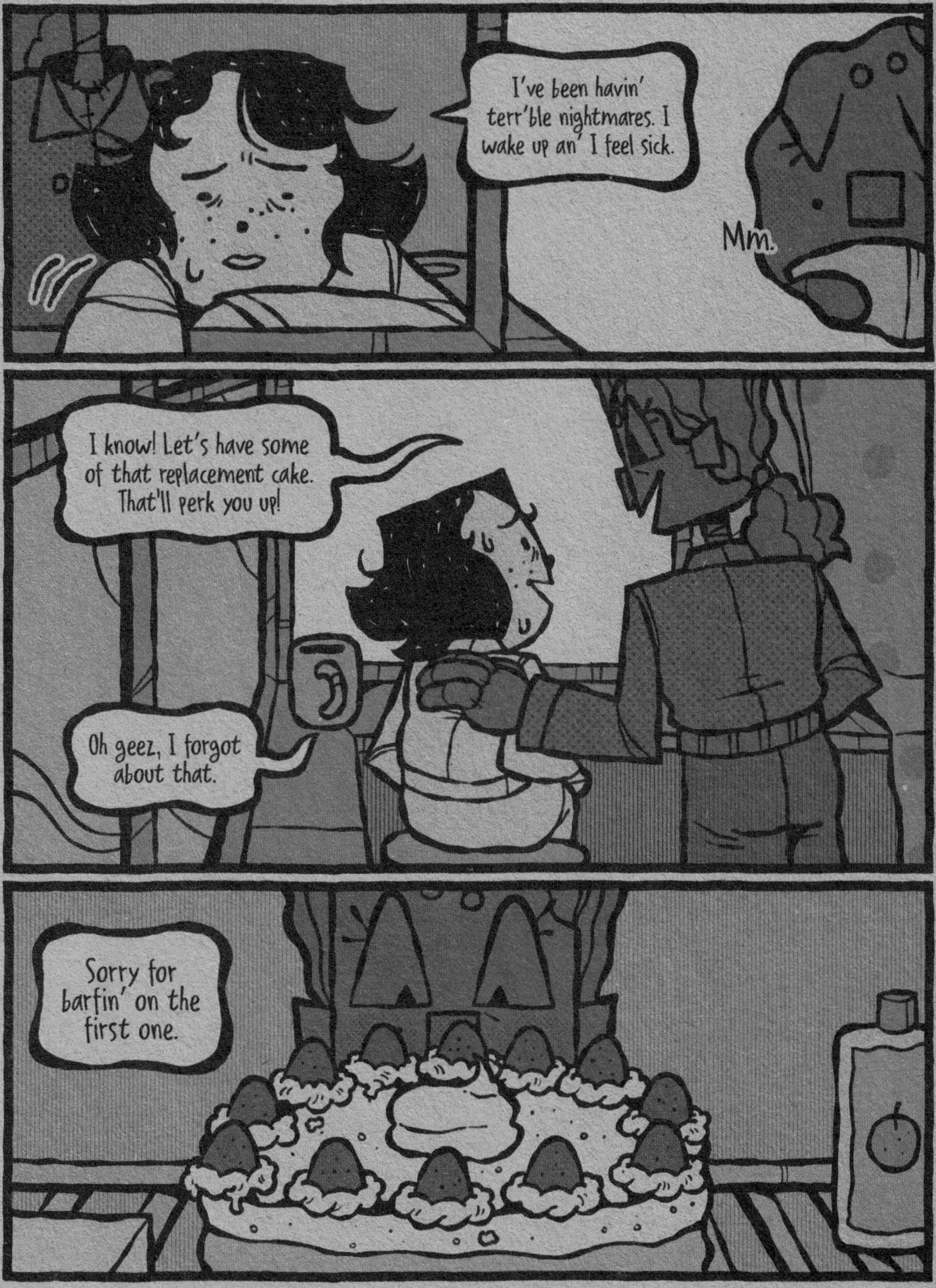
I've been havin' terr'ble nightmares. I wake up an' I feel sick.
Mm.
I know! Let's have some of that replacement cake. That'll perk you up!
Oh geez, I forgot about that.
Sorry for barfin' on the first one.

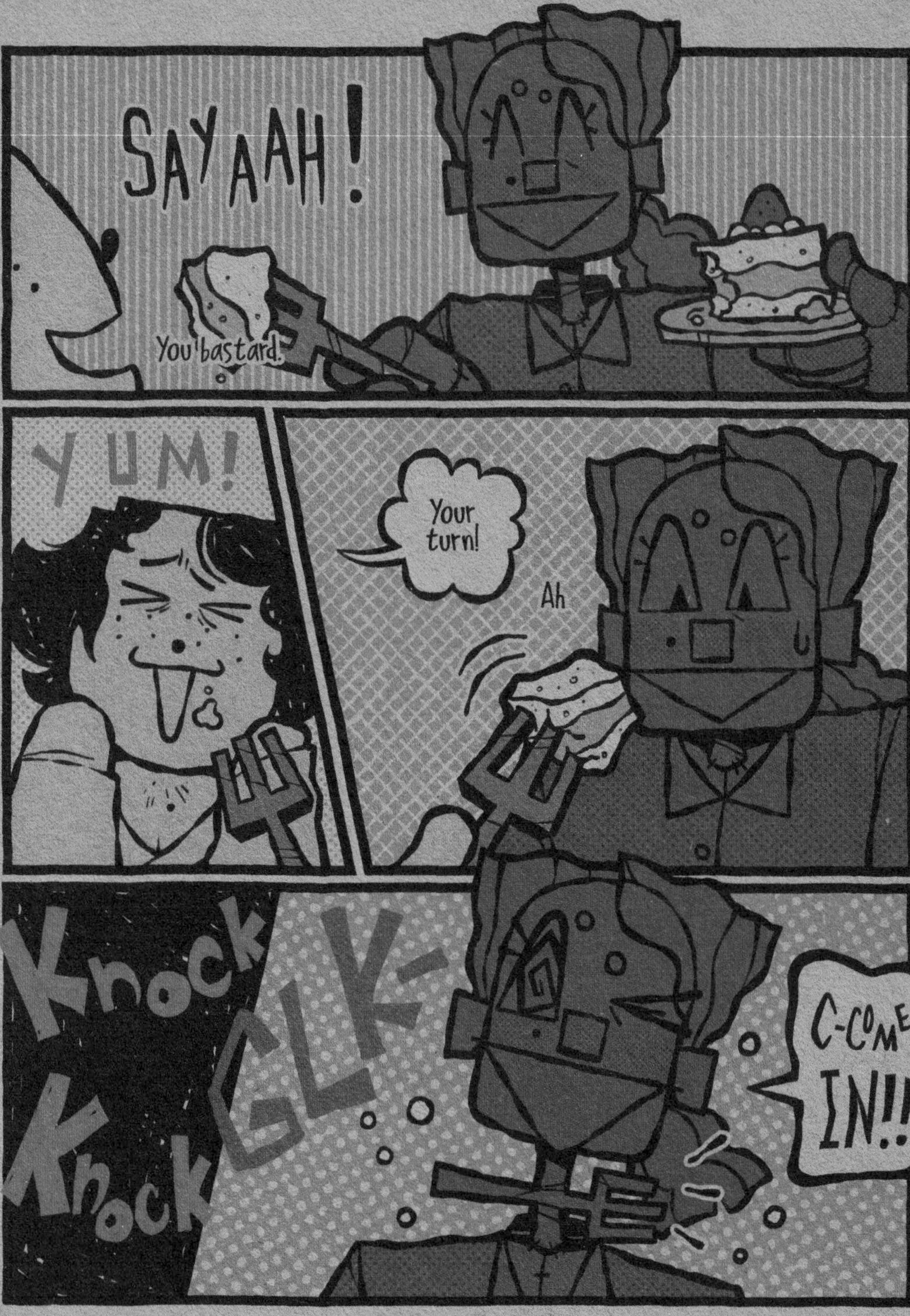
SAY AAH!
You bastard.
YUM!
Your turn!
Ah
Knock Knock
GLK-
C-COME IN!!

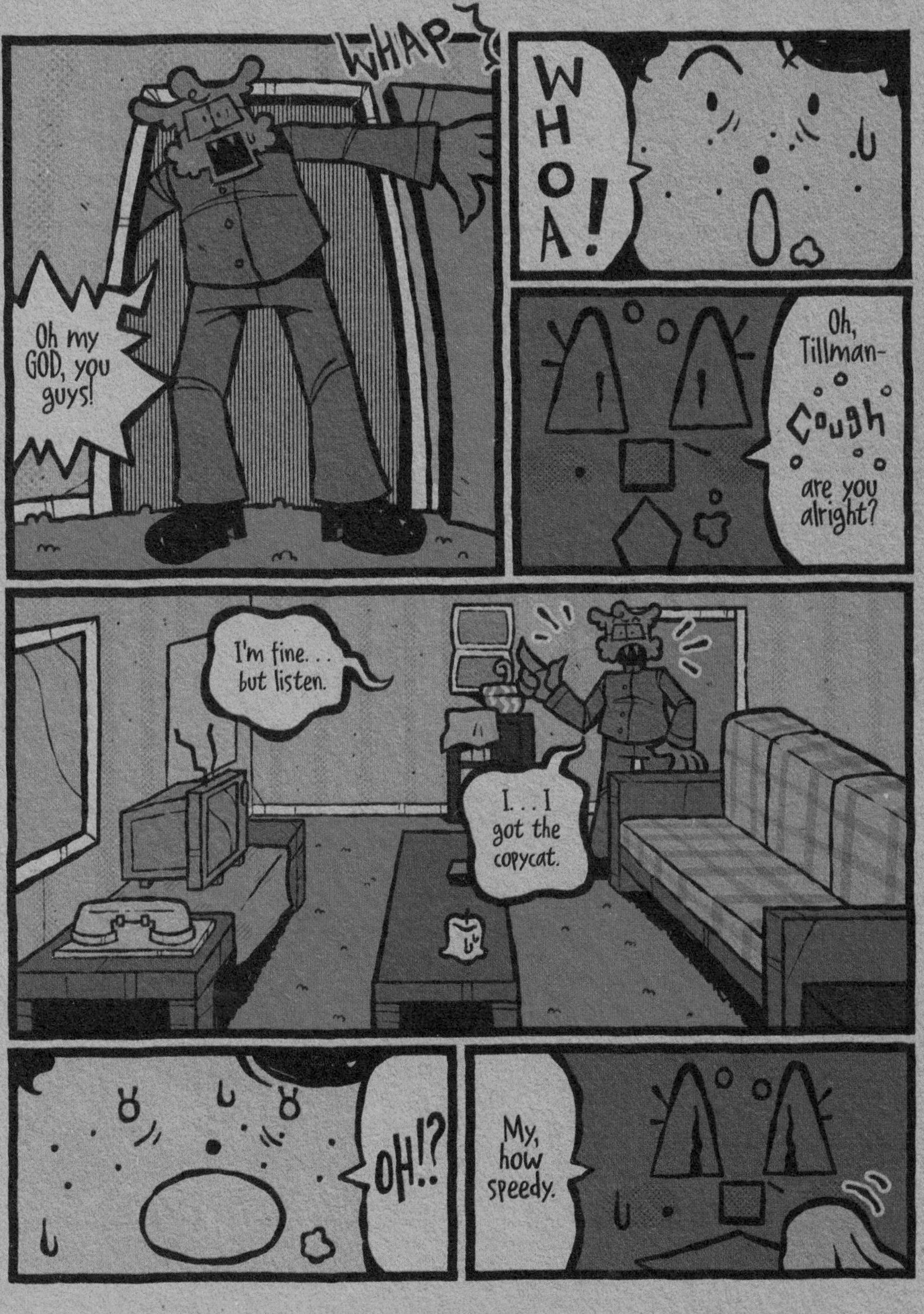
WHAP
Oh my GOD, you guys!
WHOA!
Oh, Tillman-
Cough
are you alright?
I'm fine. . . but listen.
I. . . I got the copycat.
OH!?
My, how speedy.

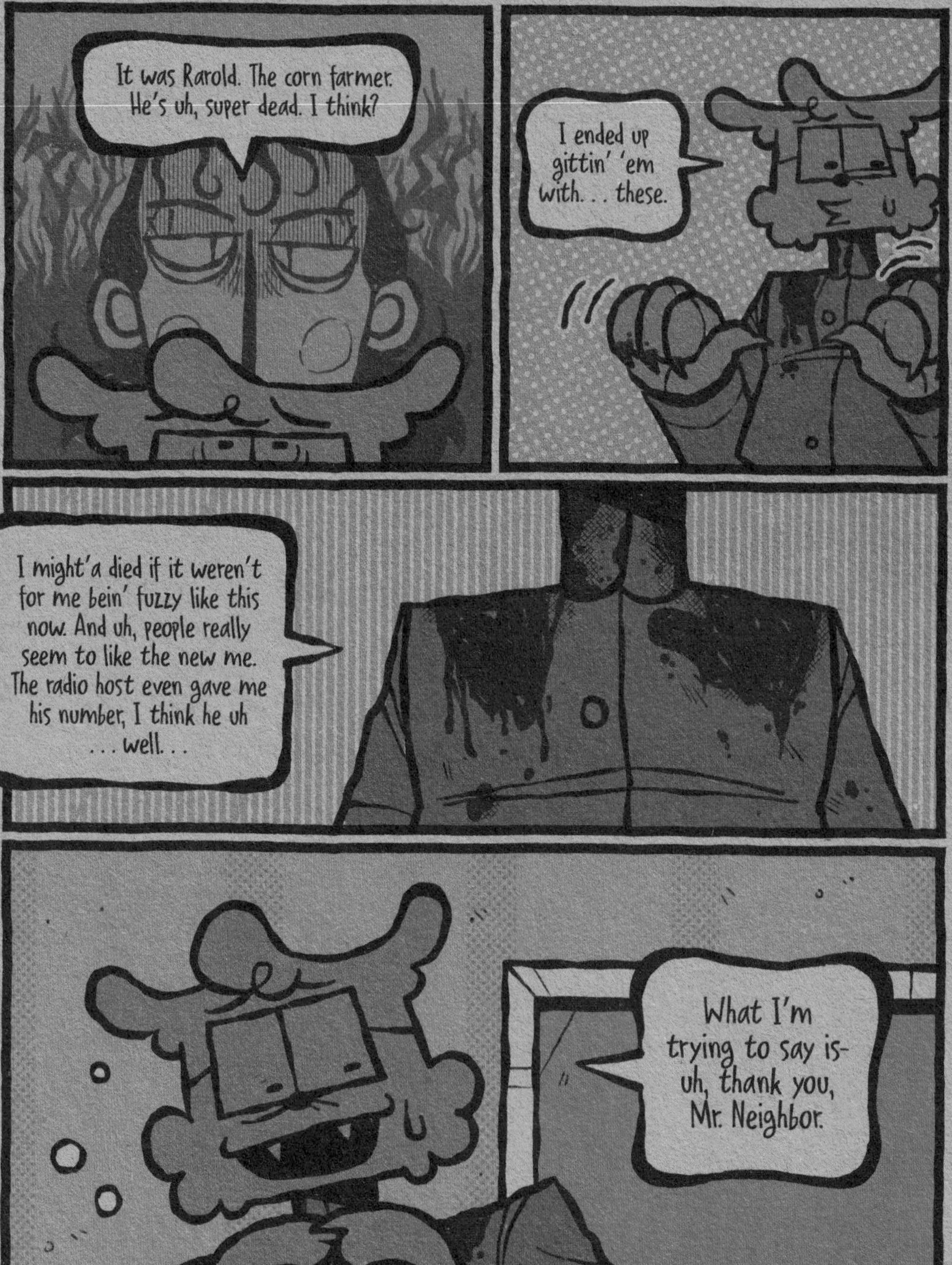
It was Rarold. The corn farmer. He's uh, super dead. I think?
I ended up gittin' 'em with. . . these.
I might'a died if it weren't for me bein' fuzzy like this now. And uh, people really seem to like the new me. The radio host even gave me his number, I think he uh . . . well. . .
What I'm trying to say is- uh, thank you, Mr. Neighbor.

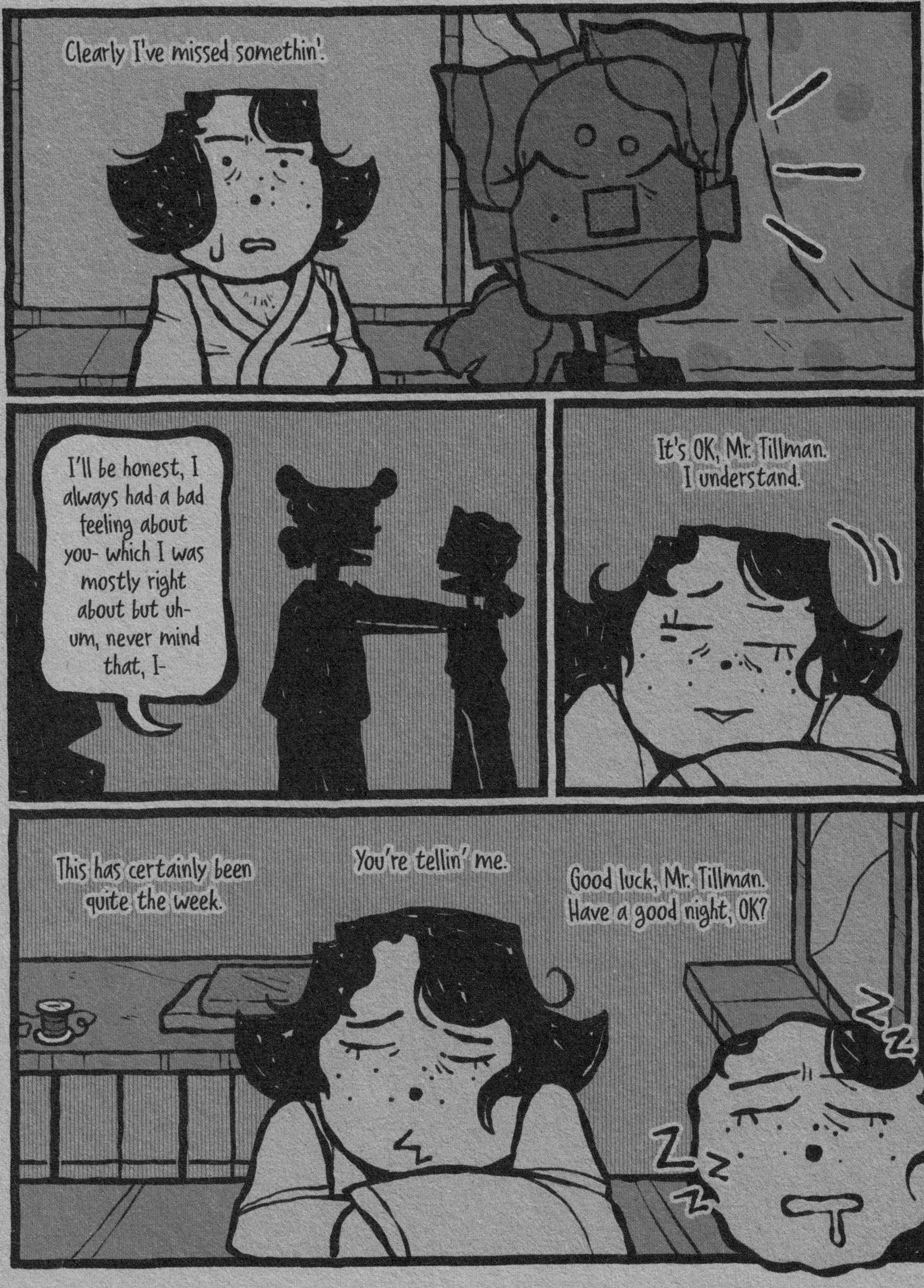

Clearly I've missed somethin'.
I'll be honest, I always had a bad feeling about you- which I was mostly right about but uh- um, never mind that, I-
It's OK, Mr. Tillman. I understand.
This has certainly been quite the week.
You're tellin' me.
Good luck, Mr. Tillman. Have a good night, OK?

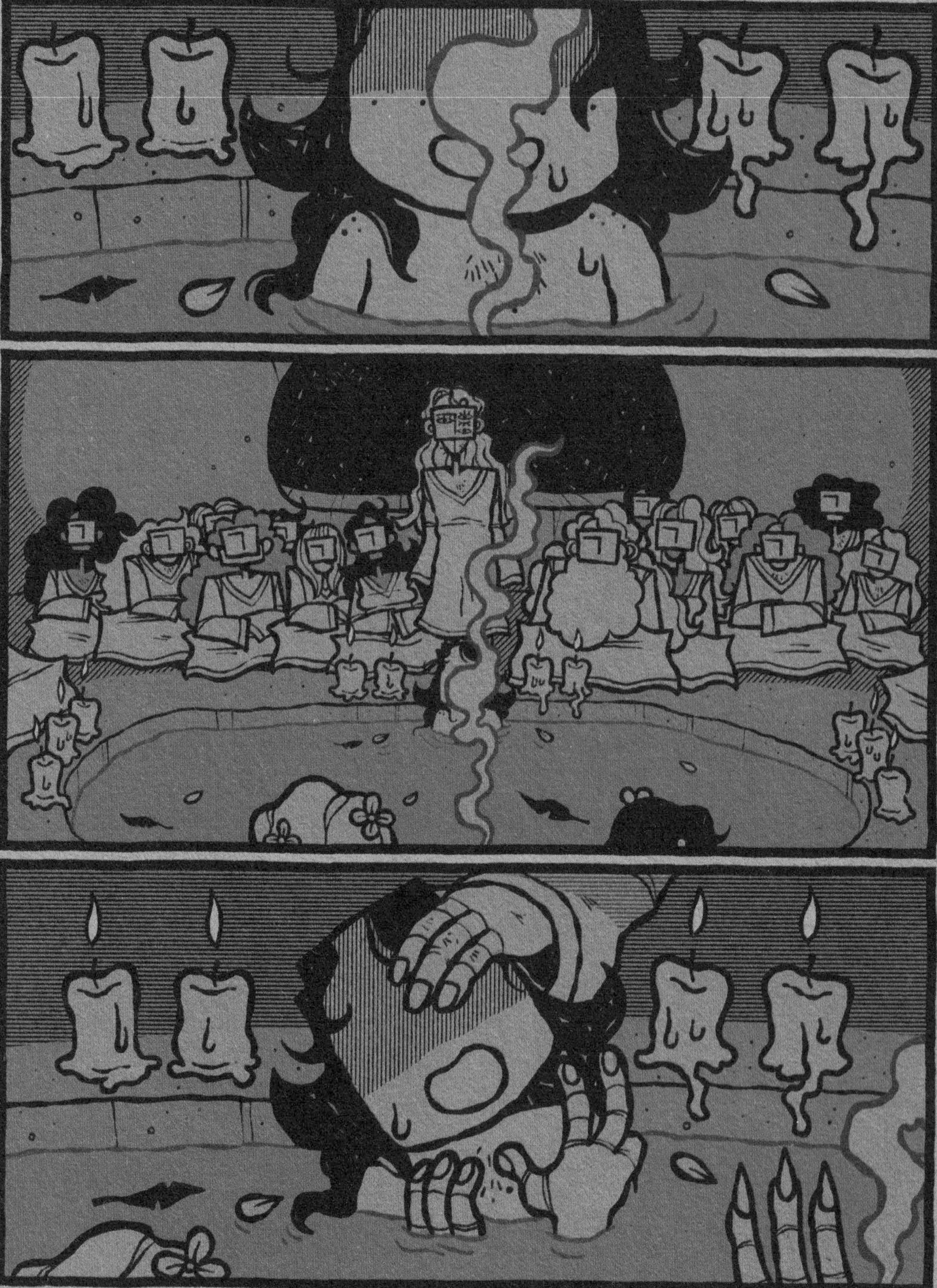

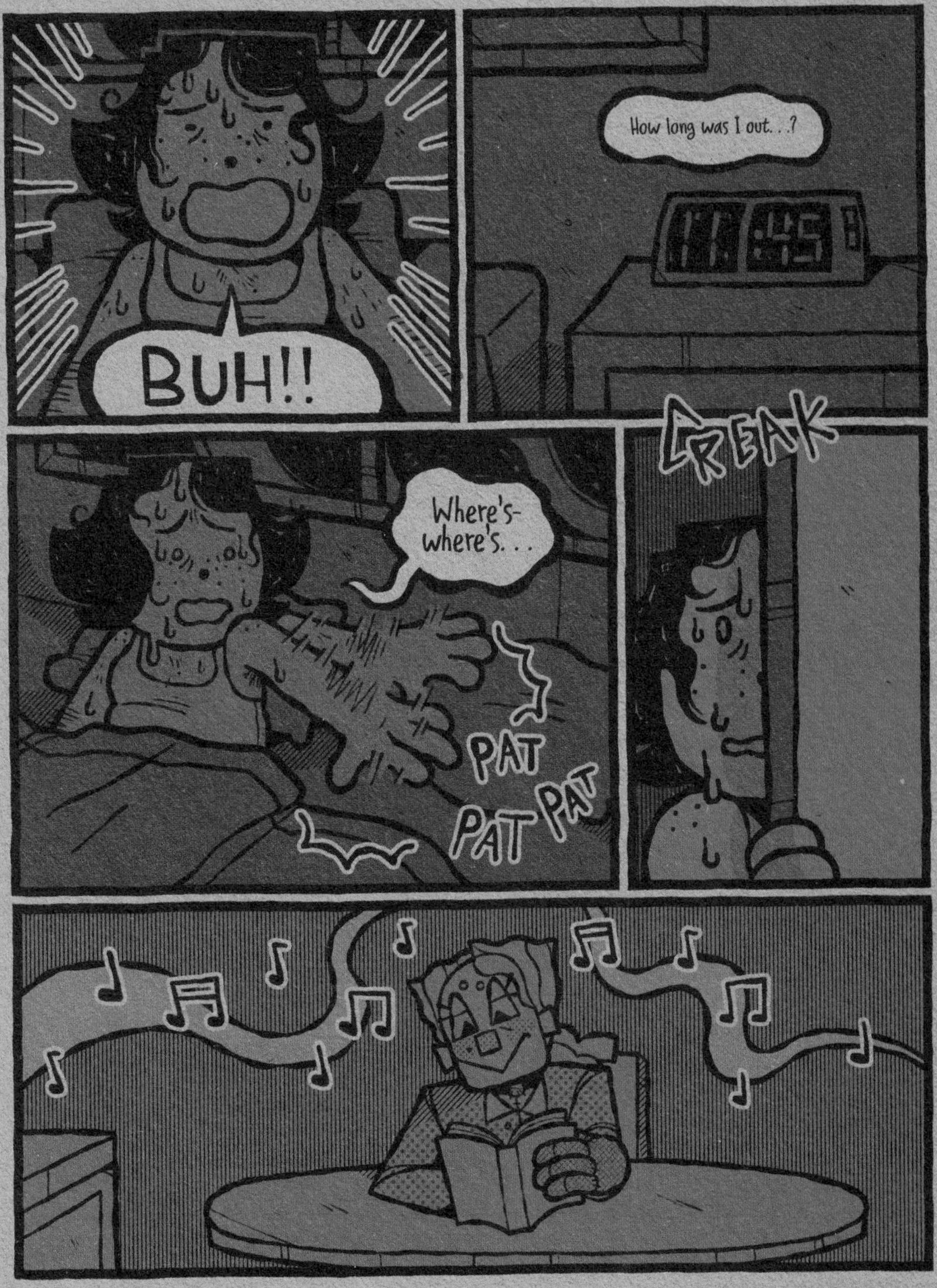
BUH!!
How long was I out...?
11:45
CREAK
Where's- where's...
PAT
PAT PAT

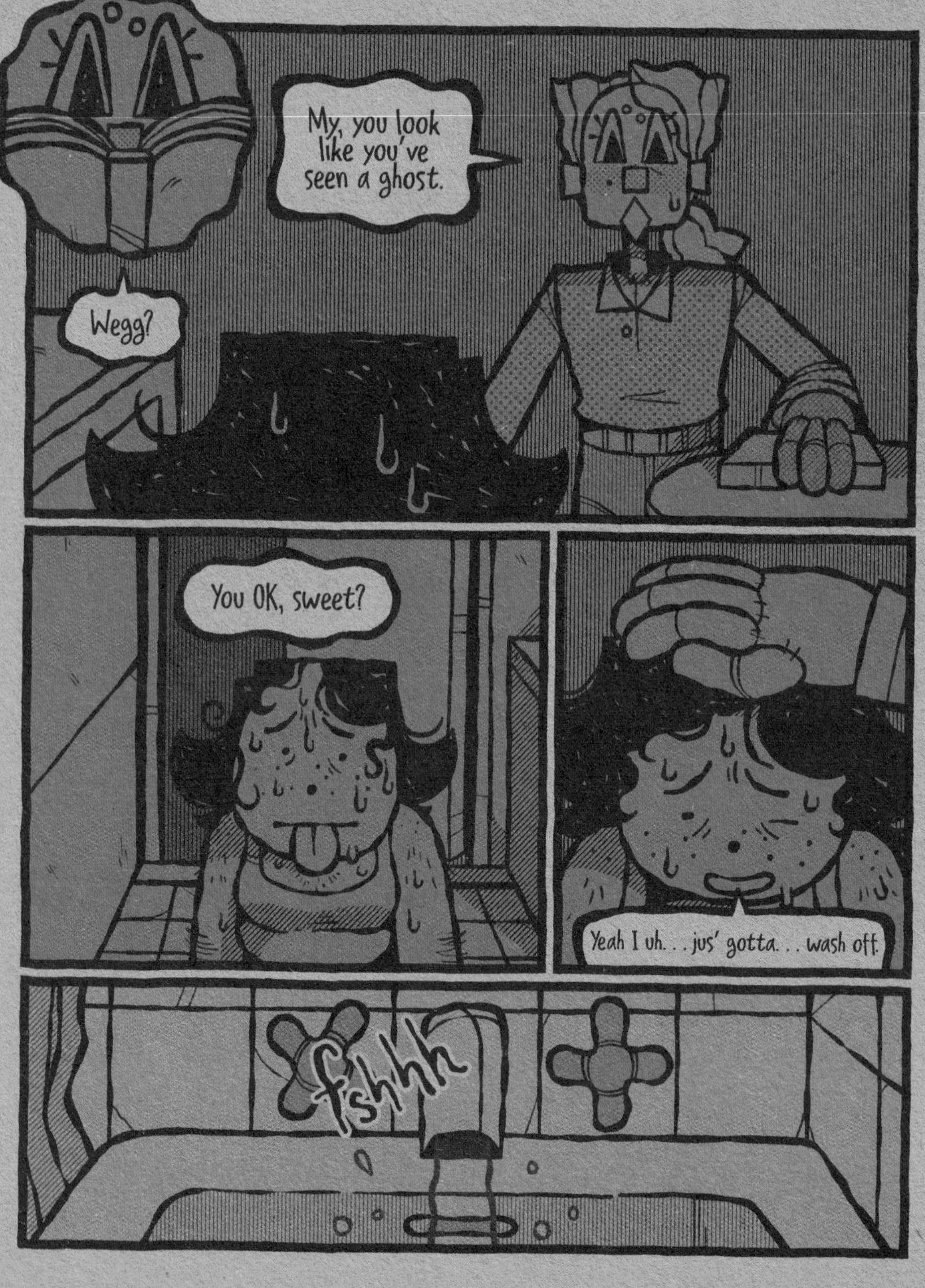
My, you look like you've seen a ghost.
Wegg?
You OK, sweet?
Yeah I uh. . . jus' gotta. . . wash off.
fshhh

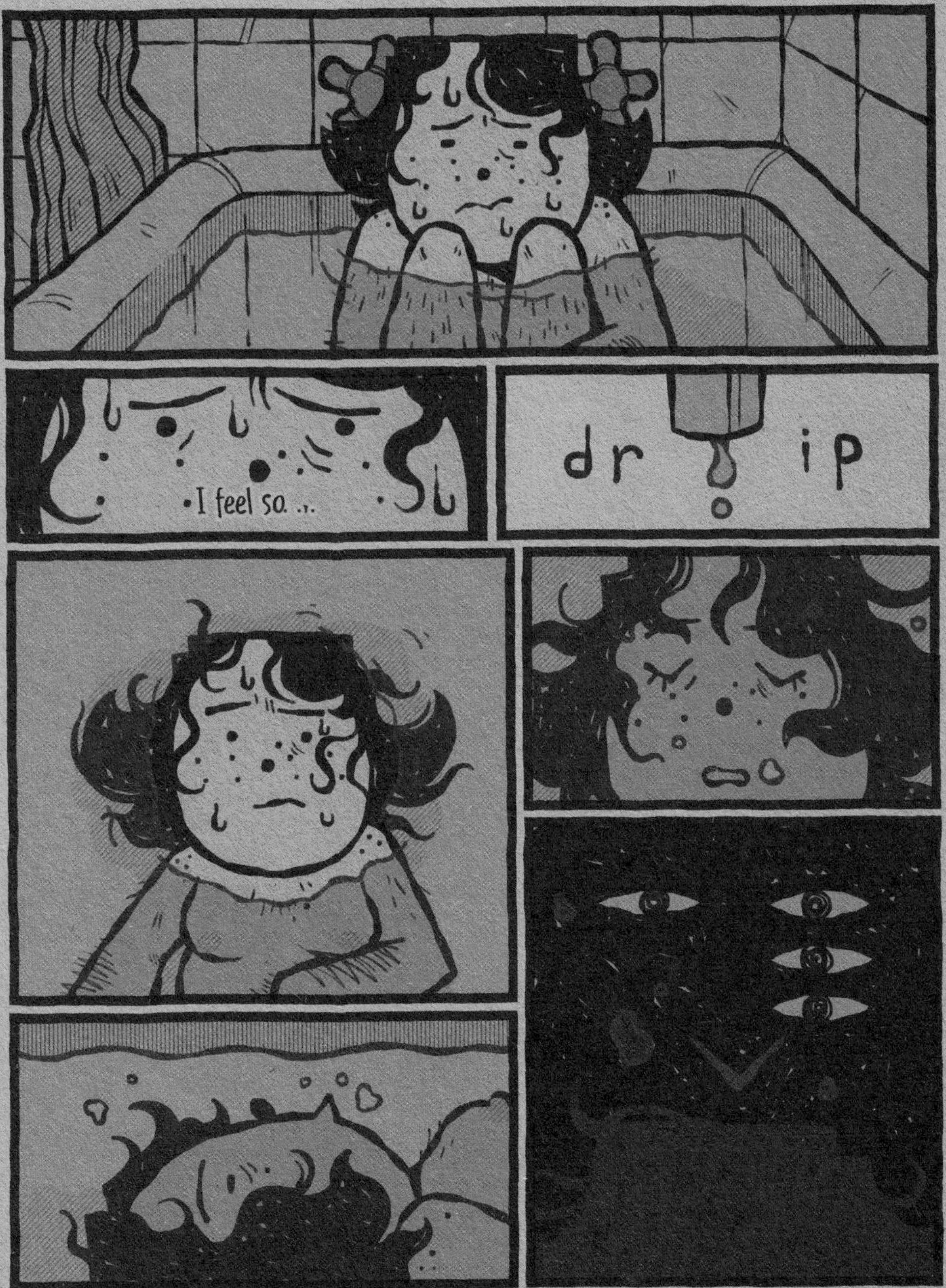
I feel so. . . .
dr ip

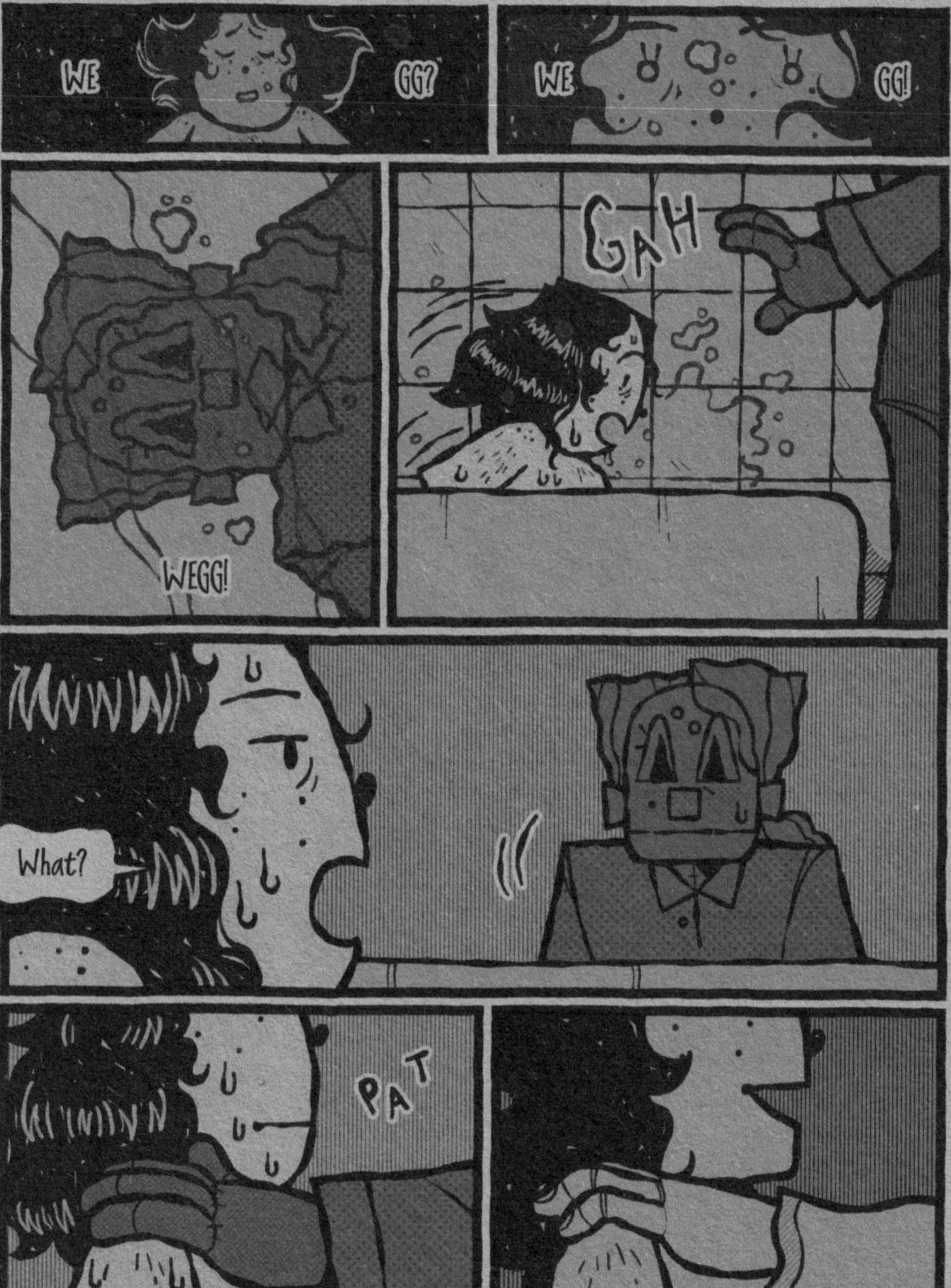

WE
GG?
WE
GG!
WEGG!
GAH
What?
PAT

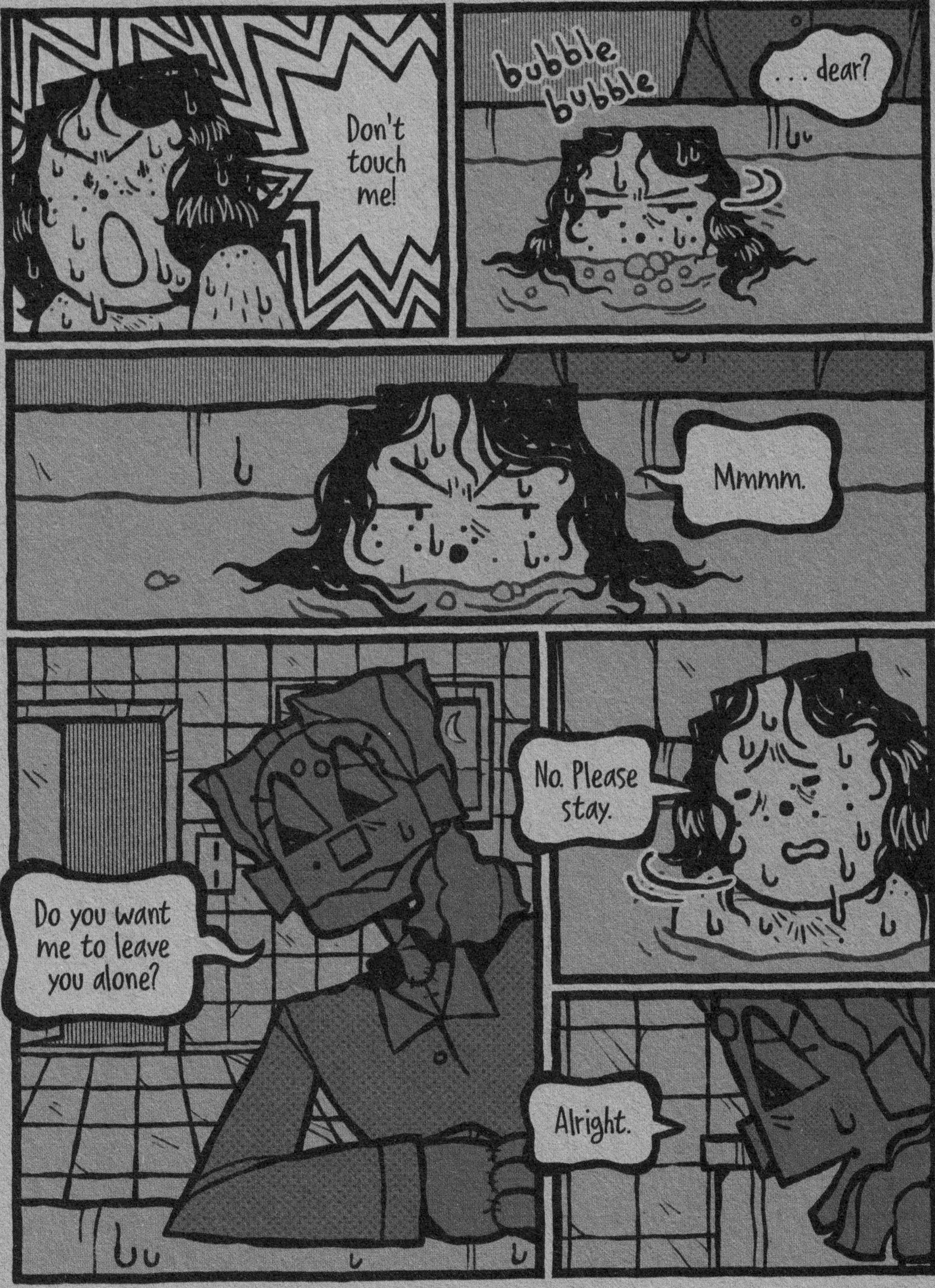
Don't touch me!
bubble bubble
. . . dear?
Mmmm.
Do you want me to leave you alone?
No. Please stay.
Alright.

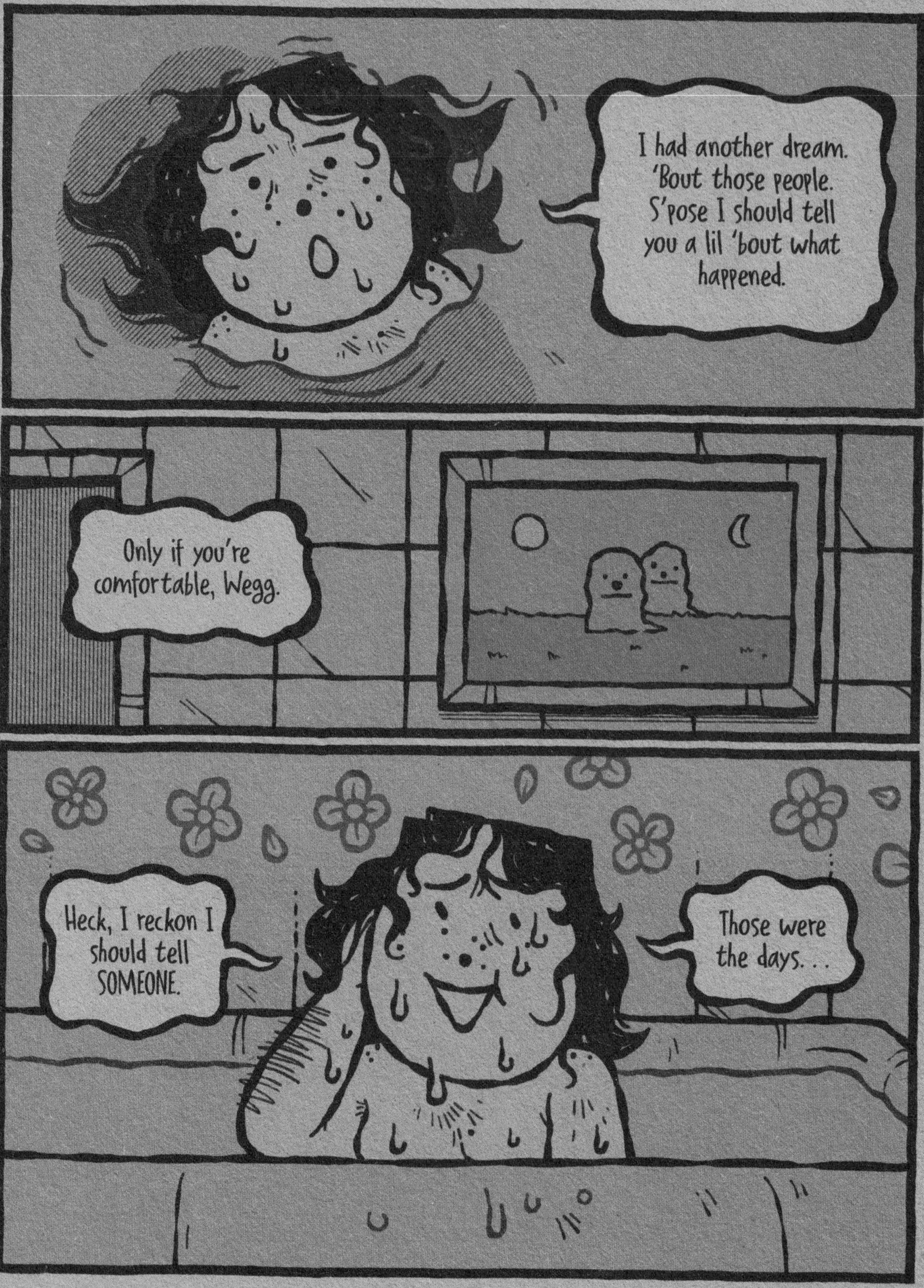
I had another dream. 'Bout those people. S'pose I should tell you a lil 'bout what happened.
Only if you're comfortable, Wegg.
Heck, I reckon I should tell SOMEONE.
Those were the days. . .

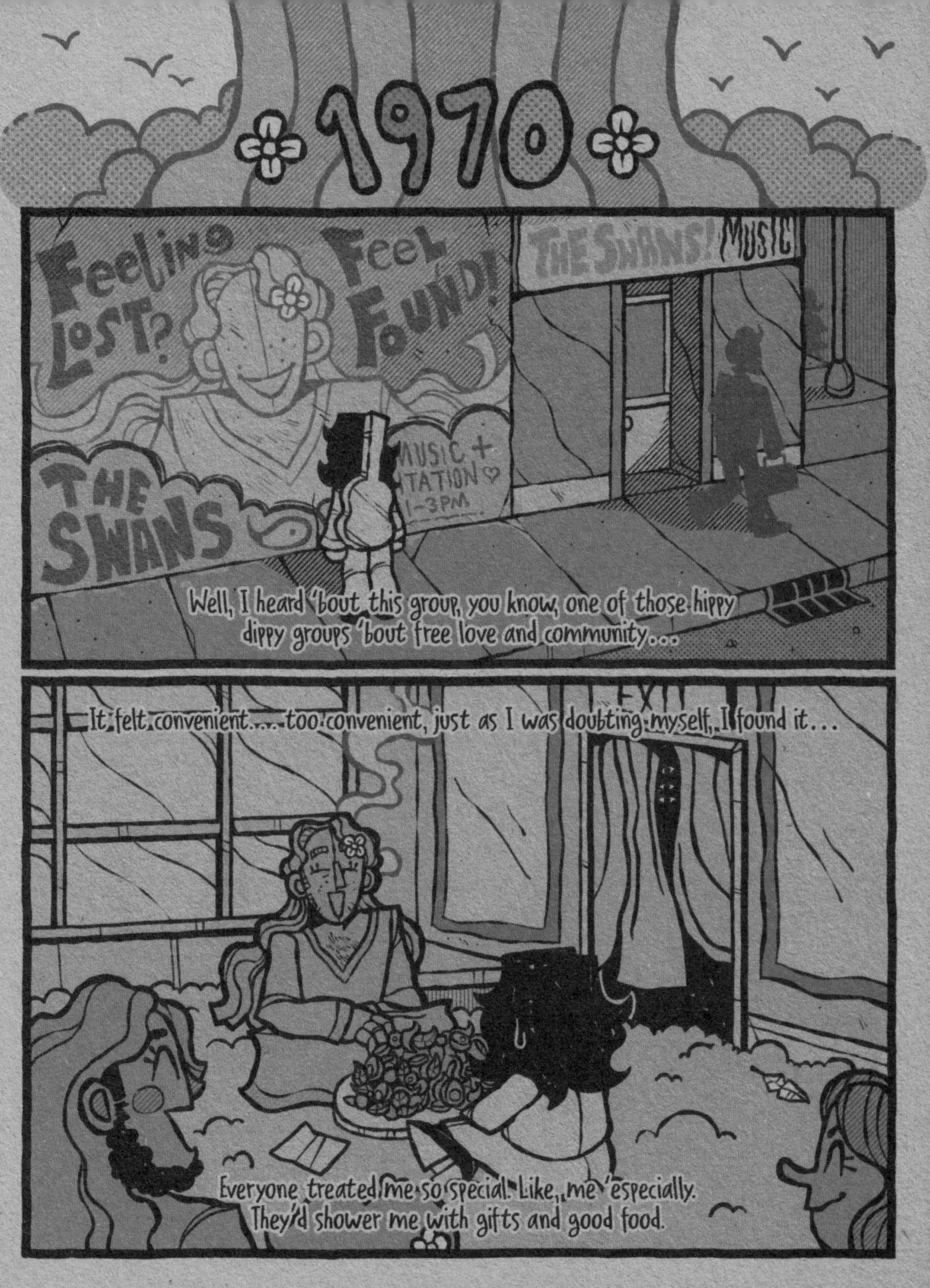
1970
Feeling Lost? Feel Found!
THE SWANS
MUSIC + ...TATION 1-3PM
THE SWANS! MUSIC
Well, I heard 'bout this group, you know, one of those hippy dippy groups 'bout free love and community...
EXIT
It felt convenient... too convenient, just as I was doubting myself, I found it...
Everyone treated me so special. Like, me 'especially.
They'd shower me with gifts and good food.

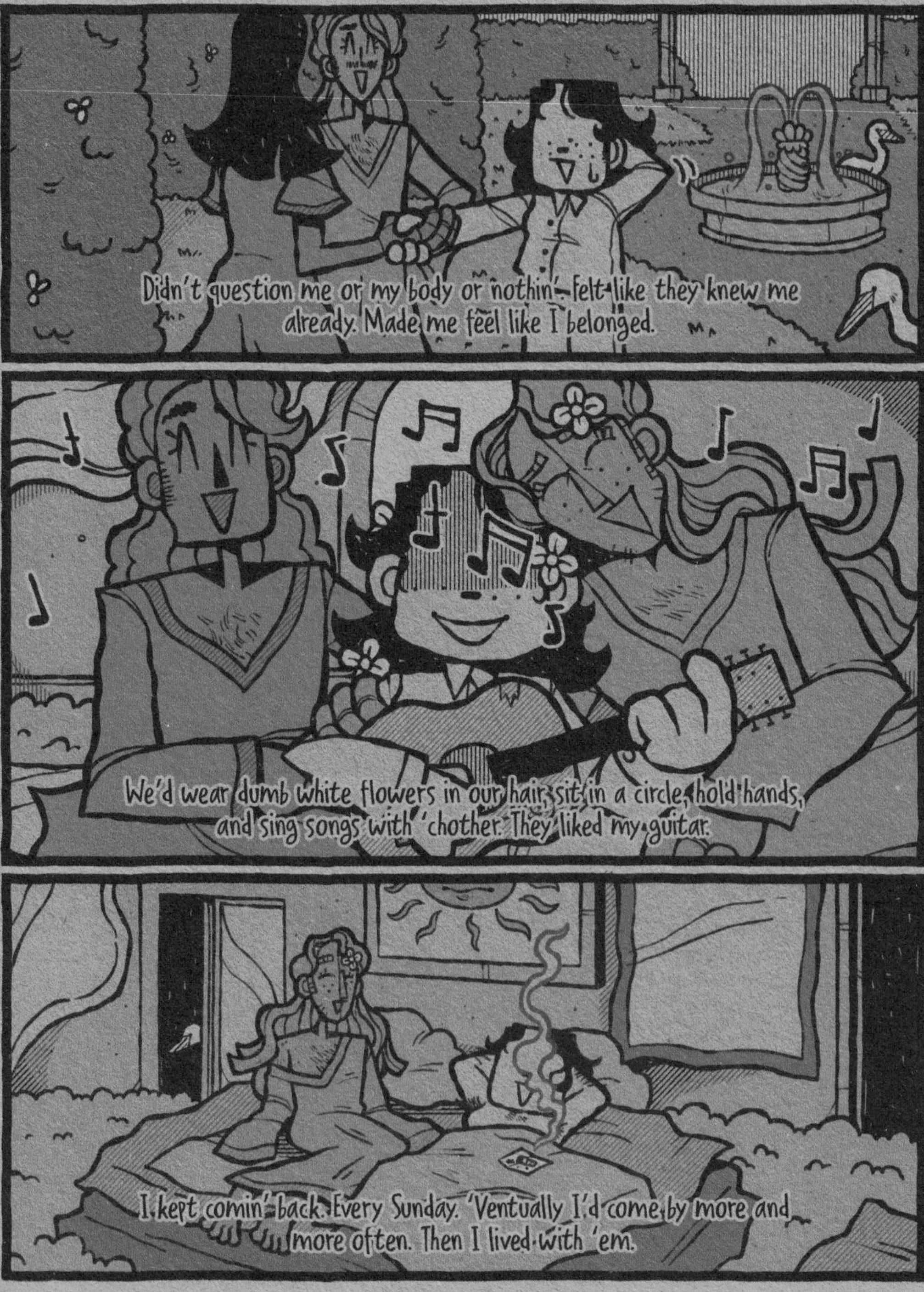
Didn't question me or my body or nothin'. Felt like they knew me already. Made me feel like I belonged.
We'd wear dumb white flowers in our hair, sit in a circle, hold hands, and sing songs with 'chother. They liked my guitar.
I kept comin' back. Every Sunday. 'Ventually I'd come by more and more often. Then I lived with 'em.

An' then... ...one day everyone was wearin' black feathers 'stead of the flowers.

Said they wanted to do some sort of... ...love ritual with me.

So they drew a huge bath for me... with just Too Many candles. Smelled nice though.

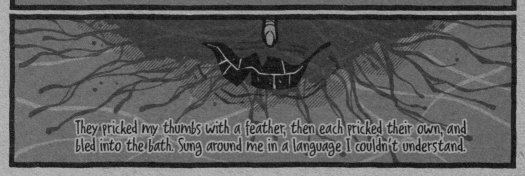

They pricked my thumbs with a feather, then each pricked their own, and bled into the bath. Sung around me in a language I couldn't understand.

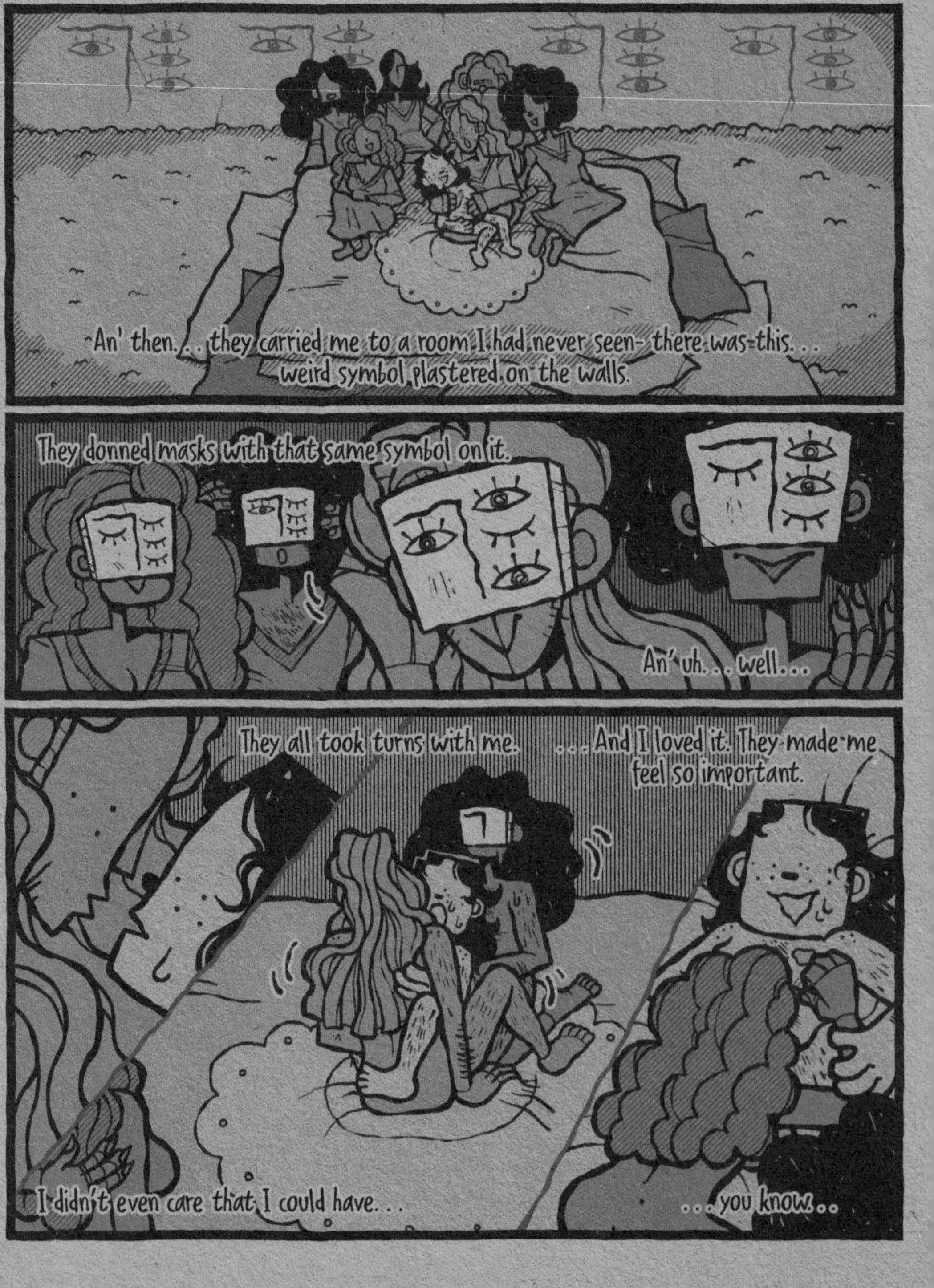
An' then. . . they carried me to a room I had never seen- there was this. . . weird symbol plastered on the walls.
They donned masks with that same symbol on it.
An' uh. . . well. . .
They all took turns with me.
. . . And I loved it. They made me feel so important.
I didn't even care that I could have. . .
. . . you know. . .

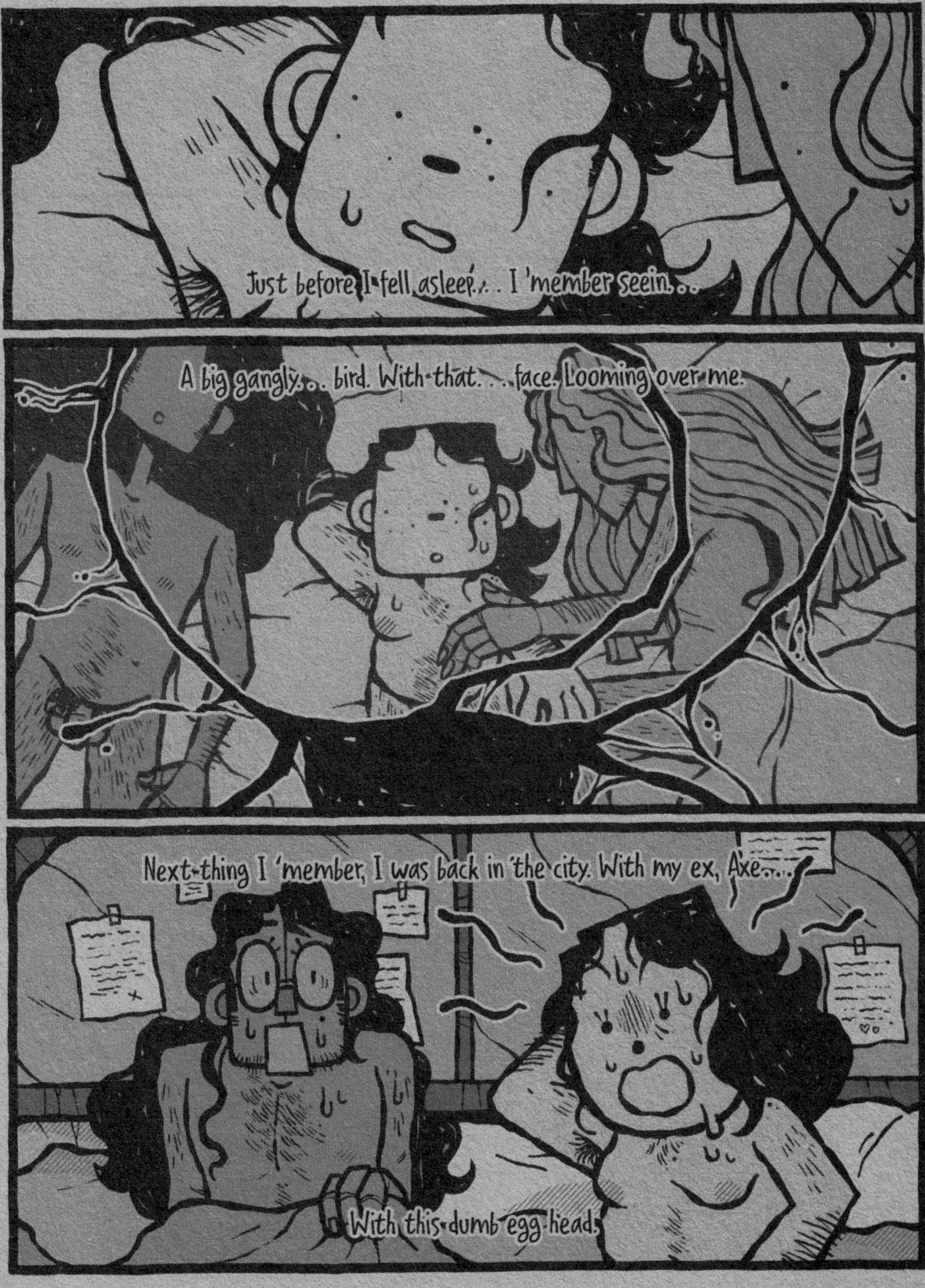
Just before I fell asleep. . . I 'member seein. . .
A big gangly. . . bird. With that. . . face. Looming over me.
Next thing I 'member, I was back in the city. With my ex, Axe. . .
With this dumb egg head.

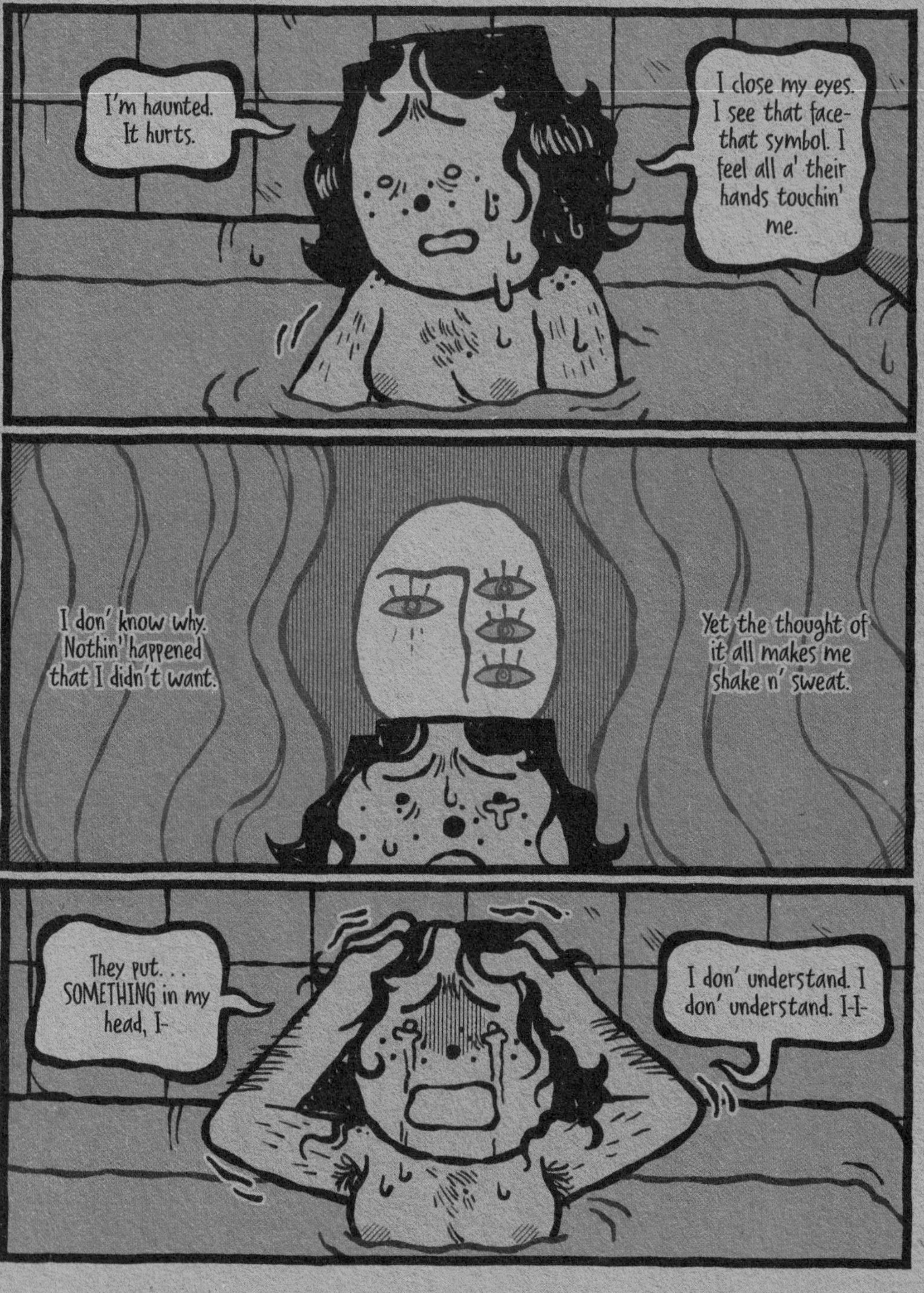
I'm haunted. It hurts.
I close my eyes. I see that face- that symbol. I feel all a' their hands touchin' me.
I don' know why. Nothin' happened that I didn't want.
Yet the thought of it all makes me shake n' sweat.
They put. . . SOMETHING in my head, I-
I don' understand. I don' understand. I-I-

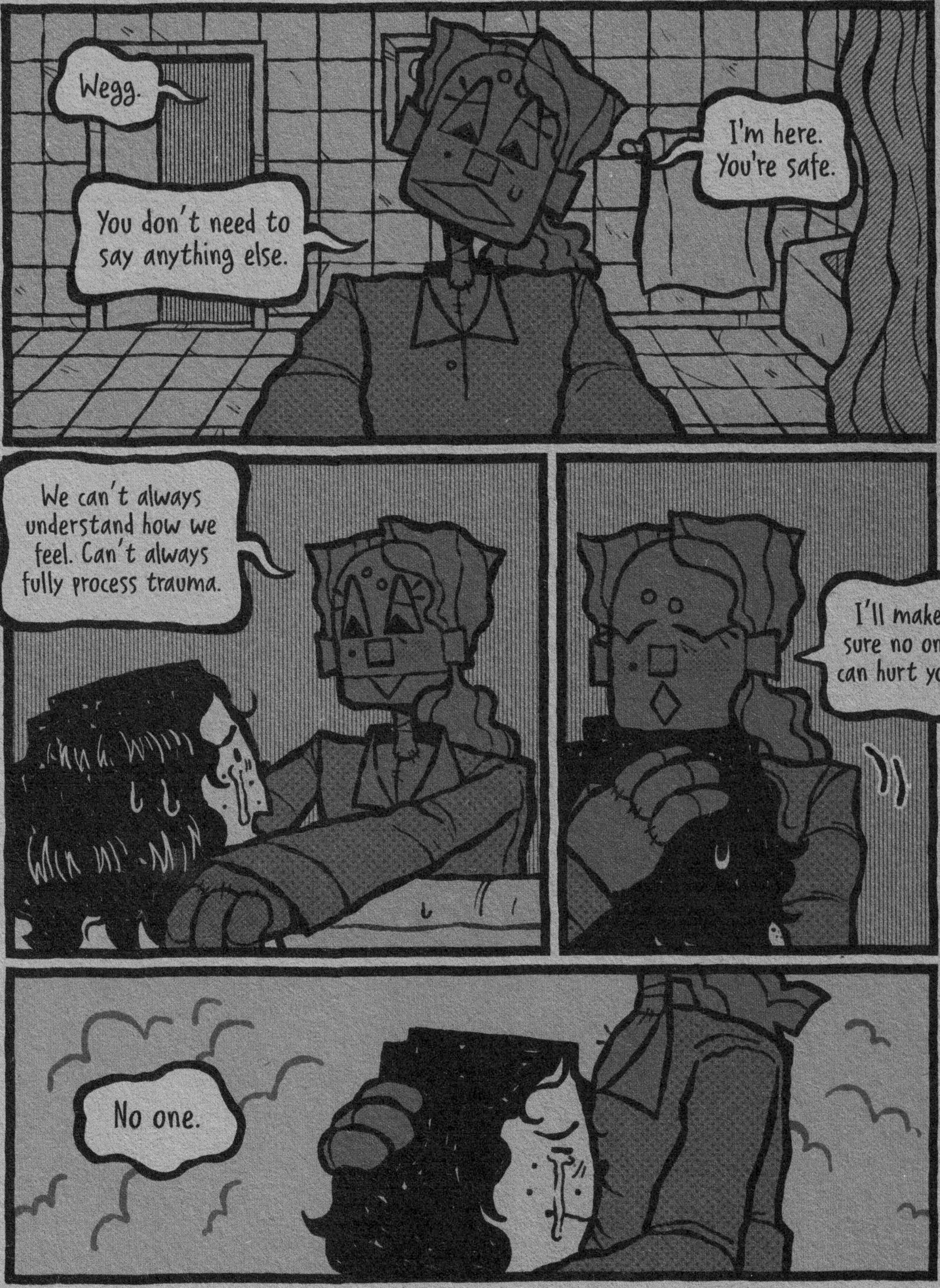
Wegg.
You don't need to say anything else.
I'm here. You're safe.
We can't always understand how we feel. Can't always fully process trauma.
I'll make sure no one can hurt you.
No one.

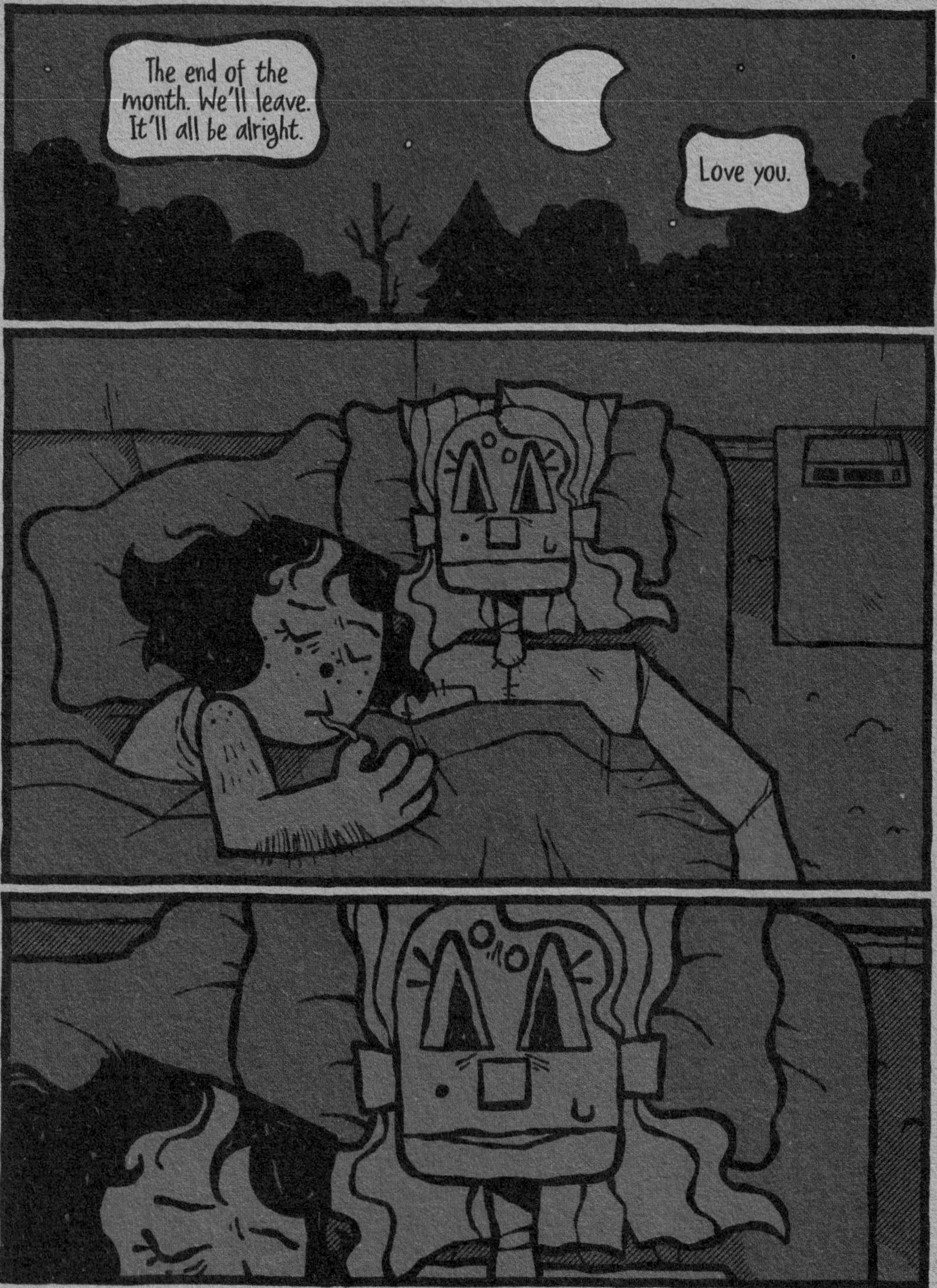
The end of the month. We'll leave. It'll all be alright.
Love you.

11, MESSIAH

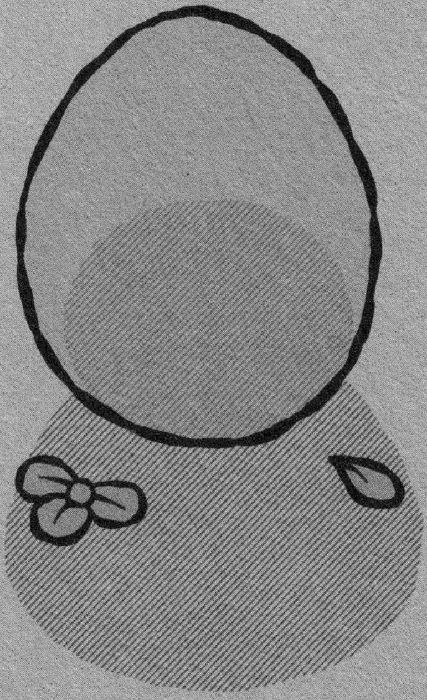

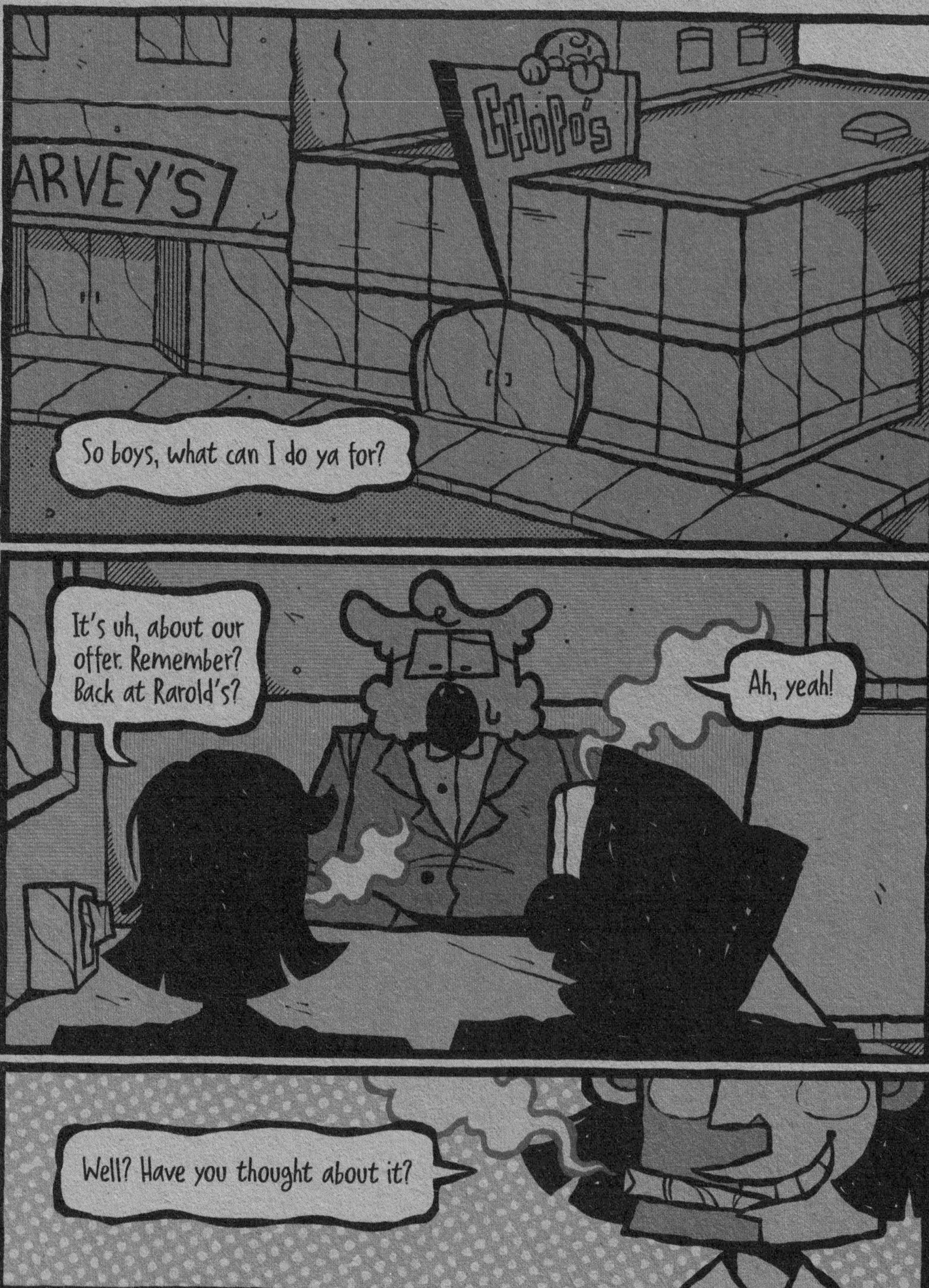

ARVEY'S
CHOPO'S
So boys, what can I do ya for?
It's uh, about our offer. Remember? Back at Rarold's?
Ah, yeah!
Well? Have you thought about it?

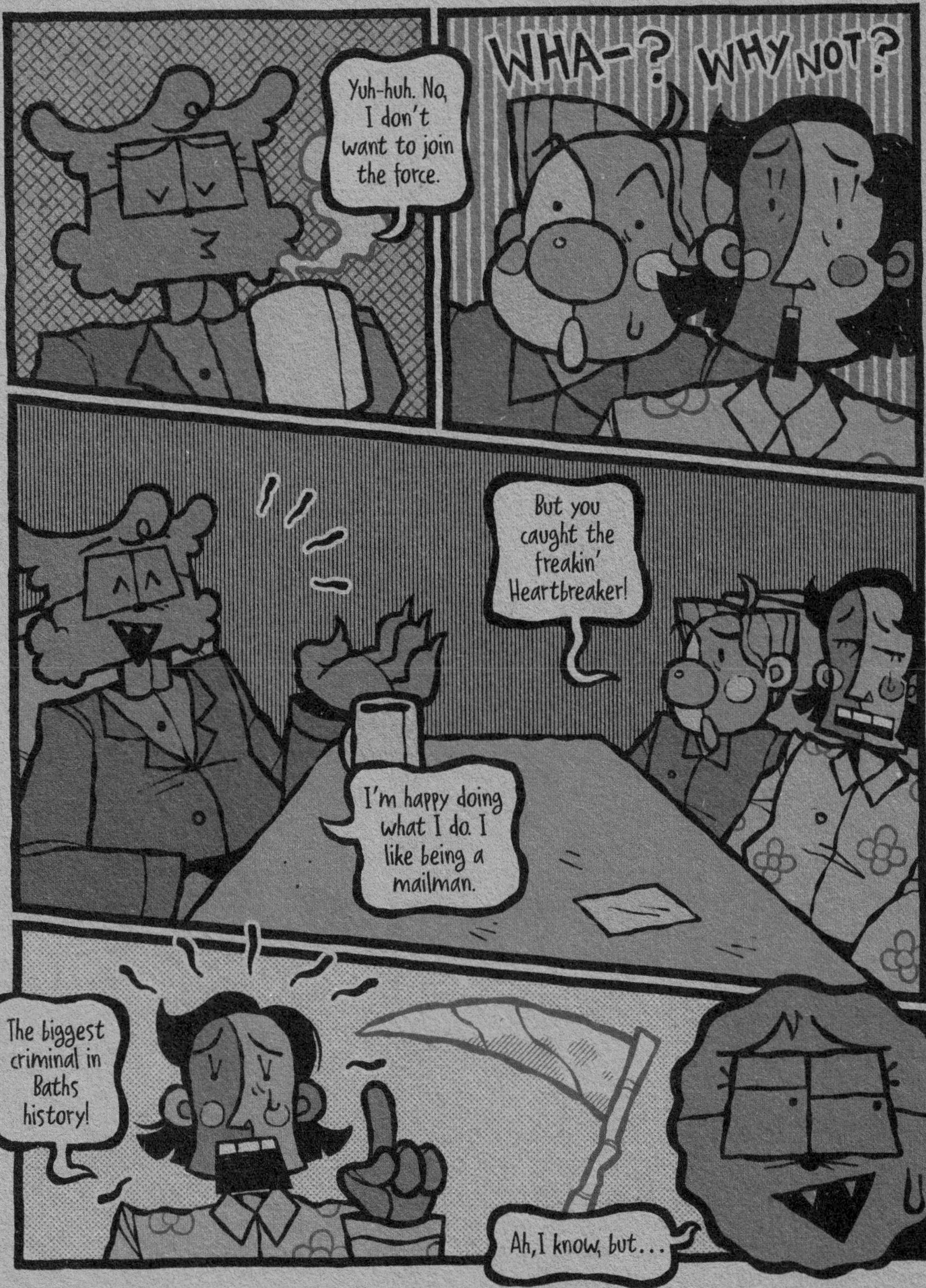
Yuh-huh. No, I don't want to join the force.
WHA-? WHY NOT?
But you caught the freakin' Heartbreaker!
I'm happy doing what I do. I like being a mailman.
The biggest criminal in Baths history!
Ah, I know, but...

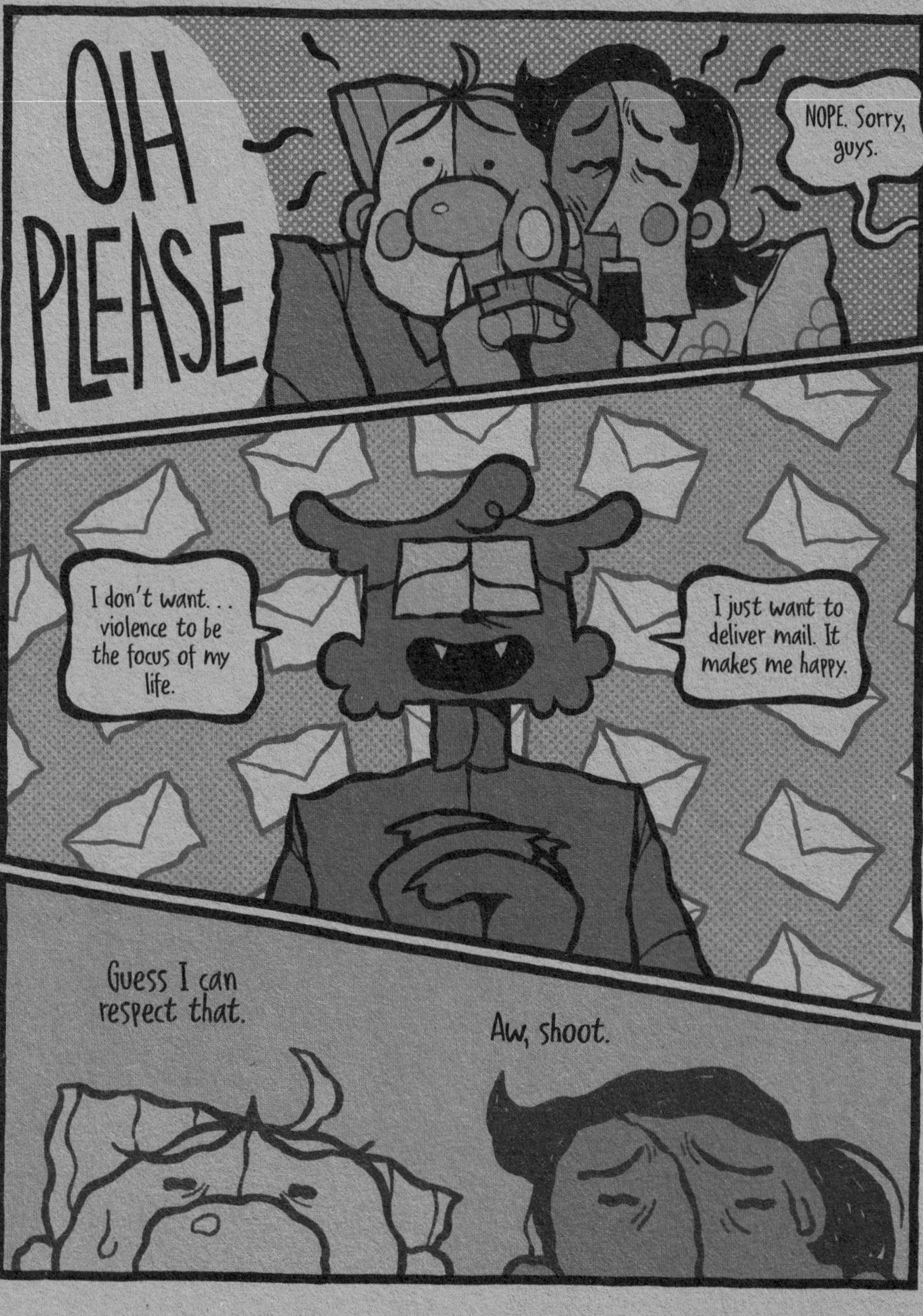
OH PLLEASE
NOPE. Sorry, guys.
I don't want. . . violence to be the focus of my life.
I just want to deliver mail. It makes me happy.
Guess I can respect that.
Aw, shoot.

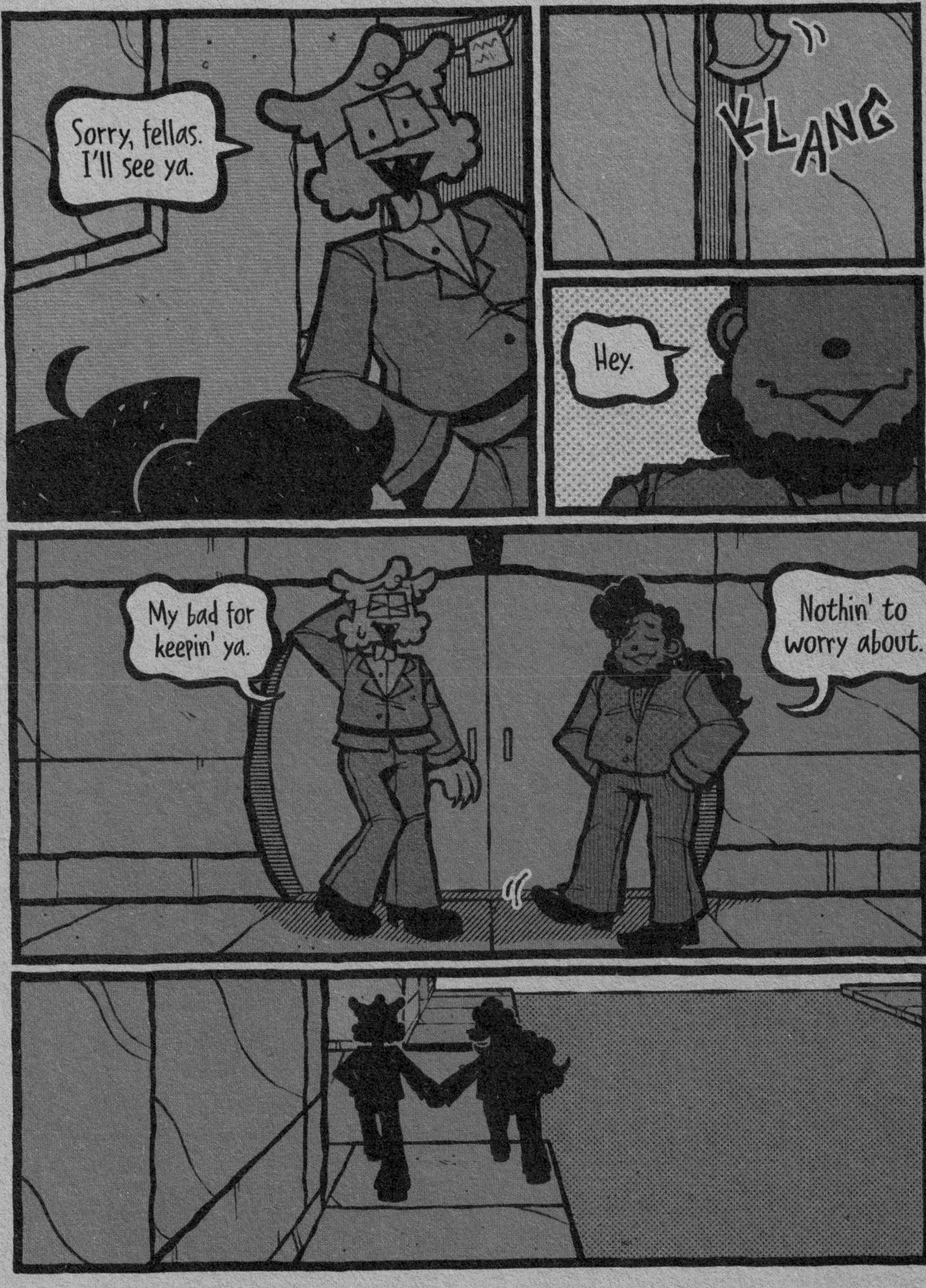
Sorry, fellas.
I'll see ya.
KLANG
Hey.
My bad for
keepin' ya.
Nothin' to
worry about.

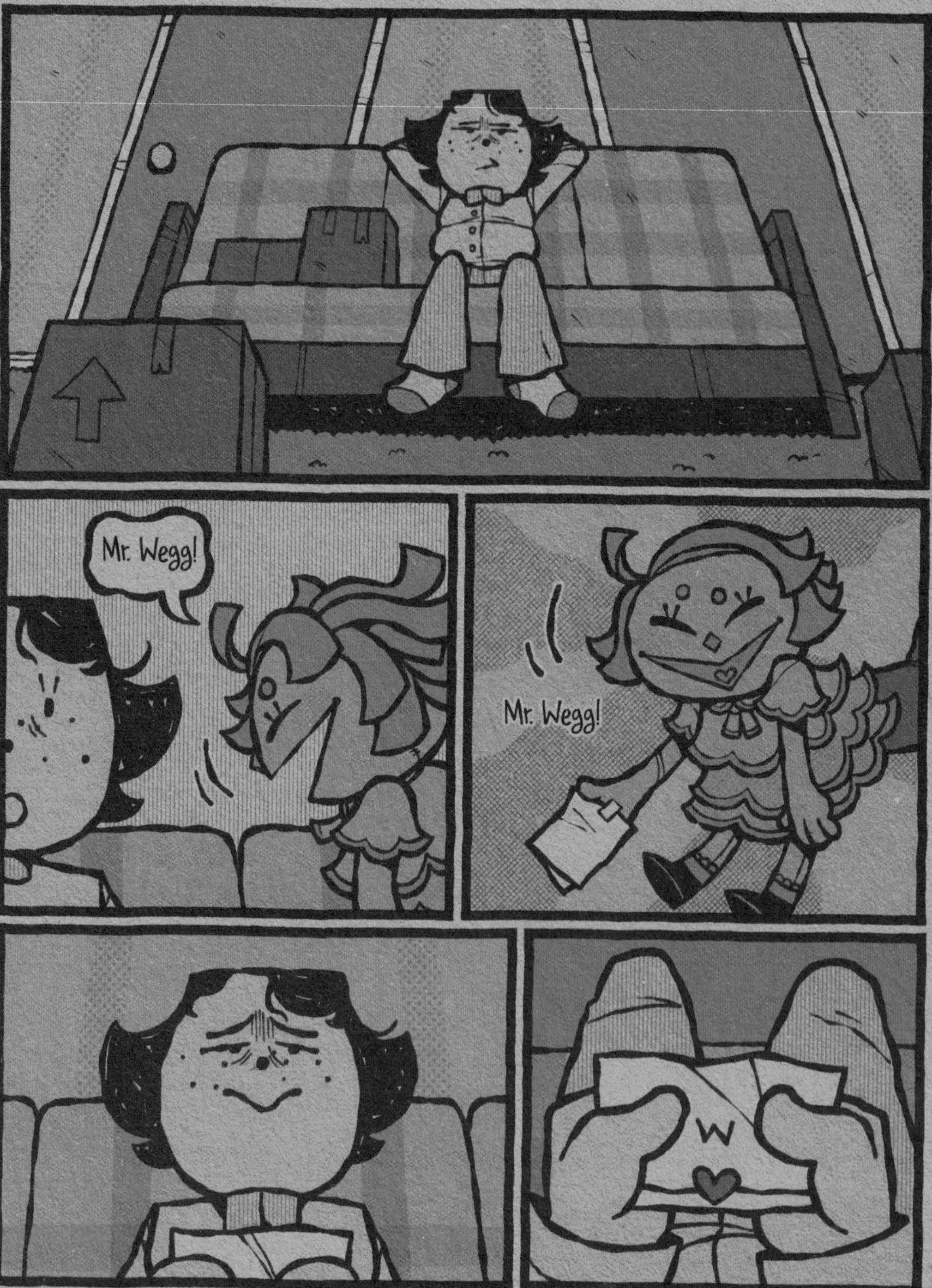
Mr. Wegg!
Mr. Wegg!
W

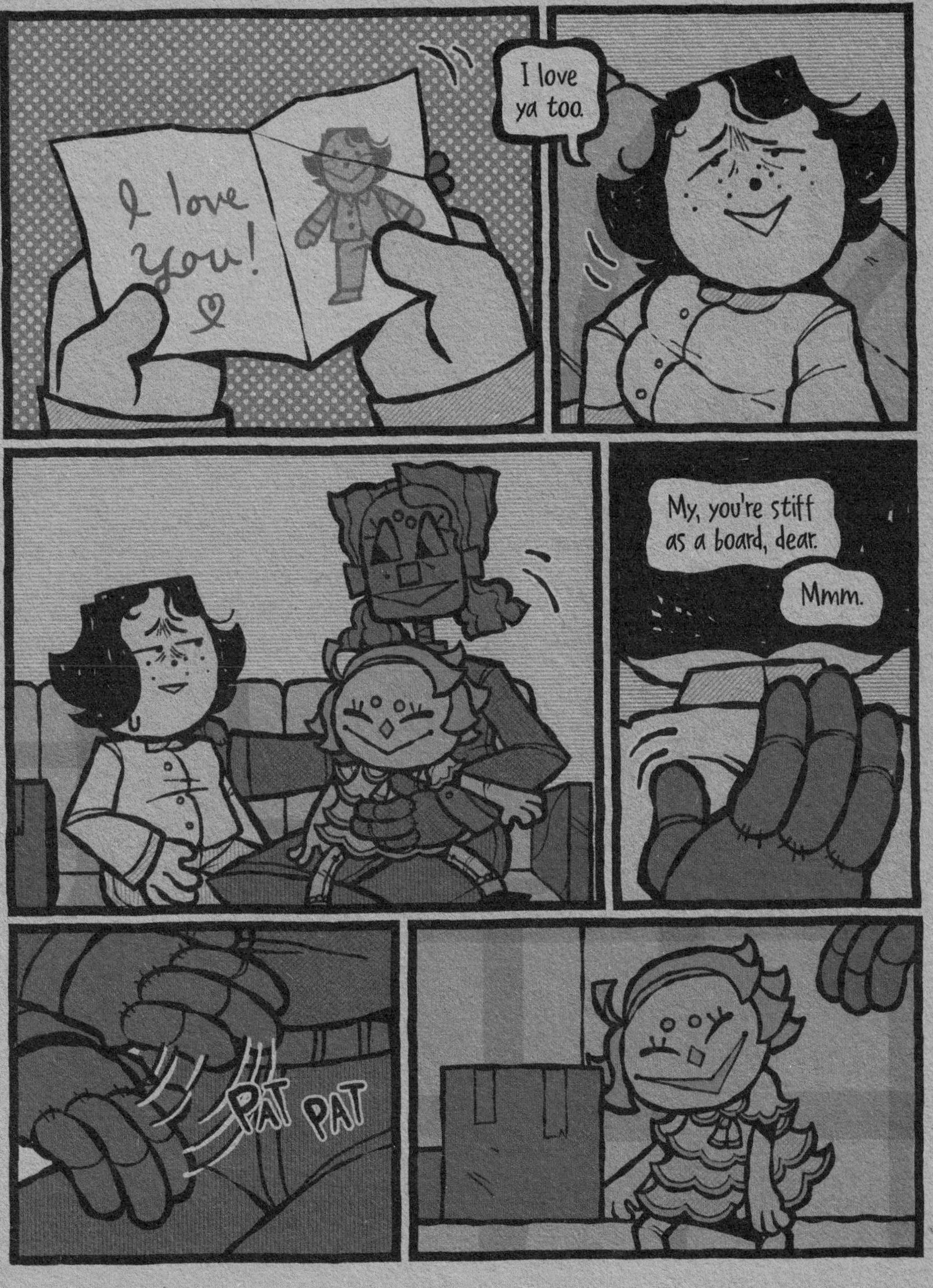
I love you!
I love ya too.
My, you're stiff as a board, dear.
Mmm.
PAT PAT

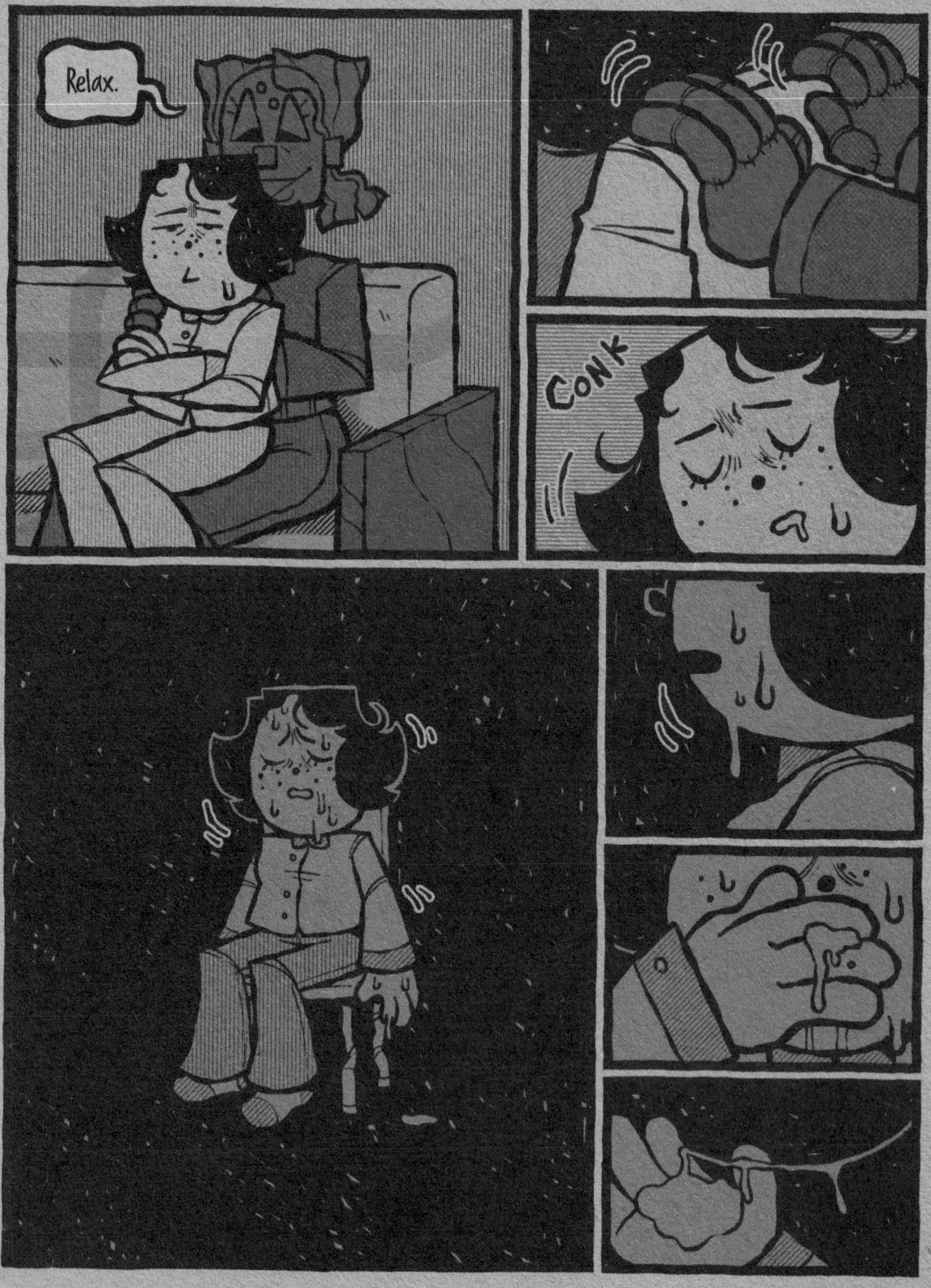
Relax.
CONK

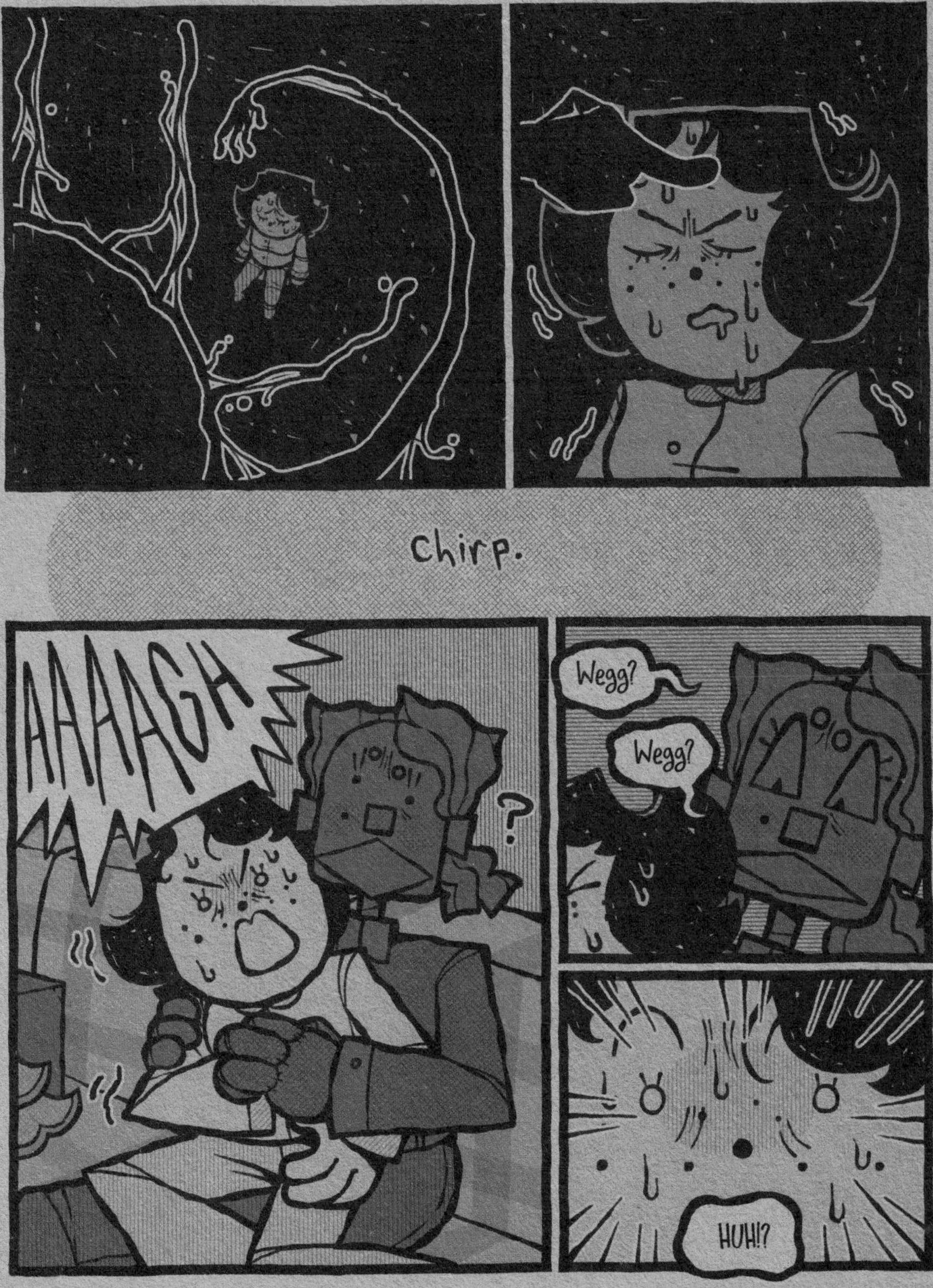
Chirp.
AAAAGH
?
Wegg?
Wegg?
HUH!?

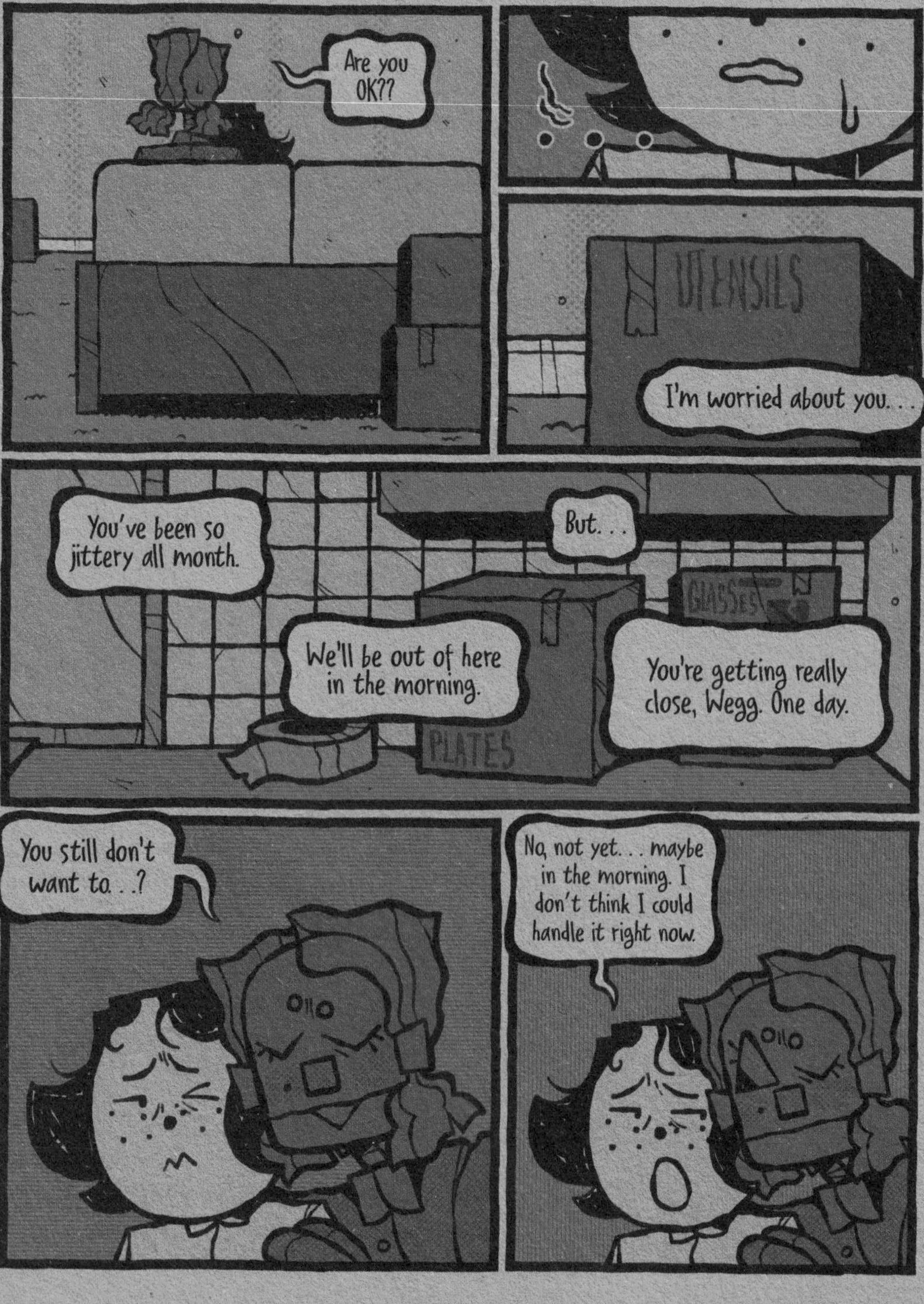
Are you OK??
I'm worried about you. . .
You've been so jittery all month.
But. . .
We'll be out of here in the morning.
You're getting really close, Wegg. One day.
You still don't want to. . ?
No, not yet. . . maybe in the morning. I don't think I could handle it right now.

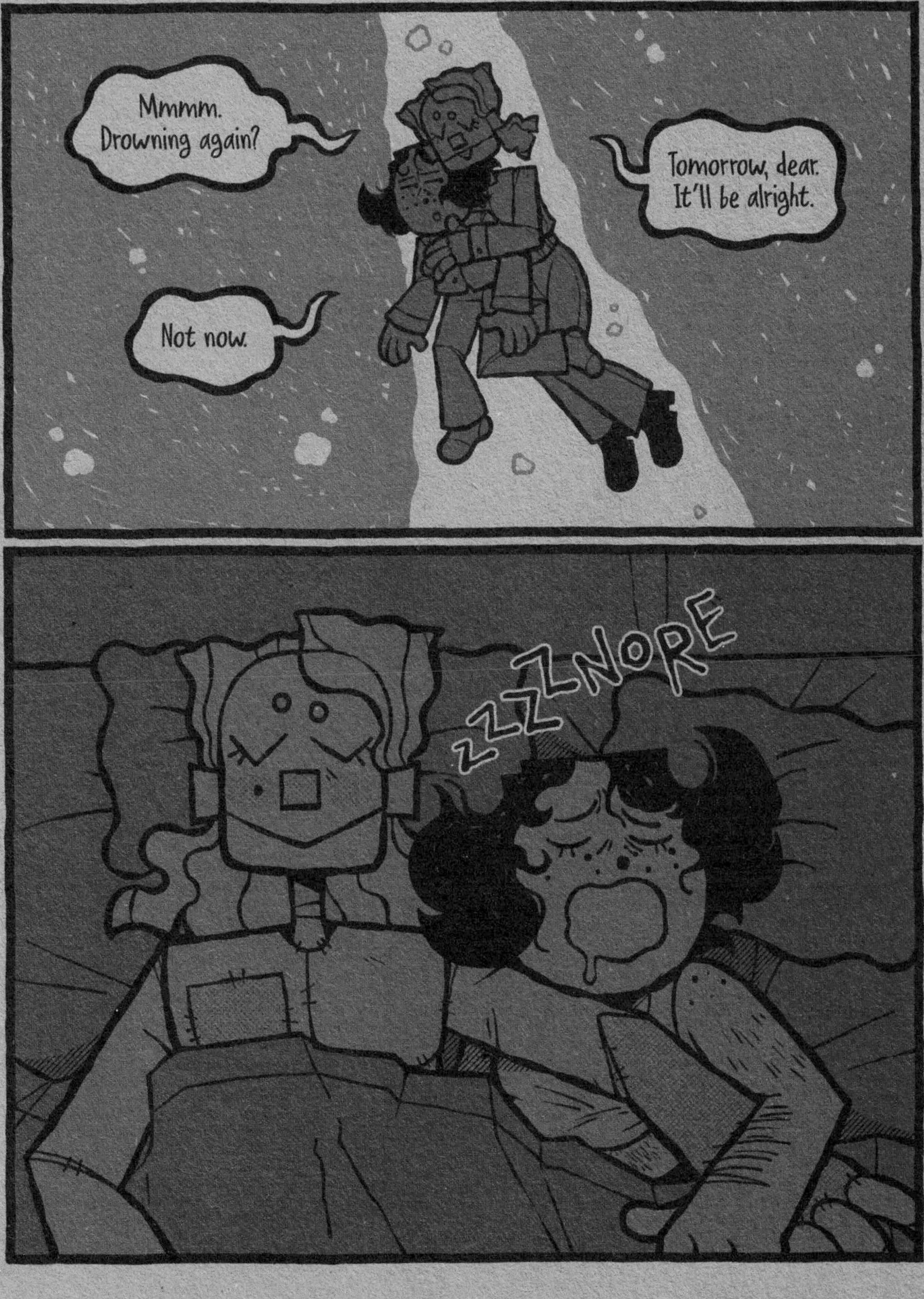
Mmmm.
Drowning again?
Tomorrow, dear.
It'll be alright.
Not now.
ZZZZNORE

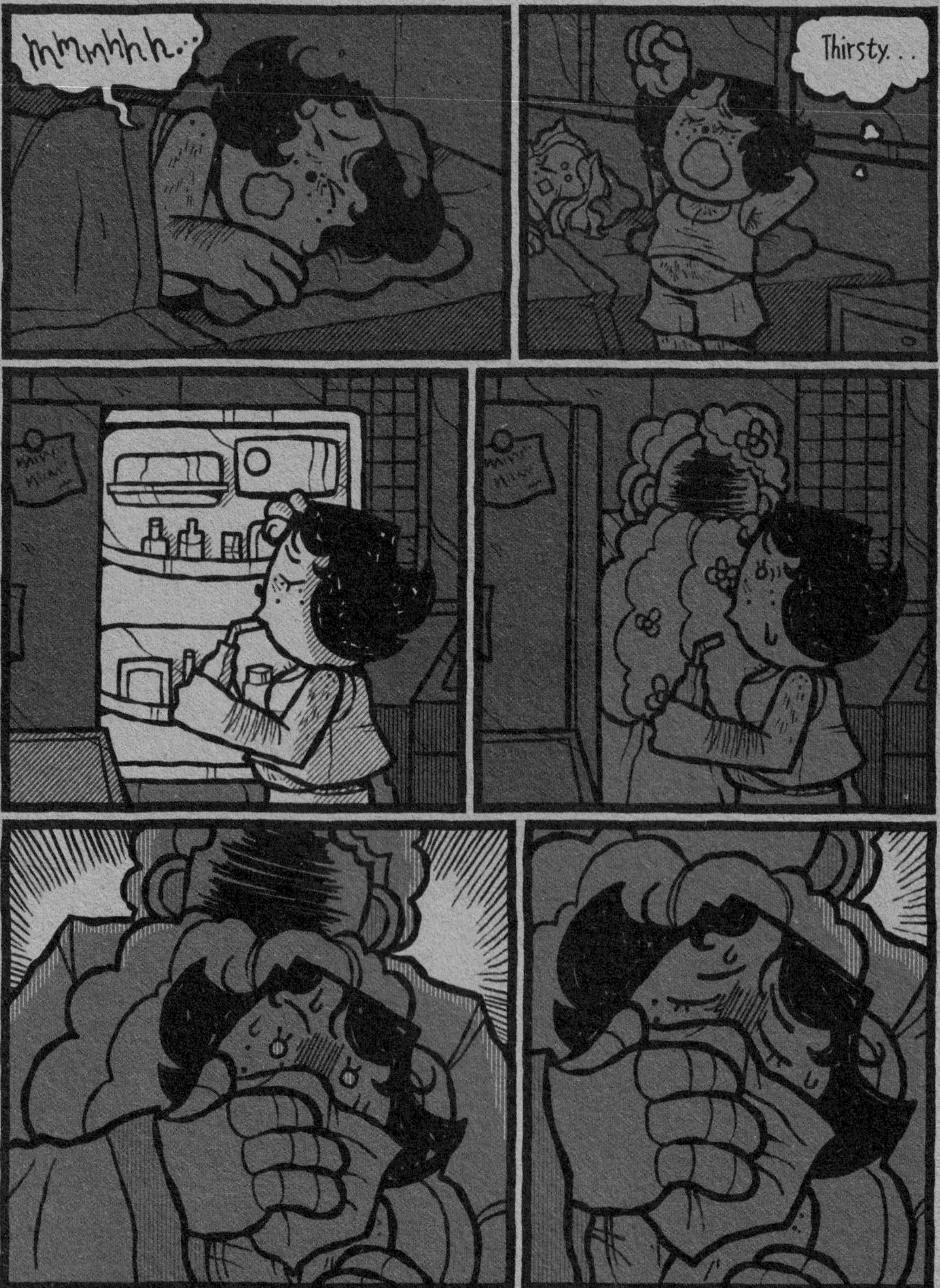
hmnhhh...
Thirsty...

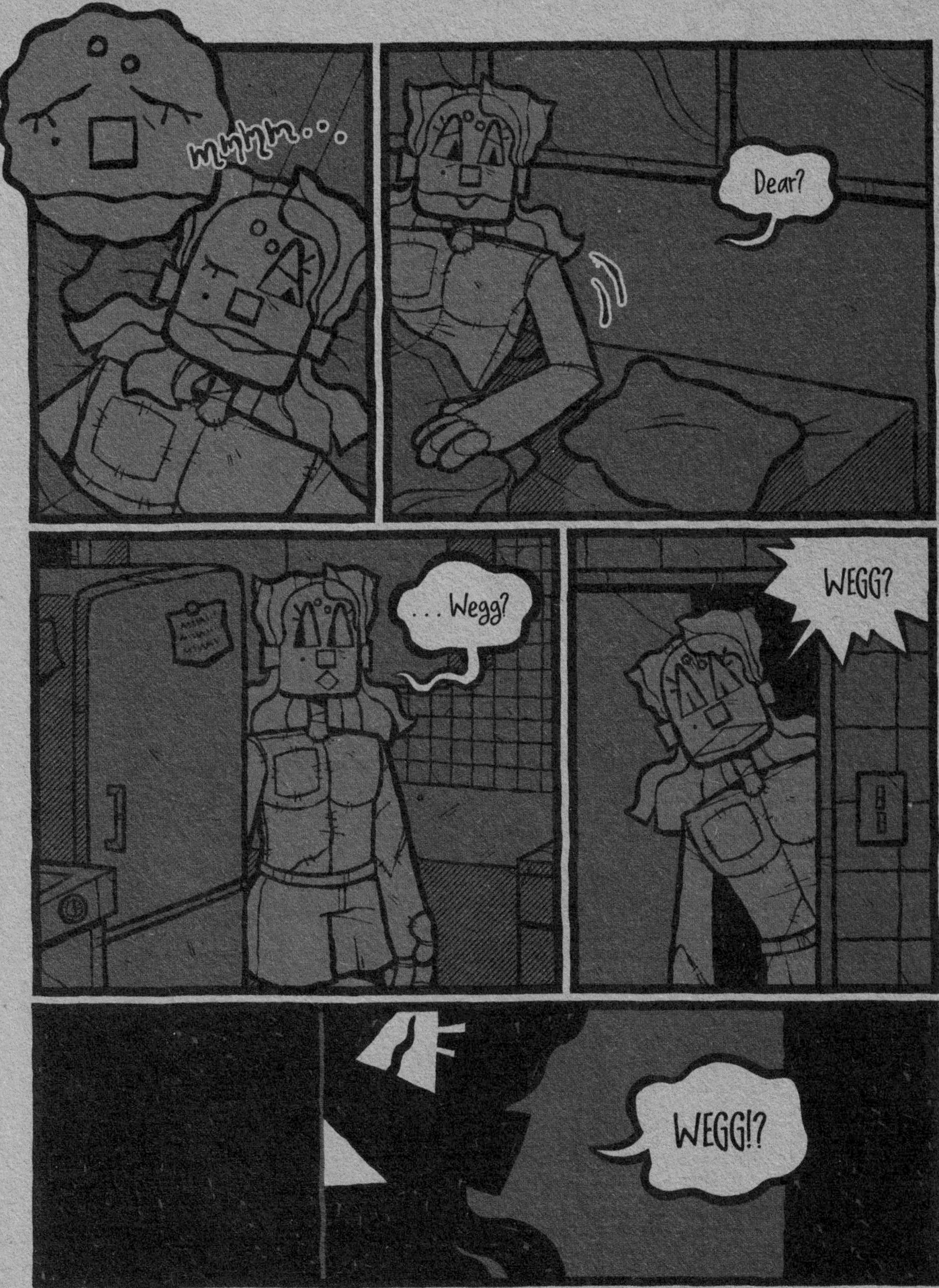
Mnmnn...
Dear?
...Wegg?
WEGG?
WEGG!?

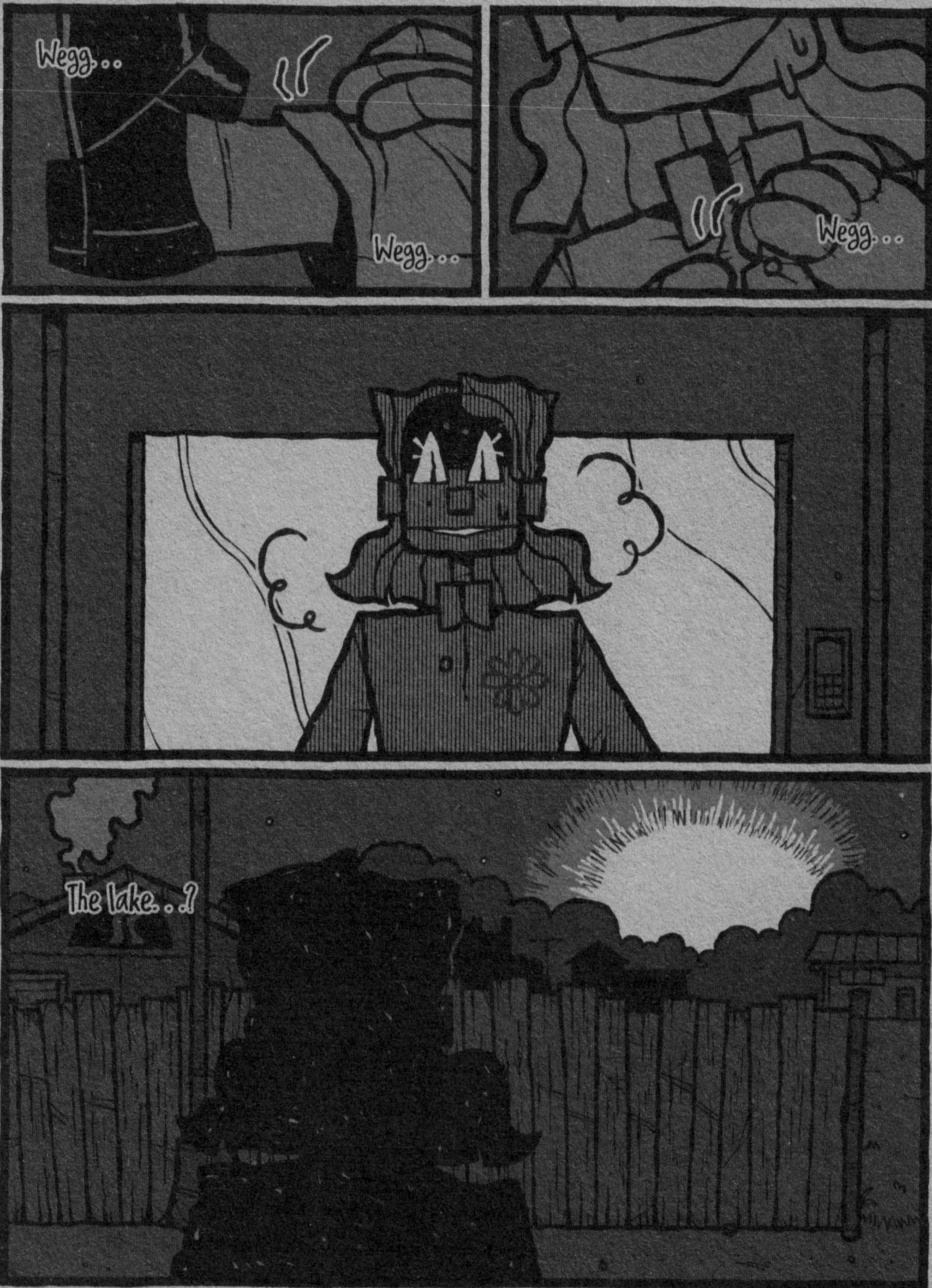
Wegg. . .
Wegg. . .
Wegg. . .
The lake. . .?

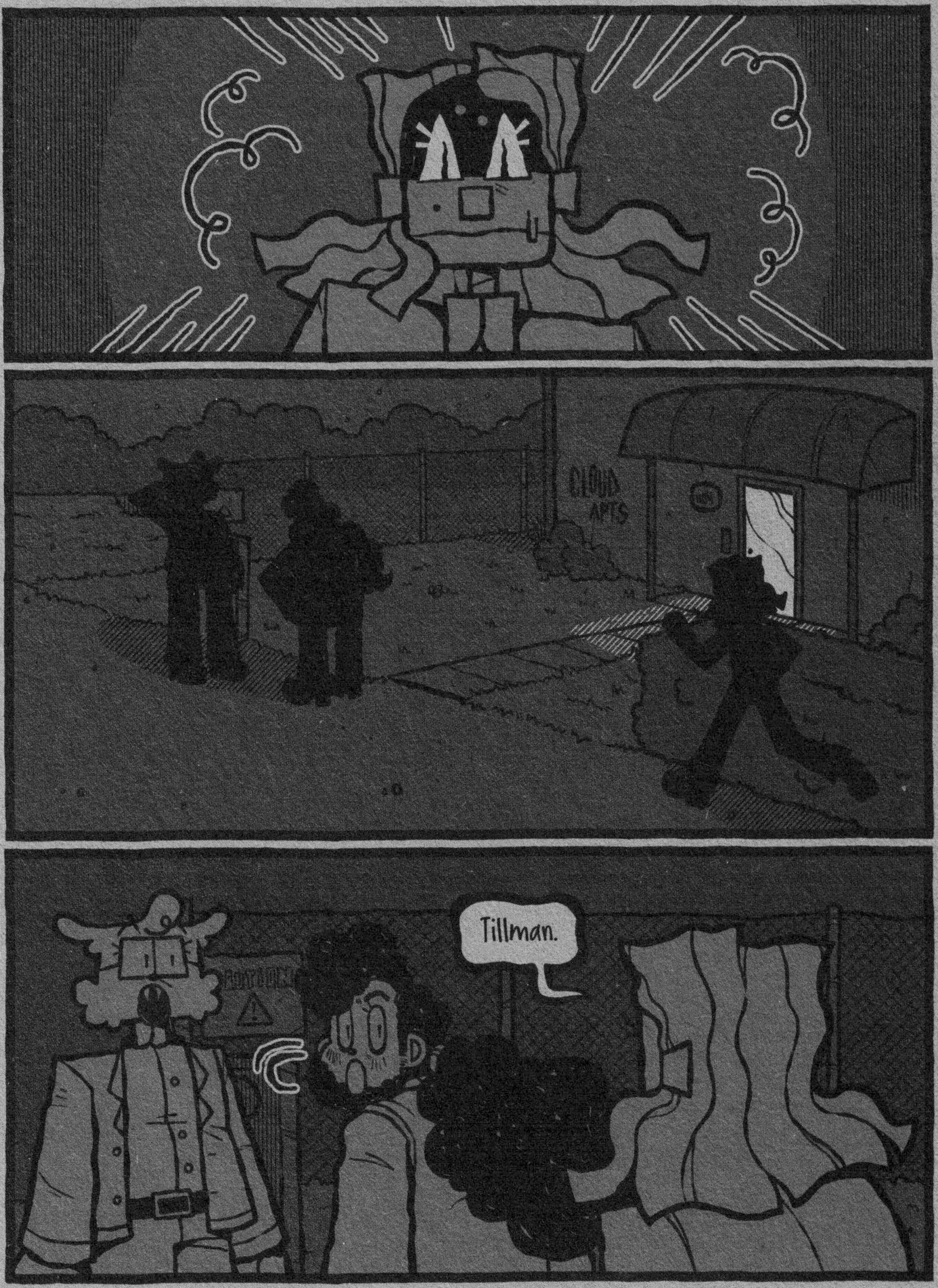
CLOUD APTS
Tillman.

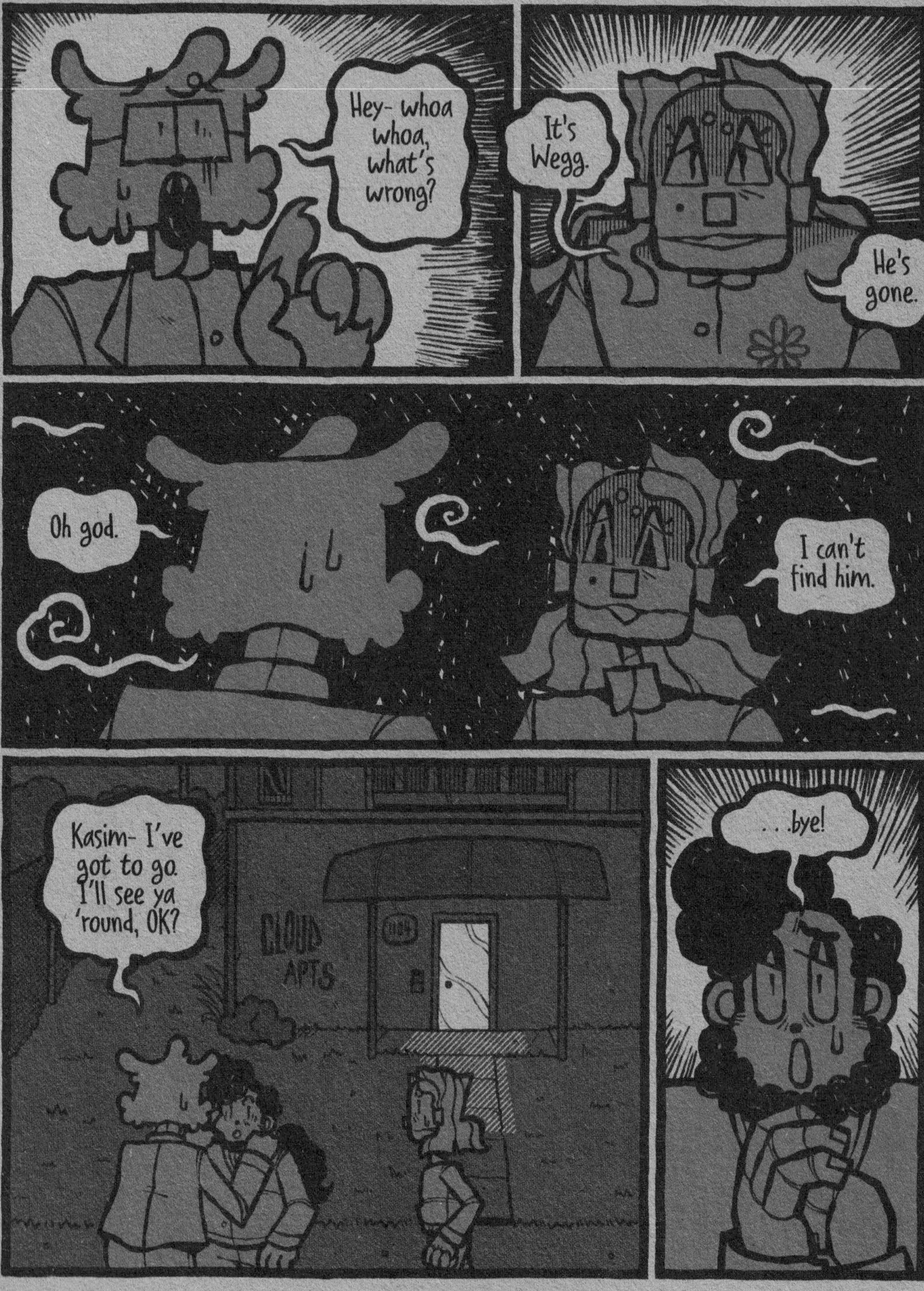
Hey- whoa whoa, what's wrong?
It's Wegg.
He's gone.
Oh god.
I can't find him.
Kasim- I've got to go. I'll see ya 'round, OK?
CLOUD APTS
. . .bye!

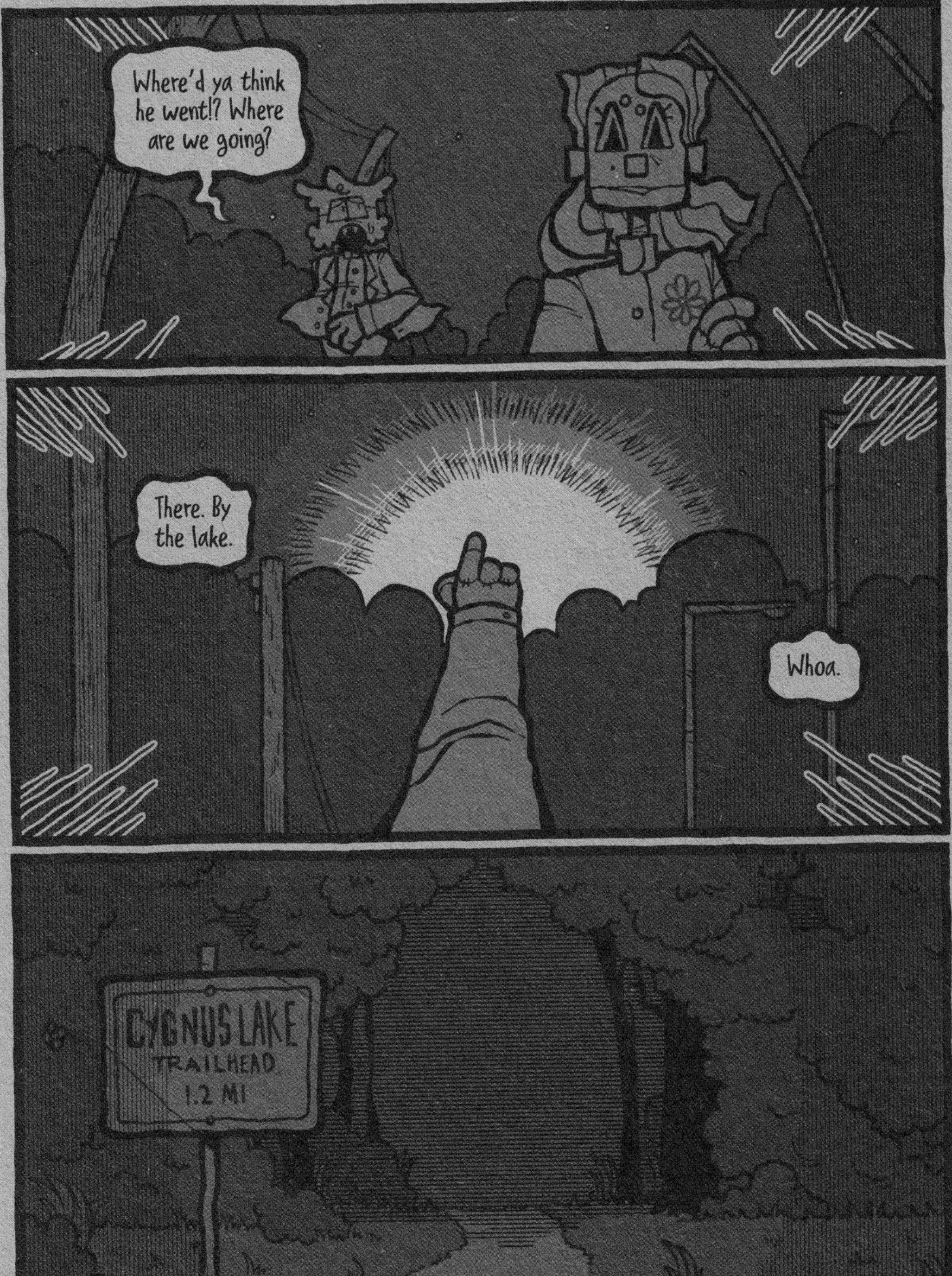
Where'd ya think he went!? Where are we going?
There. By the lake.
Whoa.
CYGNUS LAKE
TRAILHEAD
1.2 MI

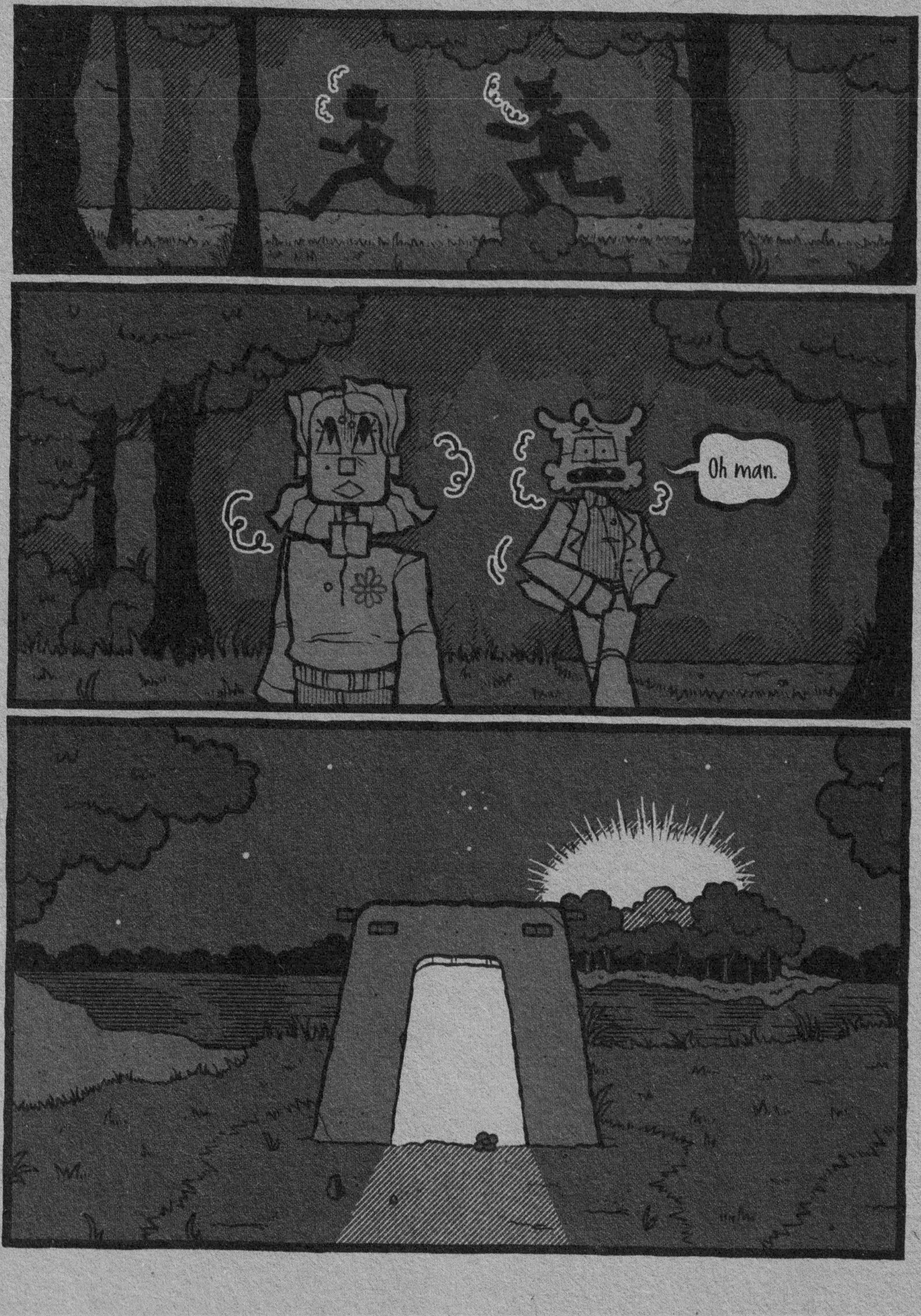
Oh man.

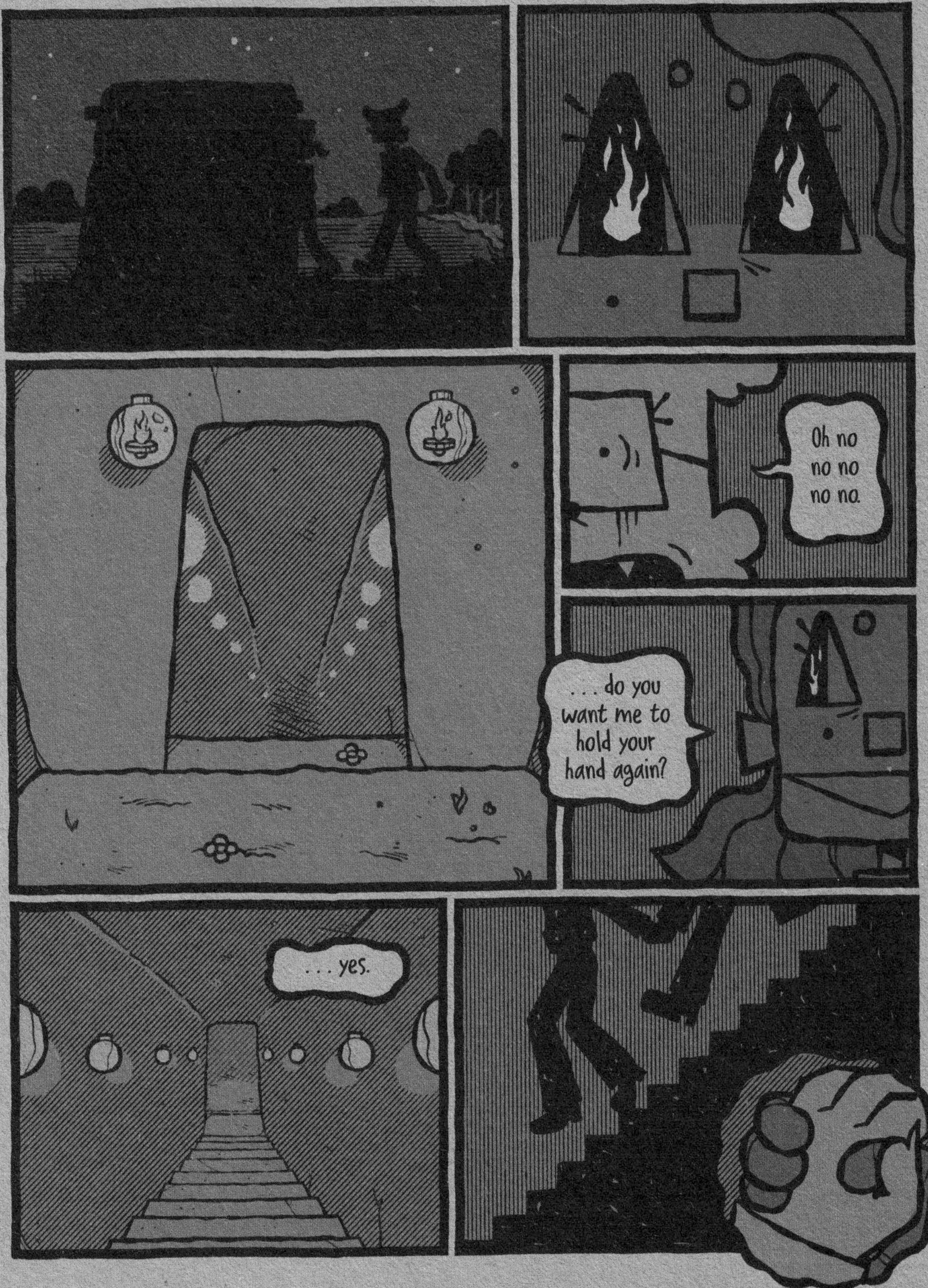

Oh no no no no no.
. . . do you want me to hold your hand again?
. . . yes.

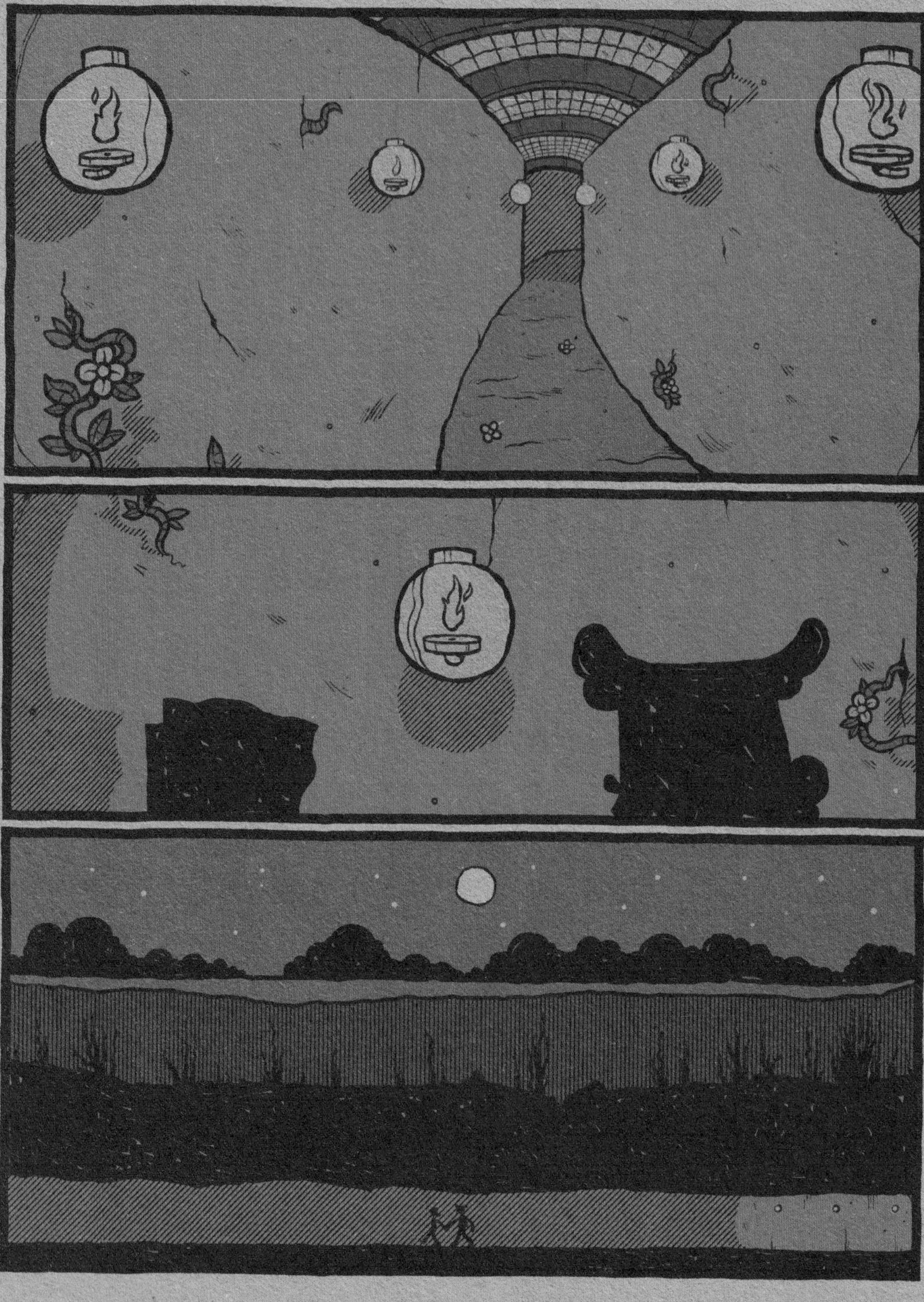

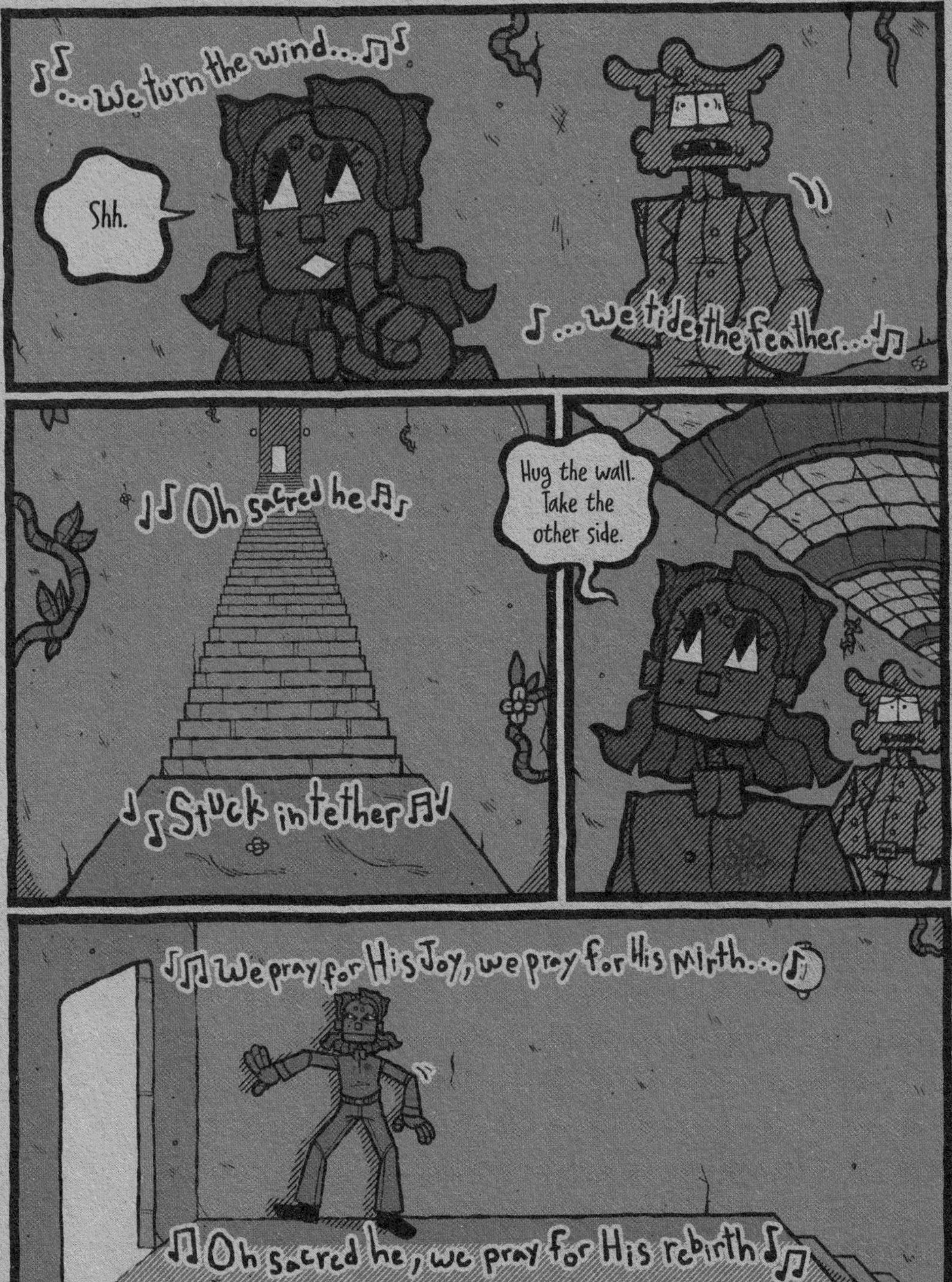
...We turn the wind...
Shh.
...we tide the feather...
Oh sacred he
Stuck in tether
Hug the wall. Take the other side.
We pray for His Joy, we pray for His Mirth...
Oh sacred he, we pray for His rebirth

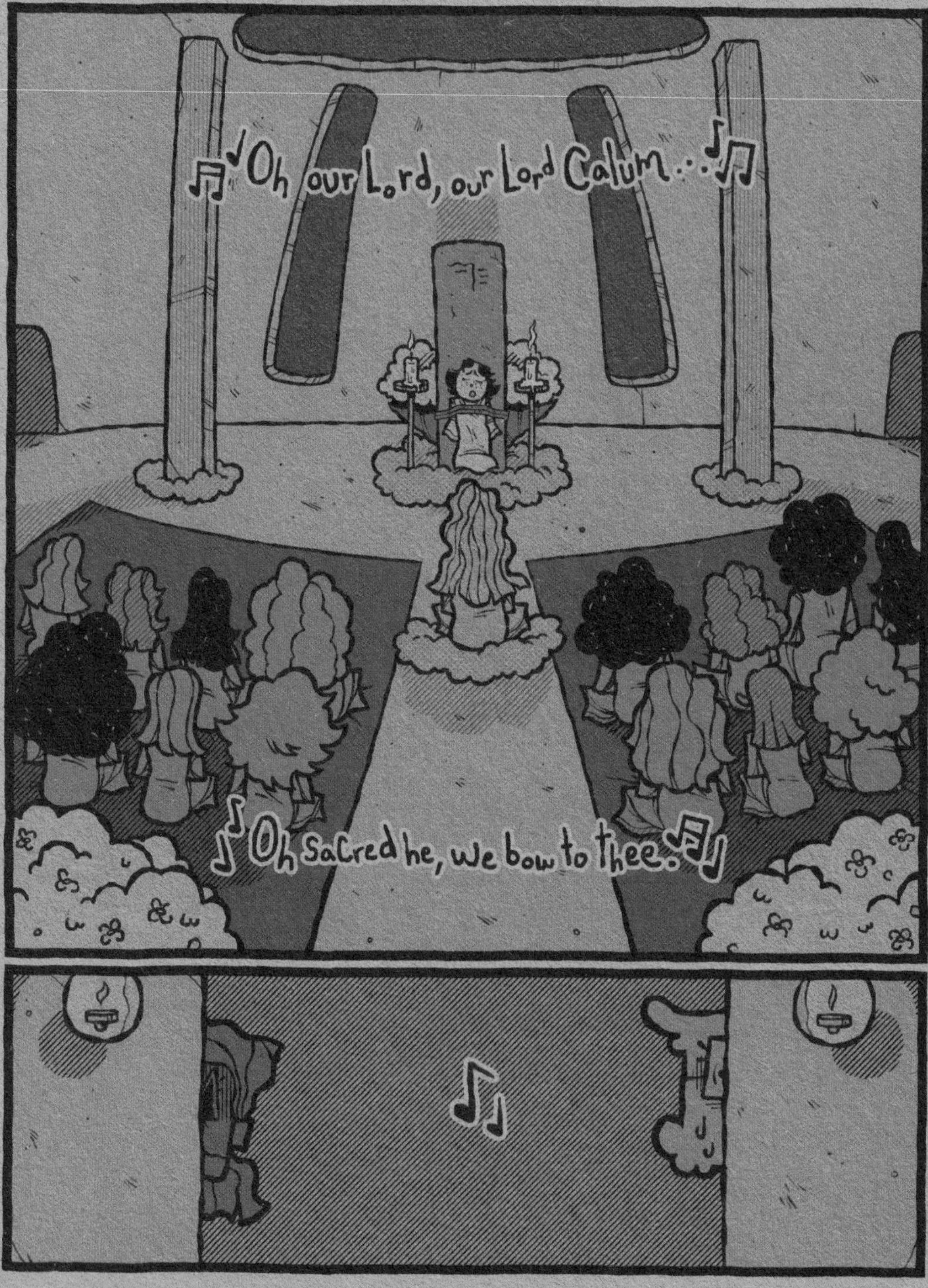
Oh our Lord, our Lord Calum...
Oh sacred he, we bow to thee.

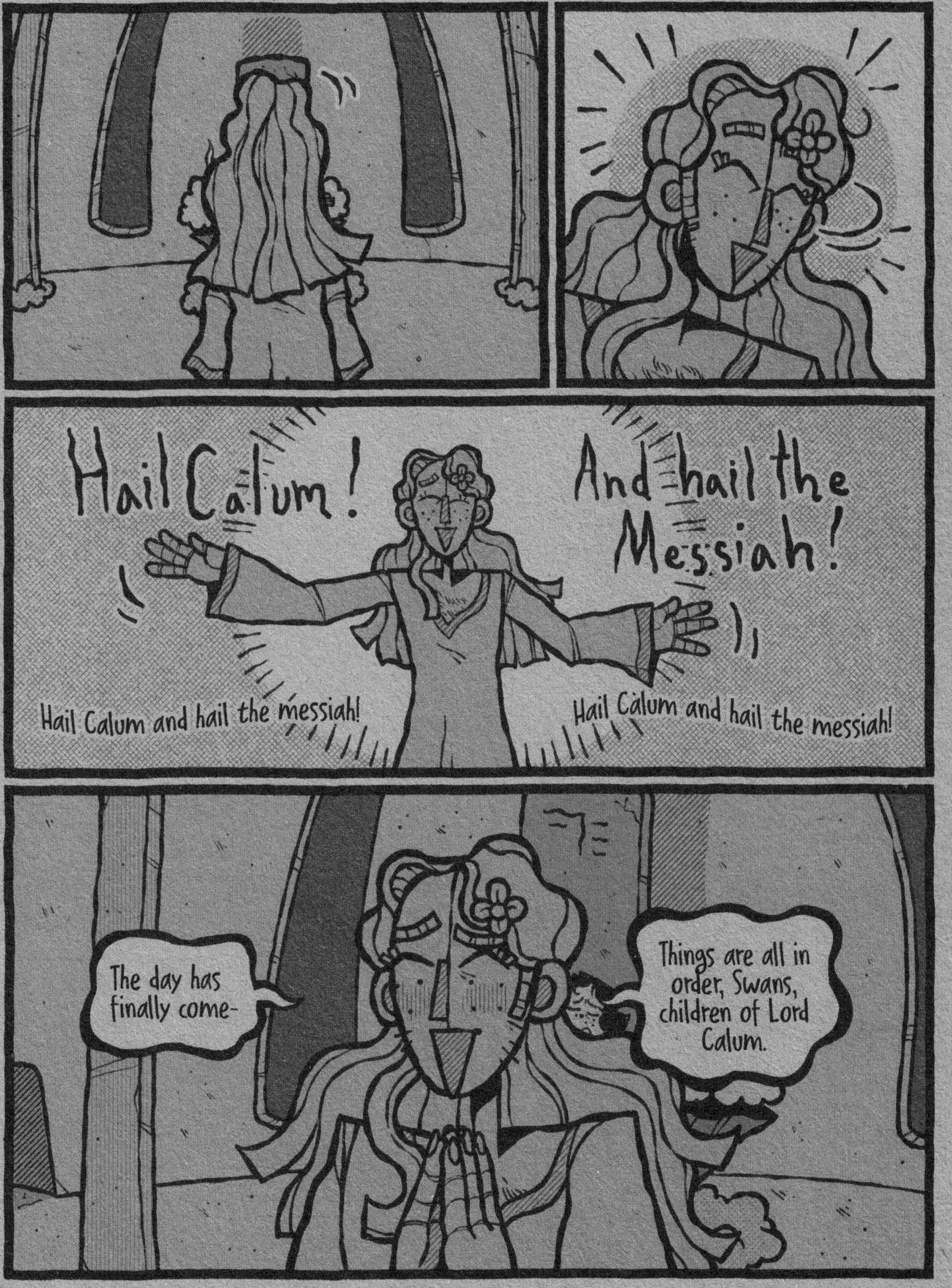
Hail Calum!
And hail the Messiah!
Hail Calum and hail the messiah!
Hail Calum and hail the messiah!
The day has finally come-
Things are all in order, Swans, children of Lord Calum.

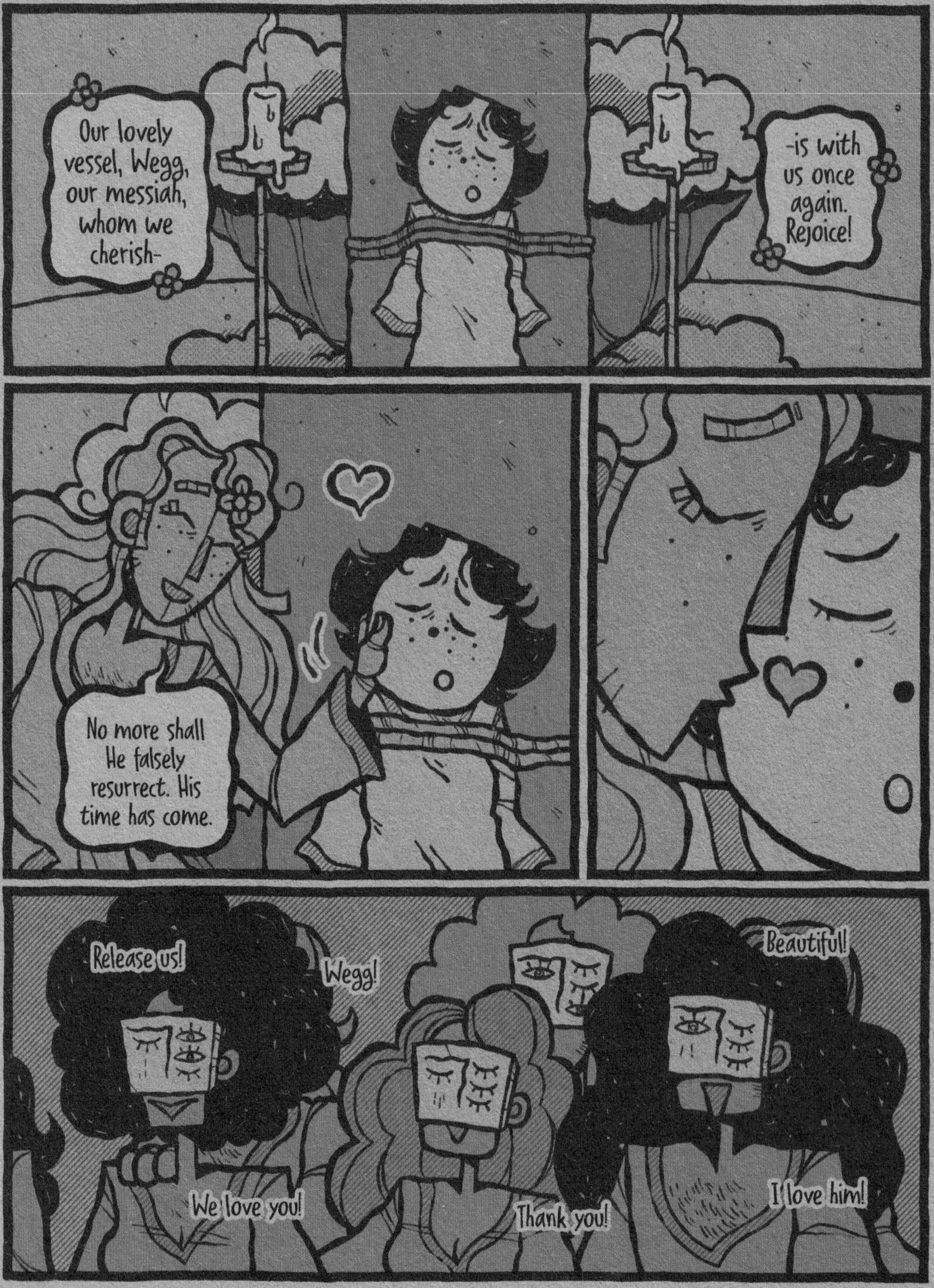
Our lovely vessel, Wegg, our messiah, whom we cherish-
-is with us once again. Rejoice!
No more shall He falsely resurrect. His time has come.
Release us!
Wegg!
Beautiful!
We love you!
Thank you!
I love him!

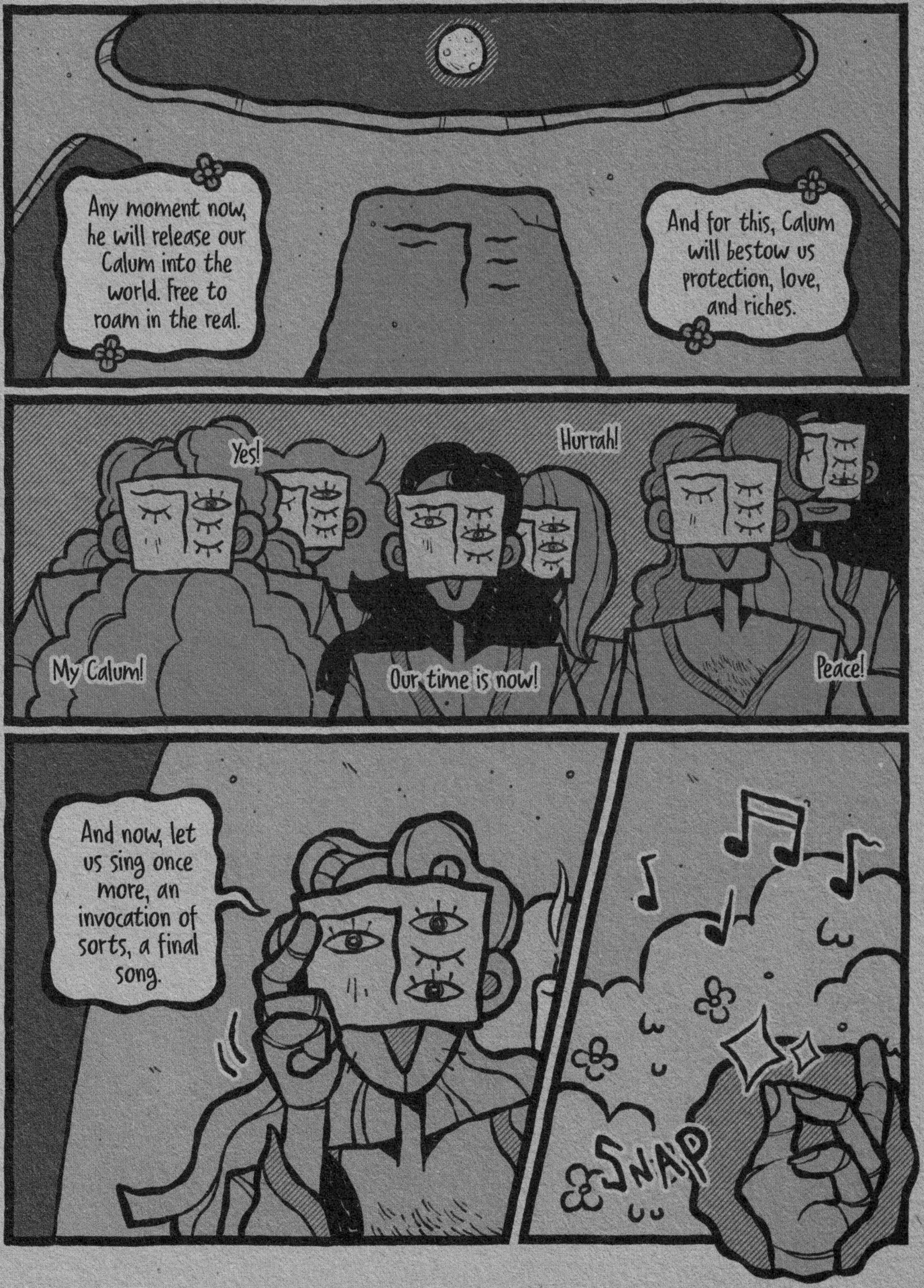

Any moment now, he will release our Calum into the world. Free to roam in the real.
And for this, Calum will bestow us protection, love, and riches.
Yes!
Hurrah!
My Calum!
Our time is now!
Peace!
And now, let us sing once more, an invocation of sorts, a final song.
SNAP

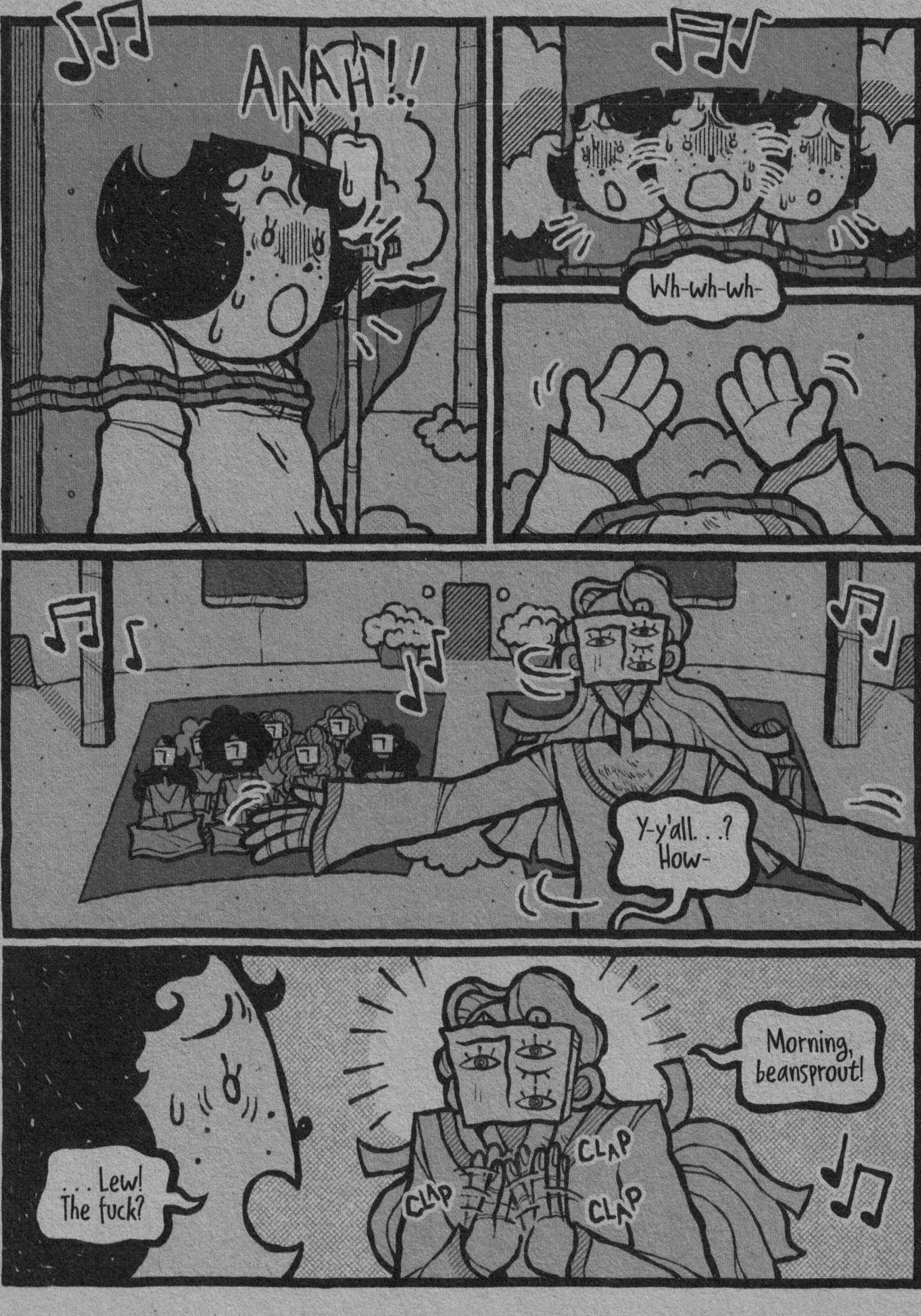
AAAH!!
Wh-wh-wh-
Y-y'all. . .?
How-
Morning,
beansprout!
CLAP
CLAP
CLAP
. . . Lew!
The fuck?

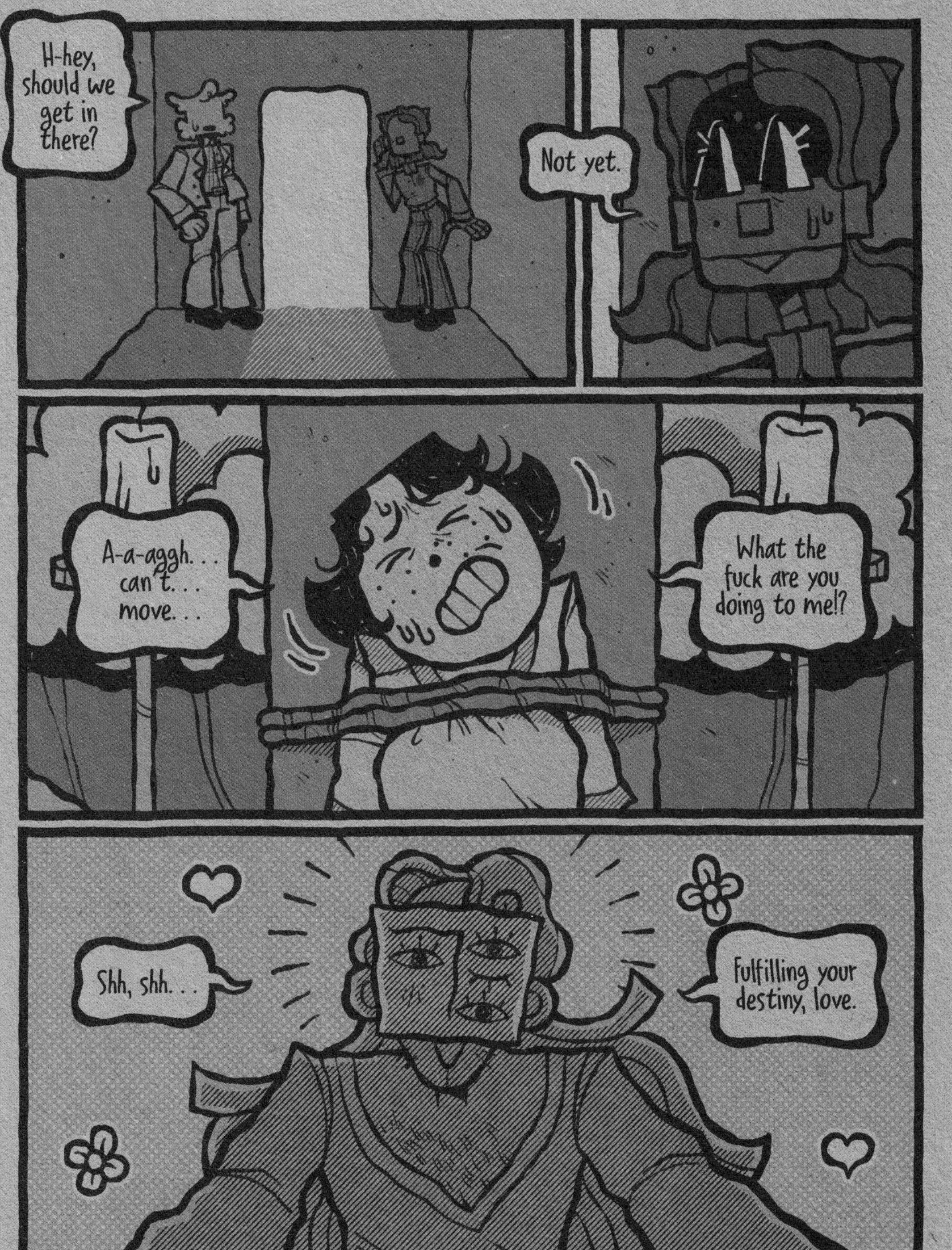
H-hey, should we get in there?
Not yet.
A-a-aggh... can't... move...
What the fuck are you doing to me!?
Shh, shh...
Fulfilling your destiny, love.

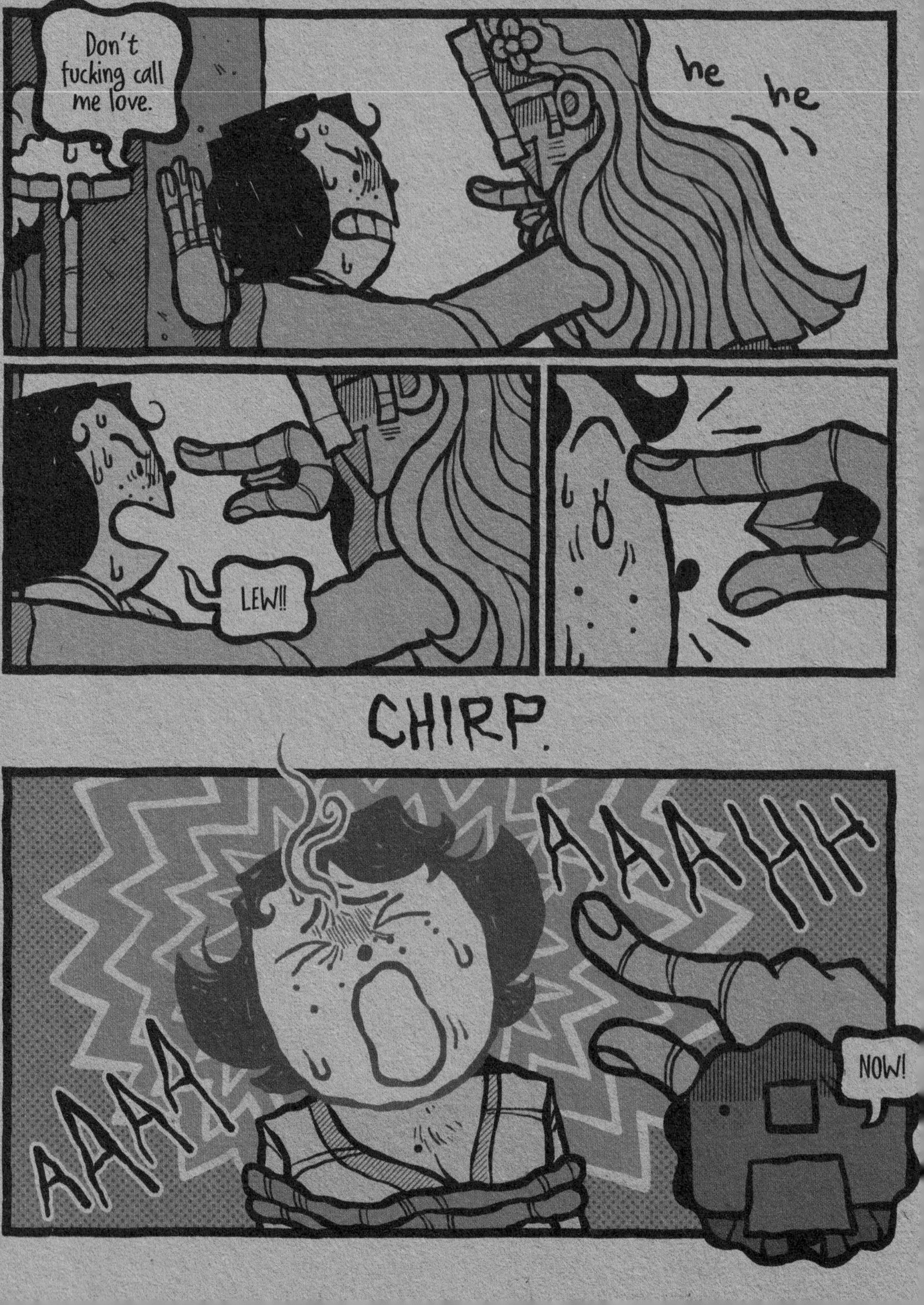
Don't fucking call me love.
he he
LEW!!
CHIRP.
AAAAAAAHH
NOW!

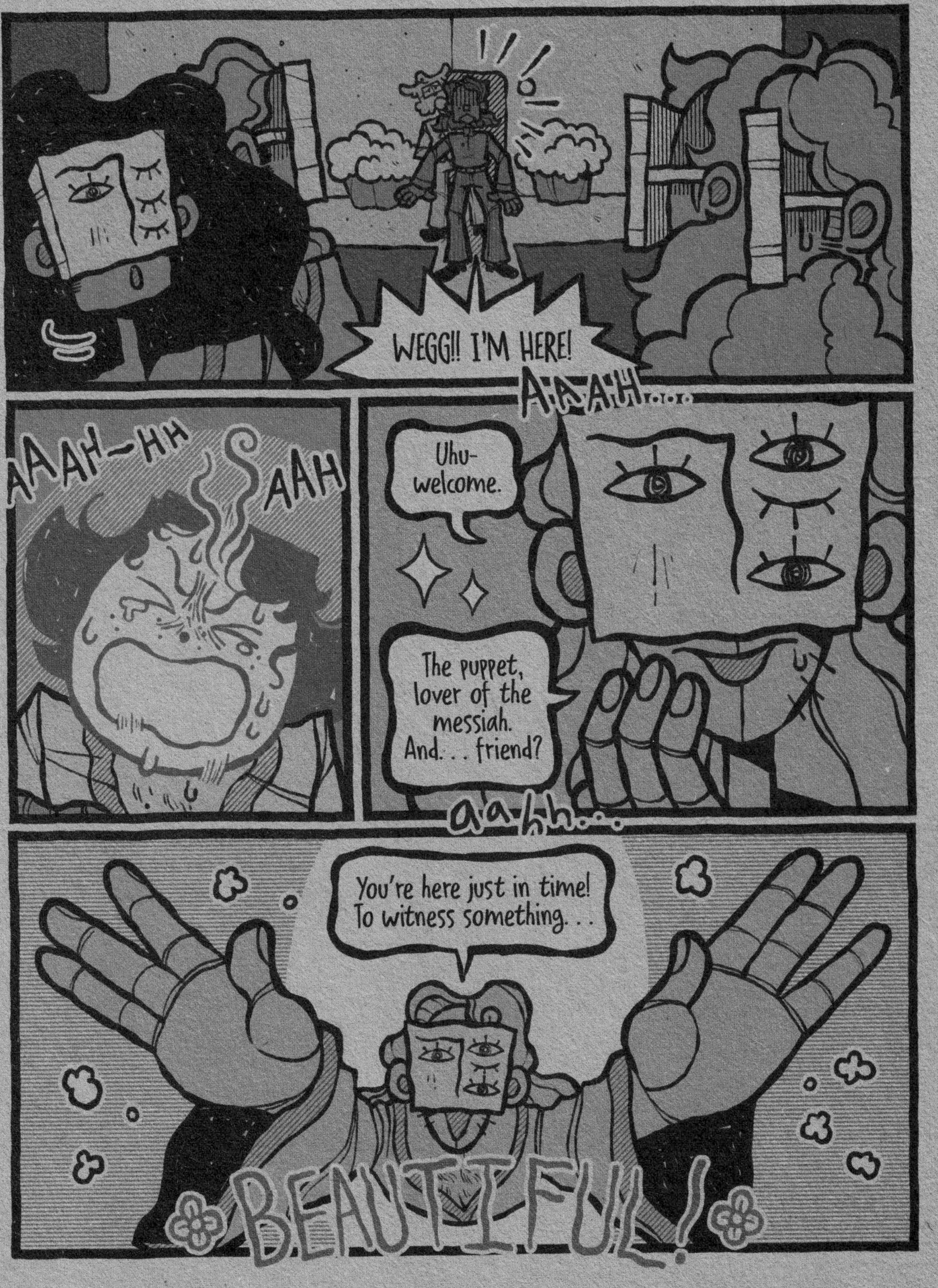
WEGG!! I'M HERE!
AAAH...
AAAH-HH
AAH
Uhu-welcome.
The puppet, lover of the messiah. And... friend?
aahh...
You're here just in time! To witness something...
BEAUTIFUL!

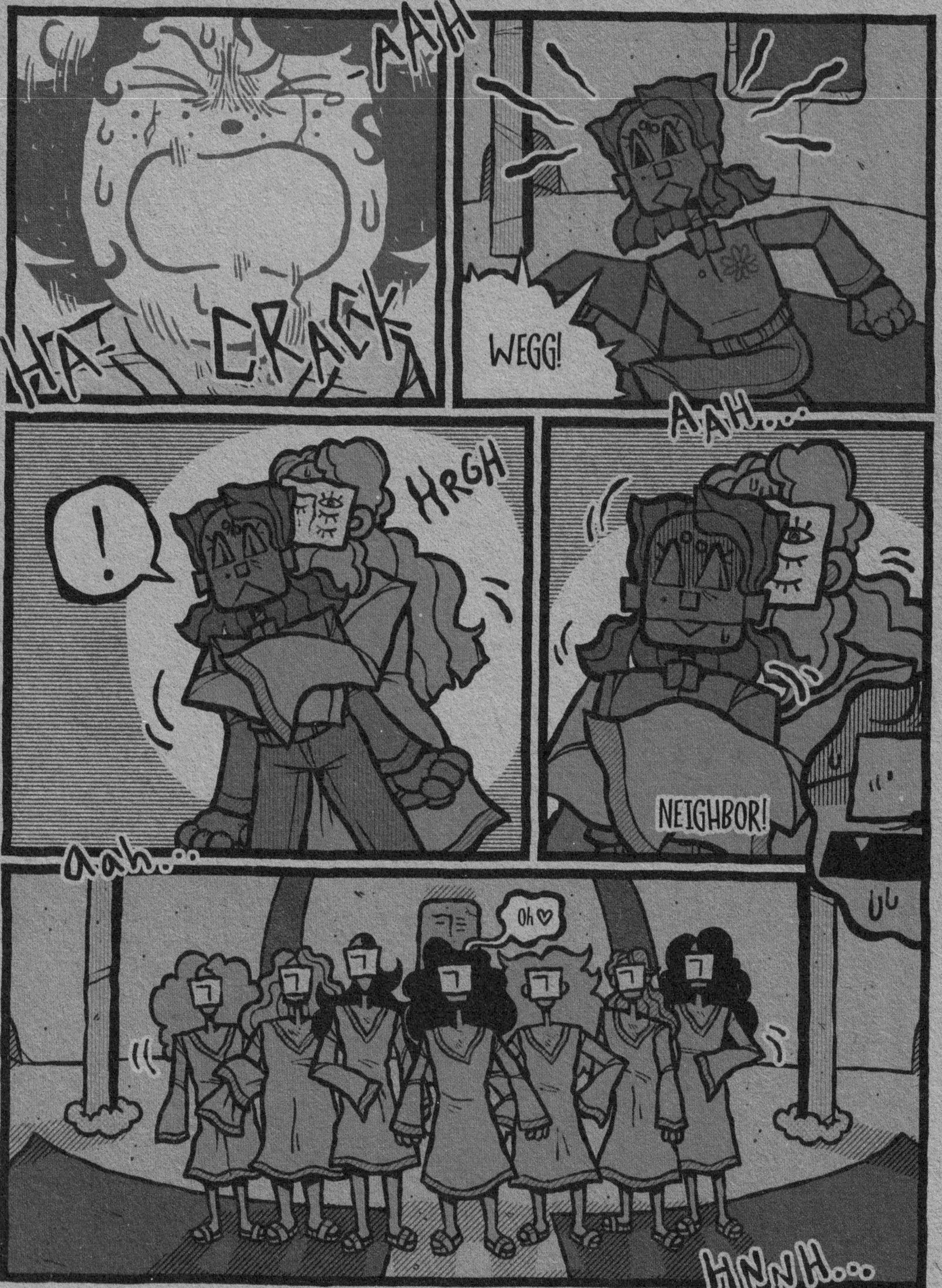
AAH
HA
CRACK
WEGG!
!
HRGH
AAH...
NEIGHBOR!
aah...
Oh♡
HNNH...

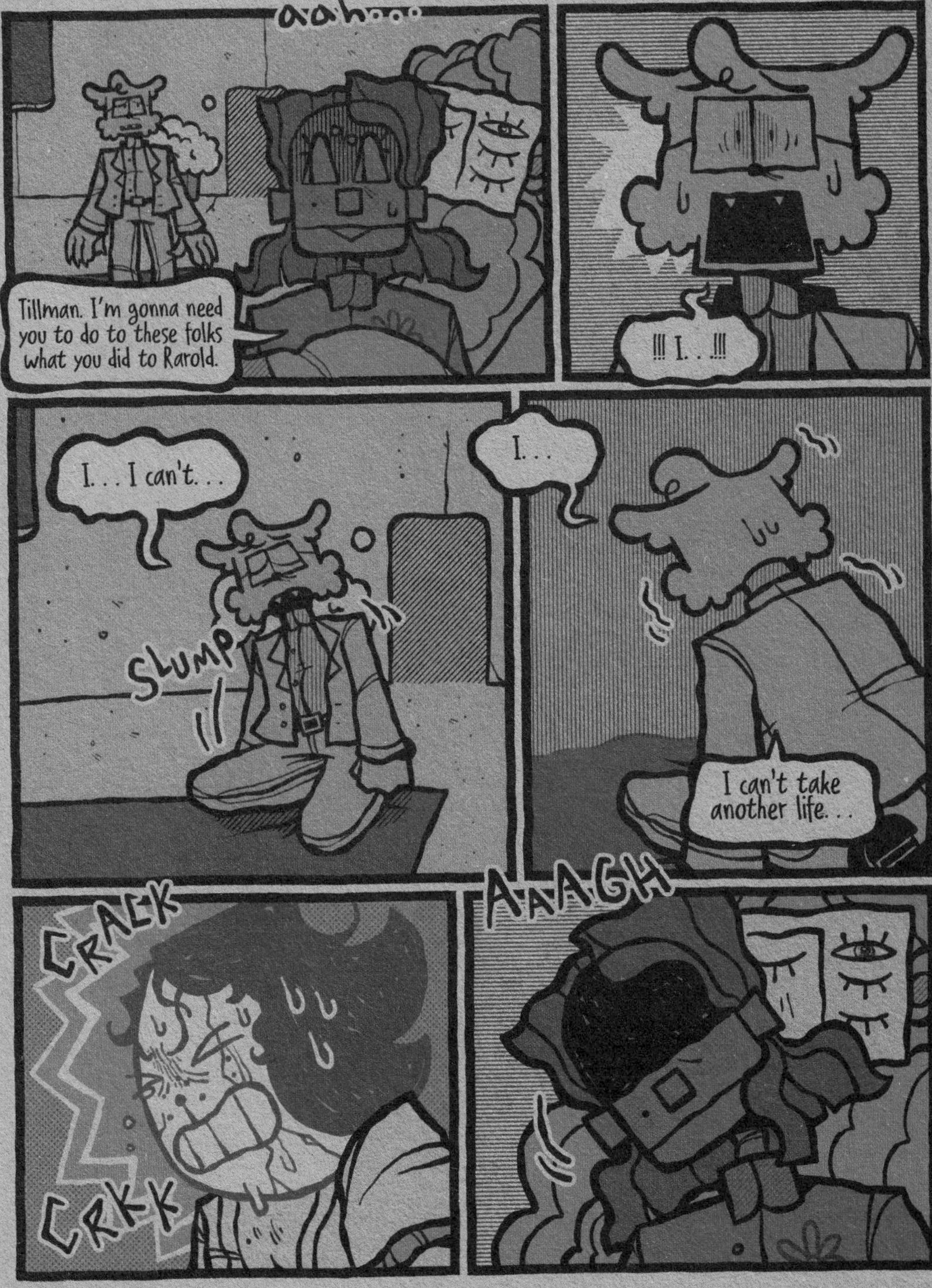
aah...
Tillman. I'm gonna need you to do to these folks what you did to Rarold.
!!! I. . .!!!
I. . . I can't. . .
SLUMP
I. . .
I can't take another life. . .
CRACK
CRKK
AAAGH

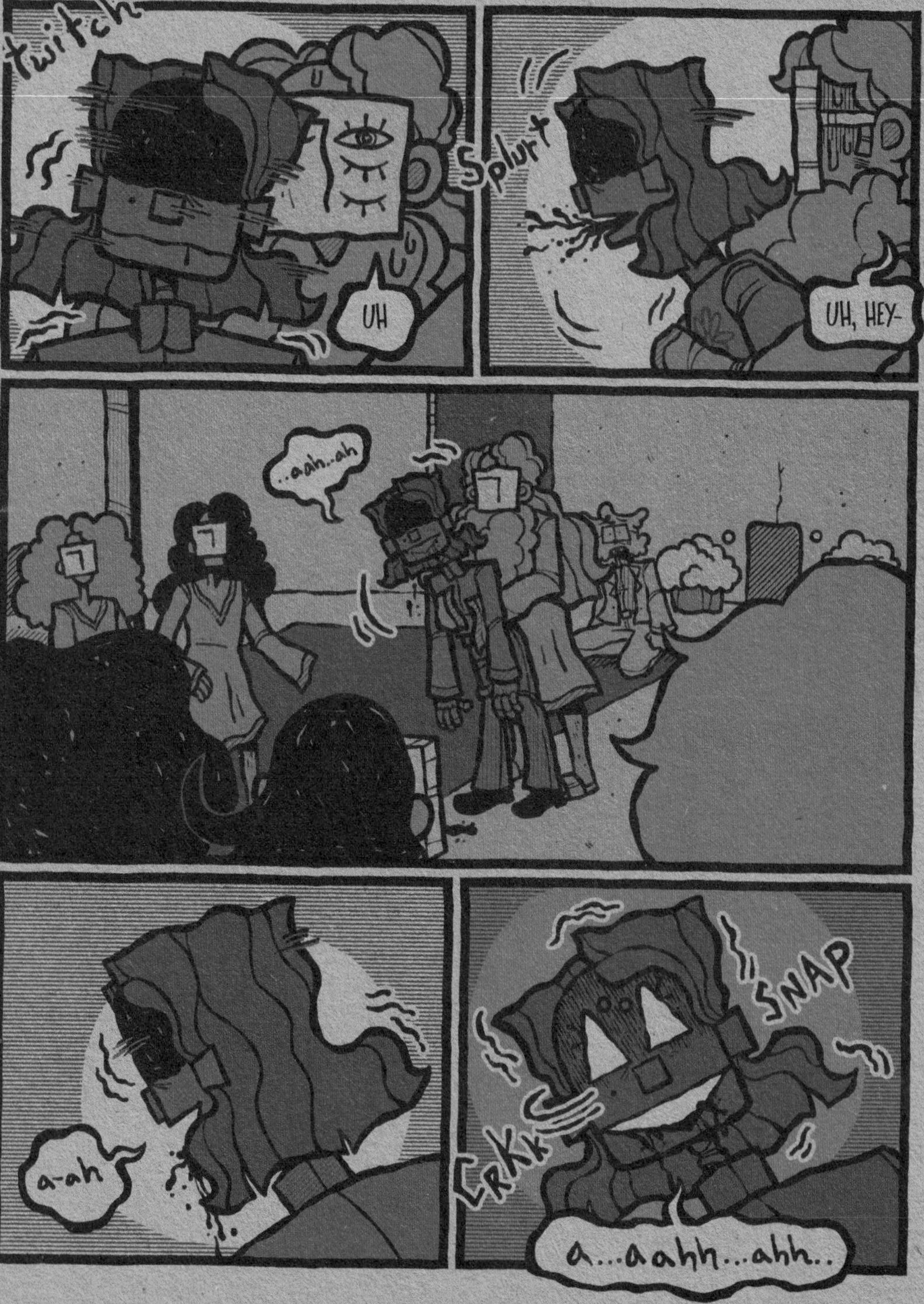
twitch
UH
Splurt
UH, HEY-
..aah..ah
a-ah
CRKK
SNAP
a...aahh...ahh..

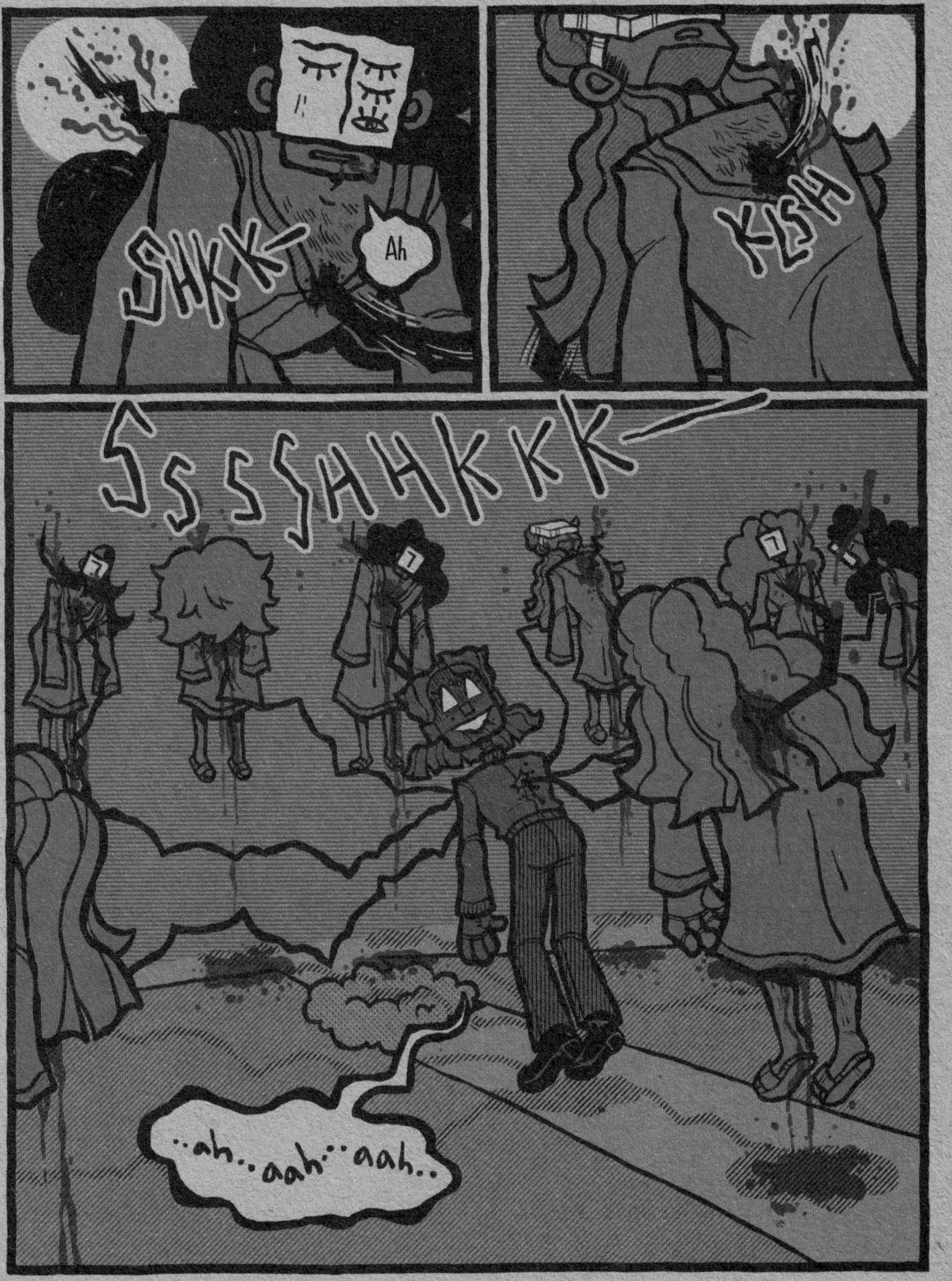
SHKK—
Ah
KLSH
SSSSAHKKK—
..ah...aah...aah..

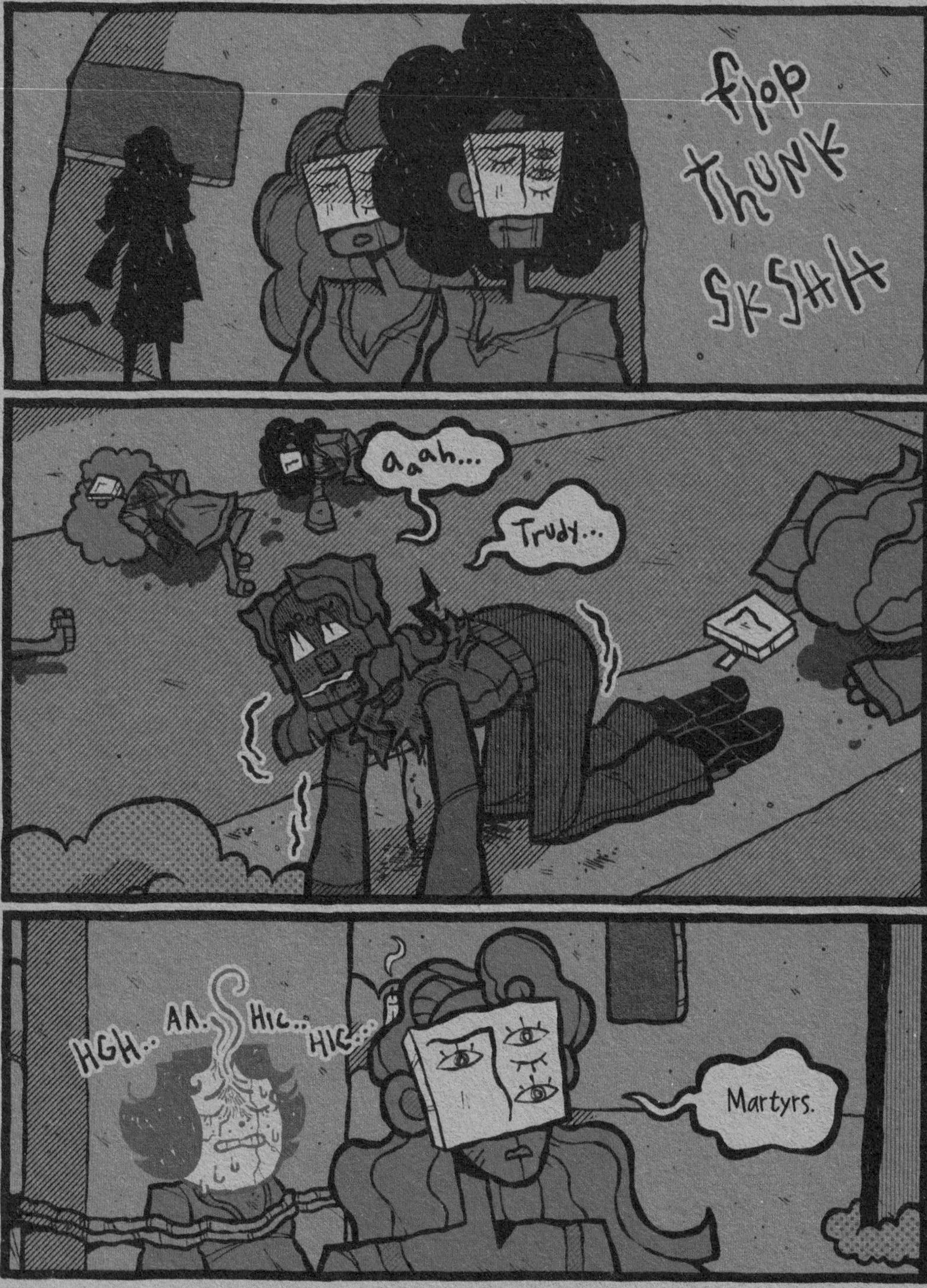
flop
THUNK
SKSHH
aaaah...
Trudy...
HGH.. AA. HIC... HIC...
Martyrs.

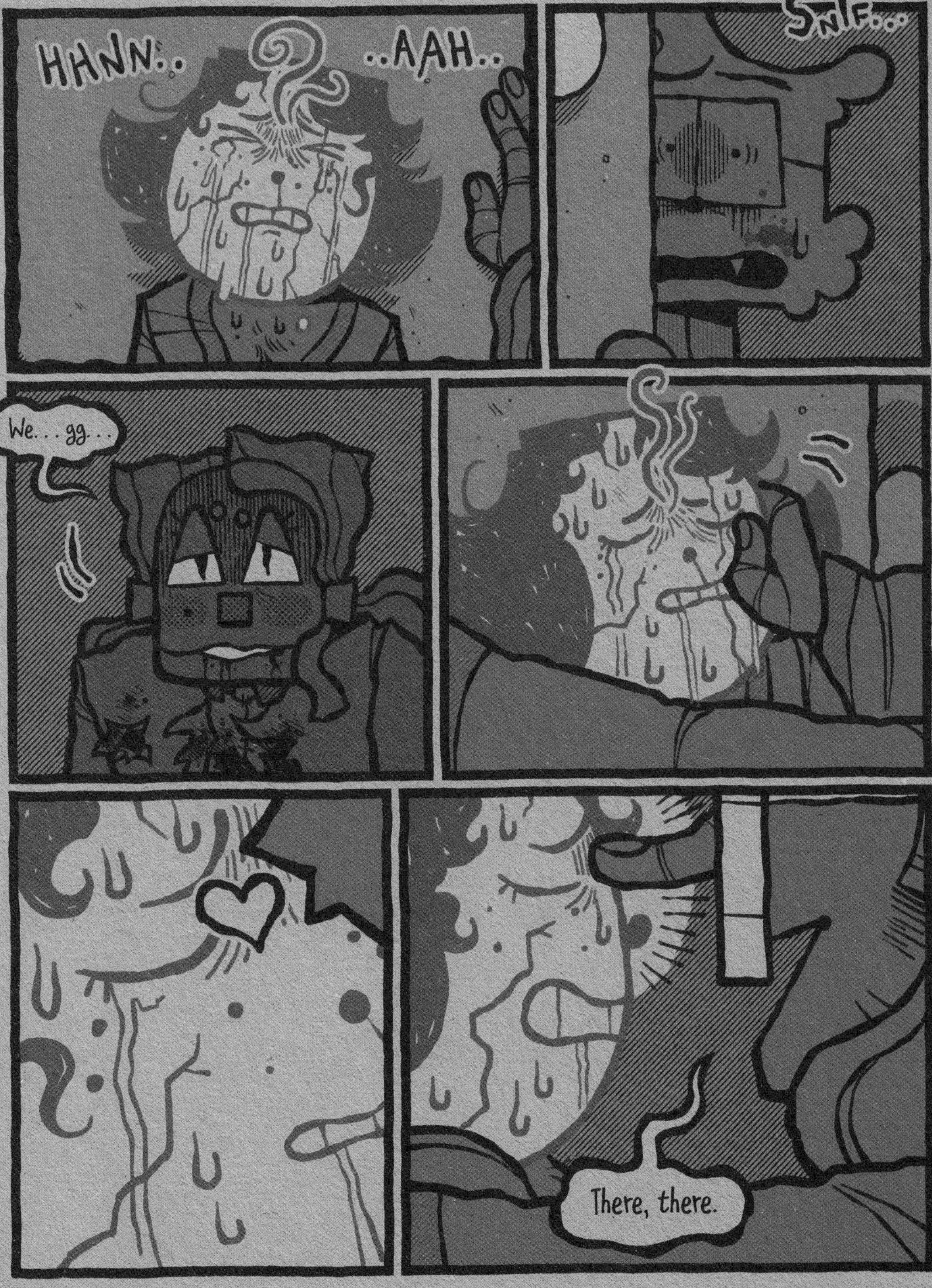
HHNN..
..AAH..
SNIF...
We...gg...
There, there.

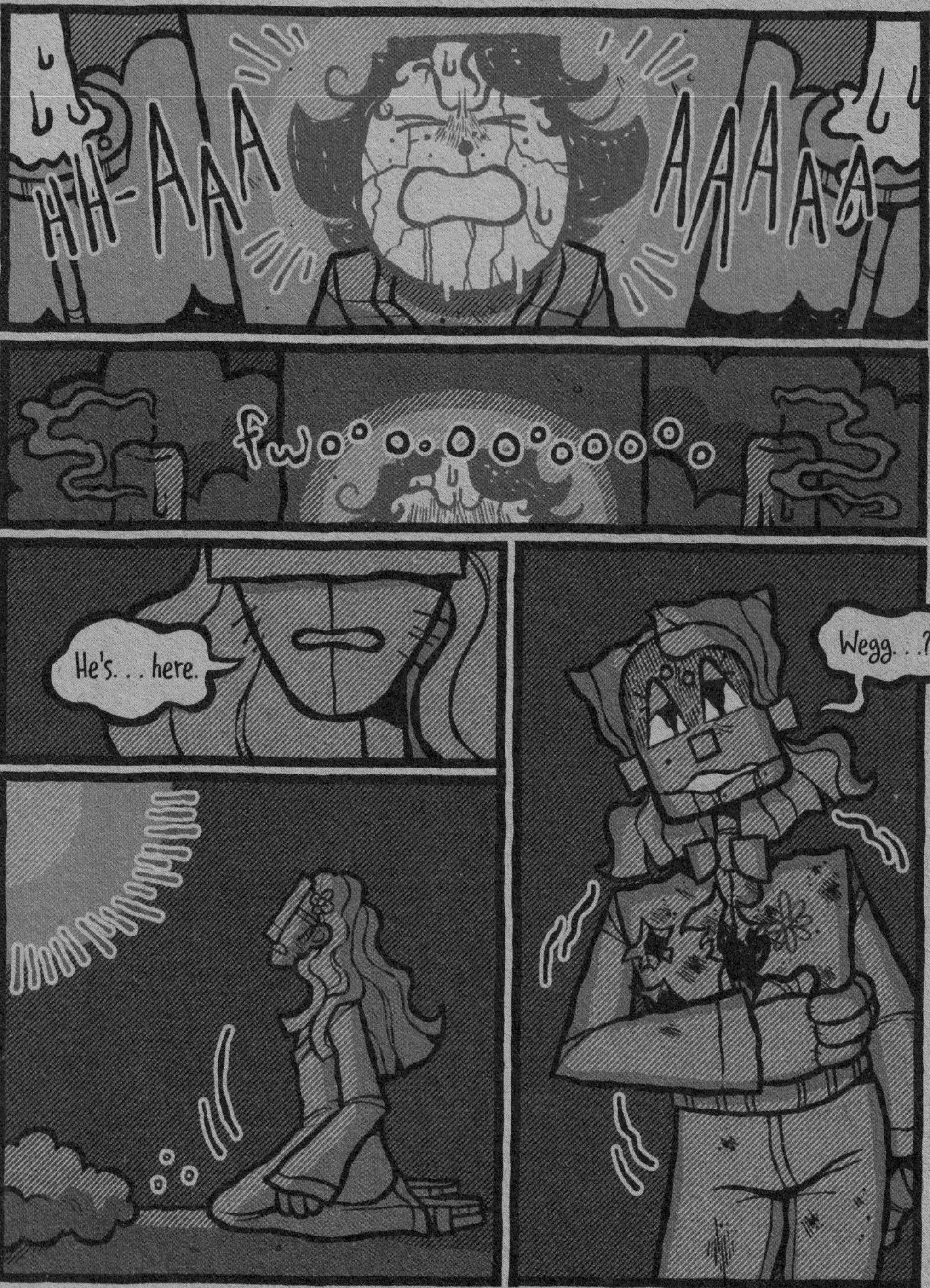
HH-AAA
AAAAA
fwoooooooooo
He's. . . here.
Wegg. . .?

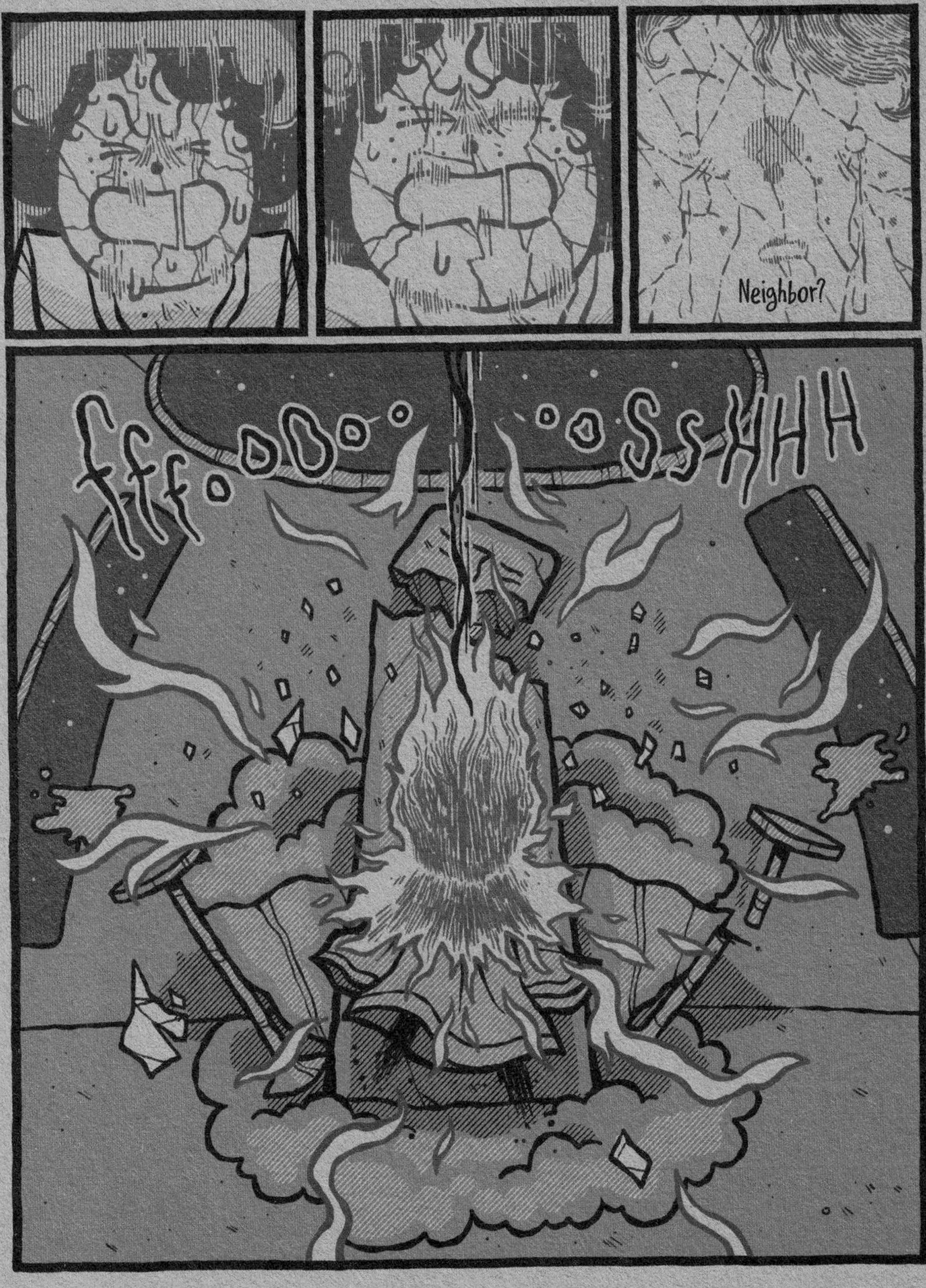
Neighbor?
fff.oOo°o °oOoSsHHH

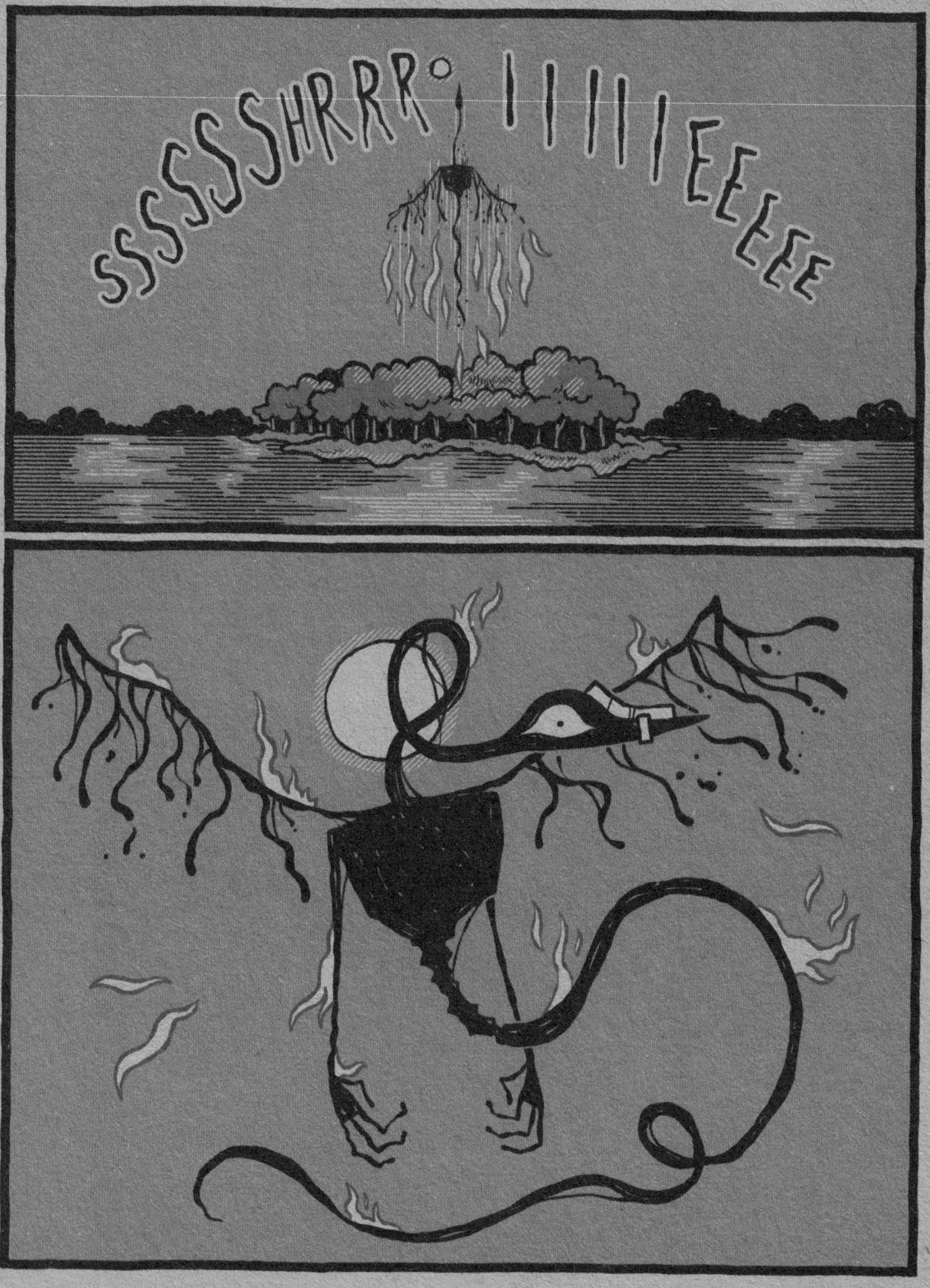
SSSSSSHRRR IIIIIEEEEE

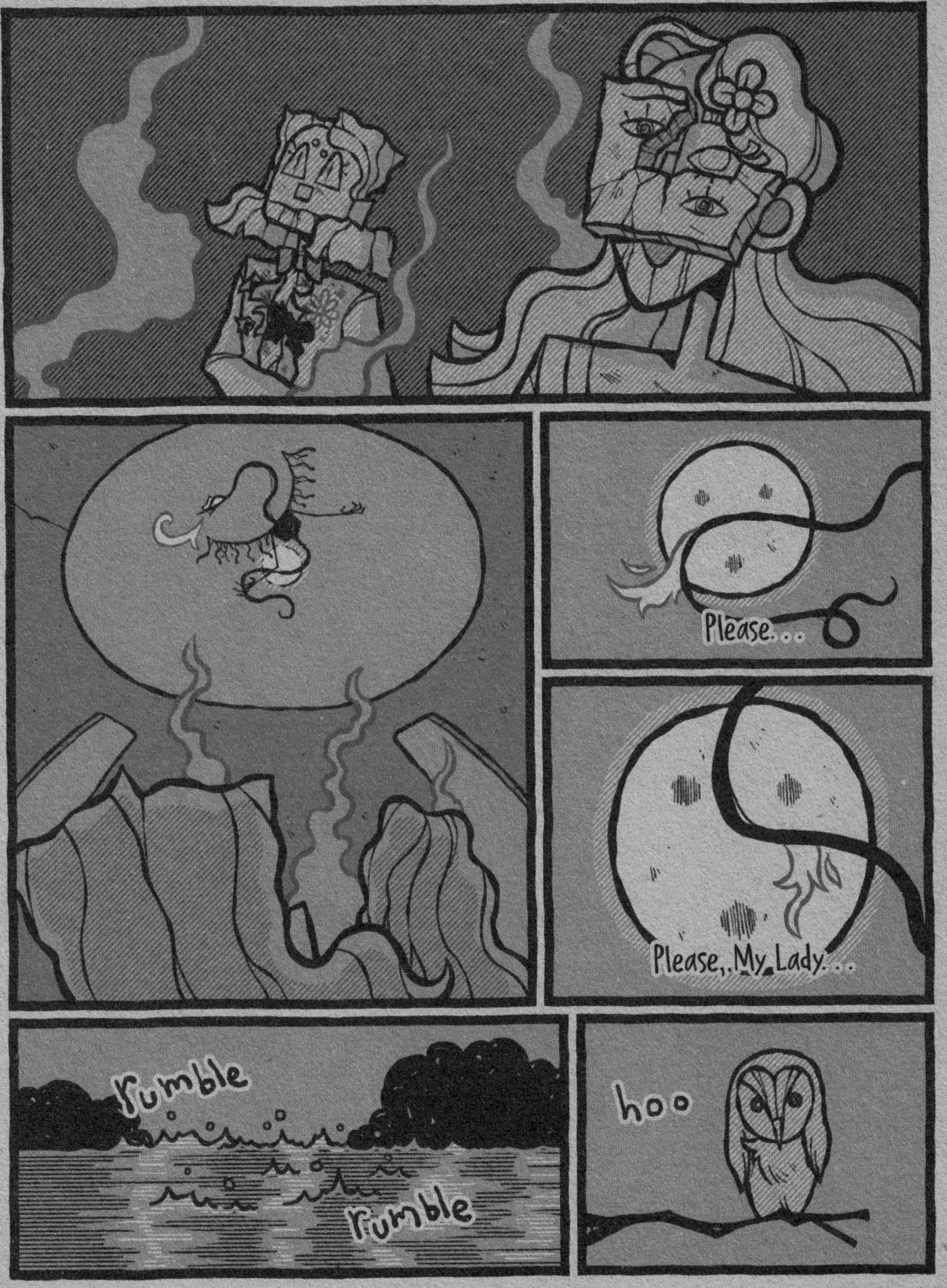

Please...
Please,. My Lady...
rumble
rumble
hoo

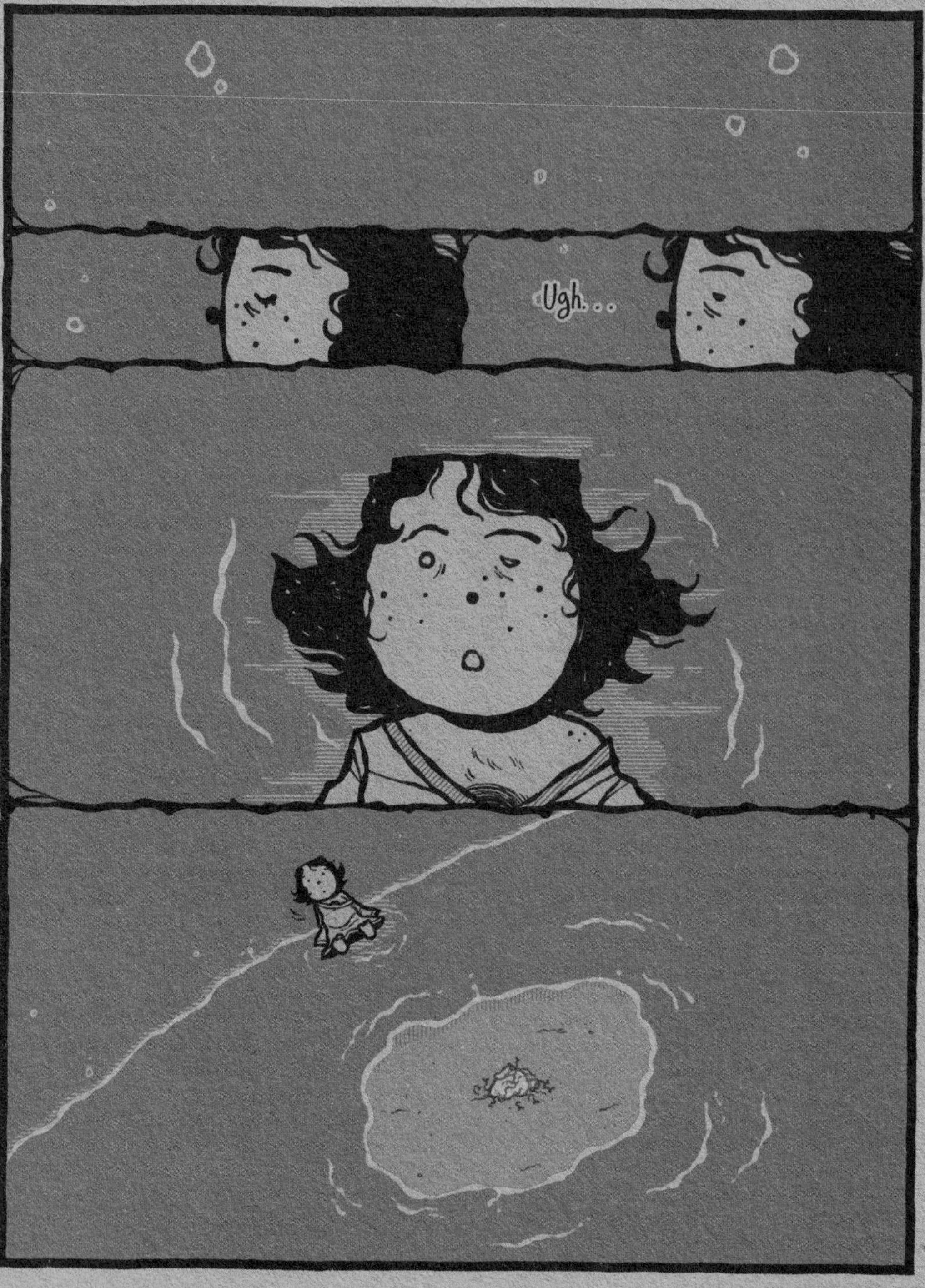
Ugh. . .

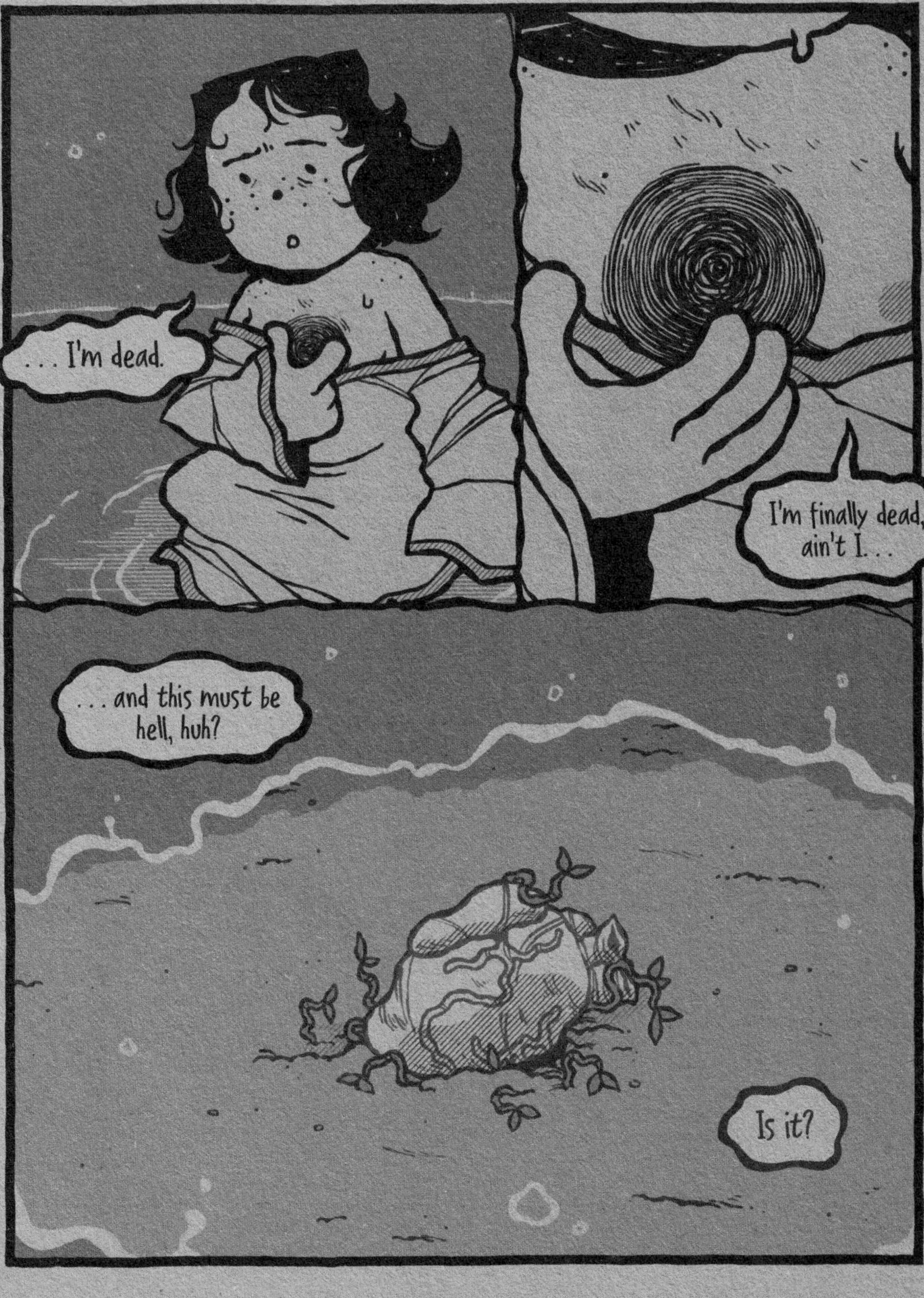
. . . I'm dead.
I'm finally dead, ain't I. . .
. . . and this must be hell, huh?
Is it?

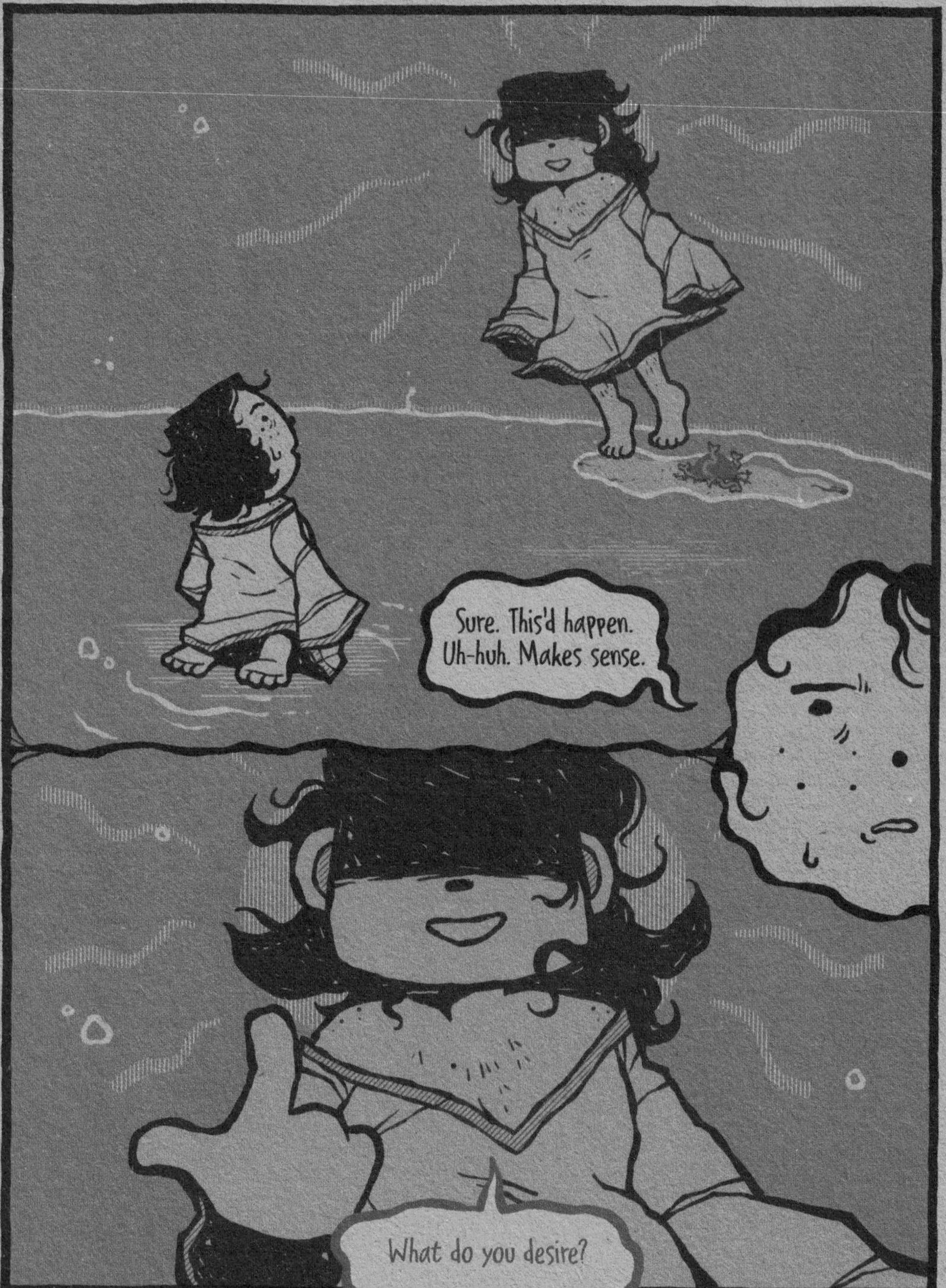
Sure. This'd happen. Uh-huh. Makes sense.
What do you desire?

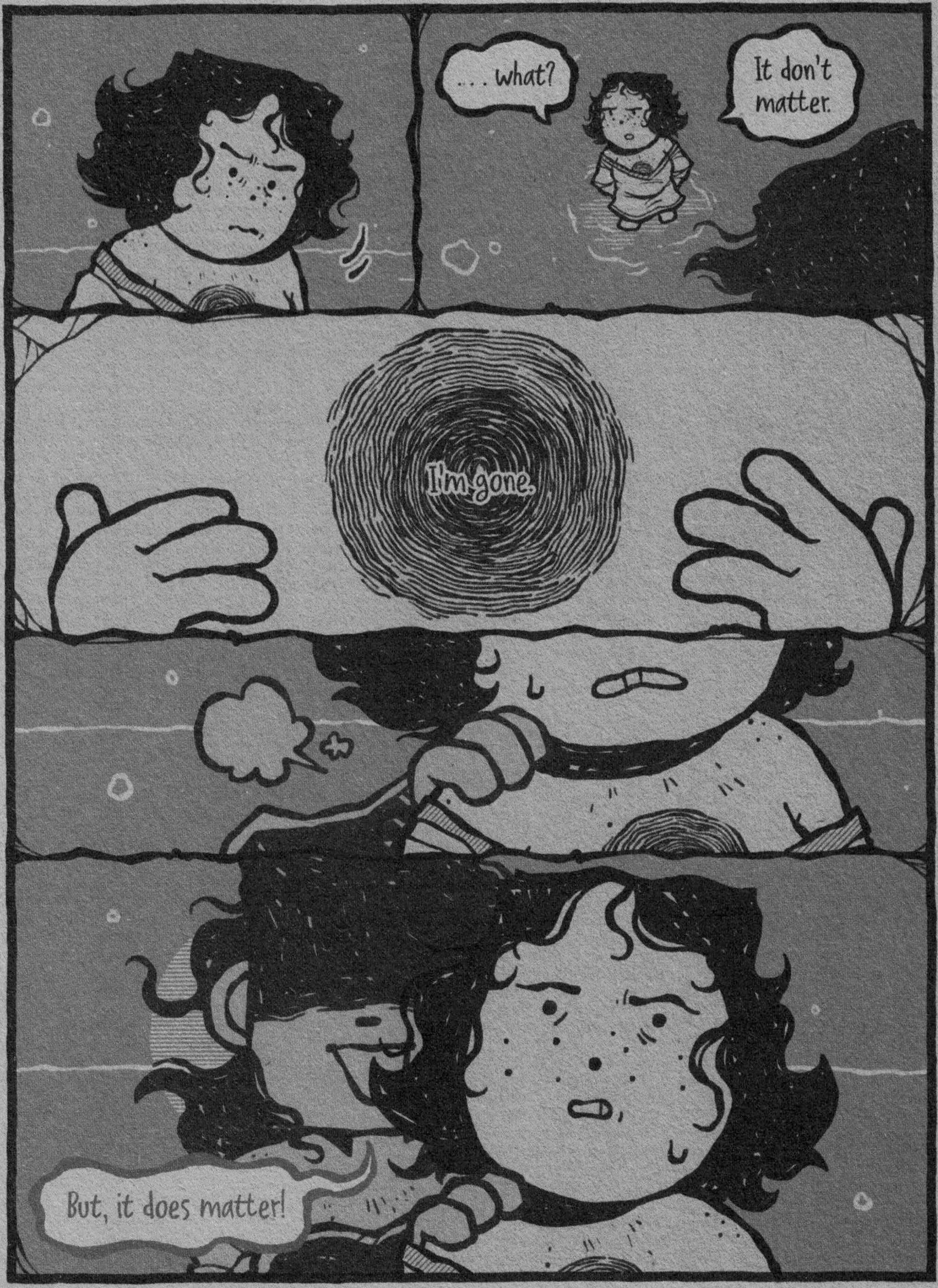
. . . what?
It don't matter.
I'm gone.
But, it does matter!

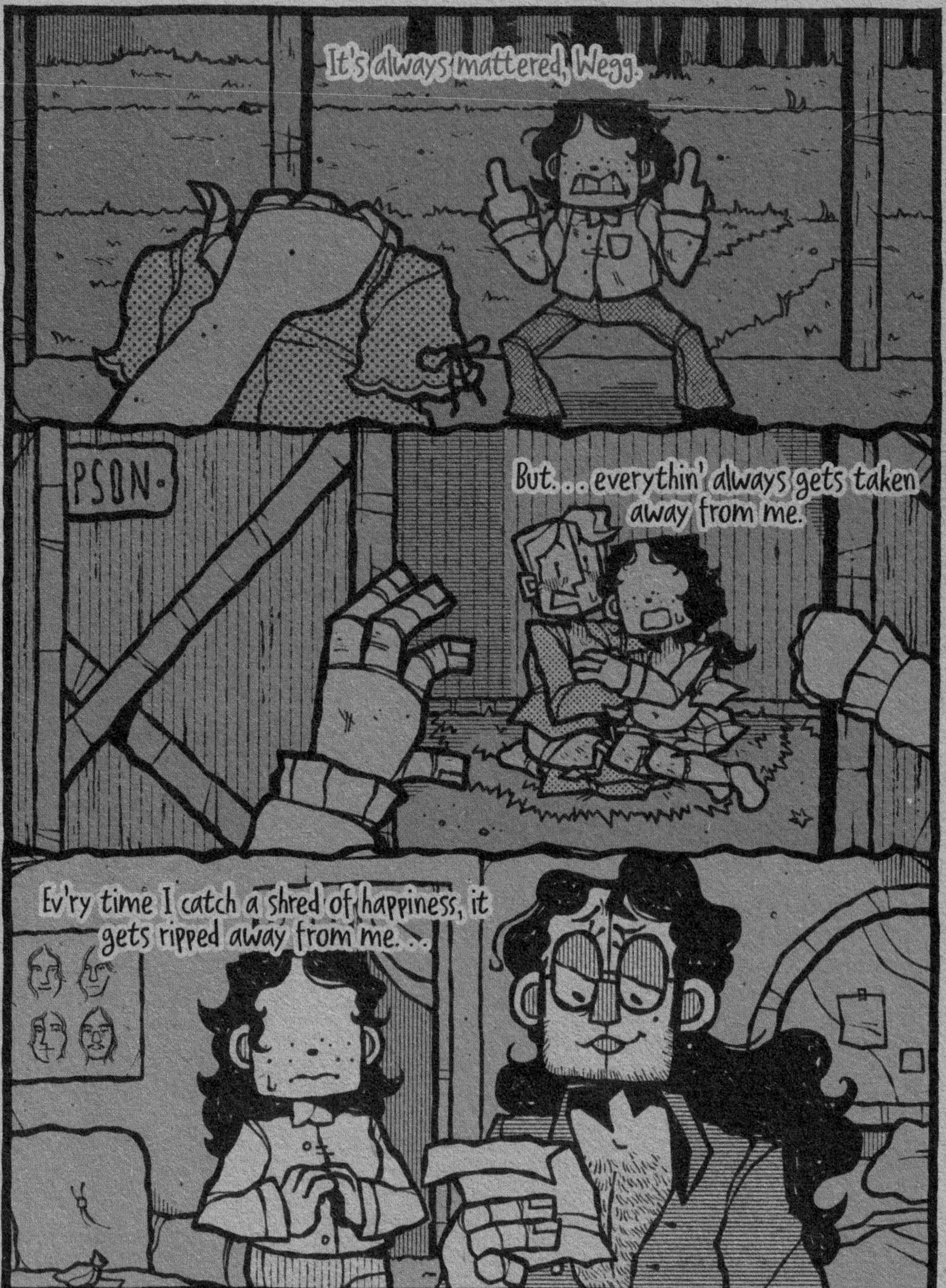
It's always mattered, Wegg.
PSON
But. . . everythin' always gets taken away from me.
Ev'ry time I catch a shred of happiness, it gets ripped away from me. . .

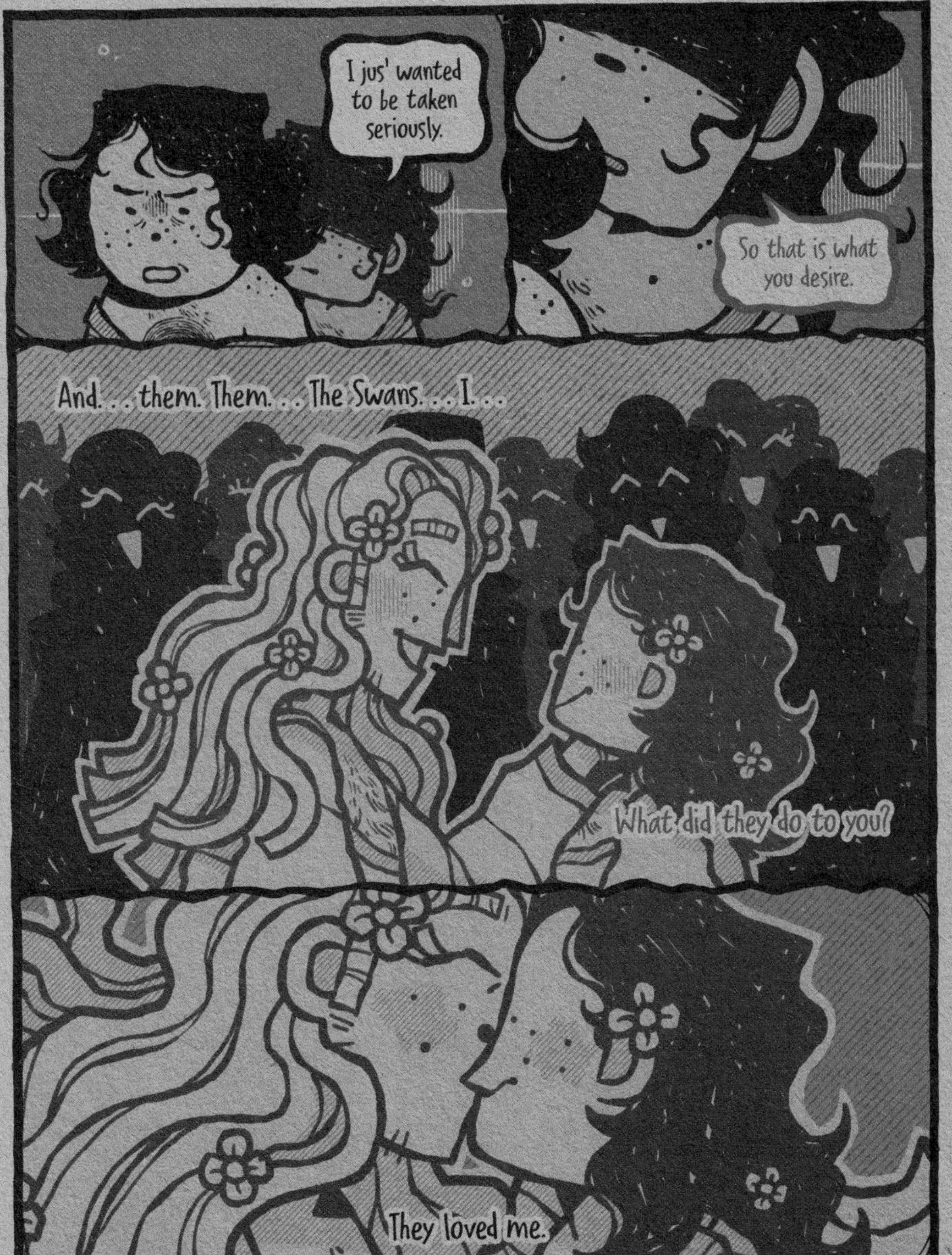
I jus' wanted to be taken seriously.
So that is what you desire.
And. . . them. Them. . . The Swans. . . I. . .
What did they do to you?
They loved me.

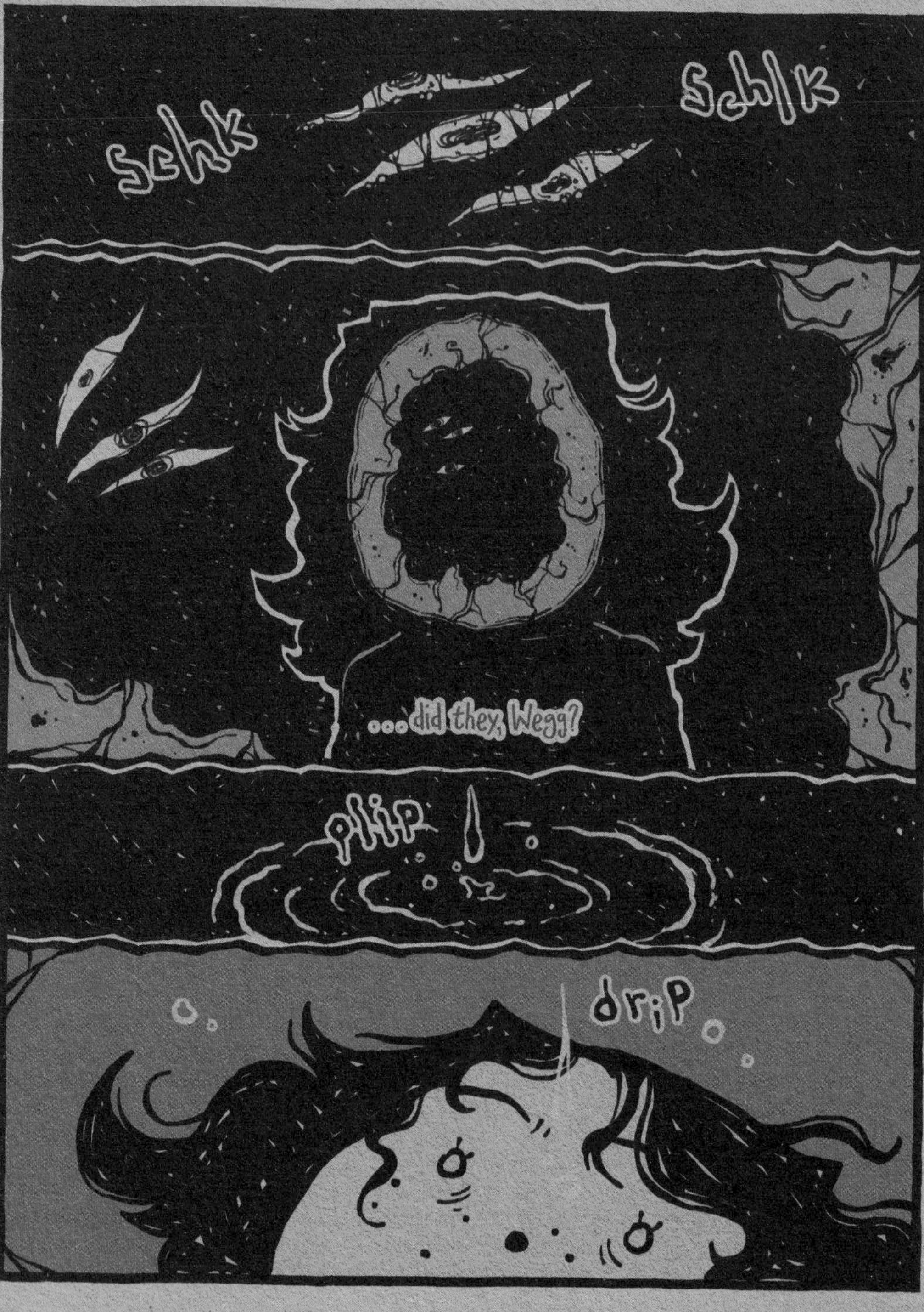
schk
schlk
...did they, Wegg?
plip
drip

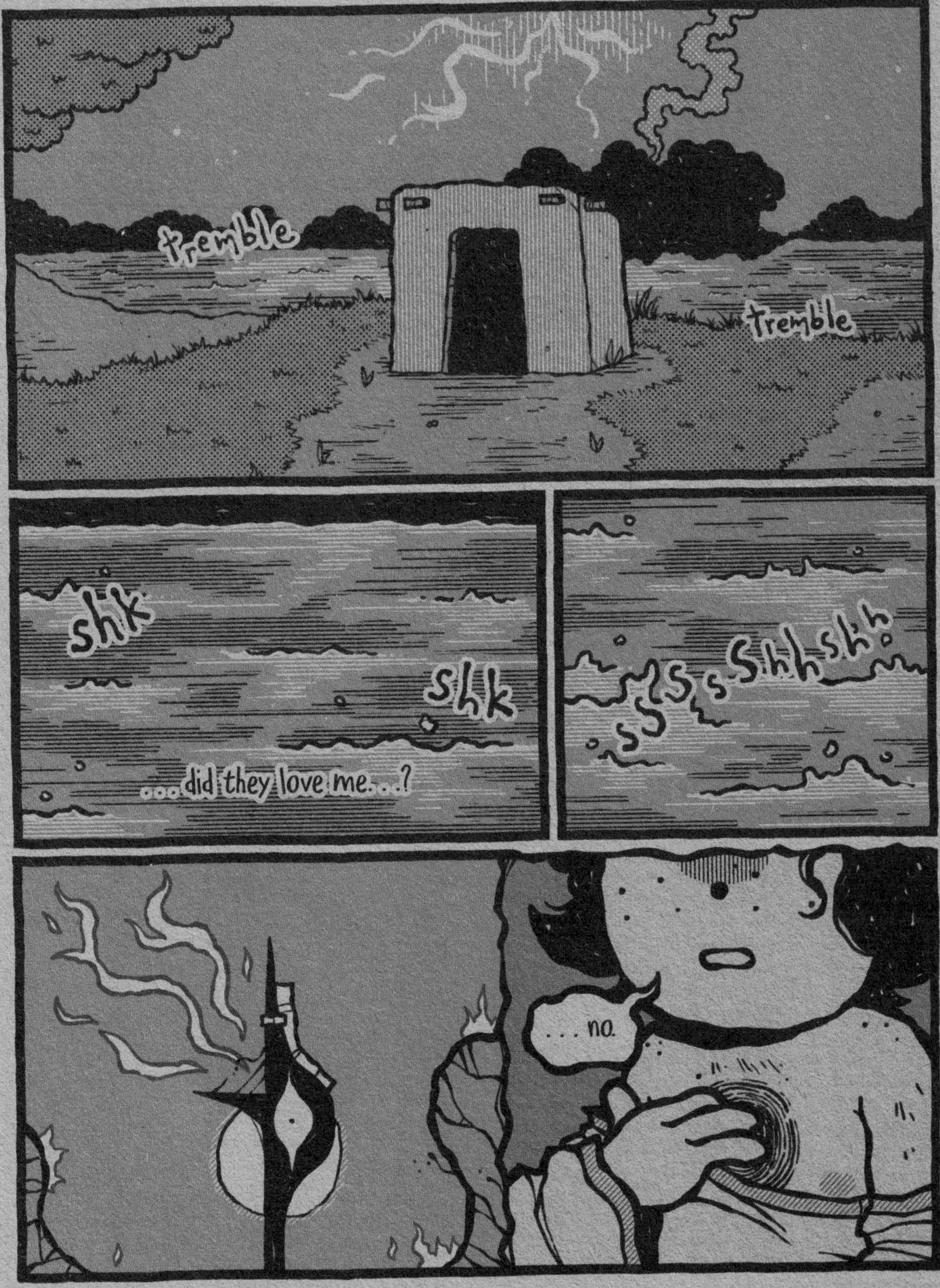

tremble
tremble
shk
shk
...did they love me...?
sssShhshh
...no.

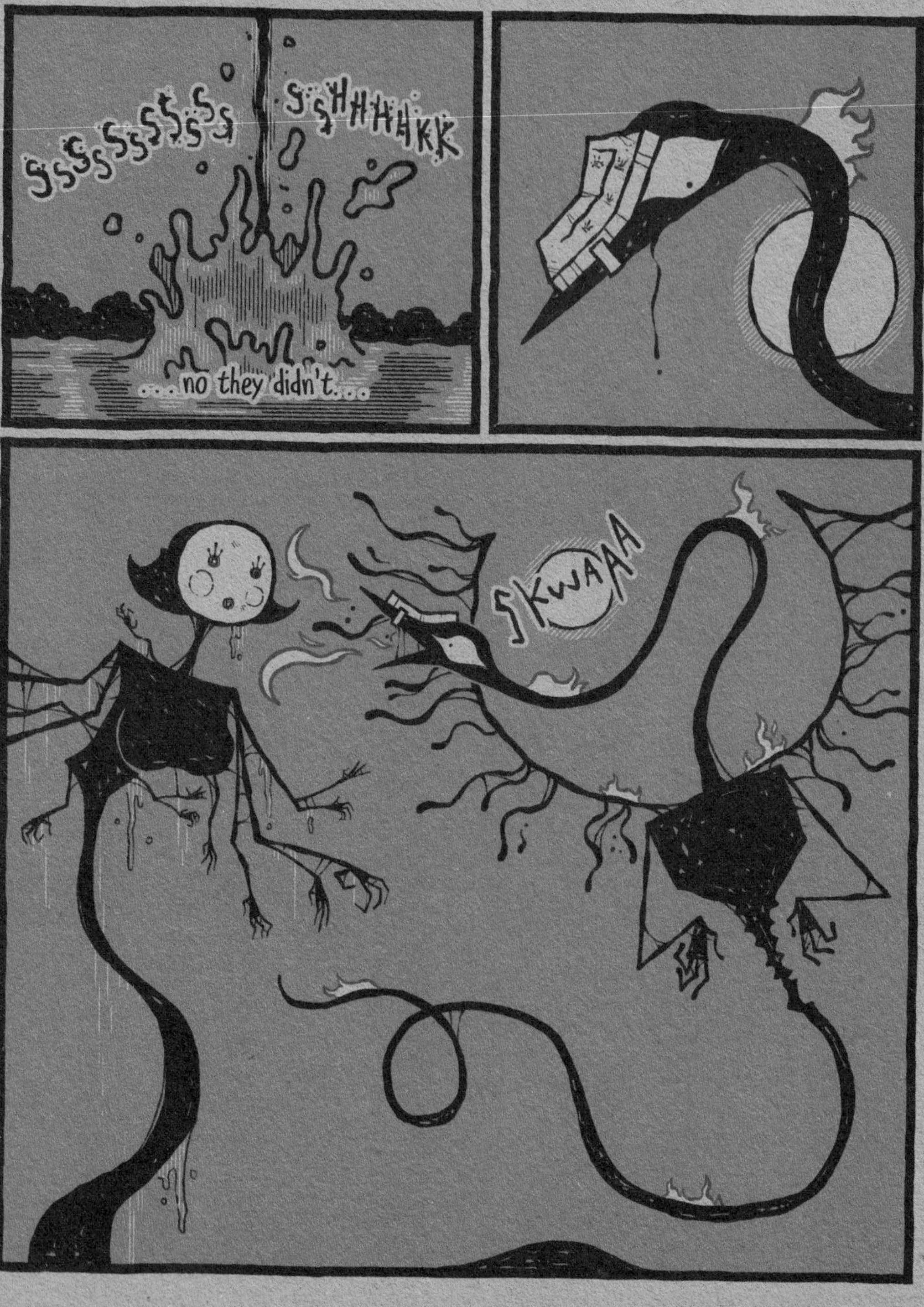
SSSSSSSSSSS
SSHHHHKK
...no they didn't...
SKWAAA

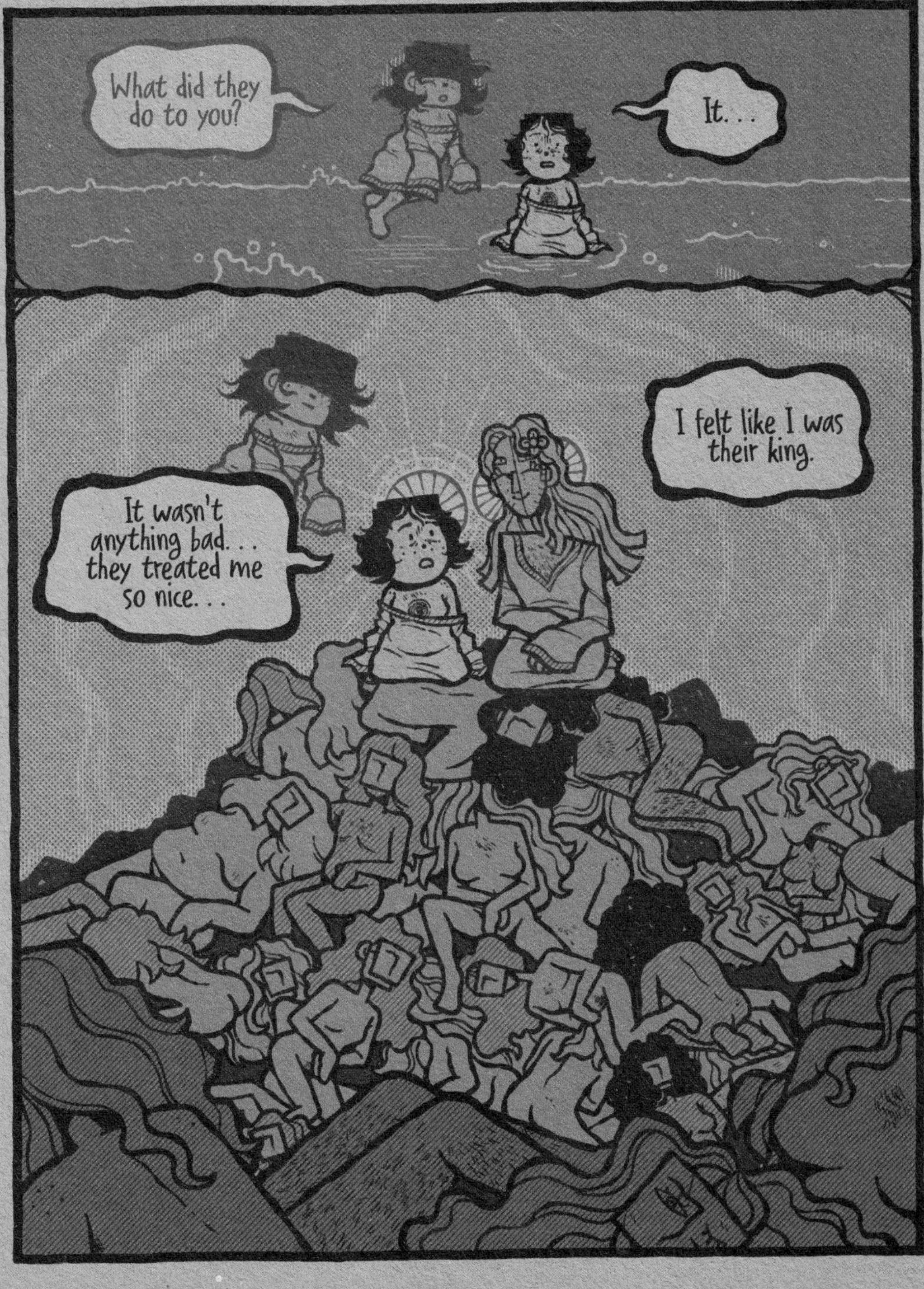
What did they do to you?
It. . .
I felt like I was their king.
It wasn't anything bad. . . they treated me so nice. . .

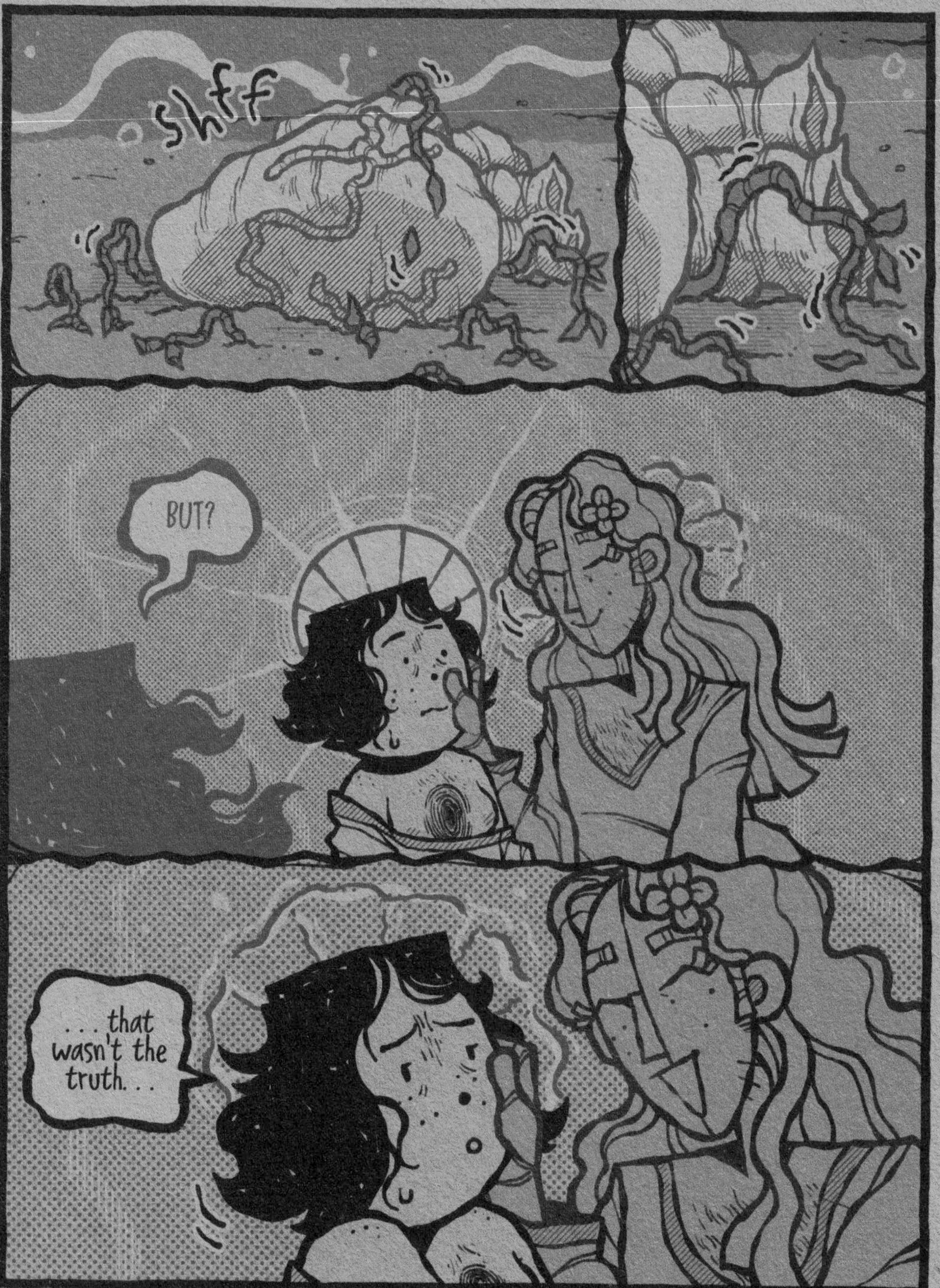
shff
BUT?
. . . that wasn't the truth. . .

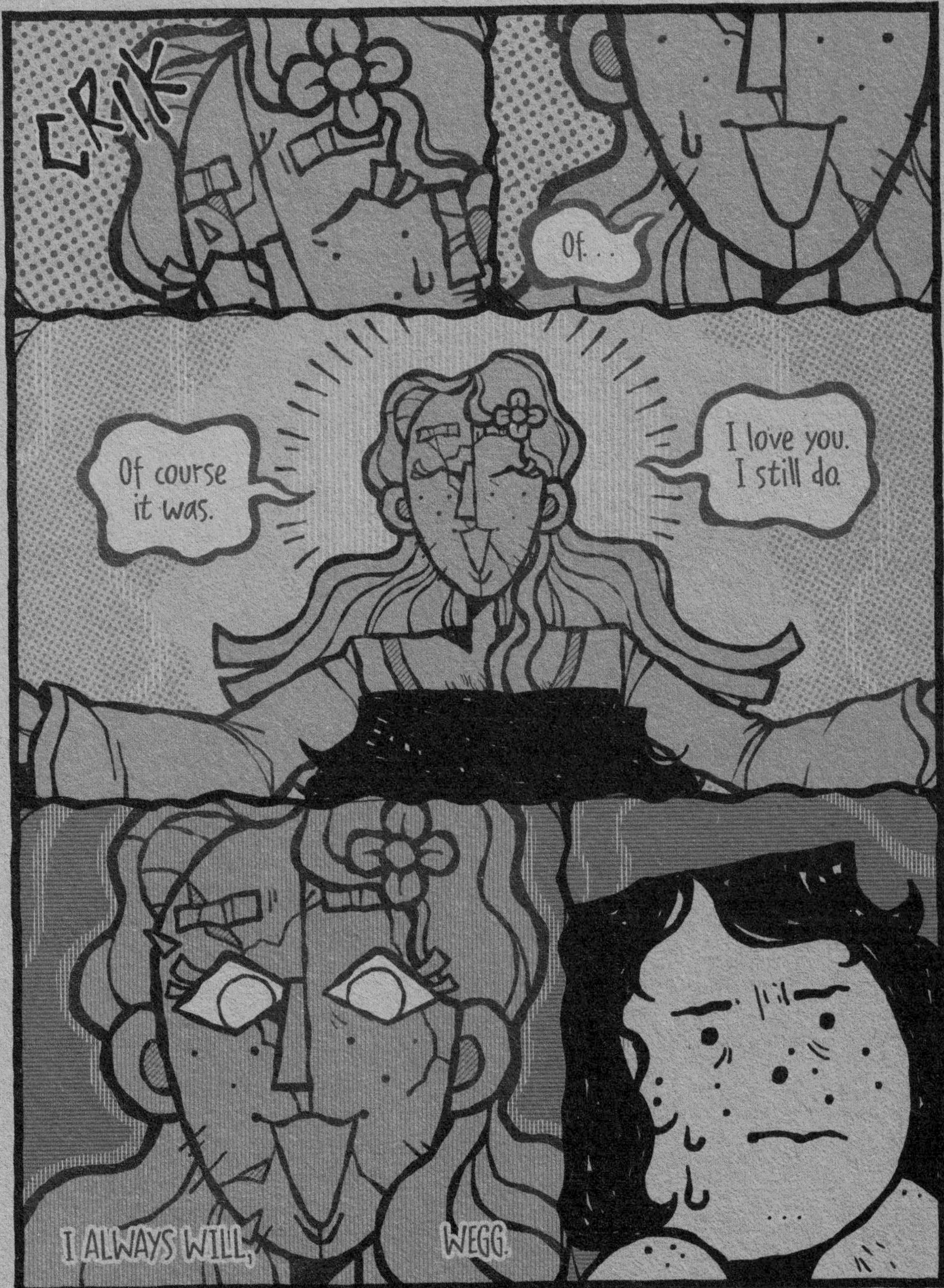
CRIK
Of...
Of course it was.
I love you. I still do.
I ALWAYS WILL,
WEGG.
...

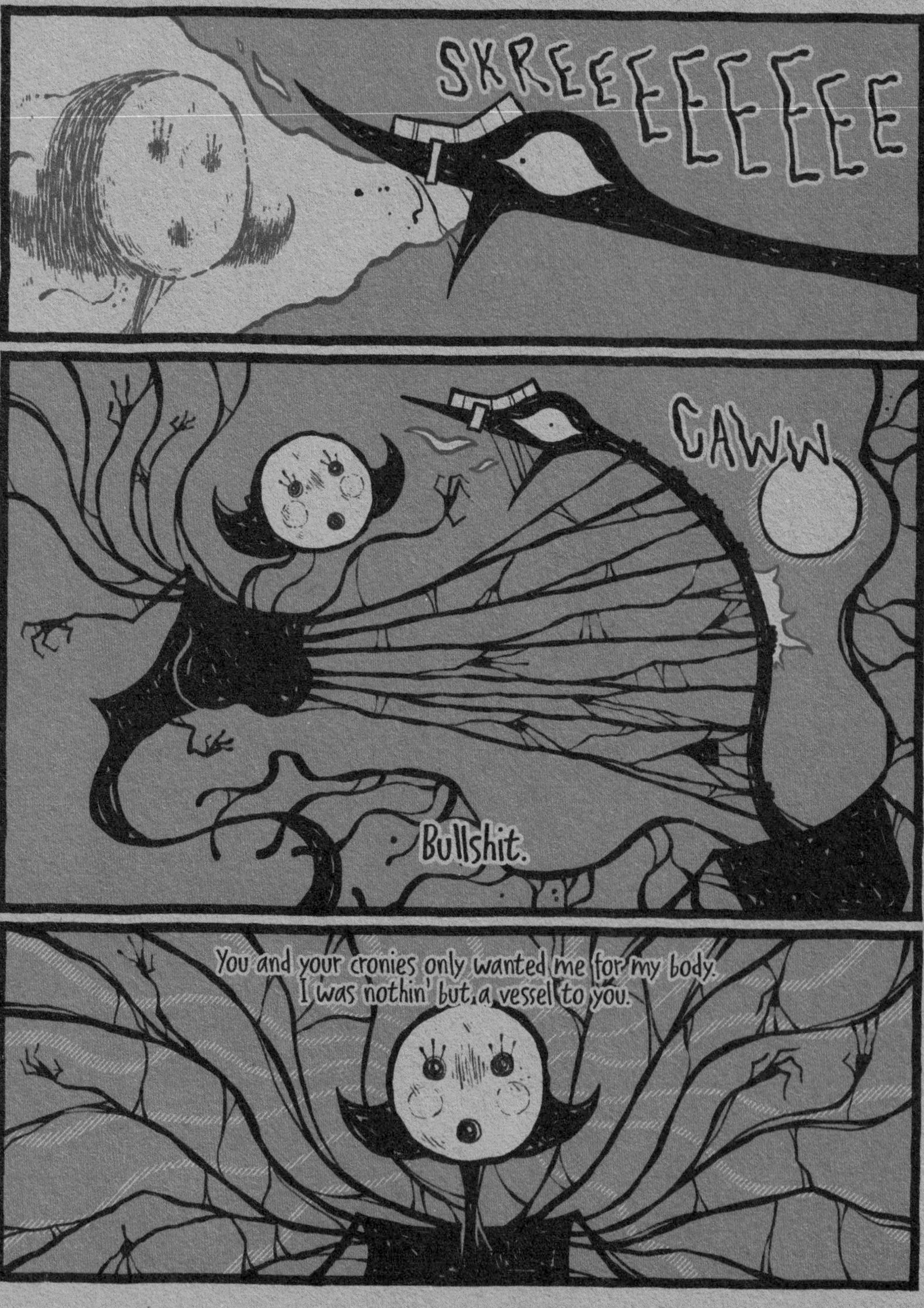
SKREEEEEEEEEE
CAWW
Bullshit.
You and your cronies only wanted me for my body.
I was nothin' but a vessel to you.

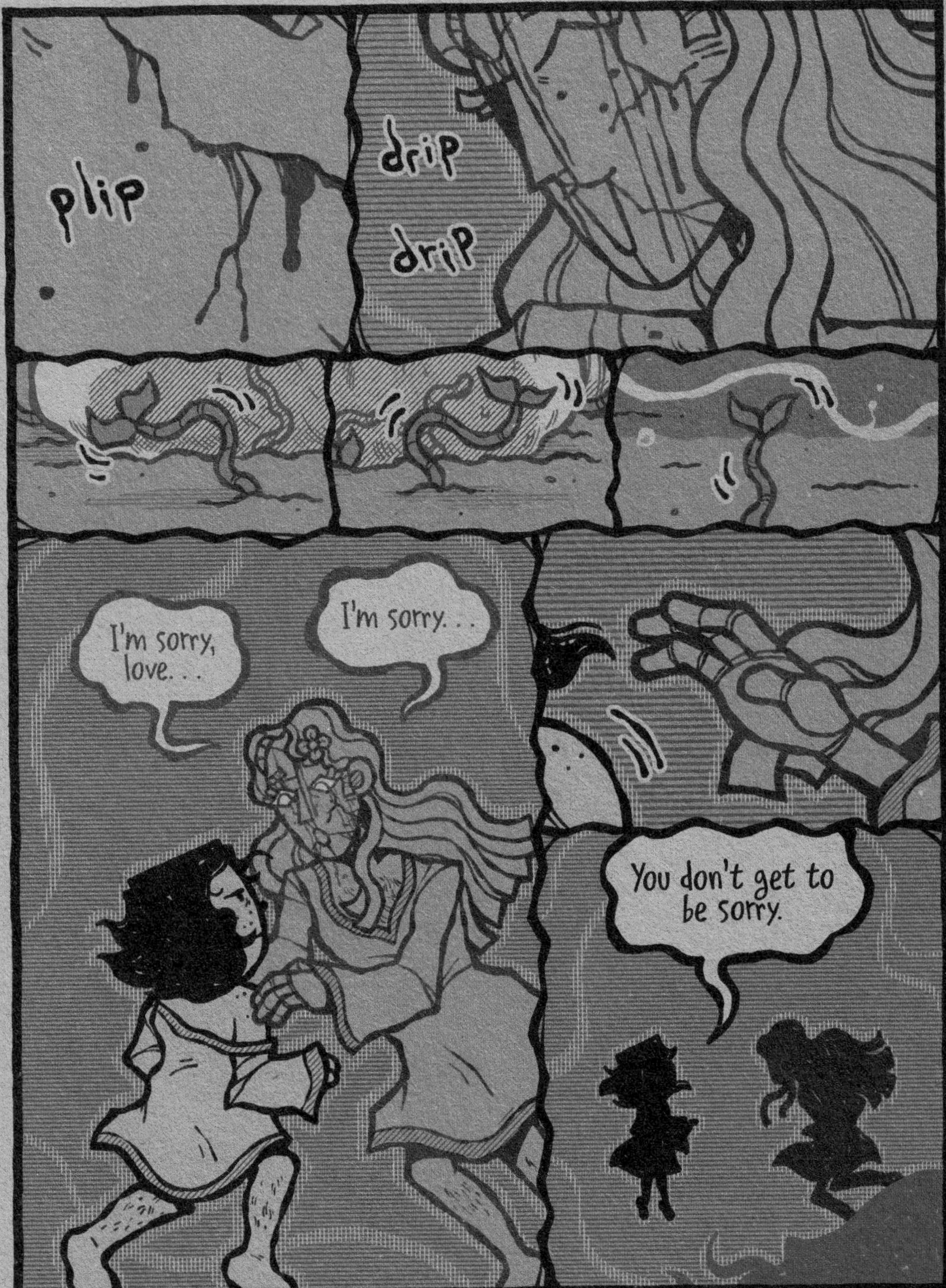
plip
drip
drip
I'm sorry, love...
I'm sorry...
You don't get to be sorry.

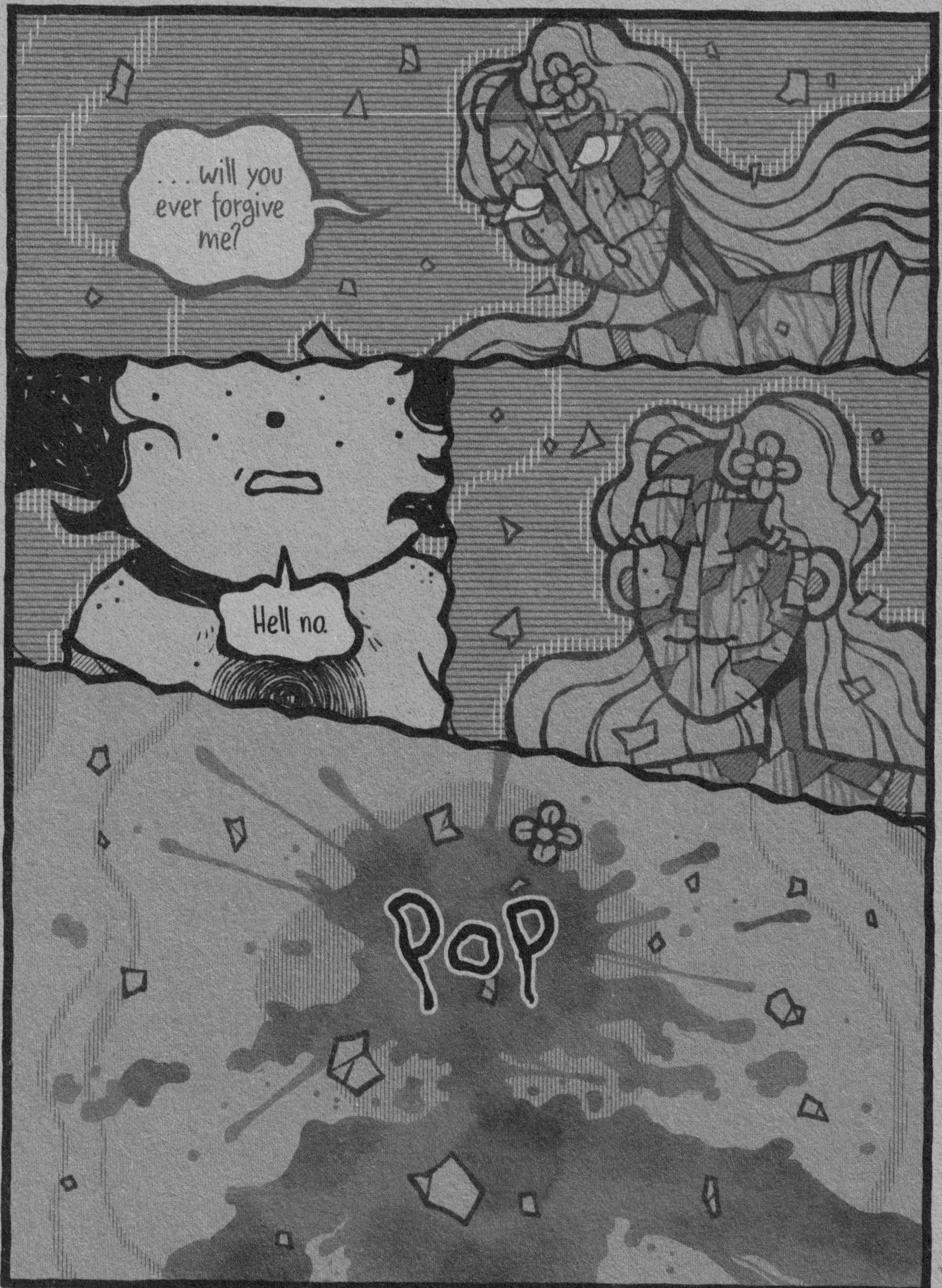
...will you ever forgive me?
Hell no.
POP

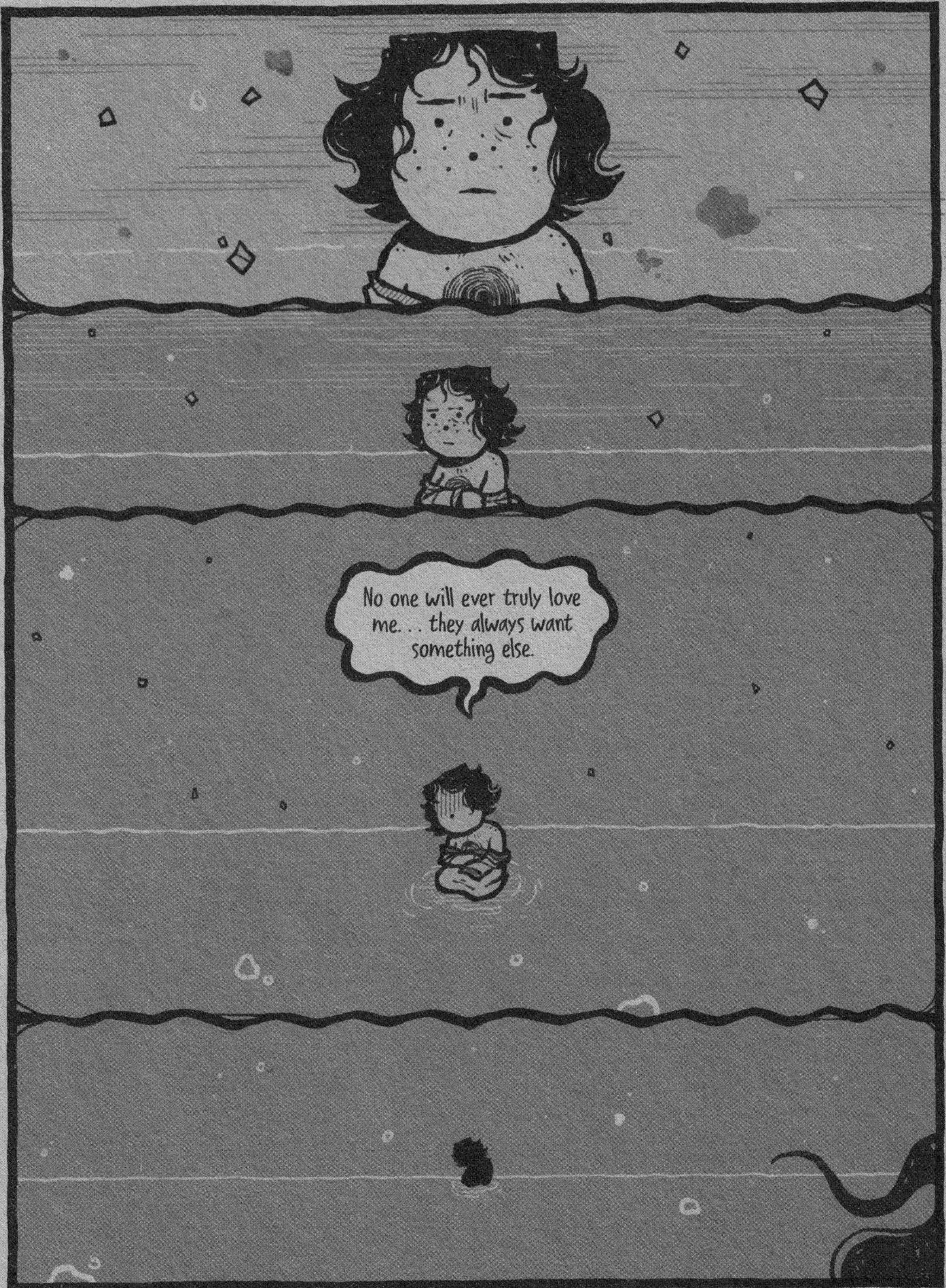
No one will ever truly love me. . . they always want something else.

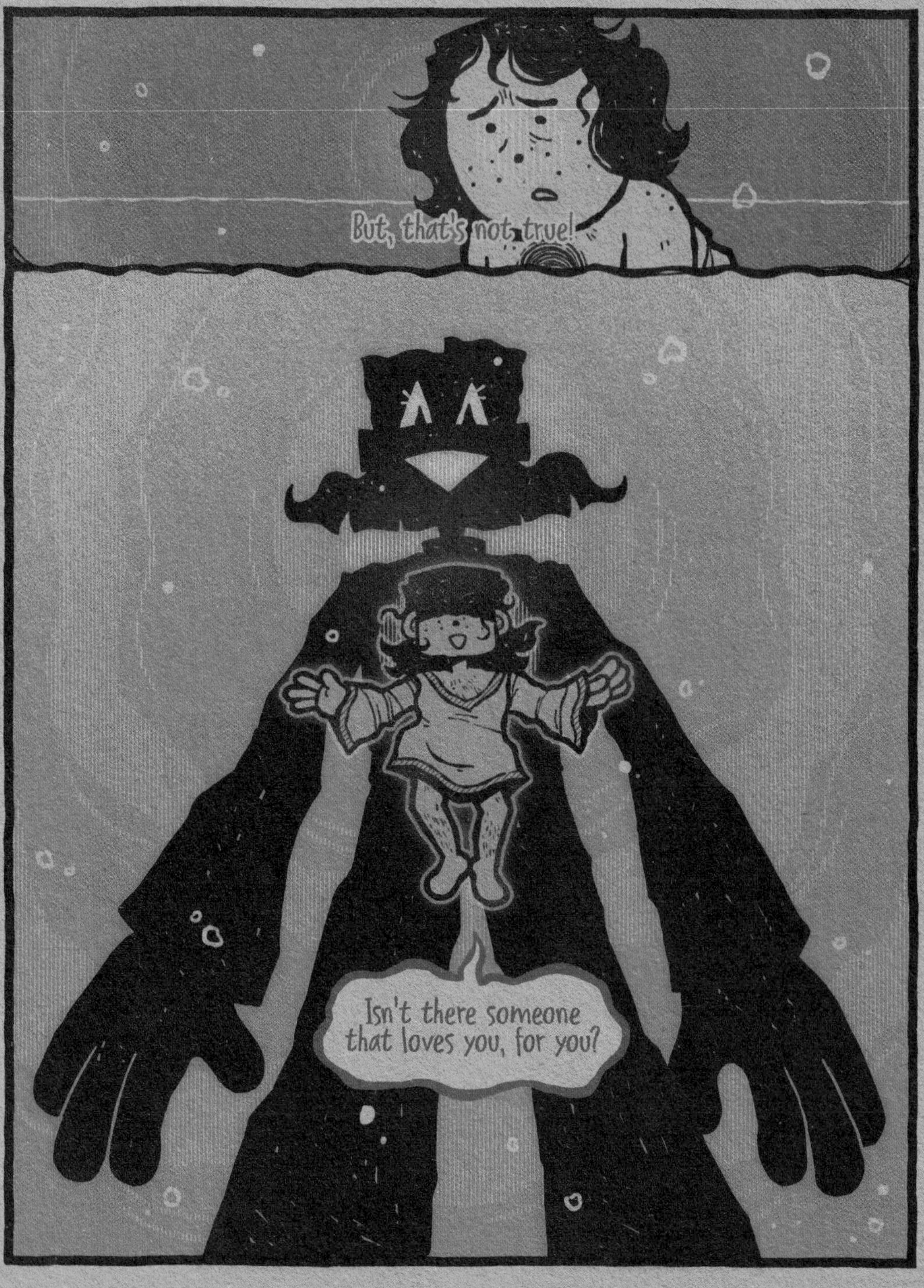
But, that's not true!
Isn't there someone that loves you, for you?

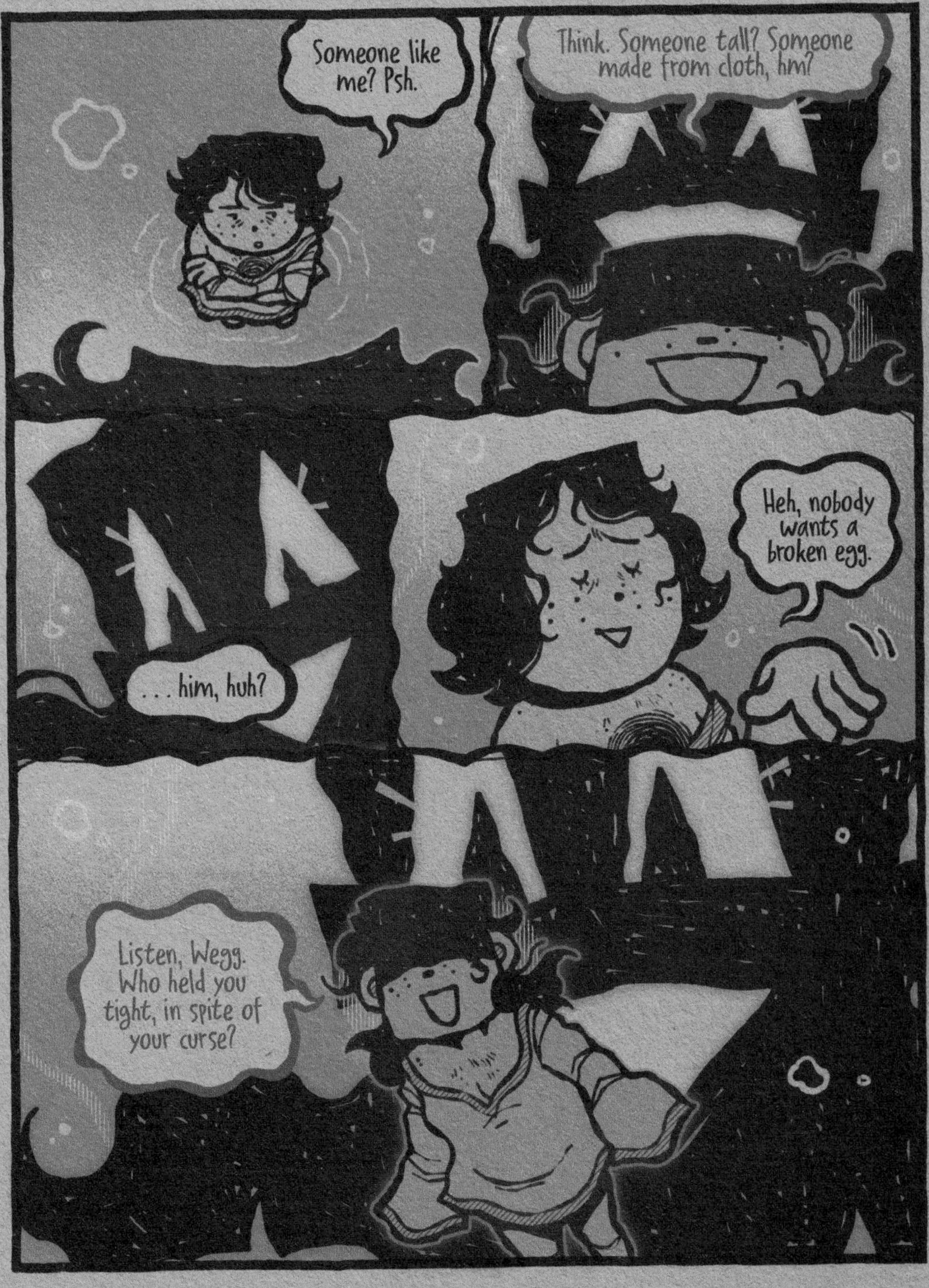
Someone like me? Psh.
Think. Someone tall? Someone made from cloth, hm?
Heh, nobody wants a broken egg.
. . . him, huh?
Listen, Wegg. Who held you tight, in spite of your curse?

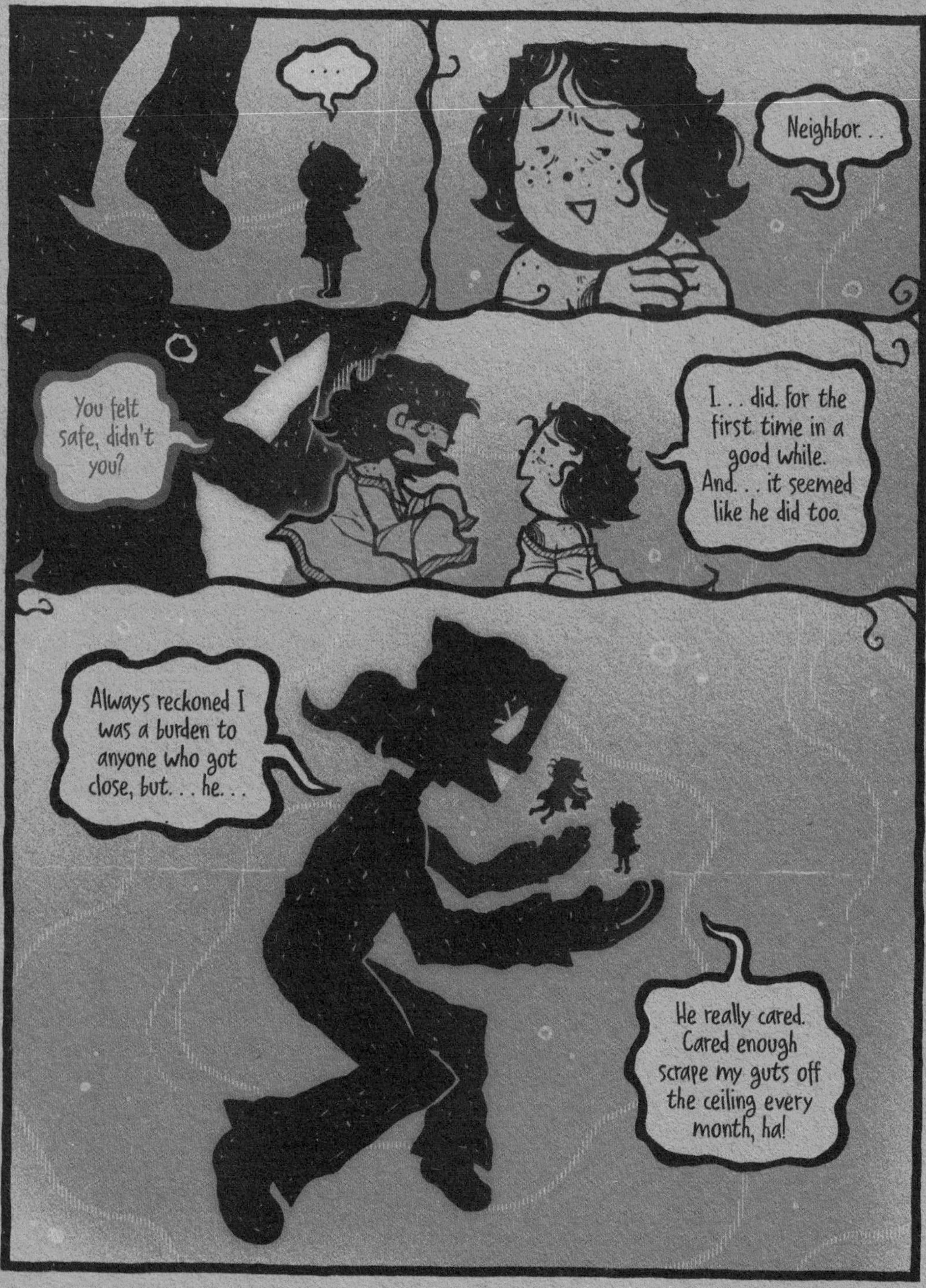
. . .
Neighbor. . .
You felt safe, didn't you?
I. . . did. For the first time in a good while. And. . . it seemed like he did too.
Always reckoned I was a burden to anyone who got close, but. . . he. . .
He really cared. Cared enough scrape my guts off the ceiling every month, ha!

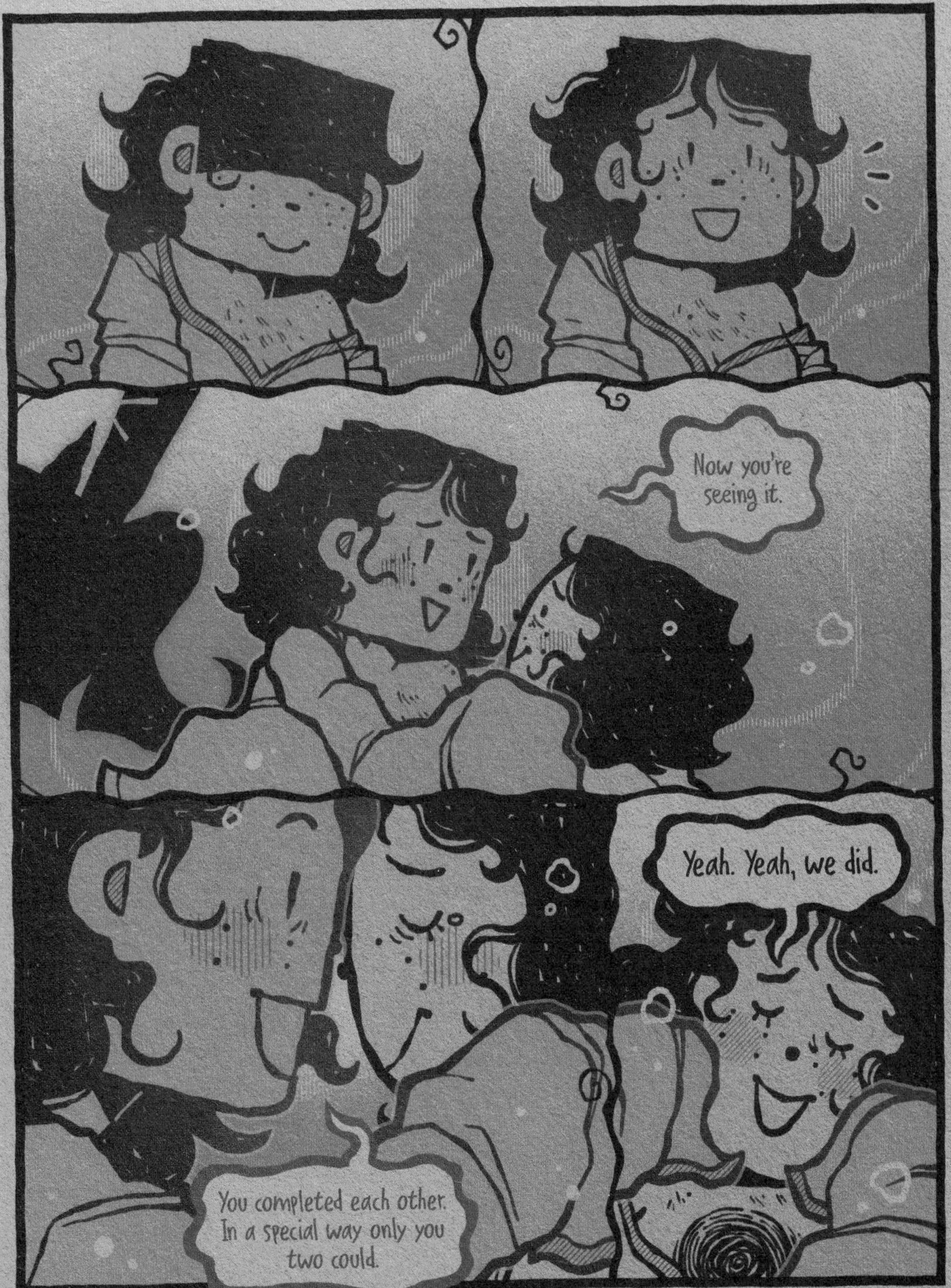
Now you're seeing it.
Yeah. Yeah, we did.
You completed each other. In a special way only you two could.

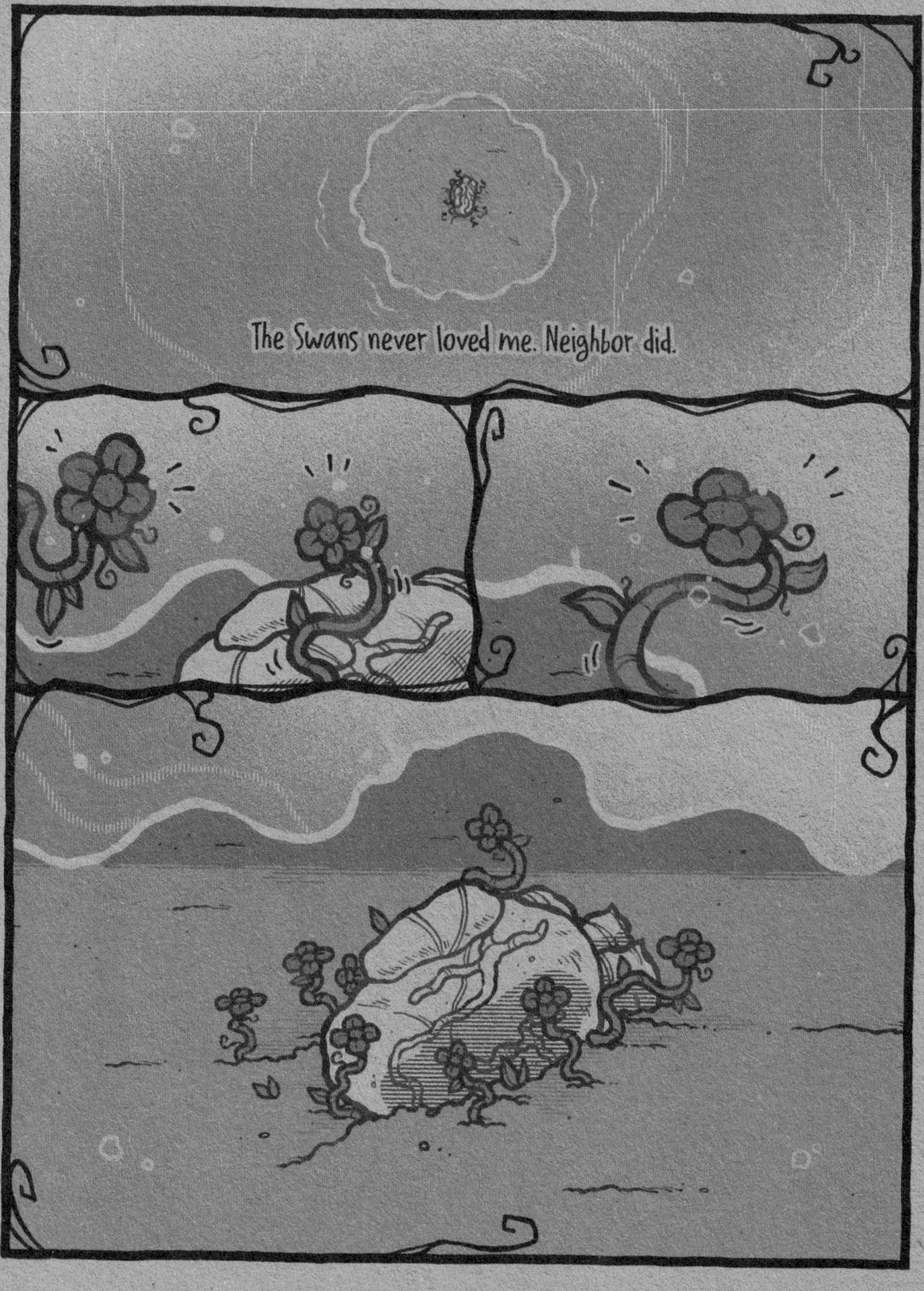
The Swans never loved me. Neighbor did.

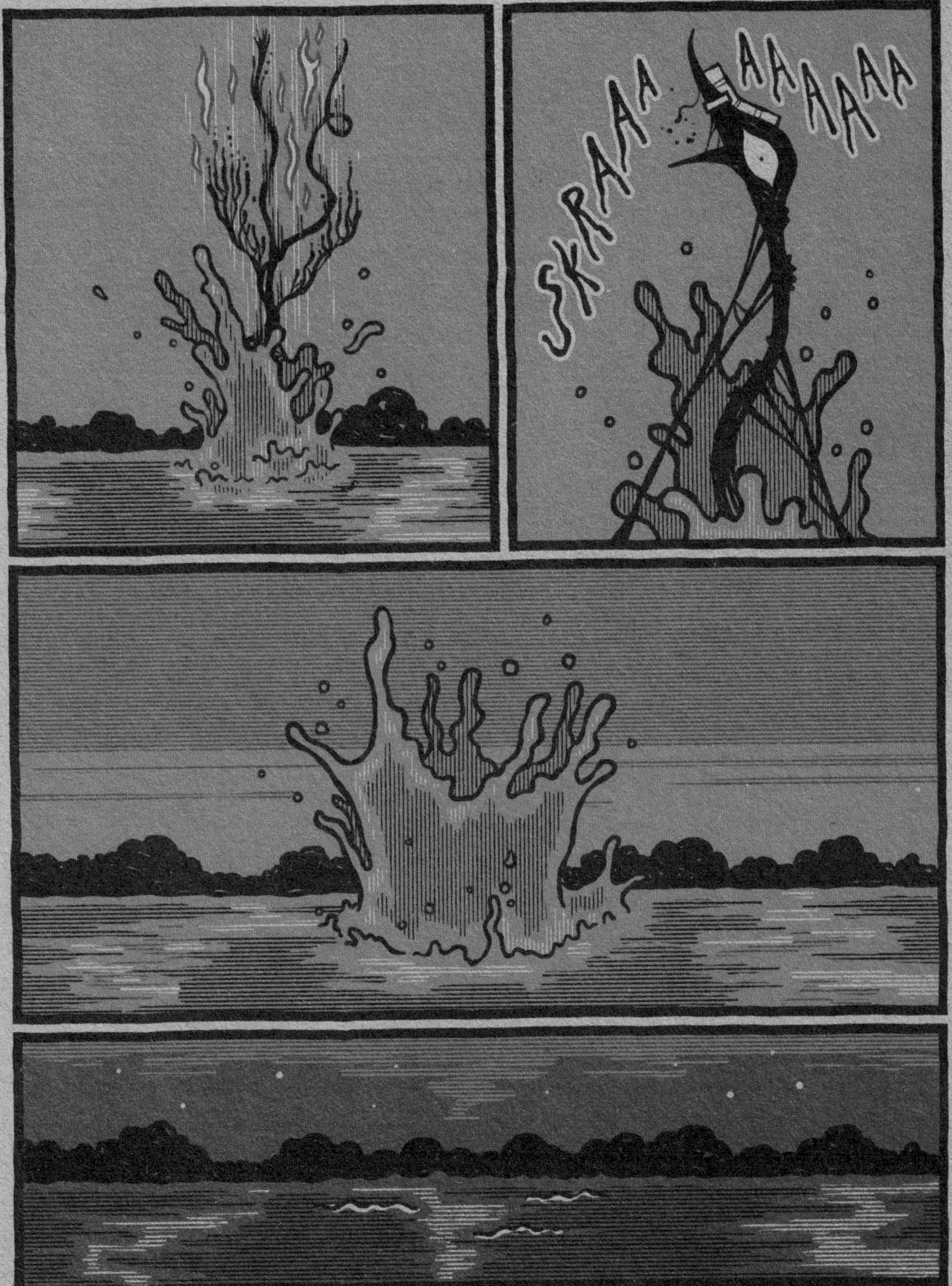
SKRAAAAAAAAA

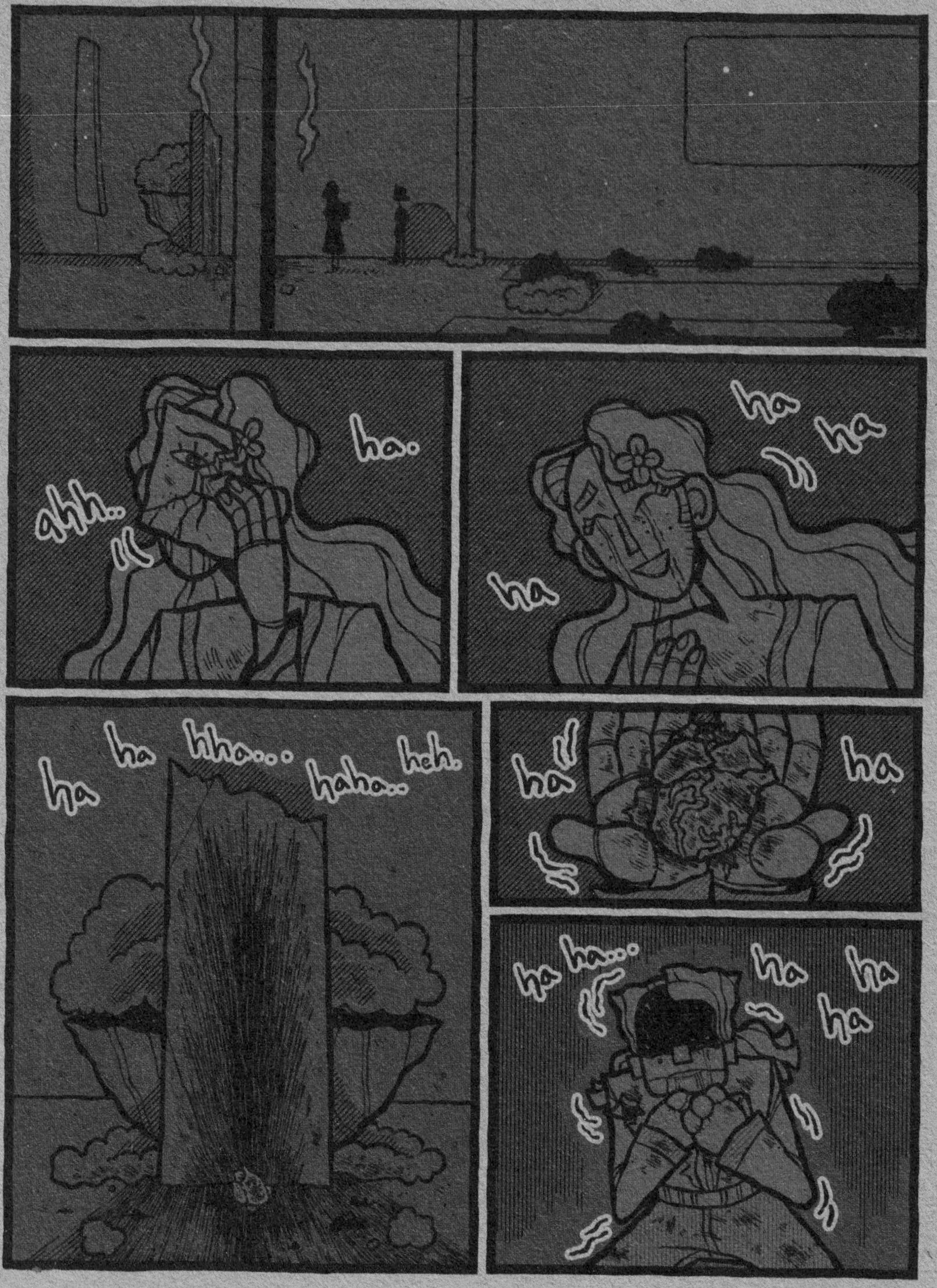
ahh..
ha.
ha
ha
ha
ha
ha
ha
hha...
haha..
heh.
ha
ha
ha ha...
ha
ha
ha

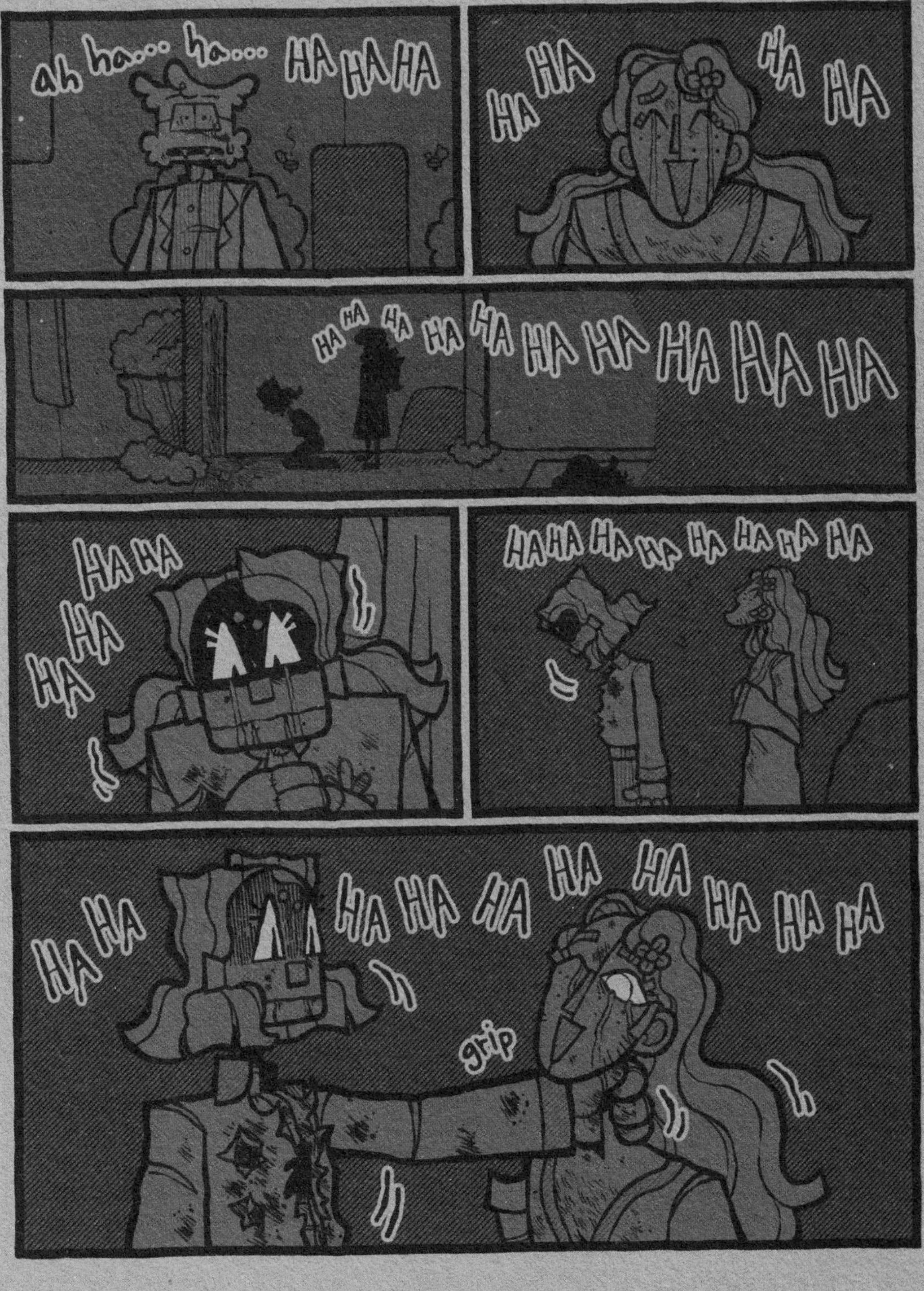
ah ha... ha... HA HA HA
HA HA HA HA
HA HA HA HA HA HA HA HA HA HA HA HA
HA HA HA HA
HA HA HA HA HA HA HA HA
HA HA HA HA HA HA HA HA HA HA HA HA
grip

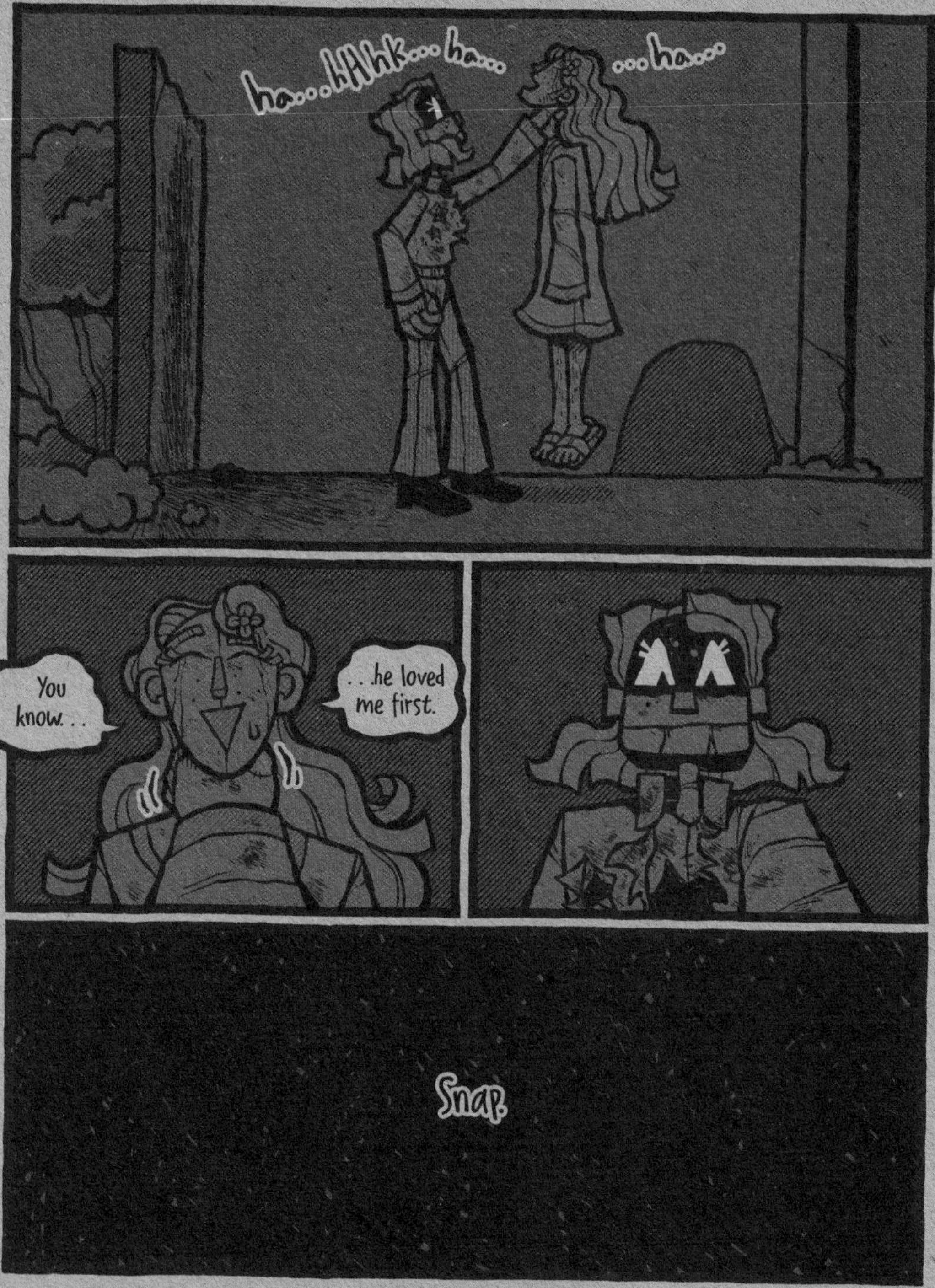
ha...hhhk...ha...
...ha...
You know. . .
. . .he loved me first.
Snap.

1975

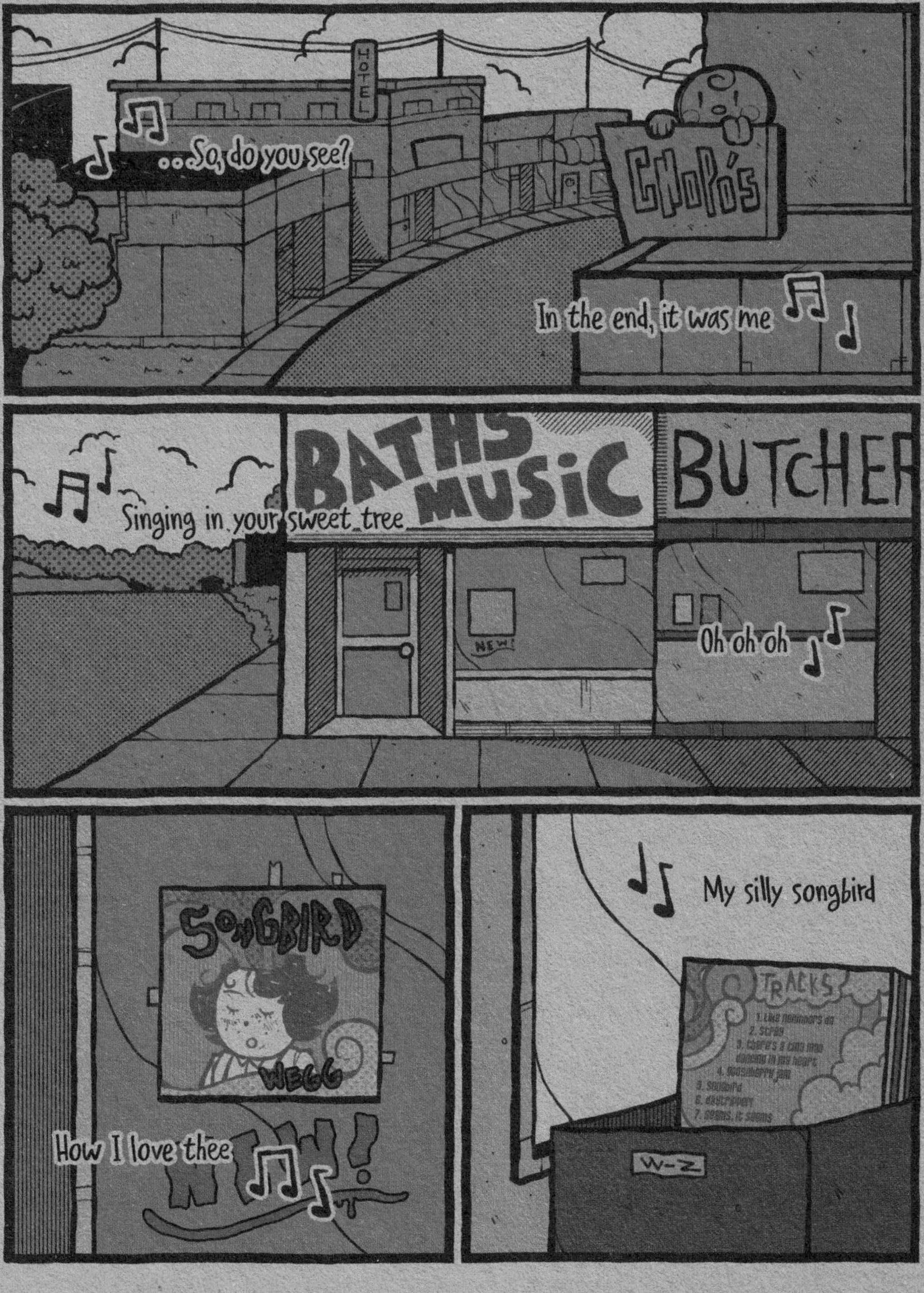
HOTEL
...So, do you see?
CHOPO'S
In the end, it was me
BATHS MUSIC
BUTCHER
Singing in your sweet tree
NEW!
Oh oh oh
SONGBIRD
WEGG
How I love thee
My silly songbird
TRACKS
W-Z

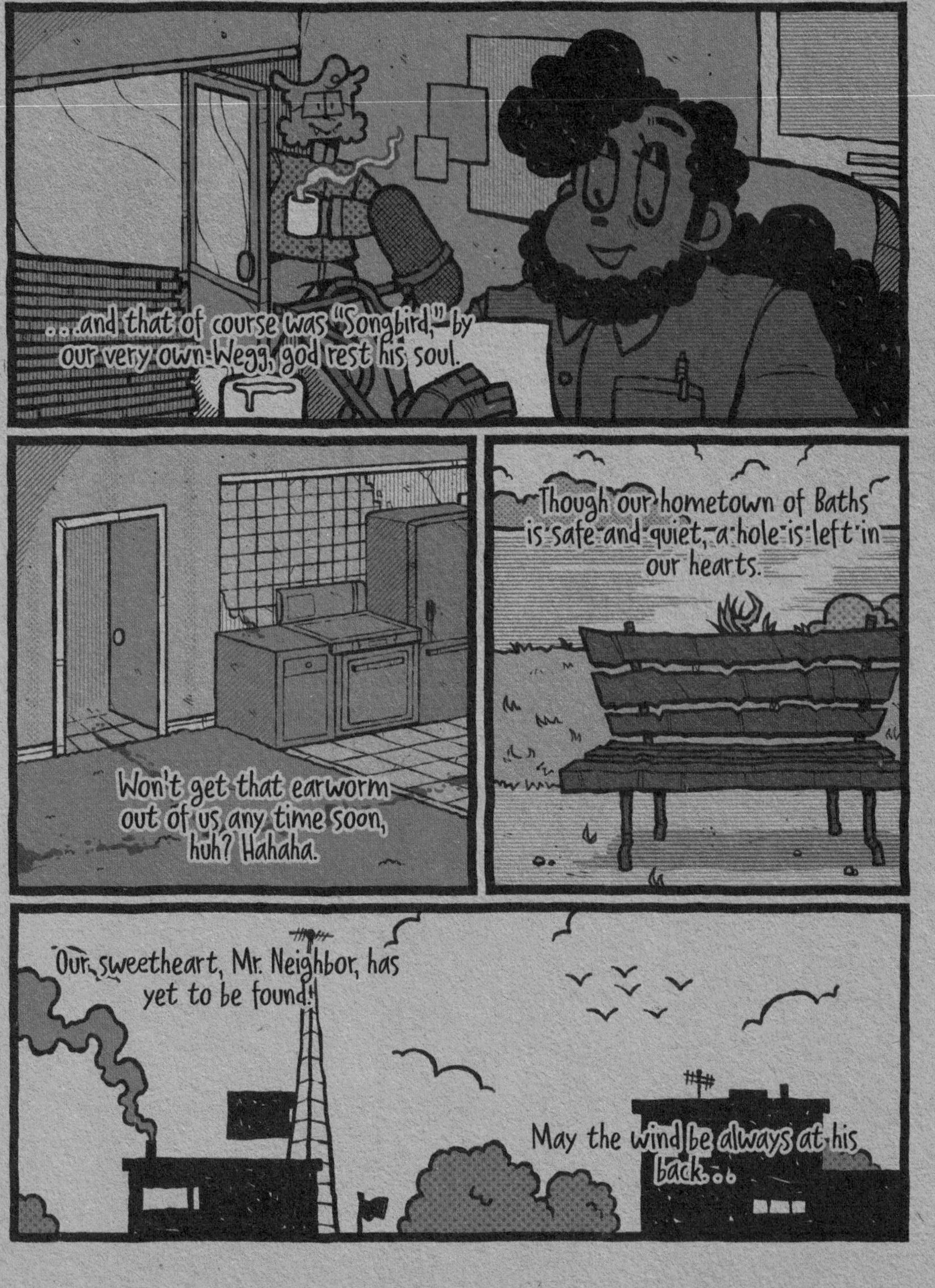
...and that of course was "Songbird," by our very own Wegg, god rest his soul.
Won't get that earworm out of us any time soon, huh? Hahaha.
Though our hometown of Baths is safe and quiet, a hole is left in our hearts.
Our sweetheart, Mr. Neighbor, has yet to be found!
May the wind be always at his back...

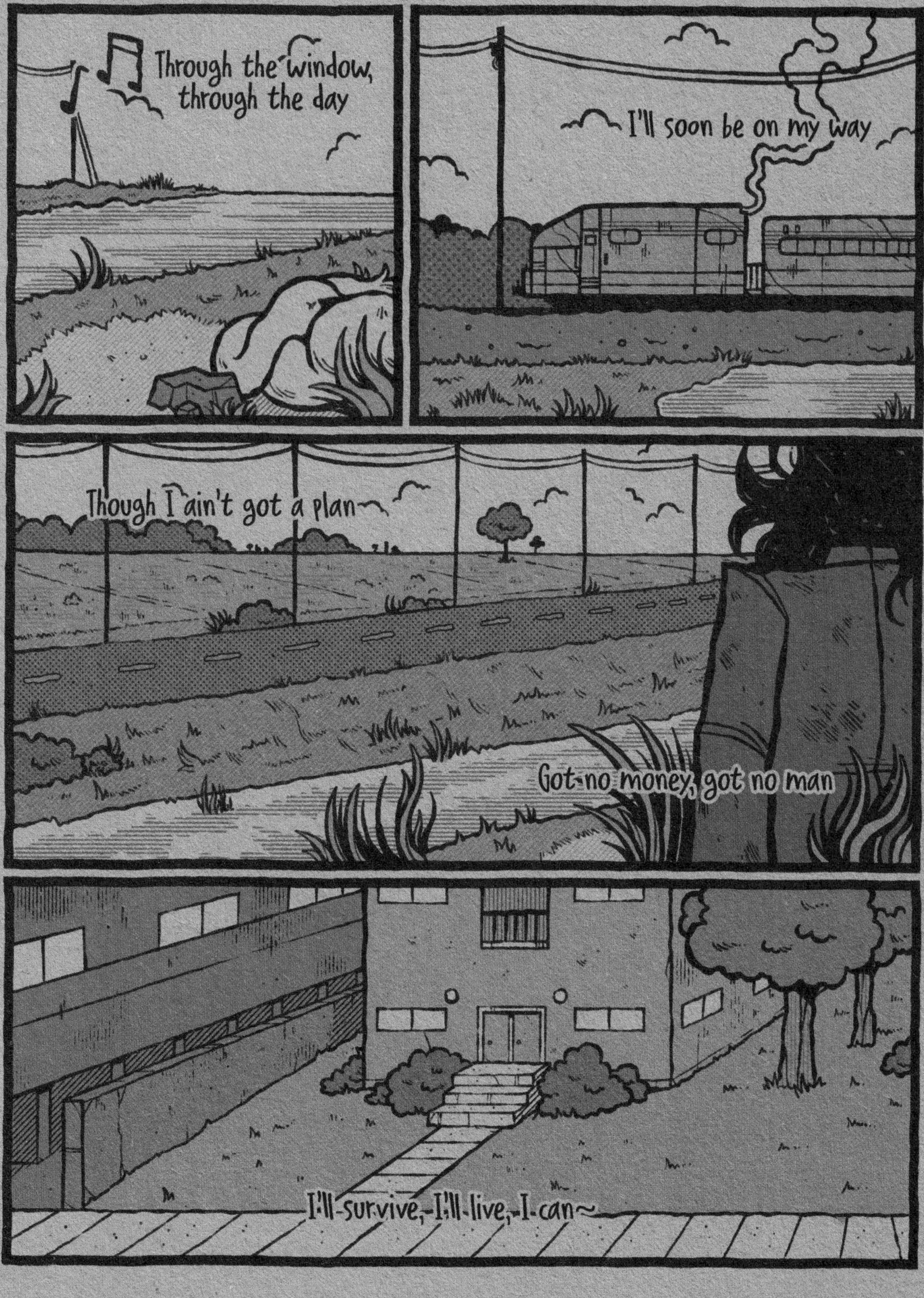
Through the window, through the day
I'll soon be on my way
Though I ain't got a plan
Got no money, got no man
I'll survive, I'll live, I can~

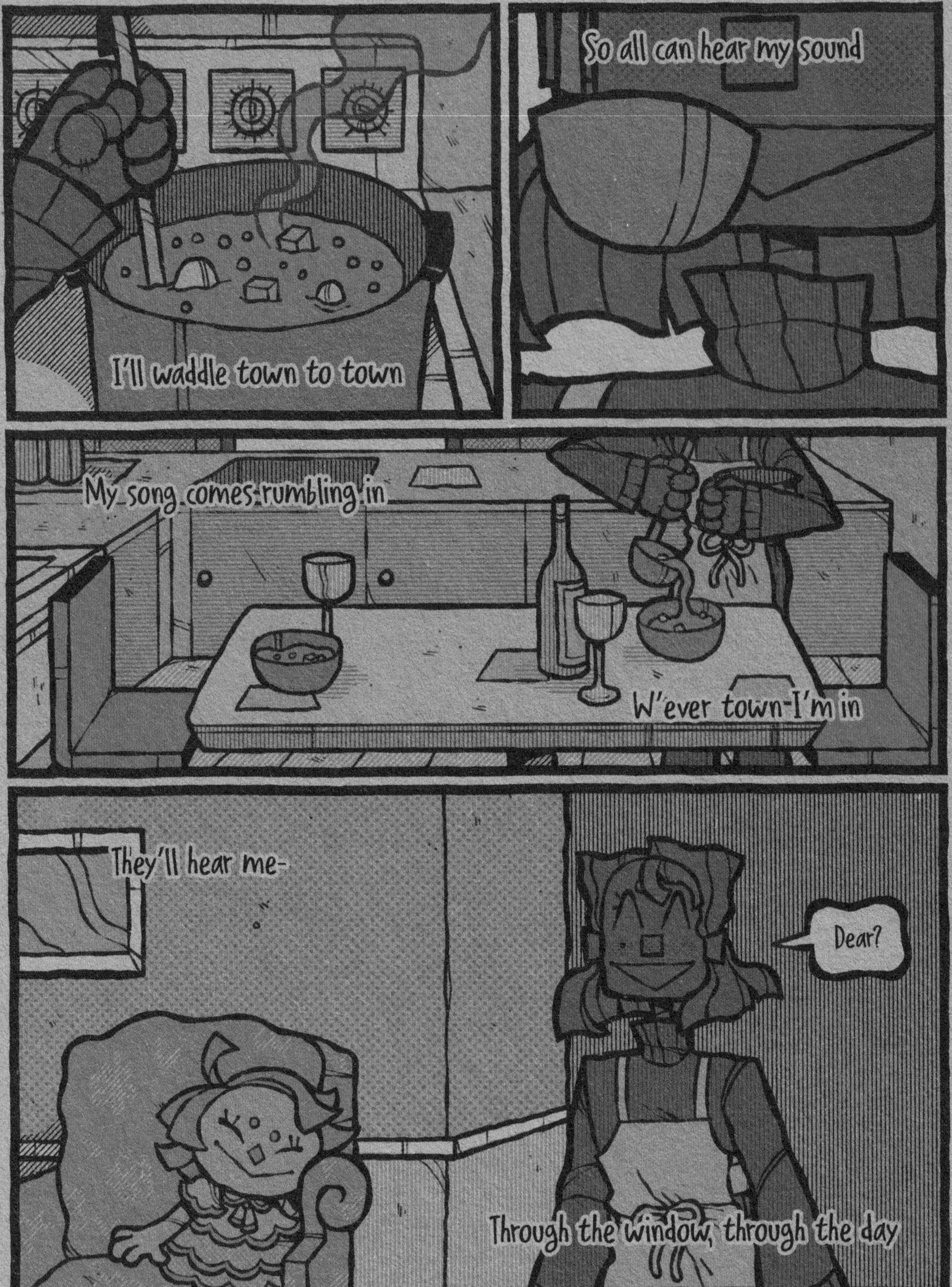
I'll waddle town to town
So all can hear my sound
My song comes rumbling in
W'ever town I'm in
They'll hear me-
Dear?
Through the window, through the day

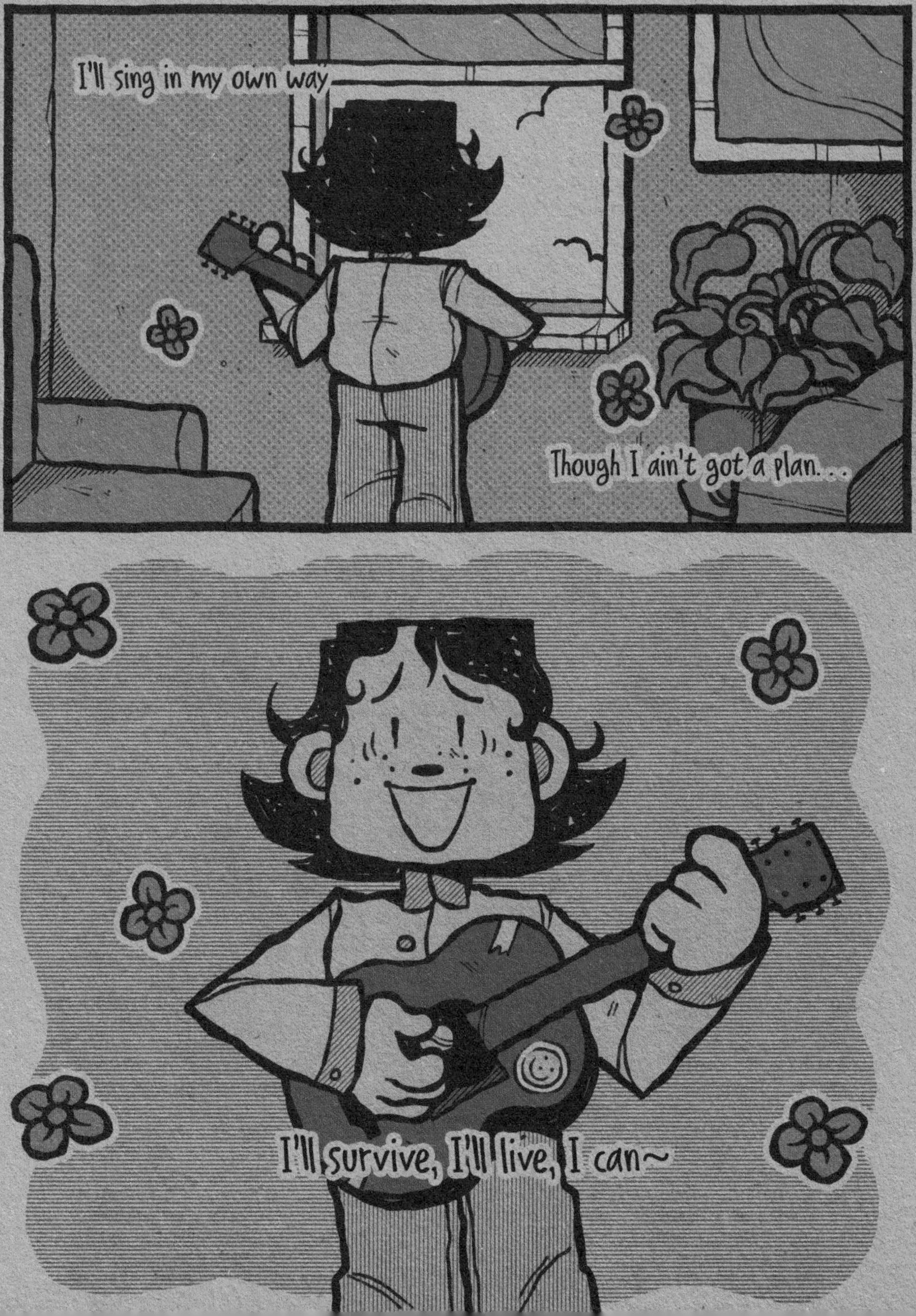
I'll sing in my own way
Though I ain't got a plan. . .
I'll survive, I'll live, I can~

THE END